# Lecture Notes in Computer Science    12066

More information about this series at http://www.springer.com/series/7409

Marié Hattingh · Machdel Matthee ·
Hanlie Smuts · Ilias Pappas ·
Yogesh K. Dwivedi · Matti Mäntymäki (Eds.)

# Responsible Design, Implementation and Use of Information and Communication Technology

19th IFIP WG 6.11 Conference on
e-Business, e-Services, and e-Society, I3E 2020
Skukuza, South Africa, April 6–8, 2020
Proceedings, Part I

 Springer

*Editors*
Marié Hattingh ⓘ
University of Pretoria
Pretoria, South Africa

Hanlie Smuts ⓘ
University of Pretoria
Pretoria, South Africa

Yogesh K. Dwivedi ⓘ
Swansea University
Swansea, UK

Machdel Matthee ⓘ
University of Pretoria
Pretoria, South Africa

Ilias Pappas ⓘ
University of Agder
Kristiansand, Norway

Matti Mäntymäki ⓘ
University of Turku
Turku, Finland

ISSN 0302-9743          ISSN 1611-3349   (electronic)
Lecture Notes in Computer Science
ISBN 978-3-030-44998-8          ISBN 978-3-030-44999-5   (eBook)
https://doi.org/10.1007/978-3-030-44999-5

LNCS Sublibrary: SL3 – Information Systems and Applications, incl. Internet/Web, and HCI

This Springer imprint is published by the registered company Springer Nature Switzerland AG
The registered company address is: Gewerbestrasse 11, 6330 Cham, Switzerland

# Preface

This book presents the proceedings of the 19th International Federation of Information Processing (IFIP) Conference on e-Business, e-Services, and e-Society (I3E 2020), which was held in Skukuza, Kruger National Park, South Africa, during April 6–8, 2020. The annual I3E conference is a core part of Working Group 6.11, which aims to organize and promote the exchange of information and co-operation related to all aspects of e-Business, e-Services, and e-Society (the three Es). The I3E conference series is truly interdisciplinary and welcomed contributions from both academics and practitioners alike.

The main theme of the 2020 conference was "Responsible design, implementation and use of information and communication technology." In line with the inclusive nature of the I3E series, all papers related to e-Business, e-Services, and e-Society were welcomed.

The age of digital transformation opens up exciting new avenues for design and application of ICTs. Yet, with the ubiquitous connectedness of a digitally transformed world, come unintended, unpredictable, and often adverse consequences for individuals, societies, and organizations – in developed and developing contexts. Security, privacy, trustworthiness, exploitation, and well-being are some of the pressing concerns resulting from new digital realities.

There is need for responsible design, implementation, and use of information systems (IS) based on critical awareness and ethical practices. As rightly put by Schultze (2017:65): "As IS researchers we need to examine our own practices – including the questions we ask, the methods we deploy and theories we adopt – to understand and critically review our world-making."

The IFIP I3E 2020 was held during April 6–8, 2020, and brought together contributions from a variety of perspectives, disciplines, and communities for the advancement of knowledge regarding responsible design, implementation, and use of information and communications technology. This was evident by our variety of keynote speakers and topics for the panel discussions. We were delighted to welcome three distinguished keynote speakers:

- Mr. James van der Westhuizen who is the founder and managing partner of KnowHouse, founded 20 years ago out of a passion to work differently with the challenge of learning and change in organizations. He is a global consultant and facilitator working across the African continent, the Middle East, Europe, and Asia.
- Prof. Irwin Brown is a full Professor and Head of the Department of Information Systems (IS) at the University of Cape Town. His research interests relate to theorizing about IS phenomena in developing countries.
- Prof. Dr. Shirish C. Srivastava is a tenured full Professor and holds the GS1 Chair on 'Digital Content for Omni Channel' at HEC Paris. His rich experience includes coaching senior executives on issues related to managing technology emerging technologies (such as big data, blockchains, and artificial intelligence), technology

enabled innovation, entrepreneurship, and managing cross-border business relationships.

The conference held two panels to facilitate discussions on important topics. The first panel on "Blockchain – hope or hype? Blockchain as a disruptive force" was chaired by Dr. Matti Mäntymäki. Blockchain is surrounded by considerable optimism and enthusiasm among businesses and academia. This enthusiasm is evidenced by the numerous calls for papers in journals and dedicated blockchain tracks in conferences. The purpose of the panel was to make sense of the actual significance of the blockchain phenomenon and provoke discussion and exchange of ideas among the I3E community. To this end, the panel paid homage to the heterogenous nature of the I3E community and invited a diverse of group of expert panellists to share their distinctive perspectives on blockchain.

The second panel, made up of a panel of editors, was chaired by Dr. Shirish C. Srivastava. The panel consisted of six journal editors from international and local (South African) publications. Each editor gave an explanation on the requirements for authors when submitting to their journal.

The Call for Papers solicited submissions in two main categories: full research papers and short research-in-progress papers. Each submission was reviewed by at least two knowledgeable academics in the field, in a double-blind process. The 2020 conference received 191 submissions. Out of the 191 papers, 91 papers were selected to be presented at the conference. Four of the accepted papers were not included in the final proceedings because the authors decided to withdraw it. Thus, the acceptance rate was 45.5%.

Following the conference, two special issues were organized for selected best papers of the I3E 2020. The two special issues are in the *International Journal of Information Management* (IJIM) and the *International Journal of Electronic Government Research* (IJEGR).

The final set of 87 full and short papers submitted to I3E 2020 that appear in these proceedings were clustered into 14 groups, each of which are outlined below.

Part I: addressing the area of Blockchain. Three papers were grouped under this theme. One of the papers proposed a framework for the adoption of blockchain whilst another reported on the application of blockchain technology in Healthcare. The third paper examined the potential disruptive impact of cryptocurrencies.

Part II of the book addressed papers on the Fourth Industrial Revolution. Nine papers were grouped under this theme. Paper details range from a systematic literature review on the incompatibility of Smart manufacturing for SMMEs to the development of models and frameworks through the application of Smart technologies. One paper included a bibliographic coupling and co-occurrence on the topic of Smart City and Economy, whilst another reported on robotic automation and the consequences for knowledge workers. The final paper reported on the co-creation for digitalization in Norwegian business clusters.

Part III of the book addressed e-Business. 12 papers were grouped under this theme. The papers presented works on online banking quality, a conceptual framework for digital entrepreneurship, mobile applications, online switching behavior, and how games are used in business. Three papers reported on systematic review of literature on eWOM, mobile shopping acceptance predictors and social commerce adoption predictors. The final paper presented a review of papers published from 2001 to 2019 by I3E.

Part IV of the book addressed Business Processes. 10 papers were grouped under this theme. The papers presented works on governance achieved through business process management, how IT is being used in Fintech Innovation, a meta model for maturity models, and a strategic model for the safeguarding the preservation of business value. In addition to these themes, papers were presented on using the story-card method for business process re-engineering, using Zachman's framework as an IS theory and a review of the Task-Technology Fit Theory.

Part V of the book addressed Big Data and Machine Learning. Seven papers were grouped under this theme. The papers presented work on using machine learning in the field of healthcare, data governance, using a deep learning neural network model to predict information diffusion on Twitter, and big data visualization tools.

Part VI of the book addresses ICT and Education. Seven papers were grouped under this theme. The papers presented work on mobile learning, new considerations for flipped classroom approach, and eModeration system considerations.

Part VII of the book addressed eGovernment. Six papers were grouped under this theme. The papers presented work on the use of social media in eParticipation, enterprise architectures in eGovernments, and eGovernment implementation framework. Other themes included were digital innovation in public organizations, implementation challenges in eProcurement, and a case from Ghana on the effects on National Health Insurance digital platform development and use.

Part VIII of the book addressed eHealth. Six papers were grouped under this theme. Papers presented work on the use of technology for diabetic patients, factors influencing community health workers, wearable devices, and a Twitter social network analysis of the South African Health Insurance Bill.

Part IX of the book addressed Security. Four papers were grouped under this theme. Papers presented work on cyber-harassment among LGBTQIA+ youth, online identity theft, cybersecurity readiness of e-tail organizations, and the ethics of using publicly available data.

Part X of the book addressed Social Media. Six papers were grouped under this theme. Papers presented works on a conceptual framework for media use behavior, metaphors of social media, credibility of online information (fake news), and problematic media and technology use.

Part XI of the book addressed Knowledge and Knowledge Management. Three papers were grouped under this theme. Papers presented work on knowledge transfer science education, a knowledge asset management implementation framework, and a conceptual knowledge visualization framework for knowledge transfer.

Part XII of the book addressed ICT for Gender Equality and Development. Nine papers were grouped under this theme. Papers presented work on the rural vs urban digital divide, socio-economic factors in Internet usage in Nigeria, and enablers and barriers of mobile commerce and banking services among elderly individuals. A methodology for addressing the second-level digital divide, gender equality in the ICT context, digital competence requirements, and the influence of culture on women's IT career choices were also presented.

Part XIII of the book addressed Information Systems for Governance. Four papers were grouped under this theme. Papers presented work on the use of machine learning on financial inclusion data for governance in Eswatini, ordinance-tweet mining to disseminate urban policy knowledge for smart governance, open technology innovation in healthcare services, and multi-stakeholder-centric data analytics governance framework.

Part XIV of the book addressed User Experience and Usability. Three papers were grouped under this theme. Papers presented work on the use of machine learning and eye tracking to predict users' ratings on the aesthetics of websites, a systematic review on designing for positive emotional responses in users of interactive digital technologies, and a methodology to compare the usability of information systems.

The success of the 19th IFIP I3E Conference (I3E 2020) was a result of the enormous efforts of numerous people and organizations. Firstly, this conference was only made possible by the continued support of WG 6.11 for this conference series and for selecting South Africa to host it in 2020, for which we are extremely grateful. We received many good-quality submissions from authors across the globe and we would like to thank them for choosing I3E 2020 as the outlet to present and publish their current research. We are indebted to the Program Committee, who generously gave up their time to provide constructive reviews and facilitate the improvement of the submitted manuscripts. We would like to thank the Department of Informatics of the University of Pretoria for their support in enabling us to host this conference. Thank you to AfricaMassive that assisted us with all the logistical arrangements with hosting the conference in Skukuza located in the Kruger National Park. Finally, we extend our sincere gratitude to everyone involved in organizing the conference, to our esteemed keynote speakers, and to Springer LNCS as the publisher of these proceedings, which we hope will be of use for the continued development of research related to the three Es[1].

February 2020

Marié Hattingh
Machdel Matthee
Hanlie Smuts
Ilias Pappas
Yogesh K. Dwivedi
Matti Mäntymäki

---

[1] Due to the global COVID-19 pandemic and the consequential worldwide imposed travel restrictions and lock down, the I3E 2020 conference event scheduled to take place in Skukuza, South Africa, was unfortunately cancelled.

# Organization

## Conference Chairs

| | |
|---|---|
| Marié (M. J.) Hattingh | University of Pretoria, South Africa |
| Machdel Matthee | University of Pretoria, South Africa |
| Hanlie Smuts | University of Pretoria, South Africa |
| Ilias Pappas | University of Adger and Norwegian University of Science and Technology (NTNU), Norway |
| Yogesh K. Dwivedi | Swansea University, UK |
| Matti Mäntymäki | University of Turku, Finland |

## Program Committee Chairs

| | |
|---|---|
| Marié (M. J.) Hattingh | University of Pretoria, South Africa |
| Machdel Matthee | University of Pretoria, South Africa |
| Hanlie Smuts | University of Pretoria, South Africa |
| Ilias Pappas | University of Adger and Norwegian University of Science and Technology, Norway |
| Yogesh K. Dwivedi | Swansea University, UK |
| Matti Mäntymäki | University of Turku, Finland |

## Keynote Speakers

| | |
|---|---|
| Irwin Brown | University of Cape Town, South Africa |
| James van der Westhuizen | KnowHouse, South Africa |
| Shirish C. Srivastava | HEC Paris, France |

## Program Committee

| | |
|---|---|
| Rami Abu Wadi | Ahlia University, Bahrain |
| Funmi Adebesin | University of Pretoria, South Africa |
| Kayode Ibrahim Adenuga | Universiti Tecknologi, Malaysia |
| Michael Adu Kwarteng | Tomas Bata University, Czech Republic |
| Augustus Barnnet Anderson | University of Ghana, Ghana |
| Bokolo Anthony Jnr. | Norwegian University of Science and Technology, Norway |
| Oluwasefunmi Arogundade | Chinese Academy of Science, China |
| Lynette Barnard | Nelson Mandela University, South Africa |
| Clara Benac Earle | Polytechnic University of Madrid, Spain |
| Khalid Benali | University of Lorraine, France |
| Djamal Benslimane | Claude Bernard University Lyon 1, France |
| Edward Bernroider | Vienna University of Economic and Business, Austria |

| | |
|---|---|
| Elmi Bester | UNISA, South Africa |
| Dzifa Bibi | University of Ghana, Ghana |
| Katja Bley | Dresden University of Technology, Germany |
| Deonie Botha | Deloitte, South Africa |
| Jacques Brosens | University of Pretoria, South Africa |
| Paul Brous | Delft University of Technology, The Netherlands |
| Peter André Busch | University of Agder, Norway |
| Andre Calitz | Nelson Mandela University, South Africa |
| Sunil Choenni | Research and Documentation Centre (WODC), Ministry of Justice, The Netherlands |
| Mahdieh Darvish | ESCP Business School, Germany |
| Dinara Davlembayeva | Newcastle University, UK |
| Carina De Villiers | University of Pretoria, South Africa |
| Marne de Vries | University of Pretoria, South Africa |
| Jules Degila | Institute of Mathematics and Physics, Benin |
| Denis Dennehy | National University of Ireland, Ireland |
| Vipin Deval | Tallinn University of Technology, Estonia |
| Christos Douligeris | University of Piraeus, Greece |
| Dirk Draheim | Software Competence Center Hagenberg, Austria |
| Alena Droit | Osnabrueck University, Germany |
| Jacobus Du Preez | University of Pretoria, South Africa |
| Edward Entee | University of Ghana, Ghana |
| Sunet Eybers | University of Pretoria, South Africa |
| Olakumbi Fadiran | UNISA, South Africa |
| Sam February | Accenture, South Africa |
| Jennifer Ferreira | Victoria University of Wellington, New Zealand |
| Blanka Frydrychova Klimova | University of Hradec Kralove, Czech Republic |
| Shang Gao | Örebro University, Sweden |
| Ping Gao | The University of Manchester, UK |
| Aurona Gerber | University of Pretoria, South Africa |
| Claude Godart | University of Lorraine, France |
| Javier Gomez | Autonomous University of Madrid, Spain |
| Anastasia Griva | Athens University of Economics and Business, Greece |
| Sara Grobbelaar | Stellenbosch University, South Africa |
| Lucas Gumbi | UNISA, South Africa |
| Hong Guo | Anhui University, China |
| Remko Helms | The Open University, The Netherlands |
| Raoul Hentschel | Dresden University of Technology, Germany |
| Grant Royd Howard | UNISA, South Africa |
| Vigneswara Ilavarasan | Indian Institute of Technology, India |
| Marijn Janssen | Delft University of Technology, The Netherlands |
| Debora Jeske | University College Cork, Ireland |
| Arpan Kar | Indian Institute of Technology, India |
| Caroline Khene | Rhodes University, South Africa |
| Eija Koskivaara | University of Turku, Finland |

| Paula Kotzé | University of Pretoria, South Africa |
| Jan H. Kroeze | UNISA, South Africa |
| Rendani Kruger | University of Pretoria, South Africa |
| Abhinav Kumar | The National Institute of Technology Patna, India |
| Amit Kumar | Kushwaha GAP, India |
| Andreas D. Landmark | SINTEF, Norway |
| Sven Laumer | Friedrich-Alexander-Universität Erlangen-Nürnberg, Germany |
| Daniel Le Roux | Stellenbosch University, South Africa |
| Hongxiu Li | Turku School of Economics, Finland |
| Lieb Liebenberg | University of Pretoria, South Africa |
| Marianne Loock | UNISA, South Africa |
| Hugo Lotriet | UNISA, South Africa |
| Mario Marais | CSIR Meraka Institute, South Africa |
| Emanuele Gabriel Margherita | Tuscia University, Italy |
| Davit Marikyan | Newcastle University, UK |
| Linda Marshall | University of Pretoria, South Africa |
| Tendani Mawela | University of Pretoria, South Africa |
| Nita Mennega | University of Pretoria, South Africa |
| Jan Mentz | UNISA, South Africa |
| Patrick Mikalef | Norwegian University of Science and Technology, Norway |
| Tshepiso Mokoena | CSIR, South Africa |
| Mathias Mujinga | UNISA, South Africa |
| Matthias Murawski | ESCP Europe Business School, Germany |
| Mohammed Khaled Mustafa | Bangladesh University of Professionals, Bangladesh |
| Mpho Mzingelwa | University of KwaZulu Natal, South Africa |
| Rennie Naidoo | University of Pretoria, South Africa |
| Alex Norta | Tallinn University of Technology, Estonia |
| Kayode Odusanya | Loughborough University, UK |
| Kwame Simpe Ofori | University of Electronic Science and Technology of China, China |
| Kingsley Ofosu-Ampong | University of Ghana, Ghana |
| Olabode Ogunbodede | Newcastle University, UK |
| Leif Erik Opland | Norwegian University of Science and Technology, Norway |
| Makoto Oya | Computer Institute of Japan, Japan |
| Niki Panteli | Royal Holloway University of London, UK |
| Savvas Papagiannidis | Newcastle University, UK |
| Zacharoula Papamitsiou | Norwegian University of Science and Technology, Norway |
| Sofia Papavlasopoulou | Norwegian University of Science and Technology, Norway |

| | |
|---|---|
| Elena Parmiggiani | Norwegian University of Science and Technology, Norway |
| Douglas Parry | Stellenbosch University, South Africa |
| Marcel Pikhart | University of Hradec Kralove, Czech Republic |
| Colin Pilkington | UNISA, South Africa |
| Komla Pillay | University of Pretoria, South Africa |
| Henk Pretorius | University of Pretoria, South Africa |
| Tania Prinsloo | University of Pretoria, South Africa |
| Maciel Queiroz | Paulista University, Brazil |
| Van Raj | UNISA, South Africa |
| Nripendra Rana | Swansea University, UK |
| Anthony Renner-Micah | University of Ghana, Ghana |
| Suzanne Sackstein | WITS University, South Africa |
| Brenda Scholtz | Nelson Mandela University, South Africa |
| Lisa Seymour | University of Cape Town, South Africa |
| Anuragini Shirish | University of Paris-Saclay, France |
| Djofack Sidonie | University of Yaounde II, Cameroon |
| Ivana Simonova | University of Jan Evangelista Purkyne, Czech Republic |
| Konstantina Spanaki | Loughborough University, UK |
| Ruan Spies | Stellenbosch University, South Africa |
| Riana Steyn | University of Pretoria, South Africa |
| Ilse Struweg | University of Johannesburg, South Africa |
| Zhaohao Sun | Federation University Australia, Australia |
| Reima Vesa Suomi | University of Turku, Finland |
| Libuse Svobodova | University of Hradec Kralove, Czechia |
| Kuttimani Tamilmani | Swansea University, UK |
| Maureen Tanner | University of Cape Town, South Africa |
| Ali Tarhini | Sultan Qaboos University, Oman |
| Temitope Oluwaseyi Tokosi | Nelson Mandela University, South Africa |
| Cathrine Tømte | University of Adger, Noway |
| Juan Carlos Torrado Vidal | Autonomous University of Madrid, Spain |
| Pieter Toussaint | Norwegian University of Science and Technology, Norway |
| Rakhi Tripathi | FORE School of Management, India |
| Valentyna Tsap | Tallinn University of Technology, Estonia |
| Pitso Tsibolane | Stellenbosch University, South Africa |
| Marita Turpin | University of Pretoria, South Africa |
| Parijat Upadhyay | IMT Nagpur, India |
| Jean-Paul Van Belle | University of Cape Town, South Africa |
| Judy van Biljon | UNISA, South Africa |
| Rogier Van de Wetering | Open University, The Netherlands |
| Thomas van der Merwe | UNISA, South Africa |
| Alta Van der Merwe | University of Pretoria, South Africa |
| J. P. van Deventer | University of Pretoria, South Africa |

| Corné Van Staden | UNISA, South Africa |
| Izak Van Zyl | Cape Peninsula University of Technology, South Africa |
| Polyxeni Vassilakopoulou | University of Agder, Norway |
| Jari Veijalainen | University of Jyvaskyla, Finland |
| Hans Weigand | Tilburg University, The Netherlands |
| Lizette Weilbach | University of Pretoria, South Africa |
| Ted White | UNISA, South Africa |
| Michael Williams | Swansea University, UK |
| Milla Wiren | University of Turku, Finland |
| Khulekani Yakobi | Nelson Mandela University, South Africa |
| Hiroshi Yoshiura | The University of Electro-Communications, Japan |
| Hans-Dieter Zimmermann | FHS St. Gallen University of Applied Sciences, Switzerland |

# Contents – Part I

**eBusiness**

## Business Processes

## Big Data and Machine Learning

## ICT and Education

# Contents – Part II

**Security**

**Social Media**

## Knowledge and Knowledge Management

## ICT and Gender Equality and Development

**Information Systems for Governance**

**User Experience and Usability**

# Block Chain

# A Framework for the Adoption of Blockchain-Based e-Procurement Systems in the Public Sector
## A Case Study of Nigeria

Temofe Isaac Akaba[1], Alex Norta[1]([✉]) [iD], Chibuzor Udokwu[1], and Dirk Draheim[2] [iD]

[1] Blockchain Technology Group, Tallinn University of Technology,
Akadeemia tee 15a, 12618 Tallinn, Estonia
{temofe.akaba,chibuzor.udokwu}@taltech.ee, alex.norta.phd@ieee.org
[2] Information Systems Group, Tallinn University of Technology,
Akadeemia tee 15a, 12618 Tallinn, Estonia
dirk.draheim@taltech.ee

**Abstract.** Public procurement constitutes a core government function for providing goods and services to citizens. The overall success of a digitized public-procurement function yields progress and economic growth for the nation. In this research, we analyze the potential of blockchain-based systems to enhance effectiveness, ease, and transparency in public procurement in the case of Nigeria and identify the current challenges facing public procurement, i.e., lack of trust and transparency among critical stakeholders in the procurement process, systems that only weakly support transaction recording and documentation, complex process structures, corruption in institutions involved in the procurement process. To address these issues, a blockchain-based framework is developed to enable interoperability of information-systems involved in the procurement process, increase citizen participation in eliciting project requirements and to enable a more transparent project monitoring and auditing. We apply the framework to a case study with respect to identifying on-chain activities that enable system interoperability, e-participation and project auditability.

**Keywords:** Blockchain · Procurement · Smart contract · Interoperability · Project-monitoring

## 1 Introduction

Public procurement is a core function of government activities that catalyzes economic growth and development, if conducted efficiently and transparently. Despite these benefits of e-procurement, developing nations, including Nigeria, still struggle with issues ranging from a lack of trust and transparency among

© IFIP International Federation for Information Processing 2020
Published by Springer Nature Switzerland AG 2020
M. Hattingh et al. (Eds.): I3E 2020, LNCS 12066, pp. 3–14, 2020.
https://doi.org/10.1007/978-3-030-44999-5_1

the important participants in the process, systems that only weakly support transaction recording and documentation, complex process structures and massive corruption in institutions within the process. The exchange of corruption money between companies and government officials to be awarded government contracts is estimated to comprise 15% of the contract value.

With respect to these challenges, an innovative approach for tracking all aspects of public procurement for trust, transparency, and ease within the system is essential. Thus, blockchain technology [25] creates a decentralized platform for validating transactions, data and information that are independent of any third party control in a verifiable, secured transparent and permanent set-up. Therefore, blockchain technology [1] has the potential to be adopted to offer solutions for public e-procurement.

In this paper, we propose a blockchain-based e-procurement framework that takes into consideration key success factors in public procurement using Nigeria as a case [3]. We commence with a thorough analysis of the procurement system in Nigeria by conducting semi-structured interviews with twelve high-level stakeholders and experts. Based on the findings of this analysis, the framework elaboration yields a set of concrete recommendations as a *concept study*, i.e., we provide a first evaluation of the framework's feasibility with application to the Nigerian case.

The remainder of the paper is structured as follows. In Sect. 2, we discuss related work and in Sect. 3, we explain details of the used research method. In Sect. 4, the case selection, subject description and results of the interviews are presented. Next, in Sect. 5, we elaborate the framework and Sect. 6 provides a mapping of the current procurement process to a blockchain-based solution. The paper finishes in Sect. 7 with a conclusion, limitations, open issues and future work.

## 2   Related Work

Public procurement is a vital part of government processes that present value for citizens [11]. The normal flow of a public procurement process includes: crafting an annual budget with the different estimated needs of government agencies, making a plan for the procurement of the items listed in the project, issuing a call for tender for interested contractors, conducting financial- and technical evaluations of participating firms and finally, the award and implementation of projects. The objective of these activities is the delivery of high-quality and timely services to citizens through public programs and -application projects.

Blockchain innovations and application are an emerging area of technology research [19,20]. Research on this technology is very diverse and previous work includes the application of blockchain in regular currencies and centralized-banking systems to curb corruption in the finance industry [16]. In [12], the authors suggest apply blockchain technology for handling and securing patient records, recording an audit trail and securing data due to its decentralized features, compare also with [4]. As another example, blockchain research related to supply-chain management focuses on reducing counterfeiting and accuracy in document-validation processes [24]. Within the context of e-Government, research in blockchain technology is explored in various fields, i.e., in the area of identity management [21] and document authentication [23], compare also with [1] versus conventional approaches such as [7], or in specialized fields such as land registration [14].

Blockchain technology application in procurement processes is on a slow but steady rise since technology infusion in this process is still vision- and experiment-oriented rather than a solution-based scientific endeavour [17]. According to [10], blockchain technology has a high potential to significantly improve procurement systems, in particular, with respect to data integration across business functions. Thus, the infusion of blockchain technology causes a positive shift in the way organizations carry out procurement, thereby creating more possibilities for growth and expansion on a global scale.

## 3 Research Methodology

We perform semi-structured interviews with twelve stakeholders and experts in public procurement, private-sector procurement, blockchain technology and advocacy for transparency and technology adoption in the Nigerian public-sector procurement. The respondents are made up of fourteen experts from relevant procurement-related organizations including the National Identity Management Commission (NIMC), private firms, civil societies and the National Assembly.

The idea for this diverse pool of respondents is to acquire a holistic compilation of ideas from a diverse set of knowledgeable stakeholders. The interview data we analyze with thematic analysis, supported by RQDA (R package for Qualitative Data Analysis)[1]. In the data analysis, we follow six well-defined steps proposed by [15].

## 4 The Case of the Nigerian Procurement System

Information about Nigeria and the procurement context, we first present in Sect. 4.1. Next, Sect. 4.2 gives the interview results.

### 4.1 Case- and Subject Description

The Nigerian government has encountered severe problems in public procurement [2,8]. According to [22], these problems have existed despite of – and even due to – the enactment of the Public Procurement Act in 2007 to ensure transparency, competitiveness, value for money and professionalism in the public-sector procurement system. The Procurement-Act guidelines demand from stakeholders the following strict rules and provides guidelines for the establishment

---

[1] http://rqda.r-forge.r-project.org/.

of an approving body, i.e., the National Council on Public Procurement, as well as a regulatory body, i.e., the Bureau of Public Procurement.

Still, the objectives of the act are in far reach due to the poor implementation of the relevant directives that can ultimately be traced to the harsh economic, social- and political environment in the country. According to [9], public procurement in Nigeria remains the most common means through which public funds have been misappropriated and stolen for personal and individual gains. Although the adoption of e-procurement is a goal, most of the functions are still operated manually and as such prone to corruption and fraud.

### 4.2 Interview Results

The interviews are structured in different sections. The first section is concerned with gaining background knowledge of the respondents to assess the validity of their responses. The other sections focus on gathering interview findings we categorize into the themes existing procurement system, stakeholder involvement and role, influencing factors for adopting blockchain-based procurement, criteria for assessing effectiveness. The project log[2] shows the detailed interview transcript for this research.

**Existing Procurement System.** The respondents express that, although the regulators aim to introduce e-procurement, the existing manual procedures are still used extensively. Furthermore, the respondents state unnecessary emphasis on rule compliance is detrimental to fair and transparent procurement processes.

Respondents mention the lack of clear structure of project planning and execution within the ministries, departments and agencies (MDAs). This structure absence renders it impossible for the Bureau of Public Procurement to install improvement plans. Approximately 50% of our respondents mention that corruption currently exists in all phases of the procurement process from project planning via bidding to the project implementation stage.

**Stakeholders Involvement.** Investigating stakeholder involvement indicates the impact on their roles and duties of adopting automating systems. To acquire a holistic understanding, we gather responses from private-sector respondents who mention that planning is a very crucial success factor of the procurement function as they perform a thorough analysis of the intended goods, services, or project. The study further explores the specific steps taken by contractors and suppliers who provide goods and services for clients who communicate via emails, or phone calls. Most respondents indicate they do not move beyond a re-order level to have stock available in the case of an emergency. In cases where the procuring entity is a large organization such as a government ministry, respondents usually place orders directly from the international manufacturers

---

[2] Project    Log    https://www.researchgate.net/publication/338102329_Interview_Transcript.

as opposed to using intermediaries. This reduces the delivery time and enables specific demand of the procuring entity to be met.

The role and involvement of the Bureau of Procurement is also explored during the research. A senior official of the Bureau mentions that, apart from acting as a regulator, the bureau also advises the government about the procurement and disposal of public goods and services. Finally, the role of civil-society organizations is considered, in particular, to monitor and track public-sector procurement, funding and financing. Two respondents who work with different civil-society organizations explain despite challenges, the government aims to ensure a more transparent and open system. With the slow progress of change, the respondents wish the government adopts technologies and systems for ease, efficiency, and transparency to meet the global standard for public procurement.

**Influencing Factors for Adopting Blockchain-Based Procurement.** In this section, we analyze the factors that hinder the effective implementation of a blockchain-based solution as well as how these issues can be addressed. The areas of a hindrance include a poor infrastructure set up, lack of political will of the government to implement necessary technology policies needed, lack of funding for a full implementation, resistance to change by public officials, and poor knowledge of blockchain technology by stakeholders involved in the process.

A number of 33% of the respondents specifically mention the epileptic power situation in Nigeria as the main challenge to fully implement blockchain technology that can not effectively run. Additionally, three respondents mention the need for political will both from the executive- and legislative arms in ensuring total compliance with the requirements needed for a functioning blockchain use. Poor technology knowledge is another challenge to adopt a blockchain system. Similarly, another respondent mentions that although these stakeholders would stall blockchains and use traditional methods of moving files to manipulate figures and engage in fraud and corruption that an advanced and digitized system restricts.

To correct these identified issues, respondents unanimously point out the need for training all procurement staff and other stakeholders to gain a better understanding of what the proposed blockchain technology entails and how it functions. One respondent particularly stresses the government ensuring maintaining and sustaining blockchain technologies.

**Criteria for Assessing Effectiveness.** It is also crucial to understand appropriate effectiveness-assessment criteria for novel blockchain-technology based systems. In summary, the following points are mentioned by the respondents: ease, transparency, affordability, communication- and feedback mechanisms, knowledge of blockchain systems and interoperability with existing databases. All respondents express the opinion that any successful new blockchain system must be easy to use and needs to support public servants in their daily routines. As the current processes are usually stressful and time consuming, a novel blockchain system is expected to solve these problems to gain full acceptance.

With respect to transparency, 67% of the respondents agree that a successful blockchain system must adequately take into account transparency and openness with respect to all aspects of the procurement process. One respondent suggests that the possibility of linking the procurement system with other national databases such as of the Corporate Affairs Commission, creates significantly more monitorable openness about the ownership of firms that win bids to execute contracts. According to the respondents, these criteria must be present and evaluated continuously to ensure that novel blockchain technology for e-procurement is active and functional.

## 5   A Framework for Blockchain-Based Procurement

Based on the findings in Sect. 4.2, we propose a novel framework that aims at enabling public organizations to implement and increase the adoption of blockchain-based procurement systems. In crafting this framework, a blockchain system is considered mainly because it possesses a shared, immutable and decentralized ledger for recording transactions and tracking assets in a network. Assets in this sense are anything of value and may be tangible, e.g., land and buildings, vehicles and machineries, or intangible such as intellectual properties, patents, copyrights, etc. These assets can be recorded, tracked and traded within a blockchain network.

The concepts of immutability, decentralization and trust renders blockchains a very transparent and efficient system for recording transactions as all relevant stakeholders maintain a level of equality and access in tracking processes. Blockchain technology provides security, ensures anonymity and enhances data integrity of transactions without any third party involved [26]. In addition, there is a time-stamp for data that is stored in a block linked to the preceding block for validation to create a chain of blocks. These features render blockchains a veritable choice for a secured and trusted system in business applications. The framework is presented as a set of recommendations in Table 1.

**Table 1.** Recommendation for blockchain implementation and -adoption in procurement processes.

| Problem category | Findings | Recommendation |
|---|---|---|
| Existing procurement system | Corruption resulting from manual processes, because existing systems involved in public procurement are not interoperable | Blockchain integration into existing systems |
| Stakeholder involvement and roles | Lack of a clear channel of communication and an effective system that can track the process | Blockchain-supported user engagement and collaboration |
| Criteria for assessing effectiveness | Lack of transparency and openness of procurement processes, affordability, feedback mechanisms, knowledge of the system | Blockchain-based project auditing and monitoring |

Three recommendations are presented and each recommendation is associated to a problem category. The first recommendation addresses the issue of corruption in existing processes due to the absence of interoperability in the systems that support the current procurement process. The proposed framework recommends using blockchain-enabled smart contracts [18] to facilitate interoperability of current systems. This results in increased automated processes and, thereby, reduces corruption cases in the procurement processes.

The second proposal involves engaging stakeholders in the procurement process and establishing clear communication channels. With roles that are clearly defined and assigned to all stakeholders, the citizens participate in eliciting service requirements before a particular project proposal is submitted. Thus, ensuring that, all stakeholders involved in the procurement processes behave according to legislation.

The final recommendation addresses the issue of assessing the effectiveness of the procurement system, processes and completed projects. The framework proposes a blockchain-based solution that is capable of tracking and monitoring the projects that are executed under the procurement. This increases the transparency and openness of the procurement processes and also provides an avenue for feedback mechanisms on executed projects.

Permissioned blockchain systems possess restrictions that limit the actions that can be taken by participants within a network to yield a strong option for future public sector application [5]. In addition, a private blockchain ensures that only parties involved in the e-procurement process can participate in the blockchain network, thereby ensuring the privacy of information, or data shared in a public procurement process. The study [13] shows how privacy can be ensured in public networks and thereby demonstrates the possibility of implementing this public procurement process in a public blockchain.

## 6 Mapping the Existing Procurement Process to a Blockchain

We apply the proposed blockchain-implementation framework presented in Sect. 5 for mapping on-chain activities for the current public procurement process. First, we present the *AS-IS* version of the procurement processes using BPMN (Business Process Model and Notation) [6] as a diagram notation and then show the activities that are executed on-chain based on our proposed framework. Section 6.1 shows the AS-IS version of the procurement process and Sect. 6.2 also comprises the on-chain activities.

### 6.1 AS-IS Procurement Process

The process begins with a procurement plan crafted by the MDA to ascertain current infrastructural and project gaps that need to be filled and provided for. Next, a budget is specified and sent to the National Assembly for appropriation. Projects that are not needed are cancelled and after the budget is passed by the National Assembly and signed into law by the executive, the projects are executed. Here, the budget is sent to the Parastatals Tender Board (PTB), or the Ministerial Tenders Board (MTB) for further checks and approval, in particular, on whether the price is within the approval thresholds. Once, the tender boards then approve the budget, a call for tender is placed in the news dailies for potential contractors. Otherwise, the budget is sent to the Bureau of Public Procurement. Once the latter receives the budget, they perform further reviews and approve if a budget is within their approval limits. Otherwise, the proposal is sent to the Federal Executive Council for further consideration and approval.

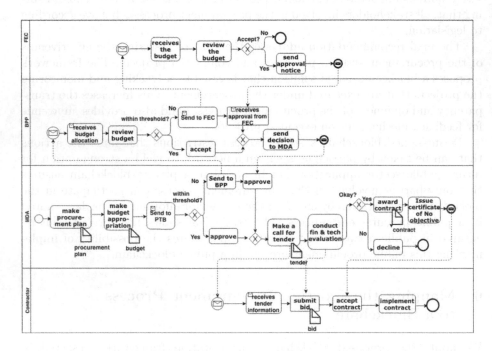

**Fig. 1.** Current AS-IS state of the public procurement process.

Once there is an approval for the project to be executed, a call for tender is issued on national dailies and contractors are expected to submit their bids. After the submission of bids, a technical- and financial evaluation is conducted, and the contract is awarded to the most qualified bidder with a certificate of no objection issued. Alternatively, the bid is declined if any irregularities are found during the technical- and financial evaluation stage. Once the process flow is completed, the project is implemented.

## 6.2   On-Chain Activities in the Procurement Process

These on-chain activities show the procurement activities that can be executed on the blockchain to achieve the goals of the recommendations in the proposed framework. First, we identify tasks in the existing process as shown in Fig. 1 that enable interoperability of all the silo systems of the organizations involved in the procurement process when they are implemented on a blockchain system. Thus, assets associated with these tasks are stored on the blockchain and accessed via the information systems of the collaborating parties. We further identify additional tasks for on-chain implementation to enable stakeholder involvement in outlining service requirements of submitted projects. Finally, we identify procurement tasks that need to be monitored on a blockchain by the citizens to increase transparency and auditability of the procurement process.

Table 2. Enabling on-chain tasks.

| Associated task | Assets stored on-chain | Stakeholders |
|---|---|---|
| *On-chain tasks enabling system interoperability* | | |
| Specify procurement plan | Procurement plan | MDA/BPP |
| Specify budget appropriation | Budget | BPP/FEC |
| Submit call to tender | Tender | All Stakeholders |
| Award contract | Contract | MDA/Contractor |
| Submit bid | Bid | MDA/Contractor |
| *Additional on-chain task enabling stakeholders engagement* | | |
| Vote on project needs | Prioritized project requirement | MDA/Citizens |
| *Additional on-chain task enabling project auditability and monitoring* | | |
| Vote on completed project | project assessment result | MDA/Citizens |

**Enabling Stakeholders Systems Interoperability:** Table 2 shows the executed tasks on blockchain and resulting assets that are also stored on-chain. This results in the interoperability of information systems of collaborating parties in the procurement process. Access to the assets are only granted to stakeholders that are associated to the task. Therefore, only a single version of an asset exists that cannot be illegally modified, or tampered by any malicious, or corrupt stakeholder in the procurement process.

**Enabling Stakeholders Engagement:** The current procurement process depicted in Fig. 1 does not show how stakeholders such as citizens are actively engaged in the procurement process. Based on our proposed framework, the citizens engage in the process by eliciting requirements included in a project. The call for tender shows the service requirements of the project and bids are submitted by contractors based on the requirements contained in the tender.

As depicted in Table 2, to engage citizens in the procurement process, an additional on-chain activity must be implemented such that citizens are able to vote on project requirements that are prioritized in the call for tender. The result of a vote is stored as an asset on the blockchain and the stakeholders involved are represented by the MDA and concerned citizens.

**Enabling Project Auditability and Monitoring:** The current procurement process does not show any activity resulting in transparent monitoring and an evaluation of completed projects. This is another main source of corruption in the existing process, since projects are not properly monitored and payments are issued to contractors that already failed to execute according to the requirements listed in the project tenders. Therefore, an additional on-chain activity is required to render the evaluation of completed projects more democratic and transparent. Using blockchain-enabled smart-contracts, citizens can track projects based on the requirements on the tender and vote 'success' when the executed projects successfully satisfy the requirements in a tender. Otherwise, the project is considered as failure. As per Table 2, further actions can be taken by the MDAs based on the citizens' project assessment result.

## 7  Conclusion

This research explores the existing public procurement processes to understand the overall structure, complexities and challenges that need to be faced in proposing a workable blockchain-based framework. Twelve high-level stakeholders and experts we interview for this purpose. The main challenges that we identify are corruption and a lack of transparency within the procurement process. An in-depth analysis reveals the underlying structural- and communication issues. On this basis, we recommend an implementation framework that aims at interoperability of all the silo systems of the involved organizations. Thus, all assets associated with crucial tasks are stored on a blockchain and accessed via the collaborating parties – creating more openness, transparency and trust.

As a further outcome, we discover that the current procurement process does not adequately support citizen engagement. For this issue, we propose an additional on-chain activity so that citizens can vote on project requirements that are prioritized during the call for a tender stage. Finally, we seek to find answers to the important aspects of project monitoring, evaluation and auditability. Our respondents mention that most of the budgeted projects are only poorly executed, or not completed at all. With respect to this, we propose an additional on-chain activity that renders the evaluation of the completed projects more democratic and transparent – by giving citizens access to track projects based on the tender requirements and allowing them to give feedback about the success, or failure based on these requirements.

A limitation of this research is the generalization power given the focus on one e-procurement case of Nigeria. Secondly, the cost of implication for the proposed blockchain-based system is also not fully considered, especially additional costs associated to blockchain activities, i.e., commonly referred to as transaction fee. As future research, we consider investigating the factors and challenges that deepen, or affect citizen involvement in the usage of blockchain technology. Secondly, the aspect of security and privacy for blockchain technology is not fully considered in this research.

# References

1. Abodei, E., Norta, A., Azogu, I., Udokwu, C., Draheim, D.: Blockchain technology for enabling transparent and traceable government collaboration in public project processes of developing economies. In: Pappas, I.O., et al. (eds.) I3E 2019. LNCS, vol. 11701, pp. 464–475. Springer, Cham (2019). https://doi.org/10.1007/978-3-030-29374-1_38
2. Adewole, A.: Governance reform and the challenge of implementing public procurement law regime across Nigerian state and local governments. Int. J. Public Adm. Manage. Res. (IJPAMR) **2**(4), 25–32 (2014)
3. Akaba, T.I.: A framework for the adoption of a blockchain-based e-procurement system: a case study of Nigeria. Master's thesis, Tallinn University of Technology, Tallinn, Estonia (2019)
4. Azogu, I., Norta, A., Draheim, A.: A framework for the adoption of blockchain technology in healthcare information management systems a case study of Nigeria. In: Proceedings of ICEGOV 2019: The 12th International Conference on Theory and Practice of Electronic Governance. ACM (2019)
5. Baliga, A.: Understanding blockchain consensus models. Persistent **2017**(4), 1–14 (2017)
6. Chinosi, M., Trombetta, A.: BPMN: an introduction to the standard. Comput. Stan. Interfaces **34**(1), 124–134 (2012)
7. Draheim, D., Koosapoeg, K., Lauk, M., Pappel, I., Pappel, I., Tepandi, J.: The design of the Estonian governmental document exchange classification framework. In: Kő, A., Francesconi, E. (eds.) EGOVIS 2016. LNCS, vol. 9831, pp. 33–47. Springer, Cham (2016). https://doi.org/10.1007/978-3-319-44159-7_3
8. Ezeh, M.E.: Public procurement reform strategies: achieving effective and sustainable outcomes. In: CIPS Pan Africa Conference. National Theatre, Accra, Ghana, pp. 21–22 (2013)
9. Fayomi, I.O.: Public procurement and due process policy in Nigeria: trust, prospects and challenges. Peak J. Soc. Sci. Humanit. **1**(4), 39–45 (2013)
10. Geissbauer, R., Weissbarth, R., Wetzstein, J.: Procurement 4.0: are you ready for the digital revolution? Strategy - part of the PwC network, 4 May 2016
11. Khan, N.: Public Procurement Fundamentals: Lessons from and for the Field (Includes A Simple Step-By-Step Generic Procurement Manual). Emerald Publishing Limited, Bingley (2018)
12. Kuo, T.T., Kim, H.E., Ohno-Machado, L.: Blockchain distributed ledger technologies for biomedical and health care applications. J. Am. Med. Inform. Assoc. **24**(6), 1211–1220 (2017)
13. Ladleif, J., Weske, M., Weber, I.: Modeling and enforcing blockchain-based choreographies. In: Hildebrandt, T., van Dongen, B.F., Röglinger, M., Mendling, J. (eds.) BPM 2019. LNCS, vol. 11675, pp. 69–85. Springer, Cham (2019). https://doi.org/10.1007/978-3-030-26619-6_7

14. Lazuashvili, N., Norta, A., Draheim, D.: Integration of blockchain technology into a land registration system for immutable traceability: a casestudy of Georgia. In: Di Ciccio, C., et al. (eds.) BPM 2019. LNBIP, vol. 361, pp. 219–233. Springer, Cham (2019). https://doi.org/10.1007/978-3-030-30429-4_15

15. Maguire, M., Delahunt B.: Doing a thematic analysis: a practical, step-by-step guide for learning and teaching scholars. AISHE-J: All Ire. J. Teach. Learn. Higher Educ. **9**(3) (2017)

16. Nicholson, J.: The library as a facilitator: how bitcoin and block chain technology can aid developing nations. Ser. Libr. **73**(3–4), 357–364 (2017)

17. Nicoletti, B.: A business model for insurtech initiatives. The Future of FinTech. PSFST, pp. 211–249. Springer, Cham (2017). https://doi.org/10.1007/978-3-319-51415-4_8

18. Norta, A.: Self-aware smart contracts with legal relevance. In: 2018 International Joint Conference on Neural Networks (IJCNN), pp. 1–8. IEEE, July 2018

19. Norta, A., Draheim, D.: In: First Workshop on Blockchains for Inter-organizational Collaboration. Proceedings of the CAiSE 2018 International Workshops, volume 316 of Lecture Notes in Business Information Processing, pp. 99–102. Springer (2018)

20. Norta, A., Leiding, B., Draheim, D., Karastoyanova, D., Pufahl, L., Schöning, S.: In: BIOC & FAiSE 2019 - Joint Workshop on Blockchains for Inter-organizational Collaboration and Flexible Advanced Information Systems. Proceedings of the CAiSE 2019 International Workshops. LNBIP, Springer (2019)

21. Norta, A., Matulevičius, R., Leiding, B.: Safeguarding a formalized blockchain-enabled identity-authentication protocol by applying security risk-oriented patterns. Comput. Secur. **86**, 253–269 (2019)

22. Olatunji, S.O., Olawumi, T.O., Odeyinka, H.A.: Nigeria's public procurement law-puissant issues and projected amendments. Public Policy Adm. Res. **6**(6), 73–85 (2016)

23. Ølnes, S., Ubacht, J., Janssen, M.: Blockchain in government: benefits and implications of distributed ledger technology for information sharing. Gov. Inf. Q. **34**(3), 355–364 (2017)

24. Toyoda, K., Mathiopoulos, P.T., Sasase, I., Ohtsuki, T.: A novel blockchain-based product ownership management system (POMS) for anti-counterfeits in the post supply chain. IEEE Access **5**, 17465–17477 (2017)

25. Udokwu, C., Kormiltsyn, A., Thangalimodzi, K., Norta, A.: The state of the art for blockchain-enabled smart-contract applications in the organization. In: 2018 Ivannikov Ispras Open Conference (ISPRAS), pp. 137–144. IEEE (2018)

26. Yli-Huumo, J., Ko, D., Choi, S., Park, S., Smolander, K.: Where is current research on blockchain technology? - a systematic review. PLoS ONE **11**(10), e0163477 (2016)

# Blockchain Technology for Empowering Patient-Centred Healthcare: A Pilot Study

Themba Makubalo, Brenda Scholtz[(✉)] [iD],
and Temitope Oluwaseyi Tokosi [iD]

Nelson Mandela University, Port Elizabeth, South Africa
Brenda.Scholtz@mandela.ac.za

**Abstract.** Patient-centred care allows patients to have complete autonomy in managing their health information and encourages patients to be proactive. Unfortunately, most patients do not have access to their complete health information as they are stored across the various institutions that they have visited over their lifetime. The purpose of this paper is to report on an investigation into developing a mobile system for patient-centered healthcare using blockchain technology. A design science research approach was used to design, develop and evaluate a prototype that implemented a three-tier architecture using blockchain. Formative evaluations of the prototype revealed that the system could successfully support patient-managed healthcare. The implications of this project would be changing the way patients and healthcare practitioners interact with each other by improving the quality of clinical encounters by allowing patients access to their health information, sharing the information with healthcare practitioners and both parties collaborating in the development of a treatment plan.

**Keywords:** Blockchain · Healthcare · Patient-centred

## 1 Introduction

South Africa plans on implementing the National Health Insurance (NHI) scheme to provide cost effective access to healthcare for all citizens. Once the scheme is in place, it is believed that the focus of the healthcare industry will shift towards preventative care and health promotion. This would require the industry to become patient-centred. Paper-based filing has major risks such as being vulnerable to damage by elements such as fire and water and medical records being lost [7]. In addition, backups are time and resource intensive and security of paper-based filing is limited to locked storage, with minimal capabilities of logging access to medical records. Various types of electronic records exist, each having a different purpose [13]. For example, an electronic medical record (EMR) typically contains detailed patient encounter information such as an encounter summary, medical history, test results, and allergy details. EMRs are owned and managed by professionals from a single institution. An electronic health record (EHR) is an aggregated collection of a patient's health information collected from multiple professionals at multiple institutions [19]. It ensures that a patient's complete medical record is available to an authorised practitioner during patient

© IFIP International Federation for Information Processing 2020
Published by Springer Nature Switzerland AG 2020
M. Hattingh et al. (Eds.): I3E 2020, LNCS 12066, pp. 15–26, 2020.
https://doi.org/10.1007/978-3-030-44999-5_2

encounters. No country in Africa has been successful in implementing a nationwide EHR system [21]. EHR and EMR are used interchangeably in the literature but the term EHR is used to refer to all electronic records for health information in this study.

## 2 Literature Overview

Paper-based filing has major risks such as being vulnerable to being damaged by elements such as fire and water; medical records being lost and creating backups requiring time and intensive resources [7]. The security of paper-based filing is limited to locked storage, with minimal capabilities of logging access to medical records. A major issue with paper-based filing is illegibility. Illegibility causes delays in treating patients as time is wasted by trying to understand what is written, contacting the author or redoing the procedure to reproduce the results. The problems associated with paper-based filing are solved with electronic records. Electronic records such as EHR use secure information systems to store and access patient health information and to ensure that the information contained is up-to-date and available when needed [13].

The challenges of implementing EHR systems are a lack of consistent supply of electricity, governmental support and the required infrastructure [21]. Despite these challenges, various vendors in SA have attempted to implement their own EHR systems, built on differing architecture which fail to interoperate with each other [21]. Disinterest stems from the belief that measurable benefits (such as finances) are better realised within their own organisation. Thus, to gain the benefits of an EHR system, patients are limited to clinical encounters with organisations that utilise the specific EHR system. This devalues the effectiveness and efficiency of patients managing their own healthcare. The biggest challenge preventing the adoption of EHR systems in the health industry is the resistance from practitioners [22].

An Accenture study on SA patients clearly indicated that electronic records are viewed as being more reliable than paper-based records [13]. It was indicated by 51% of respondents that time was wasted when having to recount their medical history to all the practitioners that they visited. Surprisingly, those with medical aid are willing to spend up to R100 extra per month to have their health records maintained electronically [13]. Muchangi and Nzuki [24] revealed that patients are not confident in using EMR systems that do not comply with established standards as they fear that their medical confidentiality and security might be compromised. Currently, the SA government lacks legislation and regulations regarding EMR implementation which has led to misuse and poor compliance by organisations [21]. Until the government develops standards for EMR, common guidelines must be followed in developing such systems.

Various technologies can be utilised to create patient-centred healthcare systems but blockchain offers a unique solution. Blockchain makes use of features (security, stability, fault-tolerance) to allow a network to remain fully functional even if a node has failed [16]. For example, each time a transaction occurs, a transaction request is transmitted to all the nodes, making each node aware of the fact as well as the time the event took place. Nodes then validate the authenticity of the block through a majority consensus and then several transactions are put together into a block. The block is then inserted into the ledger by linking to the last block that was inserted into the ledger.

Thus, as blocks are continuously inserted to the ledger, a long series of blocks is formed, hence the term blockchain. Each block is marked with a timestamp and a hash of the previous block, preventing alterations from being made to the previous block [10]. An example of blockchain is the cryptocurrency Bitcoin.

Centralised systems exhibit at least one of the following shortcomings: instability due to having a central point of failure, security shortages due to being more vulnerable to central attacks and greater potential of unethical operations due to the presence of a central authority [16]. Decentralised systems do not have a central authority. Instead, authority is shared amongst each computer (node), with each of them having equal authority [25]. Distributed systems divide computations into smaller computations to be performed by multiple nodes. Distributed and decentralised systems are highly secure as a central point to attack is lacking. This feature also makes them stable and fault-tolerant. Since each node has equal authority, unethical operations are unlikely to be performed [16]. Blockchain makes use of these features and benefits to allow the network to remain fully functional even if a node has failed.

The purpose of this paper is to report on an investigation into patient-centered healthcare and the potential of blockchain technology for supporting this system. Its contribution is the development of a blockchain technology and lessons learnt that can support other research into patient-centered healthcare.

The structure of the paper is as follows: The next section provides an overview of the design methodology adopted in the research. Section 4 illustrates the proposed requirements and design of the prototype whilst Sect. 5 discusses the design and development thereof. In Sect. 6 the pilot study protocol is explained. The formative evaluation that was conducted is highlighted in Sect. 7. In Sects. 8 and 9 a discussion of the findings and conclusions are presented.

## 3 Methodology

The project made use of the Design Science Research (DSR) methodology as proposed by [3]. This methodology creates new knowledge in a given domain through the design and creation of an innovative system that solves relevant problems or achieves substantial improvements [18]. In this study, DSR was used to examine the shortcomings of existing EHR systems and to design a mobile system that utilises blockchain technology. The five steps of DSR were iteratively conducted namely, problem awareness, suggestion, development (circumscription), evaluation and conclusion (operation and goal knowledge). A prototype was designed and developed as a proof-of-concept and the usability of the system was formatively evaluated in a pilot study.

## 4 Proposed Design

Documentation analysis is a requirement elicitation technique that collects, reviews and analyses existing documentation to gather requirements [14, 15]. These two activities formed part of the problem awareness stage of DSR in this project.

## 4.1   System and Data Requirements

The system requirements were identified from a literature review and an extant systems analysis of existing systems and then grouped into core and support components. The requirements of the first core component was to facilitate the storage of and access to a patient's health-related information. This information consists of a patient's personal information, medical practitioner information and health information. Personal information includes full name, date of birth, family history, emergency contact person(s), allergies and medical aid. The practitioners' information includes the full name of the practitioner, the profession, the medical practice number, place of work, years of experience and any malpractice claims. Information related to the patient's health consists of diagnoses, prescriptions, treatment plans and medical test results.

The requirements for the second core component is to facilitate medication adherence for patients. The purchase of prescribed medication should be logged. The data generated from the medication adherence component should be aggregated and form part of a patient's health information. The system should be able to interface with an external medication website that provides details of active ingredients, pricing etc.

The support component should facilitate communication between the two parties (patients and medical practitioners), which is achieved through a personal health community (PHC). Using a PHC gives patients control over who is a member of the community. This prevents any unwanted entities from contributing or collecting information for their own purposes. This component should also provide functionality for an Online Health Community (OHC). OHCs are an example of how social media can be incorporated into healthcare [20]. OHCs unite individuals with a shared goal or interest in healthcare. OHCs comprise of patients with a condition (such as ALS patients), a group of practitioners with a shared medical interest (such as neurologists), or a mixture of both. OHC members interact using modern communication technologies such as blogs, chats, forums, and wikis. OHCs can be classified into open and closed communities. Open OHCs are public and its contents can be accessed by anyone. All members of the community can contribute to its content.

For the data design, the data classes were based on those of the Fast Healthcare Interoperability Resources (FHIR) standard, which is a draft standard describing data formats and elements (known as "resources") and an API for exchanging electronic health records [4, 5]. The standard was created by the health level seven international (HL7) healthcare standards organisation.

In the extant systems analysis conducted in this paper, six systems were reviewed. Nine criteria were used in reviewing each system namely database, multiple users, communication, notifications, data sharing, flexible scheduling, community type, visual aids and statistics and charts. AidIT was the only system identified that provides data storage and access and is a mobile EMR system that allows patients to manage their records and facilitates the exchange of these records between patients and practitioners [8]. The AidIT system provides patients with a personal health folder that organises a patient's data into five separate categories namely: the patient's personal information (e.g. address, date of birth, photograph and information regarding his/her insurance profile); the patient's general medical history (e.g. past injuries, chronic conditions, allergies and healthcare encounters); the patient's past examinations and relevant diagnoses along with ordered lab tests and their results; the patient's current and past medication prescriptions, along with the quantity and dosage instructions required for each medication; and the patient's care plan. The patient's care plan is designed by the patient's practitioners as a list of actions to be carried out by the patient. AidT's shortcomings includes non-functionality for tracking and monitoring a patient's adherence to their medication schedule. In addition, EMR presentation does not indicate what is important and professionals can amend prior medical records which can create inconsistencies.

## 4.2   System Architecture

The system used a three-tier architecture, which consists of three layers: the application, storage and logic layer. The benefits to using a three-tier architecture is to provide security, performance and code maintenance [2]. The architecture is illustrated in Fig. 1.

The application layer is where users (patients and professionals) interact with the system to perform tasks such as registering to the system and posting messages. How the information is presented to users is also handled in this layer. The storage layer was split between a database and a blockchain network. The variability, relevance (null voids) and design of blockchain complexity of the structure of health records can limit how they would be stored in a blockchain environment. Each node in a blockchain has a replica of all information stored in the ledger. It would be impractical to have each node store all the health records as they can consume a considerable amount of space, require intensive bandwidth usage and would be wasteful on network resources.

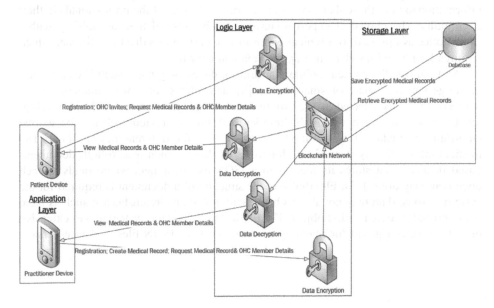

**Fig. 1.**  System architecture.

Rather, in the adopted design, the blockchain functions as an access-control manager for health records. Only the personal and professional information of patients and professionals is stored on the blockchain and the patients' health data is stored on a database with the blockchain having encrypted index pointers to the data contained in the database.

The logic layer is spread across the separate components (application, database and blockchain network). For this layer to function seamlessly, the three components must communicate with each other effectively, which is achieved by using a combination of APIs, and private-public key encryption protocols.

## 5   Design and Development

Design is iterative in nature, cycling through design–evaluation–redesign activities [15]. In DSR, iteration is an important part of the process. In this study the design and development of the system (the artefact), was iteratively designed, developed and evaluated. Two alternative wireframe prototype designs were proposed. A walkthrough evaluation was conducted on both wireframes by an expert reviewer as proposed by [1]. AdobeXD was chosen to prototype the two alternative designs as the software is a free, simple to use platform that allows for designing high fidelity wireframes that can be interacted with to simulate the system's usage. The feedback received indicated that the first wireframe was too cluttered while the second wireframe had a professional feel and made better use of hand gestures for navigation. The second wireframe design was therefore selected for further development and sample screenshots are shown in Fig. 2. A second walkthrough of the second wireframe was undertaken by a second expert reviewer. The primary feedback received was to limit the viewing of the professionals' information to only those that have been referred to by one of the professionals in their community. The choice of expert reviewers was because of their availability within short notice as opposed to a typical end-user (patient) and medical practitioner which requires lengthy ethics clearance application and approval.

Android was the chosen mobile platform for developing the system because it has the largest market share of smartphones [6], and allows for a wide audience to be reached. Java was selected as the programming language since the Android development kit is best suited to Java's libraries and Java's previous release for mobile environments makes it well suited for developing for different devices [11]. The medical information is stored in a MongoDB database, which is a NoSQL document-based database that stores its records in a JSON-like document where fields in each document may differ [23]. Flexibility in the structure of a document is required for the system as some data may not always be present in certain circumstances; such as there being no end date in a period object. The FHIR API, which the system makes extensive use of, provides support for mapping its data objects to JSON files, and vice-versa.

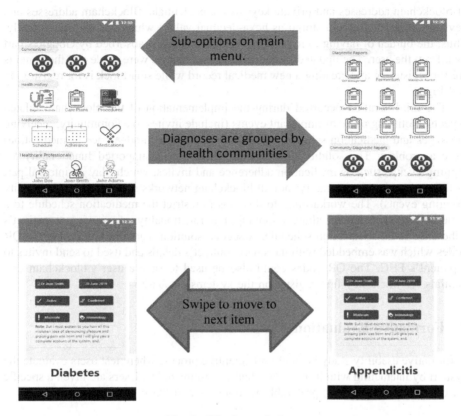

**Fig. 2.** Wireframe design.

## 6  Pilot Study

The first iteration of developing the system began with developing the two wireframes and the second wireframe was selected for implementation. The selected wireframe was able to artificially simulate how the final system could work and provided a good reference point for the development of the system. The second iteration followed soon after selecting the development environment. The major changes from the first iteration were the use of floating action buttons, making extensive use of native mobile features and incorporating labelled tabs for grouped items and efficient login credential persistence. Floating action buttons perform a primary action on a given screen [12]; these buttons appear in front of the screen's content for clear visibility and use menu icons that the user is familiar with to assist in identifying what the button's purpose is.

Android's native contacts and calendar features were utilised as a service to simplify adding emergency contacts and including reminders for medication adherence. Efficiently persisting the login credentials of the user was accomplished by incorporating Google's smart lock feature which is accessible by using permissions on Android smartphones. Persisting user credentials is very important, as the system will make use of blockchain addresses and private keys as the credentials. Blockchain addresses and keys are very lengthy and stored as hexa-decimal values which are not user-friendly. Thus, the burden of having to remember login credentials is absorbed by Google smart lock from the user. The updated system after these changes were made and the benefits are for registering and creating a new medical record while smart lock is for registration and login.

The third iteration occurred during the implementation of the blockchain related aspects. Notifying users of important events (include invites to a community; receiving messages and medication schedules, being informed of non-adherence to medication) were a problem. The solidity development environment supported functionality for logging events, such as medication adherence and invites, which play an integral part of the notification functionality; not all blockchain networks support this functionality (logging events). The workaround to this was to restrict the medication schedule to a patients' native calendar; thus, removing the functionality of viewing a patient's adherence to the medication schedule. A second solution workaround is using the QR codes which was embedded with the smart contract's details and used to send invites to a patient's PHC. The QR codes could also be used to save a user's blockchain credentials for when they first register on the systems database.

## 7 Formative Evaluation

A formative usability study is an almost scientific process where test users evaluate the system by interacting with it in a controlled environment [1]. Users are given a specific set of tasks to accomplish, preferably without the assistance of the facilitator.

### 7.1 Evaluation Objectives

The goal of the evaluation was to assess the user interaction of the system to identify any shortcomings that could be modified to provide an engaging experience for the user. Evaluation of the system served three objectives. Firstly, to identify which functionalities of the system were implemented correctly or cause the system to fail completely. The second objective was to quantify the usability of the system and gain feedback from the evaluators. The third objective was to use the feedback to make improvements to the system. The tasks to be completed by the users cover all the system's requirements. These tasks were chosen to evaluate functionality completeness, navigability, users' subjective satisfaction and user performance; such as comprehension and learnability. The users could directly interact with the system's interface by tapping buttons, swiping to move between screens or scrolling to view lists or enter data.

### 7.2 Evaluation Methodology

An expert panel of two participants was used; both were researchers in the field of Computer Science. An expert panel utilises participants who were specifically chosen to be part of the formative study [15]. The first expert was a post-doctoral researcher with a PhD in Computer Science and the second expert was a doctoral candidate. The evaluation was conducted inside a computer laboratory, which is a controlled environment allowing for the capturing of data in an accurate way without the users being distracted or interrupted by external factors, while also ensuring that the predefined tasks are performed and completed within a reasonable time frame. The participants were separated from each other and only interacted with each other when necessary. Each expert was provided with an Android smartphone to complete the tasks. One expert completed tasks related to the practitioner use cases and the other the tasks related to a patient's use cases.

The instrument used was the Post-Study System Usability Questionnaire (PSSUQ) as proposed by Lewis [9], which is a comprehensive questionnaire that provides a host of insightful information from analysing the results of the usability study. PSSUQ is comprehensive in that it provides a set of selected questions and the user does not have to add in extra comments if he/she does not want to, since the questions provide sufficient information. The questionnaire is reliable, free and addresses the usability characteristics of system usefulness, information quality, interface quality and overall satisfaction [17]. Additional questions were included to obtain the experts' views of interacting with the system. PSSUQ was the more available questionnaire during the study period because of its ability to meet the researchers study objective. A new questionnaire known as the mHealth app usability questionnaire (MAUQ) was recently developed by [26] after the completion of this study and so could not be used.

Dummy blockchain accounts were created and provided for each expert so that they were able to register their details on the system. Additional patient and practitioner accounts were provided for the experts in case of a failure of registration, creating and joining a community. The background, goals and tasks of the system were explained to the panel and they were encouraged to ask questions. Support were provided to the participants if they struggled to complete a task, and a note was made of which tasks required assistance.

## 8 Results

The results revealed that the primary concern for the system were the register (practitioner), accept community invite and update details use cases. The code that performs these use cases needs to be re-examined and may require recreating the circumstances for the failure to identify the cause of the problem and then making relevant changes to solve the problem without requiring massive changes to the remaining aspects of the system. The majority of the errors made occurred when the participants attempted a new task without a reference point as to how to successfully complete it; this is also where the facilitator was required to assist the participants in completing the task, which increased the task time. However, as the participants got used to the system, fewer errors were made, and the task times were reduced when attempting tasks that have similar steps, indicating that the system can be learnt over time.

The user satisfaction results indicated that the user interface for the patient use cases had higher satisfaction levels than that of the practitioner use cases. The patient expert perceived the consistency in the layout of the system's user interface to be the most helpful component in successfully completing tasks and found the use of icons helpful in understanding the meaning of some of the information presented to the screen. The practitioner expert perceived the system to provide poor user satisfaction due to the user interface being dis-organised and the icons being too domain specific resulting in some confusion. The practitioner expert also found it hard to keep track of the current position in the system which resulted in errors being made. The panel both mentioned that the system takes too long to respond, and that more feedback should be provided to the user when performing actions.

The major problems related to providing clarity on how to navigate the system to complete tasks, a lack of feedback from the actions the participants performed and the system's slow response time. The slow response of the system was due to having to query both the blockchain network as well as the database that stores the data. The smart contract hosted on a blockchain network contains the indices of the patient's medical records which are stored in the database. Thus, the smart contract is first queried to obtain the correct indices and then the indices are used to retrieve the medical records from the database. Converting the data from its representation in the data layer to its representation in the system layer, and vice-versa, also contributed to the lag in response from the system.

The system design made use of tabs, whereby, when a screen that requires data from the database is opened, a query to obtain all the necessary data is performed. This affected the community screen the most as all the patient's medical data must be queried before displaying the screen. A redesign of the system should thus restrict the queries to only be executed when necessary. The system's layout needs to be improved to emphasise frequently performed tasks by making the components used to complete those tasks the most prominent on the screen. Related functionality needs to be grouped together to avoid complex navigation steps being performed by users.

The system's redesign emphasised the incorporation of dialogs to the layout of the user interface while reducing the focus of using tabs. Dialogs provide a convenient method for solving most of the issues affecting the system. Dialogs are modal windows that appear at the forefront of a system's content to provide users with important information or requesting decisions that need to be made [12]. By utilising dialogs instead of tabs, only the selected type of medical information will be retrieved from the database; thus, reducing the response time as well as saving the amount of memory required to store the retrieved data. Also, all options will be clearly seen by users instead of having to scroll through tabs to get to the appropriate screen.

## 9   Discussions and Future Research

Having piloted the system and taking notes of issues experienced by the expert panel, future research study will conduct a summative usability evaluation of the system as well as provide a discussion of the results. Summative evaluations assess the success of the system accomplishing its functional requirements [17]. Unlike a formative evaluation, test users are given a list of all the tasks that can be performed using the system, which serves as a primary criterion for evaluating the system. The results will be discussed in future research output(s) where the blockchain technology app will be applied to a broader community of a larger population.

For future research and improvements, this system will be tested again on a sample population of larger size within an academic institution community. This will enable the researcher(s) assess users' satisfaction with an understanding of what patients' and medical practitioner's perceptions are of the system. All ethical considerations, applications and approvals are in processing for this second test.

# References

1. Dennis, A., Wixom, B.H., Tegarden, D.: System Analysis Design UML Version 2.0: An Object-Orientated System approach, 4th edn. Wiley, Hoboken (2012)
2. Elgendi, I., Munasinghe, K.S., Jamalipour, A.: A three-tier SDN architecture for DenseNets. In: 2015 9th International Conference on Signal Processing and Communication Systems (ICSPCS), pp. 1–7. IEEE (2015)
3. Hevner, A.R.: A three cycle view of design science research a three cycle view of design science research. Scand. J. Inf. Syst. 19(2), 4 (2007)
4. HL7.org. http://hl7.org/fhir/condition.html. Accessed 30 July 2019a
5. HL7.org. https://www.hl7.org/FHIR/. Accessed 25 Apr 2019b
6. Itfirms. https://www.itfirms.co/reasons-why-you-should-be-looking-to-develop-an-android-system-in-2018/. Accessed 06 Sept 2019
7. Kleynhans, A.: Is South Africa ready for a national Electronic Health Record (EHR)?. Doctoral dissertation: UNISA (2011)
8. Lamprinakos, G.C., Mousas, A.S., Kapsalis, P., Kaklamani, D.I., Lakovos, S.: Using FHIR to develop a healthcare mobile systemlication. In: 2014 4th International Conference on Wireless Mobile Communication and Healthcare - Transforming Healthcare Through Innovations in Mobile and Wireless Technologies (MOBIHEALTH), pp. 132–135 (2014)
9. Lewis, J.R.: Psychometric evaluation of an after-scenario questionnaire for computer usability studies: the ASQ. ACM SIGCHI Bull. 23(1), 78–81 (1991)
10. Liu, J., Li, X., Ye, L., Zhang, H., Du, X., Guizani, M.: http://arxiv.org/abs/1811.03223. Accessed 18 Aug 2018
11. Maresco, J.: https://generalassemb.ly/blog/what-is-android-development/. Accessed 06 Sept 2019
12. Material Design. https://material.io/design/components/buttons-floating-action-button.html#. Accessed 13 Sept 2019
13. Mostert-Phipps, N., Korpela, M., Pottas, D.: Improving continuity of care through the use of electronic records: a South African perspective. S. Afr. Fam. Pract. 54(4), 326–331 (2014)
14. O'Leary, Z.: The Essential Guide to Doing Your Research Project, 3rd edn. SAGE Publications Inc., Newbury Park (2017). Edited by J. Seaman
15. Preece, J., Sharp, H., Rogers, Y.: Interaction Design: Beyond Human-Computer Interaction, 4th edn. Wiley, Chichester (2015)
16. Singhal, B., Dhameja, G., Panda, P.S.: https://doi.org/10.1007/978-1-4842-3444-0. Accessed 06 Sept 2018
17. Tullis, T., Albert, B.: Measuring the User Experience, 2nd edn. Morgan Kaufmann, Waltham (2013)
18. Vaishnavi, V.K., Kuechler, W.: Design Science Research Methods and Patterns: Innovating Information and Communication Technology. CRC Press, Boca Raton (2015)

19. Vennik, F., et al.: Personal health communities: a phenomenological study of a new health-care concept. Health Expect. **18**(6), 2091–2106 (2014)
20. Aarts, J.W., Kremer, J.A., Munneke, M., Bloem, B.R., Faber, M.J., van der Eijk, M.: Using online health communities to deliver patient-centered care to people with chronic conditions. J. Med. Internet Res. **15**(6), 115–124 (2013)
21. Katurura, M.C., Cilliers, L.: Electronic health record system in the public healthcare sector of South Africa: a systematic review research methodology. Afr. J. Prim. Healthc. Fam. Med. **10**(1), 1–8 (2018)
22. Mammen, A., Weeks, R.: Electronic medical record (EMR) technology acceptance by healthcare professionals in South Africa. In: Proceedings of PICMET 2014 conference: Portland International Center of Management of Engineering and Technology; Infrastructure and Service Integration, pp. 3539–3548. PICMET, Portland (2014)
23. MongoDB. What is MongoDB? https://www.mongodb.com/what-is-mongodb. Accessed 07 Aug 2019
24. Muchangi, D., Nzuki, D.M.: Determinants of electronic health in developing countries. Int. J. Arts Commerce **3**(3), 49–60 (2014)
25. Raval, S.: Decentralized Applications - Harnessing Bitcoin's Blockchain Technology, 1st edn. O'Reilly Media, Newton (2016). Edited by T. McGovern
26. Zhou, L., Bao, J., Setiawan, I.M.A., Saptono, A., Parmanto, B.: The mHealth app usability questionnaire (MAUQ): development and validation study. JMIR mHealth uHealth **7**(4), e11500 (2019)

# Exploring the Disruptiveness of Cryptocurrencies: A Causal Layered Analysis-Based Approach

Matti Mäntymäki[1(✉)], Milla Wirén[1], and A. K. M. Najmul Islam[2]

[1] Turku School of Economics, Turku, Finland
{matti.mantymaki,milla.wiren}@utu.fi
[2] Department of Future Technologies, University of Turku,
20014 Turku, Finland
najmul.islam@utu.fi

**Abstract.** The purpose of this study is to explore whether the diffusion of cryptocurrencies represents a disruptive change and what is the potential magnitude of this change. To this end, we take disruptive innovation theory as our point of departure to scrutinize cryptocurrencies as an instance of socio-technical change. We employ Causal Layered Analysis to develop our four-layer analytical framework to conceptually examine the changes pertained by the diffusion of cryptocurrencies. We provide examples of changes company-level, industry-level as well as societal changes where cryptocurrencies have played a central role. On a company level, cryptocurrencies provide a cost-efficient means for cross-border money transfer and thus pose a significant threat to the existing intermediary-based business models. On an industry level, many central banks are experimenting with crypto- or digital currencies. On a societal level, cryptocurrencies play an important role in particularly when the traditional institutions and societal structures collapse. For example, in Venezuela's recent political and economic crisis, cryptocurrencies contributed to the development of a parallel financial system when the bolivar practically lost its value. Our study provides an analytical framework to systematically evaluate the potential disruptive nature of cryptocurrencies as well as other blockchain-based technologies.

**Keywords:** Blockchain · Cryptocurrencies · Disruption · Disruptive innovation · Causal Layered Analysis

## 1 Introduction

Since the inception of Bitcoin in 2009 [1], thousands of cryptocurrencies (also known as Altcoin) have emerged that use the blockchain technology [2, 3]. Five most valuable cryptocurrencies, Bitcoin, Etherum, XRP, Bitcoin Cash, and EOS have a total market cap of more than 200 billion USD[1]. The rapid development of blockchain or distributed ledger technologies has paved way for various Financial Technology (FinTech)

---

[1] Top 100 Cryptocurrencies by Market Capitalization https://coinmarketcap.com.

© IFIP International Federation for Information Processing 2020
Published by Springer Nature Switzerland AG 2020
M. Hattingh et al. (Eds.): I3E 2020, LNCS 12066, pp. 27–38, 2020.
https://doi.org/10.1007/978-3-030-44999-5_3

innovations. Alongside venture capitalists and FinTech startups, major banks and stock exchanges have rolled out blockchain-based products and services. Furthermore, according to Barontini and Holden [4] several central banks have established explorative as well as experimental blockchain-based initiatives as a part of the prospect for central bank-issued crypto- or digital currencies.

All in all, there is vivid debate among practitioners and academics if, or to what extent, applications of blockchain such as cryptocurrencies will have a disruptive impact on the global financial sector, central banks, or the dominant role of traditional currencies [5–10]. At the same time, however, it is largely unclear what qualifies a change to be disruptive [11–13], i.e. how to conceptually and theoretically distinguish between disruptive and more evolutionary change.

As a result, the research question this study addresses is two-fold: (1) does the diffusion of cryptocurrencies represent a disruptive change, and (2) what is the potential magnitude of this change? To this end, we build on disruptive innovation theory [14–17] to scrutinize cryptocurrencies as an instance of socio-technical change [18–22] and conceptually explore its disruptiveness through the Causal Layered Analysis [23–26].

With this paper, we make two main contributions: first we use our CLA-based analytical framework to discuss and conceptually scrutinize the disruptive potential of cryptocurrencies. Second, we discuss and present a conceptual distinction between normal and disruptive change that potentially allows identifying disruptive potential ex ante.

The paper proceeds as follows: in the second section we discuss the concept of disruptive change. Thereafter we present and discuss the CLA as a method for analyzing ongoing socio-technical change. The fourth section focuses on cryptocurrencies. In the fifth section we discuss the disruptiveness of cryptocurrencies through our CLA-based analytical framework. The sixth and final section concludes the paper.

## 2  Disruptive Change

The concept of disruption entered the management literature from innovation studies, as Christensen was puzzled about why do successful companies sometimes fail seemingly overnight [15]. The resulting answer sketched the overview of what has since become known as disruptive innovation theory. In brief, the theory posits that: (i) incumbents ignore the arrival of innovations that enter the market from niche position (originally from the low-end), (ii) incumbents overshoot their offering aims leaving room for simpler and easier offerings, and (iii) incumbents invest in sustaining innovations that fit their existing profitability, but ignore investing in potential new openings that would require new, sometimes even cannibalizing business models to become profitable [12, 16, 17, 27, 28].

Reflecting the lack of conceptual clarity surrounding what is disruptive and what type of change qualifies as disruption, Kilkki et al. [11] define disruption as "An agent is disrupted when the agent must redesign its strategy to survive a change in the environment. From the perspective of the system, disruption is an event in which a substantial share of agents belonging to the system is disrupted" (p. 276). In the realm of digital disruption, Skog et al. [29] dig deeper: they define digital disruption as

"The rapidly unfolding processes through which digital innovation comes to fundamentally alter historically sustainable logics for value creation and capture by unbundling and recombining linkages among resources or generating new ones. Skog et al. further conceptualize digital disruption to pertain three constitutive elements, namely digital innovation, digital ecosystem, and value logics. They define digital innovation as "process of combining digital and physical components to create novel devices, services or business models, bundling them to constitute and enable market offerings, and embedding them in wider sociotechnical environments to enable their diffusion, operation and use" (p. 433). Digital ecosystems in turn are "sociotechnical networks of interdependent digital technologies and associated actors that are related based on a specific context of use" (p. 433). Finally, they define value logics as "foundational rationales for designing, bundling and embedding a digital innovation to fruitfully create and capture value" (p. 434).

The focus of the disruptive innovation theory is on the market events and incumbents. The disruption is identified only ex post, through the wake of destroyed businesses. With respect to scrutinizing the actual disruptive agent, the theory contributes little: in their review of the status quo of the theory, Christensen et al. ended up in "…defining 'disruptiveness' as a relative, not absolute, phenomenon. In other words, a given innovation can be disruptive to one firm but sustaining to another firm" [17, p. 1050].

This relative nature of disruption was taken further by Schuelke-Leech [13], who explored the magnitude of disruption and proposed a two-level approach: the first order disruptions impact localized markets, whereas the second order disruptions emerge as enough of the networked first order disruptions diffuse to impact the whole market. Nevertheless, also this approach is still retrospective and does not directly facilitate anticipatory assessment of disruptive potential. In particular, we argue that disruptive change can pertain changes that take place in more than two levels. To take a multi-level perspective to disruptive change, we employ CLA [23, 24, 26] as the theoretical framework through which to scrutinize the disruptiveness effect of cryptocurrencies.

# 3    Causal Layered Analysis of Socio-Technical Change

## 3.1    Causal Layered Analysis

Previous research in futures studies has explored the possibility of forecasting discontinuities on the macro level [30], the social disruption intertwined with the diffusion of disruptive technological innovations [18], or the possibility of utilizing diverse foresight methods in identifying disruptions [31–33]. Against this backdrop, our approach to distinguishing disruptive change from normal change in the context of cryptocurrencies answers the call for understanding the multi-level nature of disruption [13]. We employ a specific futures research analytical tool, Causal Layered Analysis (CLA), which enables assessing the layered nature of diverse phenomena.

CLA [23, 34] is an analytical tool that enables viewing a phenomenon from four different perspectives conceptualized as four analytical levels. Since its introduction, the CLA has been widely adopted as an analytical aid in theorizing and as a useful tool in workshop environments, utilized in analyzing complex phenomena in a variety of fields [31, 32, 35–37]. The analytical levels of CLA are traversed up and down to understand the phenomenon on each level in addition to tracing the linkages in between them.

The first analytical level of CLA is litany. It is the imminent appearance of a phenomenon, quantitatively approachable, an issue easy to shape into a headline. For example, "Terrorism is a constant and evolving threat" [36], or "Traffic jams" (adopted from Inayatullah 2003). The litany can also be an entity like United Nations [37], or the election of Donald Trump as the president of the US [38]. While the viewpoints on the issue may differ, the phenomenon on the litany level can be easily recognized. Moreover, on the litany level the changes and solutions are fast and seemingly simple. For example, a litany level solution for traffic jams could be reducing the number of cars.

The second level of CLA is called systemic causes. Systemic causes is also the level of most analytical endeavors. For example, terrorism may be analyzed to result from lack of sufficient threat detection or to be resolved through more widely spread Western democratization [36]. Moreover, on a systemic causes level, traffic jams in turn are caused by improving living standards enabling the ownership of private cars to more individuals, or the flaws in the city planning and road infrastructure [35].

Systemic causes can be approached from several paradigmatic perspectives: positivist, constructivist, critical and utilizing diverse theoretical frameworks from institutional theory to Marxism, actor-network-theory, among others. Compared to the litany level, identifying the systemic causes is more complex. Respectively, the solutions on a systemic are complex and require more time and effort.

The third level in CLA is worldview. The worldview level stems from postmodern approaches to philosophy and sociology [23]. It takes the impact of discourses seriously and zooms into the ideologies, assumptions – to the realm of taken-for-granted that shapes social action [25]. On a worldview level, traffic jams are a consequence of industrialization, which not only mandates the ownership of a car as a symbol of social class, but also dictates work hours, which result in many people being on the streets at the same time. Fundamentally this level explores the mechanisms of meaning, the why of social action. Changes on this level, for example the development of industrial working hours or changes in symbolic value of a private car, are characteristically slow and rarely a result of intentional action [26, 35–38].

The fourth level is called myth/metaphor. The fourth level goes even deeper into meaning, and explores its origins: where do the ideologies and worldviews emerge from? The proposed answer in CLA draws from the primitive reactions, 'gut feelings', shared collective images that are difficult to even shape into conscious explanations.

For example, the myths/metaphors attributed to having a private car can stem from people's innate needs for experiencing autonomy and competence (e.g. Deci and Ryan [39] or claiming a private space [40]. While the changes on the myth/metaphor level changes can be very difficult to identify and conceptualize, the fact that CLA acknowledges the existence of this level may help recognizing and understanding events that unfold on the other three levels of analysis [31, 35–37].

## 3.2   CLA of Disruptive Change

To develop our CLA-based framework for distinguishing disruptive change from normal change we take the definition of disruption by Kilkki et al. [11] as our starting point: "An agent is disrupted when the agent must redesign its strategy to survive a change in the environment. From the perspective of a system, disruption is an event in which a substantial share of agents belonging to the system is disrupted" (p. 276). These definitions reveal two essential questions: what needs to happen for an agent to need to "redesign its strategy to survive? What needs to happen for a notable number of agents in a system to need to do the same? While there are other social, economic and environmental issues that may have an impact, here we view the role of technology.

In discussing the emergence of technology-driven social disruption, following Dosi [41], Carlsen et al. [18] note that the concept of technology includes two dimensions: first, the knowledge embedded in a field, like engineering, digital technology or biotechnology, and secondly the technological artefacts solidifying the technological knowhow into material realizations. This provides us with two levels of technological advances: developments in technological artefacts, and advances in the field level technological knowledge.

Dosi [41] elaborates on two additional levels of technological advances. According to Dosi, there are advances that change the paradigm of a given technological field within a given utility and advances that render that whole utility irrelevant through more widespread changes in the needs met with technologies. The examples of the first type of paradigm change include the shift from analogic music recording technologies to digital recordings and the subsequent transformations in distributing music. The second type of paradigm changes consists of major shifts that accompanied for example industrialization; the technologies essential in farming-based societies gave way to technologies necessary in industrial societies.

As a result, we incorporate these insights from the literature to the four levels of CLA to build our analytical framework (Table 1).

**Table 1.** CLA-based framework of the magnitude of socio-technical change

| Level in CLA | Unit of the impact of change | Technological objects of change | Magnitude of change |
|---|---|---|---|
| Litany | Technological artefacts | New artefacts, incremental innovation, radical, but bounded innovation | Normal change |
| Systemic causes | Socio-technical systems | Radical innovation that impacts infrastructures, standards, regulation, formal institutions | Firm(s) level disruption |
| Worldview | Meaning | Technological landscape, paradigm level change within utility, informal institutions | Field/industry level disruption |
| Myth/metaphor | Origins of meaning | Taken-for-grantedness of paradigm, change of utility needs | Macro-level societal transformation |

On the level of litany, the technological developments are represented in new technological artefacts resulting from either incremental innovation [15] or such boundedly radical innovations, which primarily replace one artefact with another, without impacting the overall structures or behavior. An example of the latter is for example the launch of the iPhone – while it displaced the then dominant mobile phone providers and shaped the subsequent use of phones, its diffusion built on established infrastructures and already adopted behavior. These technological innovations on the level of artefacts are by themselves not enough for initiating disruption, but merely represent the normal change – even in highly competitive market settings.

When the technological artefacts are radical enough to cause changes on the structures or in the behavior of a notable share of individuals, they have the power of supplanting such individual firms that are reliant on the structures or behavior being changed. Additionally, also the developments within a given field of technology, in the constitution of its knowhow, have a similar impact. These impacts can be represented in changes in the infrastructures, standards and regulations [42]. In short, these changes are systemic level changes and as such have the potential to disrupt a number or firms dependent on the preceding institutional settings.

On the level of worldview, the magnitude of disruption encompasses not only individual firms but industries and whole fields of operation. This requires paradigm level changes within the fields of technological knowledge: the shift from analog to digital era being a notable example [42, 43]. On this level the technological and social changes are firmly intertwined: the technological affordances drive changes not only in behavior, but also in the informal institutions, and vice versa – the changes in the informal institutions further strengthen the development trajectories of technology.

Finally, on the level of myth/metaphor, the whole of what is taken for granted changes. However, as the changes on this level unfold slowly, driven by the convergence of diverse social, economic, technological and environmental trajectories, the concept of disruption does not apply: the concept of disruption entails a level of surprise, and while we do not here delve the time dimension of disruption, slowly unfolding change, while changing the socio-economic-technological systems profoundly, is incompatible with the current use of the concept.

## 4   Cryptocurrencies

Cryptocurrencies are digital assets that are featured with strong cryptography and can be used as a medium of secure exchange [44]. They allow fast and secured peer-to-peer transactions with minimal processing fees without an intermediary such as a bank. In contrast with the traditional currencies that are controlled by central banks, cryptocurrencies use decentralized technology, especially blockchain [45]. Bitcoin, released in 2009 is the first cryptocurrency that used blockchain to record financial transactions [1]. Bitcoin was developed as a decentralized digital currency to revolutionize the traditional intermediary-based financial industry. Due to the popularity of Bitcoin, many other digital assets similar to Bitcoin were created using blockchain [2]. As of October 2019, Coinmarketcap lists altogether 2354 cryptocurrencies.

The rate of the creation of cryptocurrencies is defined by the technical system or algorithm and is hence publicly known. In the centralized banking system, central banks control the supply of the currency by printing new money. However, cryptocurrencies have been designed in such a way that the production will decrease by time for some cryptocurrencies. Moreover, a cap is set on the total amount of the currency that would be ever produced for most cryptocurrencies. For example, the cap is 21 million for Bitcoin [46]. Therefore, government, central bank or any other centralized authority cannot decide creating new units of the currency.

Use of cryptocurrencies is permissionless – that is one does not have to ask anyone to use them [3]. Transactions using cryptocurrencies are pseudonymous in nature and so as the accounts or addresses. The cryptocurrency account or address contains nothing but random characters. Thus, it is possible to check the flow of transactions, but connecting them to real world identities is not possible.

The rapid growth and diffusion of cryptocurrencies has created significant economic activity. For example, there is a fast-growing market for investors, as well as opportunities for new businesses such as mining hardware manufactures. The market hype around initial coin offerings (ICO) and tokenization has made cryptocurrencies widely known as a form of crowdfunding[2].

## 5  Disruptiveness of Cryptocurrencies

When scrutinized through the four levels of change provided by CLA, we can see that cryptocurrencies have challenged traditional currencies in number of ways. Importantly, there are indications that the monopoly of central banks in issuing currencies and controlling the monetary system has been challenged. Table 2 below summarizes the results of our conceptual analysis.

**Table 2.** Diffusion of cryptocurrencies analyzed through CLA

| Level in CLA | Unit of the impact of change | Technological objects of change | Magnitude of change |
|---|---|---|---|
| Litany | Technological artefacts | Rapid increase in the number of cryptocurrencies<br>Explosion of peer-to-peer transactions<br>Market hype around Bitcoin | Normal change |
| Systemic causes | Socio-technical systems | Incumbent financial institutions experimenting with and adopting blockchain-based technologies<br>Emergence of services for cross-border money transfer, erosion of incumbents' business<br>Regulation for cryptocurrencies emerging | Firm(s) level disruption |

(*continued*)

---

[2] https://www.cnbc.com/2018/07/13/initial-coin-offering-ico-what-are-they-how-do-they-work.html.

**Table 2.** (*continued*)

| Level in CLA | Unit of the impact of change | Technological objects of change | Magnitude of change |
|---|---|---|---|
| Worldview | Meaning | Central banks experimenting with their own crypto-/digital currencies<br>Central bank's monopoly in issuing money challenged and questioned | Field/industry level disruption |
| Myth/metaphor | Origins of meaning | Cryptocurrencies provide means to fight hyperinflation of the traditional currency (Venezuela) and establish a parallel economic system<br>Decentralized technologies enabling new forms or organizing and agency | Macro-level societal transformation |

On the level of litany, cryptocurrencies have been gaining popularity for peer-to-peer transactions. This has been partially driving by certain actors need to avoid traditional financial institutions since they typically provide information for governmental authorities. In addition, new cryptocurrencies are created at a rapid pace. Investors have been investing in cryptocurrencies with the hope for profits. Taken together, the cryptocurrency market has been constantly evolving since the birth of Bitcoin. As cryptocurrencies promise to remove central authority in the transaction, it can be seen as a threat to banks and other financial institutions, which act as the middlemen in transactions. Therefore, some governments have even banned cryptocurrencies. For example, ICOs were banned in many countries despite their popularity. Even trading cryptocurrencies is illegal in many countries such as China[3].

On the level of systemic changes, the growth of cryptocurrencies have started to challenge established companies or organizations. For example, in international money transfer, cryptocurrencies enable very cost-efficient peer-to-peer transactions and thus has the potential to decrease transaction costs by eliminating, or cutting the fees of established middlemen facilitating transactions.

Second, blockchain technologies such as cryptocurrencies typically record the transactions in a distributed ledger which cannot be changed. Therefore, it ensures trust and security without a need for a middleman involved in the transaction. Due to the anonymous nature of cryptocurrencies, it is easier for example to avoid taxation when one uses cryptocurrencies for transactions. Therefore, regulatory bodies interfered to regulate cryptocurrencies in the past years [47]. Blockchain, the underlying technology behind the cryptocurrencies has gained popularity in many other areas such as healthcare and supply-chain [48, 49]. Therefore, it has already become evident that cryptocurrencies have the potential for firm level disruption.

With respect to the worldview level of CLA, we argue that the changes associated with cryptocurrencies represent what CLA considers worldview level. This argument is supported by the fact that banks, central banks, and other financial institutions have

---

[3] https://www.coindesk.com/south-korea-will-maintain-ico-ban-after-finding-token-projects-broke-rules.

been looking for possibilities to use private or consortium blockchain as well as offering their own crypto- or digital currencies due to the possible disruption caused by cryptocurrencies.

Lastly, there is some signs that cryptocurrencies can contribute to macro-level societal changes that CLA classifies to represent the myth/metaphor level. The changes at this level are driven by the convergence of diverse social, economic, technological, and environmental trajectories. For example, cryptocurrencies, particularly Dash and Bitcoin have played a role in the recent economic and political turmoil in Venezuela. For example, due to the hyperinflation, price of one cup of coffee increased 373,233% in just 12 months. As a result, people have increasingly turned to the digital assets cryptocurrencies[4]. Many people converted their bolivars to Bitcoin or other cryptocurrencies to preserve their financial assets. Moreover, salaries have been increasingly paid in cryptocurrencies instead of bolivars. In fact, amidst the crisis, the Venezuelan government also launched its own cryptocurrency, the petro, believed to be backed by oil in order to fight the economic crisis. Taken together, the adoption of cryptocurrencies in Venezuela has skyrocketed and is seen as a way to fight the economic crisis due to the hyperinflation that collapse the value of the bolivar.

Furthermore, the emergence of blockchain technology and cryptocurrencies can be viewed as examples of the emergence of decentralized forms of organizing and thus an alternative to centralized control and authority (cf. [50]).

## 6   Discussion and Conclusion

This study was set out to explore (i) whether the diffusion of cryptocurrencies represents a disruptive change, and (ii) what is the potential magnitude of this change? To meet this objective, we built on disruptive innovation theory [15, 17] (Christensen 1997; Christensen et al. 2018) to scrutinize cryptocurrencies as an instance of sociotechnical change [13, 20–22] and employed Causal Layered Analysis [23, 26] to conceptually examine its disruptiveness.

Our contribution is twofold. First, we contribute to the evolving blockchain and cryptocurrency literature (e.g. [2, 10]; b) by evaluating the disruptive potential of cryptocurrencies with our four-layer analytical framework. In particular, our approach can be used to more systematically analyze the potential and impact of blockchain-based applications and services. As a result, we specifically contribute to the debate whether blockchain-based technologies ability to disrupt existing business models.

Second, we contributed to the disruptive innovation and disruptive change literature (e.g. [17] by using CLA as the foundation of our analytical framework, we describe the potential disruptiveness of an innovation using four layers. This provides a more detailed description of disruptiveness than the dominant two-level approach [13].

The study has a number of limitations that need to be acknowledged. At the same time, we view these limitations as immediate avenues for future research. First, this study is conceptual in nature. Therefore, future research could collect empirical

---

[4] https://www.bbc.com/news/business-47553048.

evidence to verify the applicability of CLA approach in the context of cryptocurrencies. Second, we focused only on one specific use case of blockchain technology and instance of potential disruptive change, i.e. cryptocurrencies. Thus, future research could test the applicability of our CLA-based analytical framework in other applications of blockchain technology as well as entirely different contextual domains – also within the field on information systems studies.

# References

1. Nakamoto, S.: Bitcoin: a peer-to-peer electronic cash system (2008)
2. Islam, A.K.M.N., Mäntymäki, M., Turunen, M.: Why do blockchains split? An actor-network perspective on Bitcoin splits. Technol. Forecast. Soc. Change **148**, 119743 (2019)
3. Islam, N., Mäntymäki, M., Turunen, M.: Understanding the role of actor heterogeneity in blockchain splits: an actor-network perspective of bitcoin forks. In: Proceedings of the 52nd Hawaii International Conference on System Sciences (2019)
4. Barontini, C., Holden, H.: Proceeding with Caution-A Survey on Central Bank Digital Currency. BIS Paper, no. 101, 8 January 2019
5. Caliskan, K.: Data Money: The Socio-Technical Infrastructure of Cryptocurrency Blockchains (2018). SSRN 3372015
6. Dodd, N.: The social life of Bitcoin. Theory Cult. Soc. **35**(3), 35–56 (2018)
7. Iansiti, M., Lakhani, K.R.: The truth about blockchain. Harv. Bus. Rev. **95**(1), 118–127 (2017)
8. Jun, M.: Blockchain government-a next form of infrastructure for the twenty-first century. J. Open Innov. Technol. Mark. Complex. **4**(1), 7 (2018)
9. Luther, W.J.: Cryptocurrencies, network effects, and switching costs. Contemp. Econ. Policy **34**(3), 553–571 (2016)
10. Zook, M.A., Blankenship, J.: New spaces of disruption? The failures of Bitcoin and the rhetorical power of algorithmic governance. Geoforum **96**, 248–255 (2018)
11. Kilkki, K., Mäntylä, M., Karhu, K., Hämmäinen, H., Ailisto, H.: A disruption framework. Technol. Forecast. Soc. Change **129**, 275–284 (2018)
12. Petzold, N., Landinez, L., Baaken, T.: Disruptive innovation from a process view: a systematic literature review. Creat. Innov. Manag **28**(2), 157–174 (2019)
13. Schuelke-Leech, B.-A.: A model for understanding the orders of magnitude of disruptive technologies. Technol. Forecast. Soc. Change **129**, 261–274 (2018)
14. Baiyere, A.: Discovering the Role of Information Technology In Disruptive Innovations-Enabler, Sustainer or Barrier (2016)
15. Christensen, C.M.: The Innovator's Dilemma. Harvard Business School Press, Cambridge (1997)
16. Christensen, C.M.: The ongoing process of building a theory of disruption. J. Prod. Innov. Manag. **23**(1), 39–55 (2006)
17. Christensen, C.M., McDonald, R., Altman, E.J., Palmer, J.E.: Disruptive innovation: an intellectual history and directions for future research. J. Manag. Stud. **55**(7), 1043–1078 (2018)
18. Carlsen, H., Dreborg, K.H., Godman, M., Hansson, S.O., Johansson, L., Wikman-Svahn, P.: Assessing socially disruptive technological change. Technol. Soc. **32**(3), 209–218 (2010)
19. Hayes, A.: The socio-technological lives of bitcoin. Theory Cult. Soc. **36**(4), 49–72 (2019). https://doi.org/10.1177/0263276419826218

20. McLeod, L., Doolin, B.: Information systems development as situated socio-technical change: a process approach. Eur. J. Inf. Syst. **21**(2), 176–191 (2012)
21. Sovacool, B.K., Hess, D.J.: Ordering theories: typologies and conceptual frameworks for sociotechnical change. Soc. Stud. Sci. **47**(5), 703–750 (2017)
22. Lyytinen, K., Newman, M.: Explaining information systems change: a punctuated socio-technical change model. Eur. J. Inf. Syst. **17**(6), 589–613 (2008)
23. Inayatullah, S.: Causal layered analysis: poststructuralism as method. Futures **30**(8), 815–829 (1998)
24. Inayatullah, S.: The Causal Layered Analysis (CLA) Reader. Theory and Case Studies of an Integrative and Transformative Methodology (2004)
25. Milojević, I., Inayatullah, S.: Narrative foresight. Futures **73**, 151–162 (2015)
26. Inayatullah, S., Milojevic, I.: CLA 2.0: transformative research in theory and practice (2015)
27. Gans, J.S.: Keep calm and manage disruption. MIT Sloan Manag. Rev. **57**(3), 83 (2016)
28. Lucas, H.C., Goh, J.M.: Disruptive technology: how Kodak missed the digital photography revolution. J. Strateg. Inf. Syst. **18**(1), 46–55 (2009)
29. Skog, D.A., Wimelius, H., Sandberg, J.: Digital disruption. Bus. Inf. Syst. Eng. **60**(5), 431–437 (2018)
30. Ayres, R.U.: On forecasting discontinuities. Technol. Forecast. Soc. Change **65**(1), 81–97 (2000)
31. Heinonen, S., Minkkinen, M., Karjalainen, J., Inayatullah, S.: Testing transformative energy scenarios through causal layered analysis gaming. Technol. Forecast. Soc. Change **124**, 101–113 (2017)
32. Minkkinen, M., Heinonen, S., Parkkinen, M.: Drilling and blasting to learn scenario construction: experimenting with causal layered analysis as a disruption of scenario work. World Futur. Rev. **11**(2), 110–121 (2018). https://doi.org/10.1177/1946756718774940
33. Wayland, R.: Strategic foresight in a changing world. Foresight **17**(5), 444–459 (2015)
34. Inayatullah, S.: Causal Layered Analysis: Theory, Historical Context, and Case Studies, pp. 1–52. Tamkang University Press, Taipei (2004)
35. Inayatullah, S.: Alternative futures of transport. Foresight **5**(1), 34–43 (2003)
36. Kenny, N.D.: Terrorism futures: constructing and deconstructing using causal layered analysis. In: Inayatullah, S., Milojevic, I. (ed.) pp. 235–252. Tamkang University Press, Taipei (2015)
37. Ketonen-Oksi, S.: Creating a shared narrative: the use of causal layered analysis to explore value co-creation in a novel service ecosystem. Eur. J. Futures Res. **6**(1), 1–12 (2018). https://doi.org/10.1186/s40309-018-0135-y
38. Wirén, M.: Strategizing in the new normal: implications of digitalization for strategizing and uncertainty: philosophical and managerial considerations (2018)
39. Deci, E.L., Ryan, R.M.: The "what" and "why" of goal pursuits: human needs and the self-determination of behavior. Psychol. Inq. **11**(4), 227–268 (2000)
40. Beirão, G., Cabral, J.A.S.: Understanding attitudes towards public transport and private car: a qualitative study. Transp. Policy **14**(6), 478–489 (2007)
41. Dosi, G.: Technological paradigms and technological trajectories: a suggested interpretation of the determinants and directions of technical change. Res. Policy **11**(3), 147–162 (1982)
42. Tilson, D., Lyytinen, K., Sorensen, C.: Desperately seeking the infrastructure in IS research: conceptualization of "digital convergence" as co-evolution of social and technical infrastructures. In: 2010 43rd Hawaii International Conference on System Sciences (HICSS), pp. 1–10 (2010)
43. Tilson, D., Lyytinen, K., Sørensen, C.: Research commentary—digital infrastructures: the missing IS research agenda. Inf. Syst. Res. **21**(4), 748–759 (2010)
44. Chohan, U.W.: Cryptocurrencies: a brief thematic review (2017)

45. Bech, M.L., Garratt, R.: Central bank cryptocurrencies. BIS Quarterly Review, September 2017
46. Antonopoulos, A.M.: Mastering Bitcoin: Unlocking Digital Cryptocurrencies. O'Reilly Media, Inc., Sebastopol (2014)
47. DeVries, P.D.: An analysis of cryptocurrency, bitcoin, and the future. Int. J. Bus. Manag. Commer. **1**(2), 1–9 (2016)
48. Dolgui, A., Ivanov, D., Potryasaev, S., Sokolov, B., Ivanova, M., Werner, F.: Blockchain-oriented dynamic modelling of smart contract design and execution in the supply chain. Int. J. Prod. Res., 1–16 (2019)
49. Siyal, A., Junejo, A., Zawish, M., Ahmed, K., Khalil, A., Soursou, G.: Applications of blockchain technology in medicine and healthcare: challenges and future perspectives. Cryptography **3**(1), 3 (2019)
50. Beck, R.: Beyond bitcoin: the rise of blockchain world. Computer (Long. Beach. Calif.) **51**(2), 54–58 (2018)

# Fourth Industrial Revolution

# SMME Readiness for Smart Manufacturing (4IR) Adoption: A Systematic Review

Lucas Gumbi[(✉)] and Hossana Twinomurinzi

University of South Africa, 28 Pioneer Avenue, Florida Park,
Roodepoort, South Africa
58563199@mylife.unisa.ac.za, twinoh@unisa.ac.za

**Abstract.** Smart manufacturing, Industry 4.0 and Smart Factory are phenomena regarded as a key necessity for Small, Medium and Micro Businesses (SMMEs) worldwide. Even though these 4th Industrial Revolution (4IR) phenomena are generally used interchangeably, this paper sought to identify how SMME readiness for smart manufacturing has been investigated through a systematic review. The systematic review was conducted through the lens of Nooteboom, and Tornatzky and Klein's research on technological innovation in SMMEs based on Rogers' diffusion of innovations theory. The findings reveal that there is little to no research on smart manufacturing in relation to SMMEs in low-income countries particularly the African continent. The results also show that smart manufacturing is still an emergent phenomenon with disparate definitional challenges. These definitional challenges make the adoption of smart manufacturing innovations a challenge in resource-constrained contexts; but similarly present an opportunity for new definitions and theories in such contexts. The little research often treats SMMEs homogenously and as such misses their important heterogeneous (sector or industry specific) nature. Few research studies investigate SMME awareness (adequate knowledge) or make explicit the benefits (relative advantage) of smart manufacturing. Even fewer studies are explicit on the smart manufacturing technologies that are relevant for different SMME sectors. Smart manufacturing is identified as incompatible with SMME characteristics, that is SMMEs lack expertise/skills to comprehend the complexity of smart manufacturing, and also lack financial and human resources to implement smart manufacturing. Given that awareness, relative advantage, complexity and compatibility are critical barriers for SMME smart manufacturing readiness/adoption, there is a critical need for research to focus on these factors in particular for the context of resource constrained low-income country environments.

**Keywords:** Smart manufacturing · Industry 4.0 · SMMEs · 4th Industrial Revolution · 4IR

## 1 Introduction

Smart Manufacturing is an emerging 4th Industrial Revolution (4IR) phenomena as a result of the convergence of various Information and Communication Technologies (ICT) that improve manufacturing factors such as productivity, quality, delivery and

© IFIP International Federation for Information Processing 2020
Published by Springer Nature Switzerland AG 2020
M. Hattingh et al. (Eds.): I3E 2020, LNCS 12066, pp. 41–54, 2020.
https://doi.org/10.1007/978-3-030-44999-5_4

flexibility [1–4]. Smart manufacturing relates to enabling industries and their manufacturing ecosystems to connect and adopt novel efficiency gains along their value and supply chains [5]. Smart Manufacturing as a new technological innovation is also seen as a key driver of improved manufacturing operations [6, 7] and a catalyst of manufacturing intelligence [8].

However, despite all the mentioned benefits, SMMEs are not ready for the adoption and implementation of smart manufacturing as compared to larger firms [9–12]. Jun et al. [9] attribute this to the SMME environment, their underdeveloped capabilities, and practical limitations such as cost and personnel. Muller and Voigt [10] suggest that the challenge is with SMME business model constraints, while Luff [12] and Safar et al. [11] highlight the issue of lack of resources as the primary constraint.

There have been other systematic reviews [5, 13–18] to understand the factors inhibiting smart manufacturing adoption and implementation by SMMEs. Those reviews focused on different dimensions [5, 13–16] and contextual perspectives [17, 18]. For example, Mittal et al. [5, 13, 14] focused specifically on maturity models, while Hamdi [16] and Moeuf et al. [15] focused on Enterprise Resource Planning (ERP) and organisational dimensions respectively. Nowotarski and Paslawski [17], and Sommer et al. [18] focused on Germany and the construction sector.

In this paper, the objective is to understand the level of SMME readiness/adoption for smart manufacturing and how this has been researched from the perspective of innovation. The rationale for the research objective was derived from Nooteboom [19, 20] and Tornatzky and Klein's [21] work on SMMEs underpinned by Roger's diffusion of innovations theory [22]. Building on the diffusion of innovation theory [22], Nooteboom [19, 20] identified the first stage of the SMME adoption process as awareness; adequate knowledge about the innovation to be adopted. While awareness is generally a given for large firms and technology-oriented SMMEs, it is a key barrier for technology-following and non-technological SMMEs with regard to readiness for adoption [19, 20, 23].

The adoption and diffusion of new technological innovations is contingent on three characteristics: the relative advantage (benefits) of the technological innovation, the complexity of the technological innovation and the compatibility of the technological innovation [21]. Relative advantage is the degree to which an innovation is perceived as being better than the idea it supersedes, complexity is the degree to which an innovation is perceived as relatively difficult to understand and use, while compatibility is the degree to which an innovation is perceived as consistent with the existing values, past experiences, and needs of potential adopters [21].

The systematic review specifically focuses on the context of the research (low-income or high-income country), the awareness (adequate knowledge), benefits (relative advantage), the technological innovations and readiness/adoption as important dimensions of interest. Based on the objective this review differentiates itself from previous similar reviews [5, 13–18].

The paper therefore sought to find answers from the review for the following research questions (RQ):

*RQ1: What is the state of awareness (adequate knowledge) of SMMEs in relation to smart manufacturing?*

*RQ2: What are the benefits of smart manufacturing in relation to SMMEs?*
*RQ3: Which technologies are seen as key to the concept of smart manufacturing in relation to SMMEs?*
*RQ4: What is the state of smart manufacturing readiness and adoption by SMMEs?*

The rest of the paper is structured as follows, Sect. 2 presents the review methodology. Section 3 presents the results of the review and the research gaps. The conclusions, limitations and future work are presented in Sect. 4.

## 2 Methodology

The study followed Lage and Junior's [24] systematic review protocol, and used the reporting approach of Amui et al.'s [25]. The SLR considered publications, which followed the formal introduction of Industry 4.0 that is from 2011 onwards. The time period for article selection was October 2018 to January 2019, while the analysis of the articles was from February 2019 to July 2019. A schematic representation of the adopted review protocol is shown in Fig. 1 below.

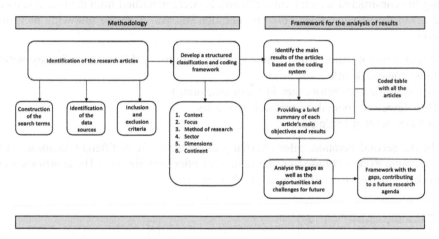

**Fig. 1.** A schematic representation for the adopted methodology and results framework for this study

### 2.1 Identification of the Research Articles

The first step was identifying the research articles through; (1) the construction of the search terms, (2) identifying the relevant data sources and (3) inclusion and exclusion criteria.

### 2.2 Construction of the Search Terms

The construction of the search terms was primarily derived from RQ1, RQ2, RQ3 and RQ4. These search strings were constructed based on the *Unit of Analysis* (SMMEs),

*Technology Artefact* (Smart Manufacturing/Industry 4.0/Smart Factory) and *Phenomenon of Interest* (Adoption/Trends/Benefits/Technologies/Issues). The full details of the 33 constructed search strings are presented in Appendix 1 found on http://dx.doi.org/10.13140/RG.2.2.19652.17285.

## 2.3   Identification of the Data Sources

Smart Manufacturing (industry 4.0) is based on the convergence of various technologies and the integration of multiple disciplines and domains such as mechanical engineering, electrical engineering, computer science and other related fields [1, 26]. The multidisciplinary nature of smart manufacturing meant that the review needed to perform the search in similar multidisciplinary research databases. The study therefore chose the four that are most commonly used by multidisciplinary researchers [27–33]; Web of Science (WoS), Academic Search Premier (ASP), ScienceDirect and Google Scholar.

## 2.4   Inclusion and Exclusion Criteria

Using the constructed search terms, 279 articles were identified from the four databases (Fig. 2) in the first iteration. This first iteration was based on the following inclusion criteria:

- Articles that mention smart manufacturing or industry 4.0 or smart factory within their content or title
- All industries or sectors (not just manufacturing)
- Peer reviewed journal or conference articles
- Articles written in English

In the second iteration, after removing duplications from different databases, 177 articles were excluded based on the review of titles and abstract. These articles were excluded based on the following exclusion criteria:

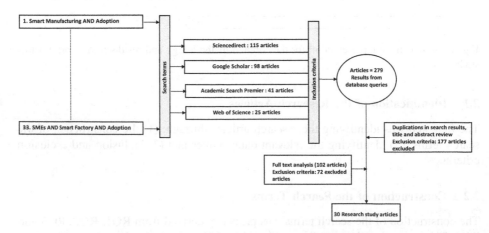

**Fig. 2.** A schematic representation of the inclusion and exclusion process

- Articles that merely mention some of the search terms, but do not solely focus on smart manufacturing, industry 4.0 or smart factory concepts
- Articles focusing on one specific application of a particular technology in relation to smart manufacturing or industry 4.0 or smart factory
- Articles that do not focus on SMMEs
- Articles that merely mention SMMEs

In the final round of the iteration process, 72 articles were excluded based on the analysis of the full text of the articles. The remainder of the articles (30 peer reviewed journals and conference papers) were determined to be relevant for this review (See Appendix 2 Table 10 on http://dx.doi.org/10.13140/RG.2.2.19652.17285 for the articles selected for this review). The primary exclusion criteria was the following:

- Articles that do not discuss any of the four study dimensions (awareness: adequate knowledge, benefits, technologies and readiness/adoption) discussed in Sect. 1 within their content

## 2.5 A Structured Classification and Coding Framework

To enable a structured and effective analysis of the body of knowledge contained within the sourced articles, a modified classification and coding framework utilizing numbers and letter codes to classify the articles was utilized (Table 1). This framework is adopted from Amui et al. [25] who developed it based on other systematic review efforts [34–38].

**Table 1.** Classification and coding framework

| Classification | Description | Codes |
|---|---|---|
| Context | High-income countries | 1A |
| | Low-income countries | 1B |
| | Not Applicable | 1C |
| Focus | Smart Manufacturing (SM) as the main theme | 2A |
| | Industry 4.0 (I4.0) as the main theme | 2B |
| | Smart Factory (SF) as the main theme | 2C |
| | SM/I4.0/SF used interchangeably | 2D |
| Method | Qualitative | 3A |
| | Quantitative | 3B |
| | Theoretical | 3C |
| | Empirical | 3D |
| | Case studies/interviews | 3E |
| | Survey | 3F |
| Sector | Manufacturing | 4A |
| | Other Sectors | 4B |
| | Not Applicable | 4C |

*(continued)*

**Table 1.** (*continued*)

| Classification | Description | Codes |
|---|---|---|
| Dimensions | **Awareness(Knowledge)** | 5A |
| | **Benefits** | 5B |
| | **Technologies** | 5C |
| | **Readiness/Adoption** | 5D |
| Origin (Continents) | America | 6A |
| | Europe | 6B |
| | Asia | 6C |
| | Oceania | 6D |
| | Africa | 6E |

# 3   Analysis and Discussion of Findings

The thirty selected research articles were coded according to Table 1, with the resultant coding results shown in Table 2 below.

## 3.1   Context and Origin

The majority of the articles focused on high-income countries (1A) in comparison to low income countries (1B) as shown in Table 2. The majority of the research studies in relation to smart manufacturing (Table 2) originated from Europe (6B) conducted by German universities and research institutions. Only one study by a Moroccan university originated from the African (6E) continent [16]. See details in Appendix 2 Table 11 on http://dx.doi.org/10.13140/RG.2.2.19652.17285.

The findings suggest that there is a research gap in this regard, and therefore a research opportunity for smart manufacturing for SMMEs in low-income countries, specifically in the African continent. The resource constrained environments of low-income country contexts often results in completely new and contrasting technological innovations as has been shown in the mobile money sector in low-income countries [39].

## 3.2   What's in a Name: Smart Manufacturing vs 4IR

In this study, no article used smart manufacturing (2A) and/or smart factory (2C) as the main theme on their own (Table 3). Both these terms were used interchangeably with Industry 4.0 as shown in Table 3. Industry 4.0 (2B) is also not used interchangeably in this study and seems to be the most preferred term (Table 3). This could be as a result of the majority of the researchers/studies emanating from Germany. The findings suggest that the manufacturing 4IR discourse has primarily been through the lens of Industry 4.0 concept applied in a non-contextual approach to country specific problems and strategic initiatives [16, 40]. However, due to definitional differences of these terms (smart manufacturing/industry 4.0/smart factory) [5], there is a research gap and a related opportunity to contextualize 4IR concepts such as smart manufacturing to country specific problems and strategic initiatives.

**Table 2.** Results of the codification framework

| Authors | Context | | | Focus | | | | Method | | | | | | Sector | | | Dimensions | | | | Origin (Continents) | | | | |
|---|---|---|---|---|---|---|---|---|---|---|---|---|---|---|---|---|---|---|---|---|---|---|---|---|---|
| | 1A | 1B | 1C | 2A | 2B | 2C | 2D | 3A | 3B | 3C | 3D | 3E | 3F | 4A | 4B | 4C | 5A | 5B | 5C | 5D | 6A | 6B | 6C | 6D | 6E |
| #1 Mittal et al. (2018a) | | | 1C | 2A | 2B | 2C | 2D | | | 3C | | | | 4A | | | 5A | | | 5D | 6A | | | | |
| #2 Ganzarain and Errasti (2016) | 1A | | | | 2B | 2C | 2D | | | | 3D | | | | | 4C | 5A | | | 5D | | 6B | | | |
| #3 Mittal et al. (2018b) | | | 1C | 2A | 2B | 2C | 2D | | | 3C | | 3E | | 4A | | | | | 5C | 5D | 6A | | | | |
| #4 Mittal et al. (2018c) | | | 1C | 2A | 2B | | 2D | | | 3C | | 3E | | 4A | | | | | 5C | 5D | 6A | | | | |
| #5 Hamidi et al. (2018) | | 1B | | | 2B | 2C | 2D | | 3B | | | | 3F | | | | 5A | | 5C | 5D | | | 6C | | |
| #6 Wang et al. (2016) | 1A | | | | 2B | | 2D | | | | 3D | | 3F | 4A | | | | | | 5D | | 6B | | | |
| #7 Moeuf et al. (2018) | | | 1C | | 2B | 2C | 2D | | | 3C | | | | | | 4C | | | 5C | 5D | | 6B | | | |
| #8 Dassisti et al. (2018) | | | 1C | 2A | 2B | | 2D | | | | | 3E | | | | 4C | 5A | | | 5D | | 6B | | | |
| #9 Andulkar et al. (2018) | 1A | | | | 2B | 2C | 2D | 3A | 3B | | | | 3F | | | 4C | 5A | 5B | 5C | 5D | | 6B | | | |
| #10 Hamzeh et al. (2018) | 1A | | | | 2B | | 2D | | | | | | 3F | | | | 5A | 5B | | 5D | | | | 6D | |
| #11 El Hamdi et al. (2018) | | 1B | | 2A | 2B | | 2D | | | | | | 3F | 4A | | | 5A | | | 5D | | | | | 6E |
| #12 Wienbruch et al. (2018) | 1A | | | | 2B | | | | | 3C | 3D | | | 4A | | | 5A | | | 5D | | 6B | | | |
| #13 Dassisti et al. (2017) | 1A | | | | 2B | | | | | 3C | 3D | | | 4A | | | 5A | | | 5D | | 6B | | | |
| #14 Bär et al. (2018) | 1A | | | 2A | 2B | 2C | 2D | 3A | | | | 3E | | 4A | | | | 5B | 5C | 5D | | 6B | | | |
| #15 Jones et al. (2018) | 1A | | | | 2B | 2C | 2D | | | | | 3E | | 4A | | | 5A | | 5C | 5D | | 6B | | | |
| #16 Colombo et al. (2015) | 1A | | | | 2B | 2C | 2D | | | 3C | 3D | | | | | 4C | | | | 5D | | 6B | | | |
| #17 Issa et al. (2017) | 1A | | | | 2B | | | | | | 3D | 3E | | 4A | | | | | 5C | 5D | | 6B | | | |
| #18 Faller and Feldmüller (2015) | 1A | | | | 2B | | | | | | 3D | | | 4A | | | | | | 5D | | 6B | | | |
| #19 Wank et al. (2016) | 1A | | | | 2B | | | | | | 3D | 3E | | | | 4C | | | | 5D | | 6B | | | |
| #20 Jäger et al. (2016) | | | | | 2B | 2C | 2D | | | | | 3E | 3F | | | 4C | | | | 5D | | 6B | | | |
| #21 Polat and Karakuş (2018) | 1A | | | | 2B | 2C | 2D | | | | | 3E | | 4A | | | 5A | | | 5D | | 6B | | | |
| #22 Nowotarski and Paslawski (2017) | | | | | | 2C | 2D | | | 3C | | | | | 4B | | | | | 5D | | | 6C | | |
| #23 Sevinç et al. (2018) | | | 1C | | 2B | 2C | | | | 3C | | 3E | 3F | 4A | | | | | | 5D | | | 6C | | |
| #24 Müller et al. (2018) | 1A | | | 2A | 2B | | 2D | 3A | | | | 3E | | 4A | | | 5A | 5B | | 5D | | 6B | | | |
| #25 Ludwig et al. (2018) | 1A | | | | 2B | | | | 3B | | | 3E | | | | 4C | | | | 5D | | 6B | | | |
| #26 Kleindienst and Ramsauer (2015) | | | 1C | | 2B | | 2D | 3A | | 3C | | | | 4A | | | | | | 5D | | 6B | | | |
| #27 Müller et al. (2017) | 1A | | | 2A | 2B | | 2D | | | | | 3E | | | | 4C | 5A | | | 5D | | 6B | | | |
| #28 Sommer (2015) | 1A | | | | 2B | | | | | 3C | | 3E | | | | 4C | 5A | | | 5D | | 6B | | | |
| #29 Modrak et al. (2018) | | | 1C | | 2B | | | | | 3C | | 3E | | | | 4C | | | 5C | 5D | | 6B | | | |
| #30 Müller and Voigt (2018) | | | 1C | | 2B | | | | 3B | | | | 3F | | | 4C | | 5B | 5C | 5D | | 6B | | | |

**Table 3.**  Usage of the 4IR terms

| 4IR concept | Code | Used as a main theme only | Used as main theme and interchangeably | No. of articles |
|---|---|---|---|---|
| Smart Manufacturing (SM) | 2A | x | x | |
| Industry 4.0 (I4.0) | 2B | √ | x | 12 |
| Smart Factory (SF) | 2C | x | x | |
| SM & I4.0 | 2A + 2B | x | √ | 6 |
| SM & SF | 2A + 2C | x | x | |
| I4.0 & SF | 2B + 2C | x | √ | 9 |
| SM & I4.0 & SF | 2A + 2B + 2C | x | √ | 3 |

### 3.3    Research Methods

The majority of the articles utilized case studies/interviews (3E) as research methods (Table 2). The case studies/interviews were in most cases used as part of the mixed research methodology approach to support conceptual/theoretical research (3C) articles (Table 2). Further analysis on the types of research methods and how they were utilized in the reviewed articles is shown in Table 4. The findings illustrate the need to create new substantive research theories that can contextualize smart manufacturing research to relate better to context specific needs.

**Table 4.**  Research methods

| Research methods | Qualitative 3A | Quantitative 3B | Theoretical 3C | Empirical 3D | Case studies/interviews 3E | Survey 3F | No. of articles |
|---|---|---|---|---|---|---|---|
| Single research method | x | x | 3 | 4 | 4 | 1 | 13 |
| Mixed research method | x | x | 9 | 3 | 13 | 6 | 17 |
| Qualitative | 4 | x | x | x | x | x | 4 |
| Quantitative | x | 4 | x | x | x | x | 4 |

### 3.4    Economic Sector

While the majority of the articles (4A) focused on the manufacturing sector, a significant number of articles (4C) studied SMMEs in a generalized manner (Table 5). Although SMMEs share a number of similarities, they are heterogeneous in nature as they operate in different sectors [41]. The findings suggest that more sector specific research needs to be done with regards to SMMEs.

**Table 5.** Economic sector

| Economic sector | Code | No. of articles |
|---|---|---|
| Manufacturing | 4A | 16 |
| Other sectors | 4B | 1 |
| Not applicable | 4C | 13 |

## 3.5    Dimensions

To answer the framed research questions posed in Sect. 1 (introduction), the four dimensions (1) awareness (adequate knowledge), (2) benefits (relative advantage), (3) technologies and (4) readiness/adoption (awareness, relative advantage, complexity and compatibility) shown in Table 1, were analyzed in accordance with the codification results of Table 2.

### Smart Manufacturing: Awareness (adequate knowledge)

RQ1 sought to establish the state of awareness (knowledge) of SMMEs in relation to smart manufacturing. While the majority of the studies (16 articles) did not mention or discuss this dimension, those articles that did mention/discuss (14 articles) this dimension did not provide any substantive details in relation to the awareness dimension (Table 6). See more details with regard to further analysis in Appendix 2 Table 12 on http://dx.doi.org/10.13140/RG.2.2.19652.17285.

The findings indicates that there is little comprehensive research focusing on investigating SMME levels of awareness in relation to smart manufacturing. Given that the awareness stage has very critical and significant implications to smart manufacturing readiness/adoption based on the innovations theory [19, 22], there is a critical need for research to focus on the awareness of SMMEs in relation to the opportunities, challenges and demands of smart manufacturing.

**Table 6.** Awareness

| Dimension: awareness | Code | No. of Articles |
|---|---|---|
| SMMEs lack awareness of smart manufacturing | 5A | 10 |
| SMMEs have adequate knowledge of smart manufacturing | 5A | 4 |
| Not discussed/mentioned | 5A | 16 |

### Smart Manufacturing (industry 4.0): Relative Advantage (Benefits)

RQ2 sought to identify the benefits (relative advantage) of smart manufacturing in relation to SMMEs. The majority of the research studies did not look into the relative advantage dimension to identify explicitly or implicitly any potential benefits of smart manufacturing for SMMEs (Table 7). Only 5 articles discussed and or identified the relative advantage of smart manufacturing (See details in Appendix 2 Table 13 on http://dx.doi.org/10.13140/RG.2.2.19652.17285).

The findings points to the need for research studies to focus on explicitly identifying the practical relative advantage of smart manufacturing for SMMEs based on concrete and comprehensive research.

**Table 7.** Benefits (relative advantage)

| Dimension: benefits (relative advantage) | Code | No. of articles |
|---|---|---|
| Potential benefits for SMMEs explicitly identified | 5B | 5 |
| Not discussed/mentioned | 5B | 25 |

## Smart Manufacturing (industry 4.0): Technologies

RQ3 sought to identify technologies that are seen as key to the concept of smart manufacturing in relation to SMMEs. The majority of the research studies identified and discussed smart manufacturing technologies from a general applications context and not specific to SMMEs or how they relate and or can be applied in SMME context (Table 8). Only 10 articles identified technologies that are seen as key to the concept of smart manufacturing in relation to SMMEs (See details in Appendix 2 Table 14 on http://dx.doi.org/10.13140/RG.2.2.19652.17285).

The findings reveals a research gap in identifying specific smart manufacturing technologies that are relevant to SMMEs from a sector or industry perspective. This research gap leaves SMMEs exposed and vulnerable to smart manufacturing anecdotes and sales pitches. The availability of empirically proven research on smart manufacturing technologies per sector and or industry would assist SMMEs which usually do not have the resources to do feasibility studies.

**Table 8.** Technologies

| Dimension: technologies (key to SMMEs) | Code | No. of articles |
|---|---|---|
| Smart manufacturing technologies for SMMEs identified/discussed | 5C | 10 |
| Not discussed/mentioned | 5C | 20 |

## Smart Manufacturing (industry 4.0): Readiness/Adoption

RQ4 sought to understand the state of smart manufacturing readiness and adoption by SMMEs based on the innovations theory [19, 22]. Readiness and adoption of smart manufacturing by SMMEs is contingent on four key dimensions (1) awareness (adequate knowledge), (2) relative advantage (benefits), (3) complexity and (4) compatibility [19, 22]. Only a few research articles looked into the issue of awareness (Table 6), relative advantage (Table 7) and complexity as shown in Table 9, while 90% of the research articles indicates that smart manufacturing is currently incompatible with SMME characteristics due to lack of expertise, skills and resources (Table 9). See detailed analysis of complexity and compatibility in Appendix 2 Table 15 on http://dx.doi.org/10.13140/RG.2.2.19652.17285.

The findings reveal that, research gaps in relation to understanding the impact of awareness, relative advantage and complexity needs to be addressed to be able to assess the state of smart manufacturing readiness and adoption by SMMEs. The findings, further reveal that compatibility seems to be emerging as one of the major factors negatively affecting smart manufacturing readiness/adoption for SMMEs. This situation may have far reaching implications in the context of low-skilled and resource constrained low-income countries.

**Table 9.** Adoption/readiness

| Dimension: adoption/readiness | No. of articles | Percentage (total articles) |
| --- | --- | --- |
| SMMEs have adequate knowledge of smart manufacturing | 4 | 13 |
| Potential benefits for SMMEs explicitly identified | 5 | 17 |
| Smart Manufacturing is complex for SMMEs to understand | 11 | 37 |
| Smart manufacturing is incompatible with SMME characteristics | 27 | 90 |

# 4 Conclusion, Limitations and Future Work

The primary objective of this work was to understand the level of SMME readiness/adoption for smart manufacturing and how this has been researched from the perspective of digital technologies innovation guided by four research questions (introduction section). Firstly, the findings suggest that smart manufacturing research on SMMEs is limited in low-income countries and also not contextualized to context specific demands such as sector and or industry specific challenges and preconditions. These includes smart manufacturing technology applications and how they relate or can be applied in SMME context. Secondly, the findings suggest that the issues of SMME awareness, relative advantage and complexity of smart manufacturing DT innovation have received very little research attention. This is critical for readiness/adoption in relation to technology-following SMMEs [20]. Lastly, SMME characteristics (lack of skills, expertise and resources) are incompatible with smart manufacturing. This renders technology-following SMMEs not ready for the adoption of smart manufacturing.

Future context specific research investigating smart manufacturing in settings such as resource constraint low-income countries, non-technology based sectors/industries such as the manufacturing and technology-following SMMEs is recommended. More research to evaluate the impact of SMME awareness, relative advantage, complexity and incompatibility of smart manufacturing for former non-technology (but now technology-following) SMMEs should also be considered in future studies.

The systematic review is limited in its time horizon and its emphasis on low-income/high-income context. Further research is needed that uses other regional aspects.

52      L. Gumbi and H. Twinomurinzi

# References

1. Kang, H.S., et al.: Smart Manufacturing: past research, present findings, and future directions. Int. J. Precis. Eng. Manuf. Green Technol. 3, 111–128 (2016). https://doi.org/10.1007/s40684-016-0015-5
2. Riddick, F., Wallace, E., Davis, J.: Variability in food production. J. Res. Natl. Inst. Stand. Technol. 121, 17–32 (2016). https://doi.org/10.6028/jres.121.002
3. Issa, A., Hatboglu, B., Bildstein, A., Bauernhansl, T.: Industry 4.0 roadmap: framework for digital transformation based on the concepts of capability maturity and alignment. Procedia CIRP. 72, 973–978 (2018). https://doi.org/10.1016/j.procir.2018.03.151
4. Zhong, R.Y., Xu, X., Klotz, E., Newman, S.T.: Intelligent manufacturing in the context of industry 4.0: a review. Engineering 3, 616–630 (2017). https://doi.org/10.1016/J.ENG.2017.05.015
5. Mittal, S., Khan, M.A., Romero, D., Wuest, T.: A critical review of smart manufacturing & Industry 4.0 maturity models: Implications for small and medium-sized enterprises (SMEs). J. Manuf. Syst. 49, 194–214 (2018). https://doi.org/10.1016/j.jmsy.2018.10.005
6. Thoben, K.-D., Wiesner, S., Wuest, T.: "Industrie 4.0" and Smart Manufacturing – a review of research issues and application examples. Int. J. Autom. Technol. 11, 4–19 (2017). https://doi.org/10.20965/ijat.2017.p0004
7. Mittal, S., Khan, M.A., Wuest, T.: Smart Manufacturing: characteristics and technologies. IFIP Adv. Inf. Commun. Technol. 492, 539–548 (2016). https://doi.org/10.1007/978-3-319-54660-5_48
8. Davis, J., Edgar, T., Porter, J., Bernaden, J., Sarli, M.: Smart manufacturing, manufacturing intelligence and demand-dynamic performance. Comput. Chem. Eng. 47, 145–156 (2012). https://doi.org/10.1016/j.compchemeng.2012.06.037
9. Jun, C., Yeon, J., Yoon, J., Hyun, B.: Applications' integration and operation platform to support smart manufacturing by small and medium-sized enterprises. Procedia Manuf. 11, 1950–1957 (2017). https://doi.org/10.1016/j.promfg.2017.07.341
10. Müller, J.M., Voigt, K.A.I.I.: Industry 4.0 - integration strategies for small and medium - sized enterprises. In: IAMOT 2017 Conference Proceedings (2017)
11. Safar, L., Sopko, J., Bednar, S., Poklemba, R.: Concept of SME business model for Industry 4.0 environment. TEM J. 7, 626–637 (2018). https://doi.org/10.18421/TEM73-20
12. Luff, P.: The 4th industrial revolution and SMEs in Malaysia and Japan: some economic, social and ethical considerations. Reitaku Int. J. Econ. Stud. 25, 25–48 (2017)
13. Mittal, S., Romero, D., Wuest, T.: Towards a smart manufacturing maturity model for SMEs (SM$^3$E). In: Moon, I., Lee, Gyu M., Park, J., Kiritsis, D., von Cieminski, G. (eds.) APMS 2018. IAICT, vol. 536, pp. 155–163. Springer, Cham (2018). https://doi.org/10.1007/978-3-319-99707-0_20
14. Mittal, S., Romero, D., Wuest, T.: Towards a smart manufacturing toolkit for SMEs 1, 155–163 (2018). https://doi.org/10.1007/978-3-319-99707-0_20
15. Moeuf, A., et al.: The industrial management of SMEs in the era of Industry 4.0. Int. J. Prod. Res. (2018). https://doi.org/10.1080/00207543.2017.1372647. 7543, 0
16. Hamdi, S.E.L.: Disposition of moroccan SME manufacturers to Industry 4.0 with the implementation of ERP as a first step. In: 2018 Sixth International Conference on Enterprise System, pp. 116–122 (2018). https://doi.org/10.1109/es.2018.00025
17. Nowotarski, P., Paslawski, J.: Industry 4.0 concept introduction into construction SMEs. In: IOP Conference Series: Materials Science and Engineering (2017)
18. Sommer, L.: Industrial Revolution - Industry 4.0: are German Manufacturing SMEs the first victims of this revolution? J. Ind. Eng. Manag. 8, 1512–1532 (2015)

19. Nooteboom, B.: Innovation and diffusion in small firms: theory and evidence. Small Bus. Econ. **6**, 327–347 (1994). https://doi.org/10.1007/bf01065137
20. Nooteboom, B., Coehoorn, C., Van Der Zwaan, A.: The purpose and effectiveness of technology transfer to small businesses by government-sponsored innovation centres. Technol. Anal. Strateg. Manag. **4**, 149–166 (1992). https://doi.org/10.1080/09537329208524089
21. Tornatzky, L., Klein, K.: Innovation characteristics and innovation adoption-implementation: a meta-analysis of findings. IEEE Trans. Eng. Manag. **29**, 28–43 (1982). https://doi.org/10.1109/TEM.1982.6447463
22. Rogers, E.M.: Difiusion of innovations. Free Press, New York (1983)
23. Gumbi, L.N., Mnkandla, E.: Investigating South African Vendors' cloud computing value proposition to small, medium and micro enterprises: a case of the City of Tshwane Metropolitan Municipality. African J. Inf. Syst. 7, 1936–282 (2015)
24. Lage Junior, M., Godinho Filho, M.: Variations of the Kanban system: literature review and classification. Int. J. Prod. Econ. **125**(1), 13–21 (2010)
25. Amui, L.B.L., Jabbour, C.J.C., de Sousa Jabbour, A.B.L., Kannan, D.: Sustainability as a dynamic organizational capability: a systematic review and a future agenda toward a sustainable transition. J. Clean. Prod. **142**, 308–322 (2017). https://doi.org/10.1016/j.jclepro.2016.07.103
26. Thoben, K.-D., Wiesner, S., Wuest, T.: "Industrie 4.0" and smart manufacturing – a review of research issues and application examples. Int. J. Autom. Technol. **11**, 4–16 (2017). https://doi.org/10.20965/ijat.2017.p0004
27. Yang, H., Tate, M., Mary Tate, V.: A descriptive literature review and classification of cloud computing research. Commun. Assoc. Inf. Syst. **31**, 35–60 (2012)
28. El-Gazzar, R.F.: A literature review on cloud computing adoption issues in enterprises. In: Bergvall-Kåreborn, B., Nielsen, P.A. (eds.) TDIT 2014. IAICT, vol. 429, pp. 214–242. Springer, Heidelberg (2014). https://doi.org/10.1007/978-3-662-43459-8_14
29. Osman Adam, I., Musah, A.: Small and Medium Enterprises (SMEs) in the cloud in developing countries: a synthesis of the literature and future research directions. J. Manag. Sustain. **5** (2015). https://doi.org/10.5539/jms.v5n1p115
30. Asatiani, A.: Why cloud? -a review of cloud adoption determinants in organizations. Twenty-Thrid ECIS **2015**, 1–17 (2015)
31. Attard, J., Orlandi, F., Scerri, S., Auer, S.: A systematic review of open government data initiatives. Gov. Inf. Q. **32**, 399–418 (2015). https://doi.org/10.1016/j.giq.2015.07.006
32. Jacsó, P.: The plausibility of computing the h-index of scholarly productivity and impact using reference-enhanced databases. Online Inf. Rev. **32**, 266–283 (2008). https://doi.org/10.1108/14684520810879872
33. Shah, S.R.U., Mahmood, K.: Review of Google scholar, Web of Science, and Scopus search results: the case of inclusive education research. Libr. Philos. Pract. 1544 (2017)
34. Fahimnia, B., Sarkis, J., Davarzani, H.: Green supply chain management: a review and bibliometric analysis. Int. J. Prod. Econ. **162**, 101–114 (2015)
35. Junior, M.L., Filho, M.G.: Production planning and control for remanufacturing: literature review and analysis. Prod. Plan. Control. **23**, 419–435 (2012). https://doi.org/10.1080/09537287.2011.561815
36. Jabbour, C.J.C.: Environmental training in organisations: from a literature review to a framework for future research. Resour. Conserv. Recycl. **74**, 144–155 (2013). https://doi.org/10.1016/j.resconrec.2012.12.017
37. Jabbour, C.J.C., Jugend, D., De Sousa Jabbour, A.B.L., Gunasekaran, A., Latan, H.: Green product development and performance of Brazilian firms: measuring the role of human and

technical aspects. J. Clean. Prod. **87**, 442–451 (2015). https://doi.org/10.1016/j.jclepro.2014. 09.036

38. Mariano, E.B., Sobreiro, V.A., do Nascimento Rebelatto, D.A.: Human development and data envelopment analysis: a structured literature review. Omega **54**, 33–49 (2015). https:// doi.org/10.1016/j.omega.2015.01.002

39. Kim, M., Zoo, H., Lee, H., Kang, J.: Mobile, Financial inclusion and development: a critical review of academic literature. In: GlobDev (2017)

40. Hamidi, S.R., Aziz, A.A., Shuhidan, S.M., Aziz, A., Mokhsin, M.: SMEs maturity model assessment of IR4.0 digital transformation. In: International Conference on Kansei Engineering & Emotion Research, pp. 721–732 (2018)

41. Alshamaila, Y., Papagiannidis, S., Li, F.: Cloud computing adoption by SMEs in the north east of England. J. Enterp. Inf. Manag. **26**, 250–275 (2013). https://doi.org/10.1108/ 17410391311325225

# Using Theories to Design a Value Alignment Model for Smart City Initiatives

Anthea van der Hoogen$^{(\boxtimes)}$ ⓘ, Brenda Scholtz ⓘ,
and Andre P. Calitz ⓘ

Department of Computing Sciences, Nelson Mandela University, Summerstrand,
Port Elizabeth 6019, South Africa
{anthea.vanderhoogen, brenda.scholtz,
andre.calitz}@mandela.ac.za

**Abstract.** Smart city initiatives are widely becoming part of the world agenda to address crises and to identify new initiatives for countries to manage resources while providing better living conditions for all citizens. The purpose of this study was to design a model to support the alignment of value in Smart City initiatives. To address this purpose, a systematic literature review (SLR) was conducted to find what Smart City initiatives have been addressed in empirical studies, and what dimensions and factors are linked to these initiatives. The SLR also identified the stakeholders in a Smart City, and what their roles should be linked to these initiatives. Six theories were identified and used to undergird the researcher's understanding of the domains of Smart Cities, value and alignment. The concepts from these theories were then used with the SLR findings to design a conceptual model for Smart City initiatives. The proposed Value Alignment Smart City Model (VASC) can be used to plan or assess Smart City initiatives. The main contribution is the alignment of value amongst stakeholders to support the success of such initiatives. Further research is required to investigate adopting the model and empirically evaluate it.

**Keywords:** Dimensions · Factors · Stakeholder roles · Value · Alignment · Theories

## 1 Introduction

Even though there is no consensus by researchers regarding the definition of a Smart City, many agree on certain aspects that can help with the understanding of what Smart City studies are about [1]. The common component of Smart Cities reported is ICT solutions that address economic, social and environmental issues to contribute to a better quality of life for the citizens [1–3]. It is found that addressing Smart City concepts and trends through initiatives can help to reach a cohesive understanding amongst cities in the world who are trying to overcome similar or different problems [1, 3]. The feasibility of Smart City initiatives is driven from the point of view that it is depending on Big Data and the Internet of Things (IoT) [1, 4]. Smart city initiatives should further incorporate technologies such as sensors where data can be collected and analysed so those who need the information can make informed decisions and manage administrative tasks [5].

© IFIP International Federation for Information Processing 2020
Published by Springer Nature Switzerland AG 2020
M. Hattingh et al. (Eds.): I3E 2020, LNCS 12066, pp. 55–66, 2020.
https://doi.org/10.1007/978-3-030-44999-5_5

Conventional and futuristic Smart City initiatives can still be classified or fit in the six dimensions namely Smart People, Smart Governance, Smart Economy, Smart Environment, Smart Mobility, and Smart Living [6]. These dimensions are said to characterise what a smart city should include and for each dimension there are factors that characterise the dimension's success [7]. A study on Smart City definitions identified certain factors on the importance of a Smart City and the information flow between the factors [7]. Their definition will be adopted for this study and states that:

*"A Smart City is based on intelligent exchanges of information that flow between its many different subsystems. This flow of information is analyzed and translated into citizen and commercial services. The city will act on this information flow to make its wider ecosystem more resource-efficient and sustainable. The information exchange is based on a smart governance operating framework designed to make cities sustainable"*. Many studies have investigated endless lists of initiatives, factors and technologies in Smart City research fields. Some studies have also addressed instruments for assessing the alignment of value and the practices of creating value [8–10]. However, few studies have assessed the perceived value by stakeholders amongst these initiatives according to the theories found for Smart Cities, theories for value and theories for alignment. The research question this study will investigate is *"What appropriate theoretical concepts can be used that will help to build a conceptual model to support the alignment of value in Smart City initiatives?"*.

The data value chain is seen as an important component within the conceptual model to ensure that data for each initiative can be identified for all the stakeholder interest. The rest of the paper starts with the research design (Sect. 2) followed, by findings from the dimensions and factors of a Smart City (Sect. 3). The stakeholders are perceived as a critical component in Smart City (Sect. 3.3). For this reason, it is even more important to identify the value created for each stakeholder that can ensure alignment between all the stakeholders' interests (Sect. 4). The proposed Value Alignment Smart City model (VASC) includes the components that can form part of a Smart City to achieve success in projects (Sect. 5). Finally, conclusions and future research are provided (Sect. 6).

## 2   Research Design

The research approach used to answer the research question was a systematic literature review (SLR) [11]. The journal articles, conference papers and reports were selected from Google Scholar, Google, and Research Gate. Only studies that cited real examples of Smart City initiatives were considered in the review. White papers and reports were excluded from the SLR. Only papers that were published between 2011 and 2018 were included, since it was shown by [12] that Smart City research started to boom from 2010 onward. The SLR started with the identification of nine Smart City dimensions from 15 initial studies (Sect. 3.1). The keywords were derived from the research question of this study and included "smart city framework", "smart city initiative", and "smart city dimension". The second round of the SLR included the identification of 39 related factors across all nine dimensions only from empirical studies included in the first round and the findings are summarized (available on request). The second round eliminated non-empirical studies and the final list of 12 studies was used as part of the analysis (available on request). The third round of the SLR helped to identify 58 stakeholder types across four stakeholder roles namely: Enabler; Provider; Utiliser and User. The final list of stakeholder types was reduced to 30 types after eliminating any duplications across the studies included in the analysis (available on request).

Finally, theories from the three domains namely Smart Cities, Value, and Alignment were investigated (Table 1). Six theories were identified as relevant and used together with the SLR findings to guide the selection of the components for the VASC model. A summary of these theories and the related components are listed in Table 1.

**Table 1.** Theoretical concepts informing the VASC model

| Domain | Theoretical concepts | Component of the VASC model |
|---|---|---|
| Smart Cities (SLR) | Hexagonal Dimension Theory [6, 13] | Original dimensions: Smart People; Smart Governance; Smart Economy; Smart Environment; Smart Mobility; and Smart Living |
| | Strategic Priority Areas Theory [14] | Extra dimensions: Smart Policy; Smart Organisation; and Smart Technology-and-ICT Infrastructure |
| | Triple Helix Model Theory [15] | Stakeholder roles and types |
| Value | Complex Value Typology Theory [16] | Five phases of benefits realisation for all stakeholders<br>Data Value Chain: data gathered and converted into beneficial information across all areas within a Smart City |
| Alignment | Strategic Perspective of Alignment [17–19] | Strategic initiatives of Smart City projects aligned to all components of the model |
| | Structural Alignment Theory [19, 20] | Alignment of roles/responsibilities of Smart City structures for all stakeholders |

The Hexagonal Dimension Theory (HDT) was selected from the Smart City domain and proposes the first six dimensions for the VASC model [6, 13]. The HDT is based on models discussing the analysis, relationships, and indicators of the six Smart City dimensions from [6]. Indicators that should be used for assessment to help determine how Smart Cities are ranked are proposed by [13, 22]. Three additional dimensions were selected as part of the VASC model, based on the Strategic Priority Areas Theory (SPAT) [14]. The additional dimensions in this study are Smart Policy; Smart Organisation, and Smart Technology-and-ICT Infrastructure [23]. The Triple Helix Model Theory (THMT) [15], emphasises the importance of the core stakeholders roles and types such as academia, industry, and government, which are key component of any national or multi-national innovation strategy and therefore any Smart City initiatives. The Complex Value Typology Theory (CVTT) was used to guide the researcher's understanding of value [16]. In this theory, value can be viewed as the nature of the benefits incurred by the stakeholders. Therefore the five phases of benefits' realisation [24], are important to be able to identify the potential benefits of all stakeholders in a Smart City initiative. Since one of the key elements of all the technologies involved in a Smart City is the data, the data value chain is extremely relevant for providing value to the stakeholders or for assessing where value is realised. The Strategic Perspective of Alignment (SPA) theory was used to guide the researcher's understanding of alignment and the Structural Alignment Type (SAT) theory was incorporated to align performance of Smart City initiatives between IT strategy and the organisational strategy [25]; as reported in [17–19]. SAT is a type of alignment based on a systematic view of a structure to ensure that strategic goals are achieved [20, 21]. The importance of having structures in place for a Smart City is important as well as to achieve the strategic goals within those structures because from these structures clear roles and responsibilities can be aligned between the stakeholders of Smart City initiatives.

## 3 Findings: Smart City Dimensions and Factors

In this section, the term dimension(s) will be used to describe the list of dimensions highlighted in Sect. 3.1. Any other aspects that are further used to describe these dimensions will be referred to as factors and these are described in Sect. 3.2.

### 3.1 Dimensions

The first round of the SLR resulted in the findings summarised in Table 2 relating to dimensions referred to in the empirical studies reviewed. The importance of considering the dimensions in a Smart City initiative was confirmed and that measures should be in place to ensure that cities continue to find smarter ways of dealing with challenges [7, 26]. The studies are listed in chronological order (Table 2). The 'x' in Table 2 represents the dimensions that are applied or mentioned in the relevant empirical study as a contributor in a Smart City and the frequency (f) of citations for each dimension is provided. The first six dimensions (D1–D6) of Smart Cities were identified by [22] and [6] and are Smart People, Smart Governance, Smart Economy, Smart Environment, Smart Mobility, and Smart Living. These were extended by three dimensions (D7–D9) proposed by [23], namely Smart Policy, Smart Organisation, and Smart Technology-and-ICT Infrastructure. Each dimension in the VASC model (Fig. 1) was classified as either a core dimension or a support dimension. Smart People (D1) and Smart Technology-and-ICT Infrastructure (D9) are classified as support dimensions to the other core dimensions (D2-D8). This classification was based on the description of Porter's value chain according to the support activities or functions in an organisation [27], where the well-known support functions in an organisation include IT and Human Resource Management. The only studies that reported on all nine dimensions were [28] and [29]. Smart economy and smart living were the top two dimensions reported on (f = 11). Smart people, smart policy and smart technology-and-ICT infrastructure are the second-highest dimensions reported (f = 10). The dimensions that were least reported on within its context of being applied within Smart Cities are smart mobility and smart organisation. Smart People (D1) is the first important dimension identified by several Smart City studies [6, 23, 28–33]. This dimension recognises that people who are stakeholders can contribute to a Smart City's success. The second last row in Table 2 indicates the total number of studies per dimension where "x" number of factors are found, i.e. not all dimensions have factors linked to each per empirical study.

**Table 2.** Comparison of studies of Smart City dimensions (Author's construct)

| Dimension (D) | D1 SMART PEOPLE | D2 SMART GOVERNANCE | D3 SMART ECONOMY | D4 SMART ENVIRONMENT | D5 SMART MOBILITY | D6 SMART LIVING | D7 SMART POLICY | D8 SMART ORGANISATION | D9 SMART TECHNOLOGY & ICT INFRASTRUCTURE | Total number of dimensions |
|---|---|---|---|---|---|---|---|---|---|---|
| [6] | x | x | x | x | x | x | | | | 6 |
| [30] | | | | | | | x | x | x | 3 |
| [37] | x | x | x | | x | x | x | x | x | 8 |
| [23] | x | x | x | x | | | x | x | x | 7 |
| [39] | x | x | x | x | x | x | | | | 6 |
| [2] | x | x | x | x | x | x | | | | 6 |
| [33] | x | x | x | x | | x | | | | 5 |
| [28] | x | x | x | x | x | x | x | x | x | 9 |
| [35] | | | x | x | | x | x | | x | 5 |
| [29] | x | x | x | x | x | x | x | x | x | 9 |
| [38] | | | | | | | x | | x | 2 |
| [36] | | | x | | | x | x | | | 3 |
| [32] | x | | x | | | | x | x | x | 5 |
| [34] | | x | | | x | x | x | | x | 5 |
| [33] | x | | | x | | x | | x | x | 5 |
| Total number of studies | 10 | 9 | 11 | 9 | 7 | 11 | 10 | 7 | 10 | |
| Total number of studies with factors | 8 | 7 | 9 | 7 | 5 | 9 | 10 | 7 | 10 | |

Some of the factors related to people are the level of qualification, affinity to lifelong learning, social and ethnic plurality, creativity, and synergies through partnerships and collaborations. The second dimension is Smart Governance (D2), which was identified as an important dimension that includes factors that drive a Smart City such as participation in decision-making, public and social services and transparent governance [6, 23, 28–31, 34]. The third dimension commonly cited in Smart City studies is Smart Economy (D3) [6, 23, 28–32, 35, 36]. This dimension refers to activities that encourage innovation, entrepreneurship spirit, productivity and international embeddedness. Seven studies reported on the importance of Smart Environment (D4) as a dimension [6, 23, 28, 29, 31, 33, 35]. This discussion relates to factors such as: attractiveness of natural conditions, environmental protection policies and being able to have sustainable resource management, and ensuring that a city is future proof (i.e. sustainable) by having a sustainability strategy to address social-economic, political and environmental aspects of a city. Interestingly, sustainable resource management and a future proof city were reported in the same seven studies as important for a Smart City. Smart Mobility (D5) is the dimension that focuses on factors involving sustainable, innovative and safe transport systems that are accessible locally, nationally and internationally [6, 28–30, 34]. The sixth dimension (D6) is Smart

Living, which includes factors such as cultural facilities, health conditions, individual safety, housing quality and education facilities. Smart Policy (D7) is the dimension that highlights the importance of a close relationship between a Smart City initiative and the city's policy and the importance of an innovative policy [28–30, 32, 34–38].

The Smart Organisation dimension was identified as the eighth dimension (D8), and is important since organisational culture and innovative leadership and management can influence the success of a Smart City [23, 28–30, 32, 33, 37]. The ninth dimension (D9) is Smart Technology and ICT-infrastructure and includes all the smart technologies that are used in a Smart City used for the collection and analysis of all related data. This is only possible when there is easy access and availability in the ICT-infrastructure [23, 28–30, 32–35, 37, 38].

## 3.2   Factors

Dimensions and factors should be incorporated in studies of Smart Cities, but provision should be made for other factors to be included when gathering data and findings of studies [22]. Each dimension of a Smart City can be categorised and ultimately measured in terms of a number of factors. From the second round of the SLR process, 39 factors (F1 to F39) were identified; however the details could not be included due to space constraints but are available on request. The studies of [39] and [2] were excluded from this analysis as they did not provide empirical evidence of the factors; therefore they are highlighted in Table 2.

A total of 12 empirical studies were therefore included in the analysis of the 39 factors. The first 31 factors identified for the first six dimensions were proposed by [6] and confirmed by other studies [23, 28–38], and the remaining eight factors were found in other studies (details available on request).

## 3.3   Stakeholder Roles and Types

Arguments show the utmost importance to involve all stakeholders in Smart City initiatives, to address the challenges of these initiatives [34, 37], and to lead to successful innovative solutions [23]. Stakeholders such as citizens, end-users, IT experts and policy experts are key to the architecture of a Smart City [30]. Understanding the needs and wants of all stakeholders will improve the citizen-government relationship [23]. A significant challenge faced by Smart Cities is to efficiently articulate the relationship between these stakeholders and the city management [29]. Four key roles for stakeholders were identified in [40], namely: enablers, providers, utilisers and users. Enablers create a vision, allocate resources, provide strategic leadership, and promote networking. Providers engage academics and professionals as innovators, provide innovative research and design (R&D) methods, augment knowledge and manage knowledge distribution systematically. Utilisers create suitable products and services, set small-scale objectives derived from the vision, learn new practices to produce accessible knowledge and innovate. Users participate in experiments, empower citizens through co-creation and produce place-based experience. The third round of the SLR identified 58 relevant stakeholder types cited in 15 studies (Table 3). In these studies, common stakeholders were recognised, however on occasions different terms were used to refer to similar stakeholder types in Smart Cities. The studies are listed in chronological order in Table 3. Six stakeholders namely, governments in other jurisdictions, non-profits, companies, schools, universities, and citizens were identified by [23]. Five stakeholder types were identified by [39], namely users, the public, administration, vendors and government. One study [41] argues that all investors (public and private) are important stakeholders. Residents and workers are amongst the stakeholders found in a Smart City [2]. It was evident in [31], that citizens are key to be engaged in Smart City projects to establish their needs, but industrial stakeholders are also important as they give the recommendations needed for new businesses. To create a sustainable city, the participation from stakeholders such as public government, NGOs, private companies and individual citizens is required [35]. Three stakeholder types were reported in [29], citizens, government, and businesses. The authors in [33], agree that citizens and government are key stakeholders. Stakeholders influencing privacy of Big Data such as data controllers, data processors, and third parties should be considered in a Smart City [38]. Open data is part of Smart Cities and the people that are involved with open data projects are stakeholders and can be used to brainstorm innovative ideas [36].

**Table 3.** Stakeholder types (Author's construct)

| Study | Stakeholder types (n = 58) |
|---|---|
| [37] | Governments; Firms; Non-profits; Citizens |
| [30] | End-users; IT experts; Policy/service domain experts; Public managers |
| [23] | Governments in other jurisdictions; Non-profits; Companies; Schools; Universities; Citizens |
| [39] | Users; Public administrations; Vendors; Government |
| [41] | Investors (public and private) |
| [2] | Residents/Citizens; Workers |
| [31] | Citizens; Industrial stakeholders |
| [28] | Performance evaluators |
| [35] | Public government; Private companies; NGOs; Citizens |
| [29] | Citizens; Government; Businesses |
| [38] | Individuals; Data controllers; Data processors; Third parties |
| [36] | Public officials; Independent developers; Technically savvy citizens; NGOs; Academic communities; Media communities |
| [32] | Industrial players; Business players; Dynamic small and medium-sized enterprises (SMEs); Building owners; Universities; Research & technology organisations; Major standardisation institutes; Government; Citizens; Local experts; External domain experts |
| [34] | Citizens; City managers; Developers; Governments |
| [33] | Citizens; Government |

They could be independent developers, technically savvy citizens, academic communities or non-governmental organisations. The co-creation process for Smart

City solutions, identified by [32], reiterates the importance of the involvement of all stakeholders (industrial and business players to external domain experts) and the alignment of value to achieving Smart City success. City managers and government should provide easy accessibility and interactions for users such as developers and citizens to open datasets [34] since this should help these users to understand the datasets and to identify ways toward sustainable open data systems.

An analysis of the definitions taken from [40] for each role was used to classify each stakeholder type according to the most relevant role. This analysis resulted in the initial list of 58 stakeholder types being reduced to 30 common types (T1 to T30) across the 15 studies and the four stakeholder roles (available on request). For example company types such as private, public, firms and SMEs were combined into one type. Two stakeholder types (city mayor and think tanks/incubators) were not identified in the studies in Table 3 but were added to the final list based on the argument of [40] that they are equally important stakeholders. Citizens as stakeholders were reported in 11 of the 15 studies, making this the most popular type reported. Six studies reported government and four studies reported companies as important. It is clear that when a city wants to co-create smart solutions, many different types of stakeholders have to be considered.

## 4  Alignment of Value for Benefits Realisation

The previous sections related to the SLR findings, it is evident that the dimensions, factors and stakeholders of a Smart City should be used to assess the benefits of a Smart City initiative. However, existing Smart City studies do not explore whether or not the benefits of initiatives are realised or whether stakeholder value is considered or aligned. It is argued that what one stakeholder might view as a successful or valuable initiative may not be considered as successful or valuable to another stakeholder. In order to finalise the model so that value can be considered, the value theory of [15] was incorporated, which equates the assessment of benefit to the concept of value [16]. For example, *"human wants, needs, and interest that are served by their realisation"* [16].

In another study of value, the authors showed the factors influencing value co-creation established by [42] and also applied by [24]. They proposed an integrated process model for co-realisation of value, and they used a government case study in Norway to validate their approach to co-realisation of IT value in a collaborative setting. In the study of [24] the value co-creation process incorporated five phases for benefits realisation to co-create IT value. Their study contributed to value theory and showed that these phases are appropriate for new, major service development in the Norwegian government. This phased approach can be adopted in Smart City initiatives to achieve alignment of stakeholder value. The first phase is Phase 1-Articulate benefits whereby the key benefit areas, Key Performance Indicators (KPI) and goals are identified and articulated amongst all stakeholders. Potential benefit areas for new services in a Smart City were also explored. Based on the THMT and studies, as many stakeholders from the roles and types should be considered and should collaborate on services in a Smart City. The second phase is Phase 2-Plan benefits realisation where the registrar (i.e. Smart City project manager) assists the service owners (i.e. stakeholders) in elaborating their ideas into a detailed benefits plan with action steps to ensure that the benefits will be realised. In Phase 3-Implement plan, the service stakeholder has to implement the plan according to the benefit plan from Phase 2. In Phase 4-Measure benefits realised, the service stakeholder has to measure the benefits according to the measurements from the benefit plan in Phase 2 and report these to the registrar. Lastly, Phase 5-Evaluate benefits gaps and needs is where the registrar evaluates all the reports from all service stakeholders and decides on corrective measures to be taken where delays in services are evident.

## 5 Discussion and Proposed Model

The proposed VASC model is shown in Fig. 1 and represents the important components of a Smart City to achieve the success of a Smart City project or initiatives. The model was designed based on the SLR findings and the six theories, relating to the domains of Smart Cities, value, and alignment. The first component is the nine dimensions of a Smart City (see Fig. 1). Each dimension has several factors for determining the success of the dimension (available on request). The second component is the four stakeholder roles, which is a key component, since if the stakeholders are not considered no Smart City initiative will be successful. In order to ensure the value or benefits derived from such initiatives, five phases should be followed and are included as the third component of the model.

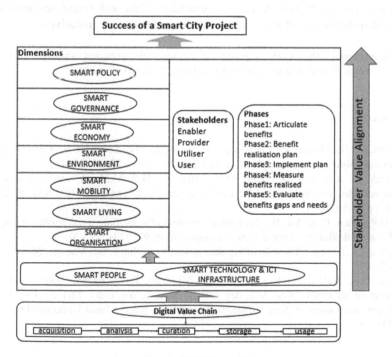

**Fig. 1.** VASC model

Finally, any Smart City initiative is dependent on the information flow that supports it. Information flow is described as a "series of steps needed to generate value and useful insights from data" [43]. To obtain value from a Smart City initiative, the data value chain is therefore a crucial consideration and is the last component in the model. The data value chain includes the entire data life-cycle and involves data acquisition, analysis, curation, storage and usage so it can be used for decision making by relevant stakeholders.

# 6   Conclusions

Smart City research has made strides to making it easier to identify smarter ways of addressing real-world problems, especially with regards to the pressures of urbanisation and resource depletion. However, consensus on the definition, required components and value for Smart Cities has yet to be reached. The theoretical perspectives explored in this study can assist researchers to move closer to such consensus. The SLR conducted focused on seeking empirical studies of Smart City projects and reviewed theories that can help to address the gaps in knowledge relating to value in Smart Cities.

The study contributes to showing real-world examples in Smart Cities, and provides a comprehensive lists of factors that can be classified for each dimension. A gap in previous research was evident relating to value alignment for Smart Cities, and this study fills this gap. The contribution is the proposed VASC model, which can be used to address how value can be aligned within a Smart City for all stakeholders and dimensions. The study was limited to secondary data and future research should therefore investigate the adoption of the model in Smart City initiatives.

**Acknowledgement.** "This work is based on the research supported wholly/in part by the National Research Foundation of South Africa (Grant Numbers: 116779)".

# References

1. Neirotti, P., De Marco, A., Cagliano, A.C., Mangano, G., Scorrano, F.: Current trends in smart city initiatives: some stylised facts. Cities **38**(April), 25–36 (2014)
2. Hamzah, H., Adnan, Y.M., Daud, M.N., Alias, A., Dali, M.M.: A smart city assessment framework. In: 8th International Real Estate Researchers Symposium (IRERS), 26–28 April 2016, pp. 1–5 (2016)
3. Lu, H.P., Chen, C.S., Yu, H.: Technology roadmap for building a smart city: an exploring study on methodology. Future Gener. Comput. Syst. **97**, 727–742 (2019)
4. Hashem, I.A.T., et al.: The role of big data in smart city. Int. J. Inf. Manage. **36**(5), 748–758 (2016)
5. Abreu, D.P., Velasquez, K., Curado, M., Monteiro, E.: A resilient Internet of Things architecture for smart cities. Ann. des Telecommun. Telecommun. **72**(1–2), 19–30 (2017)
6. Giffinger, R.: European Smart Citie: the need for a place related Understanding, Austria (2011)

7. Albino, V., Berardi, U., Dangelico, R.M.: Smart cities: definitions, dimensions, performance, and initiatives. J. Urban Technol. **22**(1), 1–19 (2015)
8. Dameri, R.P., Rosenthal-Sabroux, C.: Smart city and value creation. In: Dameri, R.P., Rosenthal-Sabroux, C. (eds.) Smart City. PI, pp. 1–12. Springer, Cham (2014). https://doi.org/10.1007/978-3-319-06160-3_1
9. Van Den Bergh, J., Dootson, P., Kowalkiewicz, M., Viaene, S.: Smart city initiatives: designing a project-level smart value assessment instrument. In: Proceedings of 19th Annual International Conference on Digital Government Research (2018)
10. Pellicano, M., Calabrese, M., Loia, F., Maione, G.: Value co-creation practices in smart city ecosystem. J. Serv. Sci. Manag. **12**(01), 34–57 (2019)
11. Kitchenham, B., Pearl Brereton, O., Budgen, D., Turner, M., Bailey, J., Linkman, S.: Systematic literature reviews in software engineering – a systematic literature review. Inf. Softw. Technol. **51**, 7–15 (2009)
12. Mora, L., Bolici, R., Deakin, M.: The first two decades of smart-city research: a bibliometric analysis. J. Urban Technol. **24**(1), 3–27 (2017)
13. Kishore, A.N.N., Sodh, Z.: Exploratory research on smart cities: theory, policy and practice, New Delhi (2015)
14. Allwinkle, S., Cruickshank, P.: Creating smarter cities: an overview. J. Urban Technol. **18** (2), 1–16 (2011)
15. Etzkowitz, H., Leydesdorff, L.: The triple helix-university-industry-government relations: a laboratory for knowledge based economic development. EASST Rev. **14**(1), 14–19 (1995)
16. Rescher, N.: Introduction to Value Theory. Prentice-Hall Inc., Englewood Cliffs (1969)
17. Avison, D., Jones, J., Powell, P., Wilson, D.: Using and validating the strategic alignment model. J. Strateg. Inf. Syst. **13**, 223–246 (2004)
18. Campbell, B., Kay, R., Avison, D.: Strategic alignment: a practitioner's perspective. J. Enterp. Inf. Manag. **18**(6), 653–664 (2005)
19. Burn, J.M., Szeto, C.: A comparison of the views of business and IT management on success factors for strategic alignment. Inf. Manag. **37**, 197–216 (2000)
20. Chorn, N.H.: The 'alignment' theory: creating strategic fit. Manag. Decis. **29**(1), 20–24 (1991)
21. Torraco, R.J., Swanson, R.A.: The strategic roles of human resource development. J. Eur. Ind. Training **18**(4), 10–21 (1995)
22. Giffinger, R., Fertner, C., Kramar, H., Kalasek, R., Milanovic, N.P., Meijers, E.: Smart Cities Ranking of European Medium-Sized Cities, pp. 13–18. Centre of Regional Science (SRF), Vienna University of Technology, Vienna (2007)
23. Alawadhi, S.: Building understanding of smart city initiatives. In: Scholl, H.J., Janssen, M., Wimmer, M.A., Moe, C.E., Flak, L.S. (eds.) EGOV 2012. LNCS, vol. 7443, pp. 40–53. Springer, Heidelberg (2012). https://doi.org/10.1007/978-3-642-33489-4_4
24. Flak, L.S., Solli-Saether, H., Straub, D.: Towards a theoretical model for co-realization of IT value in government. In: Proceedings of the 2015 48th Annual Hawaii International Conference on System Sciences, 05–08 January 2015, pp. 2486–2494 (2015)
25. Rose, K., Shuck, B., Bergman, M.: Unpacking organizational alignment: the view from theory and practice. J. Organ. Learn. Leadersh. **13**(1), 18–31 (2015)
26. Cocchia, A.: Smart and digital city: a systematic literature review. In: Dameri, R.P., Rosenthal-Sabroux, C. (eds.) Smart City. PI, pp. 13–43. Springer, Cham (2014). https://doi.org/10.1007/978-3-319-06160-3_2
27. Porter, M.E.: Competitive Advantage: Creating and Sustaining Superior Performance. Free Press, New York (1985)
28. Khatoun, R., Zeadally, S.: Smart cities: concepts, architectures, research opportunities. Commun. ACM **59**(8), 46–57 (2016)

29. Calderón, M., López, G., Marín, G.: Smart cities in Latin America. In: Ochoa, S.F., Singh, P., Bravo, J. (eds.) UCAmI 2017. LNCS, vol. 10586, pp. 15–26. Springer, Cham (2017). https://doi.org/10.1007/978-3-319-67585-5_2
30. Nam, T., Pardo, T.: Conceptualizing smart city with dimensions of technology, people, and institutions. In: Proceedings of the 12th Annual International Conference on Digital Government Research, pp. 282–291 (2011)
31. Huovila, A., Airaksinen, M., Pinto-Seppä, K.P., Penttinen, T.: Smart city performance measurement system. In: 41st IAHS World Congress: Sustainability and Innovation for the Future, 13–16 September 2016, pp. 1–11 (2016)
32. Wendt, W., Dübner, S.: Co-creation for smart city solutions – a peer-to-peer process. In: REAL CORP 2017 Proceedings, 12–14 September 2017, vol. 6, pp. 99–108 (2017)
33. Manupati, K.V., Ramkumar, M., Samanta, D.: A multi-criteria decision making approach for the urban renewal in Southern India. Sustain. Cities Soc. **42**, 471–481 (2018)
34. Yadav, P., Hasan, S., Ojo, A., Curry, E.: The role of open data in driving sustainable mobility in nine smart cities. In: 25th European Conference on Information Systems (ECIS 2017), Guimarães, Portugal, 5–10 June 2017, pp. 1248–1263 (2017)
35. Spaans, M., Waterhout, B.: Building up resilience in cities worldwide – Rotterdam as participant in the 100 Resilient Cities Programme. Cities **61**, 109–116 (2016)
36. Kassen, M.: Understanding transparency of government from a Nordic perspective: open government and open data movement as a multidimensional collaborative phenomenon in Sweden. J. Glob. Inf. Technol. Manag. **20**(4), 236–275 (2017)
37. Nam, T., Pardo, T.: Smart city as urban innovation: focusing on management, policy, and context. In: Proceedings of the 5th International Conference on Theory and Practice of Electronic Governance, pp. 185–194 (2011)
38. Garg, R., Schmitt, C., Stiller, B.: Information policy dimension of emerging technologies, 30 March 2017. https://ssrn.com/abstract=2943451. https://doi.org/10.2139/ssrn.2943451
39. Balakrishna, C.: Enabling technologies for smart city services and applications. In: Proceedings - 6th International Conference on Next Generation Mobile Applications, Services, and Technologies, NGMAST, pp. 223–227 (2012)
40. Mayangsari, L., Novani, S.: Multi-stakeholder co-creation analysis in smart city management: an experience from Bandung, Indonesia. Procedia Manuf. **4**, 315–321 (2015)
41. Monzon, A.: Smart cities concept and challenges: bases for the assessment of smart city projects. In: Helfert, M., Krempels, K.-H., Klein, C., Donnellan, B., Gusikhin, O. (eds.) Smart Cities, Green Technologies, and Intelligent Transport Systems. CCIS, vol. 579, pp. 17–31. Springer, Cham (2015). https://doi.org/10.1007/978-3-319-27753-0_2
42. Sarker, S., Sarker, S., Sahaym, A., Bjørn-Andersen, N.: Exploring value cocreation in relationships between an ERP vendor and its partners: a revelatory case study. MIS Q. **36**(1), 317–338 (2012)
43. Curry, E.: The big data value chain: definitions, concepts, and theoretical approaches. In: Cavanillas, J., Curry, E., Wahlster, W. (eds.) New Horizons for a Data-Driven Economy, pp. 29–37. Springer, Cham (2016). https://doi.org/10.1007/978-3-319-21569-3_3

# Complementary Partnerships for SMEs: A Relational Capability Maturity Model from an Ecosystem Perspective

Caro Els[1], Sara Grobbelaar[1,2(✉)] ⓘ, and Denzil Kennon[1] ⓘ

[1] Department of Industrial Engineering, Stellenbosch University,
Stellenbosch, South Africa
sssgrobbelaar@sun.ac.za
[2] DST-NRF Centre of Excellence in Scientometrics and Science,
Technology and Innovation Policy (SciSTIP), Stellenbosch University,
Stellenbosch, South Africa

**Abstract.** Inter-organisational relationships have been receiving increased attention in the context of the fourth industrial revolution. Technological advances in connectivity and digitisation are enabling vertically and horizontally integrated networks. The highly technical and dynamic environment in which various types of relationships exist requires a high level of cooperation and transparency between partners. The importance for Small and Medium Sized Organisations (SMEs) to develop and improve their relational capabilities is widely acknowledged. This research paper thus presents a tool and methodology that will enable SMEs to assess and improve these capabilities within the organisation. This paper aims to identify those requirements and practices described in the literature as conducive to sustainable relationship formation and development. A Relational Capability Maturity Model (RCMM) is proposed as a tool that will be able to address the requirements across the various functions of the organisation.

**Keywords:** Inter-organisational relationships · SMEs · Relational Capability Maturity Model · Relational capabilities

## 1 Introduction

Strong technological advances in connectivity and digitisation, are enabling integrated networks of firms, objects and systems. Transparent and flexible ecosystems are forming, cultivating dynamic, collaborative and symbiotic relationships between firms. These ecosystems are shaping new manners to create value. Increasingly, value is being created not only within firms, but rather within the rich interactions between them [1, 2]. The ecosystem perspective provides a powerful lens through which the transformation in the business landscape can be viewed, by emphasising the growing importance of relationships, partnerships, networks, alliances and collaboration [2].

'Ecosystems in a business context' is a concept derived from the biological sciences. Just as biological ecosystems consist of various interdependent species, business

© IFIP International Federation for Information Processing 2020
Published by Springer Nature Switzerland AG 2020
M. Hattingh et al. (Eds.): I3E 2020, LNCS 12066, pp. 67–78, 2020.
https://doi.org/10.1007/978-3-030-44999-5_6

ecosystems similarly consist of a variety of interdependent organisations. These dynamic and co-evolving communities create and capture new value through sophisticated models of collaboration and competition [2, 3]. Multiple players of different types and sizes are brought together to serve markets in ways that are beyond the capacity of any single organisation or any traditional industry.

The complementarity between partners have been identified as a core theme towards ecosystems value creation [4]. Shared value creation provides complementary benefits to the partners and complementary benefits are what is at the core of a sustainable partnership [5]. Small and large firms have complementary strengths and weaknesses in terms of research and development (R&D). The flexible structures and agile operations of SMEs are especially suitable for the early stages of the innovation process where ideas are created and conceptualised [5, 6]. SMEs have a relative advantage in learning and knowledge creation in emerging and risky areas [7]. Large firms on the other hand, have existing structures that are suitable for testing, documentation and operation processes that are found at the later stages of innovation [5]. The deep specialisation of SMEs can complement the service offering of large firms where they do not have the internal expertise. Large firms can in turn, expose SMEs to the critical resources and capabilities required to realise innovating ideas [2, 7].

Complementary benefits can also be found in the product or service offering of the individual firms. New and specialised capabilities are often considered a prerequisite to enable growth to new areas. While large firms usually focus on the products and services with major potential, they are able to access new capabilities from specialist firms, with less capital investment required on their own part [2, 5]. For SMEs, this means that they are able to move into the markets of the large firm without acquiring additional capabilities [8]. The advantage of partnerships with firms who have chosen to specialise in those activities, is that these firms are likely to perform the activities better. As a result, every activity is being performed by a tightly focused firm [2]. Their first-mover advantage will be enhanced, enabling them to increase their market share [8].

Another very important benefit from a partnership is in the form if organisational support. SMEs often have growth constraints due to undeveloped organisational structures and a lack of management skills [9]. Larger firms often offer their smaller partners resources such as marketing, distribution, manufacturing or training, as well as industry related know-how and expertise [10]. Large firms may even open up their contact networks to smaller partners and reference customers in the emerging industry. The reputation of the large firm usually has a positive impact on the credibility of their smaller partners. Increased credibility means that the cost of acquiring new customers or partners and sustaining existing ones will reduce [11].

Large firms often pressure smaller partners to increase its competitiveness continuously to produce high quality services or products. SMEs would often receive customer-triggered relationship requirements, resulting in the need to customise technologies and systems specifically to suit their partners [5, 12]. While these adaptations imply considerable, often non-transferable, investments by one or both parties, it simultaneously provides learning opportunities. The knowledge that SMEs acquire throughout the unique projects can be transferred to other partnerships or developed to products. In this regard, partnerships are seen as a key resource access to valuable organisational, technical and market knowledge held by key customers. This knowledge can then be used to improve and upgrade products and services, production facilities and organisational units and mechanisms [11].

For SMEs to be able to exploit the opportunities from ecosystems, the nature of the support available to SMEs require a shift in focus. The highly technical and dynamic ecosystem environment require a high level of cooperation and transparency between partners [13]. As a result, the establishment of partnerships and the development of trust simultaneously becomes increasingly critical and complex. For SMEs, who are traditionally known to suffer from severe resource constraints, creating partnerships with larger firms are becoming even more challenging [14, 15]. Partnerships between small and larger firms are often asymmetrical, and SMEs are mostly not equipped to deal with power imbalances due to their lack of resources [5].

For SMEs to be able to establish more sustainable partnerships, they require technical, organisational, and managerial capabilities that can address the challenges presented by dynamic environments and changing relationship requirements [10]. These relational capabilities enable firms to relate to other firms more successfully, contributing to both their own knowledge and to that of their relationships [16]. This paper aims to identify those requirements and practices described in the literature as conducive to sustainable relationship formation and development.

## 2  Methodology

The context of this research is centred predominately on SMEs, which can be considered to be a complex system of cultural, process, and technological components that interact with each other [17]. The research in this paper therefore followed the constructivist philosophical perspective, and was conducted primarily through an exploratory approach. Jabareen's (2009) conceptual framework analysis (CFA) method formed the foundation upon which the RCF was developed, with specific procedures modified according to the nature and requirements for this study. The CFA method is commonly used to build conceptual frameworks from multiple bodies of knowledge that belong to different disciplines [18]. Due to the ability of the CFA method to clarify conceptual linkages between different domains it was deemed an appropriated method to guide the development of the RCF. The six phases of the CFA method is summarised in Table 1.

**Table 1.** CFA methodology, adapted from Jabareen (2009)

| Phase | Description | Section |
|---|---|---|
| Phase 1: Extensive reading and categorisation of data | Read and categorise data from the spectrum of multidisciplinary literature regarding the phenomenon in question [18] | Section 3 |
| Phase 2: Identifying concepts | Read and reread the relevant data to discover concepts that are considered to be relevant to partnerships in the context of this study in some way | Section 3 |

*(continued)*

**Table 1.** (*continued*)

| Phase | Description | Section |
|---|---|---|
| Phase 3: Deconstructing and categorising concepts | Identify the main attributes, characteristics and assumptions of each concept, and categorise the concepts accordingly | Section 3 |
| Phase 4: Integrating concepts | Integrate and group together similar concepts to reduce the number of concepts | Section 4 |
| Phase 5: Synthesis | Synthesise the concepts into a theoretical framework through a repetitive and iterative process | Section 4 |
| Phase 6: Validate framework | Validate whether the proposed framework and its concepts make sense not only to the researcher but also to other scholars and practitioners | Not included in this paper |

Phase 1 was completed through a systematised literature review to provide an exhaustive review of the literature that is currently available [19]. The advantages of this method are mainly seen in its rigour and transparent process [20]. Data was collected from Scopus. The search was completed by using a combination of the keywords "business ecosystem" and "SME". The search delivered a total of 38 documents, which was then filtered through a series of criteria. After the initial screening process the final 22 documents were critically analysed (See Table 2).

**Table 2.** Systematized review criteria

| Criteria | Description |
|---|---|
| Search engine | Scopus |
| Latest search date | 31 May 2017 |
| Search terms | "SME" + "business ecosystem"; "Small business" + "business ecosystem"; and "Small firm" + "business ecosystem" |
| Publication types included | Academic journals and conference papers |
| Publication types excluded | Magazines and news articles |
| Other excluding criteria | Foreign language papers; inaccessible papers; papers not relevant to topic; and repetitive papers |

After the initial screening process the final 22 documents were critically analysed. The data analysis criteria were broken up into two sections namely (1) descriptive statistics, and (2) qualitative criteria.

Through Phase 2, an in-depth review of the research domain has resulted in a comprehensive theory base which contains a large amount of implicit knowledge that needs to be made explicit. Through this review, 114 concepts have been identified that are deemed relevant to the main research objective of this study. Following Jabareen's

(2009) CFA method as described in Table 1, each of these concepts was deconstructed into its main attributes and characteristics. This was done by labelling each of the concepts with a relevant theme that describes the attributes, characteristics of and assumptions around each. After each of the concepts has been deconstructed, Jabareen (2009) explains that the concepts should be categorised accordingly. Following the theme allocation of each concept, the concepts that share similar themes were grouped together (Phase 3).

Phase 4 of the CFA method requires the concepts that have similarities to be integrated and grouped together. The concepts were integrated by grouping together the themes that had the strongest interrelations. This phase resulted in five main themes, each addressing a critical relational issue related to SMEs in dynamic business ecosystem environments. These themes include (1) goal congruency, (2) trust, (3) collaboration, (4) flexibility, and (5) learning.

Phase 5 of Jabareen's (2009) CFA method requires the concepts to be synthesized into a conceptual framework. This means that the 37 relational capabilities were consolidated into a conceptualization that will enable firms to identify and improve these capabilities. The framework development therefore constitutes two parts. The first which concerns the appropriate structuring into a conceptual framework, and the second which concerns an appropriate methodology needed to use the framework.

## 3  Themes and Related Relational Capabilities

While the themes identified represent the requirements that SMEs must be able to meet in their B2B relationships if they operate in business ecosystems, it is necessary to convert each theme into the organisational means through which these relationship requirements can be addressed. The organisational means, referred to as relational capabilities, thus identify certain internal capabilities that SMEs would require to satisfy the relationship requirements. In total, 37 relational capabilities were identified, these are also included in Table 3.

**Table 3.** Summary of main themes and related relational capabilities

| Theme | Description | Relational capabilities |
|---|---|---|
| Goal congruency | In B2B relationships, partners work together towards reaching a common goal [21–24]. The level of goal congruency refers to the possibility for both firms to achieve their goals simultaneously [25]. According to Cuevas, Julkunen and Gabrielsson (2015), goal congruency can be viewed as a prerequisite for developing relationships of trust. If partnerships are goal congruent, the firms will view joint action as mutually beneficial [26] | (a) Establish shared relationship vision and goals; (b) Establish organisational vision and goals; (c) Developing partnering strategy; (d) Identify potential partners; (e) Uphold external reputation; (f) Attract complementary partners; and (g) Obtain market knowledge |

(continued)

**Table 3.** (*continued*)

| Theme | Description | Relational capabilities |
|---|---|---|
| Trust | Trust is widely associated with successful B2B relationships. Cooperation between partners, as well as the willingness for future collaboration, can arise directly from a strong relationship of trust. Conversely, conflict and uncertainty can be seen as a direct consequence of lack of trust [27, 28] | (a) Establish trustworthiness through behaviour; (b) Assign boundary spanner; (c) Measure relationship performance; (d) Create and sustain unique value offering; (e) Balance investment in relationships; (f) Asses relationship risk; and (g) Manage intellectual property |
| Collaboration | B2B relationships are increasingly involving the sharing of resources, allowing firms to create and share mutual benefits [29]. Firms with complementary capabilities and expertise are connected, providing the opportunity for mutually complementary action in pursuit of a common goal [30] | (a) Interpret and contextualise partner diversity; (b) Understand partner requirements; (c) Identify mutual opportunities; (d) Adapt to relationship; (e) Create joint knowledge; and (f) Leverage external resources |
| Flexibility | B2B relationships are becoming increasingly agile and adaptive as they have the need to support faster and more flexible responses to constantly changing customer needs. Due to the dynamic business environment, B2B relationships need to be resilient and anti-fragile in order to display self-organising, flexible qualities that are capable of reconfiguring and overcoming shocks and disruptions [2] | (a) Maintain adaptable and flexible organisational structure; (b) Enable product/process experimentation; (c) Encourage interdisciplinary knowledge; (d) Enable individual reflective capacity; (e) Allocate internal resources to relationship; (f) Balance relationship portfolios; and (g) Establish contracting policy |
| Learning | Knowledge and data is created and exchanged between partners, offering various opportunities for firms to learn and increase their own internal knowledge. Firms must be able to integrate new data and knowledge within their systems and incorporate it into their internal processes [31] | (a) Manage internal tacit knowledge; (b) Manage internal communication and information flow; (c) Manage tacit knowledge between partners; (d) Define communication channels between partners; (e) Externalise data and information; (f) Capture, store and retrieve data; (g) Analyse data; (h) Establish data exploitation strategy; (i) Create data security architectures; and (j) Determine relationship functional requirements |

# 4   A Relational Capability Maturity Framework

While there are various ways to measure process capabilities, the topic of capability improvement often refocuses on the content and guidelines of maturity modelling. Maturity models are well-known and widely used tools that enable users to assess the current state of maturity of capabilities in a certain domain. Maturity models further enables users to identify the strengths and weaknesses of those capabilities, and suggests an improvement plan to increase overall performance.

The concept of maturity can be traced back to quality management when Crosby (1979) introduced the idea of maturity stages building on each other [32]. One of the most recognised and most widely used maturity models today is the Capability Maturity Model Integration (CMMI®). The CMMI has its roots in the original Capability Maturity Model® for software (SW-CMM®), which was developed in 1986 in response to a request from the federal government for a method to assess the capability of their software contractors. The Software Engineering Institute (SEI) developed a process maturity framework that would help organisations improve their software processes [33, 34]. The SEI defined the CMMI as "a reference or process model of mature practices in a specified discipline, used to improve and appraise a group's capability to perform that discipline" [35].

The structure of the framework developed in this article needs to address multiple dimensions of relational capability throughout various parts of an organisation. Furthermore, complex interrelations exist between the relational capabilities. For this reason, it was decided to construct the framework along two dimensions, the organisational construct and the relational construct. The structure is largely based on the structure of the Innovation Capability Maturity Model (ICMM) as developed by [36]. The ICMM guides its users to address the maturity of innovation capability, while considering the multiple dimensions of innovation, and the different parts of the organisation that is affected. The model is also designed with the applicability and practicality factor in mind. Relational capabilities share various fundamental aspects with innovation capabilities in the sense that it is multi-dimensional, dynamic and complex. The ICMM is consequently considered to be a suitable reference to structure relational capabilities. The structure that forms the Relational Capability Framework (RCF) is displayed in Fig. 1.

## 4.1   Structure Outline

The framework is structured along three dimensions. The dimensions include (1) Relational Capability construct, (2) Organisational Construct and (3) Relational Capability Maturity. The three dimensions are summarised in Table 4.

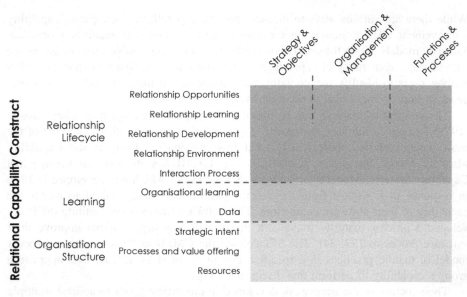

**Fig. 1.** RCF structure, adapted from [36]

**Table 4.** Three dimensions of the RCF

| *Relational capability construct* | |
|---|---|
| Relationship lifecycle | Relationships are not static, it rather evolves through a series of stages. This capability area refers to the practices, procedures and activities that are executed at the initiation of the relationship, through the growth phases of the relationship and the continuous interaction in the relationship |
| Knowledge and information | The transfer of knowledge between partners and the subsequent learning within the organisation is a fundamental part of B2B relationships. This process area addresses the capabilities to identify, acquire and manage knowledge. Also included is the organisations ability to capture, manage and utilise valuable data that is accumulated in the relationship |
| Organisational structure | The infrastructure, resources, strategy, policies and management necessary to support the relationships, and knowledge and information requirements |
| *Organisational construct* | |
| Strategy & objectives | The management response to uncertain environments, it includes the mission, vision and objectives. It provides targets and goals for the processes to steer the organisation in a particular direction |
| Organisation & management | The formal structure and governance of the organisation that is defined with the purpose of fulfilling the strategy and objectives |
| Function & processes | The activities that are performed within the organisation that drives the organisation closer to fulfilling its objectives |
| *Relational Capability Maturity* [37] | |
| Level 1: Initial | Processes are mostly ad hoc and chaotic. A stable environment to support processes are not provided |

*(continued)*

**Table 4.** (*continued*)

| Level 2: Managed | The need for relational capabilities have been identified and defined. Foundation to implement processes have been created. Process adherence is periodically evaluated |
|---|---|
| Level 3: Defined | Practices, procedures and tools have been defined and implemented. Outputs are consistent |
| Level 4: Measured | Focus is managing and improving process performance. Activities and resources are integrated and aligned within organisation. Processes are continuously monitored and evaluated |
| Level 5: Optimised | Synchronisation and institutionalisation of activities and processes. Organisation continually improves its processes based on a quantitative understanding of its business objectives and performance needs |

## 4.2 Relational Capabilities

The relational capabilities are at the core of the RCF. These capabilities were therefore categorised into the structure as it has been described in the previous section. The resulting two-dimensional face of the framework is displayed in **Error! Reference source not found.** Each of the capabilities was assigned an Organisational construct area and a Relational construct item which best defines the capability. For example, based on its representative code (RL/SO1), capability 'Establish shared relationship vision and goals' is assigned to the Strategy and objectives area as it addresses the direction in which the relationships are steered. At the same time, it is assigned to the Relationship opportunities item, as it involves searching and identifying new opportunities, as well as determining the possible implications of these opportunities. The remainder of the capabilities are distributed in a similar manner. Each of the remaining relational capabilities were similarly categorised into the structure of the framework (Table 5).

**Table 5.** Relational capability requirements categorised into construct

| Organisational construct | | Strategy & objectives | Organisation & management | Function & process |
|---|---|---|---|---|
| Relational construct | | | | |
| Relationship lifecycle | Relationship opportunities | **RL/SO1** – Establish shared relationship vision and goals | **RL/OM1** – Interpret and contextualise partner diversity | **RL/FP1** – Identify mutual opportunities |
| | Relationship development | **RL/SO2** – Create and sustain unique value offering **RL/SO3** – Leverage external resources | **RL/OM2** – Allocate internal resources to relationship | **RL/FP2** – Adapt to relationship |
| | Relationship environment | **RL/SO4** – Develop partnering strategy | **RL/OM3** – Obtain market knowledge **RL/OM4** – Uphold external reputation | **RL/FP3** – Identify complementary partners **RL/FP4** – Attract complementary partners |
| | Interaction process | **RL/SO5** – Establish contracting policy | **RL/OM5** – Assign boundary spanner | **RL/FP5** – Define communication channels between partners |

(*continued*)

**Table 5.** (*continued*)

| Organisational construct | | Strategy & objectives | Organisation & management | Function & process |
|---|---|---|---|---|
| Relational construct | | | | |
| Knowledge & information | Relationship learning | **KI/SO1** – Understand partner requirements | **KI/OM1** – Manage intellectual property<br>**KI/OM2** – Manage tacit knowledge between partners | **KI/FP1** – Create joint knowledge |
| | Organisational learning | **KI/SO2** – Manage internal tacit knowledge | **KI/OM3** – Determine relationship functional requirements | **KI/FP2** – Manage internal communication & information flow |
| | Data | **KI/SO3** – Establish data exploitation strategy | **KI/OM4** – Externalise data & information | **KI/FP3** – Create data security architectures<br>**KI/FP4** – Capture, store & retrieve data<br>**KI/FP5** – Analyse data |
| Organisational structure | Strategic intent | **OS/SO1** – Establish organisational vision and goals | **OS/OM1** – Establish trustworthiness through behaviour<br>**OS/OM2** – Balance relationship portfolios | **OS/FP1** – Enable individual reflective capacity |
| | Processes and value offering | **OS/SO2** – Maintain adaptable and flexible organisational structures | **OS/OM3** – Encourage interdisciplinary knowledge | **OS/FP2** – Enable product process experimentation |
| | Resources | **OS/SO3** – Balance investment in relationships | **OS/OM4** – Assess relationship risk | **OS/FP3** – Measure relationship performance |

## 5   Conclusion

This paper presents a model that describes the relational capabilities of small firms at three levels of detail. The 36 identified relational capabilities relates to the various aspects of the organisation through the organisational construct, providing a holistic view of the challenges associated with B2B relationships. At the same time, the granularity of the model allows that capability issues to be addressed incrementally and in part. The nature of the model is thus suitable for SMEs, for whom large, expensive and time-consuming projects are often not a feasible option. Future research to evaluate the maturity of the capability requirements in a wide range of firms is proposed. This would highlight the capability requirements as a firm develops. The aim is to enable owner-managers to improve their relational capability requirements proactively, and ultimately improve their ability to establish and sustain beneficial partnerships.

## References

1. Schlaepfer, R.C., Koch, M.: Industry 4.0: challenges and solutions for the digital transformation and use of exponential technologies. Switzerland (2015)
2. Canning, M., Kelly, E.: Business Ecosystems Come of Age. Deloitte University Press, Business Trends (2015)

3. Iansiti, M., Levien, R.: The Keystone Advantage: What the New Dynamics of Business Ecosystems Mean for Strategy, Innovation, and Sustainability. Harvard Business School Press, Boston (2017)
4. Ulaga, W.: Capturing value creation in business relationships: a customer perspective. Ind. Mark. Manag. **32**(8), 677–693 (2003)
5. Blomqvist, K.: Partnering in the dynamic environment: the role of trust in asymmetric technology. Lappeenranta University of Technology (2002)
6. Narula, R.: R&D collaboration by SMEs: new opportunities and limitations in the face of globalisation. Technovation **24**(2), 153–161 (2004)
7. Nieto, M.J., Santamaría, L.: Technological collaboration: bridging the innovation gap between small and large firms. J. Small Bus. Manag. **48**(1), 44–69 (2010)
8. Varadarajan, R., Yadav, M.S., Shankar, V.: First-mover advantage in an Internet-enabled market environment: conceptual framework and propositions. J. Acad. Mark. Sci. **36**(3), 293–308 (2008)
9. Landau, R.: Corporate partnering can spur innovation. Res. Manage. **30**(3), 21–27 (1987)
10. Teece, D.J.: Profiting from technological innovation: implications for integration, collaboration, licensing and public policy. In: The Competitive Challenge, Berkeley, pp. 187–219 (1987)
11. Bocconcelli, R., Murmura, F., Pagano, A.: Interacting with large customers: resource development in small b2b suppliers. Ind. Mark. Manag. **70**, 101–112 (2018)
12. Ngugi, I.K., Johnsen, R.E., Erdelyi, P.: Relational capabilities for value co-creation and innovation in SMEs. J. Small Bus. Enterp. Dev. **17**(2), 260–278 (2010)
13. Schröder, C.: The Challenges of Industry 4.0 for Small and Medium-sized Enterprises. Friedrich-Ebert-Stiftung, Bonn (2016)
14. Derrouiche, R., Neubert, G., Bouras, A., Savino, M.: B2B relationship management: a framework to explore the impact of collaboration. Prod. Plan. Control **21**(6), 528–546 (2010)
15. Inderst, R., Wey, C.: Buyer power and supplier incentives. Eur. Econ. Rev. **51**(3), 647–667 (2007)
16. Johnsen, R.E., Ford, D.: Interaction capability development of smaller suppliers in relationships with larger customers. Ind. Mark. Manag. **35**, 1002–1015 (2006)
17. Du Preez, N., Essman, H., Louw, L., Schutte, C., Marais, S., Bam, W.: Enterprise Engineering Textbook. Stellebosch University, Stellenbosch (2009)
18. Jabareen, Y.: Building a conceptual framework: philosophy, definitions, and procedure. Int. J. Qual. Methods **8**(4), 49–62 (2009)
19. Popay, J., Rogers, A., Williams, G.: Rationale and standards for the systematic review of qualitative literature in health services research. Qual. Health Res. **8**(3), 341–351 (1998)
20. Bonas, S., et al.: How can systematic reviews incorporate qualitative research? A critical perspective. Qual. Res. **6**(1), 27–44 (2006)
21. Archer, N., Yuan, Y.: Managing business-to-business relationships throughout the e-commerce procurement life cycle. Internet Res. Electron. Netw. Appl. Policy **10**(5), 385–395 (2000)
22. Dwyer, F.R., Schurr, P.H., Oh, S.: Developing buyer-seller relationships. J. Mark. **51**(2), 11–27 (1987)
23. Bryant, A., Colledge, B.: Trust in electronic commerce business relationships. J. Electron. Commer. Res. **3**(2), 32–39 (2002)
24. Gadde, L.E.: Activity coordination and resource combining in distribution networks - implications for relationship involvement and the relationship atmosphere. J. Mark. Manag. **20**(1–2), 157–184 (2004)
25. MacKenzie, H.F.: Partnering Attractiveness in Buyer-Seller Relationships. The University of Western Ontario, Ontario (1992)

26. Naudé, P., Buttle, F.: Assessing relationship quality. Ind. Mark. Manag. **29**(4), 351–361 (2000)
27. Pruitt, D.G.: Negotiation Behavior. Academic Press, New York (1981)
28. Morgan, R.M., Hunt, S.D.: The commitment-trust theory of relationship marketing. J. Mark. **58**(3), 20–38 (1994)
29. Kandampully, J.: B2B relationships and networks in the Internet age. Manag. Decis. **41**(5), 443–451 (2003)
30. Cunningham, M.T., Culligan, K.: Competitiveness through networks of relationships in information technology product markets. In: Paliwoda, S. (ed.) New Perspectives on International Marketing, pp. 251–275. Routledge, London (1991)
31. Herdon, M., Péntek, Á., Várallyai, L.: Digital business ecosystem prototyping for agri-food SMEs. In: HAICTA (2011)
32. Wendler, R.: The maturity of maturity model research: a systematic mapping study. Inf. Softw. Technol. **54**(12), 1317–1339 (2012)
33. Humphrey, W.S.: Three process perspectives: organizations, teams, and people. Ann. Softw. Eng. **14**(1–4), 39–72 (2002)
34. Paulk, M.C.: A history of the capability maturity model for software. Softw. Qual. Profile **1** (1), 5–19 (2009)
35. Höggerl, M., Sehorz, B.: An introduction to CMMI and its assessment procedure. In: Seminar for Computer Science (2006)
36. Essmann, H.E.: Toward innovation capability maturity. Stellenbosch University (2009)
37. SEI: CMMI® for Development, Version 1.3, Improving processes for developing better products and services. Carnegie Mellon University (2010)

# The Role of Digital Connectivity in Supply Chain and Logistics Systems: A Proposed SIMPLE Framework

Maciel M. Queiroz[1]([✉]) [iD] and Samuel Fosso Wamba[2]([✉]) [iD]

[1] Universidade Paulista (UNIP), São Paulo 04026002, Brazil
maciel.queiroz@docente.unip.br
[2] Toulouse Business School (TBS), Toulouse 31068, France
s.fosso-wamba@tbs-education.fr

**Abstract.** Industry 4.0 and its related-cutting edge technologies are generating unprecedented changes and bringing complex challenges in practically all types of business. In this context, new concepts such as digital connectivity, inter-connection, and interoperability emerged as highly disruptive approaches for logistics systems and supply chain management (SCM). To shed more light on these complexities and see how companies organized in a SCM model can adopt, implement and operate in a digital connectivity model, this study pro-poses a framework, namely SIMPLE. To develop the framework, we employed a literature review approach, focusing on recent studies published in journals. After the literature analysis, six dimensions related to digital connectivity in supply chains and logistics emerged, namely Smart, Innovative, Measurable, Profitable, Lean, and Excellence (SIMPLE). This framework brings opportu-nities for future studies, while providing important insights into the dynamics of digital connectivity in logistics and supply chains. Therefore, these SIMPLE framework dimensions should enable the actors involved in organizations' operations to interact adequately and harmoniously so as to maximize the value generated in the network.

**Keywords:** Digital connectivity · Hyperconnected · Interoperability · Interconnection

## 1 Introduction

The digital age has imposed several challenges to the organization's logistics systems and their supply chain management (SCM) [1, 2]. In this new context, digital supply chains [1] are fundamental to organizations that seek to achieve efficient processes, create business value, and gain a competitive advantage in a sustainable approach. This environment has given rise to new methods such as digital connectivity, intercon-nection, and interoperability [3], which have emerged as paradigms to be fully grasped by SCM stakeholders, which have to develop new strategies to implement critical technologies and integrate them with the SCM field [4]. The concepts of intercon-nection and interoperability clearly define the level of digital connectivity [3] of an

© IFIP International Federation for Information Processing 2020
Published by Springer Nature Switzerland AG 2020
M. Hattingh et al. (Eds.): I3E 2020, LNCS 12066, pp. 79–88, 2020.
https://doi.org/10.1007/978-3-030-44999-5_7

organization, and consequently, of the way it manages its supply chains. Interconnection in SCM refers to the connection enabled by different technologies in which supply chain partners can obtain information (mainly in real-time) from customers and SCM members and share such data while maximizing value by taking into account the personalization requirements [5].

In this study, we consider the logistics systems as a subset of SCM, according to Council of Supply Chain Management Professionals (CSCMP) "*Supply chain management encompasses the planning and management of all activities involved in sourcing and procurement, conversion, and all logistics management activities. Importantly, it also includes coordination and collaboration with channel partners, which can be suppliers, intermediaries, third party service providers, and customers. In essence, supply chain management integrates supply and demand management within and across companies*" [6]. Thus, in logistics, interoperability refers to the interaction between SCM members that is rendered possible by the use of several technologies and that fosters information sharing and the utilization of exchanged information in a set of processes [3].

However, the existing literature on digital connectivity [1, 3, 7–9] is scarce, especially in developing frameworks applicable in the logistics and SCM contexts [1]. That is, the unprecedented move in digital connectivity in the fields of logistics and SCM is yet to lure the interest of a significant number of scholars, as the related literature is still at its infancy stage, coupled with the inexistence of a framework that could help to better understand this technology, especially in the aforementioned specialized areas. This study is an attempt to enable an understanding of the various aspects of the digital connectivity at different levels (e.g., operational, tactical and strategic), and to attain this goal, it proposes a framework, namely SIMPLE.

## 2  Background

### 2.1  Industry 4.0 and Cutting-Edge Technologies that Leverage Connectivity

Industry 4.0, also known as the 4th Industrial Revolution or Advanced Manufacturing [10], and its leading technologies are provoking significant disruptions on the firm's business model. This term (Industry 4.0) was coined at the 2011 Hannover Fair, from a German Government project aimed to revitalize the country's industry [11]. With almost ten years of age, Industry 4.0 has not yet gained consensus among scholars and practitioners when it comes to a unified and acceptable definition of the concept [12]. In this study, Industry 4.0 refers to a set of cutting-edge technologies that provide connectivity, interconnection, and interoperability of humans, machines, devices, and organizations.

To support the development of the SIMPLE framework, this study highlights the following Industry 4.0 technologies (Table 1):

**Table 1.** Example of Industry 4.0 related technologies.

| Industry 4.0 technology | Example of application | Adapted from |
|---|---|---|
| Blockchain | Traceability of products in SCM | [13] |
| Artificial intelligence | Fraud detection in payment card | [14] |
| Big data analytics | Firm performance improvement | [15] |
| Physical Internet (PI) | The interplay of physical, operational, and digital interconnectivity of logistics systems | [9] |
| Internet of Things (IoT) | A framework for the analysis of the industrial internet of things | [16] |
| Cyber-physical systems | Production systems design based on cyber-physical systems knowledge tool | [17] |
| Digital platform | Platform openness in the SCM | [18] |
| Digital twin | Application for additive manufacturing in the aircraft context | [19] |
| Sensors | Application supported by big data and IoT to sustainable smart cities | [20] |
| Virtual reality | Virtual reality diffusion | [21] |
| Augmented reality | Adoption of smart glasses | [22] |
| Cloud chain | Connection of supply chain members to monitoring product lifecycle | [23] |
| Autonomous robots | Application in manufacturing processes | [24] |
| RFID | To support digital supply chains | [1] |
| M2M | Applied to support smart transactions in the electricity market | [25] |

## 3   Proposing the SIMPLE Framework

To develop and propose the SIMPLE framework, this study employed a literature review approach, focusing on recent studies published in journals. We applied an unstructured searching approach [26] using different sources, such as ScienceDirect, Emerald Insight and Taylor & Francis database, as also the reference list of the papers selected. Firstly, we used as keywords the variations of "digital Connectivity," "hyperconnected," "Interoperability," "Interconnection," and "digital supply chain." After, we used the reference list of the articles to identify other papers. After the literature analysis, six dimensions related to digital connectivity in supply chains and logistics emerged, namely Smart, Innovative, Measurable, Profitable, Lean, and Excellence (SIMPLE).

## 3.1 Smart

This dimension refers to smart applications that are used not only in internal logistics systems but also in supply chains. An example of smart applications could be explained by the use of blockchain technologies [27] to support the organization's transactions efficiently, which in turn improves the collaboration and cooperation between the members of the SCM by a tamper-proof system [28]. The "Smart" dimension has the following main sub-dimensions:

- *Develop smart logistics/SCM capabilities by using cutting-edge technologies in the operations:* it means that organizations need to develop and integrate cutting-edge technologies into their operational processes. This involves internal and external digital supply chain efforts [1].
- *Provide integration and real-time interaction with key SCM members:* for an organization to achieve effective connectivity integration through its SCM operations, it should resort to cutting-edge technologies like blockchain to enhance real-time interaction and visibility [29, 30].
- *Create integration and leverage interplay between robots and humans:* smart concepts are built on SCM activities only when robots and humans work in symbiosis [31]. To this effect, humans should develop their own education and skills to maximize operations with robots [32].

## 3.2 Innovative

Innovation should be a mandatory competency for any organization. In the context of digital connection and interoperability, innovative solutions represent a significant opportunity for making several improvements [3]. For instance, innovation in the digital age has been supported by several ICT approaches, as smart cities [33] applications (e.g., the possibility of a transportation system more connected [33]). Also, with physical internet concepts, the interconnection and interconnectivity of the organization's logistics systems and their supply chain will be more innovative [34]. This dimension has the following elements:

- *Implementation of cutting-edge technologies in logistics and supply chain activities:* The innovation processes required for implementing a particular cutting-edge technology is not trivial [4]. That is, different efforts and several partners, as also human skills are necessary [4] to achieve success or minimize the failures.
- *Improve the logistics and SCM processes by key technologies and spread in the network:* critical technologies need to support improvements not only in internal processes [35], but also throughout the whole SCM channels [36].
- *Create new products/services as a result of the connectivity's interaction in the SCM:* the interaction that is brought about by connectivity should contribute to creating innovative products and services by means of SCM. For instance, the interplay between IoT-wearable operations, an example of connectivity, is crucial to provide smarter worker care services [37].

### 3.3 Measurable

The level of interoperability [3] is an essential aspect of the digital supply chain efforts and results. It indicates the efficiency generated by cutting-edge technologies in a smart approach, as well as the results achieved in the SCM. For instance, big data applications can enable measurable information to support transportation operations [38]. The following aspects are required:

- *Design indicators for intra-organizational and operational performance in logistics by means of digital connectivity strategies:* considering the challenging landscape imposed by the digital connectivity, organizations need to develop reliable key performance indicators [39] in all business perspectives, especially within the SCM.
- *Apply indicators to measure SCM operational performance using digital connectivity strategies:* after the design of key indicators, the next challenge is to implement them [40]. This implies that traditional measures are not sufficient [41] to face the digital connection age.
- *Manage a set of key indicators about the improved processes across the supply chain networks:* to follow the digital connectivity results and improve the decision-making process, a performance measurement system (PMS) [40] is fundamental.

### 3.4 Profitable

The connectivity in the SCM context can have a substantial impact on the organization's [42], and consequently, affecting their profitability performance. Recent literature had highlights that connectivity supports the creation of internet services [43] and, consequently, could impact an organization's profitability [44]. To understand and manage these effects, the SCM members need to develop the following activities:

- *Minimize logistics costs supported by interconnection and interoperability across the SCM:* Interconnection and interoperability can minimize the costs through the entire SCM, and this may involve, for instance, PI to deliver solutions [9].
- *Leverage the operational performance gains enabled by relationships in supply chain networks and generated by interconnection and interoperability:* Interconnection and interoperability are fundamental for creating value in the SCM. For instance, cooperation between SCM members can rely on interoperability to achieve business success [45].
- *Increase profit performance with interconnection and interoperability within the supply chain networks:* Interconnection and interoperability can impact positively on the organization's profitability. In other words, the more interactions between supply chain members are performed, the more profit performance could be achieved [46].

### 3.5 Lean

Lean initiatives in the logistics and supply chain connectivity should be achieved by the implementation of a vast of cutting-edge technologies to support sustainability achievement [35]. Hence, the "lean" dimension has the following elements:

- *Promote connectivity and develop a lean relationship with cleaner stakeholders:* the lean relationship in this study refers to the collaboration between SCM members that is rendered possible by cutting-edge technologies, with a high level of responsiveness to support strategic partnerships. For instance, with IoT, lean processes in the SCM could be facilitated [46].
- *Implement different types of technologies that will be used to support lean operations:* lean technologies in the SCM can minimize waste of resources and inventories through the network while improving efficiency through the reuse of resources [47]. It is therefore clear that different types of technologies could have a good effect on production systems sustainability, and they include IoT and platforms to resource management, AI, and M2M, among others [35].
- *Implement sustainable connectivity strategies that improve the society's well-being:* sustainable connectivity strategies are related to the technologies implementation that leverage connectivity without bringing (or at least minimizing) the side effects to organizations and society. That is, the implementation of cutting-edge technologies could bring some negative impacts to society [48]. A case in point has to do with the risks of cyber-attacks associated with any technology and their side effects for the society.

## 3.6    Excellence

There is not a proper definition of connectivity excellence in the literature. In our context, connectivity excellence refers to the best practices associated with technology adoption and implementation that support real-time interactions and enable hyper-connected members in different layers of the SCM to maximize multiple values simultaneously. The connectivity excellence was considered in the framework due to its influence on the other dimensions as also be simultaneously influenced by these dimensions.

- *Leverage efficient and effective processes through the SCM:* with innovative technologies, the traditional SCM is shifting to digital supply chains [1], thereby transforming and remodeling practically all processes to gain efficiency in the network. For instance, the connectivity can lead to improved flexibility, optimized interactions with suppliers around the globe, and real-time inventories, among others [1].
- *Optimize the level of services, interconnection and interoperability in the SCM using suitable technologies:* cutting-edge connectivity is expected to significantly improve the level of services. For example, product embedding sensors would enable real-time analysis of operations and thus help optimize transaction efficiency and speed in process delivery, among others [1].
- *Improve/generate competitive advantage supported by interconnection and interoperability:* if all the dimensions of the SIMPLE framework interact harmoniously, the organization will be able to improve or generate competitive advantage. Otherwise, digital connectivity will not be operating in an optimized way. For example, by using interoperability approaches, organizations could operate efficiently in collaborative networks, reflecting on capturing value and business opportunities [3]. Figure 1 highlights the SIMPLE framework.

**Fig. 1.** SIMPLE framework.

Regarding the aforementioned characteristics of the SIMPLE framework, the following propositions emerge:

*P1. The SIMPLE framework or part of its elements is positively associated with the organization's logistics and supply chain connectivity performance.*

*P2. The interconnection and interoperability maturity level of an SCM member is positively associated with the SIMPLE framework implementation quality or part of its elements.*

*P3. The adoption and diffusion of the SIMPLE framework or part of its elements are positively related to the competitive advantage of an SCM member.*

Thus, taking account of the elements as mentioned earlier of the SIMPLE framework, it can be seen that it could help in information sharing and cost reduction. That is, with leveraging the information sharing [3] by the digital connectivity, the logistics systems and SCM should be more responsiveness, by operating with members in a more collaborative way [1]. The SIMPLE framework offers elements in terms of operational, tactical, and strategic levels to provide insights to organizations capture value considering the digital connectivity age.

# 4   Concluding Remarks, Implications, Limitations and Future Research

In this work, the SIMPLE framework was introduced in order to understand more profoundly the digital disruptions in logistics and SCM business models, in the digital connectivity era. The main contribution of this study resides in that it proposes an original framework to support and provide organizations with key insights into digital connectivity in the logistics and supply chain domain. The SIMPLE framework highlights that thanks to its six dimensions (smart, innovative, measurable, profitable, lean, and excellence), organizations can maximize their value in the network, provided that they manage such elements carefully while considering their internal and external capabilities. Therefore, these SIMPLE framework dimensions should enable the actors involved in organizations' operations to interact adequately and harmoniously to maximize the value generated in the network.

Furthermore, this work has implications from both the practitioners and theoretical perspectives. From a managerial perspective, the SIMPLE framework could be a starting point to managers and decision-makers who want to better understand the importance of an integrative tool for improved awareness and enhanced digital connectivity strategies. In terms of theory, the SIMPLE framework brings opportunities to scholars as they may want to develop empirical studies about this framework's adoption, implementation, and generalization across supply chains. Also, the three propositions that are being suggested herein could be used to develop a conceptual model to empirically test the framework. Due to the nascent status of the SIMPLE framework, the main limitation is concerned with its effectiveness in broader supply chain contexts. Therefore, opportunities for future studies may include analyzing the same framework in other industries, countries and social contexts worldwide.

# References

1. Büyüközkan, G., Göçer, F.: Digital supply chain: literature review and a proposed framework for future research. Comput. Ind. **97**, 157–177 (2018)
2. Queiroz, M.M., Pereira, S.C.F., Telles, R., Machado, M.C.: Industry 4.0 and digital supply chain capabilities. Benchmarking Int. J., vol. ahead-of-p, no. ahead-of-print (2019)
3. da Silva Serapião Leal, G., Guédria, W., Panetto, H.: Interoperability assessment: a systematic literature review. Comput. Ind. **106**, 111–132 (2019)
4. Tortorella, G.L., Fettermann, D.: Implementation of Industry 4.0 and lean production in brazilian manufacturing companies. Int. J. Prod. Res. **56**(8), 2975–2987 (2018)
5. Min, S., Zacharia, Z.G., Smith, C.D.: Defining supply chain management: in the past, present, and future. J. Bus. Logist. **40**(1), 44–55 (2019)
6. Council of Supply Chain Management Professionals (CSCMP): CSCMP's definition of supply chain management. CSCMP (2019). http://www.cscmp.org/CSCMP/Educate/SCM_Definitions_and_Glossary_of_Terms/CSCMP/Educate/SCM_Definitions_and_Glossary_of_Terms.aspx?hkey=60879588-f65f-4ab5-8c4b-6878815ef921. Accessed 30 Dec 2019
7. Tran-Dang, H., Krommenacker, N., Charpentier, P.: Containers monitoring through the Physical Internet: a spatial 3D model based on wireless sensor networks. Int. J. Prod. Res. **55**(9), 2650–2663 (2017)

8. Yang, Y., Pan, S., Ballot, E.: Innovative vendor-managed inventory strategy exploiting interconnected logistics services in the Physical Internet. Int. J. Prod. Res. **55**(9), 2685–2702 (2017)

9. Pan, S., Ballot, E., Huang, G.Q., Montreuil, B.: Physical Internet and interconnected logistics services: research and applications. Int. J. Prod. Res. **55**(9), 2603–2609 (2017)

10. Büchi, G., Cugno, M., Castagnoli, R.: Smart factory performance and Industry 4.0. Technol. Forecast. Soc. Chang. **150**, 119790 (2020)

11. Da Xu, L., Xu, E.L., Li, L.: Industry 4.0: state of the art and future trends. Int. J. Prod. Res. **7543**, 1–22 (2018)

12. Mariani, M., Borghi, M.: Industry 4.0: a bibliometric review of its managerial intellectual structure and potential evolution in the service industries. Technol. Forecast. Soc. Chang. **149**, 119752 (2019)

13. Biswas, K., Muthukkumarasamy, V., Tan, W.L.: Blockchain based wine supply chain traceability system. In: Future Technologies Conference, December (2017)

14. Ryman-tubb, N.F., Krause, P., Garn, W.: How artificial intelligence and machine learning research impacts payment card fraud detection: a survey and industry benchmark. Eng. Appl. Artif. Intell. **76**, 130–157 (2018)

15. Wamba, S.F., Gunasekaran, A., Akter, S., Ren, S.J.F., Dubey, R., Childe, S.J.: Big data analytics and firm performance: effects of dynamic capabilities. J. Bus. Res. **70**, 356–365 (2017)

16. Boyes, H., Hallaq, B., Cunningham, J., Watson, T.: The industrial internet of things (IIoT): an analysis framework. Comput. Ind. **101**, 1–12 (2018)

17. Francalanza, E., Borg, J., Constantinescu, C.: A knowledge-based tool for designing cyber physical production systems. Comput. Ind. **84**, 39–58 (2017)

18. Broekhuizen, T.L.J., Emrich, O., Gijsenberg, M.J., Broekhuis, M., Donkers, B., Sloot, L.M.: Digital platform openness: drivers, dimensions and outcomes. J. Bus. Res. (2019, in press)

19. Mandolla, C., Petruzzelli, A.M., Percoco, G., Urbinati, A.: Building a digital twin for additive manufacturing through the exploitation of blockchain: a case analysis of the aircraft industry. Comput. Ind. **109**, 134–152 (2019)

20. Bibri, S.E.: The IoT for smart sustainable cities of the future: an analytical framework for sensor-based big data applications for environmental sustainability. Sustain. Cities Soc. **38**, 230–253 (2018)

21. Laurell, C., Sandström, C., Berthold, A., Larsson, D.: Exploring barriers to adoption of virtual reality through social media analytics and machine learning – an assessment of technology, network, price and trialability. J. Bus. Res. **100**, 469–474 (2019)

22. Rauschnabel, P.A., He, J., Ro, Y.K.: Antecedents to the adoption of augmented reality smart glasses: a closer look at privacy risks. J. Bus. Res. **92**(August), 374–384 (2018)

23. Vazquez-Martinez, G.A., Gonzalez-Compean, J.L., Sosa-Sosa, V.J., Morales-Sandoval, M., Perez, J.C.: CloudChain: a novel distribution model for digital products based on supply chain principles. Int. J. Inf. Manage. **39**, 90–103 (2018)

24. Bibby, L., Dehe, B.: Defining and assessing industry 4.0 maturity levels – case of the defence sector. Prod. Plan. Control **29**(12), 1030–1043 (2018)

25. Sikorski, J.J., Haughton, J., Kraft, M.: Blockchain technology in the chemical industry: machine-to-machine electricity market. Appl. Energy **195**, 234–246 (2017)

26. de Camargo Fiorini, P., Jabbour, C.J.C.: Information systems and sustainable supply chain management towards a more sustainable society: where we are and where we are going. Int. J. Inf. Manage. **37**(4), 241–249 (2017)

27. Fosso Wamba, S., Kamdjoug, K., Robert, J., Bawack, R., Keogh, J.: Bitcoin, Blockchain, and FinTech : a systematic review and case studies in the supply chain. Prod. Plan. Control **31**(2–3), 115–142 (2020)

28. Wang, Y., Hungh, H.J., Paul, B.-D.: Understanding blockchain technology for future supply chains a systematic literature review and research agenda. Supply Chain Manag. Int. J. **24**, 62–84 (2018)
29. Korpela, K., Hallikas, J., Dahlberg, T.: Digital supply chain transformation toward blockchain integration (2017)
30. Bányai, T.: Real-time decision making in first mile and last mile logistics: how smart scheduling affects energy efficiency of hyperconnected supply chain solutions. Energies **11**(7), 1833 (2018)
31. Özdemir, V., Hekim, N.: Birth of Industry 5.0: making sense of big data with artificial intelligence, 'the internet of things' and next-generation technology policy. OMICS **22**(1), 65–76 (2018)
32. Aleksander, I.: Partners of humans: a realistic assessment of the role of robots in the foreseeable future. J. Inf. Technol. **32**(1), 1–9 (2017)
33. Tachizawa, E.M., Alvarez-Gil, M.J., Montes-Sancho, M.J.: How 'smart cities' will change supply chain management. Supply Chain Manag. Int. J. **20**(3), 237–248 (2015)
34. Ben Mohamed, I., Klibi, W., Labarthe, O., Deschamps, J.C., Babai, M.Z.: Modelling and solution approaches for the interconnected city logistics. Int. J. Prod. Res. **55**(90), 2664–2684 (2017)
35. Waibel, M.W., Steenkamp, L.P., Moloko, N., Oosthuizen, G.A.: Investigating the effects of smart production systems on sustainability elements. Procedia Manuf. **8**, 731–737 (2017)
36. Wu, L., Yue, X., Jin, A., Yen, D.C.: Smart supply chain management: a review and implications for future research. Int. J. Logist. Manag. **27**(2), 395–417 (2016)
37. Roda-Sanchez, L., Garrido-Hidalgo, C., Hortelano, D., Olivares, T., Ruiz, M.C.: OperaBLE: an IoT-based wearable to improve efficiency and smart worker care services in Industry 4.0. J. Sensors **2018**, 1–12 (2018)
38. Cottrill, C.D., Derrible, S.: Leveraging big data for the development of transport sustainability indicators. J. Urban Technol. **22**(1), 45–64 (2015)
39. Bauer, W., Hämmerle, M., Schlund, S., Vocke, C.: Transforming to a Hyper-connected Society and Economy – Towards an 'Industry 4.0'. Procedia Manuf. **3**, 417–424 (2015)
40. Ante, G., Facchini, F., Mossa, G., Digiesi, S.: Developing a key performance indicators tree for lean and smart production systems. IFAC-PapersOnLine **51**(11), 13–18 (2018)
41. Mishra, D., Gunasekaran, A., Papadopoulos, T., Dubey, R.: Supply chain performance measures and metrics: a bibliometric study **25**(3), 932–967 (2018)
42. Min, H.: Blockchain technology for enhancing supply chain resilience. Bus. Horiz. **62**, 35–45 (2018)
43. Iansiti, M., Lakhani, K.R., Mohamed, H.: It will take years to transform business, but the journey begins now. Harvard Bus. Rev. **3**, 1–11 (2017)
44. Elghannam, A., Arroyo, J., Eldesouky, A., Mesias, F.J.: A cross-cultural consumers' perspective on social media-based short food supply chains. Br. Food J. **120**(10), 2210–2221 (2018)
45. Espadinha-Cruz, P., Grilo, A.: The business interoperability decomposition framework to analyse buyer-supplier dyads. Comput. Ind. **109**, 165–181 (2019)
46. Qu, T., et al.: System dynamics analysis for an Internet-of-Things-enabled production logistics system. Int. J. Prod. Res. **55**(9), 2622–2649 (2017)
47. Despeisse, M., et al.: Unlocking value for a circular economy through 3D printing: a research agenda. Technol. Forecast. Soc. Change **115**, 75–84 (2017)
48. Conte de Leon, D., Stalick, A.Q., Jillepalli, A.A., Haney, M.A., Sheldon, F.T.: Blockchain: properties and misconceptions. Asia Pacific J. Innov. Entrep. **11**(3), 286–300 (2017)

# A Strategic Organisational Perspective of Industry 4.0: A Conceptual Model

Stefan Smuts[(✉)] , Alta van der Merwe , and Hanlie Smuts

Department of Informatics, University of Pretoria, Pretoria, South Africa
sbsmuts@gmail.com, {alta,hanlie.smuts}@up.ac.za

**Abstract.** The so-called fourth industrial revolution or Industry 4.0 (I4.0), with its potentially disruptive technologies, is changing the way we socialise, live and work and provides opportunities for organisations to innovate and disrupt. Although organisations are acknowledging the emergence of I4.0 and realise the importance of being ready for its impact, better understanding is required of the potential of I4.0 and its holistic impact on organisations. In this paper, we conducted a systematic literature review to identify all I4.0-related organisational aspects, such as an I4.0-relevant strategy, digital business model innovation, technology investment optimisation, workforce management complexity, digital eco-systems, technology-centric convergence, virtual model and physical environment linkage, value chain digitalisation and product portfolio innovation. Furthermore, we presented these I4.0 organisational aspects identified in a conceptual model based on the components of organisational strategic alignment. By using such a conceptual model, organisations can ensure that both optimisation and new opportunities enabled by I4.0 are leveraged and that a relevant, strategically aligned approach to I4.0 may be considered.

**Keywords:** Industry 4.0 · Fourth industrial revolution · Strategic alignment · Organisational context · Conceptual model

## 1 Introduction

The term Industry 4.0 was formalised in 2011 in Germany at the Hannover Messe [1–3]. *Industry 4.0* or *the fourth industrial revolution* is marked by a fast change in technologies that are changing the way we socialise, live and work [4]. Disruptive technologies emerging from I4.0, such as the internet of things (IoT), internet of services and cyber-physical systems (CPS), present new ways in which organisations can conduct business [5]. Organisations require a detailed strategic and technological plan to optimise the benefits of I4.0 and to become digital organisations [6, 7].

Although the term I4.0 is used in an organisational context, there is no accepted definition for I4.0 [4, 7–10]. Bär et al. [4] classified I4.0 as a rapid change in technology, whereas Geißler et al. [11] associated I4.0 with certain technological advancements such as IoT and CPS. Badri et al. [1] and Lezzi et al. [12] take a different view and propose that I4.0 refers to the unity of the manufacturing industry with so-called smart technologies such as IoT and CPS. Further definitions of I4.0 include "cutting-edge and disruptive technologies" [13], "end-to-end digitisation of all physical

M. Hattingh et al. (Eds.): I3E 2020, LNCS 12066, pp. 89–101, 2020.
https://doi.org/10.1007/978-3-030-44999-5_8

assets and processes" [14] and "sum of all disruptive innovations derived and implemented in a value chain to address the trends of digitalization" [8]. We need to understand what the unique I4.0 organisational aspects are and consider how these unique aspects affect strategic alignment in organisations. Therefore, the focus of this paper is on contributing to the discourse on what I4.0 is from an organisational perspective, by considering the following research question: *"What are the unique I4.0 organisational aspects and how do these unique aspects affect strategic alignment in an organisation?"* We reflect on this research question by considering an overview of I4.0, by understanding the nature of I4.0 in an organisational context and by considering the impact of strategic alignment.

In this paper we firstly provide an overview of literature in Sect. 2, followed by the research approach in Sect. 3. In Sect. 4 we present a discussion on the data analysis and findings, while Sect. 5 details the contribution of the study. Section 6 concludes the paper.

## 2   Background

Scholars report on four major industrial revolutions. As early as the 18th century, the first industrial revolution occurred [5]. With the introduction of steam-powered machines, production was decoupled from the physical limitations of humans. In the 19th century, the introduction of electricity created faster and more compact machines, leading to the second industrial revolution. The third industrial revolution was marked by the development of electronic circuits leading to assembly lines becoming more and more automated. Automation presented opportunities for optimisation of machines and processes [5]. The I4.0 is a relatively new concept first mentioned in Germany in 2011 and contrary to the other three industrial revolutions, its impact is not yet fully known [2, 7, 9]. The focus on connectivity and communication makes I4.0 intrinsically different from the other three industrial revolutions [15]. In Sect. 2.1 we give a short introduction on what I4.0 is, followed by Sect. 2.2, where we consider the organisational context of I4.0, and Sect. 2.3, in which we discuss strategic alignment.

### 2.1   Overview of I4.0

The world is experiencing revolutionary advances in science and technology [16]. In a progressively digital world, organisations have invested significantly in technologies to keep ahead of competitors and potential disruptors [17]. First-order disruption includes localised change within a market, where a particular technology is disruptive. Second-order disruption influences many industries and substantially changes societal norms and institutions, where technologies disrupt social interactions and relationships, organisational structures, institutions and public policies [18]. The aim of I4.0 is to realise improved operational efficiency and productivity [19]. This could be achieved through features such as digitisation, optimisation, production customisation, automation and adaptation [19, 20]. Furthermore, human-machine interaction enables enhanced value-added services, automatic data exchange and communication [20]. These features are also strongly associated with industrial value-adding processes, knowledge management, internet technologies and advanced algorithms [20] and applied across three areas of impact, namely integration of value chains (e.g. IoT, cloud computing, etc.), digitisation of offerings (e.g. augmented reality, smart sensors, big data analytics), and digital business models and customer access (e.g. authentication, artificial intelligence, etc.) [21, 22].

## 2.2 Organisational Context of I4.0

In order to realise I4.0 alignment, organisations need to manage multiple internal and external factors to enhance business value and create a sustainable competitive advantage [23]. Specific factors include horizontal, vertical and digital integration and areas of standardisation enabling organisations to connect to one another easily [24]. Organisations will have to manage multiple complexities, namely *complex systems,* as it is required to develop and apply new models and methods [25]; *comprehensive infrastructure* consisting of a high-quality information network and internet connectivity; *security* and *privacy,* enforcing data protection [12]; *work organisation and design,* as the roles of the employees change [26]; new and relevant *legal frameworks* [1] and the effective *use of resources* [24]. Organisational performance in this new era requires managing teams of highly specialised technical experts, as well as employees trained to operate in the new technological revolution, with specific profiles that are currently non-existent [27, 28]. In the next section we consider strategic alignment in organisations.

## 2.3 Strategic Alignment in Organisations

Organisations employ strategic planning to define direction and to guide decisions on resource allocation to pursue their strategy [29, 30]. Strategic planning provides a sense of direction, outlines measurable goals in an organisation and guides day-to-day decisions [29]. Furthermore, strategic planning is concerned with the definition of changes that may be informed by changing market conditions, competitor activity and technology advancement – typically aspects encompassed by I4.0 [29, 31]. For organisations to manage all the multiple internal and external factors described in the previous section strategically, strategic alignment must be achieved at both enterprise and departmental level [32], across four domains of strategic choices, namely strategy execution, technology potential, competitive potential and service level [31]. *Strategy execution* refers to business strategy as a driver of both organisational design choices and information system infrastructure, while *technology potential* involves the articulation of an information technology strategy in support of the selected business strategy [31, 32]. *Competitive potential* as alignment perspective is concerned with the exploitation of emerging information technology capabilities that affect key attributes of strategy, such as distinctive competencies, and it has an impact on business scope, such as new products and services, and business governance, which includes the development of new forms of relationships [31, 32]. The *service level* focuses on establishing a world-class technology organisation within an organisation and focuses on the effective use of IS resources, as well as responsiveness to the fast-changing demands of end-users and customers [31, 32]. Achieving and sustaining strategic alignment in organisations are influenced by a rapidly changing operating environment enabled by I4.0 aspects such as workforce skills and change capacity, business process automation, multiplicity of digital business models, and the variety and expectations of different customer segments [30, 32]. Therefore, I4.0 aspects must be considered across all four domains of strategic choices to achieve strategic alignment [29, 31].

## 3   Research Approach

The objective of this paper is to present the unique I4.0 organisational aspects, including the way in which these unique aspects affect strategic alignment in an organisation. In order to achieve the objective, a systematic literature review (SLR) was conducted to identify the components of a guiding conceptual model [33, 34]. The aim of an SLR is to gather, evaluate and synthesise the existing body of completed and recorded work produced by researchers, scholars and practitioners [34]. An SLR must be conducted based on a rigorous, stand-alone and systematic methodological approach [33, 35]. Specifically, we followed the methodological approach suggested by Boland, Cherry and Dickson [36], consisting of three main stages: *planning the review* (defining the research objectives and the review protocol), *conducting the review* (selecting the primary studies and extracting the data) and *reporting the review* (disseminating the report) [35, 37]. Technical reports, books and specific scientific databases were chosen for the SLR process. The databases presented in Table 1 provided access to high-quality peer-review content and were therefore chosen for the SLR. I4.0 is known by many terms, including 4IR and the 'fourth industrial revolution'. To include all references to I4.0, the search terms were chosen as: '4ir and "strategic alignment" and organisation', '"fourth industrial revolution" and "strategic alignment" and organisation"' and '"I4.0" and "strategic alignment" and organisation"'. Using all the search terms listed and only including sources from 2011 onwards, as this was the date when the term I4.0 originated, a result set of 301 papers was identified, as shown in Table 1.

**Table 1.**  Total number of papers found per database

| Database | Total papers found matching keywords | Total after first inclusion and exclusion criteria |
|---|---|---|
| ScienceDirect | 97 | 32 |
| SpringerLink | 64 | 22 |
| EBSCOhost | 31 | 16 |
| IEEE Xplore | 9 | 5 |
| Emerald Insight | 100 | 29 |
| Total | 301 | 104 |

The initial research studies extracted (301) were screened by applying specific criteria such as non-English studies, anecdotal or opinion-based papers, unobtainable papers and duplicate studies that formed part of the result set. Inclusion criteria consisted of peer-reviewed publications and technical reports relevant to the research question. After the initial search, as well as the application of inclusion and exclusion criteria, 104 publications were selected (Table 1 last column). We concluded a detailed screening of abstracts and analysis of the full text of the prospective papers, after which 35 papers were coded and themed. Sixty-nine papers were excluded based on criteria such as studies not associated with the research question, theses or dissertations and a keyword mismatch, e.g. where both "industry" and "4" appeared in a paper, but in an unrelated context.

## 4 Data Analysis and Findings

The aim of this paper is to consider the unique I4.0 organisational aspects and to reflect on the impact of these unique aspects on strategic alignment in organisations. Themes and main themes were identified in the selected studies through a two-step process: *firstly*, descriptive codes were used to identify themes [38] and *secondly*, open coding was used to identify emerging main themes [39]. Table 2 depicts the emerging themes and main themes, as well as the reference.

The first emerging theme is *external drivers*, i.e. drivers external to the organisation related to the job market and the particular market and industry sector. It is acknowledged that I4.0 may create new jobs and change current jobs to the extent that employees must either be retrained or upskilled. Job market disruptions may enforce greater worker independence, require increased workforce cognitive load, necessitate workforce augmentation and emphasise increased autonomy. Another external factor is global market and industry sector disruption. Organisations are forced to meet the ever-changing demand of consumers and must navigate the transformation of the market, industry and business sectors. Traditional markets and industries are challenged by innovations and an increased rate of change in technology. At a *strategic level*, organisations need to consider an I4.0 relevant strategy. Such a strategy brings about a potential competitive advantage gain, additional organisational value creation, organisational agility enablement and strategic objective optimisation. New technology changes the rules of the global market and therefore organisations are empowered to create new business value. As organisations embrace the new strategies and agility, there may be an organisational structural alignment trade-off where particular internal structures need to be revised to carry out the I4.0 relevant strategy. The *business value* theme highlights opportunities for business improvement, whether it is internally focused (increased effectiveness and efficiency) or related to digital business model innovation (harnessing I4.0 technologies). Internal effectiveness and efficiency improvement are fundamentally based on the value capitalisation of knowledge held in the organisation, while digital business model innovation may inherently be based on technology investment optimisation. The *workforce* emerging theme is internally focussed and deals specifically with the transformative and disruptive nature of I4.0 on the workforce of an organisation. The impact of this includes not only environmental innovation potential, productivity improvement, required skills, and education alignment, but also management complexity and workforce well-being. Complexity is created as managers must now manage teams with different skills, in agile and fast-paced environments requiring socially sustainable work systems, as well as agile environmental change response. As there is greater emphasis on collaboration and transparency, organisations must consider workplace ergonomics, workforce flexibility and motivation, change appetite and the impact on governance. Digital technologies enable environments in which workforce productivity can be improved through automation with a consequent impact on role and responsibility definition. Furthermore, productivity changes require a different skill mix, demanding essential problem-solving, critical thinking and design thinking abilities.

**Table 2.** I4.0 aspect themes and sub-themes extracted

| Main theme | Theme | References |
|---|---|---|
| External drivers | Job market disruption | [5, 22, 40–44] |
| | Market and industry disruption | [1, 4, 13, 14, 26, 42–47] |
| I4.0 relevant strategy | Competitive advantage gain | [4, 6] |
| | Organisational agility enablement | [5, 7, 22, 26, 45] |
| | Organisational structural alignment trade-offs | [26, 45, 46] |
| | Organisational value creation | [26, 45] |
| | Strategic objective optimisation | [6, 7, 12, 14, 42, 46] |
| Business value | Business opportunity improvement | [4, 7, 12, 45, 48] |
| | Digital business model innovation | [4, 5, 7, 8, 11, 13, 22, 26, 42, 46, 47] |
| | Increased entrepreneurial activity | [43, 47, 49] |
| | Knowledge management value capitalisation | [10, 25, 42] |
| | Technology investment optimisation | [40, 45] |
| Workforce | Work environment innovation | [1, 13, 25, 41, 45] |
| | Workforce education alignment | [1, 13, 22, 25, 44, 46] |
| | Workforce management complexity | [1, 5, 7, 13, 22, 25, 41, 42, 44, 46] |
| | Workforce productivity improvement | [12, 25, 41] |
| | Workforce skills qualification | [1, 5, 25, 40–44, 46] |
| | Workforce well-being improvement | [5, 41] |
| Technology | Digital eco-systems | [3, 7, 8, 12, 13, 22, 25, 46, 48, 50–52] |
| | Information technology security consideration | [42] |
| | Technology-centric convergence | [5, 12, 15, 25, 26, 42] |
| | Virtual model and physical environment linkage | [1, 7, 22, 25, 41, 50] |

(*continued*)

**Table 2.** (*continued*)

| Main theme | Theme | References |
|---|---|---|
| Customer value | Customer experience differentiation | [4, 26, 46] |
| | Customer-organisation interaction improvement | [4] |
| Process | Process optimisation | [3, 4, 7–9, 22, 25, 40, 42, 44–46, 53–55] |
| | Value chain digitalisation | [1, 4, 45, 48] |
| Data | Big data management | [3, 9, 13, 22, 25, 42, 51, 53] |
| | Data-driven decision-making | [1, 8, 10, 12, 25, 42, 53] |
| | Product and process big data generation | [11, 12] |
| Organisational change | Human-centric design transformation | [7, 8, 25, 40, 41, 53] |
| | Organisational culture change expectations | [44] |
| | Tension impact of emerging versus legacy infrastructures | [7, 26] |
| Product | Product customisation | [3, 45, 50] |
| | Product portfolio innovation | [3–11, 13, 40, 42, 43, 46, 48, 50, 53] |

From a *technology* perspective, digital eco-systems are enabled where strategy, channels, people and technology are connected within an organisation or across multiple organisations in the eco-system, emphasising security implementation concerns. As the digital technologies inform change, transformation may be based on technology-centric convergence, especially in instances where there is a blurring between virtual and physical worlds (digital twins) or where the digital world is translated to the physical one (3D printing). *Customer value*, the manner in which it is defined and how organisations view it, is centred on customer experience and the interaction between the organisation and the customer. Exceptional customer experience not only creates satisfied customers, but also leads to a competitive advantage gain. As more organisations adapt to I4.0, differentiating factors between organisations are dependent on customer experience, as improved customer satisfaction attracts more customers and retains existing ones. I4.0 presents opportunities for organisations not only to optimize their *processes,* but also to digitise their entire value chain. Changes such as manufacturing process automation and digitisation can boost manufacturing efficiency. Technologies of I4.0 can enable innovation and adoption of business processes, as well as automation of work processes. Digitisation of products, processes and systems allows organisations to gain better insight into their business operations, leading to accuracy and precision improvements, preventive step monitoring and automation of information technology innovations. Integration with the processes of other organisations becomes possible, creating improved cross-function and eco-system collaborations. Better processes lead to the evolution of business analytics and implications for lean practices.

Large volumes of *data* are one of the key characteristics of I4.0. Big data management enabling data-driven decision-making, as well as product- and process-related big data generation, requires organisations to build capabilities to process vast amounts of data. Not only must big datasets be collected by an organisation, but these datasets also need to be converted, harnessed and interpreted in near-real time in order to generate relevant insights. Furthermore, process- and product-related data analysis informs process automation opportunities, enabling advantages such as service level improvement, inventory reduction and shorter time to market. Technologies such as CPS and IoT can be used to monitor production lines and product quality. However, organisations must be aware of the impact on computational power that data-driven decision-making requires, as well as the governance, security and management of such collected data. *Organisational change* has an impact on several levels; firstly, the organisation must migrate from legacy technology to future technology with consequent impacts on processes, products, data and the workforce. New technologies create new avenues for organisations to pursue new and better *products* through product customisation and product portfolio innovation. Organisations must cater not only for the needs of the individual customer, but also encourage customer collaboration as well as creating opportunities for quality, customised products. Such flexible product portfolios offer a competitive edge, while product design, planning and production are becoming more customised as well. Product lines experience short production lifecycle changes often enabled by robotisation. However, this will require organisation of wide-ranging changes in manufacturing operations and technology, providing opportunities for product and device miniaturisation, production of products via advanced ICT and product-tracking possibilities.

## 5 An I4.0 Conceptual Model

Using the themes derived during the thematic analysis (Table 2) and the strategic alignment domains (Sect. 2.3), the I4.0 aspects derived were arranged in a conceptual model from an organisational perspective depicted in Fig. 1.

The conceptual model is built across the four domains of strategic choices, namely strategic execution, technology potential, competitive potential and service level (Sect. 2.3). The *strategy execution domain* employs business strategy as a driver of both organisational design choices and information systems infrastructure. Under strategic execution, organisations must focus on external factors, I4.0-relevant strategy and business value. Organisations need to be aware of any I4.0-induced *external factors* that can affect the organisation. Factors such as job market disruptions or market and industry disruption may present great opportunities for growth. As organisations change to I4.0-ready organisations, they need to be guided by an I4.0-relevant *strategy*. This strategy ensures future sustainability of an organisation in a global market potentially disrupted by I4.0. New processes, technology and markets have redefined *business value* in an I4.0-driven society. Organisations must reconsider business value, whether the focus is outward towards the customer or based on internal optimisation and automation, and adjust strategies accordingly.

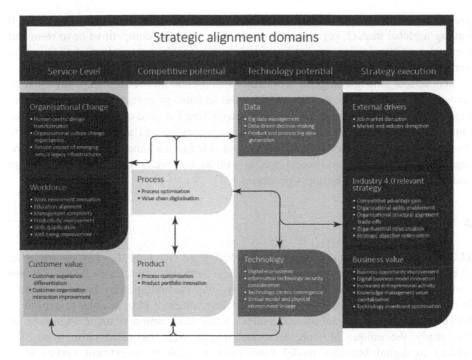

**Fig. 1.** Strategic organisational perspective of I4.0 aspects (adapted from [31])

The *technology potential domain* refers to the information technology strategy that supports the selected business strategy by considering the technologies of I4.0 and data. The disruptive nature and *technologies* of I4.0 force organisations to move towards new technologies to ensure future sustainability and competitiveness. Big data and data-driven decision-making create new opportunities for organisations to collect, analyse and use *data*. Data have a direct impact on customer value, in terms of information collected and analysed, and inform products and processes. The *competitive potential domain* as alignment perspective emphasises the use of emerging information technology capabilities that influence the business scope, such as new products and services. The *product* market is constantly innovating and implementing customisation for the individual. Organisations must adapt to this demand with innovations in products and processes, as well as consideration of the individual's need. *Process* organisations are continually optimised and digitised. This allows organisations to get products and services to market faster; however, organisations need to adopt better processes to stay competitive.

Lastly, the *service level domain* attends to establishing a world-class technology organisation within an organisation and focuses not only on the effective use of IS resources, but also on responsiveness to the fast-changing demands of end-users and customers. The technology and changes that come with I4.0 force the *workforce* to adapt in terms of productivity, skills and well-being. With new technologies and business models emerging, the focus of *customer value* is also shifting. I4.0 demands greater focus on customer interaction and experience. With the disruptive nature of I4.0 having a global impact, organisations must *change* to stay competitive or to re-invent themselves. Organisations must also be able to manage the tension impact of emerging versus legacy infrastructures.

These four strategic alignment domains also present interrelationships (denoted by arrows), as the business strategy informs the technology aspect, focusing on implementing the chosen business strategy and recognising the need to address both external and internal domains [31]. The chosen business strategy and technology opportunity also affect decisions such as product-market offering and choices pertaining to the organisational structure and workforce, as well as the specific rationale for the design and redesign of critical business processes [31].

# 6   Conclusion

I4.0 and the advancement of digital technologies are changing the way we socialise, live and work. I4.0 also provides organisations with opportunities to firstly optimise and enhance internal operations and secondly, innovate and optimise business models. It is important that organisations understand the realities of I4.0, in order to exploit its business value in an organisational context, while maintaining strategic alignment. In this study, the unique I4.0 organisational aspects were identified through an SLR related to digital business model innovation, technology investment optimisation, workforce management complexity, digital eco-systems, technology-centric convergence, virtual model and physical environment linkage, value chain digitalisation and product portfolio innovation. In order to apply these I4.0 organisational aspects, we propose a conceptual model guiding organisations on how these unique aspects affect strategic alignment in an organisation. By applying the proposed conceptual model of I4.0, a strong vision, support- and development plan and path to I4.0 can be created. By understanding such a view of I4.0, organisations can ensure that interrelationships are managed and that a relevant, fit-for-purpose approach to I4.0 may be considered in a strategically aligned manner.

As the study proposes a conceptual model, further research may be conducted to test the proposed strategic alignment model in an organisational context and real-world scenario.

# References

1. Badri, A., Boudreau-Trudel, B., Souissi, A.S.: Occupational health and safety in the industry 4.0 era: a cause for major concern? Saf. Sci. **109**, 403–411 (2018)
2. Ding, B.: Pharma Industry 4.0: literature review and research opportunities in sustainable pharmaceutical supply chains. Process Saf. Environ. Prot. **119**, 115–130 (2018)
3. Rajput, S., Singh, S.P.: Current trends in Industry 4.0 and implications in container supply chain management: a key toward make in India. In: Digital India, pp. 209–224 (2018)
4. Bär, K., Herbert-Hansen, Z.N.L., Khalid, W.: Considering Industry 4.0 aspects in the supply chain for an SME. Prod. Eng. **12**(6), 747–758 (2018)

5. Gerryts, E.W., Maree, J.G.: Enhancing the employability of young adults from socio-economically challenged contexts: theoretical overview. In: Maree, Jacobus G. (ed.) Handbook of Innovative Career Counselling, pp. 425–444. Springer, Cham (2019). https://doi.org/10.1007/978-3-030-22799-9_24

6. Özdağoğlu, A., et al.: A predictive filtering approach for clarifying bibliometric datasets: an example on the research articles related to industry 4.0. Technol. Anal. Strateg. Manage. (2019). https://doi.org/10.1080/09537325.2019.1645826

7. Ghobakhloo, M.: The future of manufacturing industry: a strategic roadmap toward Industry 4.0. J. Manuf. Technol. Manage. **29**(6), 910–936 (2018)

8. Pfohl, H., Yahsi, B., Kurnaz, T.: The impact of Industry 4.0 on supply chain. In: Kersten, W., Blecker, T., Ringle, C. (eds.) Innovations and Strategies for Logistics and Supply Chains, pp. 31–58 (2015)

9. Cieśla, B., Kolny, D.: Visual process analysis in SMEs as a support for management models on example of TOC. J. Syst. Integr. **10**(2), 19–27 (2019)

10. Junior, C.II., et al.: Performance, farmer perception, and the routinisation (RO) moderation on ERP post-implementation. Heliyon **5**(6), 1–13 (2019)

11. Geißler, A., et al.: Structuring the anticipated benefits of the fourth industrial revolution. In: Twenty-Fifth Americas Conference on Information Systems, Cancun (2019)

12. Lezzi, M., Lazoi, M., Corallo, A.: Cybersecurity for Industry 4.0 in the current literature: a reference framework. Comput. Ind. **103**, 97–110 (2018)

13. Frederico, G.F., et al.: Supply chain 4.0: concepts, maturity and research agenda. Supply Chain Manag. Int. J. (2019)

14. Turcu, C.O., Turcu, C.E.: Industrial Internet of Things as a challenge for higher education. Int. J. Adv. Comput. Sci. Appl. **9**(11), 55–60 (2018)

15. Karjalainen, J., Heinonen, S., Shaw, M.: Peer-to-peer and circular economy principles in the fourth industrial revolution (4IR) – new risks and opportunities. In: 2019 International Conference on the Domestic Use of Energy (DUE) (2019)

16. Tabarés, R.: Harnessing the power of digital social platforms to shake up makers and manufacturing entrepreneurs towards a european open manufacturing ecosystem, R.a.I. Action, Editor (2016)

17. Rocha, L., et al.: Cloud management tools for sustainable SMEs. Procedia CIRP **40**, 220–224 (2016)

18. Schuelke-Leech, B.: A model for understanding the orders of magnitude of disruptive technologies. Technol. Forecast. Soc. Change **129**(C), 261–274 (2018)

19. Lu, Y.: Industry 4.0: a survey on technologies, applications and open research issues. J. Ind. Inf. Integr. **6**, 1–10 (2017)

20. Roblek, V., Meško, M., Krapež, A.: A complex view of Industry 4.0. SAGE Open **6**(2), 1–11 (2016)

21. Khairuddin, S.M., Omar, F.I., Ahmad, N.: Digital inclusion domain in entrepreneurship: a preliminary analysis. Adv. Sci. Lett. **24**, 2721–2724 (2018)

22. Wagire, A.A.W., Rathore, A.P.S., Jain, R.: Analysis and synthesis of Industry 4.0 research landscape using latent semantic analysis approach. J. Manuf. Technol. Manag. (2018)

23. Chen, J., Yin, X., Mei, L.: Holistic innovation: an emerging innovation paradigm. Int. J. Innov. Stud. **2**(1), 1–13 (2018)

24. Crnjac, M., Veža, I., Banduka, N.: From concept to the introduction of Industry 4.0. Int. J. Ind. Eng. Manag. (IJIEM) **8**(1), 21–30 (2017)

25. Pinzone, M., et al.: A framework for operative and social sustainability functionalities in Human-Centric Cyber-Physical Production Systems. Comput. Ind. Eng. (2018)

26. Karodia, N.C.: Managing the transition to a 'digital culture': the experience of financial service firms. In: Gordon Institute of Business Science. University of Pretoria, Pretoria, p. 107 (2018)

27. Gareis, K., et al.: E-skills for jobs in Europe: measuring progress and moving ahead (2014)

28. O'Connor, B.: Digital transformation a framework for ICT literacy. In: A Report of the International ICT Literacy Panel (2007)

29. Lawrie, G., et al.: Multi-level strategic alignment within a complex organisation. J. Model. Manage. 11(4), 889–910 (2016)

30. Kaplan, R.S., Norton, D.P.: Strategy Maps: Converting Intangible Assets Into Tangible Outcomes. Harvard Business School Publishing Corp., Boston (2004)

31. Reksoatmodjo, W., et al.: Exploratory study on alignment between IT and business strategies. Gadjah Mada Int. J. Bus. 14(2), 139–162 (2012)

32. Trevor, J., Varcoe, B.: Strategy: how aligned is your organization? Harvard Bus. Rev. 1–6 (2017)

33. Biolchini, J., et al.: Systematic review in software engineering. In: System Engineering and Computer Science Department, PESC, Rio de Janeiro (2005)

34. Rouhani, B.D., et al.: A systematic literature review on enterprise architecture implementation methodologies. Inf. Softw. Technol. 2015(62), 1–20 (2015)

35. Aromataris, E., Pearson, A.: The systematic review: an overview. AJN Am. J. Nurs. 114, 53–58 (2014)

36. Boland, A., Cherry, M.G., Dickson, R.: Doing a Systematic Review: A Student's Guide. SAGE Publications, London (2014)

37. Rouhani, B.D., et al.: A systematic literature review on enterprise architecture implementation methodologies. Inf. Softw. Technol. 62, 1–20 (2015)

38. Welman, C., Kruger, F., Mitchell, B.: Research Methodology, 3rd edn. Oxford University Press Southern Africa, Cape Town (1994)

39. Leedy, P.D., Ormrod, J.E.: Practical Research: Planning and Design, 10th edn. Pearson Education Limited, New Jersey (2014)

40. Issa, A., et al.: Open innovation in the workplace: future work lab as a living lab. Procedia CIRP 72, 629–634 (2018)

41. Kadir, B.A., Broberg, O., Conceição, C.S.d.: Current research and future perspectives on human factors and ergonomics in Industry 4.0. Comput. Ind. Eng. 137 (2019)

42. Canetta, L., Barni, A., Montini, E.: Development of a digitalization maturity model for the manufacturing sector. In: 2018 IEEE International Conference on Engineering, Technology and Innovation (ICE/ITMC) (2018)

43. Ho, Y.F., Turner, J.J.: Entrepreneurial learning'– the role of university led business incubators and mentors in equipping graduates with the necessary skills set for Industry 4.0. Int. J. Educ. Psychol. Couns. 4(30), 283–298 (2019)

44. Scavarda, A., et al.: An analysis of the corporate social responsibility and the Industry 4.0 with focus on the youth generation: a sustainable human resource management framework. Sustainability 11, 1–20 (2019). 5130

45. Ooi, K.-B., et al.: Cloud computing in manufacturing: the next industrial revolution in Malaysia? Expert Syst. Appl. 93, 376–394 (2018)

46. Prifti, L.: Professional qualification in "Industrie 4.0": building a competency model and competency-based curriculum. In: Faculty Informatics. Technischen Universität München, p. 258 (2019)

47. Müller, M., Vorraber, W., Slany, W.: Open principles in new business models for information systems. J. Open Innov. Technol. Market Complex. 5(6), 1–13 (2019)

48. Ferreira, F., et al.: Industry 4.0 as enabler for effective manufacturing virtual enterprises. In: Collaboration in a Hyperconnected World, pp. 274–285 (2016)

49. Liu, Z., Stephens, V.: Exploring innovation ecosystem from the perspective of sustainability: towards a conceptual framework. J. Open Innov. Technol. Market Complex. **5**(48), 1–14 (2019)
50. Illmerab, B., Vielhaberb, M.: Virtual validation of decentrally controlled manufacturing systems with cyber-physical functionalities. Procedia CIRP **72**, 509–514 (2018). L. Wang, Editor
51. Mourtzis, D., Vlachou, E., Milas, N.: Industrial big data as a result of IoT adoption in manufacturing. Procedia CIRP **55**, 290–295 (2016)
52. Tasleem, M., Khan, N., Nisar, A.: Impact of technology management on corporate sustainability performance: the mediating role of TQM. Int. J. Qual. Reliab. Manage. **36**(9), 1574–1599 (2019)
53. Gupta, A., Modgil, S., Gunasekaran, A.: Big data in lean six sigma: a review and further research directions. Int. J. Prod. Res. (2019). https://doi.org/10.1080/00207543.2019.1598599
54. Daú, G., et al.: The healthcare sustainable supply chain 4.0: the circular economy transition conceptual framework with the corporate social responsibility mirror. Sustainability **11**, 1–19 (2019). 3259
55. Syama, N., Sharmab, A.: Waiting for a sales renaissance in the fourth industrial revolution: machine learning and artificial intelligence in sales research and practice. Ind. Mark. Manage. **2018**(69), 135–146 (2018)

# SMART City and Economy: Bibliographic Coupling and Co-occurrence

Libuše Svobodová[1]([⊠]) and Dorota Bednarska-Olejniczak[2]

[1] University of Hradec Kralove,
Rokitanskeho 62, 50003 Hradec Kralove, Czech Republic
libuse.svobodova@uhk.cz
[2] Wrocław University of Economics,
Komandorska 118-120, 53345 Wrocław, Poland
dorota.olejniczak@ue.wroc.pl

**Abstract.** Rapid development of advanced technologies and their use bear crucial influence on Smart City development. Smart economy ranks among key Smart City components. The rising awareness of the importance of Economy in Smart cities becomes a widely discussed issue and gets reflected in professional literature. The aim of the paper is to map and analyse the state of usage of current topics and terms "SMART city" and "economy" and their bibliographic coupling and co-occurrence on Web of Science. The analysis focuses on published documents and their citation, use of journals for publishing of articles, authors that have the most articles, number of published documents in countries. The reoccurrence of the most often used key words in the articles will be analysed. Analysis was done in March 2019 via VOSviewer software. The highest number of articles is presented in Smart economy in smart cities, Journal of cleaner production and Cities. USA and India are the countries with highest number of articles. Smart city, Cities, Smart cities, Governance, Innovation, Big data, Economy and Urbanization are the most often used keywords.

**Keywords:** Bibliographic coupling · Co-occurrence · Economy · SMART city

## 1 Introduction

The introduction and literature review briefly describes the potential of the study in a broad context and highlights the importance of the discussed topic. The purpose of the work and its significance are defined in this chapter. The current state of the research is reviewed carefully and key publications are cited. Then principal conclusions are formulated reflecting the main goal of the paper.

In the globalized world, there is growing concern about economic growth and economy. Development of technologies and use of ICT brings a lot of benefits to society, economy, citizens, companies, cities and next stakeholders. A lot of people use advanced technologies in their daily lives. Technologies are not used only by citizens, companies, but also by governance and cities. The phenomenon of Smart Cities has been experiencing a rising interest in the academic sphere in recent years. The first article on Smart Cities that appeared in the Web of Science database was 'Smart cities - The Singapore case' by Mahizhnan [4]. With 81 citations it is nowadays one of the most cited article on selected topic.

Graham and Aurigi [2, 3] appeared in 1997 the concept of a smart city. The possibility of using ICT tools for communicating with residents was one of the impulse. Next one was collecting data or using this data to manage the city. To state one universal definition of the concept of a smart city is difficult. The report entitled Smart Cities—Ranking of European Medium-Sized Cities [5] defined the idea of 'smart city' quite broadly. According to report "smart city is a city well performing in a forward-looking way in six characteristics [economy, people, governance, mobility, environment, and living], built on the smart combination of endowments and activities of self-decisive, independent and aware citizen". Caragliu et al. [6] defines smart city with the conditions "when investments in human and social capital and traditional (transport) and modern (ICT) communication infrastructure fuel sustainable economic growth and a high quality of life, with a wise management of natural resources, through participatory governance."

Hall et al. [31] in 2000 indicated that "a city that monitors and integrates conditions of all of its critical infrastructures, including roads, bridges, tunnels, rails, subways, airports, seaports, communications, water, power, even major buildings, can better optimize its resources, plan its preventive maintenance activities, and monitor security aspects while maximizing services to its citizen". Therefore, 'smart city' in this definition was associated with the use of ICT to support the delivery of public services.

"Unquestionably, cities are complex systems and the rapid urban growth that brings traffic congestion, pollution, and increasing social inequality may turn the city into a point of convergence of many risks (economic, demographic, social, and environmental)" [7].

"Smart cities provide major economic, social, and productivity benefits to all stakeholders. But without the right vision, plans, talent, and funding in place, smart city programmes will not reach their full potential" [1].

The issue of Smart Cities has been solved for several years. Many of the cities that have been considered successful in terms of Smart Cities will continue to have considerable place for improvement. In this topic are mostly solved technological issues, but economic view of point is not solved so often.

## 2   SMART City x Economy

"Historically, cities are considered as the highest forms of economic and sociocultural achievements in human civilization, and the location of non-primary economic activities" [8].

"When the devices start becoming smarter, it inevitably leads to a smarter ecosystem of devices. The extension of such a development forms something that is called a smart city – A whole city that uses electronics to keep the area running at high or peak efficiency. A recent whitepaper from ABI Research concludes that smart cities will see an overall economic development of 5% annually, which translates to almost $20 trillion in a decade. This again validates that smart cities are a great investment that can impact the economy in a positive way" [9].

Deloitte presents three key differentiators of a smart city [10]:

- "Quality of life
- Economic competitiveness
- Sustainability

Economic competitiveness is presented as cities have long been important centers of trade and commerce, leveraging the proximity of so many diverse citizens to help drive an innovative economy. A smart city is a business-friendly city, ensuring that jobs and tax revenue form a healthy economic platform."

Cities are as "'engines of economic growth' and dominate local and national economies." Smart City System building blocks by Kumar [11] are presented in Fig. 1.

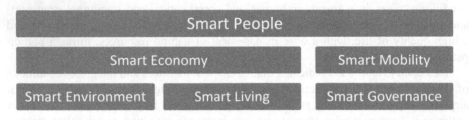

Fig. 1. Smart City System [11]

A city has many areas in which it can be managed to transform itself into a smart city. Six basic directions for action will enable it to direct its objectives along this route, according to the definition of smart cities given by Boyd Cohen [12], an urban development researcher, see Fig. 2.

Fig. 2. The six action areas of smart cities [12]

The smart economy: "it is a city that wants to position itself as a capital of the new economy and innovation as well as a centre that draws people to it" [12].

## 3   Methodology and Goal

Steps of the research are as follows. Firstly, there is the introduction to the topic. The methodological background brings the aim and goal of the study, description of the study procedure and used sources. The literature review contains basic definitions and the starting points to selected issues. The next phase deals with results from bibliographic coupling and co-occurrence of selected keywords. The final phase focuses on summarization and discussion of findings gained from the research.

The aim of the paper is to map and analyse the state of usage of current topics and terms "SMART city" and "economy" and their bibliographic coupling and co-occurrence on Web of Science. Focus will be given on documents and their citation, use of journals for publishing of articles, authors that have the most articles and number of published documents in countries. In co-occurrence will be analysed the most often used keywords in the articles. The previous studies basically focus only on a certain perspective. Visual bibliometric analysis on connected topics smart cities and economy was not founded. This study employed scoping review techniques to dissect the status quo for SMART city and economy. Our search of scientific and research sources focused on scientific sources. The bibliometric mapping study method by Leung et al. [32] and scoping review technique by Arksey and O'Malley [33] were adopted in this review-based article.

The number of co-occurrences and total strength of the co-occurrence links with other keywords for each of the selected keywords were generated in VOSviewer. Co-occurrence is the term used to describe the proximity of keywords in the title, abstract, or keyword list in publication (Van Eck and Waltman [34]) to find connections so that the research topic can be identified (Wang et al. [35]). The link indicates the strength of their occurrences. These methods were used also by Maskuriy et al. [36].

Two terms were searched 15th of March 2019 in the Web of Science database. "SMART city" AND "economy" were put into query. There were 275 articles found in all publications. There were 147 articles in journals and book chapters found in total. Then there were 128 findings in Proceedings papers, 3 in editorial material and 2 in reviews. Only articles in journals and book chapters were included into the next evaluation (Fig. 3).

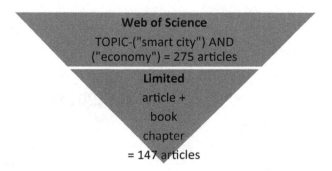

**Fig. 3.**  Selection of documents in bibliometric analysis

In case of searching the term "economics" instead of the term "economy" only 22 articles were found. Due to this reason, the term "economy" was used in the query in the next evaluation. Full record and cited references were saved as Other Reference Software and uploaded to VOSviewer. The analysis that is presented in this paper was made via VOSviewer. Analysis is made between selected sources if it is not written in another way in the text.

The article is established on secondary sources. The secondary sources provide information about smart city and economy, information gained from professional literature and databases and from professional press, from web sites, discussion at professional seminars and conferences related to smart cities and economy. Then it was necessary to select, classify and update accessible relevant information from the high number of published materials that provide the basic background about the solved issue.

## 4   Results

Graphs and tables that represent the outputs from VOSviewer are shown in this chapter. Into evaluation were taken such criteria that are interesting in publishing of the articles. The highest number of citations on document, the most often used journal for publishing this topic, authors that published the highest number of the articles, in which country is the most often solved this issue. The last one solved issue are the most often set keywords connected with the topics.

### 4.1   Bibliographic Coupling

**Documents x Number of Citations**
The minimum number of citations of a document was selected 10. Out of 147 documents, 19 documents meet the threshold. For each of the 19 documents, the total strength of the bibliographic coupling links with other documents will be calculated.

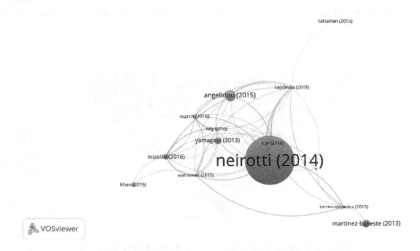

**Fig. 4.**   Bibliographic coupling – documents

The documents with the greatest total link strength will be selected. Some of the 19 items in the network are not connected with each other. The largest set of connected items consists of 14 items. Results are presented in Fig. 4. Four clusters were founded. The biggest is composed of 5 authors. Ferrara [13], Martinez-Balleste [14], Neirotti [15], Sun [16] and Torres-Sospedra [17]. The second cluster composed of 4 authors. Angelidou [18], March [19], Wiig [20] and Yamagata [21]. The third composed of Khan [22], Scuotto [23] and Walravens [24]. The last one consisted of Capdevila [25] and Tukiainen [26]. Alone are publicatons of Hens [27], Shuai [28], Das [29], Hernandez-Munoz [30] and Mahizhnan [4]. Results of number of citations are presented in Table 1. Number of citations are taken directly from Web of Science.

**Table 1.** Documents x number of citations x clusters

| Authors | Citations | Authors | Citations |
|---|---|---|---|
| Ferrara | 16 | Scuotto | 45 |
| Martinez-Balleste | 72 | Walravens | 23 |
| Neirotti | 396 | Capdevila | 22 |
| Sun | 20 | Tukianinen | 16 |
| Torres-Sospedra | 19 | Hens | 15 |
| Angelidou | 102 | Shuai | 22 |
| March | 35 | Das | 10 |
| Wiig | 10 | Hernandez-Munoz | 101 |
| Yamagata | 54 | Mahizhnan | 81 |
| Khan | 32 | | |

## Sources – Journals x Documents

Minimum number of documents of a journal is 4. Of the 98 journals only 4 meet the thresholds. Due the small number of journals were criteria reduced on 3. Only 7 from 98 sources meet the thresholds. For each of the 7 journals (see Table 2 and Fig. 5), the total strength of the bibliographic coupling links with other sources will be calculated. The journals with the greatest total link strength will be selected.

**Table 2.** Bibliographic coupling – journals (sources)

| Source | Documents | Citations | Total link strength |
|---|---|---|---|
| Journal of cleaner production | 7 | 19 | 159 |
| Cities | 7 | 562 | 154 |
| Sustainability | 5 | 6 | 88 |
| Smart economy in smart cities | 20 | 10 | 74 |
| Telematics and informatics | 3 | 28 | 58 |
| Sustainable smart cities in India: challenges and future perspectives | 3 | 0 | 40 |
| Sustainable smart cities: creating spaces for technological, social and business development | 3 | 0 | 31 |

Two clusters were found in journals (sources). By red is marked one and by green the second one.

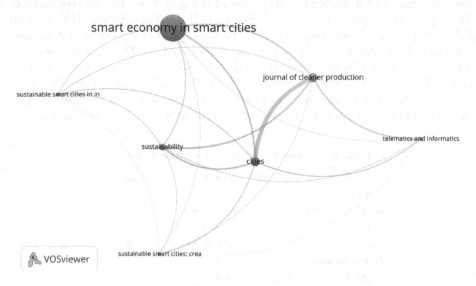

**Fig. 5.** Bibliographic coupling – sources (Color figure online)

## Authors x Documents

The minimum number of documents of an author was set at four. Only 3 authors meet the thresholds of the 403 authors. Criteria were reduced to 3 documents of an author and 7 authors meet the thresholds. In case of further reduction to 2 documents of an author, 37 meet the thresholds. The highest number of publications have Mboup, G. with 6 documents. 4 documents presented Kumar, T.M. Vinod and Mwaniki, D. 3 publications published Spruijt, W., Rodgers, T., Govada, S.S. and Alizadeh, T.

## Country x Documents

Minimum number of documents of a country was set at 5. 9 countries meet the thresholds of the 53 countries. The total strength of the bibliographic coupling links with other countries will be calculated for each of the 9 countries (see Table 3 and Fig. 6).

**Table 3.** Bibliographic coupling - country

| Country | Documents | Citations | Total link strength |
|---|---|---|---|
| Italy | 16 | 452 | 950 |
| Spain | 16 | 231 | 815 |
| USA | 18 | 46 | 774 |
| Peoples r. China | 13 | 22 | 682 |
| England | 11 | 69 | 605 |
| India | 18 | 12 | 469 |
| France | 8 | 57 | 431 |
| Australia | 8 | 20 | 337 |
| Russia | 7 | 51 | 281 |

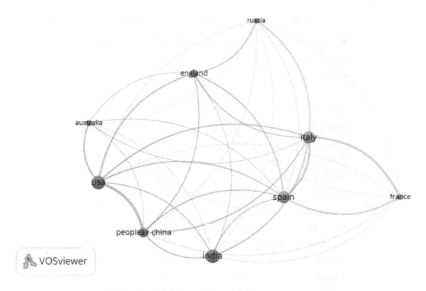

**Fig. 6.** Bibliographic coupling - country

The highest number of articles were written in USA and in India followed by Italy, Spain, Peoples Republic of China and England. The highest number of citations was done in Italy, Spain, England, France, Russian Federation and in USA.

Three clusters of countries were found in the cluster analysis. The first cluster composed of Australia, India, Peoples R. China and USA. The second cluster composed of France, Italy and Spain. The third one from England and Russia.

## 4.2 Co-occurrence

**All Keywords**
Minimum number of occurrences of a keyword was set at 6. 19 keywords meet the threshold of the 706 keyword (see Table 4 and Fig. 7). For each of the 19 keywords, the total strength of the co-occurrence links with other keywords will be calculated. The keywords with the greatest total link strength will be selected.

Internet, challenges, management, infrastructure, network, trends, urban planning, systems and sustainable development have 5 occurrences. Due better clarity will be in graph presented keywords with 6 occurrences and more.

There were identified 4 clusters. The first one composed of 7 items: cities, growth, Internet of things, model, open innovation, smart city and sustainability. Second composed of 6 items: city, economy, smart cities, technology, urban governance and urbanization. The third cluster composed of big data, future, innovation and politics. Together are also often used terms 'governance' and 'sharing economy'.

**Table 4.** Co-occurrence – all keywords

| Keyword | Occurrences | Total link strength |
|---|---|---|
| Smart city | 77 | 132 |
| Cities | 27 | 54 |
| City | 19 | 44 |
| Governance | 12 | 30 |
| Innovation | 13 | 30 |
| Smart cities | 21 | 30 |
| Economy | 9 | 29 |
| Technology | 8 | 25 |
| Big data | 11 | 21 |
| Urbanization | 9 | 21 |
| Growth | 8 | 19 |
| Sharing economy | 8 | 19 |
| Future | 6 | 18 |
| Model | 6 | 18 |
| Politics | 6 | 18 |
| Sustainability | 8 | 18 |
| Urban governance | 6 | 18 |
| Internet of things | 6 | 14 |
| Open innovation | 6 | 14 |

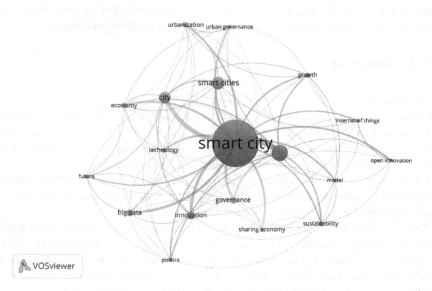

**Fig. 7.** Co-occurrence – all keywords

## 4.3  Limitations of the Study

Science, technology, and innovations are engines to drive growth and sustainable development of SMART cities all over the world.

Due to the limited number of pages and depth of the research the limitations might be found in the following areas:

- Minimum number of citations of a document was set at 10. In case that number of citation of the document will be smaller, more documents will meet the threshold. On the contrary, results will be not so well arranged.
- Number of documents in the journal was reduced due to the small number of journals (sources) with many relevant articles. The criteria were reduced to 3 papers per journal. 7 journals out of 98 sources meet the thresholds.
- Minimum number of documents of an author was set at 4. Only 3 authors out of 403 authors meet the thresholds. When the minimum number of documents by one author is reduced to 3 documents, 7 authors meet the thresholds. In case of 2 documents per author, the number of occurrences will increase.
- Minimum number of documents of a country was set at 5. Only 9 countries out of the 53 countries meet the thresholds. In case of a smaller number of documents, the number of countries meeting the thresholds will increase.
- Minimum number of occurrences of a keyword was set at 6. 19 keywords meet the threshold out of the 706 keywords. In case of smaller occurrence of a keyword, there will be higher amount of keywords.

# 5  Conclusion

Bibliographic coupling and co-occurrence measure a similarity that uses citation analysis to establish a similarity relationship between documents, authors, countries etc. A wide variety of fields may be applied in, since it helps researchers to find related research conducted in the past and to find the gap, nitch or necessities in the analysed field of study.

Topic Smart city and economy is getting its importance more and more. First article was into Web of Science included in 1999 where Mahizhnan wrote [4] that "the final goal is not just economic growth but an enhancement of the quality of life for all people, making Singapore not just a smart city but a quality city-state." The next articles were published in 2011, for ex. [30] that was with 128 citations the most cited from the publication year. The gap was in 2012 and from 2013 till 2017 numbers of articles in journals or book chapters were still rising on 52. It fall on 43 in 2018.

Neirotti, Paolo; De Marco, Alberto; Cagliano, Anna Corinna; et al. [15] with 378 citations with publication Current trends in Smart City initiatives: Some stylised facts in journal Cities recorded the highest number of citations from all authors. Hernandez Munoz et al. were cited 94 times [30], Angelidou [18] was cited 85 times and Mahizhnan [4] 79 times in database Web of Science. Sources as Cities with 562 citations, book Future Internet: Future Internet Assembly 2011: Achievements and Technological Promises with 94 citations, IEEE communications magazine with 60 citations, Applied Energy with 53 and Business Process Management Journal with 43 citations are the most often cited. Topic is the most often solved in Italy, Spain, USA and India. Smart city, cities, city, governance, innovation, smart cities, economy, technology and big data are the most often published keywords connected with topic Smart city and economy. According to above mentioned words and done analysis is Smart city also often connected with keywords technology, urbanization, growth, sharing economy, future, model, politics, sustainability, urban governance, internet of things and open innovation. The creation of smart cities is a motivator for growth, new jobs and is a productive investment in future, leading to a sustainable and environmentally friendly economy. Well-arranged pictures presented in this paper demonstrate the research achievements in the domain of the smart city and economy, which could help researchers, practitioners and mayors and politics to identify the underlying impacts from authors, journals, countries, institutions, references, and research topics.

Future research will be focused on the most frequent occurrence of keywords used in the connection of the analysed issue and their combination with more detailed description so that a wider notion on the topic could be provided.

**Acknowledgements.** This paper is supported by specific project No. 2103 "Invest-ment evaluation within concept Industry 4.0" at FIM University of Hradec Kralove, Czech Republic. The authors thank Anna Borkovcova for her help with the project.

# References

1. How smart city investment can unlock economic growth. https://www.smartcitiesworld.net/news/news/how-smart-city-investment-can-unlock-economic-growth-3566
2. Graham, S., Aurigi, A.: Urbanising cyberspace? City **2**, 18–39 (1997)
3. Graham, S., Aurigi, A.: Virtual cities, social polarization, and the crisis in urban public space. J. Urban Technol. **4**, 19–52 (1997)
4. Mahizhnan, A.: Smart cities - the Singapore case. Cities **16**(1), 13–18 (1999)
5. Giffinger, R., Fertner, C., Kramar, H., Meijers, E., Fertner, C., Kramar, H.: City-ranking of European medium-sized cities, Vienna University of Technology, Vienna (2007)
6. Caragliu, A., Bo, C.D., Nijkamp, P.: Smart cities in Europe. Urban Technol. **18**, 65–82 (2011)
7. Albino, V., Berardi, U., Dangelico, R.M.: Smart cities: definitions, dimensions, performance, and initiatives. J. Urban Technol. **2**(1), 3–21 (2015)
8. Alawadhi, S., et al.: Building understanding of Smart City initiatives. In: Scholl, Hans J., Janssen, M., Wimmer, Maria A., Moe, C.E., Flak, L.S. (eds.) EGOV 2012. LNCS, vol. 7443, pp. 40–53. Springer, Heidelberg (2012). https://doi.org/10.1007/978-3-642-33489-4_4
9. Ways Smart Cities Will Restructure The Economy (2019). https://interestingengineering.com/10-ways-smart-cities-will-restructure-the-economy
10. Smart Cities of the Future - From vision to reality. https://www2.deloitte.com/us/en/pages/consulting/solutions/smart-cities-of-the-future.html
11. Vinod Kumar, T.M., Dahiya, B.: Smart economy in smart cities. In: Vinod Kumar, T.M. (ed.) Smart Economy in Smart Cities. ACHS, pp. 3–76. Springer, Singapore (2017). https://doi.org/10.1007/978-981-10-1610-3_1
12. What is a smart city? https://smartcity.brussels/the-project-definition
13. Ferrara, R.: The Smart City and the green economy in Europe: a critical approach. Energies **8**(6), 4724–4734 (2015)

14. Martinez-Balleste, A., Perez-Martinez, P.A., Solanas, A.: The pursuit of citizens' privacy: a privacy-aware Smart City is possible. IEEE Commun. Mag. **51**(6), 136–141 (2013)
15. Neirotti, P., De Marco, A., Cagliano, A.C., et al.: Current trends in Smart City initiatives: some stylised facts. Cities **38**, 25–36 (2014)
16. Sun, J., Yan, J., Zhang, K.Z.K.: Blockchain-based sharing services: what blockchain technology can contribute to smart cities. Finan. Innov. **2**(1), 1–9 (2016)
17. Torres-Sospedra, J., Avariento, J., Rambla, D., et al.: Enhancing integrated indoor/outdoor mobility in a smart campus. Int. J. Geograph. Inf. Sci. **29**(11, SI), 1955–1968 (2015)
18. Angelidou, M.: Smart cities: a conjuncture of four forces. Cities **47**, 95–106 (2015)
19. March, H., Ribera-Fumaz, R.: Smart contradictions: the politics of making barcelona a self-sufficient city. Eur. Urban Reg. Stud. **23**(4), 816–830 (2016)
20. Wiig, A.: The empty rhetoric of the smart city: from digital inclusion to economic promotion in Philadelphia. Urban Geogr. **37**(4), 535–553 (2016)
21. Yamagata, Y., Seya, H.: Simulating a future smart city: an integrated land use-energy model. Appl. Energy **112**(SI), 1466–1474 (2013)
22. Zaheer, K., Ashiq, A., Kamran, S., et al.: Towards cloud based big data analytics for smart future cities. J. Cloud Comput. Adv. Syst. Appl. **4**(2), 1 (2015)
23. Scuotto, V., Ferraris, A., Bresciani, S.: Internet of Things applications and challenges in smart cities: a case study of IBM smart city projects. Bus. Process Manag. J. **22**(2), 357–367 (2016)
24. Walravens, N.: Mobile city applications for Brussels citizens: Smart City trends, challenges and a reality check. Telematics Inform. **32**(2), 282–299 (2015)
25. Capdevila, I., Zarlenga, M.I.: Smart city or smart citizens? The Barcelona case. J. Strateg. Manag. **8**(3), 266–282 (2015)
26. Tukiainen, T., Leminen, S., Westerlund, M.: Cities as collaborative innovation platforms. Technol. Innov. Manag. Rev. **5**(10), 16–26 (2015)
27. Hens, L., Block, C., Cabello-Eras, J.J., et al.: On the evolution of "Cleaner Production" as a concept and a practice. J. Clean. Prod. **172**, 3323–3333 (2018)
28. Shuai, W., Maille, P., Pelov, A.: Charging electric vehicles in the smart city: a survey of economy-driven approaches. IEEE Trans. Intell. Transp. Syst. **17**(8), 2089–2106 (2016)
29. Das, D.: Hyderabad: visioning, restructuring and making of a high-tech city. Cities **43**, 48–58 (2015)
30. Hernández-Muñoz, J.M., et al.: Smart cities at the forefront of the future Internet. In: Domingue, J., et al. (eds.) FIA 2011. LNCS, vol. 6656, pp. 447–462. Springer, Heidelberg (2011). https://doi.org/10.1007/978-3-642-20898-0_32
31. Hall, R.E., Bowerman, B., Braverman, J., Taylor, J., Todosow, H., Von Wimmersperg, U.: The vision of a Smart City. In: Proceedings of the 2nd International Life Extension Technology Workshop, Paris, France, 28 September 2000
32. Leung, X.Y., Sun, J., Bai, B.: Bibliometrics of social media research: a co-citation and co-word analysis. Int. J. Hosp. Manag. **66**, 35–45 (2017)
33. Arksey, H., O'Malley, L.: Scoping studies: towards a methodological framework. Int. J. Soc. Res. Methodol. Theor. Pract. **8**(1), 19–32 (2005)
34. van Eck, N.J., Waltman, L.: Visualizing bibliometric networks. In: Ding, Y., Rousseau, R., Wolfram, D. (eds.) Measuring Scholarly Impact, pp. 285–320. Springer, Cham (2014). https://doi.org/10.1007/978-3-319-10377-8_13
35. Wang, W., et al.: A bibliometric analysis of the first twenty-five years of the international journal of uncertainty, fuzziness and knowledge-based systems. Int. J. Uncertainty Fuzziness Knowl. Based Syst. **26**(02), 169–193 (2018)
36. Maskuriy, R., Selamat, A., Maresova, P., et al.: Industry 4.0 for the construction industry: review of management perspective. Economies **7**(3), 68 (2019)

# Robotic Process Automation and Consequences for Knowledge Workers; a Mixed-Method Study

Tom Roar Eikebrokk[(✉)] and Dag Håkon Olsen

Department of Information Systems, University of Agder, Kristiansand, Norway
{tom.eikebrokk, dag.h.olsen}@uia.no

**Abstract.** This paper explores an overly optimistic and tenacious claim in the literature that robotic process automation (RPA) will only free knowledge workers from mundane tasks and introduce more interesting work. We explore this claim and other consequences for knowledge workers using data from a sequential quantitative-qualitative, mixed-method study in Norway. 88 RPA users from different sectors and industries where first surveyed to identify differences in utilization and effects from RPA. Then, differences were explored in 24 in-depth interviews in the public and private sectors, including financial industry, manufacturing, and oil and gas. Results indicate that RPA is used to either layoff or not reemploy knowledge workers, but also to empower knowledge workers with more interesting tasks. Private sector was different from public sector in that private, financial companies have experienced the strongest reduction in the need for employment. RPA often lead to layoffs indirectly, and to reduced need for consultants, especially in financial companies. In contrast, public companies use RPA more for innovations in their service production from increased quality in data registration, handling of invoices, and data migration between systems. We conclude that RPA is maturing as a management tool motivated by cost reductions from reduced employment, and we suggest propositions for further research.

**Keywords:** Robotic process automation · RPA · Knowledge work · Knowledge workers

## 1 Introduction

The majority of academics occupied with knowledge workers and robotic process automation (RPA) seem to assume that automation will free knowledge workers from highly structured routine and manual tasks (e.g. [1, 14, 15] but not lead to lay-offs. For knowledge workers, the liberation from mundane tasks is especially important for their productivity [8]. As a result, this would lead to empowerment of knowledge workers who will contribute to companies through applying their convergent, divergent and creative thinking skills rather than being made obsolete. According to Drucker, the first requirement in increasing the productivity of knowledge workers is to find out what their tasks are, what they should be, and which tasks should be eliminated [8]. Since

© IFIP International Federation for Information Processing 2020
Published by Springer Nature Switzerland AG 2020
M. Hattingh et al. (Eds.): I3E 2020, LNCS 12066, pp. 114–125, 2020.
https://doi.org/10.1007/978-3-030-44999-5_10

even knowledge workers have mundane and repetitive tasks, it seems reasonable then, to assume that they will also be subjected to lay-offs following automation.

Knowledge work and knowledge workers are elusive concepts since their content often is defined as the residual after applying intelligent software via machine learning and artificial intelligence tools [2]. As the result of dynamic changes in the capability of these technologies, we see a growing number of examples of automation affecting Healthcare workers, Lawyers, Accountants and Auditors, all in areas traditionally described as characterized by knowledge work [2].

These assumptions regarding knowledge workers and lack of clarity on knowledge work itself, represent weaknesses in the literature on the applicability and consequences of robotic process automation. As a result, the motive for this study is to contribute to the literature by investigating the following research questions:

*How is RPA utilized to transform work in Norwegian companies and what can explain potential differences?*
*What are the consequences for knowledge workers affected by automation?*

The article is organized as follows. In the next section we present relevant studies in the literature on automation and knowledge work. We then describe the combination of methods used to provide information to answer our research questions, before we present results and discuss potential implications for further research and practice.

## 2 Theory

In the literature, Robotic Process Automation (RPA) has been defined as: "A pre-configured software instance that uses business rules and predefined activity choreography to complete the autonomous execution of a combination of processes, activities, transactions, and tasks in one or more unrelated software systems to deliver a result or service with human exception management" [12]. Following this definition, the result is reproduction of work done by humans by automating their tasks motivated by cost reductions, flexibility, increased speed and resource utilization, improved service capabilities and quality [17]. In the society, we see a growing number of examples of automation and RPA in many industries including the financial industry with banking, insurance and auditing [13, 18], and in public and private healthcare [20]. This development of automation can be explained by Drucker [8] who claims that the biggest challenge for companies in the 21th century whether business or non-business, will be to increase the productivity of knowledge work and knowledge workers (p. 79). Following Drucker [8], six factors define not only knowledge work, but also knowledge workers and their productivity: their tasks can be defined, they are autonomous and responsible for their own productivity, they are continuously innovating and learning, not primarily measured on quantity but rather quality, and treated as "assets" rather than "costs". These factors, following Drucker, except quality, are almost the exact opposite of what characterize manual work and the situation of the manual worker [8].

The definition of RPA above says nothing about the consequences for workers other than that their tasks are automated. Lacity and Willcocks [14] and Lacity, Willcocks and Craig [15, 16] are often cited in the academic and the practitioner literature, on their argument that RPA will liberate knowledge workers from highly structured, routine and mundane tasks so that they can focus on more interesting work. This optimistic view of the consequences, coupled with RPA's simplicity, where people with no programming skills can start applying RPA after just a few weeks of training, are probably two of the most important reasons for its growing popularity.

The general literature on automation describes a less harmonic picture. Here, the impact of task automation is described as increasingly dramatic [17]. Jobs will disappear or be redefined and new will be created [3, 7]. The driver behind automation is associated with underlying data analytics and cognitive technologies as artificial intelligence (AI), machine learning, big data, and natural language processing. Development in these technologies will enable automation of unstructured tasks that previously were impossible to automate [9]. As a result, this advancement in cognitive technologies is also challenging the concepts of knowledge work and knowledge workers.

Despite the positive prospects of RPA in the literature, there are few studies available to support the claim that knowledge workers will be freed from dreary tasks to work with more interesting tasks. Logically, when tasks are freed from the knowledge worker, it is likely that a company instead of providing knowledge workers with more interesting tasks, might need fewer knowledge workers and either lay them off or not reemploy new ones following retirement. The literature has not been able to follow pace with the advancement in technology and provides no clear guidelines on the boundaries between work and knowledge work, or between regular workers and knowledge workers. As a result, the concepts of knowledge work and knowledge workers in the literature appear as residuals after cognitive technologies and data analytics constantly push the borders of what tasks can be automated.

To sum up, the literature on RPA is scarce, unclear and lacks studies on the nature and impact of RPA in organizations and of its human and societal consequences in particular. As a result, we still see the widely cited but largely untested claim that knowledge workers will walk free from the negative consequences of automation, as being replaced or laid off. We lack empirical studies that can confirm or challenge this claim, and thus we do not know how RPA is influencing workers through their tasks in organizations, and whether and where automation might support humans or rather be taking over their jobs [11]. The development in cognitive technologies calls for further theorizing as it challenges central conceptualizations in the literature.

## 3   Research Approach

To answer our research questions, we chose a sequential quantitative-qualitative mixed method research design [6, 19] with data from Norway. A quantitative survey identified differences in the utilization of RPA that were followed up by in-dept interviews. This elicited potential explanations for the identified differences. Additional interviews were used to target effects of RPA on knowledge workers.

The survey was based on a literature review and input from three consultants on RPA, to identify functions subjected to automation: financial operations, human relations, IT, customer-oriented functions, supply chain management, shared services, and operations. The literature also identified potential effects on employment, productivity, innovation and quality. A survey instrument was then developed and included background information, experience with RPA, number of employees, sector and industry, type of functions automated (economy/finance, human relations, IT, customer support, supply chain, shared services, operations, other), and effects from RPA (downsizing, reduction in mundane tasks, reduced costs, increased productivity, increased innovation, increased service quality, general satisfaction). Response format ranged from 1 (totally disagree) to 7 (totally agree). The identification of respondents used snow-ball sampling, since no coherent database of the population exists. The responses were analyzed using SPSS version 22.

The semi-structured interviews included 24 respondents selected after the quantitative results, representing a sequential quantitative-qualitative data analysis [19]. The interviews were then taped and transcribed, and the qualitative data related to both research questions. Our mixed-method research strategy follows Creswell et al.'s [6] recommendations, where the analyses should progress in different steps related to the research questions. In interpreting the combined results, qualitative data were used to understand quantitative data and vice versa.

# 4   Results

The instrument was distributed to 438 companies receiving 88 responses (20%). 37 respondents were willing to take part in a follow-up interview. The majority of responses (65) came from private companies in the financial industry (23) and 23 responses from the public sector. Average scores indicate that downsizing is not common (2.1–3.4) but slightly more common in the financial industry (3.4) than in public (2.1) and private sectors (2.8). Reduction of mundane tasks is common in public and financial companies (6.0), and cost reductions (5.2–5.8) and productivity effects (5.6–5.9) were also reported in particular in financial companies. Innovation (5.2) and quality improvements (6.1) were more frequently reported in the public sector. The average satisfaction with RPA was positive and equally strong (5.8–5.9). See Table 1 for an overview.

Experience with RPA ranged from 0 and up to 8 or more years. Private sector (1.4) and financial industry (1, 6) report longer experience with RPA than public sector (0.7). Public sector reported less than 2 years of experience, whereas the financial industry reported close to 4 years of experience. Private sector reported short of 3.5 years.

**Table 1.** Average scores on effects of RPA in public and private sector, and financial industry.

| Organizations | Public sector | | | Private sector | | | Financial industry | | |
|---|---|---|---|---|---|---|---|---|---|
| *Responses* | *n* | *x̄* | *S* | *n* | *x̄* | *S* | *n* | *x̄* | *S* |
| Downsizing | 19 | 2.1 | 1.3 | 62 | 2.8 | 1.9 | 22 | 3.4 | 1.9 |
| Cost reductions | 19 | 5.2 | 1.7 | 63 | 5.5 | 1.6 | 22 | 5.8 | 1.5 |
| Productivity | 19 | 5.6 | 1.6 | 63 | 5.7 | 1.5 | 23 | 5.9 | 1.4 |
| Innovation | 21 | 5.2 | 1.8 | 63 | 4.9 | 1.7 | 23 | 4.6 | 1.7 |
| Quality improvements | 20 | 6.1 | 0.9 | 64 | 5.5 | 1.6 | 23 | 5.6 | 1.8 |
| Fewer mundane tasks | 20 | 6.0 | 1.3 | 64 | 5.6 | 1.8 | 23 | 6.0 | 1.7 |
| Satisfaction with RPA | 20 | 5.8 | 1.5 | 65 | 5.9 | 1.0 | 23 | 5.9 | 1.2 |
| Experience with RPA | 23 | 0.7 | 0.5 | 65 | 1.4 | 1.2 | 23 | 1.6 | 1.2 |

Independent samples t-test identified systematic differences, see Table 2. To fit the exploratory purpose, $p < 0.10$ and a two-tailed test identified systematic differences to be included in in-depth interviews.

**Table 2.** T-test to identify systematic differences between effect scores.

| Organizations | Public vs private sector | | Financial vs other | |
|---|---|---|---|---|
| Responses | Mean difference | Sig. (2 tailed) | Mean difference | Sig. (2 tailed) |
| Downsizing | −0.68 | 0.083 | 1.070 | 0.028 |
| Cost reductions | – | – | – | – |
| Productivity | – | – | – | – |
| Innovation | – | – | – | – |
| Quality improvements | 0.55 | 0.058 | – | – |
| Fewer mundane tasks | – | – | – | – |
| Satisfaction with RPA | – | – | – | – |
| Experience with RPA | −0.65 | 0.001 | 0.48 | 0.10 |

Table 2 shows average scores on significant differences in effects of RPA, satisfaction with RPA, and experience with RPA between public and private sector, and between the financial industry and other companies in general. Downsizing is less common in the public than private sector. The financial industry reports more downsizing than other companies. Quality effects are more common in public sector than in private sector, and experience with RPA is lower in the public sector than private sector, and longest in the financial industry.

Table 3 reports whether effects from RPA are related to the functions being automated. Two functions were different from functions in general – economy/accounting, and operations. Companies who automate economy/accounting functions experience less downsizing than those who automate other functions. Companies automating economy/accounting functions report significantly less experience with RPA. Companies choosing to automate operations, experience more downsizing than companies selecting other functions. The same appears for innovation, quality and reduction in mundane tasks, where companies automating operations experience higher effects than companies automating other functions. Companies automating operations are more experienced with RPA. The next section describes potential explanations for these differences, identified through in-depth interviews with selected companies that participated in the survey.

**Table 3.** T-test of systematic differences in effects from RPA between automated functions.

| Automated functions | Economy/accounting (n = 31) vs. other functions | | Operations (n = 28) vs. other functions | |
|---|---|---|---|---|
| Responses | Mean difference | Sig. (2 tailed) | Mean difference | Sig. (2 tailed) |
| Downsizing | −0.97 | 0.024 | 1.11 | 0.028 |
| Cost reductions | – | – | – | – |
| Productivity | – | – | – | – |
| Innovation | – | – | 0.69 | 0.052 |
| Quality | – | – | 0.82 | 0.004 |
| Fewer mundane tasks | – | – | 0.82 | 0.010 |
| Satisfaction with RPA | – | – | – | – |
| Experience with RPA | −0.40 | 0.085 | 0.68 | 0.014 |

Following Creswell et al. [6] it is necessary to select interviewees from survey respondents for a truly mixed method. Of 88 respondents, 37 were willing to participate in a follow-up interview, showing an interest in the topic area. Table 4 shows the distribution of interviewees in the 24 interviews conducted, including their background. The interviewees had an average of two years of experience with RPA, and three years in the finance industry. Companies primarily automate rule based and high-volume processes, consistent with the RPA literature.

Functions being automated

Back-office tasks were automated in the finance industry, particularly when RPA was first introduced. This included moving data between systems, invoice processing, updating information in legacy systems, customer management, and customer interaction tasks that customers could perform on their own. Most respondents in the finance industry had automated loan application processing, illustrated by respondent 8: "It would take weeks and days, where 10–15 people were working full time on this. [...] [It now takes] six minutes before the customer gets an offer [...] without any employees involved."

RPA was employed in various ways in private sector companies, and the respondent from the supplier industry emphasized two main areas: back-office tasks such as moving data between systems and accounting, and data retrieval from web or internal systems, where system integration or APIs were not sufficient. A respondent from the energy sector emphasized HR tasks as travel expense and payroll. The respondent from manufacturing industry reported supply chain processes, for example quality documentation and document processing. The respondent from the Oil industry reported use of RPA most extensively in finance and control. RPA was employed differently in the public sector, mostly for accounting and logistics that were not emphasized in public health enterprises. Many tasks were automated, such as HR, medical and administrative processes. Respondents from municipalities reported more traditional use of RPA in accounting and invoice processing, and data migration.

**Table 4.** Roles and affiliation of Interviewees

| Respondent | Role | Industry | Sector | RPA experience |
|---|---|---|---|---|
| 1 | Project manager | Municipality | Public | 2 years |
| 2 | RPA team leader | Health | Public | 2 years |
| 3 | Value chain coordinator | Manufacturing | Private | 3 years |
| 4 | Project manager | Oil | Private | 2 years |
| 5 | Development leader | Insurance | Private | 3 years |
| 6 | Automation architect | Bank | Private | 3 years |
| 7 | Project leader/coordinator | Energy | Private | 2 years |
| 8 | RPA analyst | Bank | Private | 3 years |
| 9 | Project manager | Bank | Private | 3 years |
| 10 | Strategic manager | Bank | Private | 3 years |
| 11 | Advisor | Health | Public | n/a |
| 12 | Process analyst/specialist | Bank | Private | 4 years |
| 13 | IT and development leader | Supplier | Private | 2 years |
| 14 | Development leader | Municipality | Public | 2 years |
| 15 | CEO | Wholesale | Private | 2 years |
| 16 | RPA team leader | Public authority | Public | 1.5 years |
| 17 | Senior advisor RPA | Health | Public | 2 years |
| 18 | RPA team leader | Energy | Private | 1.5 years |
| 19 | Development leader | Bank | Private | 2.5 years |
| 20 | Manager robotics | Bank | Private | 3.5 years |
| 21 | Business developer | IT Infrastructure | Private | 3.5 years |
| 22 | RPA manager | Energy | Private | 2 years |
| 23 | RPA advisor | Municipality | Public | 2.5 years |
| 24 | Project manager | Bank | Private | 3 years |

Work-related consequences

The finance industry stood out as a special case with longer experience with RPA, and more focused on cost reduction. The respondents pointed at the strategic focus on cost efficiency in their industry. Respondent 10 noted: "Yes, there is a lot of [downsizing] in the finance industry. There are severance packages three times a year." The strong push for cost efficiency can be related to increased competition from new entrants with a strong focus on digital transformation of the industry and the society. This has opened up for new actors, such as Apple and Facebook, where Apple launched Apple pay that forces the incumbent actors to push for more efficiency and innovation in systems solutions and business models. Norwegian banks have therefore invested significantly in new IT technology, which has increased costs and resulting in payroll cost reductions. The largest Norwegian bank (DnB) aims to reduce costs by approximately €200 millions by 2020 using RPA as one of the tools. One respondent (10) noted that his employer did not reveal the full intension behind RPA: "We got a percentage estimate of the workforce that would be replaced by this. My employer stated quite clearly that no one in Norway would be sacked as a result of this. It was a sales gimmick to make people positive." Another respondent (14) from another bank noted that the strategy of headcount reduction started before they implemented RPA – but that RPA has contributed to achieving these strategic goals: "It was a strategic decision taken before we started with RPA [...]. RPA has been a very important contributor to achieving these goals." Respondent 10 added that RPA has influenced recruiting – they do not hire new people; they employ RPA instead. Respondent 14 asserted: "We have had a quite substantial reduction in headcount, and we process higher volumes than before we started the layoffs." Both respondent 10 and 14 argued that as RPA was more employed for layoffs, the attitudes among employees become more negative. Respondent 14 noted that "People are afraid of losing their jobs [...]. Those who [work in the processes] are not always the ones that are most willing to assist [with the RPA effort]." The picture is not as dramatic in other industries. Cost reduction and efficiency were a major motivation but without significant effect on layoffs. For many companies, RPA is a way to manage growth and higher process volumes. The respondent from the energy sector noted that there was a push for both cost efficiency and digital transformation. He asserted: "It has been a strong focus on innovation. [..] There has not been a lot of innovation in this industry [...] but [we] are in a technology shift in relation to digitalization. This comes from corporate management." Respondent 5 from the manufacturing industry corroborated that digital transformation was a driver for change and noted: "we have seen that we can achieve massive cost reductions from using digital technologies. [It implies] new ways of working."

Respondent 9 from the energy industry commented on headcount reduction: "No, it is not the goal with RPA. It is more value adding work, pleasurable, less 'mouse arm' and such that are the benefits." This was supported in the manufacturing industry where respondent 6 noted: "We have not laid anyone off, and we have no intentions of doing that. [...] people have too much to do. [...] there is always something else that you can fill your days with [...] that is more value adding or reasonable." The respondent from the supplier industry reported no layoffs due to RPA because of more customers and work, and that it is too early to tell if RPA will lead to layoffs: "We grow without [hiring] new people. [...] RPA is a way to handle a part of the growth."

The major motivation in the public sector for acquiring RPA was process and service quality improvements. For health enterprises this means freeing up health workers form administrative tasks to patient care. Respondent 4 noted: "We have very little focus on [cost reduction]. [...] if you save a few hours for a Chief physician, you don't reduce his hours, and he will spend his time more effectively on the tasks that he should perform, for example with the patient. [...] for us it is more freeing up time, and to a great extent [achieving greater] quality." Respondent 13 corroborated and noted that a major goal with RPA was to increase patient security and freeing up health personnel from administrative tasks. One respondent from a municipality noted that cost efficiency was a major motivation for acquiring RPA as an inexpensive way to solve systems integration problems, and that RPA reduced the need for new employees with payroll cost reduction over time.

Consequences for knowledge workers

All companies interviewed pointed at positive consequences from more efficient work processes with fewer routine tasks, and at new and more important tasks for the company. These tasks were also more meaningful for the employees. Respondent 16 from the public sector asserts: "It has been a change in tasks where those tasks we still do are those that need human judgement, but we have got rid of those boring tasks [...] so we can concentrate on new and unsolved tasks". Respondent 15 from a wholesale company adds: "In our case, workers work more with sales tasks which leads to better market relations and increased sales – this is what makes a salesperson valuable". Respondent 19 from a bank argues: "They [workers] do other and newer tasks because it [RPA] frees up capacity to prioritize differently and learn from new insight into process and technology". Respondent 18 from an energy company also point at learning: "In those processes where we have had a full-time employee, we are working to find new alternatives for them. Out in the business units there are plenty of tasks to do, so business units are challenged to making sure that we learn to create value in new ways". Similar stories are told across industries and sectors. Companies point at the increased efficiency created by the removal of routine task, which has created opportunities to take on new tasks and to learn new skills. This means that knowledge workers are freed from mundane tasks and given new and more meaningful opportunities. Still, this is not the whole story. Most companies were reluctant in admitting that knowledge workers could lose their jobs. Rather, they argue that they meet downsizing with automation or that retirement will not be met by recruitment, as respondent 24 from a bank asserts: "We have removed tasks from the regional offices, which has made us downsize through retirement without laying people off". Respondent 22 from an energy company points to other effects: "We have some consultants in the company, so one alternative is not to hire so many of those and [thus] create more value per employee".

Respondents from the public sector and across private industries point at the communication around potential layoffs as challenging. Informant 20 from a bank reports: "Cutting costs can be done in many ways. Everybody thinks immediately that people will be fired as the only way of cutting costs. This is totally wrong because you might rather use their time to do tasks that you so far have not been able to do in the company, including new services and tasks that have been neglected for a long time. You can simply do more with the same workforce and thus save money". The difficulty of talking about layoffs was further elaborated by respondent 23 from a public company: "You cannot brag too much about how many positions you have saved up because you have to keep managers, workers and unions happy".

# 5 Discussion and Implications

This research explored how RPA are used to transform work (RQ1) and what consequences are for knowledge workers (RQ2) in Norwegian organizations. We identified several interesting issues in the quantitative phase that was further explored in the interviews, and in a combined analysis. The main contribution of our work is to refute the assertion that RPA will not lead to layoffs among knowledge workers [14]. Our findings demonstrate no reason to believe that knowledge workers are exempt from the consequences of RPA. While RPA has mainly been seen as a tool for liberating knowledge workers from tedious tasks, we found that RPA is indeed used for layoffs among knowledge workers, particularly in the finance industry. This industry has longer experience with the RPA than other industries and the public sector in our data, and it is reasonable to assume that financial companies are among the most mature RPA users. The finance industry had significantly more reduction in headcount than the other industries. The interviews showed that the reduction came from reduced hiring and layoffs, even though RPA in one instance was sold in as not leading to layoffs, but indeed used in this way eventually. This contrasts case studies of Lacity, Willcocks and Craig [15, 16] and the assertion that RPA will not lead to layoffs among knowledge workers [14]. One might ask why the myth that RPA will not lead to layoffs for knowledge workers seems so persistent? Obviously, being open with the fact that knowledge workers risk losing their jobs would create socio-political resistance against RPA. Resistance from knowledge workers is probably more challenging than resistance from regular workers, and silence to avoid resistance, combined with the likelihood that reduced need for knowledge workers emerges over time, stand out as a potential explanation for the myth. Until recently, it was perceived that jobs susceptible to automaton were in the middle of the workforce skill spectrum [9], leading to a decrease in jobs in this skill spectrum [10]. Technological development in cognitive IT technologies such as AI and machine learning enables automation of tasks that require human judgment [13, 17]. We argue that when RPA applications are programmed to access such cognitive IT applications, they can automate most knowledge worker assessments and reduce the need for most types of knowledge workers.

Studies of RPA implementation indicate that 30–50% of projects fail (Hindle et al. 2018 according to [18]) and one important reason is lack of stakeholder buy-in. We argue that it is important that management is realistic and open about the consequences of RPA adoption, and not paint an unrealistically positive picture. The management of any organization will always be looking for ways to improve the bottom line, and we argue that RPA is a handy tool for reducing personnel costs. We further conjecture that RPA will enter the management's standard toolbox as organizations become more mature RPA-users, and RPA will be used to reduce personnel costs. For organizations needing to reduce costs and improve efficiency, like businesses in the finance industry, layoffs are relevant. Thus, we raise the following proposition: P1: *As organizations gain experience with the RPA technology, they will use it more extensively for reducing personnel costs, including laying off among knowledge workers.*

The finance industry has little room for differentiation [4, 5] and experiences a strong focus on cost leadership and efficiency. It not surprising that RPA has been utilized for achieving cost reduction. We believe that the same logic applies for any industry with a low differentiation, and for companies with a cost-leadership strategy in any industry. We therefore argue that organizations or industries with little differentiation, and thus a strong focus on cost leadership, will find RPA attractive for reducing costs. We raise the following propositions: P2: *Industries with little product or service differentiation will use RPA more for reducing personnel costs, including laying off knowledge workers.* P3: *Organizations with little product or service differentiation will use RPA more for reducing personnel costs, including laying off knowledge workers.*

Second, public sector organizations had a limited focus on personnel cost reductions from RPA and instead focused on increasing service quality by freeing up personnel from administrative tasks. RPA can be a valuable tool to improve public sector services, especially in public sector health enterprises struggling to cope with a growing need for elderly healthcare in Norway as in other industrialized countries. We saw that municipalities used RPA for reducing payroll expenses, and we argue that even if organizations in the short term may use RPA to free up knowledge workers for more meaningful tasks, RPA will eventually enter management's standard toolbox, and be used to cutting personnel costs among knowledge workers. Some benefits will be achieved by giving employees new job assignments, but we argue that knowledge workers are not exempt from economic reality and may become redundant. We expect that RPA will lead to layoffs of knowledge workers, and we forward the following propositions: P4: *RPA will be used to improve service quality in the public sector.* P5: *RPA will lead to layoffs among knowledge workers in the public sector.*

Third, quantitative analysis showed that organizations with the longest experience with RPA in operations had larger effects from cost reductions, innovation, quality and reduction of mundane tasks. These findings illustrate that operational tasks are the most important application area related to the creation of products or services. In the finance industry such processes could be loan application processing, and in the manufacturing industry it could be quality documentation processing. Further research should address how RPA is utilized in various functions and look at variations in the effects.

Our exploratory study has several limitations. First, no database of companies using RPA existed at the time of study, necessitating a snowball sampling with low control with how the sample represents the population. Second, automation with RPA is highly dynamic and change as new cognitive technologies emerge, challenging our use of concepts related to automation and knowledge work.

**Acknowledgements.**    The authors will acknowledge Admir Begovic, Ole Aarsnes, Christian Thorne, and Erik Zetterquist for their work in collecting survey data and conducting the interviews.

# References

1. Aguirre, S., Rodriguez, A.: Automation of a business process using Robotic Process Automation (RPA): a case study. In: Figueroa-García, J.C., López-Santana, E.R., Villa-Ramírez, J.L., Ferro-Escobar, R. (eds.) WEA 2017. CCIS, vol. 742, pp. 65–71. Springer, Cham (2017). https://doi.org/10.1007/978-3-319-66963-2_7

2. Boulton, C.: What is RPA? A revolution in business process automation. Accessed 6 Sept 2019. https://www.cio.com/article/3236451/what-is-rpa-robotic-processautomation-explained.html (2018)
3. Brynjolfsson, E., McAfee, A.: Why workers are losing the war against machines. Atlantic **26** (2011)
4. Campbell-Hunt, C.: What have we learned about generic competitive strategy? Metaanal. Strateg. Manag. J. **21**(2), 127–154 (2000)
5. Chan Kim, W., Mauborgne, R.: Value innovation: the strategic logic of high growth. Harvard Bus. Rev. **26**(4), 22–28 (2004)
6. Creswell, J.W., Klassen, A.C., Plano Clark, V.L., Smith, K.C.: Best practices for mixed methods research in the health sciences. Bethesda (Maryland): Nat. Ins. Health **12**(4), 541–545 (2011)
7. Davenport, T.H., Kirby, J.: Just how smart are smart machines? MIT Sloan Manag. Rev. **57** (3), 21 (2016)
8. Drucker, P.: Knowledge-worker productivity: the biggest challenge. Calif. Manag. Rev. **41** (2) (1999)
9. Frey, C.B., Osborne, M.A.: The future of employment: how susceptible are jobs to computerisation? Technol. Forecast. Soc. Change **114**, 254–280 (2017)
10. Goos, M., Manning, A.: Lousy and lovely jobs: the rising polarization of work in Britain. Rev. Econ. Stat. **89**(1), 118–133 (2007)
11. Ghislieri, C., Molino, M., Cortese, C.G.: Work and organizational psychology looks at the fourth industrial revolution: how to support workers and organizations? Front. Psychol. **9**, 2365 (2018)
12. IEEE Corporate Advisory Group: IEEE Guide for Terms and Concepts in Intelligent Process Automation. IEEE. New York (2017)
13. Kokina, J., Davenport, T.H.: The emergence of artificial intelligence: how automation is changing auditing. J. Emerg. Techn. Account. **14**(1), 115–122 (2017)
14. Lacity, M., Willcocks, L.P.: What knowledge workers stand to gain from automation. Harvard Bus. Rev. **19**(6) (2015)
15. Lacity, M., Willcocks, L.P., Craig, A.: Robotic process automation: mature capabilities in the energy sector. http://eprints.lse.ac.uk/64520/1/OUWRPS_15_06_published.pdf (2015a)
16. Lacity, M., Willcocks, L.P., Craig, A.: Robotic process automation at Telefonica O2. Outsourcing Unit Work. Res. Pap. Ser. **15**(2) (2015b)
17. Marshall, T.E., Lambert, S.L.: Cloud-based intelligent accounting applications: accounting task automation using IBM watson cognitive computing. J. Emerg. Technol. Account. **15**(1), 199–215 (2018)
18. Moffitt, K.C., Rozario, A.M., Vasarhelyi, M.A.: Robotic process automation for auditing. J. Emerg. Technol. Account. **15**(1), 1–10 (2018)
19. Venkatesh, V., Brown, S.A., Sullivan, Y.W.: Guidelines for conducting mixed methods research: an extension and illustration. J. Assoc. Inf. Systems **17**(7), 435–495 (2016)
20. Wasen, K.: Replacement of highly educated surgical assistants by robot technology in working life: paradigm shift in the service sector. Int. J. Soc. Robot. **2**(4), 431–438 (2010)

# Co-creation for Digitalization: A Study of Co-creation in Norwegian Business Clusters

Dag H. Olsen[✉], Tom Roar Eikebrokk, Kristian Aspø,
and Elaine Sajets

University of Agder, Kristiansand, Norway
{dag.h.olsen,tom.eikebrokk}@uia.no

**Abstract.** There is a growing emphasis on digitalization in research and business practice. The rapid progress in digital technologies compel firms to innovate and transform their businesses. One way to improve the capacity to innovate and transform is to cooperate with others. However, there is a general lack of research on how co-creation among businesses can facilitate digitalization. This qualitative study explores how co-creation among businesses can stimulate and facilitate digitalization.

We have investigated co-creation activities involving companies in business clusters. This paper reports from a study of three business clusters in Norway. We conducted an inductive qualitative study comprising semi-structured interviews as the primary empirical data source. 12 interviews were carried out with informants from three clusters. We found that the co-creation arenas and activities in the business clusters stimulate and facilitate digitalization among the cluster companies. We also addressed the most significant drivers and barriers to co-creation to get a deeper understanding of the co-creation phenomenon.

**Keywords:** Co-creation · Clusters · Digitalization

## 1 Introduction

Digital innovation has caused disruptive changes to the economy [1], and there is rapid change in many industries due to digitalization and digital transformation [2]. The fast progress in digital technologies generates a pressure on firms to innovate and transform their businesses. Organizations need to understand how to implement digital technologies and innovative business concepts [3]. Digitalization is very challenging for most organizations who struggle with understanding the opportunities and consequences to their business [4]. The task is especially challenging for small firms due to their general lack of resources [5]. One way to develop the capability to innovate and transform is to cooperate with others [6]. Businesses are increasingly seeking multiple partners to be more successful in applying digital solutions and achieving digitalization [7]. However, instituting and effectively managing a co-creation strategy is challenging, and potentially leading to tensions between companies [8].

Our aim has been to explore how firms can co-create with other businesses to better cope with the challenges and opportunities of digitalization. We have therefore looked for arenas where firms co-create, and we conjectured that business clusters would be

© IFIP International Federation for Information Processing 2020
Published by Springer Nature Switzerland AG 2020
M. Hattingh et al. (Eds.): I3E 2020, LNCS 12066, pp. 126–137, 2020.
https://doi.org/10.1007/978-3-030-44999-5_11

appropriate arenas. Business clusters have some common elements of cooperation and common activities for the benefit of the cluster companies. We have therefore addressed how co-creation among businesses can contribute to digitalization among the cluster members. We thus raised the following research question: How does co-creation contribute to digitalization in business clusters? To answer this main research question, we raised three more specific research questions: What are the drivers for co-creation in the business clusters? what are the barriers for co-creation in the business clusters? and how does co-creation influence digitalization in the business clusters? By addressing the drivers for co-creation, we would improve our understanding of issues and activities that contributed to the co-creation of digitalization. By addressing the barriers for co-creation, we would get a better understanding of key issues that hampered the co-creation efforts. This would give us a deeper understanding of the how the co-creation activities addressed these issues in order to stimulate co-creation in the clusters.

The paper is organized as follows: The next sections present related work on co-creation. Then we present the research method, followed by the results and a discussion of potential implications for further research. Finally, we present the conclusion.

## 2 Background

The management literature has for many years acknowledged the significance of interdependence between enterprises, resulting in social relationships and networks [9, 10]. Such connections have provided the participants with the capacity to create opportunities for competitive advantage through new sources of information. A rising stream of research has conceptually described these collaborations as co-creation. This research can present substantial input to innovation processes [11]. These networks can enhance competitive power by forming shared sources of value creation through co-creation [12]. This collaboration is especially valuable when the market is dynamic, and the enterprises have limited resources for innovation. Firms collaborating in such networks contribute knowledge and resources in co-creating interpretations and responses. This co-creation relates to an array of corporate issues such as supply chain utilization, service innovations and of information technology implementation [13]. There is a dearth of research on the nature of co-creation in various contexts and how it can be managed [14, 15]. There is a need for more research on issues such as how do companies that are not suppliers or customers to each other, collaborate horizontally in business networks, and how does co-creation as a dynamic process contributes to the value-creation of the enterprises and the whole ecosystem [11].

The literature has identified various factors that influences collaboration in a cluster. Lack of resources, both human and financial, can lead to hesitation among member companies when it comes to participating in innovation [6]. Trust has also been found to have a major impact on collaboration. In a case study by Sarker, Sarker, Sahaym and Bjørn-Andersen [16], the authors found that trust, goodwill and commitment are important drivers for member companies to commit resources for generating new products and services. Other findings are issues such as lack of incentives, leadership and a clear common vision. Such issues are important barriers that must be dealt with to create a fertile co-operation environment [6]. There are many potential benefits from co-creating, and substantial benefits can come from sharing knowledge and data [6].

Knowledge sharing is seen as the heart of collaboration and can act as a driving force for change and better understanding of customer preferences [17]. Nevertheless, it is a difficult balancing act for many companies to share their knowledge without giving up competitive advantage [18]. Furthermore, we find that increased competitiveness, increased usability of collaboration tools (if done correctly) and greater focus on customer data [6, 19] are advantages that can be achieved by co-creation. In SMEs, we see that IT-facilitated collaboration between companies can increase, and it can make members more proactive. It can be a challenging task to get such a collaboration going, but it can lead to improved performance [20]. In companies with few resources and employees, IT-facilitated collaboration systems can be helpful if they cooperate [6, 20], and customer loyalty and retention may increase upon establishment of such co-creation services [17]. We argue that resources are key to realize value form co-creation [21]. We therefore adopted the resource-based view (RBV) of the firm [22, 23] as an analytical lens.

Digital transformation can be defined as a major change in how business is conducted due to digital technology [2, 24, 25]. The term digitalization usually has a more limited interpretation; it is about leveraging digital technology to modify socio-technical structures [25]. We have adopted the term digitalization, to also include minor changes to the business models. There are many definitions of digital innovation [25]. What is generally common elements is that it is perceived as something novel, and that it is based on digital technology [26, 27]. Osmundsen et al. [25] build on these definitions, and emphasizes that digital innovation is a process (to innovate) as well as an outcome, and is about "combining digital technology in new ways or with physical components that enables socio-technical changes and creates new value for adopters."

Business clusters that we know today started back in the 1950s with the production of ceramic tiles [28]. It was in a small Italian town named Sassuolo in the Emilia-Romagna area [28]. It wasn't until the early 1990s that clusters and cluster projects really came into focus through the research by Michael E. Porter [29]. This created an interest in clusters and their potential for innovation, knowledge sharing, collaboration, networking and growth [30]. Clusters can be defined as "[…] geographic concentrations of interconnected companies, specialized suppliers, service providers, firms in related industries, and associated institutions (e.g., universities, standards agencies, trade associations) in a particular field that compete but thus cooperate" [29].

We next present the research approach and the three business clusters we investigated.

## 3   Research Approach and Setting

We conducted an inductive qualitative study comprising semi-structured interviews as the primary empirical data source. 12 interviews were carried out with informants from three clusters, see Table 1 for an overview of the informants.

**Table 1.** Overview over interviewees.

| Cluster | Informant | Position | Company size | Role in cluster | Interview date | Duration |
|---------|-----------|----------|--------------|-----------------|----------------|----------|
| A | A1 | Project leader | N/A | Cluster mgmt | 02.15.2019 | 01:02 |
| A | A2 | Senior engineer | SME | Member company | 03.12.2019 | 00:58 |
| A | A3 | CTO | Large | Member company | 03.21.2019 | 01:08 |
| A | A4 | CEO | SME | Member company | 05.09.2019 | 00:54 |
| B | B1 | CEO | N/A | Cluster mgmt | 02.26.2019 | 00:44 |
| B | B2 | CEO | SME | Member company | 04.01.2019 | 00:53 |
| B | B3 | Project leader | SME | Member company | 04.11.2019 | 00:34 |
| B | B4 | Project leader | Large | Member company | 04.23.2019 | 00:35 |
| C | C1 | Member | N/A | Cluster mgmt | 04.11.2019 | 00:58 |
| C | C2 | CEO | SME | Member company | 04.02.2019 | 00:35 |
| C | C3 | CEO | SME | Member company | 04.02.2019 | 00:33 |
| C | C4 | Member | N/A | Cluster board | 04.02.2019 | 00:22 |

The interviews were mostly conducted face-to-face at the companies' sites. A few interviews were conducted over telephone. The interviews lasted from 22 min to over one hour, and they were taped and fully transcribed. The interviews were largely dialogue-based. Secondary material in the form of document studies was also utilized [31], and included information and documents available through the clusters' web pages. Due to requests for anonymity, no personal data were registered in the transcripts. The transcripts were then moved into the NVivo analysis tool. The empirical material was systematized and reduced [32], and we performed a content analysis.

Business cluster A consists of approximately 100 member companies, mainly in the energy and maritime sector. They are suppliers of technology, products and services. The cluster focuses on building competence and conducting research and training with national and international partners. The goal of the cluster is to strengthen competitiveness, improve the development of new products and services, and to apply knowledge and technology to new markets in a sustainable way. The cluster arranges and facilitates meetings, conferences and courses, in Norway as well as abroad. The cluster also runs several types of projects for cluster members.

Cluster B consists of more than 100 member companies and over 40 municipalities and other public actors. The cluster focuses on innovation, research and business development within health and welfare technology. The cluster focuses on innovation, research, development and export of products and services. Through collaboration, knowledge sharing and business development, they aim to strengthen the member companies. The cluster also aims to develop the market for health and welfare technology - both in the private and the public sector. There cluster arranges many events; it is everything from member meetings, innovation forums, conferences and courses for specific projects. They also have one innovation lab where member companies can test out various technologies.

Cluster C consists of just under 100 organizations from finance, insurance, academia and technology. The cluster focuses on financial technology, including innovation, growth and value creation. The main goal of the cluster is to make finance easy, and they work to increase export of Norwegian financial technology. The cluster organizes and facilitates several types of conferences, workshops and seminars - both in and outside Norway. In addition, there are many projects run by the cluster, where the idea for some of the projects has come from brainstorming events in the cluster.

## 4    Results

The interviews generated several drivers and barriers. The drivers and barriers emerged from the interview transcripts. Table 2 shows the drivers and barriers noted by the informants. An "x" means that the informants agree on this issue, and an "o" means that they do not fully agree on this issue. We found that the main drivers are knowledge sharing, networking and having a proficient cluster management. The main barriers are the competition between cluster companies and the costs of cluster activities for the small member businesses.

**Table 2.** Drivers and barriers for digitalization.

| Informants: | Cluster A | | | | Cluster B | | | | Cluster C | | | |
|---|---|---|---|---|---|---|---|---|---|---|---|---|
| | A1 | A2 | A3 | A4 | B1 | B2 | B3 | B4 | C1 | C2 | C3 | C4 |
| Drivers | | | | | | | | | | | | |
| Knowledge sharing | x | x | x | x | x | x | x | x | x | x | x | x |
| Networking | x | x | x | x | x | x | x | x | x | x | x | x |
| Creating visibility | | x | | | x | x | | x | | x | | |
| Access to resources | | x | | | x | | x | x | | | | |
| Insight into new markets | x | x | | | x | | | | | | | |
| Cluster management | x | x | | x | | x | x | | x | x | | |
| Barriers | | | | | | | | | | | | |
| Time | | x | x | | | x | | | x | x | x | x |
| Costs | x | o | x | | o | o | o | x | o | | x | |
| Competition | x | | x | | x | x | x | x | x | | | |
| Little activity | | x | | | x | | | x | x | | | x |

The informants from the three clusters had similar conceptions of the term digitalization. A common element among informants from cluster A was that digitalization is about employing technology to make "things simpler", for example making information more accessible. Informant A2 noted that the industry is quite conservative, making it difficult to get support for disruptive changes. Two of the informants in cluster A viewed digitalization as primarily the application of existing technologies. The focus was thus on improving rather than replacing. Informant A2 provided the following examples: automated monitoring of windmills and automated monitoring of maintenance requirements. This would be through sensors to monitor and report. Informant A1 noted that "the technology in itself is not important; it is what you can do with it for the business." Informant A1 further commented that a recent report found that enterprises with 10 to 250 employees struggle the most with digitalization – "they are big enough to make it complicated, but do not have the resources needed."

All informants in cluster B had an almost equal view of digitalization, what it implies and what opportunities this may entail in the flow of information. It was perceived to be about how to use data or digital tools to improve processes, automate processes and get different systems for talking together. Informant B2 noted that their perception of digitization depends on the context. Within the enterprise, digitization focuses on the collection and use of data to improve various health indicators among patients. Beyond this, they pointed out that they are working to make municipalities understand "how the digital data makes it much easier for them to understand things". Informant B4 corroborated this view, and he emphasized that digitalization meant "[…] how can we improve efficiency and work smarter". It was further observed that digitization was also important for management in terms of change management. Informant B1 stated that "Digital tools or digital technology give you other opportunities to do things in a completely different way." Informant B1 brought up the term disruptive as a key word for "new ways to operate your [company] that new technology enables," and pointed out that digitalization has top priority in the health sector.

Informants from cluster C emphasized process automation and application of technology as key digitalization matters. Informant C1 noted that digitalization is about "how technology can be used for a good user experience […] That's the key." Informant C4 from the cluster management also viewed customer experiences as the main focus. However, informant C4 emphasized that they need a precise definition. Informant C4 explained that "You have quite a few options then, with computing power and sensors and digital tools, to solve tasks that people had to solve [before]. That's probably the big picture digitization for me." Informant C2 explained that "Within our industry, digitalization is about creating, often moving certain tasks that have been manual over to smartphones, so that consumers can access it in better way. So, yes, it is really there to facilitate everyday life and optimize and automate processes to a large extent."

The interviews showed that the three clusters have several arenas for co-creation. The informants from cluster A emphasized arenas such as workshops, conferences, courses and co-creation projects. The project manager from the cluster administration estimated that they currently had approximately 30 cluster projects, either ongoing or about to start. Two of the informants from this cluster emphasized a test laboratory that they sponsor, where a university is the main owner. This is a lab where the cluster holds workshops with member companies, where they are exposed to emerging technologies, such as AR, VR and 3D printing. This has been seen a way to extend the member companies' scope outside the oil and gas industry. Informant A3 noted that "Then one realizes that many of these companies needed such a test lab. Then it was no longer a one-sided focus on drilling and oil exploration, it was a [quite] broader [focus]." Several informants underlined that the oil and gas industry is very conservative, and that it was very beneficial that the member companies were exposed to opportunities and challenges related to new technology. Informant A1 noted that "We also have workshops on strategy and business development […]. How will the new digital technology influence [the cluster companies]? What do they need to do today to [be] where they want to be 5 to 10 years [from now]?" We see from these examples that this cluster has many co-creation activities that encourage and support digitalization efforts among cluster companies. Table 3 shows which co-creation arenas was noted by the informants.

The informants from cluster B would use terms like building relationships and networks, and raising competencies and innovation, when describing the cluster activities. The cluster has focus on creating programs that would be beneficial for the members, efforts to raise competencies among members, arranging co-creation projects and fundraising. This cluster focuses on health technology, and it has therefore a strong relationship to the public sector, since this marked is dominated by the public healthcare system. Informant B1 asserted that: "[…] since it is about health [technology] in the public sector, we need to [focus on] developing the market too. It is quite immature. […] We work quite a lot with developing the Norwegian health industry." Informant B2 corroborated this, and he added that "[…] having the local municipalities as members meant quite a lot, since then we had a sparring partner we could learn from." We therefore conclude that the co-creation activities in this cluster clearly promotes digitalization among cluster companies.

**Table 3.** Co-creation arenas noted.

| | Cluster A | | | | Cluster B | | | | Cluster C | | | |
|---|---|---|---|---|---|---|---|---|---|---|---|---|
| | A1 | A2 | A3 | A4 | B1 | B2 | B3 | B4 | C1 | C2 | C3 | C4 |
| Hackatons | x | | | | | | | | x | | | x |
| Conferences | x | x | x | | x | x | x | x | x | x | x | |
| Courses | x | x | | | x | x | | x | x | x | | x |
| Digitalization Lab. | x | | x | | x | x | x | x | | | | |
| Seminars | x | | | | | | | | x | | x | |
| Brainstorming sessions | x | x | | | x | x | | x | x | | x | |

The informants from cluster C emphasized activities stimulating co-creation such as networking and knowledge sharing. Informant C1 noted that the cluster facilitates travels to industry conferences and gathers members for joint travels: "they dine together, have breakfast together, they attend [conference sessions] together, so [they] become good friends. [Networks] are made there". This contributes to stronger ties between people in the cluster, and it creates a stronger cluster identity and a network between people in the cluster companies. All informants emphasized the importance of networking activities for gaining deeper understanding of the challenges and opportunities related to digitalization. Informant C2 noted that they have found a business partner (in the cluster) that is proficient on machine learning, through the cluster networking activities. Informant 3 pointed out the importance of being visible in the cluster, and that the network they get access to, is very interesting, and described that this is an "investment in the future". We therefore find that significant co-creation activities were aimed at improving digital competencies and skills among cluster companies, and thus to the digitalization of these companies.

# 5  Discussion

We have explored how co-creation contributes to digitalization in three Norwegian business clusters. We found that co-creation is an important vehicle for digitalization among the individual member companies. By addressing the drivers and barriers for co-creation, we were able to achieve a better understanding of co-creation as a phenomenon, how co-creation manifests itself and the important factors related to achieving co-creation in practice. We will elaborate on the various factors below.

We conjectured that three drivers were particularly significant for achieving co-creation in the clusters. First, networking activities were perceived as a major driver for co-creation. This is consistent with the literature on business clusters (e.g. [33]), which views network building as one of the most common cluster goals. All informants in the three cases emphasized this as one of the main drivers for membership. Some companies joined the cluster to get access to new customers or partners, while others saw the cluster as an opportunity to develop new competences and capabilities. Regardless of the corporate intention, the clusters arrange various activities that facilitate networking among the members. We conjecture that such activities were essential to create arenas for co-creation. These activities could be reserved for cluster members, or they could include public institutions outside the cluster as well as members of other clusters. This is also consistent with Porter's [29] finding that involving and activating cluster members of all sizes is important for collaboration and community.

Second, related to this, we found that knowledge sharing was also a major driver for co-creation. The companies see clusters as a place to go to meet other companies in an informal setting. Informal arrangements like this have proven to lead to friendship which is important when it comes to building trust [34]. When the members of a cluster increase their trust in each other it can lead to more knowledge sharing. Networking activities create relationships and build trust between companies. This can create an arena for exchanging knowledge and experience among the cluster members. This is consistent with the literature, which points out that knowledge exchange is central in collaboration [6], and a driving force for change [17]. In our literature review, we uncovered two activities related to knowledge sharing that is consistent with our findings [35]:

- Co-inform: Common to all three clusters is the newsletter that the cluster management sends out to the cluster members by email. The newsletters convey activities and opportunities in the cluster, as well as providing information on ongoing and new projects. They also have websites where, among other things, they present the cluster members.
- Co-learn: Both Cluster A and Cluster B offer their members access to a test lab where they can access technology that they might not otherwise be able to afford. Such labs are important for companies, regardless of available resources, to test new technological trends and get access to useful knowledge. In this way they may get the ability to identify appropriate technology. Research has demonstrated that testing out new technological trends is important in order to further develop your business processes [33], and that digital technology can have a direct impact on how businesses innovate [1].

Third, we also found that cluster management was also an important driver. Many of the respondents emphasized that it was easy to get access to the cluster management. This made it easy take initiatives, for example to make request for training or to propose topics for cluster seminars. We therefore conjecture that a strong cluster management is important for initiating and supporting co-creation activities.

We identified two significant barriers. First, competition among the members is a significant barrier. We saw that informants generally are positive to sharing competence, but also that a majority of them are hesitant to share strategies or concepts where time to market is an issue. The literature also emphasizes the perils of sharing knowledge with competitors, and it may relinquish competitive advantage [18].

Second, most informants did not perceive membership costs as a significant problem, especially informants from large enterprises. However, the informants that believed that costs was an issues, felt that there should not be a membership fees for small businesses. Also, several informants from small enterprises noted that the costs of participating in cluster activities was sometimes prohibiting small member companies from participating. This is consistent with the literature, which has demonstrated that limited human and economic resources can be a significant challenge for co-creation [6]. Several informants noted that the projects could last a long time, and this would reduce the interest among the participants. The longer the time between the workshops, the higher the likelihood would be of members withdrawing from a project [25].

The activities in clusters are usually based on input from its members. Most informants noted that it was easy to get access to the cluster management, and that it was easy to propose topics for activities or projects in the clusters. It was generally perceived that it was a short way from proposing a new topic to set up a project through a brainstorming session. This can lead to digital innovation through the co-creation of new products or services [15, 25]. This supports the argument that clusters drive innovation. Sölvell et al. [33] argue that there are three critical arguments for why innovation tend to be connected with clusters: (1) the need for incremental reduction of technical and economic uncertainty, (2) the need for repeated and continuous interaction between related firms and specialized institutions (including research and education), and (3) The need for face-to-face contact in the exchange and creation of new knowledge. Our findings demonstrated that the three clusters in this study facilitate resolution of all those needs.

We saw that the clusters offered the members arenas where co-creation processes could take place. The clusters would arrange brainstorming events where members from various topical areas could discuss ideas and solutions related to perceived market needs, facilitate co-creation projects, and aid in the application for external funding. Such processes were vital to stimulate co-creation of digital innovation and digitalization in all three clusters.

Based on the findings and the discussion above, we argue that co-creation can be an important avenue for digitalization, digital innovation or digital transformation of companies. We contend that this is particularly true for the companies that have limited human and financial resources, such as small and medium sized enterprises. Such companies have limited resources to implement digital technologies and innovative business concepts. We therefore see co-creation arenas, such as business clusters, as beneficial for the digitalization of such companies.

# 6 Conclusion

This study has explored how co-creation can contribute to digitalization among companies in business clusters. We found that the co-creation arenas and activities within the business clusters stimulate and facilitate digitalization among the cluster companies. The study also addressed the most significant drivers and barriers to co-creation to get a deeper understanding of the co-creation phenomenon. Co-creation arenas, such as business clusters, can be very valuable for companies that do not have substantial resources to devote to innovation activities, such as digitalization and digital transformation.

This research has several limitations. It was performed in three clusters with a small number of informants and, therefore, has limited generalizability. Further research should explore this pertinent issue in other contexts, using the present research as a basis for subsequent quantitative studies to provide generalizable results. Such results can contribute to a better understanding about how organizations can co-create with other organizations in order to innovate and transform, and thus contributing to the theory on co-creation. This will be particularly beneficial for resource poor organizations, such as small and medium sized enterprises.

# References

1. Yoo, Y.: The tables have turned: how can the information systems field contribute to technology and innovation management research? J. Assoc. Inf. Syst. **14**(5), 227–236 (2012)
2. Hartl, E., Hess, T.: IT projects in digital transformation: a socio-technical journey towards technochange. In: Proceedings of the 27th European Conference on Information Systems, AIS Electronic Library, Stockhom-Uppsala (2019)
3. Stief, S.E., Eidhoff, A.T., Voeth, M.: Transform to succeed: an empirical analysis of digital transformation in firms. World Acad. Sci. Eng. Technol. Int. J. Soc. Behav. Educ. Econ. Bus. Ind. Eng. **10**(6), 1833–1842 (2016)
4. Bharadwaj, A., El Sawy, O.A., Pavlou, P.A., Venkatraman, N.: Digital business strategy: toward a next generation of insights. MIS Q. **37**(2), 471–482 (2013)
5. Zach, O., Munkvold, B.E., Olsen, D.H.: ERP system implementation in SMEs: exploring the influences of the SME context. Enterp. Inf. Syst. **8**(2), 309–335 (2014)
6. Eikebrokk, T.R., Lind, E., Olsen, D.H.: Co-creation of IT-value in a cluster of small enterprises. Procedia Comput. Sci. **138**, 492–499 (2018)
7. Grover, V., Kohli, R.: Cocreating IT value: new capabilities and metrics for multifirm environments. MIS Q. **36**(1), 225–232 (2012)
8. Gnyawali, D.R., Park, B.-J.R.: Co-opetition between giants: collaboration with competitors for technological innovation. Res. Policy **40**(5), 650–663 (2011)
9. Czakon, W., Kawa, A.: Network myopia: an empirical study of network perception. Ind. Mark. Manag. **73**, 116–124 (2018)
10. Grönroos, C., Voima, P.: Critical service logic: making sense of value creation and co-creation. J. Acad. Mark. Sci. **41**(2), 133–150 (2013). https://doi.org/10.1007/s11747-012-0308-3
11. Nambisan, S.: Designing virtual customer environments for new product development: toward a theory. Acad. Manag. Rev. **27**(3), 392–413 (2002)

12. Prahalad, C.K., Ramaswamy, V.: Co-creation experiences: the next practice in value creation. J. Interact. Mark. **18**(3), 5–14 (2004)
13. Kohlbacher, F.: International Marketing in the Network Economy: A Knowledge-Based Approach. Palgrave Macmillan, Basingstoke (2007)
14. Felzensztein, C., Gimmon, E., Deans, K.R.: Coopetition in regional clusters: keep calm and expect unexpected changes. Ind. Mark. Manag. **69**, 116–124 (2018)
15. Frow, P., Nenonen, S., Payne, A., Storbacka, K.: Managing co-creation design: a strategic approach to innovation. Br. J. Manag. **26**(3), 463–483 (2015)
16. Sarker, S., Sarker, S., Sahaym, A., Bjørn-Andersen, N.: Exploring value cocreation in relationships between an ERP vendor and its partners: a revelatory case study. MIS Q. **36**(1), 317–338 (2012)
17. Zainuddin, E., Gonzalez, P.: Configurability, maturity, and value co-creation in SaaS: an exploratory case study. In: Proceedings of the 32nd International Conference in Information Systems (ICIS), AIS Electronic Library (2011)
18. Yoong, P., Molina, M.: Knowledge sharing and business clusters. In: Proceedings of the Pacific Asian Conference on Information Systems (PACIS), AIS Electronic Library (2003)
19. Giesbrecht, T., Schwabe, G., Schenk, B.: Service encounter thinklets: how to empower service agents to put value co-creation into practice. Inf. Syst. J. **27**(2), 171–196 (2017)
20. Chang, H.-L., Chou, C.-Y.: Shaping proactivity for firm performance: evaluating the role of it-enabled collaboration in small and medium enterprises. In: Proceedings of the Pacific Asian Conference on Information Systems (PACIS), AIS Electronic Library (2012)
21. Schryen, G.: Revisiting IS business value research: what we already know, what we still need to know, and how we can get there. Eur. J. Inf. Syst. **22**(2), 139–169 (2013)
22. Barney, J.B.: Firm resources and sustained competitive advantage. Adv. Strat. Manag. **17**, 203–227 (2000)
23. Mata, F.J., Fuerst, W.L., Barney, J.B.: Information technology and sustained competitive advantage: a resource-based analysis. MIS Q. **19**(4), 487–505 (1995)
24. Bilgeri, D., Wortmann, F., Fleisch, E.: How digital transformation affects large manufacturing companies' organization. In: Proceedings of the 38th International Conference in Information Systems (ICIS), AIS Electronic Library (2017)
25. Osmundsen, K., Iden, J., Bygstad, B.: Digital transformation: drivers, success factors and implications. In: Proceedings of the 12th Mediterranean Conference on Information Systems (MCIS), AIS Electronic Library (2018)
26. Fichman, R.G., Dos Santos, B.L., Zheng, Z.E.: Digital innovation as a fundamental and powerful concept in the information systems curriculum. MIS Q. **38**(2), 329–354 (2014)
27. Yoo, Y., Henfridsson, O., Lyytinen, K.: Research commentary—the new organizing logic of digital innovation: an agenda for information systems research. Inf. Syst. Res. **21**(4), 724–735 (2010)
28. Porter, M.E.: Clusters and the new economics of competition. Harvard Bus. Rev. **76**(6), 77–90 (1998)
29. Porter, M.E.: Location, competition, and economic development: local clusters in a global economy. Econ. Dev. Q. **14**(1), 15–34 (2000)
30. Malmberg, A., Power, D.: True clusters: a severe case of conceptual headache. In: Asheim, B., Cooke, P., Martin, R. (eds.) Clusters and Regional Development, pp. 68–86. Taylor & Francis Group (2006)
31. Myers, M.D., Newman, M.: The qualitative interview in IS research: examining the craft. Inf. Organ. **17**(1), 2–26 (2007)
32. Miles, M.B., Huberman, A.M.: Qualitative Data Analysis: An Expanded Sourcebook. Sage, Thousand Oaks (1994)

33. Sölvell, Ö., Lindqvist, G., Ketels, C.: The Cluster Initiative Greenbook. Ivory Tower, Stockholm (2003)
34. Bergh, P., Thorgren, S., Wincent, J.: Entrepreneurs learning together: the importance of building trust for learning and exploiting business opportunities. Int. Entrep. Manag. J. 7(1), 17–37 (2011). https://doi.org/10.1007/s11365-009-0120-9
35. Waits, M.J.: The added value of the industry cluster approach to economic analysis, strategy development, and service delivery. Econ. Dev. Q. 14(1), 35–50 (2000)

# A Framework for Industrial Internet of Things

Jacques Jansen(ID) and Alta van der Merwe(✉)(ID)

Department of Informatics, University of Pretoria, Pretoria, South Africa
Jansen_CJ@outlook.com, alta@up.ac.za

**Abstract.** The Industrial Internet of Things (IIoT) is a new concept that has the potential to add value to any industrial organisation that wants to embark on the implementation thereof. Due to this newness of IoT in industrial operations, an increase in cost and maturity in terms of data handling, together with only a few implementations. There was a gap in available practical IIoT frameworks that could aid interested parties in the understanding of the constructs of IIoT and the practical implications of implementation. Within this study, we propose an Industrial Internet of Things framework intended to aid academic, technical and management persons in understanding the different considerations of the Industrial Internet of Things. This framework could also apply as a basis for implementation considerations.

**Keywords:** Cloud services · Industrial Internet of Things (IIoT) · Machine-to-machine (M2M) communication · Supervisory Control and Data Acquisition (SCADA)

## 1 Introduction

The Internet of Things (IoT) is an increasingly growing topic of interest and a regular discussion point in the information technology arena [1]. IoT could potentially change the traditional approach to the use of the internet. In the future, the goal of IoT is the unification of all "things" under a shared infrastructure, whereby network-connected sensors will be able to collect data from the surrounding environment. The collected data can then be shared across the internet to be processed and changed into meaningful information for various reasons [1].

Muntjir, Rahul and Alhumyani [2] describe the IoT as the linkage between the physical world on the one hand and the cyberworld on the other with the help of items or objects that possess sensing abilities and transmit the measured results via a network to achieve a purpose. There is an ever-increasing number of objects, from home appliances to smartphones, connecting daily to the internet or internet-like structure [3].

IoT can change the way that industrial organisations perform in terms of safety and production. Safety and production improvements would have a positive impact on any large industrial sectors; the focus was on mining operations as a significant industrial player.

Sensor prices have had a steady decline in their pricing, therefore becoming more affordable [22]. Senors are an essential part of the IIoT architecture. Parallel to the decrease in sensor prices, there have been advancements in big data handling, artificial

M. Hattingh et al. (Eds.): I3E 2020, LNCS 12066, pp. 138–150, 2020.
https://doi.org/10.1007/978-3-030-44999-5_12

intelligence and machine learning. The IIoT could only recently be implemented in industrial sectors because of this maturity and affordability of the analytics and sensors. Consequently, only a few IIoT implementations have been completed in the industrial environment [23]. Further to this, the literature on IIoT frameworks that could assist companies in implementing an industrial IIoT solution is not readily available. The unavailability of IIoT implementation frameworks presented a research gap that this research would address.

If relevant literature or guidelines in the implementation of IIoT existed on this topic, it would enable more industries to implement and leverage the advantages of IIoT in a shorter period too. The benefit of clear guidelines in the industrial sector would mean that implementations could realise some objectives of improvement on the safety and efficiency of an IIoT solution faster.

The researchers present an IIoT framework within Sect. 4 to aid technical and management persons in understanding the different considerations of the IIoT. The research was conducted to inform industries of the needed aspects to implement an IIoT solution. This framework could be used as a basis to inform technical and business decisions on the different layers of the IIoT. The IIoT framework would help product-, technical,- and business-level decisions. The IIoT framework would further aid to unlock the benefits that the IIoT could have for industrial organisations. The proposed framework could be referenced as a basis for future research on the topic.

## 2 Literature Review

### 2.1 IIoT

Muntjir et al. [2] describe the IoT as the linkage between the physical world on the one hand and the cyberworld on the other with the help of things or objects that possess sensing abilities and transmit the measured results via a network to achieve a purpose [2]. Within this definition, the basic building blocks that the IoT consists of are presented as the sensing objects used in the measurement of metrics such as flow, pressure, temperature position and vibration, and the network that communicates the result to a higher decision-making engine. The same definition applies to the IIoT domain; the only difference is that the IIoT is mostly focused on industrial applications.

The IoT is instrumental in delivering disruptive change to segments such as agriculture, healthcare, utilities and the government. The IIoT, a portion of the all-encompassing IoT, focuses on industries such as mining, oil and gas, manufacturing and utilities [4].

### 2.2 IIoT and Mining

Mining, as an industrial representer, plays an essential economic role in South Africa. The Chamber of Mines [5] showed the employee earnings within the mining sector amounted to R120 billion, with mining contributing R304.4 billion to the gross domestic product for the year 2016. The mining sector created 457,698 jobs and supported approximately 4.5 million dependents.

Statistics South Africa indicates a rapid decline in mining and mining-related activities. "Historical values of the gold index show the extent of how production has fallen. In January 1980, the index was 359.0, while the volume of gold produced was far lower in January 2015, resulting in the low index of 48.4. In other words, South Africa produced 87% less gold in January 2015 compared to the same month in 1980" [6].

Major [7] was addressing mining representatives at the Johannesburg Stock Exchange Power Hour in May when he said that "gold mining has lost a million people in 30 years". He [7] explained, "People say our gold mines are closing because of lower grade ore, but we know better than that. It is not about grades; it is about efficiencies and cost. We are taking out as many ounces of gold per employee now as we were in 1907 when we were using picks and shovels."

South Africa's gold sector that once was the world-leading gold producer needs to increase its mining production efficiency to avoid vanishing entirely by the year 2020, especially after being rated sixth in the world [7]. The statistical data from Statistics South Africa confirm Major's claim.

In assessing the status of IIoT in the industrial organisations, especially mining, the research of the company Inmersat [8] indicated that in 2017 only 12% of mining representatives had implemented IIoT solutions to a degree or a full extent. The World Economic Forum [9] predicts that the expected impact of digital transformation on the mining industry is in the region of US\$ 428 billion and US\$ 784 billion. Key contributors to the expected monetary implications could be underwritten to the potential realisation of the advantages in terms of higher production and the ability to optimise equipment, as described by Merry [10]. IIoT also has the potential to address the challenges of the South African mining industry, which O'Conner [11] has indicated to be in terms of:

- A reduction of water and energy resources
- Employee health and safety
- Improved production by the use of automation
- Decrease in waste

Within these industrial operations, there is already an abundance of data that are accumulated with sensors already implemented in existing mining operations – or better known as brownfields sites. The challenges of most of these data are stored and visible in different systems [12]. This data need horizontal integration across the value chain, vertically from the field to the control and from planning to maintenance [12]. The IIoT information could assist organisations in determining inefficiency within processes and improve the personnel work life by a reduction of effort on lesser essential aspects. This information could also assist in the identification of problems at an earlier state with subsequent business improvement.

The purpose of this research was the development of the IIoT framework that should aid technical and management persons in understanding the different considerations of the IIoT to achieve the benefits as described above.

# 3 Research Design

The study was a qualitative interpretive study where we had the benefit of a prior insight into the context of the constructs of IIoT frameworks with an understanding that it needed further investigation because of the complexity and unpredictable nature of one's knowledge of reality [13]. The prior insight was obtained with the help of literature studies on the subject matter. As part of the qualitative research design, we explored experiences through interviews and focus groups since qualitative research focuses on in-depth opinions from the participants [14].

A case study approach was used as a research strategy. The case studies used were from industrial organisations represented by mining, food and beverage and logistics companies within different locations throughout South Africa. The case studies were on successful IIoT implementations within these Industrial organisations.

The sample size in this study consisted of ten respondents and insight into the research subject was obtained through the use of an eighteen-question interview guide attached as annexure 1This interview guide These representatives drew insight into the subject matter from years of experience and involvement in different IIoT cases within South Africa industries. Three of the respondents were ICT architects, and another three were from IIoT implementation companies. Two respondents were IIoT project managers, one a representative from IIoT communication and network provider specifically for IIoT and one was a representative of an IIoT software organisation that supplies the software platforms for IIoT. Annexure 2 contains specific details on the respondents. These respondents were from different language groups and social backgrounds. Purposeful sampling was conducted, which means that we recognised and hand-picked people with specific knowledge and experience in the field under study [19].

During the analysis stage, data were coded into themes and categories where the following actions were followed to analyse the data: Interviewee data were captured via a voice recorder and transcribed via transcription software; the allocation of codes to data and similar data that were present in other transcripts received the same code as part of the analysis, writing of comments and notes; the sorting of data occurred according to themes; then grouped into the applicable themes according to the "thematising" idea of Mitchell and Jones [20]; the themes were then further explored and elaborated upon and then grouped into categories.

# 4 The IIoT Framework

From the data obtained by interviewing the IIoT experts and with reviewing of literature on IIoT three main categories with their themes emerged that was used to compile the IIoT framework as per Fig. 1: The IIoT framework. These Categories and themes are

- *The IIoT architecture:* The IIoT architecture as a category held four themes, namely the hardware and software components, the security aspects of the IIoT and the communication within the IIoT.

- *Category of implementation:* The category of implementation considered the themes of pre-implementation, implementation and post-implementation.
- *The knowledge category of IIoT:* The knowledge category of IIoT consisted of the advantages, disadvantages and training and awareness.

A discussion follows on the categories and themes that form the IIoT framework.

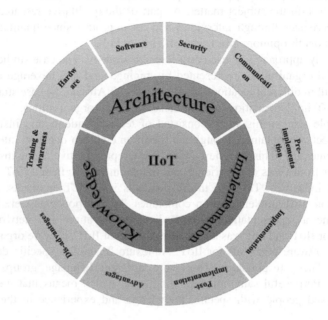

**Fig. 1.** IIoT framework

## 4.1    IIoT Architecture

The IIoT architecture, as described in the IIoT framework, is an integrated set of the components needed for the success of IIoT Without the architecture, consisting of hardware, software, security and communications, there would be no means to gain the benefits of the IIoT. Figure 2 was constructed from the architecture within the literature as described by Pena et al. [21], Boyes et al. [22] and Holdowsky et al. [25] These views were taken into account together with the responses from the interviewees in constructing the needed architecture as depicted in Fig. 2. The constructed IIoT Architecture did not take into account the suggestions of the addition of a data validation layer as described by the works of Kristofferson et al. [26]. This additional view could complement the proposed IIoT Architecture in Fig. 2.

Concerning Fig. 2, **the data generation layer** contains the measuring devices, also called things in the IIoT domain, that measure different parameters. These devices consist of hardware and software components. There could be machine-to-machine communication within the device level, and the various communication protocols are of relevance. Automation could also be within this level of IIoT. Security on this level is necessary to ensure data integrity and to prevent stoppages in the production

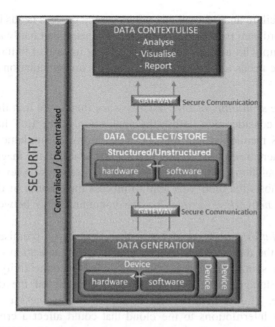

**Fig. 2.** IIoT architecture as discovered from the literature and interviews

environment. Measuring devices could communicate wirelessly with the data collect and store layer, and a high level of robustness is needed for the continuous functioning of the hardware. Data flow from this lower level to the data collect and store layer.

**The data collect and store layer** identified from the findings also consists of a hardware and software component. The hardware could be locally on the premises or make use of off-site cloud services. The hardware is used in conjunction with software to collect and store data. There is also a high level of security needed in this layer. The data could consist of structured or unstructured data and could utilise big-data sources.

Lastly, **the data contextualise layer** – be it on-site, off-site or in the cloud – presents the data in a way that the business could make sense of the data. Data become information within this layer and could be visually presented in the form of a report or a Supervisory Control and Data Acquisition (SCADA) display. Analytics could also be done within this layer as well as machine learning and pattern recognition. Conboy et al. [27] mention value-generating mechanisms. These mechanisms, in regards to analytics, could complement the data contextualisation layer in the proposed IIoT architecture.

**Hardware.** A critical consideration in the selection of the equipment in an industrial environment is hardware that can withstand the harsh production conditions. In a mining environment, the environmental factors in the mining area could be extreme heat, dust, mechanical forces and rain. For any hardware to keep functioning, it must be able to withstand these elements. It is also crucial for the device to maintain operation within an industrial environment. If the hardware were to fail, it could mean safety incidents or production losses. Equipment should be highly reliable, robust, possess a high resilience to failure and be available whenever the process needs their functioning. In certain areas, hardware redundancy is in place to ensure that hardware in a particular process is backed up with a set of standby equipment in case of failure. The following minimum hardware needs to be in place for any IIoT implementation to be successful:

- *IIoT devices.*
- Considering the *scalability of IIoT devices* when they grow into the thousands was also cited as a consideration before the application of the IIoT hardware devices. The respondees mentioned that the questions during an implementation consideration: Would there be enough technical resources to install the magnitude of sensors required in installation going into the thousands of sensors? Also, is the supporting hardware that hosts the platforms able to process the amount of data?
- *Networks and network coverage* for the communication between the different layers.
- A *hardware platform* host could be in the cloud or on-premise. This hardware platform hosts the data storage, collection and contextualisation of the data. From the findings, it should be noted that if no reliable connectivity to the cloud is available, the storage, collection and contextualisation of the data needs to be handled on-site. This is in order not to expose the business to risk if there are communication interruptions to the cloud that could affect a critical process. An example could be when a manufacturing process that moulds plastic loses connectivity to the cloud and the process halts. Consideration should be given if there is enough hardware space allocated for the storage of the information and the hosting of the services.
- *Gateway devices* that aid security solutions.

**Software.** The software platforms needed for the IIoT solution and whether these platforms could easily integrate with existing platforms should be considered. In this regard, Karschnia [23] mentions that these "things" interconnect on- and off-site to software platforms to enable remote control, monitoring and asset management using either dedicated expert teams or specialised data analysis software connected to big data lakes to add value., Interviewees indicated their experience with prior implementations is that it is essential to do a consolidation of different source data before any implementation takes place.

Within the IIoT, intelligence could move down to the instrument level. If this is the case, intelligence will be needed at the measuring device level and the ability to handle automation on the lower level. The industrial systems should be easily and frequently reprogrammable to support changing processes. Within complex industrial processes, process improvements are regularly attempted. The systems that support these processes, therefore, need to be easily adaptable.

Consideration is necessary in terms of the platforms needed for the IIoT solution and whether it would easily integrate with existing platforms. Platforms are relevant where the IIoT implementation is on an existing site.

The software should be highly reliable, robust, possess a high resilience to failure and be available whenever the process needs its functioning. System uptime is critical in industrial processes.

There is a need for a secure communications protocol and data security within any IIoT solution. **Security** is especially relevant in the IIoT environment that is reliable on the safety, security and reliability of their operations. IIoT has a higher level of security due to the critical nature of a disruption of a high-volume manufacturing process or the takedown of the electrical grid that could have an economic impact [4]. Raynor and Cotteleer [24] opine that sensor security challenges need to be kept in mind before any implementations commence. Holdowsky et al. [25] also point to the security requirements in the communications protocol that could have an impact on the safety, security and reliability within an IIoT implementation. Soldatos [28] also agrees that one of the critical concerns is the security aspect around the transmittal of information within the IIoT.

**Communication.** Raynor and Cotteleer [24] define communication as a state for the transmission of information from one place to another and then aggregating or gathering of the data from the different sources and times. The respondents mentioned that a consideration of the availability of networks and if it is possible to use these networks is available and that the industrial communication protocols be adjusted to the low-power extensive area network technology. The existing IIoT hardware and software communication platforms should not hinder the implementation of an IIoT solution. Existing networks should be considered for IIoT implementation. There was a recommendation from one of the respondents that Legislation within South Africa needs to accommodate the communications between devices. The legislation was pointed out as challenging and "communications regulators need to align their regulations concerning IIoT communications". Without reliable communication between the different levels within the IIoT, no successful implementation could take place.

In IIoT implementations, the communications should be highly reliable, robust, possess a high resilience to failure and be available whenever the process needs their functioning. Communications uptime is critical in the industrial processes, and the solution should have a low latency because of the high-speed production systems in use.

## 4.2   IIoT Implementation

**Pre-implementation.** Before implementation of any IIoT solution, there must be a need or a problem to be solved. A clear understanding of the business/user requirements and information is imperative. The business need should be supported by a clear business case that justifies the implementation of the technology and ensures that there is a return on the investment in the technology. This business requirement should be documented to ensure that the IIoT solution would support the need.

A detailed design document, based on the user requirements, should then be created before any IIoT implementation. This intricate design could direct the implementation of the IIoT solution. This design needs to consider the key performance indicators that need to be achieved as well as the available technology. The detailed design should also determine if the implementation is a new (greenfields) installation or an existing (brownfields) installation. It should be determined if the existing infrastructure and architecture are compatible with the existing infrastructure. A decision on the technology should be made. This selection of technology would need to consider the ease of serviceability and maintainability of the technology and paths should be upgraded during the life cycle. The business should have a clear vision of how the realisation would function after the implementation, and what the expectation is from the application. In terms of personnel, planning should take place for skilled staff after the installation to maintain the IIoT implementation. Consideration should be given regarding whether the solution implementation is a success. If the advantages of the IIoT implementation realise with an increase in production, would the additional product produced from a successful IIoT implementation be sellable and is there a market for it? Can the organisation's logistics accommodate the increase in the product?

Blanchette [29] emphasised the importance of thorough planning before any IIoT implementation commences. Planning was also cited as an essential factor before any IIoT rollouts could begin as there is no identification of formal IIoT guidelines.

Lueth [30] in this regard states that IIoT projects take over 18 months longer than what had initially been planned. At the base of thorough planning, Blanchette [29] iterates the creation of a baseline (as-is) situation of the organisation. The responders mentioned that the baseline should consider:

- If there are cloud services used, the presence of data analytics, the relevant needed reports for decisions and the level of automation.
- The business demographics.
- Scalability of IIoT devices when they grow into the thousands.
- Compatibility of newer equipment and systems within IIoT to function with existing or legacy systems.
- The consolidation of different source data, before implementation.
- A clear vision of where the business wants to position themselves in the future.
- A clear understanding of the needed technology to be implemented.
- Data flow mapping of where the data originates from to where it is needed.

**Implementation:** Detailed architecture is necessary when the implementation of IIoT solutions commences and needs to contain decisions on the selected technology. Change management during execution is critical to ensure that the solution is adopted and the benefits are realised. During the execution of the IIoT implementation, it is vital to use a skilled implementations team. Recommendations during the implementation of IIoT solutions from the respondents were that small achievable project milestones should be planned and pursued to ensure the IIoT implementation success. The time needed for a large scale IIoT implementation should be kept in mind.

**Post-implementation:** A review of the IIoT deliverables should take place and whether these deliverables are met. Relevant procedures and the necessary governance should be introduced to manage the IIoT infrastructure and environment.

### 4.3   IIoT Knowledge

**Training and Awareness.** There might be a lack of in-house skill for IIoT implementations and the maintenance thereof after. The lack of in-house skills for IIoT implementations poses a challenge for the organisation and consideration should be given to whether the relevant people skills needed during the implementation and after required for maintenance would be available. There might also exist a lack of appropriate skills at different levels of IIoT architecture. From the research, it could be seen that there is room for improvement in the education of companies in terms of the possibilities of Industry 4.0.

There is a need for the creation of awareness within the organisation on the management of cultural and organisational changes required with the implementation of the IIoT. These cultural and organisational changes would be a leading factor for the poor adoption of the implemented solutions if the proper change management did not occur.

Awareness and training should cater for any lack of in-house skills for IIoT implementations and the maintenance thereof after the implementation has taken place. Proper maintenance would mean that competent personnel are needed after the installation to maintain the implementation. In this regard, education for the business in terms of the possibilities of Industry 4.0 is required by the organisation to realise the potential value-adding business cases.

**Challenges.** Personnel with the appropriate experience in delivering IIoT solutions in the specific industry is needed for the implementation and maintenance of implemented solutions. Other challenges include:

- Management of cultural and organisational changes.
- Business representatives are reluctant to support the implemented solutions if the proper change management did not occur before the IIoT implementation.
- New technology introductions into the existing infrastructure and environment in terms of the connectivity, security and platforms.
- Existing infrastructure and platforms exist when implementing IIoT.
- Greenfields organisations have no challenges in terms of legacy systems.
- People skills in terms of IIoT.
- Existing communication protocols in use.
- Existing systems and hardware that are in use.
- Network connectivity challenges.

**Advantages.** The advantages described are that the IIoT has the potential to benefit industrial organisations and can complement existing technology investments. Conveniences include gaining market share, increased efficiencies, insight into business operations and insight into different aspects of the organisation.

# 5   IIoT Framework Application

The IIoT framework, as described in Sect. 4, would inform product-, technical- and business-level decisions in terms of the IIoT to unlock the benefits that the IIoT could have for industrial organisations. The following steps could be taken in applying the discovered framework to uncover the necessities needed in terms of the technical and business decisions on the different layers of the IIoT.

1. The user would ensure that there is a clear business case or need for the advantages that IIoT could offer industrial operations.
2. Following the business, the case is an assessment of the needed infrastructure (hardware and software) for any IIoT implementation.
3. After an assessment and understanding of the technical requirements needed for an IIoT solution, the user would refer to the consideration before, during and post-implementation of an IIoT initiative within the industrial environments.

# 6   Conclusion

This paper presented a discovered framework for the IIoT that could be used as a basis for IIoT implementation-specific decisions. This framework would assist mining representatives in implementations of IIoT solutions. In 2017, only 12% of mining representatives had implemented IIoT solutions to a degree or a full extent [8]. The World Economic Forum [9] predicts that the expected impact of digital transformation on the mining industry is in the region of US$428 billion and US$ 784 billion.

This framework included the needed IIoT architecture while considering the specific hardware, software, security and communication aspects. Within this framework, there was also a consideration in terms of pre-, during and post-implementation aspects and explored the advantages, disadvantages and training in terms of the IIoT. The usage of this framework would aid industrial organisations and stakeholders in terms of IIoT solutions to understand the specific considerations regarding the IIoT.

# References

1. Mitchell, B.: Introduction to the Internet of Things. https://www.lifewire.com/introduction-to-the-internet-of-things-81776. Assessed 26 Sept 2019
2. Muntjir, M., Rahul, M., Alhumyani, H.A.: An analysis of Internet of Things (IoT): novel architectures, modern applications, security aspects and future scope with latest case studies. Int. J. Eng. Res. Technol. 6(2), 422–427 (2017)
3. Storey, H.: The industrial Internet of Things. Consult.-Specif. Eng. 15(5), 1–4
4. Chan, B.: IoT for all. https://www.iotforall.com/iot-vs-industrial-iot-differences-that-matter/. Assessed 16 Jan 2019
5. Chamber of Mines South Africa: Facts and Figures. Chamber of Mines, Johannesburg. https://www.mineralscouncil.org.za/industry-news/publications/facts-and-figures/send/17-facts-and-figures/442-facts-and-figures-2016. Assessed 26 Sept 2019

6. Statistics South Africa: The Decreasing Importance of Gold. Statistics South Africa, Pretoria (2015)
7. Major, P.: Johannesburg Stock Exchange Power Hour: The State of Mining South Africa, Cádiz, 9 July
8. Inmarsat Research Programme: The future of mining. https://research.inmarsat.com/2017/the-future-of-mining/. Assessed 26 Sept 2019
9. World Economic Forum. https://www.weforum.org/. Assessed 26 Sept 2019
10. Merry, H.: IBM Internet of Things blog. https://www.ibm.com/blogs/internet-of-things/mining-industry-benefits/. Assessed 05 May 2018
11. O'Connor, C.: Challenges Facing the South-African Mining Industry. SAEE, Braamfontein (2017)
12. miningreview.com: How to master IoT challenges in mining. https://www.miningreview.com/southern-africa/iiot-challenges-mining-endresshauser/. Assessed 08 Apr 2019
13. Hudson, L., Ozanne, J.: Alternative ways of seeking knowledge in consumer research. J. Consum. Res. 14(4), 508–521 (1988)
14. Dawson, C.: Introduction to Research Methods: A Practical Guide for Anyone Undertaking a Research Project, 4th edn. How to Books, London (2009)
15. Kwon, T., Zmud, R.: Unifying the fragmented models of information system' implementation. In: Critical Issues in Information Systems Research. Wiley, New York (1987)
16. Schultze, U., Orlikowski, W.J.: A practice perspective on technology-mediated network relations: the use of internet-based self-serve technologies. Inf. Syst. Res. 15(1), 89–106 (2004)
17. Yin, R.K.: Case Study Research: Design and Methods. Applied Social Research Methods, 5th edn. Sage, Beverly Hills (1984)
18. Newman, L.: Qualitative-Quantitative Research Methodology: Exploring the Interactive Continuum. Allyn & Bacon, Carbondale (1998)
19. Creswell, J., Plano Clark, V.L.: Designing and Conducting Mixed Method Research, 2nd edn. Sage, Thousand Oaks (2011)
20. Mitchell, T., Jones, S.: Leading and co-ordinating a multi-nurse researcher project. Nurse Res. 12(2), 42–55 (2004)
21. Pena, M.D., Rodriguez-Andina, J., Manic, M.: The Internet of Things. Ind. Electron. Mag. 21(9), 1–14 (2017)
22. Boyes, H., Hallaq, B., Cunningham, J., Watson, T.: Comput. Ind. 101, 1–12 (2018)
23. Karschnia, B.: Control engineering. https://www.controleng.com/single-article/industrial-internet-of-things-iiot-benefits-examples/1da45ca93275ebd5794beb28326367c1.html. Assessed 06 Mar 2019
24. Raynor, E.M., Cotteleer, M.J.: The more things change: value creation, value capture, and the Internet of Things. Deloitte Rev. 17, 1–17 (2015)
25. Holdowsky, J., et al.: Inside the Internet of Things (IoT): a primer on the technologies building the IoT. Deloitte Insights (2019)
26. Kristoffersen, E., Aremu, O., Blomsma, F., Mikalef, P., Li, J.: Exploring the relationship between data science and circular economy: an enhanced CRISP-DM process model (2019). https://doi.org/10.13140/rg.2.2.23182.41285
27. Conboy, K., Mikalef, P., Dennehy, D., Krogstie, J.: Using business analytics to enhance dynamic capabilities in operations research: a case analysis and research agenda. Eur. J. Oper. Res. (2019). https://doi.org/10.1016/j.ejor.2019.06.051
28. Soldatos, J.: Internet of Things tutorial: introduction. KDnuggets. http://www.kdnuggets.com/2016/12/internet-of-things-tutorial-chapter-1-introduction.html. Assessed 05 May 2019

29. Blanchette, B.: Control engineering. https://www.controleng.com/single-article/how-to-implement-the-industrial-internet-of-things/6a6246ff7aee2e7498838ad0b2c02b4d.html. Assessed 05 May 2019
30. Lueth, L.K.: IOT analytics. https://iot-analytics.com/implementing-iot-technology-6-things/. Assessed 15 Jan 2019

# eBusiness

# Cybersecurity Readiness of E-tail Organisations: A Technical Perspective

Mahmood Hussain Shah[1,2,3(✉)], Raza Muhammad[1,2,3], and Nisreen Ameen[1,2,3]

[1] School of Strategy and Leadership, Coventry University, Coventry, UK
ac3559@coventry.ac.uk
[2] Department of Mathematics, Shah Abdul Latif University, Khairpur, Pakistan
[3] School of Business and Management, Royal Holloway, University of London, London, UK

**Abstract.** Cybersecurity readiness is a challenging issue for online retail businesses which are losing billions of dollars due to cyber-crimes and a lack of readiness to manage these. Therefore, research into cybersecurity readiness in the online retail industry is needed. Technical tools are the foremost measures of defence against these attacks. This study investigates cybersecurity readiness from the technical perspective in some UK online retailers. This research adopted a qualitative case study approach with semi-structured interviews for collecting data. A total of 15 interviews were conducted with an online retail company's staff and management who had responsibility for managing cybersecurity. A thematic analysis method was used to analyse the qualitative data. The research findings show that the company is facing internal and external threats to their information systems and their technical defences are not very effective at present. The company should consider investing more resources in the technical controls to prevent these attacks.

**Keywords:** Cybersecurity · Technical readiness · Organisational readiness · Network security · Cyber threats and risks

## 1 Introduction

Cybersecurity has received significant attention from researchers and professionals. It has become an integral part of business activities in all organisations regardless of their size and nature and has become particularly important for online businesses. Cybersecurity readiness can be achieved by implementing a resilient culture against cyber related threats and attacks. This culture would be useful for organisations to mitigate the impact of cyber-attacks. However, these businesses are facing cybersecurity threats/attacks from both internal and external sources [1]. Cyber threats/attacks and frauds are increasing and posing many challenges for online organisations. These challenges include externals/internals threats accidental damage and technical/organisational weaknesses.

Cyber threats include identity theft [2] and unauthorised access to an organisational network [3]. Denial of Service (DoS) attacks, malicious insiders, web-based attacks [4],

© IFIP International Federation for Information Processing 2020
Published by Springer Nature Switzerland AG 2020
M. Hattingh et al. (Eds.): I3E 2020, LNCS 12066, pp. 153–160, 2020.
https://doi.org/10.1007/978-3-030-44999-5_13

human error [3], phishing emails and inadequate security monitoring [5] are also documented threats. There are some reasons which contribute to the success of these attacks, for example, preventative equipment failures [6], lack of technical awareness [7], unauthorised access [3] and malicious employees [4]. Some basic security controls such as encryption, anti-virus software, firewalls and intrusion detection systems (IDS) suggested by Sen, Ahmed and Islam [8] could be used to prevent cyber-attacks. Unified Threat Management Systems (UTMS) provide more security to the network layer, hardware and software than standard security methods [9]. Secure authentication and authorisation systems are useful in preventing ID theft [10]. Regular assessment of security controls and monitoring of internal and external security systems may reduce the risk of cyber-attacks [11].

The aim of this research is to investigate the cybersecurity readiness, from a technical perspective, in an online retail organization, to assess how resilient its security infrastructure has been built to mitigate cyber-attacks. To achieve this aim, a qualitative case study was conducted and a total of 15 semi-structured interviews were conducted at an E-tail company in the UK. The semi-structured interviews provided an opportunity for face-to-face interactions with managers and other relevant staff. Additionally, policy documents were utilised in order to better understand the security processes in the company. Collected data was analysed using thematic analysis.

## 2   Literature Review

Cybersecurity readiness includes security policies, processes and procedures that are employed in the organisation to manage cyber threats. Furthermore, a review of cybersecurity readiness includes examinations of security functions, to check whether these functions operate in line with relevant policies, standards or procedures [12]. The importance of cybersecurity readiness has been increasingly recognised worldwide. Many leading countries have invested in their cybersecurity and have published official strategy documents for their cybersecurity; these include USA, UK, Canada, Australia, Japan, Germany and Russia [13].

Cybersecurity breaches are becoming increasingly common against companies regardless of their size and nature [14]. Cyber-attacks are malicious acts usually originating from an anonymous source that either steals, alters or destroys a specified target by hacking into a susceptible system. According to Uma and Padmavathi [15], several dimensions of cyber-attacks can be found in existing literature, but the primary objective of such attacks is to compromise the confidentiality, integrity and availability of information resources. These cyber-attacks tend to be successful due to weaknesses in technical infrastructure [16]. Due to a lack technical awareness, people become victims of cyber-attacks [7]. Therefore, this research focuses on cybersecurity readiness in the technical perspective to aid the online retail company in mitigating against potential cyber risk.

With the advancement in the technology, new methods of cyber-attacks are also emerging [14]. It is the responsibility of management to perform risk analyses and highlight flaws and vulnerabilities in the information systems, as neglecting these tasks can increase the likelihood of successful cybersecurity attacks. Therefore, online retail organisations must maintain update infrastructure to reduce the impacts of cyber-attacks in the organisation. Ultimately, these attacks affect organisations in the form of significant financial losses and reputational damage.

There are many technical threats that are possible reasons for cybersecurity breaches in online retail organisations. These include: Malware, Spam, Phishing, Spear-Phishing Attack, Denial of Service (DoS) attack, Distributed Denial of Service (DDoS), Man in Middle Attack, Hacking, Social Engineering, Spoofing, Keylogging, Cookies, Backdoor Trojan, SQL Injection and Identify Theft.

### Impact of Cyber-Attacks in Online Retail Organisations

Cybersecurity threats are a growing concern for online retail organisations. Organisations considered cyber-attacks to be the biggest threat to businesses. A recent study by Hui, Kim and Wang [17] indicated that many DDOS attacks targeted banks (24%), telecommunications companies (23%) and financial services organizations (20%), indicating they were likely financially motivated. Another survey conducted by the PWC [18] indicates that the average financial cost of cybersecurity incidents (including costs relating to business operations and data) is £857,000. The same report also pointed out that UK organisations are more reluctant in combating against cyber-attacks than peer organisations in the other countries.

### Countermeasures

The above discussion was about cybersecurity threats and attacks that affect online businesses in various forms. Effective counter measures are needed to prevent cybersecurity threats from materialising. There are several factors such as technical, organisational and human which increase the success rate of these attacks, for example, Uma and Padmavathi [15] state that there is a lack of proper understanding and technical awareness of the nature of cyber-attacks. By implementing security measures and controls, companies can help mitigate against these attacks.

Legitimate antivirus or endpoint security software along with user awareness regarding threats posed by clicking on suspicious links would be useful in mitigating cyber attacks. Organisations also use anti-spam software to limit the spam attacks, coupled with other countermeasures such as two factor authentication, web application scans, firewalls, access control, encryption and unified threat management appliances. However, the focus of this study is only cybersecurity readiness from a technical perspective and this can be achieved by proper implementation of technical controls to safeguard organisational infrastructure to mitigate the potential cyber-attacks.

## 3  Methodology

This study employs a qualitative case study approach, and focuses predominately on the perspectives conveyed by respondents, for instance, how they undertake their job roles to manage cybersecurity readiness in the online retail organisation. This approach allows the investigator to study real life events and managerial processes and it examines an existing phenomenon in depth within its real life situation [19]. This case study has been carried out in close interaction with practitioners who deal with managerial situations, so this approach is suitable to create relevant knowledge [20].

**Participant Selection and Data Gathering**

The study takes a case study based approach, using semi-structured interviews as the primary data collection method. The interview questionnaire was designed with the help of existing literature relevant to the field of information security. A pilot study was conducted with 10 academic staff in the relevant area of study and as a result, some amendments were made to the interview questions according to their suggestions. Moreover, participants were selected on the basis of their job nature and experience in the management of online security in the online retail company in the UK. A total of 15 interviews were conducted with professionals including the IT Manager, Fraud Prevention Manager and members of the Network Security Team. Face-to-face interviews lasted around 45–60 min. All interviews were audio recorded in a hand-held device to be transcribed and analysed later.

**Data Analysis**

The semi-structured interviews were transcribed manually. Furthermore, The Nvivo software was also used for the categorisation and coding of themes. This software is useful in transcribing, grouping, and coding the data. The thematic analysis method used to analyse the semi-structured interviews was proposed by Braun and Clarke [21]. Transcribed interviews were analysed using the inductive thematic analysis. This technique provides a facility to identify a set of emergent topics in the data. Each theme was carefully developed based on the analysis of transcribed text from interviews.

## 4  Results and Discussions

For this research, we conducted case study research at one large organisation. For confidentiality reasons, the case company will be referred henceforth as Company A. Company A is a leading multi-brand online retailer in the UK and Ireland, selling thousands of different brands supplied by others as well as its own brand of retail goods. In this section, we bring together the various observations from the data collected using semi-structured interviews at Company A to manage cybersecurity readiness in the technical context. Cybersecurity readiness can be achieved by implementing the following security controls (themes) which emerged from the analysis of collected qualitative data.

### (a) Access Control and Authentication

Usernames and passwords are treated commonly as authentication, but it is not a secure form of authentication because anyone can use these details and gain easy access to the systems. It is difficult for systems to recognise whether the user who has accessed system is genuine or fraudulent. Company A has two-factor authentication system to prevent unauthorised access. However, two-factor authentication is not always a secure method as cyber-criminals can violate this [22]. To make the authentication system more effective, biometric authentication systems may be used, for example, voice recognition, facial recognition and fingerprint scanning [23]. Therefore, Company A may consider biometric authentication systems to prevent unauthorised access.

### (b) Information Communication Security (ICS)

ICS helps to secure electronic communication amongst staff, third parties and customers inside and outside the company. Company A encrypts the data of customers and employees when sending it to third parties and registered post is used to send hard copies of data. Using encryption for sending and receiving information is useful for a company because it prevents modification and keeps data in its original form. This encryption method has a weakness as it does not cover the recipient of any data, as this would need Point-to-Point Encryption (P2PE). Therefore, Company A could P2PE to secure its communication channels more effectively [24]. Moreover, Public Key Infrastructure (PKI) digital signatures and Secure Sockets Layer (SSL) etc. are useful in preventing cybersecurity attacks [25]. Therefore, the company may use these for enhancing cybersecurity infrastructure.

### (c) Threat Management

Threat management is an essential component of the organisation's security process. Businesses that depend on ICT remain under threat from cyber-criminals whose motive is to steal sensitive information by infiltrating systems in different ways. Now, it is the responsibility of the organisation to manage such risks cost-effectively and minimise threats to their information systems.

Company A uses various security controls to minimise threats to information system infrastructure. Additionally, the company has professionals who constantly try to manage the security threats. However, some vulnerabilities still exist in these security controls for which Company A should assess regularly to manage security threats. This is also proposed by some researchers such as Taylor [11].

### (d) Network Security

Network security has a significant role in the information system security of online retail organisations because cyber-criminals attack the network to steal information. Cyber intrusions and attacks occur when unauthorised access is gained to networks, including theft of users' sensitive data, online economic fraud, website destruction, web application attacks and system penetration. Attackers exploit operating system vulnerabilities in web browsers, services and configurations, platform vulnerabilities in web applications, network device vulnerabilities, policy and personnel vulnerabilities in unauthorised devices [26]. Company A did face cyber-attacks, such as denial of service attacks, because of weaknesses in the network. However, encryption, anti-virus, firewalls, Intrusion Detection Systems (IDS) are useful in preventing cyber-attacks [8]. Therefore, the company should configure its firewalls to prevent denial of service attacks on the network. Firewalls are useful in preventing unauthorised access to the network and in blocking unwanted traffic into the company's network (Sen et al.) [8]. A firewall is a shield that works against dangerous communications from disseminating across any network, either from the outside world into a local system, or from one part of a local network to another. It is a useful element in network access because it can prevent unauthorised access at the boundary of a network and infrastructure.

### (e) Network Monitoring

ICT enables business processes to operate electronically and provides facilities to conduct business activities more effectively and efficiently in the digital environment.

The monitoring activities of ICT allow the company to detect vulnerabilities and respond to these appropriately by enhancing security controls. Despite such active monitoring systems, some information breaches still occur at Company A. Company A are monitoring activities inside the company and whenever unusual activity is found, they aim to resolve it immediately. The company also performs a test for vulnerabilities in its computing systems and try to fix it in the first instance. Further, the company has different teams whose work is to monitor the security processes of the company's infrastructure and prevent loopholes from being exploited. For network security, Unified Threat Management Systems (UTMS) provide more security to the network layer, hardware and software than standard detection methods because this is the combination of firewalls, pattern recognition and user authentication methods [9]. Therefore, Company A should use UTMS for effective security.

## 5   Conclusion

This paper presented the findings of the case study on cybersecurity readiness from a technical perspective, for instance, if ICT security and risk assessments are managed effectively; cybersecurity incidents in the organisation could be reduced. Therefore, the organisation should proactively asses their technical factors rather than only assessing these after an incident has occurred. A qualitative case study approach was adopted and 15 semi-structured interviews were conducted for data collection. The interviews were analysed using thematic analysis. The key areas of selected themes were discussed and confirmed by the managers and other staff members.

This research provides unique value through investigating the determinants of technical readiness. The study suggests that organisation readiness in the cybersecurity domain can be achieved by taking proactive measures such as ICT security and risk management. The results show that online organisations are lagging behind, especially in the effective implementation of up to date technical tools and measures. Although the case organisation has implemented some measures, there is still a need to explore their functionality within the organisational structure.

Like other studies, this research also has some limitations. Firstly, only a single case study was conducted in this research to evaluate the technical readiness. Secondly, only a qualitative case study approach was used for data collection. Therefore, there is a need to conduct multiple case studies to learn more about technical aspects of cybersecurity in other technical aspects, using both qualitative and quantitative methods. This study was conducted in the UK so repetition of this research in other countries would improve the research and extend results to compare and contrast the outcomes of online retailers.

## References

1. Manhart, M., Thalmann, S.: Protecting organizational knowledge: a structured literature review. J. Knowl. Manag. **19**(2), 190–211 (2015)
2. Humaidi, N., Balakrishnan, V.: Indirect effect of management support on users' compliance behaviour towards information security policies. Health Inf. Manag. J. **47**(1), 17–27 (2018)

3. Da Veiga, A.: A cybersecurity culture research philosophy and approach to develop a valid and reliable measuring instrument. Paper Presented at the Science and Information (SAI) Computing Conference, London, UK, July 13–15, pp. 1006–1015 (2016)
4. Clark, M., Harrell, C.E.: Unlike chess, everyone must continue playing after a cyber-attack. J. Invest. Compliance **14**(4), 5–12 (2013)
5. Safa, N.S., Von Solms, R.: An information security knowledge-sharing model in organizations. Comput. Hum. Behav. **57**(4), 442–451 (2016)
6. Reason, J.: Managing the Risks of Organizational Accidents. Routledge, New York (2016)
7. Pieters, W., Hadžiosmanović, D., Dechesne, F.: Security-by-experiment: lessons from responsible deployment in cyberspace. Sci. Eng. Ethics **22**(3), 831–850 (2016)
8. Sen, P., Ahmed, A., Islam, R.: A study on e-commerce security issues and solutions. Int. J. Comput. Commun. Syst. Eng. **2**(3), 425–430 (2015)
9. Kent, C., Tanner, M., Kabanda, S.: How South African SMEs address cyber security: the case of web server logs and intrusion detection. Paper Presented at the IEEE International Conference on Emerging Technologies and Innovative Business Practices for the Transformation of Societies (EmergiTech), Balaclava, Mauritius, August 3–6, pp. 100–105 (2016)
10. Sharma, A., Kansal, V., Tomar, R.: Location based services in M-commerce: customer trust and transaction security issues. Int. J. Comput. Sci. Secur. (IJCSS) **9**(2), 11–21 (2015)
11. Taylor, E.: Mobile payment technologies in retail: a review of potential benefits and risks. Int. J. Retail Distrib. Manag. **44**(2), 159–177 (2016)
12. Pereira, T., Santos, H.: A security audit framework to manage information system security. In: Tenreiro de Magalhães, S., Jahankhani, H., Hessami, Ali G. (eds.) ICGS3 2010. CCIS, vol. 92, pp. 9–18. Springer, Heidelberg (2010). https://doi.org/10.1007/978-3-642-15717-2_2
13. Klimburg, A.: National Cyber Security Framework Manual. NATO Cooperative Cyber Defence Centre of Excellence, Tallinn (2012)
14. Waly, N., Tassabehji, R., Kamala, M.: Improving organisational information security management: the impact of training and awareness. Paper Presented at the High Performance Computing and Communication & IEEE 9th International Conference on Embedded Software and Systems (HPCC-ICESS), Liverpool, UK, June 25–27, pp. 1270–1275 (2012)
15. Uma, M., Padmavathi, G.: A survey on various cyber attacks and their classification. IJ Netw. Secur. **15**(5), 390–396 (2013)
16. Shinde, P.S., Ardhapurkar, S.B.: Cyber security analysis using vulnerability assessment and penetration testing. Paper Presented at the World Conference on Futuristic Trends in Research and Innovation for Social Welfare (Startup Conclave), Coimbatore, India, 29 February–1 March, pp. 1–5 (2016)
17. Hui, K., Kim, S.H., Wang, Q.: Cybercrime deterrence and international legislation: evidence from distributed denial of service attacks. MIS Q. **41**(2), 497–572 (2017)
18. PWC: Revitalizing privacy and trust in a data-driven world: key findings from the global state of information security® survey 2018 (2018). https://www.pwc.com/us/en/cyber security/assets/revitalizing-privacy-trust-in-data-driven-world.pdf. Accessed 11 Jan 2020
19. Yin, R.K.: Case Study Research: Design and Methods. Sage Publications Ltd., London (2014)
20. Walsham, G.: Interpretive case studies in IS research: nature and method. Eur. J. Inf. Syst. **4**(2), 74–81 (1995)
21. Braun, V., Clarke, V.: Using thematic analysis in psychology. Qual. Res. Psychol. **3**(2), 77–101 (2006)
22. Srinivas, T., Vivek, G.: Cyber security: the state of the practice in public sector companies in India. Paper Presented at the International Conference on Computer and Communications Technologies (ICCCT), Hyderabad, India, December 11–13, pp. 1–5 (2014)

23. Tan, F.T.C., Guo, Z., Cahalane, M., Cheng, D.: Developing business analytic capabilities for combating e-commerce identity fraud: a study of Trustev's digital verification solution. Inf. Manag. **53**(7), 878–891 (2016)
24. Ann McGee, J., Ralph Byington, J.: Corporate identity theft: a growing risk. J. Corp. Account. Financ. **26**(5), 37–40 (2015)
25. Ray, S., Biswas, G., Dasgupta, M.: Secure multi-purpose mobile-banking using elliptic curve cryptography. Wirel. Pers. Commun. **90**(3), 1331–1354 (2016)
26. Zhao, J.J., Zhao, S.Y.: Opportunities and threats: a security assessment of state e-government websites. Gov. Inf. Q. **27**(1), 49–56 (2010)

# Consumer Mobile Shopping Acceptance Predictors and Linkages: A Systematic Review and Weight Analysis

Kuttimani Tamilmani[1]([✉]), Nripendra P. Rana[1], Yogesh K. Dwivedi[2],
and Hatice Kizgin[1]

[1] International Business, Marketing and Branding Research Centre (IBMB),
School of Management, University of Bradford, Richmond Road,
Bradford BD7 1DP, UK
kuttimani.tamilmani@gmail.com, nrananp@gmail.com,
h.kizgin@bradford.ac.uk
[2] Emerging Markets Research Centre (EMaRC), School of Management,
Swansea University Bay Campus, Swansea SA1 8EN, UK
y.k.dwivedi@swansea.ac.uk, ykdwivedi@gmail.com

**Abstract.** Mobile phones have become an integral part of human lives with majority of people using them to access product and services for their day-to-day needs. However, mobile shopping adoption across the globe is not wide or fast as expected. In addition, the research is very scant in understanding various predictors of consumer adoption towards mobile shopping. The objective of this study is to identify most significant and non-significant predictors of consumer mobile shopping acceptance. Systematic review and weight analysis on 34 mobile shopping studies revealed researchers mostly employed TAM and UTAUT model as theoretical lens. This study found an interesting revelation that extrinsic motivation variables such as social influence and perceived usefulness determine consumer mobile shopping behavioral intention during early stages. However, in later stages intrinsic motivation variables such as satisfaction and trust play crucial role to emerge as best and promising predictor of consumer continuous intention respectively.

**Keywords:** Mobile shopping · Weight analysis · Continuous intention

## 1 Introduction

Mobile technologies are the most adopted form of consumer technology across the world in 21st century with 5 billion unique mobile subscribers in 2017, which encompasses two thirds of global population [1]. The characteristics of smartphones with wireless Internet enable consumers to purchase goods and services from anywhere at any time, even in the absence wired broadband connections popularly known as mobile shopping [2]. It empowers consumer with ability to search, browse, compare, and purchase products and services through wireless handheld mobile devices. And,

M. Hattingh et al. (Eds.): I3E 2020, LNCS 12066, pp. 161–175, 2020.
https://doi.org/10.1007/978-3-030-44999-5_14

they can buy range of products and services such as electronics, apparels, housewares, books, tickets, beauty, and grocery to name a few [3–5]. The unprecedented smartphones adoption rate is in turn fuelling the mobile shopping growth to reshape the online retail environment. Leading market research firm Statista report suggests that mobile e-commerce is poised for growth globally and could possibly rake in upwards of 3.5 trillion USD constituting almost three quarters (72.9%) of all e-commerce sales [6]. Mobile phones unique characteristics enable organisations to reach right consumers anytime anywhere through mobile advertising [7, 8]. Organisation's spend on mobile advertising is on upward trajectory with a whopping amount of 105.95 billion USD in 2017 and an estimated amount of 175.64 billion USD in 2020 [9].

The above discussion underscores the central role of mobile phones as a medium for shopping to consumers and advertising to organisations respectively. Despite the potential of mobile technology, mobile readiness report on Fortune 500 companies' mobile websites revealed just one-quarter had mobile-responsiveness and majority of the companies were unprepared [10]. The majority of existing consumer on mobile shopping acceptance studies focused on intention related outcome variables such as behavioural intention [11–13], purchase intention [14, 15], and continuous intention [16, 17] rather than use behaviour. Mobile shopping adoption can be achieved at faster rate based on the learning from existing research on this topic across different countries. Existing review articles on mobile shopping mostly provide descriptive information e.g., [18, 19] without highlighting on the effective predictors necessary for successful adoption. Therefore, the objective of this study is to employ weight-analysis to synthesise existing findings on mobile shopping and identify the most/least frequently used predictors, and among these the best, worst, and promising predictors [20, 21]. This study will undertake following steps to fulfil the objective:

- Locate consumer focused mobile shopping empirical studies that employed consumer intention/use behaviour-based outcome variables.
- Conduct weight analysis on the empirical studies to understand the significant and non-significant path relationships and their performance.

The remaining sections of this paper is structured as follows: The following section i.e. Sect. 2 describes the research method employed in this study; Sect. 3 presents the findings of weight analysis and systematic literature review followed by discussion in Sect. 4 and conclusion in Sect. 5.

## 2  Research Method

This study deemed a combination of "systematic review", "Keyword search" and "weight-analysis" techniques as appropriate methodology to synthesize the existing research findings on consumer intention and usage towards mobile shopping [22–31]. It employed keyword based search in the Scopus, Web of Science, and EBSCO

Business Source complete databases with search terms such as "mobile shopping" OR "m-shopping" OR "mobile purchasing" AND "Adoption" OR "Acceptance" OR "Diffusion" OR "Usage" OR "Intention" to locate articles related to mobile shopping. The initial search from the year 2009 to 2019 resulted in 72 articles. On further screening, it was found that some of the articles were not accessible through researcher's library and numerous studies employed outcome variables other than consumer intention and usage towards mobile shopping. Such instances include but are not limited to outcome variables such as switching intention [32], loyalty [33], and patronage [34]. Therefore, studies that did not report relevant data for weight analysis were also excluded resulting in 34 final manuscripts that focussed only on consumer intention and usage as outcome variable to qualify for weight analysis.

# 3 Findings

This section presents and explains the findings from the systematic review and weight analysis.

## 3.1 Dominant Theories/Models

Researchers employed as much as thirteen unique theories/models as theoretical lens across the 34 studies to examine consumer intention and usage towards mobile shopping. Table 1 provides summary of dominant theories that are employed on two or more instances. Technology acceptance model (TAM) emerged as the most dominant theory with as much as 12 studies adapting TAM as theoretical lens by often extending the model with external constructs. For instance, Groß [35] extended TAM with perceived enjoyment and trust and found these attributes as significant predictor of consumers mobile shopping in Germany. Venkatesh, Morris, Davis and Davis [36]'s, UTAUT theory emerged as the distant second most popular theory with five research investigations. Three studies adapted Expectancy Confirmation Model making it the third most popular theoretical lens in the consumer mobile shopping acceptance arena. Multifaceted trust-risk model and theory of planned behaviour jointly occupied fourth position by serving as theoretical lens on two instances each. Furthermore, there were eight theories/models such as (1) 4P's marketing theory [16], (2) Behavioural reasoning theory [37], (3) Elaboration likelihood model [38], (4) Flow theory [39], (5) IS success model [14], (6) Stimulus-Organism-Response (SOR) framework [40], (7) Technology readiness [41], and (8) Trust transfer theory [15] that researchers employed on one instance each. Finally, there were two studies [42, 43] that did not employ any dominant theories to examine consumer mobile shopping acceptance.

**Table 1.** Dominant mobile shopping acceptance theories/models

| Theory/model | Frequency | References |
|---|---|---|
| Technology acceptance model (TAM) | 12 | Agrebi and Jallais [3]; Chen, Hsu and Lu [44]; Groß [35]; Groß [45]; Ko, Kim and Lee [5]; Lu and Su [46]; Natarajan, Balasubramanian and Kasilingam [47]; San-Martín, López-Catalán and Ramón-Jerónimo [11]; Saprikis, Markos, Zarmpou and Vlachopoulou [48]; Shang and Wu [49]; Wong, Lee, Lim, Chua and Tan [12]; Wong, Tan, Ooi and Lin [13] |
| Unified theory of acceptance and use of technology (UTAUT) | 5 | Chau, Seshadri, Broekemier and Pamornpathomkul [50]; Lu, Yu, Liu and Wei [51]; Tan and Ooi [52]; Yang and Forney [53]; Yang [54] |
| Expectancy confirmation model | 3 | Chung, Chun and Choi [17]; Hung, Yang and Hsieh [55]; Kang, Hung, Yang, Hsieh and Tang [56] |
| Multifaceted trust-risk model | 2 | Groß [57]; Marriott and Williams [58] |
| Theory of planned behaviour | 2 | Prodanova, San-Martín and Jimenez [59]; Yang [60] |

## 3.2   Weight Analysis

Weight analysis technique determines indicative predictive power of an independent variable over dependant variable. This is performed by calculating weight, which is as a ratio of total number of significant relationships between an independent and dependant variable (a) to the total number of all relationships between these two variables (b) and thus weight is calculated using formula (a)/(b) [21].

### Coding Independent and Dependent Variables

This study employed generalized coding scheme adapted from Jeyaraj, Rottman and Lacity [21], to uniformly code findings between various independent and dependant variables among the 34 consumer mobile shopping studies. The coding template comprised of 'rows' and 'columns'. Each row in the template represented one of the 34 studies, while each column represented the path relationship between an independent and a dependant variable. The intersection points between studies in a "row" and path relationship in the "column" captured the significance of the particular path relationship corresponding to that study. The coding scheme has four different values: (1) '+1' in the case where the path relationship examined was significant and hypothesized in positive direction; (2) '−1' in the case where the path relationship examined was significant and hypothesized in negative direction; (3) '0' in the case where the path relationship examined was non-significant; and (4) "Blank" when the relationship was not studied [21]. This study thoroughly examined all the hypotheses in the 34 articles to identify various dependent and independent variables that researchers employed to examine consumer mobile shopping acceptance. The examination resulted in

**Table 2.** Most frequently studied variables in mobile shopping

| Sl. no | Independent variable | Definition | Example citation(s) |
|---|---|---|---|
| 1 | Anxiety | Refers to negative emotions in cognitive states that are evoked during actual or imaginary interactions with underlying behaviour (e.g. Using mobile for shopping) [61] | Lu and Su [46]; Saprikis, Markos, Zarmpou and Vlachopoulou [48] |
| 2 | Attitude | The extent to which individuals have positive or negative evaluation about the behaviour under question [62] | Groß [45]; Gupta and Arora [37]; Yang [54]; Yang [60] |
| 3 | Compatibility | The degree to which an innovation is perceived to be consistent with the values, past experiences, and needs of potential adopters [63] | Lu and Su [46], Wong, Tan, Ooi and Lin [13] |
| 4 | Facilitating conditions | The degree to which an individual believes that an organisational and technical infrastructure exists to support use of the system [36] | Tan and Ooi [52]; Yang [54] |
| 5 | Perceived behavioural control | Individuals perception of his/her capability to performing a behaviour of interest [62] | San-Martín, López-Catalán and Ramón-Jerónimo [11], Yang [60] |
| 6 | Perceived ease of use | The degree to which a person believes that using a particular system would be free of effort [64] | Hew, Leong, Tan, Lee and Ooi [40], Natarajan, Balasubramanian and Kasilingam [47], Saprikis, Markos, Zarmpou and Vlachopoulou [48], Tan and Ooi [52] |
| 7 | Perceived enjoyment | The extent to which the activity of using a computer/particular system is perceived to be enjoyable in its own right, apart from any performance consequences that may be anticipated [65] | Natarajan, Balasubramanian and Kasilingam [47], Saprikis, Markos, Zarmpou and Vlachopoulou [48], Tan and Ooi [52], Wong, Tan, Ooi and Lin [13] |
| 8 | Perceived risk | Consumers' expectation of losses associated with purchasing and acts as an inhibitor of purchase behaviour [66] | Marriott and Williams [58], Natarajan, Balasubramanian and Kasilingam [47], Tan and Ooi [52, 12] |
| 9 | Perceived usefulness | The degree to which a person believes that using a particular system would enhance his or her job performance [64] | Natarajan, Balasubramanian and Kasilingam [47], Tan and Ooi [52], Wong, Tan, Ooi and Lin [13] |
| 10 | Personal innovativeness | The willingness of an individual to try out any new information technology [67] | Natarajan, Balasubramanian and Kasilingam [47], Saprikis, Markos, Zarmpou and Vlachopoulou [48], Wong, Tan, Ooi and Lin [13] |
| 11 | Satisfaction | The psychological or emotional state resulting from a cognitive assessment of the gap between the expectations and the actual performance of an information system [68] | Agrebi and Jallais [3], Amoroso [42], Natarajan, Balasubramanian and Kasilingam [47] |
| 12 | Social influence | The degree to which an individual perceives that important others believe he or she should use the new system [36] | Groß [45], San-Martín, López-Catalán and Ramón-Jerónimo [11], Tan and Ooi [52], Yang and Forney [53] |

(*continued*)

**Table 2.** (*continued*)

| Sl. no | Independent variable | Definition | Example citation(s) |
|---|---|---|---|
| 13 | Trust | The most important factor for establishing relationships, both of interpersonal and commercial nature between two or more parties that determine their future action [69] | Groß [35], Marriott and Williams [58], Tan and Ooi [52] |
| 14 | Trust in mobile vendor | Comprises of consumer's trusting beliefs (e.g. ability, integrity, and benevolence) and their intention to engage in a business relationship with m-vendors by providing personal information, following the m-vendor's advice, or making purchases and transferring money directly via smartphone Groß [57] | Groß [57] |

| Sl. no | Dependent variables | Definition | Example citation(s) |
|---|---|---|---|
| 1 | Behavioural intention | Represents individual intention to perform an underlying behaviour with stronger intentions leading to higher chances of performing the underlying behaviour [62] | Groß [35], Groß [45], Yang [54] |
| 2 | Continuous intention | This refers to consumers in post-purchase stage, where their consumption experience determines the future behaviour [70] | Gao, Waechter and Bai [39], Hung, Yang and Hsieh [55], Kang, Hung, Yang, Hsieh and Tang [56], Groß [57] |
| 3 | Use behaviour | The degree and manner in which customers utilise the capabilities of an underlying technology/system [71] | Groß [35], Groß [45] |

identifying 41 independent variables, five dependent variables, and 59 different path relationships among these independent and dependent variables. However, the findings of this study are limited to path relationships that are examined on two or more instances. This resulted in final 14 independent variables, three dependant variables i.e. behavioural intentional, continuous intention, and use behaviour and their 20 path relationships. Table 2 provides summary and definition of the final 14 independent variables ranging from anxiety to trust in mobile vendor and three dependent variables.

**Dominant Predictors of Mobile Shopping Acceptance**

Weight analysis classifies independent variables into two types based on the numbers of times the variable is used a predictor on a dependent variable. An independent variable is termed as 'well-utilized' predictor when examined by researchers in five or more studies. Otherwise, the independent variable is considered as an 'experimental' predictor in case of less than five examinations. Furthermore, the independent variable qualifies as the best predictor of dependant variable when they are used in five or more studies (well-utilized) and have a weight of 0.80 or more. On the other hand, independent variable can be considered as a promising predictor when it is used in less than five studies (experimental) and have perfect weight of one [21]. The summary of weight analysis findings for all the three dependant variables behavioural intentional, continuous intention, and use behaviour is depicted in Table 3.

*Well Utilized Predictors of Behavioural Intention*
Six variables fulfilled the criteria (five or more examinations) to qualify as the well utilized predictor of consumer behavioural intention towards mobile shopping. The following three predictors: perceived usefulness/performance expectancy (examined 11 times, significant 11 times), attitude (examined 8 times, significant 8 times), and social influence (examined 6 times, significant 6 times) fell under the 'best predictor' category. Since, these variables were explored five or more times and have a weight equal to or greater than 0.80. The remaining three 'well utilized' predictors 'perceived enjoyment' (examined 9 times, significant 6 times), satisfaction (examined 5 times, significant 3 times), and perceived ease of use/effort expectancy (examined 9 times, significant 4 times) having weight of 0.67, 0.60, and 0.44 respectively are termed as least effective predictor and needs further examination.

*Experimental Predictors of Behavioural Intention*
Notwithstanding the six 'well utilized' predictors behavioural intention also had seven experimental predictors such as: (1) perceived risk, (2) personal innovativeness, (3) trust, (4) compatibility, (5) anxiety, (6) facilitating conditions, and (7) perceived behavioural control. From the seven aforementioned 'experimental predictors' only two predictors such as: compatibility (examined 2 times, significant 2 times) and perceived behavioural control (examined 2 times, significant 2 times) with perfect weight of one, qualified as the promising predictors of consumer behavioural intention towards mobile shopping.

*Predictors of Continuous Intention*
There were five dominant predictors in determining consumer continuous intention towards mobile shopping. The first one is satisfaction that qualified both as a well utilized and best predictor of consumer continuous intention with significant results on all five instances of examination. The remaining four predictors such as: (1) trust (examined 3 times, significant 3 times); (2) trust in mobile vendor (3) perceived risk (examined 2 times, significant 2 times); and (4) perceived usefulness/performance expectancy (examined 2 times, significant '0' times) each with less than five examinations emerged as 'experimental predictors'. The first three 'experimental predictors' of continuous intention (trust, trust in mobile vendor, and perceived risk) also qualified as promising predictor perfect weight of one. Meanwhile, perceived usefulness/performance expectancy emerged as the as least effective predictor of continuous intention.

*Predictors of Use Behaviour*
Use behaviour comprised of only two experimental predictors with less than five examination such as 'satisfaction' (examined 2 times, significant 2 times) and 'behavioural intention' (examined 2 times, significant 2 times). This indicates researchers scarcely employed use behaviour as outcome variable in consumer mobile shopping acceptance research. Both the experimental predictors qualified as the promising predictors of use behaviour with perfect weight of one.

**Table 3.** Weight analysis summary approach adapted from Jeyaraj, Rottman and Lacity [21]

| SN | Independent variable | DV | Sig (a) | Non-Sig | Total (b) | Weight (a/b) |
|---|---|---|---|---|---|---|
| 1 | Perceived usefulness/performance expectancy | BI | 11 | 0 | 11 | 1.00 |
| 2 | Perceived ease of use/effort expectancy | | 4 | 5 | 9 | 0.44 |
| 3 | Perceived enjoyment | | 6 | 3 | 9 | 0.67 |
| 4 | Attitude | | 8 | 0 | 8 | 1.00 |
| 5 | Social influence | | 6 | 0 | 6 | 1.00 |
| 6 | Satisfaction | | 3 | 2 | 5 | 0.60 |
| 7 | Perceived risk | | 3 | 1 | 4 | 0.75 |
| 8 | Personal innovativeness | | 2 | 1 | 3 | 0.67 |
| 9 | Trust | | 2 | 1 | 3 | 0.67 |
| 10 | Compatibility | | 2 | 0 | 2 | 1.00 |
| 11 | Anxiety | | 1 | 1 | 2 | 0.50 |
| 12 | Facilitating conditions | | 1 | 1 | 2 | 0.50 |
| 13 | Perceived behavioural control | | 2 | 0 | 2 | 1.00 |
| 14 | Satisfaction | CI | 5 | 0 | 5 | 1.00 |
| 15 | Trust | | 3 | 0 | 3 | 1.00 |
| 16 | Trust in mobile vendor | | 2 | 0 | 2 | 1.00 |
| 17 | Perceived risk | | 2 | 0 | 2 | 1.00 |
| 18 | Perceived usefulness/performance expectancy | | 0 | 2 | 2 | 0.00 |
| 19 | Satisfaction | UB | 2 | 0 | 2 | 1.00 |
| 20 | Behavioural intention | | 2 | 0 | 2 | 1.00 |

[**Legend:** BI: Behavioural Intention; CI: Continuous Intention; DV: Independent Variable; Non-Sig: Number of non-significant path values; Sig (a): Number of significant path values; UB: Use Behaviour]

## 4    Discussion

Literature synthesis on consumer mobile shopping acceptance studies reveal that researchers to date have mostly employed theories such as TAM and UTAUT. These theories were originally developed in the organisational context with major focus on individual employee characteristics and their motivation in using underlying technologies to improve job related outcomes. In addition, perceived usefulness similar to performance expectancy (11 studies) and perceived ease of use (9 studies) similar to effort expectancy the two independent variables of technology acceptance model (TAM) emerged as the most utilized variables emphasising TAM's dominance in individual adoption research. Besides individual characteristics from dominant technology acceptance theories, researchers have scarcely employed theories such as IS success model e.g., [16, 72] and flow theory e.g., [39, 52] to evaluate impact of system characteristics such as system quality, information quality, and system flow experience on consumer mobile shopping acceptance. The preceding discussion reveals researches mostly deployed theories developed in the organisation context as theoretical lens and seldom employed consumer-focused theories such as extended unified theory of acceptance and use of technology (UTAUT2) to examine mobile shopping acceptance.

The weight analysis findings reveal an interesting pattern that the role and relevance of various attributes depend upon the time period when the consumer starts using the underlying technology. The best predictors of consumer behavioural intention, which refers to early and potential users of technology are perceived usefulness, attitude, and social influence. This is followed by compatibility and perceived behavioural control that emerged as most promising predictors with all significant results for early mobile shopping users. However, attributes such as satisfaction, trust, and perceived risk emerged as least effective predictors of consumer behavioural intention. The plausible explanation could be early users haven't utilized the technology enough and/or bought product/service to evaluate their satisfaction, trust, and risk level of both the platform and vendors.

Interestingly, for consumers in the post-purchase stage, 'satisfaction' emerged as the single most well utilized and best predictor of their continuous intention. In addition, attributes such as trust, perceived risk, and trust in mobile vendor emerged as the promising predictor with all significant results. This underscores the significant role of both the platform and vendors in sustaining the existing consumers and influencing their continuous intention for future transactions. The emergence of variables such as Trust in mobile vendor as promising predictor only for continuous intention and not for behavioural intention further validates the role of product/service providers in improving the longevity of consumers towards mobile shopping. Surprisingly, perceived usefulness/performance expectancy that was best predictor of behavioural intention became least effective predictor of consumer continuous intention towards mobile shopping. The plausible explanation for this pattern comes from Hung, Yang and Hsieh [55] study that extended Expectation-Confirmation model with Trust to examine consumer continuous intention towards mobile shopping. The study results among 244 consumers found that extrinsic motivation variable perceived usefulness became non-significant determinant of continuous intention over time. However, during repurchasing activities, intrinsic motivation variable 'trust' explained the most variance on consumer continuous intention towards mobile shopping followed by Satisfaction. Finally, both Satisfaction and Behavioural intention the two predictors of Use behaviour emerged as promising predictor with all significant results. The preceding discussion indicates Use behaviour is sparingly examined as outcome variable in consumer mobile shopping acceptance. This pattern is understandable as consumer mobile shopping is still at nascent stages of acceptance in many parts of the world and researchers are trying to measure the intention rather than actual behaviour [20]. However, Wu and Du [73] meta-analysis on BI and UB caution the notion of IS researchers considering BI as surrogate of UB. Because, individual's use behaviour towards technology cannot be measured without assessing their actual system usage. Furthermore, Wu and Du [73] cautioned research community that they should be circumspect of studies that measure only behavioural intention without investigating use behaviour. Figure 1 depicts the resultant model emerging from weight analysis on mobile shopping empirical studies.

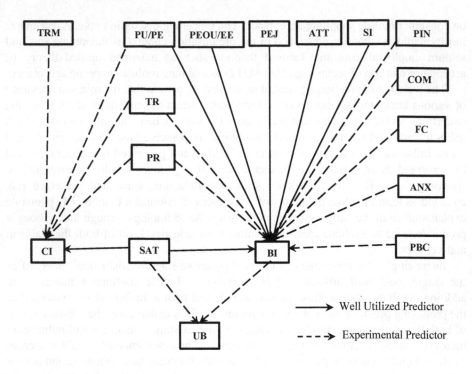

[LEGEND: **ANX:** Anxiety; **AT:** Attitude; **BI:** Behavioural Intention; **COM:** Compatibility; **CI:** Continuous Intention; **FC:** Facilitating Conditions; **PBC:** Perceived Behavioural Control; **PEOU/EE:** Perceived Ease of Use/ Effort Expectancy; **PEJ:** Perceived Enjoyment; **PR:** Perceived Risk; **PU/PE:** Perceived Usefulness/ Performance Expectancy; **PIN:** Personal Innovativeness; **SAT:** Satisfaction; **SI:** Social Influence; **TR:** Trust; **TRMV:** Trust in Mobile Vendor; **UB**: Use Behaviour]

**Fig. 1.** Emergent model of mobile shopping weight-analysis

## 5    Conclusion

This study identified various predictors of consumer mobile shopping acceptance and their linkage by synthesising findings from extant literature through weight analysis. The findings emerging from this study is important for future researchers in this domain and practitioners alike. Weight analysis results found among fourteen unique independent variables (Table 3) only four emerged as the best predictor three on behavioural intention (perceived usefulness, attitude, and social influence) and one on continuous intention (Satisfaction). This is followed by five promising predictor two on behavioural intention (compatibility, perceived behavioural control) and three on continuous intention (trust, trust in mobile vendor, and perceived risk), which are more likely candidates to emerge as best predictor in future. Therefore, researchers should continue using promising predictors while investigating consumer mobile shopping acceptance alongside the best predictors. The remaining five final independent variables perceived ease of use, perceived enjoyment, personal innovativeness, anxiety, and facilitating conditions emerged only as least effective predictors on consumer mobile shopping acceptance endogenous variables. Perceived ease of use one of the core construct of TAM, despite being the second most frequently used predictor produced the most non-significant results. Therefore, researchers should be more cautious while operationalizing this type of construct in their research model. They should make necessary adaptations and/or omit irrelevant constructs such as least effective predictors from the model depending upon context rather than having obligation to replicate all the constructs in underpinning model/theory. Moreover, the review found almost half - 47% studies in consumer mobile shopping arena employed theories developed under organisational context such as TAM and UTAUT. Therefore, future researchers should employ more consumer focussed theories such as UTAUT2.

Notwithstanding the precautionary measures taken for coding and analysis, the findings of this study is not without its limitations. First the studies involved for weight analysis were limited only to three databases such as Scopus, Web of Science, and EBSCO Business Source complete restricting the total number of empirical studies available for weight analysis. In future, researchers should widen their search horizon to more databases that will increase the number of studies available for analysis and minimize publication bias. Second, weight analysis does not take sample size into consideration like meta-analysis and cannot provide true effect size in a path relationship. In future, researchers should try to combine meta-analysis with weight analysis to calculate the true-effect size of path relationships. Third, this research included studies that employed intention and use related outcome variables pertaining to consumer mobile shopping acceptance. In future, researchers should include all outcome variables to provide comprehensive overview on various outcomes measured in consumer mobile shopping acceptance arena and their predictors. Finally, this study included only quantitative studies that reduced final number of studies available for analysis. Future studies should include both qualitative and quantitative studies in weight analysis.

# References

1. GSMA Intelligence: Global Mobile Trends 2017. https://www.gsmaintelligence.com/research/?file=3df1b7d57b1e63a0cbc3d585feb82dc2&download. Accessed 01 June 2019
2. Tan, G.W.-H., Lee, V.-H., Wong, C.-H., Ooi, K.-B.: Mobile shopping: the new retailing industry in the 21st century. Encyclopedia of E-Commerce Development, Implementation, and Management, pp. 1448–1460. IGI Global (2016)
3. Agrebi, S., Jallais, J.: Explain the intention to use smartphones for mobile shopping. J. Retail. Consum. Serv. **22**, 16–23 (2015)
4. Cheng, Y.-H., Huang, T.-Y.: High speed rail passengers' mobile ticketing adoption. Transp. Res. Part C Emerg. Technol. **30**, 143–160 (2013)
5. Ko, E., Kim, E.Y., Lee, E.K.: Modeling consumer adoption of mobile shopping for fashion products in Korea. Psychol. Mark. **26**, 669–687 (2009)
6. Statista: Mobile E-commerce is up and poised for further growth. https://www.statista.com/chart/13139/estimated-worldwide-mobile-e-commerce-sales/. Accessed 01 July 2019

7. Maneesoonthorn, C., Fortin, D.: Texting behaviour and attitudes toward permission mobile advertising: an empirical study of mobile users' acceptance of SMS for marketing purposes. Int. J. Mob. Mark. **1**, 66–72 (2006)
8. Yang, K.C.: Exploring factors affecting consumer intention to use mobile advertising in Taiwan. J. Int. Consum. Mark. **20**, 33–49 (2007)
9. Statista: Mobile advertising spending worldwide from 2007 to 2022. https://www.statista.com/statistics/303817/mobile-internet-advertising-revenue-worldwide/. Accessed 01 Aug 2019
10. McCorkindale, T., Morgoch, M.: An analysis of the mobile readiness and dialogic principles on Fortune 500 mobile websites. Public Relat. Rev. **39**, 193–197 (2013)
11. San-Martín, S., López-Catalán, B., Ramón-Jerónimo, M.A.: Mobile shoppers: types, drivers, and impediments. J. Organ. Comput. Electr. Commer. **23**, 350–371 (2013)
12. Wong, C.H., Lee, H., Lim, Y.H., Chua, B.H., Tan, G.: Predicting the consumers' intention to adopt mobile shopping: an emerging market perspective. Int. J. Netw. Mob. Technol. **3**, 24–39 (2012)
13. Wong, C.H., Tan, G.W.H., Ooi, K.B., Lin, B.: Mobile shopping: the next frontier of the shopping industry? An emerging market perspective. Int. J. Mob. Commun. **13**, 92–112 (2014)
14. Chen, L.Y.: Antecedents of customer satisfaction and purchase intention with mobile shopping system use. Int. J. Serv. Oper. Manag. **15**, 259–274 (2013)
15. Zhou, T.: An empirical examination of the determinants of mobile purchase. Pers. Ubiquit. Comput. **17**, 187–195 (2013)
16. Chen, H.-J.: What drives consumers' mobile shopping? 4Ps or shopping preferences? Asia Pac. J. Mark. Logist. **30**, 797–815 (2018)
17. Chung, D., Chun, S.G., Choi, H.Y.: Empirical study on determinants for the continued use of mobile shopping apps. Issues Inf. Syst. **17**, 34–43 (2016)
18. Shankar, V., Kleijnen, M., Ramanathan, S., Rizley, R., Holland, S., Morrissey, S.: Mobile shopper marketing: key issues, current insights, and future research avenues. J. Interact. Mark. **34**, 37–48 (2016)
19. Marriott, H.R., Williams, M.D., Dwivedi, Y.K.: What do we know about consumer m-shopping behaviour? Int. J. Retail Distrib. Manag. **45**, 568–586 (2017)
20. Tamilmani, K., Rana, N.P., Dwivedi, Y.K.: Mobile application adoption predictors: systematic review of UTAUT2 studies using weight analysis. In: Al-Sharhan, S.A., et al. (eds.) I3E 2018. LNCS, vol. 11195, pp. 1–12. Springer, Cham (2018). https://doi.org/10.1007/978-3-030-02131-3_1
21. Jeyaraj, A., Rottman, J.W., Lacity, M.C.: A review of the predictors, linkages, and biases in IT innovation adoption research. J. Inf. Technol. **21**, 1–23 (2006)
22. Tamilmani, K., Rana, N.P., Dwivedi, Y.K.: Use of 'habit' is not a habit in understanding individual technology adoption: a review of UTAUT2 based empirical studies. In: Elbanna, A., Dwivedi, Y.K., Bunker, D., Wastell, D. (eds.) TDIT 2018. IAICT, vol. 533, pp. 277–294. Springer, Cham (2019). https://doi.org/10.1007/978-3-030-04315-5_19
23. Tamilmani, K., Rana, N.P., Dwivedi, Y.K., Sahu, G.P., Roderick, S.: Exploring the role of 'price value' for understanding consumer adoption of technology: a review and meta-analysis of UTAUT2 based empirical studies. In:Twenty-Second Pacific Asia Conference on Information Systems Japan (2018)
24. Tamilmani, K., Rana, N.P., Dwivedi, Y.K.: A systematic review of citations of UTAUT2 article and its usage trends. In: Kar, A.K., et al. (eds.) I3E 2017. LNCS, vol. 10595, pp. 38–49. Springer, Cham (2017). https://doi.org/10.1007/978-3-319-68557-1_5

25. Tamilmani, K., Rana, N.P., Alryalat, M.A.A., Al-Khowaiter, W.A., Dwivedi, Y.K.: Social media research in the context of emerging markets: an analysis of extant literature from information systems perspective. J. Adv. Manag. Res. **15**, 115–129 (2018)
26. Dwivedi, Y.K., Rana, N.P., Jeyaraj, A., Clement, M., Williams, M.D.: Re-examining the unified theory of acceptance and use of technology (UTAUT): towards a revised theoretical model. Inf. Syst. Front. **21**, 719–734 (2019)
27. Ismagilova, E., Slade, E.L., Rana, N.P., Dwivedi, Y.K.: The effect of electronic word of mouth communications on intention to buy: a meta-analysis. Inf. Syst. Front. 1–24 (2019). https://doi.org/10.1007/s10796-019-09924-y
28. Dwivedi, Y.K., Ismagilova, E., Rana, N.P., Weerakkody, V.: Use of social media by b2b companies: systematic literature review and suggestions for future research. In: Pappas, I.O., Mikalef, P., Dwivedi, Y.K., Jaccheri, L., Krogstie, J., Mäntymäki, M. (eds.) I3E 2019. LNCS, vol. 11701, pp. 345–355. Springer, Cham (2019). https://doi.org/10.1007/978-3-030-29374-1_28
29. Ismagilova, E., Slade, E., Williams, M.: Persuasiveness of eWOM communications: literature review and suggestions for future research. In: Dwivedi, Y.K., et al. (eds.) I3E 2016. LNCS, vol. 9844, pp. 354–359. Springer, Cham (2016). https://doi.org/10.1007/978-3-319-45234-0_32
30. Waseem, D., Biggemann, S., Garry, T.: Value co-creation: the role of actor competence. Ind. Mark. Manag. **70**, 5–12 (2018)
31. Juntunen, M., Ismagilova, E., Oikarinen, E.-L.: B2B brands on Twitter: engaging users with a varying combination of social media content objectives, strategies, and tactics. Ind. Mark. Manag. (2019). https://doi.org/10.1016/j.indmarman.2019.03.001
32. Chang, H.H., Wong, K.H., Li, S.Y.: Applying push-pull-mooring to investigate channel switching behaviors: M-shopping self-efficacy and switching costs as moderators. Electron. Commer. Res. Appl. **24**, 50–67 (2017)
33. Groß, M.: Mobile shopping loyalty: the salient moderating role of normative and functional compatibility beliefs. Technol. Soc. **55**, 146–159 (2018)
34. Aldás-Manzano, J., Ruiz-Mafé, C., Sanz-Blas, S.: Exploring individual personality factors as drivers of M-shopping acceptance. Ind. Manag. Data Syst. **109**, 739–757 (2009)
35. Groß, M.: Exploring the acceptance of technology for mobile shopping: an empirical investigation among Smartphone users. Int. Rev. Retail Distrib. Consum. Res. **25**, 215–235 (2015)
36. Venkatesh, V., Morris, M.G., Davis, G.B., Davis, F.D.: User acceptance of information technology: toward a unified view. MIS Q. **27**, 425–478 (2003)
37. Gupta, A., Arora, N.: Understanding determinants and barriers of mobile shopping adoption using behavioral reasoning theory. J. Retail. Consum. Serv. **36**, 1–7 (2017)
38. Kim, M.J., Chung, N., Lee, C.-K., Preis, M.W.: Dual-route of persuasive communications in mobile tourism shopping. Telemat. Inform. **33**, 293–308 (2016)
39. Gao, L., Waechter, K.A., Bai, X.: Understanding consumers' continuance intention towards mobile purchase: a theoretical framework and empirical study–a case of China. Comput. Hum. Behav. **53**, 249–262 (2015)
40. Hew, J.-J., Leong, L.-Y., Tan, G.W.-H., Lee, V.-H., Ooi, K.-B.: Mobile social tourism shopping: a dual-stage analysis of a multi-mediation model. Tour. Manag. **66**, 121–139 (2018)
41. Celik, H., Kocaman, R.: Roles of self-monitoring, fashion involvement and technology readiness in an individual's propensity to use mobile shopping. J. Syst. Inf. Technol. **19**, 166–182 (2017)
42. Amoroso, D.L.: The importance of institution-based trust in mobile adoption with online shopping applications. Int. J. Technol. Diffus. (IJTD) **4**, 1–26 (2013)

43. Kim, C., Li, W., Kim, D.J.: An empirical analysis of factors influencing M-shopping use. Int. J. Hum.-Comput. Interact. **31**, 974–994 (2015)
44. Chen, Y.-M., Hsu, T.-H., Lu, Y.-J.: Impact of flow on mobile shopping intention. J. Retail. Consum. Serv. **41**, 281–287 (2018)
45. Groß, M.: Heterogeneity in consumers' mobile shopping acceptance: a finite mixture partial least squares modelling approach for exploring and characterising different shopper segments. J. Retail. Consum. Serv. **40**, 8–18 (2018)
46. Lu, H.-P., Su, P.Y.-J.: Factors affecting purchase intention on mobile shopping web sites. Internet Res. **19**, 442–458 (2009)
47. Natarajan, T., Balasubramanian, S.A., Kasilingam, D.L.: The moderating role of device type and age of users on the intention to use mobile shopping applications. Technol. Soc. **53**, 79–90 (2018)
48. Saprikis, V., Markos, A., Zarmpou, T., Vlachopoulou, M.: Mobile shopping consumers' behavior: an exploratory study and review. J. Theor. Appl. Electron. Commer. Res. **13**, 71–90 (2018)
49. Shang, D., Wu, W.: Understanding mobile shopping consumers' continuance intention. Ind. Manag. Data Syst. **117**, 213–227 (2017)
50. Chau, N.N., Seshadri, S., Broekemier, G., Pamornpathomkul, S.: An exploratory study of mobile shopping behaviors of young adults in Thailand. J. Internet Commer. **17**, 339–355 (2018)
51. Lu, J., Yu, C.-S., Liu, C., Wei, J.: Comparison of mobile shopping continuance intention between China and USA from an espoused cultural perspective. Comput. Hum. Behav. **75**, 130–146 (2017)
52. Tan, G.W.-H., Ooi, K.-B.: Gender and age: do they really moderate mobile tourism shopping behavior? Telemat. Inform. **35**, 1617–1642 (2018)
53. Yang, K., Forney, J.C.: The moderating role of consumer technology anxiety in mobile shopping adoption: differential effects of facilitating conditions and social influences. J. Electron. Commer. Res. **14**, 334 (2013)
54. Yang, K.: Determinants of US consumer mobile shopping services adoption: implications for designing mobile shopping services. J. Consum. Mark. **27**, 262–270 (2010)
55. Hung, M.-C., Yang, S.-T., Hsieh, T.-C.: An examination of the determinants of mobile shopping continuance. Int. J. Electron. Bus. Manag. **10**, 29 (2012)
56. Kang, C.-R., Hung, M.-C., Yang, S.-T., Hsieh, T.-C., Tang, S.-M.: Factors affecting the continued intention of mobile shopping. In: 2010 IEEE International Conference on Industrial Engineering and Engineering Management, pp. 710–713. IEEE (2010)
57. Groß, M.: Impediments to mobile shopping continued usage intention: a trust-risk-relationship. J. Retail. Consum. Serv. **33**, 109–119 (2016)
58. Marriott, H.R., Williams, M.D.: Exploring consumers perceived risk and trust for mobile shopping: a theoretical framework and empirical study. J. Retail. Consum. Serv. **42**, 133–146 (2018)
59. Prodanova, J., San-Martín, S., Jimenez, N.: Are you technologically prepared for mobile shopping? Serv. Ind. J. 1–23 (2018). https://doi.org/10.1080/02642069.2018.1492561
60. Yang, K.: Consumer technology traits in determining mobile shopping adoption: an application of the extended theory of planned behavior. J. Retail. Consum. Serv. **19**, 484–491 (2012)
61. Bandura, A.: Social Foundation of Thought and Action: A Social-Cognitive View. Prentice Hall, Englewood Cliffs (1986)
62. Ajzen, I.: The theory of planned behavior. Organ. Behav. Hum. Decis. Process. **50**, 179–211 (1991)
63. Rogers, E.: Diffusion of Innovations. Free Press, New York (1995)

64. Davis, F.D.: Perceived usefulness, perceived ease of use, and user acceptance of information technology. MIS Q. **13**, 319–340 (1989)
65. Davis, F.D., Bagozzi, R.P., Warshaw, P.R.: Extrinsic and intrinsic motivation to use computers in the workplace. J. Appl. Soc. Psychol. **22**, 1111–1132 (1992)
66. Peter, J.P., Ryan, M.J.: An investigation of perceived risk at the brand level. J. Mark. Res. **13**, 184–188 (1976)
67. Agarwal, R., Prasad, J.: A conceptual and operational definition of personal innovativeness in the domain of information technology. Inf. Syst. Res. **9**, 204–215 (1998)
68. Oliver, R.L.: Measurement and evaluation of satisfaction processes in retail settings. J. Retail. **57**, 25–48 (1981)
69. McKnight, D.H., Chervany, N.L.: What trust means in e-commerce customer relationships: an interdisciplinary conceptual typology. Int. J. Electron. Commer. **6**, 35–59 (2001)
70. Bhattacherjee, A.: Understanding information systems continuance: an expectation-confirmation model. MIS Q. **25**, 351–370 (2001)
71. DeLone, W.H., McLean, E.R.: Information systems success: the quest for the dependent variable. Inf. Syst. Res. **3**, 60–95 (1992)
72. Chen, L.Y.: The quality of mobile shopping system and its impact on purchase intention and performance. Int. J. Manag. Inf. Technol. **5**, 23 (2013)
73. Wu, J., Du, H.: Toward a better understanding of behavioral intention and system usage constructs. Eur. J. Inf. Syst. **21**, 680–698 (2012)

# Social Commerce Adoption Predictors: A Review and Weight Analysis

Prianka Sarker, Laurie Hughe[⊠], Yogesh K. Dwivedi,
and Nripendra P. Rana

Emerging Markets Research Centre (EMaRC), School of Management,
Swansea University Bay Campus, Swansea SA1 8EN, UK
{937449, d. l. hughes, y. k. dwivedi}@swansea. ac. uk,
ykdwivedi@gmail. com, Nrananp@gmail. com

**Abstract.** Social commerce is a rapidly growing platform of e-commerce that utilises social media and online social interaction to build brand awareness and increase sales. Buying and selling through social media can create a reliable and sustainable platform for buyers and vendors, offering an alternative platform to traditional online approaches. Research on social commerce began to achieve traction in 2006 and has grown since with a significant focus from academics who have offered new insight to many of the key topics. This study seeks to offer an additional contribution to the literature by analysing the predictors of consumer adoption of social commerce from existing studies by employing a weight analysis technique. The analysis considered seven dependent variables (along with their best and worst predictors) that are most frequently examined and are relevant to consumer adoption. The review presented in this study suggests that the intention to purchase is the most frequently examined dependent variable and that *trust* in the social commerce context is a key factor.

**Keywords:** Social commerce · Weight analysis · Literature review

## 1 Introduction

Development and growth of social media platforms (such as Facebook, Twitter, LinkedIn and Instagram) have given rise to a new business model for e-commerce, frequently known as social commerce. Social commerce utilises web 2.0 technology and a specially designed infrastructure to support online communications and user contributions to assist in the acquisition of products and services [1]. Social commerce technologies are not only delivering a platform for communication between consumers to vendors as well as consumers to consumers but also creating significant challenges for scholars that have led to the development and validation of new models and theories. According to e-commerce marketing statistics, 74% of online consumers are relying on social media to guide their purchases, and 60% of businesses have gained new customers through social media within the US [2]. This highlights the importance of social media for facilitating information diffusion and augmenting towards further growth of e-commerce. Social commerce has proved to be an essential platform for online shoppers where consumers can view the product, read reviews, analyse key

© IFIP International Federation for Information Processing 2020
Published by Springer Nature Switzerland AG 2020
M. Hattingh et al. (Eds.): I3E 2020, LNCS 12066, pp. 176–191, 2020.
https://doi.org/10.1007/978-3-030-44999-5_15

information and browse special offers [3]. The use of social commerce drives an active engagement that regularly presents relevant product content within the consumer's news feed and social media interactions. In this way, consumers can interact with others using likes, comments and tagging posts within their friend network. Moreover, social commerce can help to generate loyal and sustainable customers via word of mouth and by supporting other customers to make timely buying decisions [4]. There are six dimensions of social commerce that create a sustainable social commerce platform: social shopping; rating and review; recommendation and referrals; forums and communities; social media optimisation; social ads and applications [5]. Due to emerging social commerce applications and increasing interest in this topic, researchers have conducted the number of studies to offer an additional contribution and facilitate wider adoption of social commerce platforms. However, in this study, we analyse the role of several different antecedents of social commerce intention and adoption that have been examined within the literature. The analysis revealed that the effect of such antecedents has been inconsistent across different studies in terms of significance and coefficient relationships between independent and dependent variables. No study has yet to conduct a consolidated view of the effect of various antecedents of social commerce intention, use behaviour and other related dependent variables. Also, no study has an attempt to understand the value of the relationships of social commerce adoption. The research model is one of the essential parts of the research. Therefore, it is also essential to understand various independent and dependent variables. However, this study based on social commerce, the research focuses on independent/dependent variables and relationship that influence social commerce adoption. The study is providing a robust view of the variables that will be supportive of creating a concrete research model. The objectives of this study are to summarise the relationships and analyse the weight of the relationship using the weight analysis technique. This study to gain new insight into the various predictors of social commerce related dependent variables including *intention, trust, satisfaction, attitude and urge to buy impulsively.*

To develop the objectives, this study undertook the following steps: (1) Identify empirical studies that utilised different models, and associated antecedents (predictors) for understanding consumer adoption of social commerce, (2) Conduct a weight analysis using results from exiting studies to determine the importance of various predictors. This paper is structured as follows. Section 2 of this paper briefly describes the research method employed to conduct this study. Section 3 then presents the results from the weight analysis, and the paper is concluded within Sect. 4.

## 2  Research Method

The literature has highlighted several types of review studies for a deeper understanding of this area. This review studies were attempt weight analysis method, investigated the theories and model and conducted adoption researches. This studies based on: specific journals e.g. [6–9]; methods e.g. [10]; theories and models e.g. [11–15] and topics e.g. [16–29]. Searches were undertaken using Scopus database the following set of keywords: "Social commerce" "S-Commerce" OR "F–Commerce" AND title ABS Key "Adoption" OR "Acceptance" OR "Usage" OR "Use Behaviour"

OR "Intention" OR "Purchase". We make sure the keywords are included in abstracts or title or keywords of the journal paper. This search returned 166 articles. Therefore, we eliminated the conference paper, internet and newspaper blogs and only considered journal articles. Then we separated qualitative and quantitative studies and used quantitative studies for applying weight analysis technique. However, 68 studies were not related to social commerce adoption. Finally, we focus on 73 journal articles which are related to social commerce adoption and published from 2006 to 2019.

## 3  Weight Analysis

Weight analysis is a practical approach to calculate the importance of predictors. Weight analysis determines the inductive and predictive power of an independent variable over the dependent variable. This technique helps to rank the variables to understand the most important and least important relationships. Also, this technique supports to calculate each relationship, significant level and the predictors' weight. In this study, the weight analysis technique finds out different relationships that influence social commerce adoption. Therefore, the independent and dependent variables, which are the most important aspects of developing a perfect adoption model. Using weight analysis, we summarised all the relationships and segregated based on significant and non-significant relationship. Therefore, the weight result indicated the value of the relationships. Therefore, all the relationships, variables and weight values will be helpful for the researcher to choose appropriate variables to develop a suitable research model for further studies. The weight analysis approach employed within this study was adopted from Jeyaraj et al. [30] and Tamilmani et al. [31] where the analysis of the weights of each relationship is developed from the dependent and independent variables. This study has selected the following most frequently examined dependent variables: Intention to purchase, Trust, Social commerce intention, Behavioural intention, Urge to buy impulsively, Attitude and Satisfaction. Each of the listed tables that present the weight analysis calculates the antecedents of a specific dependent variable, the total number of times a particular relationship has been examined and how many times each relationship is found to be significant and non-significant. The weight columns present the weight analysis of each of the relationships. The weight analysis provides four different values: (a) "+1" indicate the significant relationships between independent and dependent variables and hypothesised in positive direction, (b) "−1" indicate the non-significant relationships between independent and dependent variables and hypothesised in negative direction, (c) "0" suggest that the relationship of independent and dependent variable is insignificant, (d) "Blank" when the relationships were not examined [31]. Of the 73 articles examined, 251 are unique and can be described as exhibiting significant relationships and 32 were categorised as non-significant relationships. These relationships were aligned to the following seven dependent variables: *intention to purchase (Table 1), trust (Table 2), behavioural intention (Table 3), social commerce intention (Table 4), satisfaction (Table 5), urge to buy impulsively (Table 6) and attitude (Table 7).*

## 3.1    Intention to Purchase

Table 1 lists 32 out of 73 studies and highlights 108 individual relationships. The study found 63 independent variables which were aligned to the dependent variable - *Intention to purchase*. However, identical relationships that were examined in five or more studies are considered as strong utilised relationships and independent variables and were considered to be the best predictor of the dependent variable. Additionally, less than four of the relationships were considered as experimental variables with a weight of 0.80 or above., Independent variables could be considered as a promising predictor when used in less the five studies and have the perfect weight of 1 [31]. In this study, the best predictor found *trust* as an independent variable utilised maximum time with *purchase intention* (examined eight times) with all studies finding a significant

**Table 1.**  Weight analysis summary for intention to purchase

| IV | Sig | Citation | Non-Sig | Citation | Total | Weight |
|---|---|---|---|---|---|---|
| Trust | 8 | Kim and park [32]; Hajli et al. [33]; Makmor et al. [34]; Adwan [35]; Hajli et al. [36]; Faratin and Rodríguez [37]; Lee and Choi [38]; Zhao et al. [39] | 0 | | 8 | 1 |
| Familiarity | 4 | Adwan [35]; Hajli et al. [36]; Ng [40]; Gibreel et al. [41] | 0 | | 4 | 1 |
| Recommendations and referrals | 2 | Makmor and alam [42]; Mikalef et al. [43] | 1 | Li et al. [51] | 3 | 0.66 |
| Trust toward member | 2 | Farivar et al. [44]; Chen and Shen [45] | 0 | | 2 | 1 |
| Brand trust | 2 | Zhao et al. [39]; Erdoğmuş [46] | 0 | | 2 | 1 |
| Social presence | 2 | Adwan [35]; Hajli et al. [36] | 0 | | 2 | 1 |
| Swift guanxi | 2 | Lin et al. [47]; Yang [48] | 0 | | 2 | 1 |
| Familiarity | 2 | Hajli et al. [36]; Gibreel et al. [41] | 0 | | 2 | 1 |
| Informational support | 1 | Makmor and Alam [42] | 1 | Li et al. [51] | 2 | 0.5 |
| Perceived commerce risk | 0 | | 2 | Farivar et al. [44] Gan et al. [50] | 2 | 1 |
| Social commerce constructs | 1 | Hajli et al. [49] | 1 | Li et al [51] | 2 | 0.5 |
| Usefulness | 1 | Lee and Choi [38] | 1 | Gibreel et al. [41] | 2 | .50 |

**The following constructs had been tested by only one study and their effect was significant with resulting weight of 1:** Trust toward website; Mutual understanding; Relationship Harmony; Reciprocal favour; Trust in social network community; Closeness; WOM Content; Observe Consumer Purchase; Positive Valence WOM; Negative valence WOM; Social Desire; Commercial Desire; Good Friend; Simple friend; Non-reportable stranger; Re-routable stranger; Community commitment; Trust towards community; Trust in product recommendation; Brand engagement; Form factor; Intention to search; Para social interaction; EWOM information; Intuitive evaluation; Social identity; Rating and Reviews; Socializing; Product selection; Trust in sellers; Usage behaviour; System trust towards social commerce apps; Utilitarian value; Social value; Hedonic value; Social commerce information seeking; Innovativeness; Guanxi elements; Perceived value; Customers' experience; Discount rate; Social media product browsing; Positive; Observing consumer purchasing; Heuristic factors; Systemic factors; Attitude; Trust in sellers; Forums and Communities; Attitude towards eWOM; EWOM engagement; Social commerce information seeking

**The following constructs had been tested by only one study and their effect was nonsignificant with resulting weight of 0:** Perceived ease of use; Income; Emotional support; Information availability; Customer loyalty; Particularized trust towards social commerce members; Electronic inventiveness; Scarcity of time; Scarcity of quality; Provisional coupon

effect. *Familiarity* has been utilised in four instances and all have found significant. Five independent variables occur in two *instances with buying intention, and those are Recommendations and referrals, Trust toward member, brand trust, social presence and Swift Guanxi* with weight "0". Additionally, 74 independent variables have occurred with a weight of "1". *Recommendations and referrals* have been utilised three times and found to be significant in two studies and non-significant in one study with a weight "0.66". *Informational support, perceived commerce risk, social commerce construct* and *usefulness* analysis with *intention to buy* found two non-significant relationships. The weight result found "0.50" in three of those relationships. Finally, ten relationships found non-significant with weight "0" (See Table 1).

## 3.2   Trust

Table 2 represents 24 studies and 52 relationships on the subject of *trust*. The study found six significant relationships among *information quality* and *trust*. Additionally, five studies found significant associations between *relationship quality* and *trust*. However, three independent variables: *emotional support, social presence, familiarity* have occurred four times with *trust* and found significant relationships. The weighted analysis of the above relationships results "1" and were found as best predictors. Four hypotheses (Reputation, communication, size and WOM referrals) appeared twice and found significant relationships with weight "1". The product price has found one significant and one non-significant relationship with the weight result "0.50". The 19 independent variables found highlighted a relationship towards *trust* and found a significant correlation with weight "1". Finally, two more relationships found to be non-significant with a weight result "0" which are the worst predictors in the study.

**Table 2.**  Weight analysis summary for trust

| IV | Sig | Citation | Non-Sig | Citation | Total | Weight |
|---|---|---|---|---|---|---|
| Information quality | 6 | Lu et al. [52]; Faratin and Rodríguez [37]; Lin et al. [24]; Kim and Noh [34]; Shanmugam et al. [32]; Li et al. [51] | 0 | | 6 | 1 |
| Relationship quality | 5 | Liang and Turban [1]; Zhang et al. [54]; Hajli [55]; Sheikh et al. [56]; Tajvidi et al. [57] | 0 | | 5 | 1 |
| Emotional support | 4 | Makmor et al. [34]; Lin et al. [47]; Shanmugam et al. [53]; Li [51] | 0 | | 4 | 1 |
| Social presence | 4 | Adwan [35]; Li et al. [51]; Hajli [58]; Lu et al. [52] | 0 | | 4 | 1 |

*(continued)*

**Table 2.** (*continued*)

| IV | Sig | Citation | Non-Sig | Citation | Total | Weight |
|---|---|---|---|---|---|---|
| Familiarity | 4 | Gibreel et al. [41]; Hajli [32]; Adwan [35]; Li [51] | 0 | | 4 | 1 |
| Reputation | 2 | Lu et al. [52]; Kim and Noh [59] | 0 | | 2 | 1 |
| Communication | 2 | Lu et al. [52]; Kim and Noh [59] | 0 | | 2 | 1 |
| Size | 2 | Lu et al. [52]; Kim and Noh [59]. | 0 | | 2 | 1 |
| Word-of-Mouth referrals | 2 | Lu et al. [52]; Gibreel et al. [41] | 0 | | 2 | 1 |
| product price | 1 | Yahia et al. [60] | 1 | Gibreel et al. [41] | 2 | .50 |

**The following constructs had been tested by only one study and their effect was significant with resulting weight of 1:** Internal similarity, External similarity, Closeness, Social presence of interaction with sellers, Perception of others, Trust in sellers, Susceptibility reviews, General credibility, Perceived Security, E-WOM information, Perceived security, Perceived ease of use, Trust in product, Symbolic value, Feedback, Interactivity, Social Commerce Constructs, Transaction Safety

**The following constructs had been tested by only one study and their effect was nonsignificant with resulting weight of 0:** Persuasiveness, Economic Feasibility

## 3.3 Behavioural Intention

Table 3 presents 11 studies on *behavioural intention* as the dependent variable. The literature analysis found 26 significant relationships among various independent variables with *behavioural intention* and six non-significant relationships. The best predictor is perceived usefulness which was appeared in six studies with the weight "1". Perceived ease of use hypnosis in four studies with significant relationship and one study found non-significant relationship that weight ".080". Risk appeared in three studies and weight "0.66". Three studies quantified the factors - effort expectancy, facilitating conditions and social influence with *behavioural intention* as significant and defined one as non-significant with weight result "0.50". The worst relationship found among Perceived connective affordances and *behavioural intention* with weight result "0".

**Table 3.** Weight analysis summary for behavioural intention

| IV | Sig | Citation | Non-Sig | Citation | Total | Weight |
|---|---|---|---|---|---|---|
| Perceived usefulness | 6 | Williams [61]; Biucky et al. [62]; Hajli et al. [58]; Featherman [63]; Shin et al. [66]; Tello et al. [64] | 0 | | 6 | 1 |
| Perceived ease of use | 4 | Kim and Noh [59]; Hajli [58]; Biucky et al. [62]; Featherman and Hajli [63] | 1 | Williams [61] | 5 | .80 |
| Risk | 2 | Biucky et al. [62]; Tello et al. [64] | 1 | Featherman and Hajli [63] | 3 | .66 |
| Effort expectancy | 1 | Gatautis and Medziausiene [65] | 1 | Sheikh et al. [68] | 2 | .50 |
| Facilitating conditions | 1 | Gatautis and Medziausiene [65] | 1 | Sheikh et al. [68] | 2 | .50 |
| Social influence | 1 | Gatautis and Medziausiene [65] | 1 | Sheikh et al. [68] | 2 | .50 |
| Perceived enjoyment | 2 | Shin [66]; Akman and Mishra [67] | 0 | | 2 | 1 |
| Subjective norm | 2 | Featherman and Hajli [63]; Shin [66] | 0 | | 2 | 1 |

**The following constructs had been tested by only one study and their effect was significant with resulting weight of 1:** Learning and training, perceived hedonic affordances, perceived utilitarian affordance, Innovativeness, Convenience, Perceived Social pressure, Perceived satisfaction, Perceived awareness, perceived Ethics, Trust perception person, The website's reputation, Website visual and design, Attitude, Social commerce constructs, Price saving orientation, Hedonic motivations, Habit, Performance expectancy

**The following constructs had been tested by only one study and their effect was non-significant with resulting weight of 0:** Perceived connective affordances

## 3.4    Social Commerce Intention

*Social commerce intention* quantified as dependent variables appeared in 11 studies with 40 relationships. However, 35 relationships were found to be significant, and five relationships defined as non-significant. Table 4 lists various independent variables with the relationship between *social commerce intentions*. Social support with *social commerce intention* was found to be the best predictors. The relationships have appeared in five studies with weight "1". Therefore, Flow, relationship quality, website quality and social presence appeared three times with significant relationships. Informational support, trust towards community and emotional support found twice with significant relationships as well. However, all the relationships are weight "1" which is found as best predictors. Finally, the worst predictors are Habit, forums and communities, recommendations and referrals, perceived interactivity and perceived personalization with *social commerce intention* found the negative relationship and weight "0."

**Table 4.** Weight analysis summary for social commerce intention

| IV | Sig | Citation | Non-Sig | Citation | Total | Weight |
|----|-----|----------|---------|----------|-------|--------|
| Social support | 5 | Liang and Turban [1]; Hajli [55]; Zhang et al. [54]; Sheikh et al. [28]; Hajli and Sims [74]; Hajli [55]; Liang et al. [69]; Zhang et al. [54] sheikh et al. [56]; Hajli and Sims [70] | 0 | | 5 | 1 |
| Flow | 3 | Zhang et al. [71]; Molinillo et al. [72]; Bhat and Singh [73] | 0 | | 3 | 1 |
| Relationship quality | 3 | Hajli [55]; Liang et al. [69]; sheikh et al. [56] | 0 | | 3 | 1 |
| Web site quality | 3 | Liang and Turban. [1]; Molinillo et al. [72]; Bhat and Singh [43] | 0 | | 3 | 1 |
| Social presence | 3 | Zhang et al. [71]; Molinillo et al. [72]; Bhat and Singh [43] | 0 | | 3 | 1 |
| Informational support | 2 | Molinillo et al. [72]; Lal [74] | 0 | | 2 | 1 |
| Trust towards community | 2 | Lal [74]; Goraya et al. [75] | 0 | | 2 | 1 |
| Emotional support | 2 | Molinillo et al. [72]; Bhat and Singh [43] | 0 | | 2 | 1 |

**The following constructs had been tested by only one study and their effect was significant with resulting weight of 1:** Social commerce constructs, Rating and reviews, Community commitment, Trust towards Members, Service quality, Perceived Sociability, Trust in Platform, Ease of navigation, Hedonic motivation, Perceived ease of use, facilitating conditions, Trust in the s-vendor

**The following constructs had been tested by only one study and their effect was non-significant with resulting weight of 0:** Perceived personalization, Perceived interactivity, Recommendations and Referrals, Forums and Communities, Habit

### 3.5 Satisfaction

Nine studies used satisfaction as dependent variables and are presented in Table 5. In this study we found 19 significant relationships and one non-significant relationship. The study found the best predictors are Social support, utilitarian, hedonic, relationship quality and confirmation that appeared twice. However, the relationships are found significant with weight "1". Information quality with satisfaction appeared once as a significant and once as a non-significant predictor and found the weight "0.50". Moreover, Perceived usefulness, trust, service quality, system quality, physical environment quality, outcome quality, interaction quality, perceived risk has relationship with satisfaction and result significant with weight "1". This study did not find any non-significant relationships within the literature.

**Table 5.**  Weight analysis summary for satisfaction

| IV | Sig | Citation | Non-Sig | Citation | Total | Weight |
|---|---|---|---|---|---|---|
| Social support | 2 | Gan et al. [50]; Osatuyi et al. [76] | 0 | | 2 | 1 |
| Utilitarian | 2 | Gan et al. [50]; Osatuyi et al. [76] | 0 | | 2 | 1 |
| Hedonic | 2 | Gan et al. [50]; Osatuyi et al. [76] | 0 | | 2 | 1 |
| Relationship quality | 2 | Liang and Turban [1]; Zhang et al. [54] | 0 | | 2 | 1 |
| Confirmation | 2 | Hew et al. [77, 78] | 0 | | 2 | 1 |
| Information quality | 1 | Vongsraluang and Bhatiasevi [79] | 1 | Cho and Son [80] | 2 | 0.5 |

**The following constructs had been tested by only one study and their effect was significant with resulting weight of 1:** Perceived usefulness, trust, Service quality, system quality, physical environment quality, outcome quality, interaction quality, perceived risk

## 3.6   Urge to Buy Impulsively

Urge to buy impulsively was referenced in six different studies with 12 significant relationships and one non-significant relationship. Table 6 presents the urge to buy impulsively as dependent variables with Hedonic shopping value and impulsiveness as independent variables. Both of the relationships appeared twice and found significant predictors with weight "1". However, the independent variables such as *consumer attitude, arousal, pleasure, affective trust in recommender, serendipity information, scarcity, para social interaction* and *perceived enjoyment* relationship with the *urge to buy impulsively* found significant with weight "1". Therefore, the worst predictor is *utilitarian shopping* value with weight "0".

**Table 6.** Weight analysis summary for urge to buy impulsively

| IV | Sig | Citation | Non-Sig | Citation | Total | Weight |
|---|---|---|---|---|---|---|
| Hedonic shopping value | 2 | Chung et al. [81]; Xiang et al. [82] | | | 2 | 1 |
| Impulsiveness | 2 | Chung et al. [81]; Xiang et al. [82] | | | 2 | 1 |

**The following constructs had been tested by only one study and their effect was significant with resulting weight of 1:** Consumer attitude, arousal, Pleasure, Affective trust in recommender, Serendipity information, Scarcity, Para social interaction, Perceived enjoyment

**The following constructs had been tested by only one study and their effect was non-significant with resulting weight of 0:** Utilitarian shopping value

### 3.7 Attitude

Table 7 has listed consumer *attitude* towards social commerce. Five studies used *attitude* as a dependent variable. In this study, the best predictor is perceived enjoyment with *attitude* that appeared in two studies and found significant relationships. However, *Usefulness, Ease of use, Social interaction, Vendor trust, Social networking site trust, Systemic factors, Heuristic factors, Perceived benefit, Trust in the initiator, Peer norm, Trustworthiness* and *Attractiveness with attitude* weight "1".

**Table 7.** Weight analysis summary for attitude

| IV | Sig | Citation | Non-Sig | Citation | Total | Weight |
|---|---|---|---|---|---|---|
| Enjoyment | 2 | Shin [66]; Cho and Son [80] | 0 | | 2 | 1 |

**The following constructs had been tested by only one study and their effect was significant with resulting weight of 1:** Usefulness, Ease of use, Social interaction, Vendor trust, Social networking site trust, Systemic factors, Heuristic factors, Perceived benefit, Trust in the initiator, Peer norm, Trustworthiness, Attractiveness

## 4  Discussion and Conclusion

This study conducted a weight analysis technique to determine the importance of various predictors of consumer adoption of social commerce. However, it is essential that a robust research model needs reliable variables, and this study provided a summary of those variables. The results revealed the most important independent and dependent variables that influence social commerce adoption. Using weight analysis technique, the study finds out the different value of the predictors. The study found Trust, behavioural intention, social commerce intention, urge to buy impulsively, satisfaction and attitude that used in maximum studies that influence social commerce. The weight analysis has identified the best, moderate and worst predictors of consumer adoption for social commerce. The analysis of this study found that Trust to purchase intention, information quality with Trust, social support with social commerce intention and satisfaction, informational quality with behavioural intention, perceived enjoyment with attitude and hedonic shopping value with the urge to buy are the best predictors. There is no study without limitation. However, this study points out some limitation and recommend future step for the scholar to take forward this study. Firstly, the study has considered journal papers. Therefore, future research could involve conference papers to minimise publication bias. Secondly, the study did not include any control variables. However, future research can separately analyse them and can showcase their impact on the independent/dependent variables. Thirdly, this study considers the essential variables and relationship that influence social commerce adoption. However, some other variables appeared in less study. A future study could involve those for a better view. Lastly, the study considered the weight analysis method. Therefore, Future research can extend this study further using a different method such as Meta-analysis with the combination of weight analysis.

# References

1. Liang, T.P., Ho, Y.T., Li, Y.W., Turban, E.: What drives social commerce: the role of social support and relationship quality. Int. J. Electron. Commer. **16**(2), 69–90 (2011)
2. Oragui, D.: Social Commerce: 8 Benefits for Your Business **30**(2), 1–3(2019). Blog. salesandorders.com.blog.salesandorders.com/social-commerce-benefits
3. Search Engine Journal. 15 Must-Have Features for Ecommerce Sites (2019). searchenginejournal.com/ecommerce-guide/must-have-website-features
4. Stephen, A.T., Toubia, O.: Deriving value from social commerce networks. J. Mark. Res. **47**(2), 215–228 (2010)
5. Shadkam, M., O'Hara, J.: Social commerce dimensions: the potential leverage for marketers. J. Internet Bank. Commer. **18**(1), 1–14 (1970)
6. Avison, D.E., Dwivedi, Y.K., Fitzgerald, G., Powell, P.: The beginnings of a new era: time to reflect on 17 years of the ISJ. Inf. Syst. J. **18**(1), 5–21 (2008)
7. Dwivedi, Y.K., Kuljis, J.: Profile of IS research published in the European journal of information systems. Eur. J. Inf. Syst. **17**(6), 678–693 (2008)
8. Dwivedi, Y.K., Lal, B., Mustafee, N., Williams, M.D.: Profiling a decade of Information Systems Frontiers' research. Inf. Syst. Front. **11**(1), 87 (2009)
9. Dwivedi, Y.K., Kiang, M., Williams, M.D., Lal, B.: Profiling electronic commerce research published in the journal of electronic commerce research. J. Electron. Commer. Res. **9**(2), 77–91 (2008)
10. Choudrie, J., Dwivedi, Y.K.: Investigating the research approaches for examining technology adoption issues. J. Res. Pract. **1**(1), 1 (2005)
11. Dwivedi, Y.K., Rana, N.P., Jeyaraj, A., Clement, M., Williams, M.D.: Re-examining the unified theory of acceptance and use of technology (UTAUT): towards a revised theoretical model. Inf. Syst. Front. **21**(3), 719–734 (2019)
12. Sarker, P., Kizgin, H., Rana, N.P., Dwivedi, Y.K.: Review of theoretical models and limitations of social commerce adoption literature. In: Pappas, I.O., Mikalef, P., Dwivedi, Y.K., Jaccheri, L., Krogstie, J., Mäntymäki, M. (eds.) I3E 2019. LNCS, vol. 11701, pp. 3–12. Springer, Cham (2019). https://doi.org/10.1007/978-3-030-29374-1_1

13. Weerakkody, V., Dwivedi, Y.K., Irani, Z.: The diffusion and use of institutional theory: a cross-disciplinary longitudinal literature survey. J. Inf. Technol. **24**(4), 354–368 (2009)
14. Williams, M.D., Rana, N.P., Dwivedi, Y.K.: The unified theory of acceptance and use of technology (UTAUT): a literature review. J. Enterp. Inf. Manag. **28**(3), 443–488 (2015)
15. Williams, M.D., Dwivedi, Y.K., Lal, B., Schwarz, A.: Contemporary trends and issues in IT adoption and diffusion research. J. Inf. Technol. **24**(1), 1–10 (2009)
16. Alalwan, A.A., Rana, N.P., Dwivedi, Y.K., Algharabat, R.: Social media in marketing: a review and analysis of the existing literature. Telematics Inform. **34**(7), 1177–1190 (2017)
17. Duan, Y., Edwards, J.S., Dwivedi, Y.K.: Artificial intelligence for decision making in the era of Big Data–evolution, challenges and research agenda. Int. J. Inf. Manag. **48**, 63–71 (2019)
18. Dwivedi, Y.K., Rana, N.P., Tajvidi, M., Lal, B., Sahu, G.P., Gupta, A.: Exploring the role of social media in e-government: an analysis of emerging literature. In: Proceedings of the 10th International Conference on Theory and Practice of Electronic Governance (pp. 97–106). ACM (2017)
19. Dwivedi, Y.K., Kapoor, K.K., Chen, H.: Social media marketing and advertising. Mark. Rev. **15**(3), 289–309 (2015)
20. Dwivedi, Y.K., Venkitachalam, K., Sharif, A.M., Al-Karaghouli, W., Weerakkody, V.: Research trends in knowledge management: analyzing the past and predicting the future. Inf. Syst. Manag. **28**(1), 43–56 (2011)
21. Hughes, L., Dwivedi, Y.K., Misra, S.K., Rana, N.P., Raghavan, V., Akella, V.: Blockchain research, practice and policy: applications, benefits, limitations, emerging research themes and research agenda. Int. J. Inf. Manag. **49**, 114–129 (2019)
22. Irani, Z., Gunasekaran, A., Dwivedi, Y.K.: Radio frequency identification (RFID): research trends and framework. Int. J. Prod. Res. **48**(9), 2485–2511 (2010)
23. Ismagilova, E., Slade, E., Rana, N.P., Dwivedi, Y.K.: The effect of characteristics of source credibility on consumer behaviour: a meta-analysis. J. Retail. Consum. Serv. (2019). https://doi.org/10.1016/j.jretconser.2019.01.005
24. Ismagilova, E., Hughes, L., Dwivedi, Y.K., Raman, K.R.: Smart cities: advances in research—an information systems perspective. Int. J. Inf. Manag. **47**, 88–100 (2019)
25. Kapoor, K.K., Tamilmani, K., Rana, N.P., Patil, P., Dwivedi, Y.K., Nerur, S.: Advances in social media research: past, present and future. Inf. Syst. Front. **20**(3), 531–558 (2018)
26. Kapoor, K.K., Dwivedi, Y.K., Williams, M.D.: Rogers' innovation adoption attributes: a systematic review and synthesis of existing research. Inf. Syst. Manag. **31**(1), 74–91 (2014)
27. Kapoor, K.K., Dwivedi, Y.K., Williams, M.D.: Innovation adoption attributes: a review and synthesis of research findings. Eur. J. Innov. Manag. **17**(3), 327–348 (2014)
28. Rana, N.P., Dwivedi, Y.K., Williams, M.D.: A meta-analysis of existing research on citizen adoption of e-government. Inf. Syst. Front. **17**(3), 547–563 (2015)
29. Shiau, W.L., Dwivedi, Y.K., Lai, H.H.: Examining the core knowledge on facebook. Int. J. Inf. Manag. **43**, 52–63 (2018)
30. Jeyaraj, A., Rottman, J.W., Lacity, M.C.: A review of the predictors, linkages, and biases in IT innovation adoption research. J. Inf. Technol. **21**(1), 1–23 (2006)
31. Tamilmani, K., Rana, N.P., Dwivedi, Y.K.: Mobile application adoption predictors: systematic review of UTAUT2 studies using weight analysis. In: Al-Sharhan, S.A., et al. (eds.) I3E 2018. LNCS, vol. 11195, pp. 1–12. Springer, Cham (2018). https://doi.org/10.1007/978-3-030-02131-3_1
32. Kim, S., Park, H.: Effects of various characteristics of social commerce (s-commerce) on consumers' trust and trust performance. Int. J. Inf. Manag. **33**(2), 318–332 (2013)

33. Hajli, N., Shanmugam, M., Powell, P., Love, P.E.: A study on the continuance participation in on-line communities with social commerce perspective. Technol. Forecast. Soc. Change **96**(2), 232–241 (2015)
34. Makmor, N., Alam, S.S., Aziz, N.A.: Social support, trust and purchase intention in social commerce era. Int. J. Supply Chain Manag. **7**(5), 572–581 (2018)
35. Al-adwan, A.S.: Novel research framework for social commerce purchase intentions. J. Theor. Appl. Inf. Technol. **96**(14), 28–29 (2018)
36. Hajli, N., Sims, J., Zadeh, A.H., Richard, M.O.: A social commerce investigation of the role of trust in a social networking site on purchase intentions. J. Bus. Res. **71**(1), 133–141 (2017)
37. Faratin, P., Rodríguez-Aguilar, J.A.: Agent-Mediated Electronic Commerce VI: Theories for and Engineering of Distributed Mechanisms and Systems (2006)
38. Lee, H., Choi, J.: Why do people visit social commerce sites but do not buy? the role of the scarcity heuristic as a momentary characteristic. KSII Trans. Internet Inf. Syst. **8**(7), 125–127 (2014)
39. Zhao, J.D., Huang, J.S., Su, S.: The effects of trust on consumers' continuous purchase intentions in C2C social commerce: a trust transfer perspective. J. Retail. Consum. Serv. **50**(2), 42–49 (2019)
40. Ng, C.S.P.: Intention to purchase on social commerce websites across cultures: a cross-regional study. Inf. Manag. **50**(8), 609–620 (2013)
41. Gibreel, O., AlOtaibi, D.A., Altmann, J.: Social commerce development in emerging markets. Electron. Commer. Res. Appl. **27**(2), 152–162 (2018)
42. Makmor, N.B., Alam, S.S.: Attitude towards social commerce: a conceptual model regarding consumer purchase intention and its determinants. Int. J. Econ. Res. **14**(15), 431–441 (2017)
43. Mikalef, P., Giannakos, M.N., Pappas, I.O.: Designing social commerce platforms based on consumers' intentions. Behav. Inf. Technol. **36**(12), 1308–1327 (2017)
44. Farivar, S., Turel, O., Yuan, Y.: A trust-risk perspective on social commerce use: an examination of the biasing role of habit. Internet Res. **27**(3), 586–607 (2017)
45. Chen, J., Shen, X.L.: Consumers' decisions in social commerce context: an empirical investigation. Decis. Support Syst. **79**(1), 55–64 (2015)
46. Erdoğmuş, İ.E., Tatar, Ş.B.: Drivers of social commerce through brand engagement. Procedia-Soc. Behav. Sci. **207**, 189–195 (2015)
47. Lin, J., Yan, Y., Chen, S.: Understanding the impact of social commerce website technical features on repurchase intention: a Chinese guanxi perspective. J. Electron. Commer. Res. **18**(3), 225–226 (2017)
48. Yang, X.: Consumers' decisions in social commerce: the role of guanxi elements. Asia Pac. J. Mark. Logistics **25**(2), 243–245 (2019)
49. Hajli, N.: Social commerce constructs and consumer's intention to buy. Int. J. Inf. Manag. **35**(2), 183–191 (2015)
50. Gan, C., Wang, W.: The influence of perceived value on purchase intention in social commerce context. Internet Res. **27**(4), 772–785 (2017)
51. Li, C.Y.: How social commerce constructs influence customers' social shopping intention? an empirical study of a social commerce website. Technol. Forecast. Soc. Chang. **45**(2), 342–345 (2017)
52. Lu, B., Fan, W., Zhou, M.: Social presence, trust, and social commerce purchase intention: an empirical research. Comput. Hum. Behav. **56**(2), 225–237 (2016)
53. Shanmugam, M., Sun, S., Amidi, A., Khani, F., Khani, F.: The applications of social commerce constructs. Int. J. Inf. Manag. **36**(3), 425–432 (2016)

54. Zhang, K.Z., Benyoucef, M., Zhao, S.J.: Building brand loyalty in social commerce: the case of brand microblogs. Electron. Commer. Res. Appl. **15**(1), 14–25 (2016)
55. Hajli, M.N.: The role of social support on relationship quality and social commerce. Technol. Forecast. Soc. Change **87**(1), 17–27 (2014)
56. Sheikh, Z., Yezheng, L., Islam, T., Hameed, Z., Khan, I.U.: Impact of social commerce constructs and social support on social commerce intentions. Inf. Technol. People **32**(1), 68–93 (2019)
57. Tajvidi, M., Richard, M.O., Wang, Y., Hajli, N.: Brand co-creation through social commerce information sharing: the role of social media. J. Bus. Res. (2018)
58. Hajli, M.: An integrated model for e-commerce adoption at the customer level with the impact of social commerce. Int. J. Inf. Sci. Manag. **22**(1), 77–97 (2012)
59. Kim, S., Noh, M.J.: Determinants influencing consumers' trust and trust performance of social commerce and moderating effect of experience. Inf. Technol. J. **11**(10), 1369–1380 (2012)
60. Yahia, I.B., Al-Neama, N., Kerbache, L.: Investigating the drivers for social commerce in social media platforms: importance of trust, social support and the platform perceived usage. J. Retail. Consum. Serv. **41**(2), 11–19 (2018)
61. Williams, M.D.: Social commerce and the mobile platform: payment and security perceptions of potential users. Comput. Hum. Behav. (2018)
62. Biucky, S.T., Harandi, S.R.: The effects of perceived risk on social commerce adoption based on tam model. Int. J. Electron. Commer. Stud. **8**(2), 173–196 (2017)
63. Featherman, M.S., Hajli, N.: Self-service technologies and e-services risks in social commerce era. J. Bus. Ethics **139**(2), 251–269 (2016)
64. Mendoza-Tello, J.C., Mora, H., Pujol-López, F.A., Lytras, M.D.: Social commerce as a driver to enhance trust and intention to use cryptocurrencies for electronic payments. IEEE Access **6**, 50737–50751 (2018)
65. Gatautis, R., Medziausiene, A.: Factors affecting social commerce acceptance in Lithuania. Procedia-Soc. Behav. Sci. **110**, 1235–1242 (2014)
66. Shin, D.H.: User experience in social commerce: in friends we trust. Behav. Inf. Technol. **32**(1), 52–67 (2013)
67. Akman, I., Mishra, A.: Factors influencing consumer intention in social commerce adoption. Inf. Technol. People **30**(2), 356–370 (2017)
68. Sheikh, Z., Islam, T., Rana, S., Hameed, Z., Saeed, U.: Acceptance of social commerce framework in Saudi Arabia. Telematics Inform. **34**(8), 1693–1708 (2017)
69. Li, Q., Liang, N., Li, E.Y.: Does friendship quality matter in social commerce? an experimental study of its effect on purchase intention. Electron. Commer. Res. **18**(4), 693–717 (2018)
70. Hajli, N., Sims, J.: Social commerce: the transfer of power from sellers to buyers. Technol. Forecast. Soc. Change **94**(1), 350–358 (2015)
71. Zhang, H., Lu, Y., Gupta, S., Zhao, L.: What motivates customers to participate in social commerce? the impact of technological environments and virtual customer experiences. Inf. Manag. **51**(8), 1017–1030 (2014)
72. Molinillo, S., Liébana-Cabanillas, F., Anaya-Sánchez, R.: A social commerce intention model for traditional e-commerce sites. J. Theor. Appl. Electron. Commer. Res. **13**(2), 80–93 (2018)
73. Bhat, I.H., Singh, S.: Intention to participate on social commerce platform: a study on E-commerce websites. Acad. Mark. Stud. J. **22**(4), 1–10 (2018)
74. Lal, P.: Analyzing determinants influencing an individual's intention to use social commerce website. Fut. Bus. J. **3**(1), 70–85 (2017)

75. Goraya, M.A.S., Jing, Z., Shareef, M.A., Imran, M., Malik, A., Akram, M.S.: An investigation of the drivers of social commerce and e-word-of-mouth intentions: elucidating the role of social commerce in e-business. Electron. Mark. **34**(3), 1–15 (2019)

76. Osatuyi, B., Qin, H.: How vital is the role of effect on post-adoption behaviours? an examination of social commerce users. Int. J. Inf. Manag. **40**(2), 175–185 (2018)

77. Hew, J.J., Lee, V.H., Ooi, K.B., Lin, B.: Mobile social commerce: the booster for brand loyalty? Comput. Hum. Behav. **59**(2), 142–154 (2016)

78. Hew, J.J., Leong, L.Y., Tan, G.W.H., Ooi, K.B., Lee, V.H.: The age of mobile social commerce: an artificial neural network analysis on its resistances. Technol. Forecast. Soc. Change **32**(2), 45–46 (2017)

79. Vongsraluang, N., Bhatiasevi, V.: The determinants of social commerce system success for SMEs in Thailand. Inf. Dev. **33**(1), 80–96 (2017)

80. Cho, E., Son, J.: The effect of social connectedness on consumer adoption of social commerce in apparel shopping. Fashion Text. **6**(1), 14–15 (2019)

81. Chung, N., Song, H.G., Lee, H.: Consumers' impulsive buying behavior of restaurant products in social commerce. Int. J. Contemp. Hosp. Manag. **29**(2), 709–731 (2017)

82. Xiang, L., Zheng, X., Lee, M.K., Zhao, D.: Exploring consumers' impulse buying behavior on social commerce platform: the role of parasocial interaction. Int. J. Inf. Manag. **36**(3), 333–347 (2016)

83. Ali, S.Y., Hussin, A.R.C., Ghazali, M.: Antecedents and consequences of ewom in social commerce. J. Theor. Appl. Inf. Technol. **96**(1), 22–24 (2018)

84. Bai, Y., Yao, Z., Dou, Y.F.: Effect of social commerce factors on user purchase behaviour: an empirical investigation from renren. com. Int. J. Inf. Manag. **35**(5), 538–550 (2015)

85. Braojos, J., Benitez, J., Llorens, J.: How do social commerce-IT capabilities influence firm performance? theory and empirical evidence. Inf. Manag. **56**(2), 155–171 (2019)

86. Ng, C.S.P.: Intention to purchase on social commerce websites across cultures: a cross-regional study. Inf. Manag. **50**(8), 609–620 (2013)

87. Wang, Y., Yu, C.: Social interaction-based consumer decision-making model in social commerce: the role of word of mouth and observational learning. Int. J. Inf. Manag. **37**(3), 179–189 (2017)

88. Ko, H.C.: Social desire or commercial desire? the factors driving social sharing and shopping intentions on social commerce platforms. Electron. Commer. Res. Appl. **28**(2), 1–15 (2018)

89. Cheng, X., Gu, Y., Shen, J.: An integrated view of particularized trust in social commerce: an empirical investigation. Int. J. Inf. Manag. **45**(3), 1–12 (2019)

90. Yang, X.: Consumers' decisions in social commerce: the role of guanxi elements. Asia Pac. J. Mark. Logistics **25**(2), 243–245 (2019)

91. Hassan, M., Iqbal, Z., Khanum, B.: The role of trust and social presence in social commerce purchase intention. Pak. J. Commer. Soc. Sci. **12**(1), 111–135 (2018)

92. Yeon, J., Park, I., Lee, D.: What creates trust and who gets loyalty in social commerce? J. Retail. Consum. Serv. **50**(2), 138–144 (2019)

93. Yusuf, A.S., Che Hussin, A.R., Busalim, A.H.: Influence of e-WOM engagement on consumer purchase intention in social commerce. J. Serv. Mark. **32**(4), 493–504 (2018)

94. Fu, S., Xu, Y., Yan, Q.: Enhancing the parasocial interaction relationship between consumers through similarity effects in the context of social commerce: evidence from social commerce platforms in China. J. Strateg. Mark. **27**(2), 100–118 (2017)

95. Tarmedi, E., Sulastri Sumiyati, S., Dirgantari, P.D.: Factors affecting customer trust and their impact on customer behavioural intention: a study of social commerce in Indonesia. Pertanika J. Soc. Sci. Humanit. **23**(2), 35–36 (2018)

96. Tang, J., Zhang, P.: The impact of atmospheric cues on consumers' approach and avoidance behavioural intentions in social commerce websites. Comput. Hum. Behav. (2018)
97. Amelina, D., Zhu, Y.Q.: Investigating effectiveness of source credibility elements on social commerce endorsement: the case of instagram in indonesia. In: PACIS, p. 232 (2016)
98. Lin, C.S., Wu, S.: Exploring antecedents of online group-buying: social commerce perspective. Hum. Syst. Manag. 34(2), 133–147 (2015)
99. Tariq, A., Wang, C., Tanveer, Y., Akram, U., Akram, Z.: Organic food consumerism through social commerce in China. Asia Pac. J. Mark. Logistics 31(1), 202–222 (2019)
100. Ju, J., Ahn, J.H.: The effect of social and ambient factors on impulse purchasing behaviour in social commerce. J. Organ. Comput. Electron. Commer. 26(4), 285–306 (2016)

# Digital Entrepreneurship in Business Enterprises: A Systematic Review

Samuel Anim-Yeboah, Richard Boateng(✉) [iD],
Emmanuel Awuni Kolog [iD], Acheampong Owusu [iD],
and Ibrahim Bedi

University of Ghana Business School, Box LG 78, Accra, Ghana
Richboateng@ug.edu.gh

**Abstract.** This study systematically reviews extant contemporary literature on digital entrepreneurship in peer-reviewed journal articles over six years (2013–2018) from six journal databases. It involved a systematic literature review of 101 papers from 53 journals focusing on the publication outlets, yearly trends, themes, and associated theoretical and conceptual approaches, methodologies, sources and geographical distribution of digital entrepreneurship research. The findings suggest that extant literature mostly lacked sound theoretical underpinnings. More work adopting appropriate and proven theoretical approaches is needed. Most of the reviewed papers also focused mainly on issues relating to the technology itself than those relating to the enterprise or the entrepreneur. The capabilities and capacities of enterprises, as well as the strategies in implementing digital technologies and harnessing the opportunities of digitalization, are key issues that have not hitherto received much attention. The study contributes to the understanding of the conceptualization of the digital entrepreneurship phenomenon. Future research should consolidate the understanding of the field, with models and frameworks that recognize digital entrepreneurship as an academic research field in its own right, and also consider the impact of enterprise capabilities and capacities on digital entrepreneurship.

**Keywords:** Digital technology · Digital entrepreneurship · Business enterprise · Systematic review

## 1 Introduction

Digital entrepreneurship is generally defined as the pursuit of business or economic opportunities based on the use of digital technologies [9], and this definition is adopted for this study. The entrepreneurs involved in the digital entrepreneurship are then described as digital entrepreneurs while the resulting ventures or firms, which provide economic and social value for themselves or their communities, are referred to as digital enterprises [9, 50]. Although researchers and policymakers have widely used the term 'digital entrepreneurship', its conceptualisation remains elusive, with very little evidence of scholarship in the field [50].

There is a growing interest in digital entrepreneurship since it is considered to be the ultimate and contemporary trend in entrepreneurship development due to the rapid

© IFIP International Federation for Information Processing 2020
Published by Springer Nature Switzerland AG 2020
M. Hattingh et al. (Eds.): I3E 2020, LNCS 12066, pp. 192–203, 2020.
https://doi.org/10.1007/978-3-030-44999-5_16

development of digital technologies and the emerging digital economy [20]. Bog-danowicz [2] also emphasises the renewed and increasing interest in digital entrepreneurship and calls for empirical evidence [24].

Despite the increased interest in digital entrepreneurship and technology-based innovations, there has been limited clarification of the concept from different perspectives and conceptualisations. Moreover, there has also been a lack of contextual and conceptual development and discussion of the concept of digital entrepreneurship, as most prior research examined only the sporadic phenomena associated with it [42, 50]. Furthermore, some critical and fundamental issues about digital entrepreneurship currently remain unresolved in the literature. These include how digital technologies transform entrepreneurship, how digital entrepreneurship predicts performance outcomes, and how digital entrepreneurship differs from traditional entrepreneurship [48, 50]. Meanwhile, not much has been done in terms of reviewing the body of literature and research trends in digital entrepreneurship, so the need for conceptualisations in the field is much desired [34].

Furthermore, there is a dearth in knowledge regarding the detailed classification of digital technology-enabled entrepreneurship and enterprises, making it difficult to appreciate the current level of understanding and boundaries of the original concept [36, 41]. Additionally, the current conceptualisation of digital entrepreneurship is considerably diverse. While some researchers have opted for a broad conceptualisation of digital entrepreneurship as a combination of digital technology and entrepreneurship innovation [1, 14], others have limited the concept to the attainment of entrepreneurship goals with digital technological applications [44].

It is essential to review achievements and studies to date, regarding what has been done, what needs to be revisited and what is still missing in the field, in order to better appreciate and promote the development of digital entrepreneurship on the academic and research front [33]. A review of studies on the concept of digital entrepreneurship is necessary to evaluate the current understanding of, and complementary perspectives on, how the digital technology revolution has permeated entrepreneurship and innovation [22].

Hence, compelled by the challenges posed by the development of the digital entrepreneurship concept, particularly in the IS research environment, this study seeks to provide a systematic review of the extant literature on digital entrepreneurship. The study will identify and describe the major issues, themes, trends, distribution, and focus of research on the concept. It will also examine the methodological and theoretical approaches to past studies on the concept, identify the limitations and gaps in the literature, and offer recommendations for future research. The resulting review is expected to serve as a one-stop source, offering insight into what has been accomplished so far, what is currently being done, and what challenges and opportunities lie ahead, in terms of research on digital entrepreneurship. The study, therefore, addresses the following questions to achieve this:

1. What are the major trends, characteristics, and distribution of research work on digital entrepreneurship?
2. What major issues and themes are being focused on and discussed in digital entrepreneurship research?

3. What theoretical, conceptual, and methodological, approaches are being used to address digital entrepreneurship research?
4. What are the limitations and gaps in the extant literature on digital entrepreneurship?

This study seeks to systematically review research articles concerning digital entrepreneurship in peer-reviewed journals from six major journal databases, over six years. The next section presents the methodology employed, while the third section presents the findings and discussions. The fourth section elaborates the limitations and gaps identified, followed by the conclusion and contribution.

## 2  Methodology

The study was conducted as a systematic literature review (SLR) of extant studies on the conceptualisation of digital entrepreneurship [37]. The searches for articles were conducted in six electronic databases for which the researcher had full-text access: ScienceDirect/Elsevier, Emerald, AIS Library, Sage, Springer, and Taylor and Francis. Although these databases may not exhaustively list all relevant journals, they, however, cover a reasonable portion of the existing database for IS journals. As Levy and Ellis, [29] noted in their guide to a systematic approach to a literature review in IS, it is better to use multiple databases in conducting literature searches, since the IS domain is multidisciplinary and IS literature outlets are highly diversified. Quality IS literature is dispersed through-out hundreds of databases and some of the databases used in this study, being multidisciplinary, are among those recommended by Levy and Ellis, [29] as useful for IS research. Moreover, most journals in these databases are globally top-ranked IS journals [4]. Against this backdrop, the list of databases above was a fair and adequate representation of the relevant IS databases suited for digital entrepreneurship study, which is a multidisciplinary subject.

The searches were conducted using "digital innovation" and "digital entrepreneurship" as search terms. Other keywords included "digital enterprise," "digital economies," "digital technologies," and "innovative technologies." The search was limited to articles published between January 2013 and August 2018, resulting in 175 papers or articles, that were downloaded.

The exclusion criteria applied included the delimiting of the papers to peer-reviewed research articles, and hence, conference papers and book chapters were excluded from the study, in addition to stock reviews. The articles were also restricted to those concerning business entrepreneurship and business enterprises, and thus, all articles concerning policy, education, and social entrepreneurship were eliminated. After the papers had been identified and elicited, they were sorted and cross-checked to eliminate duplications.

Ultimately, 101 articles from 53 journals were selected. The selected papers were then classified based on the publishing journal, year of publication, digital technology issues and themes, theoretical and conceptual approaches and frameworks, research methodologies and methods, data sources and levels of analysis. The data collected on the various classifications were analysed and summarized using descriptive statistics.

## 3 Findings and Discussions

### 3.1 Publication Databases and Journals

Regarding the distribution of the articles in the databases, it was found that Emerald hosted the majority of the publications, followed by ScienceDirect, Springer Link, and Taylor and Francis. Sage and AIS Library, by contrast, had small numbers of journals and articles, with particularly the AIS Library having the least. Such observation may be explained by the fact that, because digital entrepreneurship researches straddle multidisciplinary fields, it may be expected that libraries and databases that accommodate multidisciplinary fields will have more articles on digital entrepreneurship [29]. Moreover, apart from the AIS Library, which contains papers specifically related to IS, the other libraries (Emerald, ScienceDirect, Taylor and Francis, Springer Link and Sage) contain papers from several different fields [29].

In terms of the number of articles per journal, *the Journal of Small Business and Enterprise Development* had the highest number of 11 (10.9%) articles and is followed by *Technological Forecasting and Social Change* with 9 (8.9%) articles. The *Information and Management journal* had 5 (4.9%) articles, *Journal of Business Research* and the *Journal of Information Technology* had 4 (4.0%) articles each, while the *Journal for Innovation and Entrepreneurship, Journal of Strategic Marketing, Small Business Economics journal* and the *Journal of Open Innovation, Technology, Market and Complexity* had 3 (3.0%) articles each. Twelve (12) of the journals had 2 (2.0%) articles each while the rest of the journals, thirty-two (32) in all, had 1 (1.0%) article each.

The focal areas for many of the journals from which the papers were obtained included information systems (IS), information technology (IT), innovation, business, entrepreneurship, management, marketing, human relations, governance, regulation, operation, production, knowledge, planning, strategy, gender, and other diverse fields. These focal areas suggest the suitability of the journals for digital entrepreneurship research, which is a multidisciplinary concept that is applied in different scientific and academic fields. It further corroborates the observation that digital entrepreneurship is multidisciplinary in perspective [5, 45, 47].

### 3.2 Year of Publication

The distribution of the publications by year (Fig. 1) shows an increasing trend of articles on digital entrepreneurship from January 2013 to August 2018. Throughout the period under study, the number of papers published continually increased from six papers in 2013 to 33 papers in 2018 (up to August only), representing more than five-fold increment. Apart from an insignificant drop from six in 2013 to five in 2014, the increment was consistent, as the number of papers increased to 13 in 2015, 14 in 2016, 30 in 2017, and 33 in 2018. This trend shows that the number of publications is likely to increase further in the future.

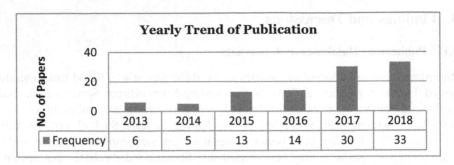

**Fig. 1.** Trends in the publication by year (N = 101)

This trend shows a growing interest in digital entrepreneurship, not only in practice and policy but also in research, which affirms Kelestyn and Henfridsson's [27] claim. Considering the proliferation of digital technology and information technology (IT) based business, the increase in digital entrepreneurship research is expected to continue for several years [19, 27, 30].

### 3.3    Focus and Categories of Research Issues and Themes

The study identified several issues of focus in the papers reviewed. These issues were grouped into four categories as (i) those that focused directly on the technology involved (73 papers), (ii) those that focused on the relationships and interactions with the technology (58 papers) (iii) those that focused directly on the enterprise (53 papers), and (iv) those that focused on the entrepreneur (13 papers).

The *technology-focused issues* concerned digital technologies like mobile technology, e-business platforms, social media, cloud computing, big data, crowdsourcing, internet, enterprise systems, and blockchain [49]. Some of the technology-focused articles, however, did not indicate any specific technologies but mentions digital technologies or ICT in general. The *interaction-focused issues* comprised access, adoption, impact, role, influence, possession, trust, and use of digital technology. The *enterprise-focused issues* involved demographics, business model, innovation, transformation, performance, productivity, profitability, value, expansion, growth, convergence, ecosystems, incubations, start-ups, cooperation, competition, internationalisation, marketing, stakeholder collaboration, success factors, and strategic orientation. The *entrepreneur-focused issues* encompassed behaviour, gender, competence, perception, positions, and management.

Given that digital entrepreneurship is ICT-driven [35], it was not surprising that the technology-focused issues (from 73 papers) dominated the various issues addressed. The distribution of the themes within the technology focussed issues shows that most of the papers, 33 articles (32.7%) did not specify the exact technology theme. Specifically, the dominant technology theme identified from the publications on digital entrepreneurship included e-business platforms with 12 (11.9%) papers and social media platforms with 10 (9.9%) papers. Other digital platforms and mobile technology reflected in 4 (4.0%) papers each while cloud computing had 3 (3.0%) papers. The enterprise systems and blockchain were considered in 2 (2.0%) papers, whereas internet service, big data, and crowdsourcing reflected in 1 (1.0%) paper each. The e-Business, social media, other digital platforms, and mobile application are all expected to feature as main themes in publications on digital entrepreneurship due to their popularity. Of the 58 papers that focused on issues of the interactions with technology, 17 (16.8%) focused on influence, 13 (12.9%) on adoption, 11 (10.9%) on impact, 7 (6.9%) on use, 6 (5.9%) on role, 2 (1.6%) on trust and 1 (1.0%) each on access to and possession of the technology. Whereas, out of the 53 papers with enterprise-focused issues 17 of them focused on business model, innovation and transformation; 10 on business growth, expansion, performance, success factors and return on investment; 7 on ecosystems, incubation and sharing economy, 6 on competition, convergence, collaboration and cooperation; 5 on enterprise processes, institutional and social interactions; 4 on enterprise state, demographics, boundaries and employment; and 4 on marketing and strategy. Meanwhile, of the 13 papers focusing on entrepreneur related issues, 5 focused on the entrepreneur's perspectives, perceptions and behaviour; 3 on entrepreneur's gender, race and class; 3 on entrepreneurial competence and another 3 on ownership and management. These constitute the trending issues that dominate contemporary discussions and study of digital entrepreneurship.

### 3.4 Theoretical and Conceptual Approaches

Regarding the use of specific theories or concepts, the findings show that 57 (56.4%) of the papers had no theory or concept underpinning it, while 44 (43.6%) had theories or frameworks. Of the 44 papers that were underpinned by theories or concepts, 35 (34.6%) used single theories, while 9 (8.9%) combined two or three theories. Meanwhile, 14 (13.9%) of the 35 papers that used single theory or concept and 1 (1.0%) of the nine papers that combined theories or concepts utilized the author's frameworks. This implies that only 29 (28.7%) of the papers, comprising 21 (20.8%) of the 35 papers with single theory and 8 (7.9%) of the nine papers with combined theories, utilized known and established theories or concepts.

In all 28 different known and established theories and concepts were employed. The Dynamic Capability theory was used in 4 papers, while the Resource-Based View was used in 3 papers. Diffusion of Innovation, Institutional Theory, Technology Acceptance Model, Technology Organization and Environment framework, Theory of Planned Behavior, and the Trust Theory were used in two papers each, while each of the remaining 20 theories was used in one paper each. The theory-based studies focused on enterprise-related issues such as business model, value, process, innovation, and transformation, as well as competition, expansion, marketing, and strategic orientation. The review also shows that some of the studies with no theories could have been underpinned with applicable theories in IS literature such as social theories, socio-technical theories, institutional theories and the Task-Technology Fit (TTF) theoretical framework which could explain the assumptions on which many of the publications were conducted [6, 38, 43].

These theories and concepts that were used by the papers reflect the wide application of different theories and concepts in digital entrepreneurship for different purposes, depending on the focus of the research, which emphasizes the multidisciplinary nature of digital entrepreneurship with a diversity of research approaches. With fewer papers, 29 (28.7%) in all, utilizing 28 different established theories and concepts also suggests the newness of the knowledge area in research. For studies in digital entrepreneurship to gain prominence in the IS research landscape, further work based on grounded, appropriate, and credible theoretical approaches should be considered.

Among the theories used, the most dominant was the social theories approach with 25 (24.8%) papers, followed by the socio-technical theories approach with 11 (10.9%) papers and the technical theories approach with 5 (4.9%) papers. The dominance of social theories could be due to the social nature of entrepreneurship studies. Many of the studies that used social theories focused on ICT adoption and impact [11, 18, 39], while others used the theories to explain the influence and impact of ICT on business [8, 12, 40]. From the review, it also emerged that studies that adopted the socio-technical theories approach focused on the influence of ICT in business [6], the extent of ICT adoption, and barriers to its adoption [38]. The theories applied in the publications reviewed are popular and prominent in IS research.

### 3.5   Research Methodology Used and Trend

Regarding the classification of the publications by the research methodology employed, four distinct groups emerged, namely, those that used mixed methods, qualitative methodology, quantitative methodology, and those with no defined methodology. Regarding the distribution, the results show the almost equal distribution for studies using qualitative (41 (40.6%) papers) and quantitative methodologies (39 (38.6%) papers), which were the dominant approaches. Just a few papers used mixed methods 3 (3.0%), while a reasonable number did not use any defined methodology 18 (17.8%).

Of the 41 quantitative papers, 22 (21.8%) were based on theories, of which 15 (14.9%) were established theories. Whereas, of the 39 qualitative papers, 17 (16.8%) were based on theories, of which 12 (11.9%) were established theories. Having 83 (82.2%) of the papers with both quantitative and qualitative methodologies almost equally shared suggest that the digital entrepreneurship research is becoming more mature with proven methodologies. The 18 studies that were not underpinned by any defined methodology were made of 16 reviews, and two content analysis papers and most did not have any theory as well. Moreover, with 13 of the 18 no defined methodology and review papers published in 2017 and 2018, it goes to suggest the growing interest in exploring the research already done in the area of digital entrepreneurship.

It was further observed that both quantitative and qualitative methodologies have increased in use in recent years (Fig. 2). The increasing use of qualitative methodology suggests the subjection of digital entrepreneurship to exploratory research, being a new field, while the increasing dominance of quantitative methodology also reveals the simultaneous development of statistical rigor and analysis [21, 39]. According to Creswell [7], qualitative methods are commonly used in fields that are new and require more exploratory research designs, hence the observed trend reflects the attractiveness of digital entrepreneurship as a new area of research.

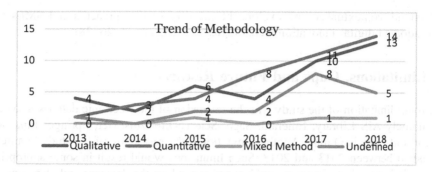

Fig. 2. The yearly trend of research methodology

## 3.6 Data Sources, Research Methods and Levels of Analysis

The data sources used in the publications included secondary sources, primary sources, and some undefined sources. The results indicate that about two-thirds, 68 (67.3%) of the papers used data from primary sources, whereas about a quarter, 27 (26.7%) of the papers used secondary data sources. The data sources available for a study largely depend on the availability of previous studies on the topic and the research approach employed. The survey and case study research approaches tend to employ primary sources [12, 31, 32], whereas most reviews tend to rely on secondary sources [10, 46].

Based on the results of the study, survey and case study were the two dominant methods used, which resulted in the use of primary data sources for many of the papers. Meanwhile, the data sources and methods used are also influenced by the level of research development in the field of inquiry [25]. In relatively new areas of research, obtaining secondary data or the adoption of a literature review approach may be hampered. The limited use of secondary data sources in many of the works published in this area reflects the relative newness of the field. This assertion is also reflected in the research approach that was employed in the study. From the results, it is clear that the most widely used methods were a survey, case study, literature review, and interviews. The use of the case studies and interviews suggest that more exploratory and descriptive questions are being asked at the same time that rigor is being sought through surveys. The greater use of the research approaches mentioned above, compared to others, suggests that many of the papers were focused on discovering and describing phenomena related to digital entrepreneurship [25]. Interestingly of the 35 papers that used a case study or interview methods, 21 of them have no theory base, which further emphasizes the exploratory and descriptive purposes. The focus of such papers included adoption, impact, influence and use of digital technologies like social media, e-business, enterprise systems and crowdsourcing [15, 28].

Research methods, approaches, and data sources used may also be entirely dependent on the level of analysis that the researcher intends to perform [3]. The results show that many of the studies were conducted at the micro-level, with very few at the macro- and meso- levels, which suits entrepreneurship research [25]. The current focus on organizational level noted in the study may be explained by the fact that many of the studies are applied studies that do not simply seek to advance knowledge, but also to understand, contextualize and explore the practices of entrepreneurs and SMEs that have adopted digital innovation technologies [13, 16, 17, 23, 26, 38].

## 4 Limitations, Gaps and Future Research

The main limitation of the study was the restriction of the electronic databases to only six, namely AIS Library, Emerald, Sage, ScienceDirect/Elsevier, Springer Link, and Taylor and Francis Online. Another limitation is the restriction of the study to articles published between 2013 and 2018. Such limitations would result in some appropriate articles being eluded. Future research could expand on the database and also consider other forms of digital entrepreneurship.

Only a few of the studies discussed had sound theoretical underpinnings. A major gap identified, is the limited use of theoretical and conceptual frameworks that would bring the concept of digital entrepreneurship up to par with major areas of academic inquiry in IS research. Meanwhile, for studies in digital entrepreneurship to acquire some eminence in the IS research purview, more work adopting appropriate and proven theoretical approaches is needed. Few papers focused on issues relating to the enterprise while much fewer papers focused on the entrepreneur. Future research should consider the drivers and motivation of the entrepreneur for digital entrepreneurship. The capabilities and capacities of enterprises, as well as the strategies in implementing digital technologies and harnessing the opportunities of digitalization, are key issues that have not hitherto received much attention.

Future research should consolidate the understanding of the field, with models and frameworks that recognize digital entrepreneurship as an academic research field in its own right, and also consider the impact of enterprise capabilities and capacities on digital entrepreneurship.

## 5 Conclusion and Contribution

There is an arguable case for acknowledging digital entrepreneurship as a distinct field that has attracted considerable scholarly attention in recent years. As a multidisciplinary and multi-sectoral subject, research on digital entrepreneurship encompasses many fields. Owing to the broad range of research within the scope of digital entrepreneurship, the understanding of the concept is diffuse and open to misinterpretation.

The paper provides guidance for researchers with insight into the conceptualization of digital entrepreneurship as a multidisciplinary research field. It will also help academicians understanding a holistic view of available research and the developing trend in digital entrepreneurship. This paper contributes to information systems research by describing and classifying the published literature in digital entrepreneurship and by pointing out the gaps where further research is most needed. Furthermore, the paper provides a framework that may provide a conceptual structure for future studies in digital entrepreneurship.

# References

1. Beckman, C.M., Eisenhardt, K., Kotha, S., Meyer, A., Rajagopalan, N.: The role of the entrepreneur in technology entrepreneurship. Strateg. Entrepreneurship J. 6(3), 203–206 (2012)
2. Bogdanowicz, M.: Digital entrepreneurship barriers and drivers-the need for a specific measurement framework. Institute for Prospective Technological Studies, European Commission, Joint Research Centre (JRC) Technical report, EUR 27679 EN (2015). https://doi.org/10.2791/3112
3. Bryman, A., Bell, E.: Business Research Methods. Oxford University Press, Oxford (2015)
4. CABS: Acad. J. Guide (AJG). Chart. Assoc. Bus. Schools (2018). https://charteredabs.org/academic-journal-guide-2018/
5. Carlborg, P., Kindström, D., Kowalkowski, C.: The evolution of service innovation research: a critical review and synthesis. Serv. Ind. J. 34(5), 373–398 (2014)
6. Chandna, V., Salimath, M.S.: Peer-to-peer selling in online platforms: a salient business model for virtual entrepreneurship. J. Bus. Res. 84, 162–174 (2018)
7. Creswell, J.W.: Research Design: Qualitative, Quantitative, and Mixed Methods Approaches, 2nd edn. Sage, Thousand Oaks (2003)
8. Daniel, E.M., Domenico, M.D., Sharma, S.: Effectuation and home-based online business entrepreneurs. Int. Small Bus. J. 33(8), 799–823 (2015)
9. Davidson, E., Vaast, E.: Digital entrepreneurship and its socio-material enactment. In: 43rd Hawaii International Conference on System Sciences (HICSS) 2010, pp. 1–10. IEEE (2010)
10. David-West, O., Umukoro, I.O., Onuoha, R.O.: Platforms in Sub-Saharan Africa: start-up models and the role of business incubation. J. Intell. Cap. 19(3), 581–616 (2018)
11. Durkin, M., McGowan, P., McKeown, N.: Exploring social media adoption in small to medium-sized enterprises in Ireland. J. Small Bus. Enterp. Dev. 20(4), 716–734 (2013)
12. Dutot, V., Bergeron, F.: From strategic orientation to social media orientation: improving SMEs' performance on social media. J. Small Bus. Enterp. Dev. 23(4), 1165–1190 (2016)
13. Ensign, P.C., Farlow, S.: Serial entrepreneurs in the Waterloo ecosystem. J. Innov. Entrepreneurship 5(1), 20 (2016)
14. Ferreira, J.J.M., Ferreira, F.A.F., Fernandes, C.I.M.A.S., Jalali, M.S., Raposo, M.L., Marques, C.S.: What do we [not] know about technology entrepreneurship research? Int. Entrepreneurship Manag. J. 12(3), 713–733 (2016). https://doi.org/10.1007/s11365-015-0359-2
15. Foroudi, P., Gupta, S., Nazarian, A., Duda, M.: Digital technology and marketing management capability: achieving growth in SMEs. Qual. Mark. Res.: Int. J. 20(2), 230–246 (2017)
16. Fu, X., Mohnen, P., Zanello, G.: Innovation and productivity in formal and informal firms in Ghana. Technol. Forecast. Soc. Change 131, 315–325 (2018)
17. Garcia-Murillo, M., Velez-Ospina, J.A.: ICTs and the informal economy: mobile and broadband roles. Digital Policy Regul. Gov. 19(1), 58–76 (2017)
18. George Wynn, M., Turner, P., Lau, E.: E-business and process change: two case studies (towards an assessment framework). J. Small Bus. Enterp. Dev. 20(4), 913–933 (2013)
19. Giones, F., Brem, A.: Digital technology entrepreneurship: a definition and research agenda. Technol. Innov. Manag. Rev. 7(5), 44–51 (2017)
20. Hafezieh, N., Akhavan, P., Eshraghian, F.: Exploration of process and competitive factors of entrepreneurship in digital space: a multiple case study in Iran. Educ. Bus. Soc.: Contemp. Middle Eastern Issues 4(4), 267–279 (2011)

21. Haghighi, N.F., Hajihoseini, H., Nargesi, G.R., Bijani, M.: Gap analysis of current and desired states of entrepreneurship development components in the field of ICTs in Iran. Technol. Soc. **54**, 101–110 (2018)

22. Hanna, R., Rohm, A., Crittenden, V.L.: We're all connected: the power of the social media ecosystem. Bus. Horiz. **54**(3), 265–273 (2011)

23. Hartmann, P.M., Zaki, M., Feldmann, N., Neely, A.: Capturing value from big data–a taxonomy of data-driven business models used by start-up firms. Int. J. Oper. Prod. Manag. **36**(10), 1382–1406 (2016)

24. Hull, C.E.K., Hung, Y.T.C., Hair, N., Perotti, V., DeMartino, R.: Taking advantage of digital opportunities: a typology of digital entrepreneurship. Int. J. Netw. Virtual Organ. **4**(3), 290–303 (2007)

25. Ireland, R.D., Reutzel, C.R., Webb, J.W.: Entrepreneurship research in AMJ: what has been published, and what might the future hold? Acad. Manag. J. **48**(4), 556–564 (2005)

26. Kabongo, J.D., Okpara, J.O.: ICT possession among Congolese SMEs: an exploratory study. J. Small Bus. Enterp. Dev. **21**(2), 313–326 (2014)

27. Kelestyn, B., Henfridsson, O.: Everyday digital entrepreneurship: the inception, shifts, and scaling of future-shaping practices. In: Proceedings of the 35th International Conference on Information Systems (ICIS 2014). Auckland, New Zealand (2014)

28. Kuester, S., Konya-Baumbach, E., Schuhmacher, M.C.: Get the show on the road: go-to-market strategies for e-innovations of start-ups. J. Bus. Res. **83**, 65–81 (2018)

29. Levy, Y., Ellis, T.J.: A systems approach to conduct an effective literature review in support of information systems research. Inf. Sci. J. **9**, 181–212 (2006)

30. Miniaoui, H., Schilirò, D.: Innovation and entrepreneurship for the growth and diversification of the GCC economies, MPRA Paper No. 71898 (2016). https://mpra.ub.uni-muenchen.de/71898/. Accessed 20 Nov 2018

31. Mohajerani, A., Baptista, J., Nandhakumar, J.: Exploring the role of social media in importing logics across social contexts: the case of IT SMEs in Iran. Technol. Forecast. Soc. Change **95**, 16–31 (2015)

32. Moghavvemi, S., Mohd Salleh, N.A., Standing, C.: Entrepreneurs adoption of information system innovation: the impact of individual perception and exogenous factors on entrepreneur's behavior. Internet Res. **26**(5), 1181–1208 (2016)

33. Mosey, S., Guerrero, M., Greenman, A.: Technology entrepreneurship research opportunities: insights from across Europe. J. Technol. Transf. **42**(1), 1–9 (2017)

34. Nambisan, S.: Digital entrepreneurship: toward a digital technology perspective of entrepreneurship. Entrepreneurship Theory Pract. **41**(6), 1029–1055 (2017)

35. Ngoasong, M.Z.: Digital entrepreneurship in a resource-scarce context: a focus on entrepreneurial digital competencies. J. Small Bus. Enterp. Dev. **25**(3), 483–500 (2018)

36. Ngoasong, M., Paton, R., Korda, A.: Impact investing and inclusive business development in Africa: a research agenda. The Open University, Milton Keynes, IKD Working Paper, No. 76 (2015). http://oro.open.ac.uk/42157/1/ikd-working-paper-76.pdf. Accessed 18 Dec 2018

37. Okoli, C.: A guide to conducting a standalone systematic literature review. Commun. Assoc. Inf. Syst. **37**(43), 879–910 (2015)

38. Panayiotou, N.A., Katimertzoglou, P.K.: Micro firms internet adoption patterns: the case of the Greek jewellery industry. J. Enterp. Inf. Manag. **28**(4), 508–530 (2015)

39. Sarmah, B., Sharma, S., Gupta, S.: Antecedents of e-business adoption intention: an empirical study. Int. J. Innov. Sci. **9**(4), 417–434 (2017)

40. Sedera, D., Lokuge, S., Grover, V., Sarker, S., Sarker, S.: Innovating with enterprise systems and digital platforms: a contingent resource-based theory view. Inf. Manag. **53**(3), 366–379 (2016)

41. Shemi, A.P., Procter, C.: E-commerce and entrepreneurship in SMEs: the case of myBot. J. Small Bus. Enterp. Dev. **25**(3), 501–520 (2018)
42. Shen, C.H., Chen, S.C., Hsiao, H.C., Chang, J.C., Chou, C.M., Chen, C.P.: Can the entrepreneurship course improve the entrepreneurial intentions of students? Int. Entrepreneurship Manag. J. **11**(3), 557–569 (2015)
43. Tumbas, S., Berente, N., Seidel, S., vom Brocke, J.: The 'digital facade' of rapidly growing entrepreneurial organizations. In: Proceedings of the International Conference on Information Systems (ICIS 2015), Fort Worth, Texas (2015)
44. Wallin, A., Still, K., Henttonen, K.: Entrepreneurial growth ambitions: the case of finnish technology start-ups. Technol. Innov. Manag. Rev. **6**(10), 5–16 (2016)
45. Whittington, D.: Digital Innovation and Entrepreneurship. Cambridge University Press, Cambridge (2018)
46. Xiao, X., Califf, C.B., Sarker, S., Sarker, S.: ICT innovation in emerging economies: a review of the existing literature and a framework for future research. J. Inf. Technol. **28**(4), 264–278 (2013)
47. Yoo, Y., Henfridsson, O., Lyytinen, K.: Research commentary—the new organizing logic of digital innovation: an agenda for information systems research. Inf. Syst. Res. **21**(4), 724–735 (2010)
48. Yunis, M., Tarhini, A., Kassar, A.: The role of ICT and innovation in enhancing organizational performance: the catalyzing effect of corporate entrepreneurship. J. Bus. Res. **88**, 344–356 (2018)
49. Zalan, T.: Born global on blockchain. Rev. Int. Bus. Strategy **28**(1), 19–34 (2018)
50. Zhao, F., Collier, A.: Digital entrepreneurship: research and practice. In: Proceedings of the 9th Annual Conference of the EuroMed Academy of Business, 2016, Warsaw, Poland (2016)

# Assessing the Role of Trust in Merchant Adoption of Mobile Payments in Ghana

Eunice Yeboah, Richard Boateng ⓘ, Acheampong Owusu(✉) ⓘ,
Eric Afful-Dadzie, and Joshua Ofori-Amanfo

University of Ghana Business School, Box LG 78, Accra, Ghana
aowusu@ug.edu.gh

**Abstract.** Encouraged by the crucial need to understand merchant adoption of mobile payment, this study explores the role trust play in the adoption of mobile payment by merchant and the enablers for merchant's trust in mobile payment systems. This was done by Conceptualising the characteristics of the service provider and technology characteristics as the two dimensions that could influence merchant adoption of mobile payments. The study was done through the lenses of the Technology Acceptance Model (TAM) and the Trust-Theoretic Model and adopted a qualitative approach where two merchants were selected from the health sector. The findings demonstrate that the role of merchant trust is very critical for adoption due to m-payment technology and security risk. Hence, sufficient trust-building structures in mobile payment space are essential for the adoption of mobile payment by merchants. Moreover, the findings indicate mobile service provider characteristics and the mobile technology characteristics are both imperative toward building trust in mobile payment systems for merchants' adoption. The study also found that the trust of both technology and service provider has a far more critical influence on merchants' adoption of mobile payments than perceived usefulness or ease of use. The study, therefore, recommends that service providers should consider the opportunity to nurture merchant trust because merchant trust acts as a fundamental enabler for the adoption of mobile payments. Other implications are also discussed.

**Keywords:** Merchants · Adoption · M-payments · Trust · Ghana

## 1 Introduction

Mobile technology evolution and the extensive diffusion of mobile phones in performing several functions and tasks, has led to the phenomenal growth in the ownership of mobile phones globally. Notable among these everyday tasks is the use of mobile phones in making payments for goods and services without the need for cash or participation of banking institutions (Liébana-Cabanillas and Lara-Rubio 2017; Dahlberg et al. 2015; Chandra et al. 2010). This rising interest in mobile payment usage from the consumer to the merchants has become a strategic tool that facilitates positive business outcomes (Congdon 2016). Further, this innovative payment solution is considered a bedrock for competitive advantage, productivity, and growth, providing a way for businesses to achieve efficiency (Hsiao 2019). The high penetration of mobile

© IFIP International Federation for Information Processing 2020
Published by Springer Nature Switzerland AG 2020
M. Hattingh et al. (Eds.): I3E 2020, LNCS 12066, pp. 204–215, 2020.
https://doi.org/10.1007/978-3-030-44999-5_17

payments within society, its accessibility and ease of use has led to experts classifying mobile payments as the potential payment of choice (Liébana-Cabanillas and Lara-Rubio 2017; Cabanillas et al. 2016). This makes mobile payments deployment relevant to the growth and development of businesses across the world (Oliveira et al. 2016). More importantly in developing countries, the mobile payment revolution is transforming households and businesses by providing a business solution to small and medium-sized businesses as well as mobile phone-related financial services to the underserved population, and help developing economies leapfrog poor non-existing payment infrastructure (Asongu et al. 2018).

Arguably, it is fascinating to observe that earlier studies on mobile payment have not fully explored the various factors that influence the behavioural intention of merchants to adopt mobile payment technology (Cabanillas et al. 2016; Dahlberg et al. 2015). Current studies on mobile payments have mostly explored technology and consumer adoption especially their implementation (Miao and Jayakar 2016; Madan and Yadav 2016). While consumer adoption studies are important in understanding mobile payments systems, researchers are of the view that an investigation of consumer adoption in isolation will not provide a full understanding of mobile payments (Dahlberg et al. 2015).

Trust, which is an essential adoption enabler in different IS situations, has not been adequately looked at in the environment of merchant adoption of mobile payment. However, mobile payments, transactions can occur among unknown entities, since mobile payments are regarded as a type of an online transaction completed over a mobile network and an accepted progression from electronic payment systems. This makes trust a significant facilitator for the merchant adoption of mobile payment (Rouibah et al. 2016). Therefore, this study seeks to understand the merchant adoption of m-payment systems and explore the trust-theoretic perspective to examine the enablers of merchant trust in mobile payment systems (Mallat 2007). The questions underpinning the study are: what is the enabler of merchant trust and what is the role of merchant trust in m payment adoption. The remainder of this paper is structured as follows: The next section reviews the literature on mobile payments and briefly discusses the theoretical underpinnings. The third section presents the conceptual framework guiding the study; the section that follows details the methodology employed. Subsequently, the findings are analysed, and discussions of the findings presented. Finally, the paper concludes with specific contributions and directions for future research.

## 2   Literature Review

### 2.1   Merchant Adoption of M-Payment Systems

The most critical step for technology acceptance and success in technological innovations such as mobile payments is for the intended users to take the initially vital step of adoption. The vibrant nature of evolving technologies and the dynamic circumstances calls for the basic question in adoption "what factors affect the intended user to adopt various technologies?" Because research on IT innovation adoption is extensive, this fundamental question is examined from various dimensions such as technological, and security features, individual adopters, organisations and environment (Miao and Jayakar 2016; Dahlberg et al. 2015; Madan and Yadav 2016). Generally, scholars have used different theories to explain the adoption of innovation in technology. The study used literature on "trust" in combination with the Technology Acceptance Model (TAM) to establish a trust-theoretic model for payment adoption. TAM has been extensively used in studying IS adoption behavior (Hsiao 2019; Upadhyay and Jahanyan 2016; Merhi 2016; Shanko et al. 2016). The theory stipulates that individual's adoption of an innovation in an information system is dependent on the intention of the individual to use the system and an extent to which a customer accept that adopting an innovation will improve his effectiveness and job performance (Davis 1993; Liébana-Cabanillas et al. 2017).

Generally, using TAM is appealing in the sense that it is empirically robust, with excellent measurement qualities and dependable instruments (Davis 1993; Aboobucker and Bao 2018). Several innovation studies have validated the instructive supremacy of TAM for technology acceptance which is proven for multiple IS types (Davis 1993; Davis et al. 1989). The two key belief concepts of PU and PEOU in the theory might not sufficiently explicate the effect of additional usage issues that can influence individual intention to adopt (Davis 1993; Moon and Kim 2001). However, limited studies have examined "trust" as an additional concept. Nevertheless, trust is a fundamental concern in the mobile payment context due to the apprehensions associated with the mobile service provider and the environmental uncertainties associated with mobile technology. Chandra et al. (2010) examined trust in consumer adoption of mobile payment and the role of trust by contextualising the trust antecedents to the m-payment situation proposing a trust-theoretic m-payment adoption model. Drawing from Chandra et al. (2010), the study contextualises the antecedents of trust in mobile payment situation to merchant adoption based on the trust-theoretic m-payment adoption model.

**Merchant Trust in Mobile Payments.** The concept of trust has attracted a considerable amount of research due to its significant role in information systems research, especially in the e-commerce environment. Mobile payments, which are a kind of online transaction, involve virtuality, anonymity and temporal and spatial separation, which can lead to considerable uncertainty and risk. Therefore, trust is very relevant for mobile payment technology adoption. According to Zhou (2013) merchants usually have concerns about security when it comes to the use of mobile payment. Nevertheless, merchants consider trust in payment services providers and the security of mobile payment solutions as necessary criteria for the adoption of mobile payment. Therefore, it is necessary to integrate trust in examining the merchant adoption of mobile payments (Zhou 2013). Therefore, in the mobile payment environment, the two enablers of merchant trust consist of trust in provider of mobile service as well as trust in technology-enhanced by characteristics of the service provider and characteristics of the mobile technology (Chandra et al. 2010; Broutsou and Fitsilis 2012).

## 2.2 Mobile Service Provider (MSP) Characteristic

Always, there is an affiliation between the mobile payment service provider characteristics and merchant trust as shown in Fig. 1. This can be likened to the concept of the "halo effect". The concept of the halo effect is based on the explanation that an individual's perception or views about a product or a person is based on previous experiences and the sort of interpretation which leads to cognitive bias. For instance, one can explain that Apple's other products are successful and people have confidence in it, due to the positive influence and how successful iPod was (Chong et al. 2018; Wilcox 2008). Thus, merchant perceptions on MSP as fair and honest translates to beliefs and trust for the mobile payment system controlled by the MSP. Research demonstrates that based on the halo effect, merchant trust has a positive relationship with the perceived reputation of the provider of the service, which leads to trusting beliefs in the merchant.

Therefore Proposition 1: The reputation of mobile service providers influences the level of trust the merchant has in mobile payments.

Similarly, opportunism is evident when implied and obvious possibilities around pre-determined conduct are fraudulently abused (Chong et al. 2018; John 1984). Regarding mobile payment transactions, the service provider plays a vital role, provider opportunism can be inferred as dishonest happenings such as altering information, revealing personal customer data, or deliberately unfulfilling responsibilities and promises. Therefore, merchant trust for the m-payment transaction will reduce when there is perceived opportunism. (Chong et al. 2018; Xin et al. 2013).

Thus, we propose that Proposition 2: The level of merchant trust in mobile payment systems will be reduced when there is perceived opportunism.

## 2.3 Mobile Technology Characteristics

Confidentiality and Safety concerns hamper merchant adoption of an online and wireless channel for a commercial transaction (Bhuvana and Vasantha 2017). Because of the shared domain of online information which merchants may be reluctant to adopt until they are convinced of self-assurance in the safety feature of the technology (Osakwe and Okeke 2016). In the mobile payment environment, merchants have to entrust all their account details, to MSPs and other players in the mobile payment context. Owing to the merchant's lack of control and uncertainties associated with mobile payment transactions makes merchants perceive environmental risks (Bhuvana and Vasantha 2017; Osakwe and Okeke 2016).

So, we propose that Proposition 3: The level of merchant trust in mobile payment systems are affected by Perceived environmental risk.

Nevertheless, the threat posed by mobile payment systems in comparison to traditional payment methods, stern from the technological uncertainties using the open technological infrastructure for transactions (Bhuvana and Vasantha 2017). Building suitable legal and technological safeguards can be accomplished through the development of institutional-based trust through technical procedures such as encryption of data and additional legal actions that avert confidentiality and monetary losses as a means of structural assurance for the mobile environment (McKnight et al. 2002). In other words, if a merchant perceived a very useful structural assurance, it will increase the level of merchant trust in mobile payment systems. Zhou (2013) and Dahlberg et al. (2015) have demonstrated that reducing the risk associated with the transaction would probably lead to the increasing adopting of mobile payments as a mode of transaction. Hence, we propose that Proposition 4: The level of merchant trust in the mobile payment system is positively influenced by perceived structural assurance.

### 2.4    Adoption Intention of Mobile Payment Based on Merchant Trust

Studies have confirmed that trust is dependent on the agency of an IT to perform a definite task (Lizcano et al. 2019; Teo et al. 2005). Regarding the mobile payment scenario, the skill is considered as the capability credence, which enables the merchants to trust that the mobile payment is suitable in attaining the anticipated objective and hence execute the intended level of performance. (Broutsou and Fitsilis 2012; Pavlou 2003). Similarly, in different online settings, individual trust is an essential element of perceived usefulness in mobile payment environment due to the uncertainties involved in such transactions and the impersonal nature of the mobile internet environment. Hence, we propose that Proposition 5: Perceived usefulness will positively influence merchant trust in mobile payment systems.

However, if there is low merchant trust in the system, it will drive the merchant to be anxious with the transactional routines (Teo et al. 2005). Which can lead to individual spending more time and effort in comprehending the system leading to systems usage challenge (Pavlou 2003; Moqbel and Bartelt 2016). Merchant trust in m-payment systems is related to perceived ease of use of m payment systems. As a result, we propose that Proposition 6: the extent of merchant trust in m-payment systems is related to perceived ease of use. Proposition 7: Merchant trust in m payment systems will positively influence merchant adoption of mobile payment.

According to Yang et al. (2012), the TRA indicates that 'an individual's intention to adopt an IS innovation is influenced by attitude and subjective norms, which are shaped by behavioral and normative beliefs of an individual. Trust then becomes an essential behavioral belief that generates positive attitudes to influence intention to adopt mobile payment systems, when trust is positive it is likely that merchants will likely have an intention to adopt the mobile payment system. Henceforth, merchants will adopt m-payment systems that are easy to use and will be perceived as useful. There are several benefits of M-payment systems to merchants irrespective of place and time, self-regulating transactions, which leads to effective payment transactions to the merchant. Thus, leading to an expectation that because merchant regards the mobile payment as a useful tool in achieving their purpose, they will adopt. Therefore, we propose that Proposition 8: Merchant adoption of mobile payment is positively influenced by Perceived ease of use. Proposition 9: Perceived usefulness of the m-payment systems is connected to merchant adoption of m-payment systems.

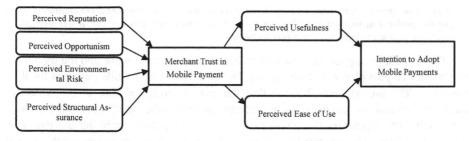

**Fig. 1.** Conceptual framework Source: Adopted from (Chandra et al. 2010)

# 3 Methodology

The study adopted an exploratory approach to help bring a deeper understanding of the issues under study (Saunders et al. 2012). As such, a case study was used as the research method. A case study is considered suitable for this study grounded on Yin's (2009) assertion of a case study where "why and how" questions are asked. In addition, case studies help in areas where the researcher does not have much control over the situation or where the issues under investigation are new and there is not much theory to explain issues adequately (Yin 2009). Empirical research on merchant adoption of mobile payments is spiral, in this case, the phenomenon is new and needs an in-depth understanding from the perspective of a developing country experience. The descriptive case study approach was used to enable theory to guide the data collection process (Yin 2009); as a result, the trust-theoretic stance and Technology Acceptance Model (TAM) were reviewed as the theory underpinning the case study design (Chandra et al. 2010). Face to face interview was used as a data collection method. The interview guide consisted of both open and close-ended questions. According to Walsham (1993) and Yin (2009) case study research has no universally accepted number of cases. It can be a single case or multiple cases. This research was based on a case study of two merchants from the service sector in the health industries. The case was strategically selected to enhance its external validity but not based on statistical consideration. The case was analyzed using Miles and Huberman's (2013) approach to data analysis.

# 4 Results and Discussion of Findings

## 4.1 Mobile Service Provider Characteristics

From the case finding it was established that the respondents selected the current service provider because of its brand reputation and the requisite credibility and infrastructure to deliver a reputable mobile payment service to merchants. The issue of mobile service providers' reputation was an essential trust-building mechanism in merchant adoption of mobile payment.

> *"It is an international company with a lot of reputation. They are credible to provide payment services, besides there is no known scandal against the service provider for all the years they have been operating the mobile money platform".* The CEO of a pharmaceutical retail shop

*"My service provider, is listed on the Ghana stock exchange which makes them credible and for the period I have worked with them their services have not failed so far, it has worked well".:* Director of operations in a private health facility.

These findings suggest that merchants depend on the brand name and the reputation of the service provider as risk-mitigating factors in adopting mobile payment for their business. The interviewees believe that the risk is mitigated due to the levels of authorization that the provider has in place to ensure that the rightful persons are either authorizing or originating the transaction or the exact person receiving the payment. For every transaction, you receive a message to confirm the transaction and this serves as a record to trace your transaction. Again, the respondents believe that, because there is a regulator who regulates and monitors the operations of a service provider, it will push them to do the right thing.

*"I believe people do what is inspected not what is expected. We have not experienced a situation where the service provider has used our information for their selfish interest. This is because all transaction comes with notification messages to confirm the transaction".* As mention by the Operations director.

These findings suggest merchants trust that, service providers have the ability and benevolence needed to provide the necessary service experience. This is because of their technological infrastructure and the legal structures that bind their operations. The merchants believe that their service providers will work within a regulated legal framework so they can be trusted to do the right things.

However, further, exploring the data retrieved from the merchants revealed that they are suspicious their service providers can behave opportunistically. This is in relation to merchant information and does not trust that their information could be safe with the service provider, because it is possible that service providers could give out personal information to the third party.

*As intimated by the CEO "Sometimes you receive unsolicited information from the third party and you wonder how and where they get the information, which makes you think that, your service provider may have given merchant information to a third party".*

This makes merchants unsure of the security of their information with the service provider, which they think could be detrimental to the business when given to your competitor. These findings suggest that the extent of merchant trust in mobile payment is influenced by the service provider reputation, however, the merchant perception of mobile service providers opportunism can reduce the level of merchant trust in M payment. These finding support propositions 1 and 2 in the model.

These findings confirm earlier findings by Chandra et al. (2010) and Xin et al. (2013) on how features of the service provider and mobile payment vendor characteristics can affect trust in mobile payment adoption.

## 4.2   Mobile Technology Characteristics

On findings pertaining to mobile technology characteristics, it was discovered from the case findings that, the inherent technological risk associated with mobile payments has an influence on the adoption intention of merchants. According to the respondent, using mobile payment as a merchant comes with a huge risk because mobile payment operates in a wireless environment, people can steal information from the provider.

*"Since it is an IT platform someone can hack into the system and delete or modify information for reasons best known to them, this makes it risky but because of its advantages it is worth the risk."* As intimated by the CEO.

This assertion by merchants portrays mobile payment as potentially having significant technological risk. As such, merchants are skeptical about their information with the service provider because mobile payment is a wireless network and is susceptible to hacker attacks and intruders, which can affect transactional security. Merchants were particularly concerned about privacy, security, fraud, payment transaction errors and potential loss of cash. As a result, they did not always feel very confident in using the mobile payment for their transactions. The merchants interviewed think that mobile payment can be trusted but the risk associated with it, impacts negatively on their trust and influence their attitude which they consider a barrier to adoption of mobile payment.

*"We get all kind of calls supposedly coming from providers but it turns out to be intruders who are able to generate codes, that should be coming from service providers which are a little bit suspicious if merchant information ends up with third parties"* As alluded by the operations director

*"I think the encryptions back to back are not strong enough because fraudsters are able to wipe people's wallet without knowing the merchant code. I don't feel safe with the telecom company because they do not understand the banking rudiment; I will feel safe if these services are run by the banks"* a statement by the operations Director

This finding is similar to earlier findings on the relationship between risk and trust (see Pavlou 2003; Osakwe and Okeke 2016; Bhuvana and Vasantha 2017). These findings support proposition 3 in the model. Additionally, the findings from the case study demonstrate that merchants are able to build confidence and sufficient trust in mobile payment systems because of structural assurance such as encryption, authentication and third-party certifications by their service providers. For example, the use of message authentication code, assures merchants and their clients that information is not tampered during transferring via networks. This ensures confidentiality, anonymity, and integrity (see Yang and Lin 2016; Xin et al. 2013). This, to a large extent, ensures the safety of the system. *"I know that when I initiate a transaction nobody will be able to intercept it midway has and it gets to its destination because there is encryption for a transaction"* as intimated by the CEO.

The efficient application of these technical controls helps build trust mechanisms for mobile payment systems which improve merchants' trust and confidence in mobile payment adoption intention. Further, the case findings show that proof of transactions, recipient, and assurance of user's identity helps to secure mobile payment environment without fear of compromise. This finding is also supported by our 4th proposition which states that the level of merchant trust in mobile payment systems is influenced by perceived structural assurance.

## 4.3    Perceived Usefulness

It was identified from the case findings that merchants interviewed use the payment platform to pay their suppliers and receive payment from their clients. According to them, the companies strategically adopted mobile payment to improve the effectiveness of their business and to meet their customers' needs profitably. More importantly, the findings suggest that because the payment system is convenient and useful the merchants are prepared to ignore the risk associated with the transaction.

> *"The use of mobile payment has helped reduced outstanding debts because clients are able to fall on mobile payment at any time". "Since it is an IT platform someone can hack into the system and delete or modify information for reasons best known; to them, this makes it risky but because of its advantages it is worth the risk."* Both respondents confirmed their usefulness.

This finding is similar to what Yang et al. (2012) found that in online payment, uncertainty risk is more or less ignored by consumers pursuing convenience and usefulness of online payment. This finding supports proposition 9 which suggests that perceived usefulness of mobile payments is associated with merchant adoption. However, this same finding points to the fact that merchant trust of mobile payment systems does not depend on perceived usefulness which means that the proposition 7 is not supported because it states that merchants trust in mobile payment systems will influence merchant adoption but the findings indicate that adoption of mobile payment does not necessarily depend on trust because trust may not signify usefulness.

## 4.4    Perceived Ease of Use

Finally, findings from the case study suggest that the functionality of the mobile payment interface by service providers through a mobile device is relatively simple and easy to navigate. They are of the view that using mobile payments for their transactions on a mobile device does not require much. The ease with which they are able to operate and understand the procedures produces a lot of confidence and builds trust that they have control of their transactions. This finding is consistent with (Lu et al. 2011). It was also observed through the case findings that merchants primarily use mobile payments to receive payments and to pay for their bills. It was evident that the level of education of merchants interviewed played a significant role in enhancing their technological literacy of mobile payment functions. Both respondents had a post-graduate degree and their staff a minimum of diploma degree.

> *"I am knowledgeable in all forms of electronic payment, be it internet or mobile hence mobile payment interface is easy" "We have dedicated staff who are knowledgeable in technology and are put in charge to do the mobile transactions"* As commented by the merchants

This finding supports propositions 6 and 8 which indicates that the level of merchant trust in mobile payment systems has a positive influence on perceived ease of use and that merchant adoption of mobile payment is positively influenced by perceived ease of use.

## 5   Conclusion and Recommendation

The study set out to explore the role of trust in merchant adoption of m-payment systems as well as the enablers for merchant's trust in mobile payment systems through the conceptualization of the service provider and the technology characteristics as the two dimensions that could influence merchant adoption of mobile payments. Arguably, the role of merchant trust is very significant for adoption, because of the technological risk and lack of merchant control (Yang et al. 2012; Xin et al. 2013). Hence, a sufficient trust-building mechanism is essential for merchants to adopt mobile payment. More-over, the characteristics of the service provider of mobile payment and the mobile technology features are both imperative to build trust in mobile payment systems for merchants' adoption. The study also found that the trust of both technology and service provider has a far more critical influence on merchants' adoption of mobile payments than perceived usefulness or ease of use.

### 5.1   Implications of the Study

**Implication for Theory.** This study contributes to the information system literature, by establishing a relationship between merchant trust and adoption intention because merchant's acceptance and use of mobile payments is growing in recent times. Hence it is imperative to appreciate the effect of trust and how service providers can implement these technologies. These new theoretical insights will help researchers to better understand merchants trust-related antecedents and their influence on technology adoption in the context of merchant adoption of mobile payments.

**Implication for Practice.** Service providers should consider the opportunity to nurture and build merchant trust because merchant trust acts as a fundamental enabler for the adoption of mobile payments.

### 5.2   Limitation of the Study

The study has some limitations, it concentrated on a few variables and only done in the context of Ghana and targeted merchants who have already adopted mobile payment. Future research could compare merchants who have not yet adopted the technology with those who have adopted in context with a similar characteristic.

## References

Asongu, S.A., Nwachukwu, J.C., Orim, S.M.I.: Mobile phones, institutional quality and entrepreneurship in Sub-Saharan Africa. Technol. Forecast. Soc. Change **131**(November 2016), 183–203 (2018). https://doi.org/10.1016/j.techfore.2017.08.007

Aboobucker, I., Bao, Y.: What obstruct customer acceptance of internet banking? Security and privacy, risk, trust and website usability and the role of moderators. J. High Technol. Manag. Res. **29**(1), 109–123 (2018)

Bhuvana, M., Vasantha, S.: A Structural Equation Modeling (SEM) approach for mobile banking adoption-a strategy for achieving financial inclusion. Indian J. Public Health Res. Dev. 8(2), 175–181 (2017)

Broutsou, A., Fitsilis, P.: Online trust: the influence of perceived company's reputation on consumers' trust and the effects of trust on intention for online transactions. J. Serv. Sci. Manag. 5(04), 365 (2012)

Chandra, S., Srivastava, S.C., Theng, Y.-L.: Evaluating the role of trust in consumer adoption of mobile payment systems: an empirical analysis. Commun. Assoc. Inf. Syst. 29, 561–588 (2010). 27 Article

Chong, A.Y.L., Lacka, E., Boying, L., Chan, H.K.: The role of social media in enhancing Guanxi and perceived effectiveness of E-commerce institutional mechanisms in online marketplace. Inf. Manag. 55(5), 621–632 (2018)

Congdon, S.: What's in your wallet: addressing the regulatory grey area surrounding mobile payments. Case W. Res. JL Tech. Internet 7, 95 (2016)

Dahlberg, T., Guo, J., Ondrus, J.: A critical review of mobile payment research. Electron. Commer. Res. Appl. 14(5), 265–284 (2015)

Davis, F.D.: User acceptance of information technology: system characteristics, user perceptions and behavioral impacts. Int. J. Man-Mach. Stud. 38(3), 475–487 (1993)

Davis, F.D.: Perceived usefulness, perceived ease of use, and user acceptance of information technology. MIS Q. 13(3), 318–339 (1989)

Davis, D., Bagozzi, R.P., Warshaw, P.R.: User acceptance of computer technology: a comparison of two theoretical models. Manag. Sci. 35(8), 982–1003 (1989)

Hsiao, M.H.: Mobile payment services as a facilitator of value co-creation: a conceptual framework. J. High Technol. Manag. Res. 30(2), 100353 (2019)

John, G.: An empirical investigation of some antecedents of opportunism in a marketing channel. J. Market. Res. 21, 278–289 (1984)

Liébana-Cabanillas, F., Lara-Rubio, J.: Predictive and explanatory modeling regarding adoption of mobile payment systems. Technol. Forecast. Soc. Chang. 120, 32–40 (2017)

Liébana Cabanillas, F., Slade, E., Dwivedi, Y.: Time for a different perspective: a preliminary investigation of barriers of merchants' adoption of mobile payments (2016)

Liébana-Cabanillas, F., Ramos de Luna, I., Montoro-Ríos, F.: Intention to use new mobile payment systems: a comparative analysis of SMS and NFC payments. Econ. Res. 30(1), 892–910 (2017)

Lu, Y., Yang, S., Chau, P.Y., Cao, Y.: Dynamics between the trust transfer process and intention to use mobile payment services: a cross-environment perspective. Inf. Manag. 48(8), 393–403 (2011)

Lizcano, D., Lara, J.A., White, B., Aljawarneh, S.: Blockchain-based approach to create a model of trust in open and ubiquitous higher education. J. Comput. High. Educ. 31, 1–26 (2019)

Madan, K., Yadav, R.: Behavioural intention to adopt mobile wallet: a developing country perspective. J. Indian Bus. Res. 8(3), 227–244 (2016). https://doi.org/10.1108/JIBR-10-2015-0112

Mallat, N.: Exploring consumer adoption of mobile payments - a qualitative study. J. Strateg. Inf. Syst. 16, 413–432 (2007)

McKnight, D.H., Choudhury, V., Kacmar, C.: Developing and validating trust measures for e-commerce: an integrative typology. Inf. Syst. Res. 13(3), 334–359 (2002)

Merhi, M.I.: Towards a framework for online game adoption. Comput. Hum. Behav. 60, 253–263 (2016)

Miao, M., Jayakar, K.: Mobile payments in Japan, South Korea and China: cross-border convergence or divergence of business models? Telecommun. Policy 40(2–3), 182–196 (2016)

Miles, M.B., Huberman, A.M., Saldana, J.: Qualitative Data Analysis: A Methods Sourcebook. SAGE Publications, Incorporated, Thousand Oaks, California (2013)

Moqbel, M.A., Bartelt, V.L.: Open data discourse: consumer acceptance of personal cloud: Integrating trust and risk with technology acceptance model. Trans. Replication Res. 2, 1–8 (2016)

Moon, J.W., Kim, Y.G.: Extending the Tam for a World-Wide-Web context. Inf. Manag. 38(4), 217–230 (2001)

Oliveira, T., Thomas, M., Baptista, G., Campos, F.: Mobile payment: understanding the determinants of customer adoption and intention to recommend the technology. Comput. Hum. Behav. 61, 404–414 (2016)

Osakwe, C.N., Okeke, T.C.: Facilitating mCommerce growth in Nigeria through mMoney usage: a preliminary analysis. Interdisc. J. Inf. Knowl. Manag. 11, 115–139 (2016)

Pavlou, P.A.: Consumer acceptance of electronic commerce—integrating trust and risk with the technology acceptance model. Int. J. Electron. Commer. 7(3), 101–134 (2003)

Rouibah, K., Lowry, P.B., Hwang, Y.: The effects of perceived enjoyment and perceived risks on trust formation and intentions to use online payment systems: new perspectives from an Arab Country. Electron. Commer. Res. Appl. 19, 33–43 (2016)

Saunders, M., Lewis, P., Thornhill, A.: Research Methods for Business Students, 6th edn. Pearson Education Limited, Noida (2012)

Shanko, G., Negash, S., Bandyopadhyay, T.: Mobile healthcare services adoption. Int. J. Netw. Virtual Organ. 16(2), 143–156 (2016)

Teo, E., Fraunholz, B., Unnithan, C.: Inhibitors and facilitators for mobile payment adoption in Australia: a preliminary study. In: International Conference on Mobile Business (ICMB 2005), pp. 663–666. IEEE, July 2005

Upadhyay, P., Jahanyan, S.: Analyzing user perspective on the factors affecting use intention of mobile based transfer payment. Internet Res. 26(1), 38–56 (2016)

Walsham, G.: Interpreting Information Systems in Organizations, vol. 19. Wiley, Chichester (1993)

Wilcox, J.: The iPhone Halo Effect. Apple Watch—eweek.com, 22 August 2008. http://blogs. eweek.com/applewatch/content/mac_os_x/the_iphone_halo_effect.html

Xin, H., Techatassanasoontorn, A.A., Tan, F.B.: Exploring the influence of trust on mobile payment adoption (2013)

Yang, J.H., Lin, P.Y.: A mobile payment mechanism with anonymity for cloud computing. J. Syst. Softw. 116, 69–74 (2016)

Yang, S., Lu, Y., Gupta, S., Cao, Y., Zhang, R.: Mobile payment services adoption across time: an empirical study of the effects of behavioral beliefs, social influences, and personal traits. Comput. Hum. Behav. 28(1), 129–142 (2012)

Yin, R.K.: Case Study Research, Design and Methods, 3rd edn. Sage Publications, Newbury Park (2009)

Zhou, T.: An empirical examination of continuance intention of mobile payment services. Decis. Support Syst. 54(2), 1085–1091 (2013)

# The Influence of Price Comparison Websites on Online Switching Behavior: A Consumer Empowerment Perspective

Michael Adu Kwarteng[1,2]([📧]) [iD], Abdul Bashiru Jibril[1,2] [iD],
Elsamari Botha[1,2] [iD], and Christian Nedu Osakwe[1,2] [iD]

[1] Faculty of Management and Economics, Tomas Bata University in Zlin,
Mostni 5139, 76001 Zlin, Czech Republic
{Kwarteng, Jibril}@utb.cz, emc@usb.ac.za,
chriso@sun.ac.za
[2] University of Stellenbosch Business School, Stellenbosch, South Africa

**Abstract.** While online price comparison websites have burgeoned, there is scant understanding of how they influence online consumer behavior. This study addresses this gap in the literature by investigating the influence of price comparison websites on online switching behavior, and also suggests some additional factors that may be considered when looking at this relationship. We argue that shopper innovativeness, their perceived usefulness of the ad, and their customer service experience consciousness are important factors to consider when evaluating the impact of price comparison websites on eSwitching behavior. We also argue that the most appropriate theoretical lens through which to investigate this relationship is that of the consumer empowerment paradigm. A conceptual model is proposed and tested. Our analysis of 345 sample respondents finds that perceived usefulness of ads and customer service experience expectations are important enablers to price comparison websites use. Similarly, we find that shopper innovativeness and customer service expectations, in addition to price comparison websites use, are significant enablers to eSwitching behaviour. However, contrary to prediction, we find that shopper innovativeness has little to no influence on shoppers' use of price comparison websites; we also observed similar patterns concerning the link between the perceived usefulness of online ads and eSwitching behaviour. In conclusion, our research contributes to better understanding the influence of price comparison websites on online switching behavior, and the factors that might influence this relationship.

**Keywords:** Consumer empowerment · Customer service experience
consciousness · eSwitching · Online ads · Price comparison websites · Shopper
innovativeness

# 1   Introduction

While online price comparison websites have burgeoned, there is scant understanding of how they influence online consumer (eSwitching) behavior. This study addresses this gap in the literature by investigating the influence of price comparison websites on online switching behavior. While Osakwe and Chovancová (2015) examined female shoppers' perceptions towards the use of price comparison websites, Jung et al. (2014) examined work shoppers' response to price comparison websites, and Pourabedin *et al.* (2016) investigated the role of customer value and attitudes in online channel switching behavior, there are no studies to the authors' knowledge that investigates the relationship between eSwitching behavior and price comparison websites. The emerging question, therefore, is whether the use of price comparison websites can lead to eSwitching behavior. This study by addressing this question seeks to close the void in our understanding concerning the relationship between price comparison websites and eSwitching behavior. This study also suggests some additional factors that may be considered when looking at this relationship.

Accordingly, and based on a survey of existing research (Broniarczyk and Griffin 2014; Hudders et al. 2019; Osakwe and Chovancova 2015; Xu et al. 2013; Zhang et al. 2012), it is argued that shoppers' innovativeness, their perceived usefulness of online ads, and their customer service experience consciousness are important factors to consider when evaluating the impact of price comparison websites on eSwitching behavior and this forms the overarching objective of our paper. We also argue that the most appropriate theoretical lens through which to investigate this relationship is that of the consumer empowerment paradigm (e.g. Broniarczyk and Griffin 2014; Camacho et al. 2014; Kucuk 2009). In other words, by employing the consumer empowerment paradigm, this paper's objective is to investigate the relationship between (the use of) price comparison websites and eSwitching behavior in addition to the investigation of the determinants behind these phenomena, which we have identified above.

Altogether, this allows us to contribute to the literature on online shopping in at least two important ways. First, is that we contribute to the online shopping literature particularly concerning the presentation of evidence that the use of price comparison websites, especially with regard to young and existing online shoppers, significantly empowers shoppers to engage in eSwitching behavior. The second contribution pertains to the investigation of the determinants behind the perceived use of price comparison websites in addition to the investigation of the empirical question on the determinants of eSwitching behavior. In particular, we find that shoppers' traits primarily customer experience consciousness and innovativeness are enablers to eSwitching behavior, while positive perceptions towards the use of online ads as well as customer experience consciousness engender the use of price comparison websites.

Because it is commonly known that young adults, especially student population, are usually heavy users of online services and in general more receptive to emerging technologies (see also Yoo and Donthu 2001), we chose to test the study hypotheses using a (university) student sample; which is also consistent with studies on consumer switching in the technology context (e.g. Bhattacherjee et al. 2012). At the same time, it is worth noting that our sample is primarily made up of experienced internet users and who are familiar with online shopping. Taken together, this empirical context is appropriate for our investigation.

The following literature review addresses each of these constructs in turn, before suggesting the theoretical model that was tested. This is followed by a brief overview of the methodology, and findings of an exploratory study to test the model. We conclude with a short discussion of these findings.

# 2  Literature Informing Hypotheses Development

## 2.1  Consumer Empowerment Paradigm

The consumer empowerment paradigm in marketing is an important extension of the psychological empowerment construct, long studied, in the psychology literature (cf. Zimmerman 1995; Cattaneo and Chapman 2010). Camacho et al. (2014:294), while citing previous research, describe empowerment as "strategies or mechanisms that equip people with sufficient knowledge and autonomy to allow them to exert control over a certain decision". Similarly, it has been noted in the marketing literature that "empowerment requires mechanisms for individuals to gain control over issues that concern them, including opportunities to develop and practice skills necessary to exert control over their decision making" (Pires et al. 2006, p. 938). In light of previous discussions and among them Broniarczyk and Griffin (2014), Kucuk (2009), and Pires et al. (2006), the current investigation argues that this paradigm can help us gain understanding into the perceived use of price comparison websites and eSwitching behaviour in particular among existing shoppers. In general, the internet equips users with the tool to gain access to credible and quality information and this by implication confers more power and freedom of choice to users and in this case online shoppers. Moreover, since it is known that customers often rely on expert advice (in this instance, price comparison websites) when making purchase decisions (Camacho et al. 2014), such advice - well-intentioned – can dramatically reduce switching cost. One of the benefits of comparison tools and in this case price comparison websites is that they offer shoppers a range of choices (Broniarczyk and Griffin 2014), thus allowing shoppers to shop across stores. Online switching behaviour (or eSwitching) is considered to be a possible outcome of this process. Similarly, since it is has been suggested in the literature that digital ads may be an important source of consumer empowerment today (Hudders et al. 2019), it is considered therefore to play an influential role in shoppers' behavioural tendencies to use price comparison websites and to consequently eSwitch. Consequently, the following hypothesis is proposed:

*H1: Price comparison websites' perceptions positively influence eSwitching behaviour.*

At the same time, it is known that intrapersonal factors, described as "how people think about themselves and includes domain-specific perceived control and self-efficacy, motivation to control, perceived competence, and mastery" (Zimmerman 1995, p. 588), is a key aspect of empowerment. Accordingly, we consider intrinsic factors, or more precisely traits, like the customer service experience and consumer/ shopper innovativeness, to be strong propelling force for price comparison websites use and eSwitching behaviour. Before discussing each of these in turn, we turn to eSwitching behaviour.

## 2.2    eSwitching Behaviour

The reasons why customers engage in switching intentions and/or behaviour remains an important topic in the literature to this day (Bhattacherjee et al. 2012; Fan and Suh 2014; Gopta et al. 2004; Malhotra and Malhotra 2013; Mosavi et al. 2018; Pourabedin et al. 2016). Multiple reasons exist for this kind of behaviour (Chuang and Tai 2016; Keaveney 1995; Malhotra and Malhotra 2013; Mosavi et al. 2018; Zhang et al. 2012) but a factor often identified as a key determinant is the attractiveness of alternatives (Chuang and Tai 2016; Xu et al. 2013; Zhang et al. 2012). In the context of this study, consumers might easily switch between online stores when it is believed they can get better price deals elsewhere. Price comparison websites lower the barriers to switching by offering such alternatives in one central place, with links that could easily navigate to said alternatives. Because price comparison websites are price aggregators, it offers the opportunity for shoppers to easily know the prices of each competing online stores and this consequently reduces switching cost. This study hypothesized (see H1) that these price comparison websites directly influence eSwitching behavior. The following section describes the former.

## 2.3    Price Comparison Websites

Comparison shopping can be defined as "the practice of comparing the prices of items from different sources to find the best deal" (Hajaj et al. 2015: 563). Price comparison websites provide the online alternative to this and we, therefore, define online price comparisons as *the online tool that allows for the comparison of item prices from different sources to find the best deal.* The use of price comparison websites has been acknowledged as an important search information tool, which has strong potential to alter shopping behaviour both in the online and offline environment (Bodur et al. 2015; Broeckelmann and Groeppel-Klein 2008, Osakwe and Chovancová 2015; Passyn et al. 2013). Osakwe and Chovancová (2015:597) describe price comparison websites as "a near-frictionless marketing intermediary that can drive down online shoppers' search costs".

Because shoppers can easily compare prices of similar firms and/or brands in a matter of seconds, the active use of price comparison websites not only reduces search costs but also empowers shoppers to buy from firms offering the best deal. This study argues that the greater the perceived usefulness of price comparison websites, the more it is expected that shoppers will use the information available on these sites in their pre- and post-purchase decisions. It, therefore, acts as a key mediator in the relationship between key influencing factors and online switching behavior. From a consumer empowerment perspective, it is pertinent to consider how these websites influence the relationship between eSwitching and shopper innovativeness, perceived usefulness of an ad and the consumers' service experience consciousness. Each of these now discussed in turn.

## 2.4   Shopper Innovativeness

Consumer/shopper innovativeness, or what some scholars may well refer to as variety seeking propensity, is a well-researched concept in the literature (e.g. Agarwal and Prasad 1998; Bhattacherjee et al. 2012; Xu et al. 2013; Mishra 2015). In this instance and following prior literature (Agarwal and Prasad 1998; Bhattacherjee et al. 2012), we define shopper innovativeness as *a trait reflecting the willingness on the part of the shopper to experiment and/or try out any new products or range of services*. Moreover, because consumer innovativeness has been implied in the internet browser context to positively relate to switching intentions among a similar sample of respondents like this study (Bhattacherjee et al. 2012), it stands to reason, that both the relationship between shopper innovativeness and eSwitching behavior, and its relationship to price comparison website perceptions begs investigation. Hence, we proposed that:

*H2: Shopper innovativeness positively influences eSwitching behavior.*
*H3: Shopper innovativeness is positively related to price comparison website perceptions.*

## 2.5   Customer Service Experience Consciousness

The role of customer service experience is well researched in academic and business literature (Berry et al. 2002; Khan et al. 2015; Meyer and Schwager 2007; Osakwe and Chovancová 2015). However, its relationship to online switching behavior and price comparison websites remains underdeveloped in empirical research. Service experience consciousness reflects a trait among shoppers who are highly demanding in service encounters, and thus tend to exhibit a higher dissatisfaction threshold. This trait, for example, has been reported to be an important enabler to customer-perceived use of price comparison websites (Osakwe and Chovancová 2015), and is therefore included in the proposed conceptual model:

*H4: Customer service experience consciousness is positively related to price comparison website perceptions.*

We extend this research by arguing that since this set of shoppers invests a significant amount of cognitive, emotional and even intellectual resources into service interactions/encounters with the firm, they are therefore more demanding, difficult to please and more likely to move from one store to another in search for better services at all times. Customer service experience consciousness has already been identified as a trait reflecting the likelihood of a customer to become highly dissatisfied with service encounters and since customer dissatisfaction has been linked to switching intentions in prior research (e.g. Fan and Suh 2014), it can be posited therefore that customer service experience consciousness and eSwitching behavior are related. Moreover, following previous research (Keaveney 1995; Liang et al. 2013), we argue that service inconvenience, impolite behavior on the part of service personnel, and occurrence of core service and service encounter failures will be less tolerated by those scoring high in customer service experience consciousness and thus in this case impacting eSwitching behavior. Consequently, the following hypothesis has been developed:

*H5: Customer service experience consciousness is positively related to eSwitching behavior.*

The final construct, from an empowered customer perspective, we felt pertinent to include in the study is that of the perceived usefulness of online ads.

### 2.6  Perceived Usefulness of Online Ads

Consumers' attitudinal response to advertisements in general and online ads, in particular, is mixed (Le and Vo 2017; Shavitt et al. 1998; Schlosser et al. 1999), yet it is considered an important contributing factor when investigating online consumer behavior (Ducoffe and Carlo 2000; Mehta 2000; Osakwe and Chovanocva 2015; Paliwoda et al. 2007). Some consumers have ill-feelings about online ads, others may be indifferent to online ads, while some have positive perceptions about online ads. In theory, however, ads are often meant to inform consumers and offer choices which they can easily choose from. Online ads, therefore, empower consumers concerning his/her buying decisions (cf. Ducoffe and Curlo 2000). Therefore, in this instance, online ads can confer significant power to consumers (Hudders et al. 2019), especially when it is perceived to be informative and valuable. In an online services context, strong perceptions towards online ads provide fertile ground for shoppers to become increasingly price-sensitive (Osakwe and Chovancová 2015). This may be particularly true with regard to the use of price comparison websites. This study, therefore, extends this line of the suggestion by including eSwitching behaviour as an alternative outcome of online ads' perceived usefulness. Consequently, the following hypotheses were developed:

*H6: Customers' perceived usefulness of ads positively influences their perception of price comparison websites.*
*H7: Customers' perceived usefulness of ads positively influences their eSwitching behavior.*

The above literature review and proposed hypotheses can be summarized in the theoretical model proposed in Fig. 1. This model extends prior research (e.g. Osakwe and Chovancová 2015) by our assessment of enablers to the perceived use of price comparison websites and eSwitching behavior, especially concerning young and existing online shoppers.

The methodology used to test the proposed model is outlined in the following section.

## 3  Empirical Study

### 3.1  Survey Data and Method

More specifically, student sample was used in the study because this is an important consumer segment for studying online behaviour and has also been extensively employed in the literature (Fan and Suh 2014; Hong 2015; Ozok and Wei 2010; Wu et al. 2011). This study recruited participants from one of the state universities in the

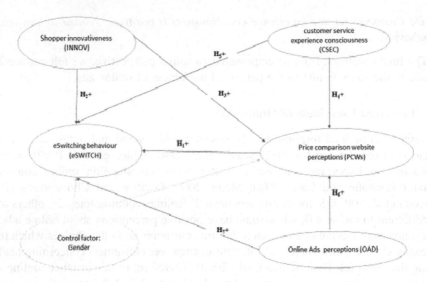

**Fig. 1.** Empirical model

Czech Republic using a convenience-based sampling approach which we consider to be most practical in this case. This study uses both online and self-administered surveys, nevertheless, most of the completed responses were from the self-administered questionnaire. Because we wanted to ensure that those who participated in the study have fairly good internet experience with online purchases, in the end – particularly after deleting responses from six non-online shoppers - we had in total 345 valid responses. Therefore, the empirical focus is on existing online shoppers.

The majority of sample respondents were female (59%), aged between 17–24 (80%), and undergraduates (66%). In this study, statistical analyses were performed using both IBM SPSS and WarpPLS (Kock 2017). Finally, the research constructs - except for demographics - were measured using a five-point scale (ranging from completely disagree to completely agree).

## 3.2   Construct Measurement Validation

In order to improve the face and construct validity of the research constructs, constructs were adapted constructs from the literature. In particular, the measures for customer service experience consciousness, perceptions regarding the use of online ads and price comparison websites were based on Osakwe and Chovancová (2015), while the measure for consumer innovativeness was based on Daghfous et al. (1999) and finally the measure for eSwitching was modified from Kim et al. (2006) in addition to reading from the broader literature.

The research hypotheses were tested by using the PLS-path modeling technique and precisely using mode A algorithm. The inspected composite reliability scores were as follows: 0.85 (online ads perceptions/OAD), 0.84 (price comparison websites use/PCWs), 0.80 (shopper innovativeness/INNOV), 0.71 (customer service experience consciousness/CSEC), and 0.74 (eSwitching behavior/eSWITCH). At the same time, all indicator loadings and weights were statistically significant at $p < 0.01$, besides all the indicator loadings but two exceeded the 0.6 scores required for this kind of exploratory work. In terms of convergent validity, average variance extracted (AVE) scores range from 0.59 (OAD), 0.58 (PCW), 0.58 (INNOV), 0.46(CSEC), to 0.49 (eSWITCH). Although not reported here, following Fornell and Larcker (1981) discriminant validity was established for the constructs.

## 4  Structural Model

Model fit and quality criteria were inspected based on SRMR and R-squared contribution ratio (RSCR). We obtained 0.09 (SRMR value and thus acceptable since it is less than 0.1) and RSCR scores of 0.99 (which approximates to the ideal cut-off value of 1) (Kock 2017).

Regarding the hypothesized relationships, there is evidence for all but two (see Table 1 for details). Notably, the control variable i.e. gender neither statistically impacted price comparison websites use nor eSwitching. Finally, model predictive power concerning shoppers' use of PCW was 14%, whereas for eSwitching it was 30%; meaning that the empirical model explains about 14% and 30% variations in the use of price comparison websites and eSwitching respectively.

**Table 1.** Structural Model statistics

| Hypothesis | β (t-ratios) | p-values | Significant/Not |
|------------|--------------|----------|-----------------|
| H1 | .19 (3.26) | <.01 | Yes |
| H2 | .36 (6.31) | <.01 | Yes |
| H3 | .04 (.51) | .30 | Not |
| H4 | .29 (4.58) | <.01 | Yes |
| H5 | .26 (4.88) | <.01 | Yes |
| H6 | .20 (4.36) | <.01 | Yes |
| H7 | .03 (.49) | .31 | Not |

## 5  Short Discussion and Conclusion

This study has been able to identify antecedent factors leading to switching behaviour in the context of service and in particular in online stores beyond the usual suspects in the literature, for instance, attitudes towards switching (cf. Pourabedin et al. 2016). Through the consumer empowerment paradigm, we find, not surprisingly, the perceived use of price comparison websites relates strongly with eSwitching. This novel finding in some ways mirrors the conclusion in past research about the role that search-intentions play in customers' channel switching (Gopta et al. 2004). The point is that shoppers who use price comparison websites mainly use it for bargain hunting. This suggests that to reduce this positive effect on online switching behaviour, online retail merchants, particularly with a focus on young shoppers, will need to do more in the area of sales promotion and loyalty coupons as this might be one of the most effective ways to reduce the incidence of eSwitching and even customer churn.

Also, we find that a higher possession of the following traits in shoppers namely innovativeness and their perception of the customer service experience empowers these shoppers to engage substantively in online switching behavior. Shopper innovativeness had the greatest impact on eSwitching. Since it has been suggested that individuals who are more likely to experiment with new ideas and/or products are more prone to switching (Bhattacherjee et al. 2012; Xu et al. 2013) and perceived innovativeness of the services provider inhibits customer switching intentions (Malhotra and Malhotra 2013), the study's finding, therefore, is a reinforcement to extant research.

Because shoppers who possess a higher level of service experience conscientiousness than others may be more prone to service dissatisfaction, the finding, therefore, mirrors previous discussions about the role of customer dissatisfaction in customer switching behaviour (cf. Chuang and Tai 2016; Fan and Suh 2014). Moreover, as predicted and consistent with previous research (Osakwe and Chovancová 2015), this study finds that positive perceptions concerning online ad usefulness, in addition to service expectations, increasingly empower shoppers to use price comparison websites.

Although this study initially proposed that consumer innovativeness and perceived use of price comparison websites are strongly related, evidence, however, shows it to be marginal, at best. Therefore, further research is needed to explore not only this insignificant finding but even further the supported research evidence reported in this paper. In other words, there is a need for more analysis on the research issues discussed in this work because until they are reassessed our findings are at best preliminary and limited to a specific sample. Furthermore, since the strength of relationships was never hypothesized, it is important therefore for future analysis to validate the assumption that shopper innovativeness, compared to others, has the strongest impact on online switching behaviour. Meanwhile, an important limitation of this analysis is that it was conducted using a student population and so makes it difficult to generalize beyond the target population. This consequently reinforces our call for further research on this topic. Finally, this study despite its limitations has added to the customer switching behaviour literature in addition to the heavily under-researched research stream of price comparison websites through the demonstration of the antecedents for eSwitching and shoppers use of price comparison websites based on the consumer empowerment paradigm.

**Acknowledgement.** This work was supported by the Internal Grant Agency of FaME through TBU in Zlín No. IGA/FaME/2020/002; and further by the financial support of research project NPU I no. MSMT-7778/2020 RVO - Digital Transformation and its Impact on Customer Behaviour and Business Processes in Traditional and Online markets.

# References

Agarwal, R., Prasad, J.: A conceptual and operational definition of personal innovativeness in the domain of information technology. Inf. Syst. Res. **9**(2), 204–215 (1998). https://doi.org/10.1287/isre.9.2.204

Berry, L.L., Carbone, L.P., Haeckel, S.H.: Managing the total customer experience. MIT Sloan Manag. Rev. **43**(3), 85–89 (2002)

Bhattacherjee, A., Limayem, M., Cheung, C.M.K.: User switching of information technology: a theoretical synthesis and empirical test research. Inf. Manag. **49**, 327–333 (2012). https://doi.org/10.1016/j.im.2012.06.002

Bodur, O., Klein, N.M., Arora, N.: Online price search: impact of price comparison sites on offline price evaluations. J. Retail. **91**(1), 125–139 (2015). https://doi.org/10.1016/j.jretai.2014.09.003

Broeckelmann, P., Groeppel-Klein, A.: Usage of mobile price comparison sites at the point of sale and its influence on consumers' shopping behaviour. Int. Rev. Retail Distrib. Consum. Res. **18**(2), 149–166 (2008). https://doi.org/10.1080/09593960701868266

Broniarczyk, S.M., Griffin, J.G.: Decision difficulty in the age of consumer empowerment. J. Consum. Psychol. **24**(4), 608–625 (2014). https://doi.org/10.1016/j.jcps.2014.05.003

Camacho, N., de Jong, M., Stremersch, S.: The effect of customer empowerment on adherence to expert advice. Int. J. Res. Mark. **31**, 293–308 (2014). https://doi.org/10.1016/j.jcps.2014.05.003

Cattaneo, L.B., Chapman, A.R.: The process of empowerment: a model for use in research and practice. Am. Psychol. **65**(7), 646–659 (2010). https://doi.org/10.1037/a0018854

Chuang, Y.F., Tai, Y.F.: Research on customer switching behavior in the service industry. Manag. Res. Rev. **39**(8), 925–939 (2016). https://doi.org/10.1108/MRR-01-2015-0022

Daghfous, N., Petrof, J.V., Pons, F.: Values and adoption of innovations: a cross-cultural study. J. Consum. Mark. **16**(4), 314–331 (1999). https://doi.org/10.1108/07363769910277102

Ducoffe, R.H., Curlo, E.: Advertising value and advertising processing. J. Mark. Commun. **6**(4), 247–262 (2000). https://doi.org/10.1080/135272600750036364

Fan, L., Suh, Y.-H.: Why do users switch to a disruptive technology? An empirical study based on expectation-disconfirmation theory. Inf. Manag. **51**(2), 240–248 (2014). https://doi.org/10.1016/j.im.2013.12.004

Fornell, C.G., Larcker, D.F.: Evaluating structural equation models with unobservable variables and measurement error. J. Mark. Res. **18**(1), 39–50 (1981). https://doi.org/10.1177/002224378101800104

Gopta, A., Su, B.-C., Walter, Z.: An empirical study of consumer switching from traditional to electronic channels: a purchase-decision process perspective. Int. J. Electron. Commer. **8**(3), 131–161 (2004). https://doi.org/10.1080/10864415.2004.11044302

Hajaj, C., Hazon, N., Sarne, D.: Improving comparison shopping agents? Competence through selective price disclosure. Electron. Commer. Res. Appl. **14**(6), 563–581 (2015). https://doi.org/10.1016/j.elerap.2015.08.006

Hong, I.B.: Understanding the consumer's online merchant selection process: the roles of product involvement, perceived risk, and trust expectation. Int. J. Inf. Manag. **35**(3), 322–336 (2015). https://doi.org/10.1016/j.ijinfomgt.2015.01.003

Hudders, L., Van Reijmersdal, E., Poels, K.: Editorial: digital advertising and consumer empowerment. Cyber Psychol.: J. Psychosoc. Res. Cyberspace **13**(2) (2019). https://doi.org/10.5817/cp2019-2-xx

Jung, K., Cho, Y.C., Lee, S.: Online shoppers' response to price comparison sites. J. Bus. Res. **67**, 2079–2087 (2014). https://doi.org/10.1016/j.jbusres.2014.04.016

Keaveney, M.: Customer switching behavior in service industries: an exploratory study. J. Mark. **59**(2), 71–82 (1995)

Khan, I., Garg, R.J., Rahman, Z.: Customer service experience in hotel operations: an empirical analysis. Procedia – Soc. Behav. Sci. **189**, 266–274 (2015). https://doi.org/10.1016/j.sbspro.2015.03.222

Kim, G., Shin, B., Lee, H.G.: A study of factors that affect user intentions toward email service switching. Inf. Manag. **43**(7), 884–893 (2006). https://doi.org/10.1016/j.im.2006.08.004

Kock, N.: WarpPLS 6.0 user manual. ScriptWarp Systems, Laredo, Texas (2017)

Kucuk, U.S.: Consumer empowerment model: from unspeakable to undeniable. Direct Mark.: Int. J. **3**(4), 327–342 (2009). https://doi.org/10.1108/17505930911000892

Le, T.D., Vo, H.: Consumer attitude towards website advertising formats: a comparative study of banner, pop-up and in-line display advertisements. Int. J. Internet Mark. Advert. **11**(3), 202–217 (2017). https://doi.org/10.1504/IJIMA.2017.085654

Liang, D., Ma, Z., Qi, L.: Service quality and customer switching behavior in China's mobile phone service sector. J. Bus. Res. **66**(8), 1161–1167 (2013). https://doi.org/10.1016/j.jbusres.2012.03.012

Malhotra, A., Malhotra, C.K.: Exploring switching behavior of us mobile service customers. J. Serv. Mark. **27**(1), 13–24 (2013). https://doi.org/10.1108/08876041311296347

Mehta, A.: Advertising attitudes and advertising effectiveness. J. Advert. Res. **40**(3), 67–72 (2000). https://doi.org/10.2501/jar-40-3-67-72

Meyer, C., Schwager, A.: Understanding customer experience. Harvard Bus. **85**(2), 117–126 (2007)

Mishra, A.A.: Consumer innovativeness and consumer decision styles: a confirmatory and segmentation analysis. Int. Rev. Retail Distrib. Consum. Res. **25**(1), 35–54 (2015). https://doi.org/10.1080/09593969.2014.911199

Mosavi, S.M., Sangari, M.S., Keramati, A.: An integrative framework for customer switching behavior. Serv. Ind. J. **38**, 15–16 (2018). https://doi.org/10.1080/02642069.2018.1428955

Osakwe, C.N., Chovancová, M.: Exploring online shopping behaviour within the context of online advertisement, customer service experience consciousness and price comparison websites: perspectives from young female shoppers in the Zlinsky region. Acta Universitatis Agriculturae Et Silviculturae Mendelianae Brunensis **63**(2), 595–605 (2015). https://doi.org/10.11118/actaun201563020595

Ozok, A.A., Wei, J.: An empirical comparison of consumer usability preferences in online shopping using stationary and mobile devices: Results from a college student population. Electron. Commer. Res. **10**(2), 111–137 (2010). https://doi.org/10.1007/s10660-010-9048-y

Passyn, K.A., Diriker, M., Settle, R.B.: Price comparison, price competition, and the effects of ShopBots. J. Bus. Econ. Res. **11**(9), 401–416 (2013). https://doi.org/10.19030/jber.v11i9.8068

Paliwoda, S., Marinova, S., Petrovici, D., Marinov, M.: Determinants and antecedents of general attitudes towards advertising. Eur. J. Mark. **41**(3/4), 307–326 (2007). https://doi.org/10.1108/03090560710728354

Pires, G.D., Stanton, J., Rita, P.: The internet, consumer empowerment and marketing strategies. Eur. J. Mark. **40**(9/10), 936–949 (2006). https://doi.org/10.1108/03090560610680943

Pourabedin, Z., Foon, Y.S., Chatterlee, R.S., Ho, S.Y.: Customers' online channel switching behavior: the moderating role of switching cost. Information **19**(7B), 2961–2970 (2016)

Schlosser, A.E., Shavitt, S., kanifer, A.: Survey of internet users' attitudes toward internet advertising. J. Interact. Mark. **13**(3), 34–54 (1999). https://doi.org/10.1002/(SICI)1520-6653(199922)13:3%3c34:aid-dir3%3e3.0.CO;2-r

Shavitt, S., Lowrey, P., Haefner, J.: Public attitude toward advertising: more favorable than you might think. J. Advert. Res. **38**(4), 7–22 (1998)

Wu, K., Zhao, Y., Zhu, Q., Tan, X., Zheng, H.: A meta-analysis of the impact of trust on technology acceptance model: investigation of moderating influence of subject and context type. Int. J. Inf. Manag. **31**(6), 572–581 (2011). https://doi.org/10.1016/j.ijinfomgt.2011.03. 004

Xu, X., Li, H., Heikkilä, J., Liu, Y.: Exploring individuals' switching behaviour: an empirical investigation in social network games in China. In: The 26th Bled eConference, Bled, pp. 141–153 (2013). https://doi.org/10.1007/978-3-642-39808-7_8

Yoo, B., Donthu, N.: Developing a scale to measure the perceived quality of an internet shopping site (Sitequal). Q. J. Electron. Commer. **2**(1), 31–46 (2001)

Zhang, K.Z., Cheung, C.M., Lee, M.K.: Online service switching behavior: the case of blog service providers. J. Electron. Commer. Res. **13**, 184–197 (2012)

Zimmerman, M.A.: Psychological empowerment: issues and illustrations. Am. J. Commun. Psychol. **23**(5), 581–599 (1995). https://doi.org/10.1007/BF02506983

# Online Banking Service Quality:
# A South African E-S-QUAL Analysis

Mathias Mujinga(✉) iD

School of Computing, University of South Africa, Johannesburg, South Africa
mujinm@unisa.ac.za

**Abstract.** Technologically, competition is fierce in the banking industry, as such, banks need to offer cutting-edge technology and still make sure the banking solutions provided keep customers satisfied, as customers could switch between banks with minimum inconvenience. Electronic service quality measures the level of satisfaction deliver to bank customers through online banking digital solutions. This paper provides an investigation of electronic service quality based on customers' perceptions in South Africa. The paper presents findings based on quantitative data from 184 online banking customers using E-S-QUAL measurement scale. The results show that banks are meeting customer expectations of service quality delivery, although there is room for improvement. The study has practical implications to financial institutions in South Africa, as it highlights areas of attention to improve service quality delivered to online banking customers.

**Keywords:** Service quality · E-S-QUAL · Online banking · South Africa

## 1  Introduction

Retail banking allows customers to change from one bank to the other with ease. As such, the business model of financial institutions depends on customer satisfaction realised through customer loyalty and retention [1]. Improved service quality is one such mechanism of ensuring customer satisfaction [1]. In the context of banking, service providers need to consistently meet and exceed customer expectations for both face-to-face and online banking delivery models. Consequently, customer satisfaction needs a holistic approach and banks are continuously looking for ways to attract new customers and retain existing customers. In South Africa's cash-based economy [2] – meaning that a significant amount of transactions still relies on cash rather than cashless means such as money transfers and credit card services. Hence, advances in technology still need to be coupled by in-branch operational advancements as well to fully satisfy the customer base.

Wilson et al. [3] further acknowledges service quality as a major factor in gaining competitive advantage and maintaining customer satisfaction. This paper investigated the retail-banking customers' perceptions on the quality of service of online banking. The following research questions are posed in this study:

*What are the perceptions of retail banking customers on the service quality of online banking as delivered by the South African banks?*

© IFIP International Federation for Information Processing 2020
Published by Springer Nature Switzerland AG 2020
M. Hattingh et al. (Eds.): I3E 2020, LNCS 12066, pp. 228–238, 2020.
https://doi.org/10.1007/978-3-030-44999-5_19

A brief background of customer satisfaction is presented followed by a discussion of the South African banking sector. The literature review discusses service quality and E-S-QUAL measurement scale. Then data collection is followed by data analysis and lastly, the paper presents the study limitations and further research ideas followed by the conclusion.

## 2 Customer Satisfaction

Customer loyalty and retention is strongly dependent on customer satisfaction especially in the services industry [4]. As such, customer satisfaction is critical in ensuring business goals are achieved. The achievement of goals the customer set out to achieve without limitations results in customer satisfaction [5], which is key to customer retention [6]. However, Rauyruen and Miller [7] identified factors that impact customer satisfaction, in addition to contextual and personal aspects, price, product quality and service quality also plays a role. According to Hallowell [8], profitability of banks depends on customer loyalty derived from customer satisfaction. Service quality, customer satisfaction, and customer loyalty in retail banking are linked together [9]. Mihelis et al. [10] linked customer satisfaction to excellence that can be applied to any organisation. Customer satisfaction requires organisations to not only match customer expectations but exceed them in order to promote customers retention [11].

## 3 Retail Banking in South Africa

South Africa is home to a number of retail banks, these include banks that are locally owned and controlled, and branches and subsidiaries of foreign banks. There are 71 banks operating in South Africa according to the South African Reserve Bank (SARB). Like in many other countries, the banking industry in South Africa is dominated by a few major banks [12] and these banks account for 89% of the market share although this has been decreasing lately [13].

The fourth industrial revolution in South Africa has revolutionise how we conduct our banking. This has led to the introduction of purely digital banks such as Tyme-Bank, Bank Zero, and Discovery Bank, just to mention a few [14]. Columinate [15] highlighted the extent of how South Africa lags behind in online banking adoption. Online banking services consists of a variety of transactions such as checking account balances, bill payments, buying prepaid services (electricity and airtime), inter-account transfers, and new account applications, to mention but a few. Among the benefits of online banking, users identified service convenience, while security was identified as the main concern [16].

The European Union (EU) had one of the highest online banking adoption rates of 49% of the total population back in 2017 [17]. Norway had the highest rate of 93% in 2018 [18]. The Middle East and Africa have an online banking adoption rate of 8.8%, which is far lower than the average global rate of 28.7% from 2012 data [19]. Although a higher uptake of online banking can be expected in developed countries that already have a higher internet penetration rate, the South African rate of uptake is alarmingly lower than the global average given that internet penetration rate is 54% [20].

South Africa has a national policy guideline on digitisation that includes the provision of egovernment services. However, private organisations such as banks are self-regulating concerning technological advancements as these are driven by customer needs, business cases, and maintaining a competitive edge. Moreover, the South African economy is still cash-based, as the majority of the population still has no access to financial credit services [21].

## 4   Service Quality

Parasuraman et al. [22] defined service quality as the customer's perception of the degree to which the service delivered meets the customer's expectations. Parasuraman et al. [23] contends that service quality is essentially perceived quality as it comes from a comparison between actual service and expected service performance. Hence, service quality plays a critical role in maintaining an organisation's competitive edge [5]. The authors further indicated that the level of the quality of service provided had a positive effect on an organisation's financial performance. An improved competitive advantage leads to increased market share through customer loyalty [24].

There are a number of measurement models of service quality. These include SERVQUAL and SERVPERF scales for offline service quality measurement. SERVQUAL is a gap-based scale that compares customers' perceptions and expectations [25], while SERVPERF performance-based scale [26], an improvement of the SERVQUAL. In the context of South Africa, retail banks need to improve service quality based on SERVQUAL dimensions [27]. For online services, Parasuraman et al. [22] developed the E-S-QUAL and E-RecS-QUAL scales for measuring service quality in electronic service quality delivered by the electronic service provider and electronic recovery for ecommerce returns, respectively. eTailQ is used to assess the quality of retail electronic commerce [28]. The E-S-QUAL scale was chosen for this study to measure service quality in online banking, the model has been used extensively in similar settings for a number of years since the development of the scale. E-S-QUAL measurement scale has been applied in online banking across different regions including Turkey [29], Northern Cyprus [30], Australia [31], and China [32].

The original electronic service quality (E-S-QUAL) scale is a 22-item scale consisting of four dimensions to measure online service quality. The dimensions are efficiency, fulfilment, system availability, and privacy. Efficiency measures how effective the website responds to customer needs. Fulfilment deals with timeous and accuracy of service delivery through digital channels. System availability is concerned about the system downtime, while privacy measures how the system protects customers' information. Given the increasing introduction of online services, a new scale was necessary to measure service quality delivered through online services – hence the emergence of E-S-QUAL. Kenova and Jonasson [33] developed an online banking E-S-QUAL scale with these dimensions, service performance, website characteristics, communication, and efficiency. Yaya et al. [34] evaluated a number of studies that used E-S-QUAL scale and found that the scale is still relevant although some improvements are needed as technology advances, especially regarding its application in different environments.

# 5 Methodology

The E-S-QUAL measurement scale was used in a quantitative survey research. The survey was administered through Google Forms online tool with invitations sent to potential respondents using mediums that include email, social media, and online forums. The target population and inclusion criteria were retail banking customers that use online banking in South Africa.

The demographic section of the survey collected data on four independent variables. The measurement scale items were measured based on a 5-point Likert scale that range from strongly disagree (1) to strongly agree (5). Based on convenience sampling technique, the sample came from a wide range of different income levels, qualifications, and age groups. In the end the study obtained 184 valid and usable responses from retail banking customers across South Africa. The scale used in this study is an adaptation of the original E-S-QUAL that consists of 4 dimensions and 23 statements. The statements gather customer perceptions that investigate the actual service quality experienced by customers. The adaptation was necessary to align the dimensions to online banking, as some of the original questions were deemed irrelevant in that context.

# 6 Data Analysis

Using IBM SPSS 25 statistical tool, descriptive and inferential was conducted to analyse the quantitative data. First, descriptive statistics reports on the frequencies of the biographic information provided by the respondents followed by the scale reliability test. The inferential statistical analysis section reports on group comparisons using independent samples and correlation of E-S-QUAL constructs based on demographic groups.

Table 1 shows the frequencies for each category of the variables that were included in the survey. Gender of respondents was split down the middle at 50% each. A large proportion (40.2%) of respondents were aged between 30–39 years, with all income groups evenly represented at around 15% except for highest income earners group at 22.8%. FNB was the most represented bank with 37% of respondents.

Experience in using online banking was measured using the number years users have been using the service, users with 5 years or more accounted for the highest percentage with 22.8%, while novices those that have been using the service for less than a year accounted for 16.3%. Most users access online banking once a week (45.1%), while mobile devices are used by most used (39.1%) followed by the use of both mobile devices and desktop computers with 36.4%.

**Table 1.** Descriptive statistics (N = 184)

| Variable | Category | Frequency | Percentage | Cum. Percentage |
|---|---|---|---|---|
| Gender | Male | 92 | 50.0 | 50.0 |
| | Female | 92 | 50.0 | 100.0 |
| Age | Younger than 20 years | 9 | 4.9 | 4.9 |
| | 20–29 years | 45 | 24.5 | 29.3 |
| | 30—39 years | 74 | 40.2 | 69.6 |
| | 40—49 years | 31 | 16.8 | 86.4 |
| | 50 years or older | 25 | 13.6 | 100.0 |
| Income | Less than R10 000 | 27 | 14.7 | 14.7 |
| | R10 000–R19 999 | 26 | 14.1 | 28.8 |
| | R20 000–R29 999 | 29 | 15.8 | 44.6 |
| | R30 000–R39 999 | 29 | 15.8 | 60.3 |
| | R40 000–R49 999 | 31 | 16.8 | 77.2 |
| | R50 000 or more | 42 | 22.8 | 14.7 |
| Bank | FNB | 68 | 37.0 | 37.0 |
| | S. Bank | 30 | 16.3 | 53.3 |
| | ABSA | 26 | 14.1 | 67.4 |
| | Nedbank | 23 | 12.5 | 79.9 |
| | Capitec | 37 | 20.1 | 100.0 |
| Experience | Less than 12 months | 30 | 16.3 | 16.3 |
| | 1–4 years | 64 | 34.8 | 51.1 |
| | 5 years or more | 90 | 48.9 | 100.0 |
| Use frequency | Every day | 56 | 30.4 | 30.4 |
| | Once a week | 83 | 45.1 | 75.5 |
| | Once a month | 45 | 24.5 | 100.0 |
| Device | Mobile device | 72 | 39.1 | 39.1 |
| | Desktop computer | 45 | 24.5 | 63.6 |
| | Both | 67 | 36.4 | 100.0 |

**Table 2.** Lowest mean E-S-QUAL scores

| Item | Mean |
|---|---|
| The bank's website contains just the basics and is simple to use | 3.98 |
| The bank's website does not share my personal information with other websites or third parties | 3.94 |
| The bank's website does not crash | 3.91 |
| The bank notifies you in advance when the website will be unavailable | 3.79 |

The mean E-S-QUAL statistics show that the overall mean for all respondents' average scores for the 23 items is 4.19 with a standard deviation of 0.762. On face value, 4.19 out of a possible perfect score of five indicates that users are generally satisfied with the quality of service delivered by service providers.

Table 2 shows the lowest scoring questions relative to the rest of the questions in the survey that are below mean score of four. These questions show that users are unhappy with online banking websites containing more than the basic information relevant to online banking. Also of concern is the sharing of personal information provided to banks by users with third parties. The other two lowest scoring items relates to the system availability, specifically website crashing and timeous notification of system downtime.

However, further analysis is warranted to determine the statistical significance of the difference in mean E-S-QUAL values based on moderating variables that were investigated during the study. To ensure internal consistency, the scale was tested for reliability using Cronbach's Alpha. The reliability was found to be 0.969 based on the instruments' standardised items, which is acceptable as the minimum threshold for reliability is 0.70 [35]. Further reliability tests on individual constructs of the E-S-QUAL measurement scale (Table 3) were also above the threshold value.

**Table 3.** Instrument reliability

| Item | No of items | Cronbach's Alpha |
| --- | --- | --- |
| Efficiency | 8 | 0.921 |
| Fulfilment | 4 | 0.828 |
| Privacy | 5 | 0.887 |
| System availability | 6 | 0.851 |
| Whole instrument | 23 | 0.969 |

## 7 Inferential Statistical Analysis

The study collected data on moderating factors to enable the investigations based on group comparisons. The moderating factors include gender, age, income, experience, use_frequency, device, and bank. Inferential statistical analyses conducted include independent samples t-tests, one-way ANOVA, and Pearson correlation.

### 7.1 Independent Samples T-Tests

Independent samples *t*-tests allow for comparison of variables that can be categorised into dichotomous groups. Gender was the only dichotomous variable that could be analysed using independent t-tests. Hence, the hypothesis that male and female respondents have the same E-S-QUAL mean values was tested. The study conducted independent samples *t*-tests using both the *Levene's test for equality of variances* and the *t-test for equality of means* with a $p$-value of Levene's test of 0.347. Given that the Levene's test is greater than the acceptable threshold of 0.05, the study accepts the null hypothesis and concludes that the variance in E-S-QUAL values for males and females was equal. Hence, the difference was statistically insignificant, which meant that we had to consider the output of *equal variance assumed* in order to *test for equality of means*.

## 7.2   One-Way ANOVA

One-way ANOVA means analysis of variance was performed for variables with more than two groups to determine the significance of statistical differences in mean values. F denotes the test statistic for one-way ANOVA. Table 4 provides one-way ANOVA F- and p-values, including *post hoc tests* for group comparisons.

The findings show that the mean E-S-QUAL values for different groups in the variables age, experience, income, and use_frequency have no significant differences. This is because the significance (p values) are all above the 0.05 threshold. Hence, the study accept the null hypothesis that the means are not different.

The results also show that there was some significant difference in the mean values based on the respondents' bank as indicated by F value of 3.644 at 0.007 significance level ($p < 0.01$). However, the differences are not significant when comparing each bank against the other based on multiple comparisons that showed no significant p values both at 0.01 and at 0.05 level. This implies that users' perceived service quality is influenced by the bank of choice but no significant influence when comparing each of the investigated banks against each other.

**Table 4.** One-way ANOVA: E-S-QUAL mean scores

| Factor | df | F | Sig. | Post hoc tests (multiple comparisons) | |
|---|---|---|---|---|---|
| Age | 4 | 0.585 | 0.674 | None | $p > 0.05$ |
| Experience | 2 | 1.171 | 0.312 | None | $p > 0.05$ |
| Income | 5 | 0.625 | 0.681 | None | $p > 0.05$ |
| Use frequency | 2 | 1.999 | 0.138 | None | $p > 0.05$ |
| Bank | 4 | 3.644 | 0.007 | None | $p < 0.05$ |
| Device | 2 | 9.253 | 0.000 | Mobile vs both PC vs both | $p < 0.05$ |

The choice of device between mobile, desktop computer, or both devices indicated that E-S-QUAL values depends on the device of choice – with *F* value of 9.253 at 0.000 significant level ($p < 0.01$). Multiple group comparisons, both comparisons between mobile device vs both devices and PC vs both devices showed significant means difference at the 0.05 level. Hence, the device used to access online banking has influence on how the user perceives the quality of service delivered by the bank.

## 7.3   Correlations

To determine the strength and direction of relationships between the dependent variable E-S-QUAL values and independent moderating variables Pearson correlation analysis was conducted. The Pearson correlation is a number between −1 and +1 that indicates the degree of the relation among two or more variables. Table 5 has correlation analysis results with the relations that are noted for discussion formatted in bold, as they are significant at 0.05 level.

   Pearson correlation values that are below 0.3 are considered weak, between 0.3 and .05 are moderate with 0.5 to 1 considered strong [35]. Using this interpretation, Table 5 has only four moderate relationships as follows: age-income, income-experience, income-use_frequency, and income-device. A positive coefficient means that there is a direct relation between the two variables, meaning that as one variable increases, the other increases [36]. Age-income have a moderate positive relationship, meaning as age of users increases so does their income. The same trend is noted for both income-experience and income-device relations. High-income earners tend to make use of both mobile and desktop computer to access online banking and are generally more satisfied with the service quality. On the other hand, the relations between income-use_frequency have a moderate negative relationship. This implies that as income increases the frequency at which users access online banking decreases. Interestingly, only device has any notable correlation with E-S-QUAL mean values, that is, a very weak positive relationship. This leads to the conclusion that E-S-QUAL is not influenced by any of the variables investigated since no medium or strong relationships exist at 0.05 level, albeit a very weak one with device. The rest of the bold relationships in Table 5 are weak and no strong relationships exists.

**Table 5.** Correlation between moderating variables

| | | Gender | Age | Income | Experience | Use frequency | Device |
|---|---|---|---|---|---|---|---|
| Gender | Pearson correlation | 1 | | | | | |
| | Sig. (2-tailed) | | | | | | |
| Age | Pearson correlation | −.031 | 1 | | | | |
| | Sig. (2-tailed) | .681 | | | | | |
| Income | Pearson correlation | −.264** | .420** | 1 | | | |
| | Sig. (2-tailed) | .000 | .000 | | | | |
| Experience | Pearson correlation | −.059 | .262** | .468** | 1 | | |
| Use frequency | Sig. (2-tailed) | .427 | .000 | .000 | | | |
| | Pearson correlation | .213** | .131 | −.311** | −.253** | 1 | |
| Device | Sig. (2-tailed) | .004 | .076 | .000 | .001 | | |
| | Pearson correlation | −.156* | .167* | .407** | .251** | −.291** | 1 |
| | | .034 | .024 | .000 | .001 | .000 | |

# 8  Limitations and Further Research

The E-S-QUAL scale need updating as electronic service quality has evolved since 2005 the year of its first introduction. For instance, the scale is heavy on infrastructure reliability in meeting customer needs. The scale lacks emphasis on new aspects in online customer satisfaction such as user experience and electronic satisfaction. These can be considered for further research to assist in the evolution of E-S-QUAL. A larger sample would also make the generalisation of findings across the whole population of online banking users. This also allows the reporting to include bank names without unwarranted prejudice. Further research is needed to also include current aspects such as user experience of online banking that affect customer satisfaction and provide a holistic service quality assessment. Also of consideration as future work is a qualitative study that investigates new constructs by asking online banking users what services they need, instead of an evaluation of the currently provided services. Moreover, measurements based on customer perceptions are highly subjective, which requires some caution in generalisation of such findings.

# 9  Conclusion

E-S-QUAL essentially measures the extent to which online users are satisfied with the service quality delivered by the service provider. The study analysed the mean E-S-QUAL values to determine the existence of any significant differences in mean scores across moderating variables. The average mean E-S-QUAL scores for individual respondents across the sample showed that users are generally satisfied with the service quality of online banking. The exception were four questions that had mean scores of below four with two lowest scores concerning system availability. Inferential statistical results show that there are insignificant differences in mean scores based on independent samples $t$-tests, one-way ANOVA, and Pearson correlation analyses. Using Levene's test, gender showed no statistical significance, as this was the only variable with dichotomous values. One-way ANOVA tests identified the variable device as the only variable that has influence on E-S-QUAL scores, while all other variables tested had no influence customers' perceptions of online banking service quality. This suggest banks need to offer online banking through a variety of devices, in order to optimise service quality to improve customer satisfaction.

Overall, the study accept the null hypothesis and concludes that the difference in E-S-QUAL mean values are statistically insignificant for all moderating variables. This means banks can take holistic approaches in improving service quality that does not target specific demographic groups but the whole customer base in addressing service quality problems. The significance of electronic service quality measurement is to identify areas for improvement and encourage wide usage of digital channels. Especially, considering huge investments financial institutions are making in digital channels. This allows for higher return on investment on digital solutions while reducing in-branch operational costs for banks.

# References

1. Rahman, M.S., Khan, A.H., Haque, M.M.: A conceptual study on the relationship between service quality towards customer satisfaction: servqual and Gronroos's service quality model perspective. Asian Soc. Sci. **8**(13), 1227–1232 (2012)
2. Hull, E., James, D.: Introduction: popular economies in South Africa. Ocean Coast. Manag. **82**(1), 1–19 (2012). https://doi.org/10.1017/SOOO1972011000696
3. Wilson, A., Zeithaml, V.A., Bitner, M.J., Gremler, D.D.: Services Marketing: Integrating Customer Focus Across the Firm, 3rd edn. McGraw Hill, London (2012)
4. Oliver, R.L.: Whence consumer loyalty? J. Market. **63**(1999), 33–44 (1999). https://doi.org/10.2307/1252099
5. Paul, J., Mittal, A., Srivastav, G.: Impact of service quality on customer satisfaction in private and public sector banks. Int. J. Bank Mark. **34**(5), 606–622 (2016). https://doi.org/10.1108/ijbm-03-2015-0030
6. Kottler, P., Keller, K.L.: Marketing Management, 15th edn. Pearson Pretice Hall, New Jersey (2016)
7. Rauyruen, P., Miller, K.E.: Relationship quality as a predictor of B2B customer loyalty. J. Bus. Res. **60**(1), 21–31 (2007). https://doi.org/10.1016/j.jbusres.2005.11.006
8. Hallowell, R.: The relationships of customer satisfaction, customer loyalty, and profitability: an empirical study. Int. J. Serv. Ind. Manag. **7**(4), 27–42 (1996). https://doi.org/10.1108/09564239610129931
9. Ngo, V.M., Nguyen, H.H.: The relationship between service quality, customer satisfaction and customer loyalty: an investigation in Vietnamese retail banking sector. J. Compet. **8**(2), 103–116 (2016). https://doi.org/10.7441/dokbat.2016.43
10. Mihelis, G., Grigoroudis, E., Siskos, Y., Politis, Y., Malandrakis, Y.: Customer satisfaction measurement in the private bank sector. Eur. J. Oper. Res. **130**(2), 347–360 (2001). https://doi.org/10.1016/s0377-2217(00)00036-9
11. Hoffmann, A.O.I., Birnbrich, C.: The impact of fraud prevention on bank-customer relationships: an empirical investigation in retail banking. Int. J. Bank Mark. **30**(5), 390–407 (2012)
12. BusinessTech: Battle of the banks: how SA's big five banks compare. https://businesstech.co.za/news/banking/182873/battle-of-the-banks-how-sas-big-five-banks-compare/. Accessed 5 Apr 2018
13. Fin24: Big five SA banks losing market share. https://www.fin24.com/Companies/Financial-Services/big-five-sa-banks-losing-market-share-20160525. Accessed 5 Apr 2018
14. IT Web: Digital newcomers to disrupt South African banking. https://www.itweb.co.za/content/kLgB1MeJbZXq59N4. Accessed 20 Feb 2019
15. Van Zyl, G.: FNB rated SA's 'top internet banking provider. http://www.fin24.com/Tech/News/FNB-rated-SAs-top-internet-banking-provider-20150507. Accessed 20 Nov 2017
16. Mujinga, M., Eloff, M.M., Kroeze, J.H.: Online banking users' perceptions in South Africa: an exploratory empirical study. In: Proceedings of IST-Africa 2016 Conference, Durban, South Africa, 11–13 May 2016, pp. 1–7 (2016)
17. Statista: Online Banking Penetration in Selected European Markets in 2016. https://www.statista.com/statistics/222286/online-banking-penetration-in-leading-european-countries/. Accessed 20 Nov 2017
18. Statista. Online banking penetration in Norway from 2005 to 2018. https://www.statista.com/statistics/380892/online-banking-penetration-in-norway/. Accessed 20 Feb 2019

19. Statista: Global online banking penetration in April 2012, by region. https://www.statista.com/statistics/233284/development-of-global-online-banking-penetration/. Accessed 6 Nov 2017

20. Internet World Stats: Internet World Stats. http://www.internetworldstats.com/stats.htm. Accessed 15 Aug 2017

21. Maziya, M., Zwane, T.: Financial inclusion is more than just access to credit. https://mg.co.za/article/2017-11-03-financial-inclusion-is-more-than-just-access-to-credit. Accessed 20 Feb 2019

22. Parasuraman, A., Zeithaml, V.A., Malhotra, A.: E-S-QUAL - a multiple-item scale for assessing electronic service quality. J. Serv. Res. **7**(3), 213–233 (2005). https://doi.org/10.1177/1094670504271156

23. Parasuraman, A., Zeithaml, V.A., Berry, L.L.: A conceptual model of service quality and its implications for future research. J. Mark. **49**(Fall 1985), 41–50 (1985). https://doi.org/10.1177/002224298504900403

24. Siu, N.Y., Mou, J.C.: Measuring service quality in internet banking: the case of Hong Kong. J. Int. Consumer Market. **17**(4), 99–116 (2005). https://doi.org/10.1300/j046v17n04_06

25. Parasuraman, A., Zeithaml, V.A., Berry, L.L.: SERVQUAL: a multiple-item scale for measuring consumer perceptions of service quality. J. Retail. **64**(1), 12–40 (1988)

26. Cronin Jr., J.J., Taylor, S.A.: Measuring service quality: a reexamination and extension. J. Mark. **56**(3), 55–68 (1992). https://doi.org/10.2307/1252296

27. Mujinga, M.: Retail banking service quality measurement: SERVQUAL gap analysis. In: 2019 Conference on Information Communications Technology and Society (ICTAS), Durban, South Africa, 6–8 March 2019, pp. 1–6 (2019)

28. Wolfinbarger, M., Gilly, M.C.: eTailQ: dimensionalizing, measuring and predicting etail quality. J. Retail. **79**(3), 183–198 (2003). https://doi.org/10.1016/s0022-4359(03)00034-4

29. Akinci, S., Atilgan-Inan, E., Aksoy, S.: Re-assessment of E-S-Qual and E-RecS-Qual in a pure service setting. J. Bus. Res. **63**(3), 232–240 (2010)

30. Karatepe, O.M., Yavas, U., Babakus, E.: Measuring service quality of banks: scale development and validation. J. Retail. Consum. Serv. **12**(5), 373–383 (2005). https://doi.org/10.1016/j.jretconser.2005.01.001

31. Herington, C., Weaven, S.: E-retailing by banks: e-service quality and its importance to customer satisfaction. Eur. J. Mark. **43**(9/10), 1220–1231 (2009). https://doi.org/10.1108/03090560910976456

32. Sun, Q., Wang, C., Cao, H.: Applying ES-QUAL scale to analysis the factors affecting consumers to use internet banking services. In: 2009 IITA International Conference on Services Science, Management and Engineering, Zhangjiajie, China, 11–12 July 2009, pp. 242–245 (2009)

33. Kenova, V., Jonasson, P.: Quality online banking services. Jonkoping International Business School (2006)

34. Yaya, L.H.P., Marimon, F., Casadesús, M.: The expert experience in adopting the ES-QUAL scale. Total. Qual. Manag. Bus. Excel. **28**(11–12), 1307–1321 (2017). https://doi.org/10.1080/14783363.2015.1135728

35. Pallant, J.: SPSS Survival Manual: A Step by Step Guide to Data Analysis using IBM SPSS, 5th edn. McGraw-Hill Education, Berkshire (2013)

36. Antonius, R.: Interpreting Quantitative Data with IBM SPSS Statistics, 2nd edn. Sage Publications, London (2013)

# The Characteristics of Digital Entrepreneurship and Digital Transformation: A Systematic Literature Review

Joshua Antonizzi and Hanlie Smuts[(✉)] [iD]

Department of Informatics, University of Pretoria, Pretoria, South Africa
ul5052682@tuks.co.za, hanlie.smuts@up.ac.za

**Abstract.** The characteristics of digital entrepreneurship and digital transformation and how they are related, is complex and important to understand in this digital age. Such an understanding of digital entrepreneurship is perceived as a key pillar for economic growth, job creation and innovation. However, a number of issues regarding digital entrepreneurship and digital transformation are prevalent, inhibiting digital entrepreneurs to optimise the advantages that digital entrepreneurship contributes towards business value. Therefore, the aim of this research paper is to investigate digital entrepreneurship and digital transformation, their characteristics and inter-relationships. Data extracted and analysed through a structured analysis process, recognises and discusses the characteristics of digital entrepreneurship and digital transformation. The characteristics are reported by employing the Dynamic Capabilities Theory as the structure. By understanding the characteristics of digital entrepreneurship and digital transformation, individuals and organisations may either create new business ventures or transform existing businesses through the development of novel digital technologies or the innovative application of such technologies.

**Keywords:** Digital entrepreneurship · Digital transformation

## 1 Introduction

Entrepreneurship, in its simplest form, can be described as self-employment [1]. Digital entrepreneurship, on the other hand, diverges from this definition seeing as it involves entrepreneurial pursuits which occur on a digital platform [2]. Digital entrepreneurs have a reliance on digital media tools and Information Technology (IT) in the pursuit of entrepreneurial prospects [2]. Digital entrepreneurship ensues when an asset owned by a business, a service performed by a business or a fundamental element of a business has been digitised [3]. Digital entrepreneurship expands on the traditional notion of entrepreneurship in the sense that it includes a set of participants which is constantly evolving and is highly diverse [4]. This moves away from the traditional, established participant to a more ever-changing assemblage of participants who possess their own, and differing, competencies, aspirations, and, ultimately, purposes [3, 4].

Furthermore, digital entrepreneurship is deeply entrenched in digital opportunity [5]. The rate of technological development is at an all-time, ever-increasing high, and

© IFIP International Federation for Information Processing 2020
Published by Springer Nature Switzerland AG 2020
M. Hattingh et al. (Eds.): I3E 2020, LNCS 12066, pp. 239–251, 2020.
https://doi.org/10.1007/978-3-030-44999-5_20

digital entrepreneurs are mindful of the opportunities that this growth is creating [5, 6]. To capitalise on these opportunities, entrepreneurs are looking towards digital transformation. Digital transformation can be defined as companies who alter their operations, and, in broader terms, it can also refer to the persistent change of our civilization through the use of technology [6, 7]. Digital transformation involves the redesign of business practices to incorporate digital technology within all facets of the business [7]. Digital entrepreneurs are offered significant opportunity through the use of digital networking capabilities. These opportunities present themselves through users of digital mediums who can now be offered support, can respond to messages and can offer constructive criticism and suggestions which organisations can utilize [3].

However, there are a number of concerns surrounding digital entrepreneurship and digital transformation. Using business processes and capabilities to achieve the wants of customers is of paramount importance to up-and-coming companies and their digital entrepreneurs [3, 8]. Digitisation spanning all functions and operations of a business can be considered more and more difficult the larger the organisation [3, 8]. The practice of large companies updating obsolete and outdated business systems to modernized, digital systems can be problematic owing to the irregularities found within these systems [9]. Other challenges related to digital transformation point to occurrences where existing business models generate sufficient profit to ward off the need for establishing new, digitised products and services for clients to purchase [10].

Consequently, the main purpose of this study is to explore the following primary research question: *"What are the characteristics of the relationship between digital entrepreneurship and digital transformation?"* By considering such a digital entrepreneurship scope, digital entrepreneurs may optimise the advantages that digital transformation brings towards achieving business value.

The remainder of the paper is structured as follows: in Sect. 2 we provide the background to the study presenting an overview of digital entrepreneurship (Sect. 2.1), digital transformation (Sect. 2.2), and their interrelationship (Sect. 2.3). The approach to this study is discussed in Sect. 3, where after we provide an overview of the findings in Sect. 4. In Sect. 5, we present the framework for digital entrepreneurship enabled through digital transformation and we conclude the study in Sect. 6.

## 2   Background

The nature of digital entrepreneurship based businesses is that of both IT and traditional business knowledge. This translates to entrepreneurs requiring both technical and business-related knowledge and skills, which is a duel-mastery, and not easily acquired [11, 12]. Two types of entrepreneurs are prevalent [11, 13]. The first type of entrepreneur is that of the research-based entrepreneur that commercialises original technological discoveries. The second kind of entrepreneur is an imitative entrepreneur that develops present markets by assembling available organisational resources [13]. Digital entrepreneurs have been found to have a reliance on digital media tools and Information Technology (IT) in the pursuit of entrepreneurial prospects [11]. As a result, the digital economy is suffering as digital entrepreneurs are intensifying the rivalries between industry participants [14]. This means that digital entrepreneurs can fall within the classification of research-based or imitation entrepreneurs, who simply make use of digital media in the pursuit of other, broader entrepreneurial opportunities [11, 12].

Scholars cite a number of barriers that prevent this pursuit of entrepreneurial opportunities; excessive amounts of data which cannot be properly processed, a distinct lack of training on business knowledge and digital skills, disproportionate competition and competitor-drenched markets as well as a lack of investor interest or inability to attain capital [15]. Finally, exorbitant cost to start-up and the inability to keep up with disruption factors and costs, needs to be addressed when considering digital entrepreneurship [15, 16].

In the next sections we explore digital entrepreneurship and digital transformation in more detail, as well as the relationship between these two concepts.

## 2.1 Digital Entrepreneurship

Digital entrepreneurship can be defined as entrepreneurial opportunities being created and pursued through the use of technological platforms and other information communicating equipment [2, 14]. Therefore, digital entrepreneurship may fall within many categories of business [1, 5]. As technology advances and cultivates, so too will these categories (e.g. marketing, sales, products, distribution, stakeholder management, operations) and new categories can potentially be fashioned [1, 11].

Another characteristic regarding digital entrepreneurship is that it is multi-faceted and is a combination of business-, knowledge- and institutional entrepreneurship working symbiotically [14]. *Business entrepreneurship* is a form of entrepreneurship which is most commonly heard-of and discussed. It explains the practice of seeking out or identifying business opportunities which can be exploited [17]. These practices include new product or service creation, raw material identification and use, new industry creation, new forms of business and more [18]. *Knowledge entrepreneurship* is categorised by the identification and quest for information or knowledge-based prospects and encompasses the expansion of existing knowledge-bases as well as the development of new ones [19]. *Institutional entrepreneurship* characterises the actions of entrepreneurs who make use of resources in the pursuit of creating new organisations or upgrading old ones [20]. Digital entrepreneurship is subsequently a combination of the above three entrepreneurial practices. Digital entrepreneurs synergistically combine business, institutional and knowledge entrepreneurship and this combination forms the basis of being able to take traditional practices, such as the business categories listed above, and alter them digitally [14, 21].

Owing to the fact that digital entrepreneurship is fundamentally based on digital enablement, digital transformation is presented in the next section.

## 2.2 Digital Transformation

All around the world, companies across all industries are comprehending the importance of digital transformation to the sustainability of their profits and their continued existence and prosperity [6]. Therefore, business functions, such as sales, marketing, human resources, operations, finance, research and development and customer support need to be transformed into the digital environment [7]. Gale and Aarons [22] studied companies which had undergone digital transformation and found that they are able to gain competitive advantages by simultaneously lowering their expenses, innovating and becoming more organized and competent. Additionally, true mastery of an organisation's supply-chain activities will arise from digital transformation [23]. As a result of this digital transformation necessity, companies need to design and create strategies in order to make digital transformation possible [6, 7]. A digital business strategy can be described as a corporate strategy designed, created and implemented making use of digital resources to create new and unexploited worth [24].

There are 4 interrelated business transformation strategies, namely: use of technologies, changes in value creation, structural changes as well as financial aspects [25, 26]. *Use of technologies* speaks to an organisation's technological drive and desire to transform and determines an organisation's opinions about a new IT factor, as well as that particular organisation's willingness and capacity to use it. *Changes in value creation* describes the effect of digital transformation strategies on the value chains, which presently existed within an organisation and determines the level at which the digitised processes are different from the existing, traditional methods. *Structural changes* form the foundation of an organisation's ability to transform digitally and make use of new technologies to change their value creation, while *financial aspects* refers to the requirement of funding and capital that is required for digital transformation to take place [25, 26].

Much like the relationship between the above four strategies, digital transformation has a strong, growing relation with digital entrepreneurship. This relationship is explored in the following section.

## 2.3 Digital Entrepreneurship and Digital Transformation Interrelationship

In order to understand the difference between digital entrepreneurship and digital transformation, the supply-side and the demand-side of entrepreneurship needs to be clarified [27]. The *supply-side* of entrepreneurship encompasses the human element of entrepreneurship. That is, the people who are suitable to take-on entrepreneurial roles and positions. The *demand-side* encompasses those aforementioned positions; new positions which are available to those entrepreneurs who are willing and able to fill them [27]. This typifies the necessary and present relationship between digital entrepreneurship and digital transformation - digital entrepreneurs can take on roles and responsibilities created through digital transformation, or could create digital transformation themselves [21]. As a result, new disruptive growth for businesses leads to an increase in opportunity for digital entrepreneurs.

Two strategies were developed towards growing new disruptive businesses [28]: firstly, creating a new market as the foundation for the disruption and secondly, disrupting business models which are held by industry leaders. *New market creation* involves identifying a product or service which satisfies a need which people have, but neither have the time, the energy, the drive nor the resources to do it. It is less complicated and more cost-effective to attract customers who are purchasing nothing than it is to poach or sway customers who are loyal to existing companies or competitors. *Disrupting business models* propose that if a new market cannot be created, an alternative possibility is to enter an existing market and to disrupt it instead [28].

The next section presents an overview of the research methodology followed for this research paper.

# 3 Research Approach

The objective of this paper is to investigate digital entrepreneurship and digital transformation, their characteristics and inter-relationships. In order to achieve this objective, a systematic literature review (SLR) was conducted in order to provide a thorough, impartial amalgam of a number of studies relevant to the topic being researched, collated within one document [29]. An SLR process comprises of 3 consecutive stages: (1) planning, (2) execution and (3) result analysis [30]. *Planning* involves defining the research objectives and the manner in which the review will be carried out. *Execution* points to the study selection and the data collection, while *result analysis* encompasses the data synthesis and results discussion [29, 30]. The *planning* phase was guided by the aim of the research study, namely, to propose a digital entrepreneurship framework enabled by digital transformation. Technical reports, academic books and specific scientific databases were chosen for the SLR process. The sources considered are shown in Table 1 in the *database* column as they hold the most important and highest impact full-text journals and conference proceedings in the digital technologies field.

**Table 1.** Total number of papers found per database

| Database | Entrepreneurship | Transformation | Total |
|---|---|---|---|
| EBSCOhost | 13 | 40 | 53 |
| Emerald Insight | 16 | 17 | 33 |
| Google Scholar | 30 | 30 | 60 |
| IEEE Xplore | 15 | 15 | 30 |
| SAGE | 2 | 1 | 3 |
| Springer Link | 59 | 15 | 74 |
| Total | 135 | 118 | 253 |

The following keywords were used to find relevant studies: for Digital Entrepreneurship included ("Digital Entrepreneurship" OR "Digital Business" OR "Digital Entrepreneur*" OR "Digital (NEAR/2) era") AND (skills OR frame* OR strat* OR review OR func* OR fail* OR barriers OR characteristics) NOT transformation. For Digital Transformation the search terms included ("Digital Transformation" OR "Transform* digital" OR "strategic transform*") AND (strat* OR adopt* OR benefits OR barriers OR practices) NOT Entrepreneurship. The initial search produced a list of 253 papers as shown in Table 1.

The research studies were screened through the application of specific criteria to exclude papers such as studies not associated with the research questions, non-English studies, anecdotal or opinion-based papers and duplicate studies that formed part of the result set. Criteria for inclusion of sources consisted of peer-reviewed publications (journal papers, conference proceedings, books, case studies, book chapters) and technical reports.

After the initial search, the application of exclusion and inclusion criteria, the detailed screening of abstracts and analysis of the full-text of the prospective papers, 30 papers were identified for detailed analysis.

## 4   Data Analysis and Findings

Data was extracted from the selected papers based on the objective of this study, which is to consider the characteristics of digital entrepreneurship and digital transformation. Characteristic in the context of this paper refer to any distinguishing feature or attribute of an item [31]. These distinguishing features or attributes were extracted and reported in Table 2 together with the number of times the same theme occurred (frequency count). For each characteristic identified, the source is indicated.

*Self-employment* refers to an individual's aspiration of working for him/herself as a freelance employee or the owner of a business, rather than for an employer. Self-employment is viewed as freedom from traditional work assignments, work hours and undesirable working conditions. *Work satisfaction* alludes to the measure of person's satisfaction with their job. Work satisfaction could be an important cornerstone of any person's reason to choose what industry to work in, which job they seek or how strongly they wish to be an entrepreneur. *Entrepreneurship* is a practice which people are drawn to, one which offers the potential for freedom, money, power and personal purpose. Entrepreneurs across all industries, disciplines and practices, have certain *traits* which set them aside from the rest of the work force such as business opportunity identification and exploitation, vision and overcoming potential barriers. Entrepreneurship can come from a range of areas and *opportunities*. This particular characteristic was identified from entrepreneurship stemming from circumstances which allowed for entrepreneurship to arise and flourish. These opportunities come in the form of new markets, technological advancements, deficiencies in need satisfaction, price-point vulnerabilities and a variety of other sources which lead to entrepreneurship in multiple forms.

From a digital transformation perspective, *digitisation* allows for better relationships. Critical to the success of almost all organisations globally is their ability to create, maintain and prioritise relationships, and even more so for entrepreneurs. These are relationships between the entrepreneur and other organisations within and outside of their market, their suppliers, their employees and, most importantly, with their customers; prioritising communication channels with their customer base have significant competitive advantages over their competitors. Digitisation facilitates communication, making it pivotal to the continuing success of an entrepreneur therefore, understanding digitisation is critical. Digitisation, however, does not mean success is automatically and easily attainable. While digitisation offers a range of opportunities to

**Table 2.** Characteristic and reference

| Characteristic | Source |
|---|---|
| Self-employment | [15, 32] |
| Work satisfaction | [32] |
| Entrepreneurship prospect | [27] |
| Entrepreneurial traits | [15–18, 27, 33] |
| Entrepreneurship can come from opportunity | [3, 14–18, 20, 21, 27, 33–38] |
| Digitisation allows for better relationships | [9, 22, 23, 25, 34, 35, 39] |
| Digitisation does not mean success is clear and easy to entrepreneurs | [16] |
| Employee involvement is crucial | [40] |
| Knowledge management | [19] |
| Traditional organisational structures may slow progress | [9, 23, 41] |
| E-strategies bolster competitive advantage | [42] |
| Entrepreneurship aspiration | [20, 37] |
| Business intelligence can facilitate entrepreneurship and transformation | [43] |
| Disruption comes from new market creation | [14, 15, 17, 22, 28, 33, 34, 38] |
| Disruption comes from existing markets | [17, 20, 25, 28, 37, 38, 40, 44] |
| Production competence comes from technology | [25, 34, 45, 46] |
| Costs of technology | [22, 37, 45, 46] |
| Technology adoption | [25, 34, 45, 46] |
| Technology improves compatibility and working between organisations | [9, 35] |
| Understanding digitisation is critical | [3, 21, 22, 24, 25, 39, 40, 44] |
| Digitisation allows for virtual teamwork | [21, 35] |

entrepreneurs, enacting it is not a guarantee of success to entrepreneurs. There is also an array of other issues which need to be carefully considered, managed and mitigated. There are resource issues, social issues, network requirements, market availability and competitors which will constantly keep entrepreneurs vigilant, regardless of how digitised their organisation has become. *Employee involvement* is also important as having the best technology, processes, strategies, operations, partners and opportunities in a market cannot add any value if the company has no one to endorse all of these aforementioned strengths. The benefits of any technology can only be realised when it is being truly accepted and utilised. User acceptance of technologies and the influences on user attitudes, customer engagement and business operations have been widely researched, and is a key characteristic enabling digital entrepreneurship.

*Knowledge management* involves the creation, control and use of all forms of knowledge throughout an organisation. This is knowledge of systems, customers, employees, strategies, threats, opportunities, and any other form of information which an organisation can be sustained and improved using. Managing and effectively distributing knowledge throughout an organisation is crucial to both maintaining success as well as pioneering expansion. Traditional organisations are heavily structured, rigid bodies which possess a great deal of hierarchy. Upper management and associated strategists decide on the direction of the organisation and dictate that direction to subordinates. This may *slow down progress* drastically compared to fast-paced, new-age companies. E-strategies bolster *competitive advantage*. As we move further and further into the digital age, e-business strategies are becoming cardinal to successful operations, sustenance and development of all organisations, especially those which primarily operate within the digital realm. Organisations which employ e-strategies are experiencing advantages over competitors who are not engaging in strategies of a similar nature. *Adoption* can be increased or reduced based on a number of factors. There is a broad spectrum of reasons organisations are either excited or reluctant to adopt new technologies and practices. These reasons include cost, competitive advantage, learning curves, training, revenue potential and all other factors which are relevant to adoption. Entrepreneurship can also come from within. While entrepreneurship is primarily associated with private, self-employed individuals starting companies, it is important to note that entrepreneurship can arise from within an existing organisation. Emerging markets allow for entrepreneurs to go from being employees within an organisation to becoming self-sufficient entrepreneurs, creating new businesses within those markets.

*Business intelligence* can facilitate entrepreneurship and transformation. Entrepreneurship and transformation is impossible to achieve without data, and more information and, most importantly, knowledge. Business intelligence is the driver behind entrepreneurship and transformation. Business intelligence offers information on technology, applications, processes, dashboards and other key tools entrepreneurs require to be successful and organisations require to successfully transform themselves. *Disruption* comes from *new market* creation. The creation of a new market is a common occurrence when investigating disruptive companies. Creating a new market, which solves the needs of customers across a variety of existing markets, can be crucial to incumbent organisations sustaining their success. Organisations creating new markets and obtaining a large share of that market, while negatively impacting on the performance of organisations in other, related markets, can cause a great deal of disruption. *Disruption* comes from *existing* markets. Disruption from within already-established markets is an alternative, but equally common, approach to causing disruption for organisations which are incumbent to that market. When there is a number of organisations operating within and profiting from the same market, competitor activity may disrupt the market they know and capitalize off of, could be fundamentally changed. *Production competence* comes from technology. The ability of an organisation to produce competently is based on a variety of mechanisms. And technology is at the centre of these mechanisms. Maintaining production competence in industries where competitors are constantly improving their technology can be harmful to organisations who are not improving their technology. There are a number of barriers to the initial adoption of technology as well as to improving existing technology, but the challenges of these changes could be outweighed by the negative effects that the failure to change carries.

*Costs of adoption* are a primary negative. There is a multitude of possible reasons why organisations do not want to adopt new technologies, techniques or operating methods. Chief among these reasons is that of cost. The inordinate costs associated with both adopting new technologies or operational methods, as well as improving on existing technology or operational methods, is the principal reason organisations are reluctant to digitally transform. Technology improves *compatibility and working* between organisations. Communication, mutual operation and successful interactions between organisations is facilitated and improved by technology. Traditional channels of business are supplemented with technology, where organisations which rely on each other have superior means of communication and operational efficiency stemming from their use of supporting technology. Digitisation allows for *virtual teamwork*. Traditionally, employees would have face-to-face interactions with one another at a physical workplace. However, owing to digitisation, organisations are now able to create virtual teams, which have the potential to span a city, a country, or the globe. As a result, teams can cooperate with one another at anytime from anywhere in the world without having to physically meet. This allows for new perspective, ways of working, problem solving and round-the-clock working on the same projects as well as more flexibility and employee freedom.

## 5 Digital Entrepreneurship and Digital Transformation Characteristics

In order to report the findings of the SLR, we utilised the Dynamic Capabilities Theory which refers to the "ability to integrate, build, and reconfigure internal and external competencies to address rapidly-changing environments" [47: 9]. The dynamic capabilities approach emphasises organisational and strategic capabilities to realise competitive advantage and consists of three main components of capabilities: (1) to sense and shape opportunities and threats (sensing), (2) to seize opportunities (seizing), and (3) to maintain competitiveness through enhancing, combining, protecting, and, when necessary, reconfiguring the organisation's intangible and tangible assets ("transforming" or "shifting") [47]. By mapping the characteristics identified (Table 2) to the 3 main components of the dynamic capabilities based on the definitions and scope of each, the particular feature and attribute set of digital entrepreneurship and digital transformation are depicted in Table 3.

The aim of this paper was to consider the characteristics of digital entrepreneurship and digital transformation as they are not mutually exclusive (Sect. 2.3). Characteristics pertinent to *sensing and shaping* opportunity includes the creation of self-employment through prospects based on an entrepreneurs' drive to succeed. Digital transformation in this instance provides opportunities to create new markets or to optimise existing collaborations and the understanding of digitisation may shape additional prospects. Digitisation enables digital entrepreneurship and digital transformation. The management, and the successful implementation thereof, is what allows for lucrative digital

**Table 3.** Digital entrepreneurship and digital transformation characteristics mapped to dynamic capabilities [47]

| Sensing | Seizing | Transforming or shifting |
|---|---|---|
| Self-employment | Entrepreneurship can come from opportunity | Work satisfaction |
| Entrepreneurship prospect | Traditional organisational structures may slow progress | Entrepreneurial traits |
| Entrepreneurship aspiration | E-strategies bolster competitive advantage | Digitisation allows for better relationships |
| Disruption comes from new market creation | Disruption comes from existing markets | Digitisation does not mean success is clear and easy to entrepreneurs |
| Technology improves compatibility and working between organisations | Production competence comes from technology | Employee involvement is crucial |
| Understanding digitisation is critical | | Knowledge management |
| | | Business intelligence can facilitate entrepreneurship and transformation |
| | | Cost of technology |
| | | Technology adoption |
| | | Digitisation allows for virtual teamwork |

entrepreneurship and digital transformation to take place. Characteristics relevant to *seizing* opportunity are based on an entrepreneurs' ability to exploit prospects that may be derived from existing market- or digital transformation strategies. The potential of technology in improving productivity also presents opportunity. Technology is employed, in some form or another, by incumbent organisations which dominate markets, start-ups, entrepreneurs and by those who are transforming organisations. The fact that traditional organisations may slow down progress is highlighted as a characteristic to be aware of in a digital entrepreneurship endevour. Characteristics applicable to *maintaining competitiveness* include features pertaining to an entrepreneur profile such as traits, work satisfaction, relationships, collaboration, technology adoption and the management of knowledge. The facilitative role of data and business intelligence on entrepreneurship and transformation, must be considered and the cost of adoption is a characteristic highlighting potential drawbacks to be cognisant of.

Table 3 illustrates that a number of characteristics need to be considered in order to achieve digital entrepreneurship enabled through digital transformation, signifying the relationship existing between them. By taking the characteristics into account, both organisations as well as individuals can consider creating new business ventures or transform existing enterprises by creating, or making use of, innovative technologies.

## 6 Conclusion

The purpose of this paper was to consider the characteristics of digital entrepreneurship and digital transformation. After investigating and analysing entrepreneurship and digital transformation to determine a clearer understanding of what these concepts entail, a SLR was conducted. Twenty-one characteristics were identified and presented using the Dynamic Capabilities Theory, illustrating the key features and attributes of digital entrepreneurship and digital transformation.

By referencing the data from this study, both individuals and companies can garner a firmer grasp on what these concepts entail and how they can add value to intellectual and practical knowledge. This paper contributed by highlighting a number of key characteristics which exist for each digital entrepreneurship and digital transformation, with focus on how these characteristics relate. By making use of the proposed conceptual framework, individuals and organisations alike can either start new companies or adapt existing ones to be aligned with the digital age.

As this study focused on identifying the characteristics of digital entrepreneurship and digital transformation, the proposed findings may be tested in a real-world situation within and organisation, with entrepreneurs or with an idea incubator and accelerator. Through such a process, the proposed characteristic set may be enriched.

## References

1. Gohmann, S.F.: Institutions, latent entrepreneurship, and self-employment: an international comparison. Entrep. Theory Pract. **36**(2), 295–321 (2012)
2. Giones, F., Brem, A.: Digital technology entrepreneurship: a definition and research agenda. Technol. Innov. Manag. Rev. **7**(5), 44–51 (2017)
3. Kraus, S., et al.: Digital entrepreneurship: a research agenda on new business models for the twenty-first century. Int. J. Entrep. Behav. Res. **25**, 353–375 (2019)
4. Autio, E., et al.: Digital affordances, spatial affordances, and the genesis of entrepreneurial ecosystems. Strat. Entrep. J. **12**(1), 72–95 (2018)
5. Richter, C., et al.: Digital entrepreneurship: innovative business models for the sharing economy. Creat. Innov. Manag. **26**(3), 300–310 (2017)
6. Hess, T., et al.: Options for formulating a digital transformation strategy. MIS Q. **15**(2), 123–139 (2016)
7. Bounfour, A.: Digital Futures, Digital Transformation. PI. Springer, Cham (2016). https://doi.org/10.1007/978-3-319-23279-9
8. Boneva, M.: Challenges related to the digital transformation of business companies. In: Proceedings of the 6th International Conference Innovation Management, Entrepreneurship and Sustainability. University of Economics, Prague. pp. 101–114 (2018)
9. Zhu, K., et al.: Innovation diffusion in global contexts: determinants of post-adoption digital transformation of European companies. Eur. J. Inf. Syst. **15**, 601–616 (2006)

10. Dutot, V., Van Horne, C.: Digital entrepreneurship intention in a developed vs. emerging country: an exploratory study in France and the UAE. Transnatl. Corp. Rev. **7**(1), 79–96 (2015)
11. Rashidi, R., et al.: Presenting a butterfly ecosystem for digital entrepreneurship development in knowledge age. In: 7th International Conference on Application of Information and Communication Technologies. IEEE, Baku (2013)
12. Najda-Janoszka, M.: Matching imitative activity of high-tech firms with entrepreneurial orientation. J. Entrep. Manag. Innov. **9**(1), 52–67 (2012)
13. Darnihamedani, P., Hessels, J.: Human capital as a driver of innovation among necessity-based entrepreneurs. Int. Rev. Entrep. **14**(1), 1–23 (2016)
14. Davidson, E., Vaast, E.: Digital entrepreneurship and its sociomaterial enactment. In: Proceedings of the Annual Hawaii International Conference on System Sciences, pp. 1–10. IEEE (2010)
15. Rindova, V., Barry, D., Ketchen, D.J.J.: Entrepreneuring as emancipation. Acad. Manag. Rev. **34**, 477–491 (2009)
16. Dy, A.M., Martin, L., Marlow, S.: Emancipation through digital entrepreneurship? A critical realist analysis. Organization **25**, 585–608 (2018)
17. Cuervo, Á., Ribeiro, D., Roig, S.: Entrepreneurship: concepts, theory and perspective. Introduction. In: Cuervo, Á., Ribeiro, D., Roig, S. (eds.) Entrepreneurship. Springer, Heidelberg (2007). https://doi.org/10.1007/978-3-540-48543-8_1
18. Shane, S., Venkataraman, S.: The promise of entrepreneurship as a field of research. Acad. Manag. Rev. **25**, 217–226 (2000)
19. Rowley, J.: From learning organisation to knowledge entrepreneur. J. Knowl. Manag. **4**, 7–15 (2000)
20. Maguire, S., Hardy, C., Lawrence, T.B.: Institutional entrepreneurship in emerging fields: HIV/Aids treatment advocacy In Canada. Acad. Manag. J. **47**, 657–679 (2004)
21. Hull, C.E., et al.: Taking advantage of digital opportunities: a typology of digital entrepreneurship. Int. J. Netw. Virtual Organ. **4**, 290–303 (2007)
22. Gale, M., Aarons, C.: Digital transformation: delivering on the promise. Lead. Lead. **2018**, 30–36 (2018)
23. Bowersox, D.J., Closs, D.J., Drayer, R.W.: The digital transformation: technology and beyond. Supply Chain Manag. Rev. **9**, 22–29 (2005)
24. Bharadwaj, A.S., et al.: Digital business strategy: toward a next generation of insights. MIS Q. **37**, 471–482 (2013)
25. Matt, C., Hess, T., Benlian, A.: Digital transformation strategies. Bus. Inf. Syst. Eng. **57**, 339–343 (2015)
26. Kane, G.C., et al.: Strategy, not technology, drives digital transformation. MIT Sloan Manag. Rev. (2015). https://sloanreview.mit.edu/projects/strategy-drives-digital-transformation/
27. Thornton, P.H.: The sociology of entrepreneurship. Annu. Rev. Sociol. **25**, 19–46 (1999)
28. Christensen, C.M., Johnson, M.W., Rigby, D.K.: Foundations for growth: how to identify and build disruptive new businesses. MIT Sloan Manag. Rev. **43**, 22–32 (2002)
29. Aromataris, E., Pearson, A.: The systematic review: an overview. AJN Am. J. Nurs. **114**, 53–58 (2014)
30. Rouhani, B.D., et al.: A systematic literature review on enterprise architecture implementation methodologies. Inf. Softw. Technol. **62**, 1–20 (2015)
31. Characteristic. BusinessDictionary.com. http://www.businessdictionary.com/definition/characteristic.html. Accessed 05 Jan 2020
32. Blanchflower, D.G., Oswald, A.J.: What makes an entrepreneur? J. Labor Econ. **16**, 26–60 (1998)

33. Bogdanowicz, M.: Digital entrepreneurship barriers and drivers the need for a specific measurement framework (2015)
34. Ebert, C., Duarte, C.H.C.: Digital transformation. IEEE Softw. **35**, 16–21 (2018)
35. Hair, N., et al.: Market orientation in digital entrepreneurship: advantages and challenges in a Web 2.0 networked world. Int. J. Innov. Technol. Manag. **9**, 18 (2012)
36. Liao, A., Hull, C.E., Sriramachandramurthy, R.: The six facets model of technology management: a study in the digital business industry. Int. J. Innov. Technol. Manag. **10**, 1–24 (2013)
37. Minniti, M., Lévesque, M.: Entrepreneurial types and economic growth. J. Bus. Ventur. **25**, 305–314 (2010)
38. Nambisan, S.: Digital entrepreneurship: toward a digital technology perspective of entrepreneurship. Entrep. Theory Pract. **41**, 1029–1055 (2017)
39. Berman, S.J.: Digital transformation: opportunities to create new business models. Strat. Lead. **40**, 16–24 (2016)
40. Schuchmann, D., Seufert, S.: Corporate learning in times of digital transformation: a conceptual framework and service portfolio for the learning function in banking organisations. Int. J. Autom. Comput. **8**, 31–39 (2015)
41. Christensen, C.M., Verlinden, M., Westerman, G.: Disruption, disintegration and the dissipation of differentiability. Ind. Corp. Change **11**, 955–993 (2002)
42. Lee, G.-G., Bai, R.-J.: Organizational mechanisms for successful IS/IT strategic planning in the digital era. Manag. Decis. **41**, 32–42 (2003)
43. Nerkar, A.D.: Business Analytics (BA): Core of Business Intelligence (BI). Int. J. Adv. Eng. Manag. Sci. **2**, 2176–2178 (2016)
44. Piccinini, E., et al.: Transforming industrial business: the impact of digital transformation on automotive organizations. In: Thirty Sixth International Conference on Information Systems, pp. 1–20 (2015)
45. Chambers, C.: Technological advancement, learning, and the adoption of new technology. Eur. J. Oper. Res. **152**, 226–247 (2004)
46. Resca, A., Za, S., Spagnoletti, P.: Digital platforms as sources for organizational and strategic transformation: a case study of the midblue project. J. Theor. Appl. Electron. Commer. Res. **8**, 71–84 (2013)
47. Teece, D., Peteraf, M., Leih, S.: Dynamic capabilities and organizational agility: risk, uncertainty, and strategy in the innovation economy. Calif. Manag. Rev. **58**(4), 13–35 (2016)

# Mapping the Intellectual Progress in e-Business, e-Services and e-Society from 2001 to 2019

Zacharoula Papamitsiou[⊠] and Patrick Mikalef

Norwegian University of Science and Technology, Trondheim, Norway
{zacharoula.papamitsiou,patrick.mikalef}@ntnu.no

**Abstract.** This study aims to identify the conceptual structure and the thematic progress in e-Business, e-Services and e-Society and to elaborate on backbone/emerging topics in the field from 2001 to 2019. To address this objective, this paper employs hierarchical clustering, strategic diagrams and network analysis to construct the intellectual map of the I3E community and to visualize the thematic landscape in this field, using co-word analysis. Overall, a total of 835 papers from the proceedings of the e-Business, e-Services and e-Society (I3E) conference, and the respective 2574 author-assigned keywords, were included in the analyses. The results indicate that the community has significantly focused in areas like technology adoption models, Social Media, e-Government and business models; sentiment analysis and m-payments are peripheral themes, yet topics like cloud computing and Open Data are emerging. The analysis highlights the shift of the research interest throughout the past decades, and the rise of new topics, comprising evidence that the field is expanding and evolving. Limitations of the approach and future work plans conclude the paper.

**Keywords:** Co-word analysis · Bibliometrics · Conceptual mapping · e-Services

## 1 Introduction

The subject area of e-Business, e-Services and e-Society has delved into the topic of digitalization with regards to different facets of how we live, work, and conduct business [8]. Since the early 2000s when the dot com period hit its peak, the research interest has centered on the opportunities, challenges and implications that novel digital technologies introduce. The proliferation of such technologies, coupled with the rapid adoption of computer-based systems and the investments in network infrastructures, created a new wave of opportunities on digitalized processes [1, 22]. Along this progression, research has focused on issues related to each transition, examining obstacles of adoption from the individual to the industry level, value generating mechanisms, and the anticipated and unanticipated effects of integrating these technologies in everyday life.

Now that the field counts 18 years, based on the number of the e-Business, e-Services and e-Society (I3E) conferences being organized, it is a good time to analyze its past and current state. Doing so will allow researchers to understand the evolution of the field over the past two decades and identify the challenges and opportunities that lie ahead. The most appropriate way to examine all publications presented in the conferences throughout these years is by applying a methodology that quantifies the core topics, the marginal contributions, the under-developed themes, and the forthcoming ideas that worth investing on, as well as how these topics are related and move between these states during the last 18 years. The main objective of this work is to capture, interpret and understand the big picture in the I3E domain from a *quantified* viewpoint. The research presented in this paper is a *mapping study* of the I3E field; it is a review that seeks to identify, not results, but linkages, shows the internal dynamics and structure of the domain, and pinpoints the *topics with impact in the given discipline*.

Towards facilitating this objective, this paper employs co-word analysis, and examines the associations and networks among concepts, ideas, and issues that have contributed to the evolution of the field to date [5]. Co-word analysis allows for and supports the identification of key patterns and trends that point to particular changes in research topics (e.g., emerging or declining interests) or specific research directions (e.g., paradigm shifts), using a graph of key-terms [11], *extracted directly from the metadata of the papers*. Considering this, the present study maps the intellectual progress of the e-Business, e-Services and e-Society landscape, as reflected in the records of I3E conferences. The proceedings of this event provide a solid foundation to the related work published to date. During the past 18 years, considerable work has been published, allowing us to observe where the field currently stands, what are the challenges and opportunities the researchers are facing, and what are the potential driving forces in the near future. Accordingly, this work mainly contributes as follows:

- brings new insights on the intellectual mapping and progress of the area of I3E;
- raises awareness of the community on the mature, under-developed, emerging, or declining research themes;
- highlights individual topics as popular, core or backbone topics within the discipline.

## 2  Background and Related Work

The community of I3E is inherently diverse at the intersection of digital technologies, business, social sciences, big data, artificial intelligence, and network infrastructures [1, 8]. Digital services can make a global impact and therefore, the understanding of the economic, technical, and social aspects of service development and innovation is a demand [16]. The quantity and quality of the research activity within this community has been the topic to a variety of literature reviews, aiming to evaluate the research progress, impact and societal value, from different viewpoints (e.g., [9, 12, 26, 27]).

For instance, persuasiveness of electronic Word-of-Mouth (eWOM) communications has received much attention from scholars because it can affect consumers' purchase attitudes, intention, decisions, and hence sales. A dedicated review of existing literature on the topic offered an overview of the determinants of eWOM persuasiveness, identified gaps in current research and provided directions for future research [12].

Another study reviewed inclusive eGovernment strategies and socially-aware eGovernment policies, and highlighted the need for a better understanding of the role of new intermediaries as actors that can impact the qualities of the citizens' and public-sector relationships [26]. The results recognized the usefulness of placing the inter-mediaries in an institutional framework and the authors proposed an agenda for future research.

More recently, the emergence and extended discussions about blockchain and what it can offer to businesses in relation to consumers (B2C), businesses (B2B) and gov-ernments (B2G) were under the lens of a systematic literature review of 40 articles from business, management and accounting peer review journals [9]. The findings demon-strate the role of blockchain as a facilitator of instant payments, trusted interfaces and traceability of goods for the consumers. Specifically, businesses can be benefited from blockchain in terms of machine-to-machine transactions, accounting, business process management and provenance traceability. New business opportunities also arise in government sector such as digital storage, authentication and maintenance of records, smart trust codification and new market for digital payment services and global commerce [9].

In another systematic review of 71 articles, social media applications over the marketing context were explored [2]. The study synopsized the main themes and trends, including the role of social media on advertising, the eWOM, customers' relationship management, and firms' brands and performance.

Apparently, despite the several literature reviews in the field, they are sparse and there is no previous attempt – to the best of our knowledge – that maps the field as a whole. As I3E is a highly diverse and continuously evolving field, it is important to (a) identify and understand its core foundations that might contribute to reinforcing the community's identity; (b) detect under-represented or under-developed themes that require attention for their inclusion and success; (c) highlight research gaps in bridging theory and practice; and (d) find challenges and opportunities that hold the promise for improving the digitization processes. As the digitalization process and its outcomes in the 21st century accelerate transformation and the creation of sustainable societies, offering tremendous opportunities for revising current business methods and practices [22], there is a critical need for understanding and evaluating the field as a whole.

# 3  Methodology

## 3.1  Data Collection

The data analyzed in this study were downloaded from the I3E Springer proceedings between 2001 and 2019. Overall, 835 peer-reviewed papers were produced within the community of I3E and published to-date. The keynote speeches, prefaces to the con-ference-, or track proceedings, as well as the papers that did not contain any keywords, were excluded from the analysis. From the collected papers, the author-assigned keywords were extracted from the metadata of each paper and were used as a *unit of analysis*. The keywords used for the description of the content of a publication can be seen as the basic *building blocks* of the structure of a research field; an article's keywords provide an adequate summary of its content, and thus can be utilized to reduce a large space of descriptors (i.e., article text) to a network graph of smaller related spaces (i.e., keywords) [6]. Although when authors choose keywords to describe their work those keywords can either be very generic or very specific, still, those keywords are human annotations on the content of the papers, reflecting human judgement and perspective. The idea is to understand the conceptual structure and evolution of a field directly from the interaction between keywords: if two keywords co-occur within a paper, then the two topics they represent are related; higher co-word frequency implies stronger correlation in keywords pairs, further suggesting that two keywords are related to a specific theme [6]. The 835 papers are distributed per year of publication as shown in Fig. 1.

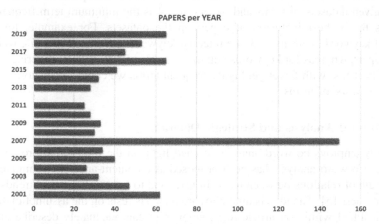

**Fig. 1.** Number of I3E publications per year for the period 2001–2019.

## 3.2 Data Pre-processing

From the 835 published papers, the 531 had author-assigned keywords. Specifically, 2574 keywords (M = 4.85 per article) were identified in total. The retrieved author-assigned keywords were manually pre-processed and standardized through merging words that convey similar meaning (e.g., "electronic government" and "e-Gov" were merged into "eGovernment"), fixing misspelled keywords (e.g., "goverment"), following a common spelling for UK and US terms (e.g., "behaviour" and "behavior"), and filtering broadly used terms (e.g., "IoT" and "Internet of Things"; "WoM" and "Word of Mouth") - following the approach recommended in [11, 17], in a non-invasive manner. Keywords appearing in singular and plural forms of nouns and gerunds were also merged. At the end of this pre-processing, 1732 keywords (67.3% of the original dataset) were identified as *unique* and were subjected to further analysis. In order to be able to apply this method, papers from more than 5 years of research are required.

The Kolmogorov Smirnoff test shown that the frequency of keywords follows a power-law distribution with an alpha of 1.87. Due to this heavy-tailedness, the research landscape of I3E is a *scale-free network*, with small number of popular terms acting as "*hubs*": they connect different topics, capture major research directions and influences in the field, and shape its intellectual structure [11]. A scale-free network also suggests that major research themes can be detected with small subset of popular terms. A previous analysis in the HCI research field demonstrated that less than 100 keywords are enough to describe the intellectual progress of a field [17]. Thus, in the present study we decided to include only those keywords that appear more than four times ($n \geq 4$) in the period 2001–2019. This decision was grounded on two facets: (a) the frequency of a term reflects its significance for a research community, i.e., the higher the frequency is, the more often the term attracts the researchers' attention/interest; and (b) the retained 65 keywords (total frequency = 646, 37.3% of the total unique keywords) cover 461 (86.8%) of the 531 articles (with keywords) published. Furthermore, for the given datasets of terms and papers, n = 4 is the minimum term frequency that achieves the highest inclusion of papers in the datasets. For example, for author-assigned keywords with $n \geq 3$, the retained keywords are N = 150 and cover 88.9% of the papers, whereas for keywords with $n \geq 5$, N = 57 keywords, covering 72.3% of the papers. Thus, with fewer yet highly frequent terms we could satisfactorily describe the I3E network of terms.

### 3.3   Co-word Analysis and Strategic Diagram

This study employs co-word analysis to shed light on the intellectual progress in the I3E field. Co-word analysis has been proposed as a content-analysis technique to map the strength of relations between terms in texts and to trace patterns and trends in term associated-ness [5]. The idea behind co-word analysis rests on the assumption that key-terms identified within an article (e.g., keywords) can adequately describe and communicate the content of that article; the co-occurrence of at-least two keywords in the same article indicates a linkage between the topics, i.e., a "*theme*" [4]. The main units of analysis are *keywords*, *clusters* (i.e., sets of keywords) and *keyword networks* [17].

Co-word analysis is applied to reduce the broad network of keywords into a smaller network of related topics using graph theory [7]. Graphs consist of nodes that represent the keywords, and links that represent the interactions between the nodes. Given a network of keywords, a combination of clustering, network analysis and strategic diagrams is used to model the conceptual structure of a field and to characterize it [4]. The graph theory concepts employed are *centrality* (i.e., the strength of the links from one research theme or cluster to others, indicating its significance in the development of the community [17]) and *density* (i.e., the coherence of a cluster and a measure of a theme's development [10]). Combining centrality and density allows for the creation of two-dimensional *strategic diagrams* [4] (Fig. 2): the position of a cluster in the diagram corresponds to the importance of the cluster in the whole network (i.e., centrality – *x-axis*) in relation to how well the theme of this cluster is developed (i.e., density –*y-axis*).

As one can observe, *Quadrant I (Q1)* holds the motor themes (i.e., mainstream themes) that have strong centrality and high density. *Quadrant II (Q2)* contains themes

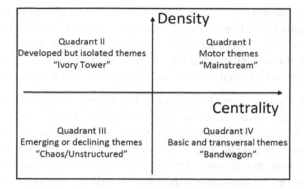

**Fig. 2.** Number of I3E publications per year for the period 2001–2019.

that are internally well-structured but have weak external ties. These research themes are more specialized and peripheral to the mainstream work that is central in the research field. *Quadrant III (Q3)* includes the themes with low density and low centrality, that are either emerging, or disappearing. Finally, *Quadrant IV (Q4)* covers basic and transversal themes of considerable significance to the entire research network, i.e., central to the community, with potential to become important to the field as a whole.

### 3.4 Data Analysis

To identify the major research themes in the I3E domain, hierarchical clustering analysis on a correlation matrix with the retained terms was performed, using the Ward's method with Squared Euclidean Distance as the distance measurement [19]. The supervised clustering method allows to maintain content validity and cluster fitness for the highest number of clusters [11, 17]. Each cluster represents a research theme or sub-field. The co-word network was further analyzed using the following measures:

- **Keywords:** set of terms that constitute a cluster;
- **Size:** number of keywords in the cluster;
- **Frequency:** how many times all keywords (in a cluster) appear in the dataset;
- **Co-word frequency:** how many times at-least two keywords (from a cluster) appear in the same paper. Computing this results in a symmetrical co-occurrence matrix [15]: values in the diagonal cells are term frequencies, and values in non-diagonal cells are co-word frequencies. High frequency of co-occurrence between terms indicates connection between the topics they represent;
- **Transitivity:** how tightly connected is the cluster (the *clustering coefficient*), i.e., how close the keywords are to being a "clique". Transitivity is the frequency of loops of length three in the cluster; a loop of length three is a sequence of nodes $x, y, z$ such that $(x, y)$, $(y, z)$ and $(z, x)$ are edges of the graph [25]. The value range is $[0, 1]$;
- **Centrality:** the degree of interaction of a theme with other parts of the network, i.e., how many other clusters a cluster connects to [4]; Centrality refers to a group of metrics that aim to quantify the "importance" of a particular node (or cluster) within a

network (e.g., betweenness centrality, closeness centrality, eigenvector centrality, degree centrality) [20]. Here we used betweenness centrality (C), with $0 \leq C \leq 1$;

- **Density:** how cohesive is the cluster of terms, i.e., the number of direct ties observed for the cluster divided by the maximum number of possible ones [4]. Density is graph-dependent and can be any positive real number [14].

Based on the clustering results, we plotted the strategic diagram for the years 2001–2019 to visualize the cohesion and maturity of the I3E themes [4, 17]. In addition, a keyword network graph was created from the keywords list. In this graph, each keyword is represented as a node, and the keywords that co-appear on a paper are linked together. By creating associations between keywords, multiple networks associated with different themes are also created. In this case, bridges are built between the nodes of keywords, to allow communication and information flow between isolated regions in the whole network. Those nodes are known as *structural holes* [21]. Keywords acting as structural holes serve as a "backbone" of a network: if removed, the network will lose its cohesion and will disintegrate into separated and unconnected concepts. Thus, the network's core-periphery structure needs to be computed, to determine which nodes are part of a densely connected core (i.e., with a higher number of bridges), or a sparsely connected periphery [24]. Core nodes are reasonably well-connected to peripheral nodes, while peripheral nodes are sparingly connected to a core node or to each other. A node belongs to a core only if it is well-connected to other core nodes and to peripheral nodes [24]. A follow-up core-periphery analysis was performed to spot the core research topics from the perspective of the whole network. In this analysis, keywords were categorized according to their popularity, coreness (i.e., connectedness with other topics) and constraint (i.e., backbone). The whole approach is illustrated in Fig. 3.

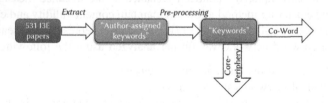

**Fig. 3.** Research methodology.

## 4 Results

### 4.1 Mapping of the Field

The analysis on the retained 65 author-assigned keywords led to 14 clusters (labeled as C1–C14, in Table 1), with each cluster representing a research theme or a sub-field. In order (a) to better understand the relative "position" of these clusters within the overall I3E field (i.e., what is the distance from each other in terms of cohesion and maturity of research themes they correspond to); and (b) to create the conceptual structure of the I3E discipline, we constructed strategic diagrams (plots) using the centrality and density of each cluster [4, 17]. The overall results can be seen in reading Fig. 4 and Table 1 together. In the plots, both axes are centralized to the average centrality and average density respectively (i.e., 0.247, 1.361). The overall network's density was 0.667.

As it can be observed from Fig. 4, one motor theme (*Mainstream theme*), represented by cluster C5 (i.e., literature review, TAM, adoption) is detected using the human descriptors (keywords) of the papers. In other words, the field is in general fragmented, with only one theme having received substantial attention from the community, in terms of human annotations. Furthermore, in Fig. 4, the author-assigned keywords indicate that the community has few internally well-structured research themes, yet with weak external ties (*Ivory Towers*), acting as peripheral nodes to the global network (i.e., connect only to core nodes, yet not necessarily to mainstream topics only), and classified in clusters C2, C3 and C4 (e.g., mPayments, Digital Payment, Twitter, Sentiment Analysis, UTAUT2, Perceived Risk). Those topics appear to have high-density, i.e., the clustering coefficient is high and the topics within each of the cluster are very well connected to each other, but they lack strong ties with topics that are external to them. The following-up core-periphery analysis will provide insight on that issue.

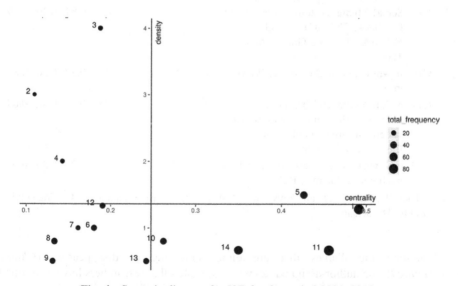

**Fig. 4.** Strategic diagram for I3E for the period 2001–2019.

**Table 1.** Clusters of topics in I3E for the period 2001–2019.

| Q | ID | Keywords (the most frequent in bold) | Size | FrEquation[a] | CW-Fr.[a] | T[a] | C[a] | D[a] |
|---|---|---|---|---|---|---|---|---|
| Q1 | C5 | **adoption**, literature review, TAM, India, use | 5 | 45 | 82 | 0.90 | 0.43 | 1.50 |
| Q2 | C2 | **m-payments**, digital payment | 2 | 10 | 20 | N/A | 0.11 | 3.00 |
| Q2 | C3 | twitter, **sentiment analysis** | 2 | 18 | 27 | N/A | 0.19 | 4.00 |
| Q2 | C4 | **UTAUT2**, information systems, perceived risk | 3 | 16 | 28 | 1.00 | 0.14 | 2.00 |
| Q2-Q3 | C12 | **Big Data**, data quality, information sharing | 3 | 26 | 27 | 1.00 | 0.19 | 1.33 |
| Q3 | C6 | **eWOM**, motivation, e-Services, information seeking, online reviews | 5 | 28 | 39 | 0.87 | 0.18 | 1.00 |
| Q3 | C7 | **Cloud Computing**, **SaaS**, eBusiness models, business intelligence | 4 | 17 | 23 | 1.00 | 0.16 | 1.00 |
| Q3 | C8 | **Open Data,** benefits, usability, evaluation, AHP, public services | 6 | 33 | 41 | 0.81 | 0.13 | 0.80 |
| Q3 | C9 | **SME**, mobile devices, marketing, technology adoption, CRM | 5 | 28 | 28 | 0.33 | 0.13 | 0.50 |
| Q3 | C13 | **business model**, strategy, value, information technology | 4 | 29 | 30 | 0.33 | 0.24 | 0.50 |
| Q4 | C1 | **Social Media**, customer engagement, Facebook, SNS, ICT, Social Networks, Use and Gratification Theory | 7 | 86 | 108 | 0.87 | 0.49 | 1.29 |
| Q4 | C10 | **privacy**, Social Commerce, WoM, trust | 4 | 35 | 44 | 0.87 | 0.26 | 0.80 |
| Q4 | C11 | **e-Commerce**, collaboration, interoperability, interorganizational system, security, supply chain, e-Business, web services, QoS | 9 | 86 | 93 | 0.53 | 0.46 | 0.67 |
| Q4 | C14 | **e-Government**, Smart Cities, artificial intelligence, Internet, B2B | 6 | 61 | 62 | 0.33 | 0.35 | 0.67 |

[a]**Freq**: Total frequency of all keywords; **CW-Fr**: Co-word Frequency; **T**: Transitivity; **C**: Centrality; **D**: Density

Regarding the themes that are either emerging or disappearing (*Chaos/Unstructured*), the author-assigned keywords revealed that researchers have developed a considerable number of topics with – in a sense – "marginal" interest in the I3E network, classified in clusters C6, C7, C8, C9, C12 and C13 (e.g., eWOM, online Reviews, motivation, information Seeking, eServices, Cloud Computing, SaaS, Business Intelligence, eBusiness models, Open Data, information technology), as illustrated in Fig. 4. The term "marginal" here is used to describe both the cases of "close-to-disappearing" and "nearly rising" topics, i.e., topics that either tend to no-longer attract major interest, or they have recently started to attract attention, but have not yet been well-developed.

Finally, a substantial number of transversal themes *(Bandwagon)* have been detected as well, i.e., themes that are strongly linked to specific research interests throughout the network yet are only weakly linked *together*. These are categorized in the clusters C1 (e.g., customer engagement, facebook, social media, use and gratification theory, social networks), C10 (e.g., social commerce, WoM, trust, privacy) C11 (e.g., eCommerce, interoperability, interorganizational system, security, supply chain, eBusiness, web services, QoS) and C14 (e.g., IoT, Smart Cities, artificial intelligence, eGovernment, b2b).

## 4.2   Keywords Network Map

A network of keywords demonstrates the relationships among different themes; to better understand and visualize the interactions between the research themes in Table 1, network analysis was used to create a granular map of the keywords. Figure 5 displays the results. Each node in the graph represents a keyword that is linked to other keywords that appear on the same paper. The size of the nodes is proportional to the frequency of the keywords, the color of the node corresponds to the cluster the keyword has been classified in, and the thickness of the links between the nodes is proportional to the co-occurrence correlation for that pair of keywords. To reduce visual clutter, a centralized subset of the complete network is illustrated, omitting isolated nodes and keywords with less than 3 strong ties, that would lead to a highly disconnected network.

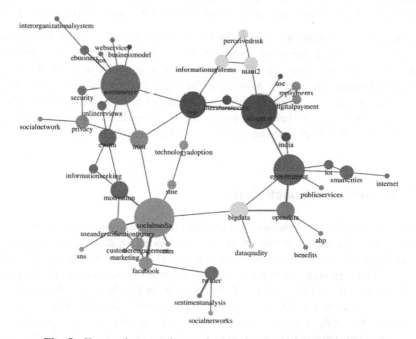

**Fig. 5.** Keywords network map for I3E for the period 2001–2019.

**Table 2.** Summary of popular, core and backbone topics of I3E in 2001–2019.

| # | Popular topic | Frequency | Core Topic | Coreness | Backbone topic | Constraint |
|---|---|---|---|---|---|---|
| 1 | **Social Media** | 51 | **Social Media** | 0.45 | **Social Media** | 0.19 |
| 2 | **e-Government** | 37 | **e-Commerce** | 0.30 | **TAM** | 0.19 |
| 3 | **e-Commerce** | 36 | **TAM** | 0.29 | **Trust** | 0.21 |
| 4 | **Big Data** | 18 | **Adoption** | 0.28 | **Big Data** | 0.21 |
| 5 | Business Model | 17 | **e-Government** | 0.27 | **e-Commerce** | 0.22 |
| 6 | **Adoption** | 15 | **Trust** | 0.25 | **Adoption** | 0.23 |
| 7 | e-Business | 15 | **Big Data** | 0.22 | **e-Government** | 0.23 |
| 8 | **Trust** | 13 | Facebook | 0.13 | Motivation | 0.24 |
| 9 | Smart Cities | 12 | Open Data | 0.09 | Literature Review | 0.26 |
| 10 | **TAM** | 12 | Twitter | 0.09 | Technology adoption | 0.26 |

Finally, core-periphery analysis was performed to identify the core research topics, from a whole-network perspective, as individual keywords, regardless of the cluster they belong to. The analysis yielded 10 topics in each of the categories (Table 2):

- **Popularity:** how frequently a keyword is used;
- **Coreness:** how connected is a keyword with other topics; value range: [0–1];
- **Constraint:** how connected is a keyword with other *otherwise distinct* topics (i.e., if the topic creates a backbone of the field); constraint is measured on a [0–1] scale.

High core value indicates a topic that is well connected to other topics. Lower constraint suggests a keyword that brings together otherwise isolated topics ("bridges"). Burts constraint (i.e., Constraint) [3] is commonly used for this purpose (accurately speaking, the lack of it, because the larger the constraint, the less structural opportunities a node may have for bridging structural holes). Topics with high Popularity and Coreness and low Constraint can be considered as driving forces for advancements in the field: without these topics, the field of I3E would be completely fragmented.

## 5   Discussion and Conclusions

The I3E conference on e-Business, e-Services and e-Society has grown and evolved over the years. The mere fact that the conference has managed to keep and expand its active community of researchers for almost two decades, demonstrates that the field is of increased and growing relevance. The objective and contribution of this paper is twofold: (a) to have a methodological contribution in the field (i.e., the method presented in this paper has not been employed in this research domain before); and (b) to demonstrate and apply a quantified (objective) methodology that is beyond the qualitative (subjective) perspective of a systematic literature review, aiming to shed light to the maturation of the field throughout the past two decades and to map the research streams in the field, how they are connected, and detect those that would benefit for more focus or integration. The analysis conducted in this study highlighted the major themes that have dominated the researchers' interest, as well as those that are likely to be the core focus of future studies. The co-word analysis of the I3E proceedings to date revealed some interesting findings regarding the progression of the field as a whole.

In coherence with the title of the conference, the three main (i.e., motor) themes have been on e-business (i.e., *e-commerce*), e-services (i.e., *e-government*) and e-society (i.e., *social media*) as is depicted in Fig. 5, and in line with previous systematic literature reviews [2, 26]. The underlying topic that has linked these three focus areas has been *adoption models*, examining the factors concerning individuals, users and organizations intention to adopt such systems, also noted in previous studies [8, 1]. This trend also indicates the maturity of these technologies, with substantial research still concerning why and how adoption of emerging digital technologies can be enhanced.

An intriguing finding is the emergence of *big data* as a linkage between the main three pillars (Figs. 4 and 5). Research themes that fall within the "Chaos/Unstructured" quadrant will attract attention in the years to come: as more and more people are moving from the adoption of digital technologies to the routinization in everyday life, so is the amount of generated data increasing. This has led to a surge of research on the potential of big data analytics for extracting actionable insight confirming previous findings [22].

As seen from the network map (Fig. 5), big data – in particular with relevance to e-government and social media – is an area with much future interest, also highlighted in [13]. The use of user generated data, and the integration with social media platforms offers an interesting perspective into the generated insight, the services that can be built based on this insight, as well as the implications and ethical issues that accompany such ventures. Big data and business analytics ecosystems may pave the way towards digital transformation and sustainable societies [23]. Furthermore, the strong link between e-commerce and social media (Table 1), denotes the increased prevalence of social commerce efforts over the last years (e.g., [18]). We witness an increased number of social media platforms featuring commercial aspects, with some notable examples being Facebook and Instagram. As more vendors utilize these platforms, trust emerges as a core aspect [9], both regarding the sales side and the products featured on these, as well as on the data exchanged and utilized for marketing and sales promotions [8]. Recent events (e.g. the Cambridge Analytica scandal) surfaced issues about privacy violation and use of data by third-parties which have come to the attention of the general population. As social media and e-commerce vendors become increasingly more integrated, data sharing and ownership issues will be brought in the spotlight of research/practice.

While these are some of the major trends that can be detected throughout an analysis of the field covered by the I3E conference, there are many more sub-fields that are likely to be fruitful areas for future research. Our ambition was to illustrate some of these as well as to identify the core areas that have received the center light of attention by researchers over the past two decades. Our analysis indicates that the three pillars of the I3E conference are becoming increasingly more fussed, and that future research is likely to bridge all three domains to derive important research and practical knowledge.

# References

1. Al-Sharhan, S.A., et al. (eds.): I3E 2018. LNCS, vol. 11195. Springer, Cham (2018). https://doi.org/10.1007/978-3-030-02131-3
2. Alalwan, A.A., Rana, N.P., Algharabat, R., Tarhini, A.: A systematic review of extant literature in social media in the marketing perspective. In: Dwivedi, Y.K., et al. (eds.) I3E 2016. LNCS, vol. 9844, pp. 79–89. Springer, Cham (2016). https://doi.org/10.1007/978-3-319-45234-0_8
3. Burt, R.S.: Structural holes and good ideas. Am. J. Sociol. **110**(2), 349–399 (2004)
4. Callon, M., Courtial, J.P., Laville, F.: Co-word analysis as a tool for describing the network of interactions between basic and technological research: the case of polymer chemsitry. Scientometrics **22**(1), 155–205 (1991)
5. Callon, M., Courtial, J.P., Turner, W.A., Bauin, S.: From translations to problematic networks: an introduction to co-word analysis. Inf. (Int. Social Science Council) **22**(2), 191–235 (1983)
6. Cambrosio, A., Limoges, C., Courtial, J., Laville, F.: Historical scientometrics? Mapping over 70 years of biological safety research with coword analysis. Scientometrics **27**(2), 119–143 (1993)
7. Cobo, M.J., López-Herrera, A.G., Herrera-Viedma, E., Herrera, F.: Science mapping software tools: review, analysis, and cooperative study among tools. J. Am. Soc. Inf. Sci. Technol. **62**(7), 1382–1402 (2011)
8. Douligeris, C., Polemi, N., Karantjias, A., Lamersdorf, W. (eds.): I3E 2013. IAICT, vol. 399. Springer, Heidelberg (2013). https://doi.org/10.1007/978-3-642-37437-1
9. Grover, P., Kar, A.K., Vigneswara Ilavarasan, P.: Blockchain for businesses: a systematic literature review. In: Al-Sharhan, S.A., et al. (eds.) I3E 2018. LNCS, vol. 11195, pp. 325–336. Springer, Cham (2018). https://doi.org/10.1007/978-3-030-02131-3_29
10. He, Q.: Knowledge discovery through co-word analysis. Libr. Trends **48**, 133–159 (1999)
11. Hu, C.P., Hu, J.M., Deng, S.L., Liu, Y.: A co-word analysis of library and information science in china. Scientometrics **97**(2), 369–382 (2013)
12. Ismagilova, E., Slade, E., Williams, M.: Persuasiveness of ewom communications: literature review and suggestions for future research. In: Dwivedi, Y.K., et al. (eds.) Social Media: The Good, the Bad, and the Ugly, pp. 354–359. Springer, Cham (2016). https://doi.org/10.1007/978-3-319-45234-0_32
13. Janssen, M., et al. (eds.): I3E 2015. LNCS, vol. 9373. Springer, Cham (2015). https://doi.org/10.1007/978-3-319-25013-7
14. de Laat, M., Lally, V., Lipponen, L., Simons, R.J.: Investigating patterns of interaction in networked learning and computer-supported collaborative learning: arole for social network analysis. Int. J. Comput.-Support. Collab. Learn. **2**(1), 87–103 (2007)
15. Leydesdorff, L., Vaughan, L.: Co-occurrence matrices and their applications in information science: extending ACA to the web environment. J. Am. Soc. Inf. Sci. Technol. **57**(12), 1616–1628 (2006)
16. Li, H., Mäntymäki, M., Zhang, X. (eds.): I3E 2014. IAICT, vol. 445. Springer, Heidelberg (2014). https://doi.org/10.1007/978-3-662-45526-5
17. Liu, Y., Goncalves, J., Ferreira, D., Xiao, B., Hosio, S., Kostakos, V.: CHI 1994–2013: mapping two decades of intellectual progress through co-word analysis. In: Proceedings of the 32rd Annual ACM Conference on Human Factors in Computing Systems, pp. 3553–3562. ACM, New York (2014)

18. Mikalef, P., Pappas, I.O., Giannakos, M.N., Sharma, K.: Determining consumer engagement in word-of-mouth: trust and network ties in a social commerce setting. In: Kar, A.K., et al. (eds.) I3E 2017. LNCS, vol. 10595, pp. 351–362. Springer, Cham (2017). https://doi.org/10.1007/978-3-319-68557-1_31
19. Murtagh, F., Legendre, P.: Ward's hierarchical agglomerative clustering method: which algorithms implement ward's criterion? J. Classif. **31**(3), 274–295 (2014)
20. Newman, M.E.: A measure of betweenness centrality based on random walks. Soc. Netw. **27**(1), 39–54 (2005)
21. Nielsen, A.E., Thomsen, C.: Sustainable development: the role of network communication. Corp. Soc. Responsib. Environ. Manag. **18**(1), 1–10 (2011)
22. Pappas, I.O., Mikalef, P., Dwivedi, Y.K., Jaccheri, L., Krogstie, J., Mäntymäki, M. (eds.): I3E 2019. LNCS, vol. 11701. Springer, Cham (2019). https://doi.org/10.1007/978-3-030-29374-1
23. Pappas, I.O., Mikalef, P., Giannakos, M.N., Krogstie, J., Lekakos, G.: Big data and business analytics ecosystems: paving the way towards digital transformation and sustainable societies. IseB **16**(3), 479–491 (2018). https://doi.org/10.1007/s10257-018-0377-z
24. Rombach, P., Porter, M.A., Fowler, J.H., Mucha, P.J.: Core-periphery structure in networks (revisited). SIAM Rev. **59**(3), 619–646 (2017)
25. Schank, T., Wagner, D.: Approximating clustering-coefficient and transitivity. Universität Karlsruhe, Fakultät für Informatik (2004)
26. Sorrentino, M., Niehaves, B.: Intermediaries in e-inclusion: a literature review. In: 2010 43rd Hawaii International Conference on System Sciences, pp. 1–10 (2010)
27. Tamilmani, K., Rana, N.P., Prakasam, N., Dwivedi, Y.K.: The battle of brain vs. heart: a literature review and meta-analysis of hedonic motivation use in UTAUT2. Int. J. Inf. Manag. **46**, 222–235 (2019)

# Weight Analysis of the Factors Affecting eWOM Providing Behavior

Elvira Ismagilova[1(✉)], Yogesh K. Dwivedi[2], Nripendra P. Rana[1],
Uthayasankar Sivarajah[1], and Vishanth Weerakkody[1]

[1] Faculty of Management, Law and Social Sciences,
University of Bradford, Bradford, UK
{e.ismagilova,n.p.rana,u.sivarajah,
v.weerakkody}@bradford.ac.uk
[2] Emerging Markets Research Centre, School of Management,
Swansea University, Swansea, UK
y.k.dwivedi@swansea.ac.uk

**Abstract.** Electronic word of mouth (eWOM) significantly affects the consumer decision-making process. A number of studies investigated why consumers provide eWOM communications. Existing literature has contradicting factors regarding factors affect eWOM providing behaviour. This study aims to evaluate factors affecting eWOM providing behaviour by performing a systematic review and weight analysis of existing research outputs. Based on the result of weight analysis it was found that the best predictors of eWOM providing behaviour are involvement, self-enhancement, and trust in web eWOM services. Scholars can use the results of this study when making decisions regarding the inclusion of factors in their research. Practitioners can pay more attention to the best predictors.

**Keywords:** eWOM, weight analysis · Literature review · eWOM providing behaviour

## 1 Introduction

Electronic word of mouth (eWOM) significantly affects the consumer decision-making process [1, 2]. eWOM is defined as "the dynamic and on-going information exchange process between potential, actual, or former consumers regarding a product, service, brand, or company, which is available to a multitude of people and institutions via the Internet" [3].

An increasing number of researchers and practitioners have started paying attention to eWOM communications [4–6]. A number of studies investigated factors affecting eWOM providing behaviour [7–10]. Existing studies in this area have reported conflicting results on the effect of factors affecting eWOM providing behaviour. For instance, Luarn et al. [11] found that altruism does not affect eWOM providing behaviour, while Cui et al. [12] found that altruism has a significant positive effect on eWOM providing behaviour. Another study by Shen et al. [13] by using surveys found that economic incentives do not have any significant impact on eWOM providing

© IFIP International Federation for Information Processing 2020
Published by Springer Nature Switzerland AG 2020
M. Hattingh et al. (Eds.): I3E 2020, LNCS 12066, pp. 266–275, 2020.
https://doi.org/10.1007/978-3-030-44999-5_22

behaviour, while Son et al. [14] found the opposite results-economic incentives positively affect individual's behaviour to provide eWOM. The mixed findings on the factors affecting eWOM providing behaviour can lead to confusion for scholars and practitioners.

Thus, it is crucial to conduct a review of existing studies on eWOM providing behaviour and perform weight analysis. Thus, the aim of this research is to examine factors affecting eWOM providing behaviour by performing a systematic review and weight analysis of existing research findings. Conducting weight analysis will help to investigate the predictive power of the independent variables on the dependent variables, by taking into account the number of times a relationship has been previously studied. The model developed through the weight analysis will help eWOM practitioners and scholars to focus on more influential factors of eWOM providing behaviour.

The remaining part of the paper is organised in the following way. Section 2 focuses on the method which was used for this study. Section 3 will present the literature review. After, the findings from weight analysis are presented and discussed in Sect. 4. Section 5 presents a conclusion followed by the limitations of this study and directions for future research.

## 2 Literature Search Method

To perform weight analysis peer-reviewed journal articles on eWOM communications were collected from bibliographic database Scopus, which is one of the world's largest abstract and citation databases of peer-reviewed literature. The searched keywords were selected after consulting the experts and included "Online review", "Online reviews", "Electronic word-of-mouth", "Electronic word of mouth", "eWOM", "Internet word-of-mouth", "Internet word of mouth", "iWOM", "Online word-of-mouth", "Online word of mouth", "Virtual word-of-mouth". As a result, more than 500 articles were identified published from 2000 untill 2018. Articles that did not focus on eWOM providing behaviour and did not have empirical findings were excluded, leaving 54 research papers relevant for this research.

## 3 Literature Synthesis

An extensive number of studies investigated factors affecting eWOM providing behaviour. The studies were conducted in different contexts (e.g. SNS, opinion platforms, online review websites), countries (e.g. USA, China, Spain), using different products and services as examples (e.g. laptop, restaurants, hotels) [9, 15–18]. Additionally, studies used various methods for data collection such as surveys or data mining [19, 20]. Studies applied a number of theories to study factors affecting eWOM providing behaviour such as social exchange theory, motivational theory and Uses and Gratification theory to name a few [17]. Based on the literature review 21 factors which affect eWOM providing behaviour were identified (see Table 1).

**Table 1.** Factors affecting eWOM providing behaviour

| Construct | Definition | Number of studies | Representative studies |
|---|---|---|---|
| Influence of others | Influence by the behaviours and practices of other users | 6 | [7, 8] |
| Information influence | Capacity to accept information from another knowledgeable person to select a product or brand | 4 | [9, 10] |
| Tie strength | The depth of a relationship between source and information seeker. Variables included: tie strength, social interaction tie, perceived social relationships | 7 | [21, 22] |
| Homophily | The degree to which two or more individuals who interact are similar in certain attributes (e.g. beliefs, education, social status) | 3 | [9, 15] |
| Economic incentive | Getting economic benefits (e.g. money, web coupons, free delivery). Variables included: economic incentive, remuneration, extrinsic reward, open market reward | 12 | [13, 14] |
| Altruism | The aim of increasing welfare of one or more person(s) other than oneself | 8 | [11, 12] |
| Self-enhancement | Presenting themselves positively, sharing information to look good | 12 | [12, 23] |
| Satisfaction in helping other customers | Pleasant consumption fulfilment which happens as a result of helping other customers | 4 | [17, 18] |
| Opinion seeking | Behaviour focused on looking for eWOM communications | 3 | [24, 25] |
| Opinion leadership | A domain-independent, trait-like set of personality characteristics that are stable over time and across respondent groups. Opinion leaders shape public opinion by selectively conveying mass media messages to their social networks | 3 | [25, 26] |
| Community identity | Sense of belonging to the virtual (online) community. Variables included: community identification, social identification | 3 | [20, 27] |
| Reciprocity | Benefit for individuals to engage in social exchange; a person who offers help to others is expecting returns in the future | 2 | [19, 20] |

(*continued*)

Table 1. (*continued*)

| Construct | Definition | Number of studies | Representative studies |
|---|---|---|---|
| Information usefulness | The degree to which the information assists consumers in making their purchase decisions | 3 | [28, 29] |
| Affective commitment | Affective (emotional) commitment derived from emotional attachment to, identification with, and involvement in an entity | 2 | [30, 31] |
| Normative commitment | Motivated by the actor's moral obligation that s/he must fulfil | 2 | [30, 31] |
| Involvement | The degree of psychological identification and emotional ties the receiver has with the product/service | 8 | [12, 32] |
| Customer satisfaction | A condition that happens as a result of a pleasant consumption fulfilment | 8 | [16, 33] |
| Loyalty | Overall attachment with a favourable attitude manifested by repeated purchasing | 3 | [14, 16] |
| Perceived risk | The uncertainty a consumer has in making a purchase decision | 3 | [18, 34] |
| Brand loyalty | Favourable attitude toward the brand | 2 | [35, 36] |
| Trust in web eWOM services | The subjective belief that a party will fulfil their obligations | 4 | [20, 37] |

To determine the strength of the relationships between constructs, weight analysis was conducted by dividing the number of significant relationships by the total number of analysed relationships between studied independent and dependent variables. For example, the relationship between economic incentive and engaging in eWOM communications was examined 13 times and was significant eight times. As a result, the weight significance of a relationship between these two constructs is calculated by dividing 8 by 13, which gives 0.615. If weight is equal to 1 it indicates that the relationship between two constructs is significant across all studies, while a weight equal to 0 shows this relationship is non-significant throughout all examined studies (Jeyaraj et al. [39]; Rana et al. [40]). Table 2 presents the weight analysis of all 21 relationships included in this study.

Researchers [38–40] classify predictors as follows: a predictor is 'well-utilised' if examined five or more times, otherwise it is considered as 'experimental'; a predictor is a 'best predictor' if its weight is greater or equal to 0.8 and it has been examined more than five times but is a 'promising predictor' if it has been examined less than 5 times and has a weight of 1.

**Table 2.** Results of weight analysis

| Independent variable | Number of significant relationships | Number of non-significant relationships | Total number of relationships | Weight |
|---|---|---|---|---|
| Satisfaction in helping other customers | 4 | 0 | 4 | 1.000 |
| Opinion seeking | 3 | 0 | 3 | 1.000 |
| Opinion leadership | 4 | 0 | 4 | 1.000 |
| Information usefulness | 4 | 0 | 4 | 1.000 |
| Affective commitment | 3 | 0 | 3 | 1.000 |
| Normative commitment | 3 | 0 | 3 | 1.000 |
| Loyalty | 3 | 0 | 3 | 1.000 |
| Perceived risk | 3 | 0 | 3 | 1.000 |
| Trust in web eWOM services | 5 | 0 | 5 | 1.000 |
| Self-enhancement | 12 | 1 | 13 | 0.923 |
| Involvement | 7 | 1 | 8 | 0.875 |
| Brand loyalty | 2 | 1 | 3 | 0.667 |
| Economic incentive | 8 | 5 | 13 | 0.615 |
| Altruism | 5 | 4 | 9 | 0.556 |
| Customer satisfaction | 5 | 4 | 9 | 0.556 |
| Influence of others | 3 | 3 | 6 | 0.500 |
| Tie strength | 4 | 4 | 8 | 0.500 |
| Community identity | 2 | 2 | 4 | 0.500 |
| Homophily | 1 | 2 | 3 | 0.333 |
| Reciprocity | 1 | 2 | 3 | 0.333 |
| Information influence | 1 | 4 | 5 | 0.200 |

*Note:* Dependent variable is eWOM providing behavior

The following predictors of intention to provide eWOM communications fall within the category of best predictor: involvement (examined 8 times, significant 7 times), self-enhancement (examined 13 times, significant 12 times), and trust in web eWOM services (examined 5 times, significant 5 times). All of these predictors were explored five or more times and have a weight equal to or greater than 0.80.

Predictors such as information usefulness (examined 4 times, significant 4 times), affective commitment (examined 3 times, significant 3 times), normative commitment (examined 3 times, significant 3 times), loyalty (examined 3 times, significant 3 times), perceived risk (examined 3 times, significant 3 times), opinion seeking (examined 3 times, significant 3 times), and opinion leadership (examined 4 times, significant 4 times) are considered as promising predictors of intention to engage in eWOM communications. Although these relationships were found to be significant across all examined studies, Jeyaraj et al. [39] suggest that these types of experimental variables need more testing to be categorised as best predictors.

Even though none of the studied relationships between predictors and intention to engage in eWOM was found to have a weight of '0', some of the well-utilised independent constructs are considered to be least effective predictors, such as influence of others (examined 6 times, significant 3 times), tie strength (examined 8 times, significant 4 times), information influence (examined 5 times, significant once), economic incentive (examined 13 times, significant 8 times), altruism (examined 9 times, significant 5 times), and customer satisfaction (examined 9 times, significant 5 times). It is proposed by Jeyaraj et al. [39] that justification for continuing to examine such predictors should be convincing. Nevertheless, it may be premature to exclude such predictors given that eWOM providing behaviour research is still emerging as far as the empirical aspects and solid theoretical foundations of this research are concerned. Out of the total 21 examined relationships only nine were found to be studied five or more times (influence of others, tie strength, information influence, economic incentive, altruism, involvement, self-enhancement, customer satisfaction, and trust in web eWOM services), which proposes that eWOM research is still not that well developed. Moreover, some researchers propose that weight analysis may not be a sufficient reason to exclude any variables from further analysis (Rana et al. [40]). None of the predictors was found to be the worst predictors of intention to engage in eWOM communications.

## 4  Discussion

Taking into account the increasing number of studies on eWOM providing behaviour, it is important to discuss and analyse their collective findings. Figure 1 presents the diagrammatic representation of the factors affecting eWOM providing behaviour with their corresponding weight based on the results of weight analysis. The findings suggest the best predictors such as involvement, self-enhancement, and trust in web eWOM services should be included in eWOM research. Promising predictors such as should be included in future empirical research to evaluate their overall performance.

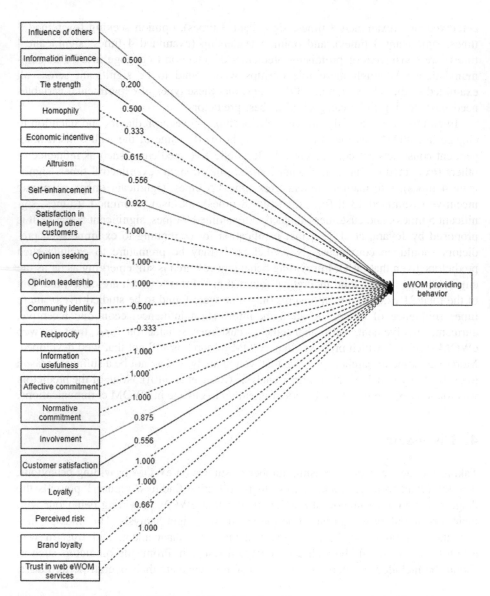

**Fig. 1.** Factors affective eWOM providing behaviour Note: - - -> experimental predictors; →
well-utilised predictors.

## 5    Conclusion and Limitations

The aim of this research was to examine factors affecting eWOM providing behaviour
by conducting weight analysis of existing research findings. The weight analysis was
performed by identifying a number of significant and non-significant relationships
between studied variables.

The current study provides some implications for researchers and practitioners. This research provided a framework for future research identifying factors affecting eWOM providing behaviour. Scholars can use the results of this study when making decisions regarding the inclusion of factors in their research. Practitioners can pay more attention to the best predictors- involvement, self-enhancement, and trust in web eWOM services.

The current research has a number of limitations. First, this study only conducted weight analysis without performing meta-analysis which could strengthen those findings of weight analysis and evaluate the significance of the studies relationships [41]. It is advised that future research performs meta-analysis on factors affecting eWOM providing behaviour. Second, this study only used the Scopus database for the collection of study. This can affect the number of research outputs available for weight analysis, the coverage and representativity of the sample considered in the analysis. Thus, future research should employ other available datasets (e.g. web of science, Google Scholar, EBSCO).

# References

1. Dwivedi, Y.K., Kapoor, K.K., Chen, H.: Social media marketing and advertising. Market. Rev. **15**, 289–309 (2015)
2. Alalwan, A.A., Rana, N.P., Dwivedi, Y.K., Algharabat, R.: Social media in marketing: a review and analysis of the existing literature. Telematics Inform. **34**, 1177–1190 (2017)
3. Ismagilova, E., Dwivedi, Y.K., Slade, E., Williams, M.D.: Electronic Word of Mouth (eWOM) in the Marketing Context: A State of the Art Analysis and Future Directions. Springer, Heidelberg (2017). https://doi.org/10.1007/978-3-319-52459-7
4. Rathore, A.K., Ilavarasan, P.V., Dwivedi, Y.K.: Social media content and product co-creation: an emerging paradigm. J. Enterprise Inf. Manag. **29**, 7–18 (2016)
5. Shareef, M.A., Mukerji, B., Dwivedi, Y.K., Rana, N.P., Islam, R.: Social media marketing: comparative effect of advertisement sources. J. Retailing Consumer Serv. **46**, 58–69 (2019)
6. Shiau, W.-L., Dwivedi, Y.K., Yang, H.S.: Co-citation and cluster analyses of extant literature on social networks. Int. J. Inf. Manag. **37**, 390–399 (2017)
7. Choi, J.H., Scott, J.E.: Electronic word of mouth and knowledge sharing on social network sites: a social capital perspective. J. Theoret. Appl. Electron. Commer. Res. **8**, 69–82 (2013)
8. Christodoulides, G., Michaelidou, N., Argyriou, E.: Cross-national differences in e-WOM influence. Eur. J. Market. **46**, 1689–1707 (2012)
9. Saleem, A., Ellahi, A.: Influence of electronic word of mouth on purchase intention of fashion products in social networking websites. Pak. J. Commer. Soc. Sci. (PJCSS) **11**, 597–622 (2017)
10. Wu, L., Mattila, A.S., Wang, C.-Y., Hanks, L.: The impact of power on service customers' willingness to post online reviews. J. Serv. Res. **19**, 224–238 (2016)
11. Luarn, P., Chiu, Y.-P., Yang, J.-C.: An exploratory study of the motives engaged in the dissemination of social word-of-mouth via mobile device. In: 2014 47th Hawaii International Conference on System Sciences, pp. 1033–1042. IEEE (2014)
12. Cui, J., Wang, L., Feng, H., Teng, Y.: Empirical study of the motivations of E-WOM spreading on online feedback system in China. In: PACIS, p. 251 (2014)

13. Shen, W., Cai, J., Li, L.: Electronic word-of-mouth in China: a motivational analysis. In: 2011 International Conference on E-Business and E-Government (ICEE), pp. 1–6. IEEE (2011)

14. Son, J.-E., Kim, H.-W., Jang, Y.-J.: Investigating factors affecting electronic word-of-mouth in the open market context: a mixed methods approach. In: PACIS, p. 167 (2012)

15. Hansen, S.S., Lee, J.K.: What drives consumers to pass along marketer-generated eWOM in social network games? Social and game factors in play. J. Theoret. Appl. Electron. Commer. Res. **8**, 53–68 (2013)

16. Lee, J., Lee, J.-N., Tan, B.C.: The contrasting attitudes of reviewer and seller in electronic word-of-mouth: a communicative action theory perspective. Asia Pac. J. Inf. Syst. **23**, 105–129 (2013)

17. Tong, Y., Wang, X., Tan, C.-H., Teo, H.-H.: An empirical study of information contribution to online feedback systems: a motivation perspective. Inf. Manag. **50**, 562–570 (2013)

18. Zhang, Y., Lv, T.: Analysis of the relationship between involvement and the internet word-of-mouth. In: 2010 2nd IEEE International Conference on Network Infrastructure and Digital Content, pp. 1018–1024. IEEE (2010)

19. Cheung, C.M., Lee, M.K.: What drives consumers to spread electronic word of mouth in online consumer-opinion platforms. Decis. Support Syst. **53**, 218–225 (2012)

20. Horng, S.-M.: A study of active and passive user participation in virtual communities. J. Electron. Commer. Res. **17**, 289–311 (2016)

21. Niu, H., Wang, X., Sun, N.: Influences of external incentives on consumers' positive electronic word-of-mouth intention. Mark. Sci. Innov. Econ. Dev. 236–244 (2010)

22. Wolny, J., Mueller, C.: Analysis of fashion consumers' motives to engage in electronic word-of-mouth communication through social media platforms. J. Market. Manag. **29**, 562–583 (2013)

23. Hennig-Thurau, T., Gwinner, K.P., Walsh, G., Gremler, D.D.: Electronic word-of-mouth via consumer-opinion platforms: what motivates consumers to articulate themselves on the internet? J. Interact. Market. **18**, 38–52 (2004)

24. Nagy, A., Kemény, I., Szűcs, K., Simon, J., Kiss, V.: Are opinion leaders more satisfied? Results of a SEM model about the relationship between opinion leadership and online customer satisfaction. Soc. Econ. **39**, 141–160 (2017)

25. Sun, T., Youn, S., Wu, G., Kuntaraporn, M.: Online word-of-mouth (or mouse): an exploration of its antecedents and consequences. J. Comput.-Mediated Commun. **11**, 1104–1127 (2006)

26. Kucukemiroglu, S., Kara, A.: Online word-of-mouth communication on social networking sites: an empirical study of Facebook users. Int. J. Commer. Manag. **25**, 2–20 (2015)

27. Yoo, C.W., Sanders, G.L., Moon, J.: Exploring the effect of e-WOM participation on e-Loyalty in e-commerce. Decis. Support Syst. **55**, 669–678 (2013)

28. Frasquet, M., Ruiz-Molina, M.-E., Molla-Descals, A.: The role of the brand in driving online loyalty for multichannel retailers. Int. Rev. Retail Distrib. Consum. Res. **25**, 490–502 (2015)

29. Huang, L., Shao, J., Wang, W.: Research on the relationships between hotel internet word-of-mouth and customers' behavior intention based on trust. In: 2013 6th International Conference on Information Management, Innovation Management and Industrial Engineering, pp. 250–254. IEEE (2013)

30. Jin, X., Xiang, L., Lee, M.K., Cheung, C.M., Zhou, Z., Zhao, D.-T.: Electronic word-of-mouth contribution continuance in online opinion platforms: the role of multiple commitments. In: PACIS, p. 149 (2010)

31. Li, C.-H., Chang, C.-M.: The influence of trust and perceived playfulness on the relationship commitment of hospitality online social network-moderating effects of gender. Int. J. Contemp. Hospitality Manag. **28**, 924–944 (2016)

32. De Meyer, C., Petzer, D.: Product involvement and online word-of-mouth in the South African fast food industry. READINGS BOOK 205 (2013)
33. Lii, Y.-S., Lee, M.: The joint effects of compensation frames and price levels on service recovery of online pricing error. Manag. Serv. Qual.: Int. J. **22**, 4–20 (2012)
34. Tirunillai, S., Tellis, G.J.: Does chatter really matter? Dynamics of user-generated content and stock performance. Market. Sci. **31**, 198–215 (2012)
35. Rialti, R., Zollo, L., Pellegrini, M.M., Ciappei, C.: Exploring the antecedents of brand loyalty and electronic word of mouth in social-media-based brand communities: do gender differences matter? J. Glob. Market. **30**, 147–160 (2017)
36. Yeh, Y.-H., Choi, S.M.: MINI-lovers, maxi-mouths: an investigation of antecedents to eWOM intention among brand community members. J. Market. Commun. **17**, 145–162 (2011)
37. Nusair, K., Hua, N., Ozturk, A., Butt, I.: A theoretical framework of electronic word-of-mouth against the backdrop of social networking websites. J. Travel Tourism Market. **34**, 653–665 (2017)
38. Ismagilova, E., Slade, E.L., Rana, N.P., Dwivedi, Y.K.: The effect of electronic word of mouth communications on intention to buy: a meta-analysis. Inf. Syst. Front. 1–24 (2019). https://doi.org/10.1007/s10796-019-09924-y
39. Jeyaraj, A., Rottman, J.W., Lacity, M.C.: A review of the predictors, linkages, and biases in IT innovation adoption research. J. Inf. Technol. **21**, 1–23 (2006)
40. Rana, N.P., Dwivedi, Y.K., Williams, M.D.: A meta-analysis of existing research on citizen adoption of e-government. Inf. Syst. Front. **17**, 547–563 (2015)
41. Dwivedi, Y.K., Rana, N.P., Jeyaraj, A., Clement, M., Williams, M.D.: Re-examining the unified theory of acceptance and use of technology (UTAUT): towards a revised theoretical model. Inf. Syst. Front. **21**, 719–734 (2019)

# An Intelligent Marketspace Mobile Application for Marketing Organic Products

Oluwasefunmi 'Tale Arogundade[1]([⊠]) [ID], Adebayo Abayomi-Alli[1] [ID],
Kayode Adesemowo[2] [ID], Taiwo Bamigbade[1], Modupe Odusami[3] [ID],
and Victor Olowe[1]

[1] Federal University of Agriculture, Abeokuta, Nigeria
{arogundadeot, abayomiallia, olowevio}@funaab.edu.ng,
bamigbadetaiwo@gmail.com
[2] Nelson Mandela University, Port Elizabeth, South Africa
kadesemowo@soams.co.za
[3] Covenant University, Ota, Nigeria
modupe.odusami@convenantuniversity.edu.ng

**Abstract.** Sustainable food security (Sfs) desires not only that people always
have passage to ample and nutritious food, but also that this food be formed with
minimum environmental impact. This research is aimed at developing a mobile
application for marketing organic farm products with the functionality of
automated geo-location services, preferred goods delivery services, easy access
to different organic farm produce. The mobile user platform consists of the
Presentation, Business, Data and Data storage which is a slight variation of the
Model-View-Controller architecture. It also takes into deep awareness the
configuration, security and communications aspect as these are the underlying
factors for the robustness of mobile application. The Presentation Tier consists
of the user interface and the logic used to navigate around the user interface
meaningfully. It modifies and shows information into a human distinct pattern.
The Business Logic tier is essentially efficient for information transfer between
the user interface and the database of the project. The last layer of the three-
tiered architecture is the Data Access tier, which is made up of the Database
servers. The application was implemented in Java, SQLite (local) and PHP for
the backend server and Amazon Web Services for cloud infrastructure. Farmers
were engaged in cursory testing. Users find the application concept very
interesting.

**Keywords:** Access · Geolocation · Marketspace · Model view · Orgafamob ·
Organic farming · Pragmatism · Sustainable food

## 1 Introduction

Agriculture is the main factor for the survival of humans and it also provides food, fuel
and other services in line with ecosystems. It plays an important function in economic
development and it is an essential source of livelihood. Agriculture is also a crucial
origin of environmental downgrading, adding to climate variation, decreasing fresh-
water resources, detracting soil fertility and contaminating the environment over

M. Hattingh et al. (Eds.): I3E 2020, LNCS 12066, pp. 276–287, 2020.
https://doi.org/10.1007/978-3-030-44999-5_23

fertilizer and pesticide [1, 2]. Essentially, food production relies on the lofty natural resources it is derogating. Sfs therefore not only requires that all people always have access to sufficient and nutritious food, but food be formed with minimal environmental brunt. Hence, sustainable agricultural development desires that agriculture face the demands of the present without negotiating the capability of future generations to tourney their own demands [3]. Achieving these goals by current Agriculture practices has not been very successful. Today, Agriculture is not only a dominating factor of environmental degradation, it is a major force compelling the Earth System beyond the 'safe-operating space' for humanity [4, 5].

Knowing that we have not achieve Sf s today and given the fact that we will probably need to double food production by 2050 so that we can feed 9 billion people with rising demand for meat and dairy products [6], there is a drastic need for changes in the food system. We need to increase the production of food in the right locations at fair prices, protecting livelihoods to farmers and reducing the environmental cost of agriculture. Recently, the market for organic food (ORF) has increased, and call for fair sustainable farming.

It is worth mentioning that this research is aimed at developing a mobile application for marketing organic farm products with the functionality of automated geo-location services, preferred goods delivery services, easy access to different organic farm produce. Although a considerable amount of study can be found in the literature which identifies the attitude of dairy farmers towards organic farming [7, 8], economic and social implications of organic agriculture [9], these did not take mobile and real-time, geo-location into due consideration. The contributions of this work are:

- Ensuring real time information delivery on changing trends and key discoveries in the organic farm produce.
- Providing organic farmers cultivating crops with an e-commerce platform for easy facilitation of their business.
- Enabling practicing organic farmers form a cluster around themselves thereby empowering them with the benefits that comes with economics of scale.

The paper is organized in the following way. Section 2 comprises of related works in the area of organic farming and mobile applications that has been developed to improve the availability of organic products. Section 3 deals with the requirement analysis and design methodology of the proposed mobile application. In Sect. 4, we detail the implementation of the mobile application for organic market Space. Finally, Sect. 5 includes our conclusion.

## 2 Literature Review and Related Works

In this section, we discuss the economic and social meanings of organic Agriculture, and the usage of ICT and mobile technology in Agriculture.

## 2.1    Economic and Social Implications of Organic Agriculture (OA)

The advantage of OA for micro farmers is reliant on organic yields, the cost of organic production, and the size of the organic price choice [10]. In [11], economic impact of organic farming in livelihoods of farmers of Nepal was explored. Binta and Barbier in [2], carried out a comparative study on the economic and environmental performances of organic and conventional horticultural farming systems in the Niayes region in Senegal.

Health has been one of the major reasons consumers purchase organic goods [12, 13] so much as safety, quality and taste [14–17] are very imperative motivations for purchasing ORF. In marketing and promoting organic ORF, eating pleasure (particularly tastiness) is now the main argument, followed by health and then environmental benefits [18, 19]. It is surprising to discover that consumers appear to be relatively incognizant of the constructive impact that OA has on the environment [20].

Results showed that economically, farmers were found satisfied and encouraged to expand their organic business. Although, there is limited market for ORF in the region unlike the conventional farming however, investment in agro-ecological research, organic management can greatly improve it. Especially through the establishment of a local market for organic crops. Hence, [21] explained that the study put out by the Maine Organic Farmers and Gardeners Association (MOFGA) indicates that these farms are contributing to Maine's economy positively.

## 2.2    ICT and Mobile Technology in Agriculture

A short introduction of the implications of ICTs in agricultural sector was presented in [22]. The authors demonstrated the fact that there are large number of ICT-enabled services which can improve many processes in the agricultural sector. In [23] the impact of proliferation of ICTs was investigated, due to the growth of mobile technologies, in order to know if it has actually had any significant impact on Agriculture. It was confirmed that ICTs play a significant role in enhancing agricultural production. Study [24] presented a research that assessed the traits, diversity and impacts of ICTs used in African agriculture. The key challenges hindering more widespread use of the technologies were also highlighted by the author. The study in [24], vividly reveals that ICTs are making impact in increasing productivity and marketing of products but there are still several constraints for adequate utilization by the farmers. Hence, there is likelihood that combination of mobile technologies with other ICT platforms such as mass media, will have exponential impact on agriculture. Study in [25] on the influence of ICT in agriculture, (in developing countries), in respect of opportunities and challenges, found that one of the major benefits of ICT in agricultural sector is the improvement of market activities.

Finally, it is merit observing that the motivation of buyers to buy ORF are interest and sentimental federation of organic goods with realness and reminiscence taste of the past. However, the loss of adequate provision of ORF [18] and, above all, its higher price is often a strong obstacle to the purchase of ORF. Also, the inadequacy of information on the meaning of ORF [26], coupled with diverse of ways to label organic products has affected the purchasing power of organic products. Despite the fact that organic farming looks quite comforting for consumers, the response of farmers to the concept is not at an alarming rate. Only a minority of farmers, especially in dairy areas, are in favour of organic farming.

# 3 Methodology

The Orgfarmob, is underpinned by pragmatism philosophy as it seeks to provide practical solutions and outcomes [27]. It follows the build and process methods from a design research point of view [28, 29], rather than design science research methodology strategy. Given the emphasis on practical solutions, the logical design, presented as the design process, is the primary focus of this paper: the development of *orgfarmob marketspace*. It starts off tilting towards inductive approach to discern better the nature of the problem within the context (organic farmers in Nigeria) and guide towards gathering requirement [27].

Before proceeding with 'requirement analysis', 'architectural framework' and 'design and use-case design considerations', we quickly outline the orgfarmob marketspace build and process approach. In line with our pragmatic approach, we built on aspects of the framework for computing research methods [29]. We only utilized aspects that we required and applicable to our study. The following were considered:

## 3.1 Framework for Computing Research

- What do we want to achieve?

  a. (Find out what is happening) – the authors wished to achieve a better understanding of the use and application of ICT mobile development in organic farming (in Nigeria), starting with the western part of Nigeria.
  b. (Develop something that works) – the authors will embark on developing a mobile tool, orgfarmob' to understudy and assist organic farmers.

- Where did the data come from?

  c. (Read) – the authors will literatures on organic farming and ICT in agriculture.
  d. (Observe, Ask) – the authors will engage with and get opinions from organic farming practitioners in western part of Nigeria.
  e. (Model) – the authors will conceptualise and utilize UML to model practical design model covering user activity, admin activity, entity- relationship and sequence.
  f. (Where to collect) – the authors will collect and collate relevant requirement and design data from the field and conceptual analysis.

- What did they do with the data?

    g. (Identify themes, Identify trends) – the authors will use the collated information to better understand organic farming and use of ICT in organic farming.
    h. (Create frameworks/taxonomy/prototype) – the authors will in the first iteration design an architectural framework for orgfarmob. Thereafter, in iterative manner, the author will prototype the orgfarmob application.

- Had they achieved their goal?

    i. (Evaluate results, Draw conclusions) – the authors, having gain understanding and developed working prototype, will now be better placed to analyse and iteratively finetune the design and build (soft- ware development).
    j. (identify limitation) – the authors will draw from the design and development process what are the bounds of limits and/or how prior studies can be extended or critique.

Flowing from the framework for computing research approach, this study was carried out through source of opinions from organic agriculture practitioners, some web materials, survey of organic farmers in Nigeria and the world at large through the internet and personal interview of organic farming practitioner.

The Unified Modelling Language (UML), Meta model elements are arranged diagrammatically. Several diagrams are used for distinct purpose based on the angle from which you are viewing the system. The various views are called "architectural views". These architectural views enable the organization of knowledge, and diagrams allow the communication of knowledge. Then knowledge itself is contained in the model or set of models that focuses on the problem and solution. Figure 1 depicts the architectural view of the proposed study. The given implementation model is majorly categorized into two broad categories which are the mobile user platform and the remote infrastructure.

## 3.2   Architectural Framework

The mobile user platform consists of the Presentation, Business, Data and Data storage which is a slight variation of the Model-View-Controller architecture. It also takes into deep awareness the configuration, security and communications aspect as this are the underlying factors for the robustness of the mobile application. The Presentation Tier consists of the user interface and the logic used to navigate around the user interface meaningfully. It converts and displays information into a human legible form. The Business Logic tier is mainly responsible for information exchange between the user interface and the database of the project.

The last layer of the three-tiered architecture is the Data Access tier, which consists of the Database servers. The updates of the information and server communication exist here.

## 3.3   Design and Use-Case Design Considerations

In line with the pragmatic approach of this paper, the logical design is the critical and main design process [30]. The software coding thereafter results in the developed prototype which is the first instance of validation of the design process.

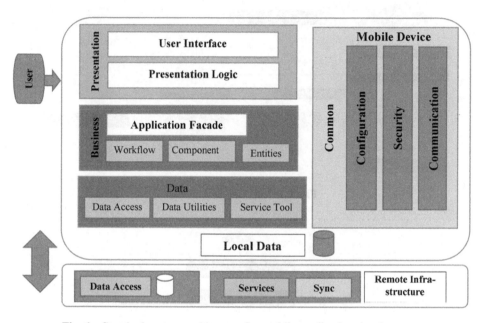

**Fig. 1.** Standard system architecture for mobile application development

Figure 2 depicts the User Activity Diagram and the Admin Activity Diagram of the proposed study is shown in Fig. 3.

Activity diagram, an important diagram in UML, was used to conceptualised and express driving aspects of the system. It is essentially a flowchart that depict the flow from one activity to another.

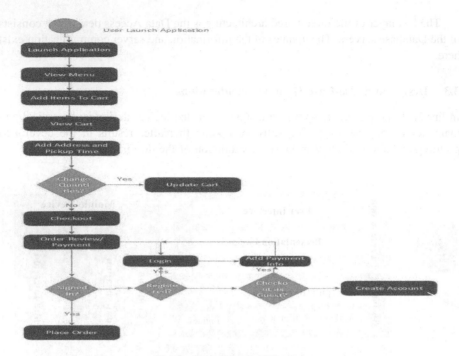

**Fig. 2.** User Activity Diagram

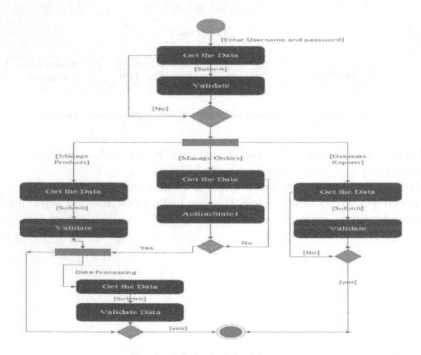

**Fig. 3.** Admin Activity Diagram

## 3.4  Entity Relationship and Sequence Diagram

The Entity-Relationship Diagram (ERD) shows the relationships of entity sets stored in a database as depicted in Fig. 4.

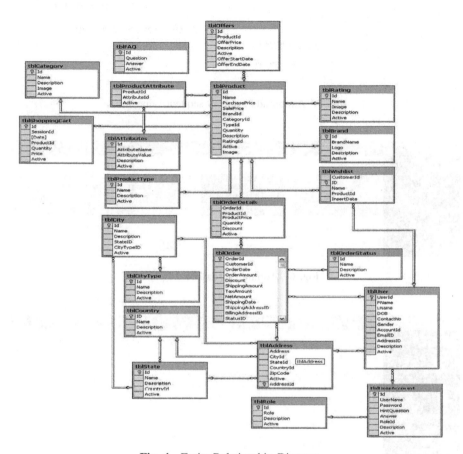

**Fig. 4.**  Entity-Relationship Diagram

Sequence diagrams, also called event diagrams, with only one instance shown in Fig. 5, describe interactions among classes in terms of an exchange of messages over time. Due to space constraint, we couldn't show the sequence diagrams for each of the interactions and communications between the entities involved in the system.

## 4  Results and Discussion

In this section, we only discuss some of the modules incorporated into the mobile application to achieve the objectives of this research work. The result thus far, which flows from the framework for computing research and use-case approaches is a web and mobile application management system for organic farming.

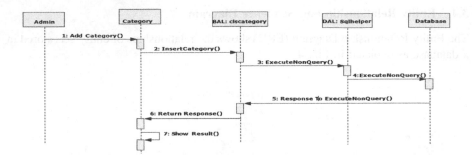

**Fig. 5.** Admin add category sequence diagram

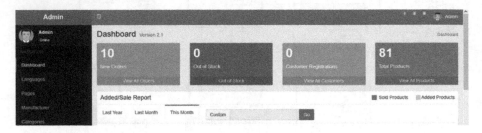

**Fig. 6.** Admin user dashboard page

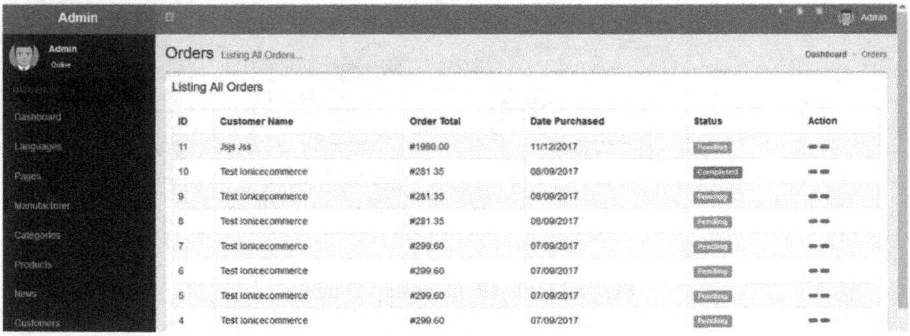

**Fig. 7.** Listing order page

Figure 6 outline the Admin-User dashboard page: part of the backend module to view every activity from the aspect of ordered products to the order management, user management, and mobile application management and so on. The listing order page, Fig. 7, is the module used to view new ordered products, processed products and processing products. Also, on this page, administrators can manage order status. Sample cart and shopping market place are shown in Fig. 8. Readers should note that due to paper length constraint, several application interfaces are not included.

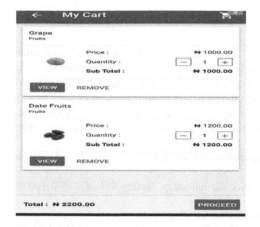 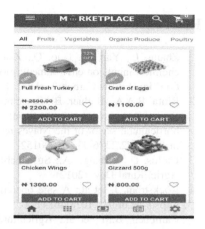

**Fig. 8.** Sample Cart and shopping market place pages

## 5   Conclusion

This study was carried out through source of opinions from professionals in organic agriculture, literature review, some web materials, survey of organic farmers (primarily in Nigeria), and personal interview of organic farming practitioners.

Orgfarmob marketspace is a mobile application that helps in the process of Buying and Selling of Organic products, gives them access to e-commerce platform and gives them information about the registered cooperative bodies based on geolocation and the aspect of organic farm produce. The system was model with UML.

The main contribution to knowledge of this project is the framework for computer research approach to the conceptualisation and design of real-time, geo-location information delivery system that enables practicing organic farmers to empower themselves and leverage on economics of scale. It provides organic farmers cultivating crops with an e-commerce platform for easy facilitation of their business. It enables practicing organic farmers form a cluster around themselves thereby empowering themselves with the benefits that comes with economics of scale.

### 5.1   Future Direction

In future iteration, usability, acceptance and observation studies are planned. This will be followed by longitudinal studies over a three-to-five years period. Economic consideration might be considered: contingent valuation, hedonic pricing. The authors hope to develop a reference ontology, based on the architectural framework, to assist body of knowledge in the use of mobile application in organic farming.

# References

1. Zhang, L., Yan, C., Guo, Q., Zhang, J., Ruiz-Menjivar, J.: The impact of agricultural chemical inputs on environment: global evidence from informetrics analysis and visualization. Int. J. Low-Carbon Technol. **13**, 338–352 (2018). https://doi.org/10.1093/ijlct/cty039
2. Binta, B.A.A., Barbier, B.: Economic and environmental performances of organic farming system compared to conventional farming system: a case farm model to simulate the horticultural sector of the Niayes region in Senegal. J. Hortic **02**, 1–10 (2015). https://doi.org/10.4172/2376-0354.1000152
3. Cioloş, D., Piebalgs, A.: Sustainable agriculture for the future we want. Eur. Commiss. Agric. Rural Dev. (2012)
4. Rockström, J., et al.: A safe operating space for humanity. Nature **461**, 472–475 (2009). https://doi.org/10.1038/461472a
5. Campbell, B.M., et al.: Agriculture production as a major driver of the earth system exceeding planetary boundaries. Ecol. Soc. **22**, 8 (2017). https://doi.org/10.5751/ES-09595-220408
6. Foley, J.A., et al.: Solutions for a cultivated planet. Nature **478**, 337–342 (2011). https://doi.org/10.1038/nature10452
7. Nandi, R., Bokelmanna, W., Nithya, V.G., Dias, G.: Smallholder organic farmer's attitudes, objectives and barriers towards production of organic fruits and vegetables in India: a multivariate analysis. Emirates J. Food Agric. **27**, 396–406 (2015). https://doi.org/10.9755/ejfa.2015.04.038
8. Rana, S., Hasan, M.H., Alam, M.S., Islam, M.S.: Farmer attitude towards organic vegetable cultivation in Rangunia Upazila, Chittagong, Bangladesh. J. Biosci. Agric. Res. **14**, 1151–1156 (2017). https://doi.org/10.18801/jbar.140117.141
9. Torres, J., Valera, D., Belmonte, L., Herrero-Sánchez, C.: Economic and social sustainability through organic agriculture: study of the restructuring of the citrus sector in the "Bajo Andarax" district (Spain). Sustainability **8**, 918 (2016). https://doi.org/10.3390/su8090918
10. Ton, P.: Productivity and profitability of organic farming systems in East Africa. IFOAM OSEA Proj. 1–60 (2013)
11. Banjara, R.K., Paudel, M.: Economic impact of organic farming; cases from the farmers of Nepal. Adv. Soc. Sci. Res. J. **2**, 187–194 (2015). https://doi.org/10.14738/assrj.211.1617
12. Shafie, F.A., Rennie, D.: Consumer perceptions towards organic food. Procedia - Soc. Behav. Sci. **49**, 360–367 (2012). https://doi.org/10.1016/j.sbspro.2012.07.034
13. Wang, X., Pacho, F., Liu, J., Kajungiro, R.: Factors influencing organic food purchase intention in developing countries and the moderating role of knowledge. Sustainability **11**, 209 (2019). https://doi.org/10.3390/su11010209
14. Lucas, M.R., et al.: Quality, Safety and Consumer Behaviour Towards Organic Food in Germany and Portugal (2008)
15. Monaco, E.: Consumers Buy Organic Food for Taste and Health Reasons, Not Ethics, Study Shows. https://www.organicauthority.com/buzz-news/study-shows-consumers-buy-organic-food-for-taste-and-health-reasons-not-ethics. Accessed 15 Dec 2019
16. Chiciudean, G., Harun, R., Ilea, M., Chiciudean, D., Arion, F., Ilies, G., Muresan, I.: Organic food consumers and purchase intention: a case study in Romania. Agronomy **9**, 145 (2019). https://doi.org/10.3390/agronomy9030145
17. Gschwandtner, A.: The organic food premium: a local assessment in the UK. Int. J. Econ. Bus. **25**, 313–338 (2018). https://doi.org/10.1080/13571516.2017.1389842

18. Lee, W.J., Shimizu, M., Kniffin, K.M., Wansink, B.: You taste what you see: do organic labels bias taste perceptions? Food Qual. Prefer. **29**, 33–39 (2013). https://doi.org/10.1016/j.foodqual.2013.01.010

19. Lee, M., Hwang, J., Yoe, H.: Agricultural production system based on IoT. In: 2013 IEEE 16th International Conference on Computational Science and Engineering, pp. 833–837. IEEE (2013). https://doi.org/10.1109/CSE.2013.126

20. Meemken, E.-M., Qaim, M.: Organic agriculture, food security, and the environment. Annu. Rev. Resour. Econ. **10**, 39–63 (2018). https://doi.org/10.1146/annurev-resource-100517-023252

21. Beach, J.: Organic Farming in Maine (2011)

22. Salampasis, M., Theodoridis, A.: Information and communication technology in agricultural development. Procedia Technol. **8**, 1–3 (2013). https://doi.org/10.1016/j.protcy.2013.11.001

23. Chavula, H.K.: The role of ICTs in agricultural production in Africa. J. Dev. Agric. Econ. **6**, 279–289 (2014). https://doi.org/10.5897/JDAE2013.0517

24. Kiambi, D.: The use of information communication and technology in advancement of African agriculture. Afr. J. Agric. Res. **13**, 2025–2036 (2018). https://doi.org/10.5897/AJAR2018.13300

25. Saidu, A., Clarkson, A.M., Adamu, S.H., Mohammed, M., Jibo, I.: Application of ICT in agriculture: opportunities and challenges in developing countries. Int. J. Comput. Sci. Math. Theory. **3**, 8–18 (2017)

26. Hamzaoui-Essoussi, L., Zahaf, M.: The organic food market: opportunities and challenges. In: Reed, M. (ed.) Organic Food and Agriculture - New Trends and Developments in the Social Sciences. InTech (2012). https://doi.org/10.5772/30155

27. Saunders, M.N.K., Lewis, P., Thornhill, A.: Understanding research philosophy and approaches to theory development. In: Research Methods for Business Students, pp. 128–170. Pearson, Harlow (2019)

28. Amaral, J.N., et al.: About Computing Science Research Methodology. Edmonton, Alberta, Canada (2011). https://doi.org/10.1.1.124.702

29. Holz, H.J., Applin, A., Haberman, B., Joyce, D., Purchase, H., Reed, C.: Research methods in computing. In: Working Group Reports on ITiCSE on Innovation and Technology in Computer Science Education - ITiCSE-WGR 2006, p. 96. ACM Press, New York (2006). https://doi.org/10.1145/1189215.1189180

30. Alwadain, A.S.A.: A model of enterprise architecture evolution (2014). http://eprints.qut.edu.au/71204/

# How Corporates in South Africa Are Using Serious Games in Business

Shiraz Amod and Sumarie Roodt[✉]

University of Cape Town, Rondebosch, Cape Town 7700, South Africa
sumarie.roodt@uct.ac.za

**Abstract.** It has been shown that serious games are useful in the military, healthcare, and education sectors. Meanwhile corporate interest in serious gaming in business has rapidly grown internationally. However the level of awareness and adoption of serious gaming among South African corporates in business is still unclear.

This interpretive study explores South African corporate awareness of serious gaming in business and the barriers to its adoption. Semi-structured interviews were used to collect qualitative data from managers in Johannesburg Stock Exchange-listed companies. Eight participants were interviewed across four different industries. Data analysis was guided by the general inductive approach.

The absence of serious gaming adopters among the participants, and the general lack of awareness of serious gaming in business were identified as the most salient features. The analysis suggests that corporates currently use technologies related to serious games (e-learning, collaborative tools, and simulation tools), and that there is a demand for the greater promotion and use of serious gaming.

While the findings provide new insights into the level of serious gaming awareness, caution should be exercised when attempting to generalize these findings due to the small sample and the scarcity of prior research.

**Keywords:** Serious games · Serious gaming · Corporate · Barriers to adoption · Awareness · Digital Game-Based Learning · Commercial off the shelf · Serious games in business

## 1 Introduction

The contribution offers a novel understanding on the adoption and potential use of serious games in corporate business environments. Serious games use the artistic medium of games to deliver a message, teach a lesson, or provide an experience. A serious game is an "interactive computer application, with or without significant hardware component that has a challenging goal, is fun to play and engaging, incorporates some scoring mechanism, and supplies the user with skills, knowledge or attitudes useful in reality" (Bergeron 2006). Studies abound that show the application of serious games in the entertainment, military, healthcare, and education sectors (Levin 2010; Smith 2007; Zyda 2005). However, there are limited studies on the application within the corporate sector. The field of serious games is relatively new and

© IFIP International Federation for Information Processing 2020
Published by Springer Nature Switzerland AG 2020
M. Hattingh et al. (Eds.): I3E 2020, LNCS 12066, pp. 288–298, 2020.
https://doi.org/10.1007/978-3-030-44999-5_24

therefore, limited research has been conducted in this area (Azadegan et al. 2012; Levin 2010). Few studies exist about the application of serious games in the South African business context. Therefore, the study serves to raise corporate awareness of serious games and the potential applications in the context of South Africa business.

## 2 Literature Review

### 2.1 Definitions

Serious games involve a broader spectrum of uses than Digital Game-Based Learning (Breuer and Bente 2010; Connolly et al. 2012; Michael and Chen 2006). DGBL is a term used in the domain of education as it involves the use of digital games primarily for learning purposes (Breuer and Bente 2010; Susi et al. 2007). Serious gaming relates to the concepts of virtual worlds and DGBL (Connolly et al. 2012; Susi et al. 2007). DGBL found in education involves applying digital games primarily for learning purposes (Breuer and Bente 2010; Susi et al. 2007). Virtual worlds are "computer-simulated, usually 3-D, representations that allow avatars to interconnect and communicate in relatively lifelike environments" (Ives and Junglas 2008). These environments persist; continue to exist and undergo changes even when players are not present (Cox 2000; Ives and Junglas 2008). Serious games have their own virtual world in which players play the game (Breuer and Bente 2010; Levin 2010). Serious games can be divided into two broad categories: commercial off the shelf (COTS) games, and games developed specifically for educational or corporate purposes (Azadegan and Riedel 2012; Graafland et al. 2012). COTS involves re-purposing an existing game to harness the power of serious games without the risk and expense of developing a bespoke serious game that may not be sufficiently engaging (Connolly et al. 2012). Both categories of serious games are included in this study.

### 2.2 Application of Serious Games

Three broad application areas of serious games in business exist: (1) conducting training in a simulated environment; (2) as a platform for collaboration; and (3) as a tool for demonstrations and education (Fernandes et al. 2012; Herrlich 2007; Ives and Junglas 2008; Levin 2010; Michael and Chen 2006).

Training conducted with serious games, especially in simulated environments is prevalent (Michael and Chen 2006; Susi et al. 2007). Games offer a simulated environment in which training exercises can be performed, much like real-life training simulations (Graafland et al. 2012; Susi et al. 2007). There are benefits of using serious games over traditional forms of training. Serious games present a safe environment for performing training (Graafland et al. 2012; Oliveira et al. 2012). The simulation of a real life activity allows skills to be fine-tuned through practice in a risk-free environment without consequence (Graafland et al. 2012; Oliveira et al. 2012). Serious games can also be deployed as a collaborative platform among multiple people (Bozanta et al. 2012; Fernandes et al. 2012; Oliveira et al. 2012). Using the internet as a communication medium enables serious games to provide Multi-User Virtual Environments

(MUVEs) in the form of virtual worlds (Bozanta et al. 2012). The MUVEs provide a virtual environment that players can communicate and collaborate to jointly achieve their goals (Fernandes et al. 2012). Collaboration enables people in different locations to collaborate effectively without needing to travel or for expensive teleconferencing technologies to be purchased (Bozanta et al. 2012; Fernandes et al. 2012; Levin 2010). Serious games are also employed for demonstrations and education (Herrlich 2007; Levin 2010). Serious games provide unique immersive environments that teach complex material (Susi et al. 2007). Serious games aid marketing and performing demonstrations of products or services (Herrlich 2007; Levin 2010). COTS games have been suitable for this purpose because of their low cost, fast implementation, and high level of engagement ("flow") (Herrlich 2007; Rankin and Shute 2010).

### 2.3   Barriers to Adoption of Serious Games

The application of serious games is new, especially in a business context (Azadegan et al. 2012). Companies which are unaware of serious games will not adopt them, and those which are aware of the concept, but not of the benefits are equally unlikely to adopt serious games (Azadegan et al. 2012). Perceptions of employees and managers towards games heavily influence the likelihood of adoption (Azadegan et al. 2012; Ives and Junglas 2008). Games perceived as easy and not contributing to training or promoting the company's purpose, will not be adopted (Azadegan et al. 2012; Ives and Junglas 2008). Based on the work by Azadegan et al. (2012) in the area of serious game adoption in businesses, four categories of barriers are identified: barriers with familiarity about serious games (familiarity barriers), financial barriers, barriers in terms of the practicality of serious games (practicality barriers), and the level of Information Technology facilities and support (IT facilities and support barriers) (Azadegan et al. 2012).

## 3   Materials and Methods

The primary research question asks, "What is the state of use of serious games by South African corporations in a business context?" Secondary questions asked include: *(1) What is the level of awareness of serious games within South African corporates? (2) What uses for serious games are South African corporates embracing? (3) What barriers are preventing the adoption of serious games by South African corporates?*

   In-depth semi-structured interviews were conducted with corporate managers, who were prepared with a briefing on serious games before answering related questions on awareness and adoption. The work follows the study on the adoption of serious games in corporate training in the United Kingdom (Azadegan et al. 2012). The sample consists of eight South African corporations across a range of four industries that includes; Financial Services, Retail, Insurance, and Construction. A qualitative analysis of the interview transcripts was conducted via a thematic analysis. Thematic analysis was performed using open coding and then axial coding to assess the most common uses and barriers to adoption of serious games in South African corporations. To avoid biased results comparative analysis was only performed on the questions that were consistently posed to all subjects.

# 4 Results and Data Analysis

Interviews were conducted with eight participants from different South African corporations for this study. For a description of the sample data, the characteristics of the participants are summarized (See Table 1).

**Table 1.** Overview of participants

| Name | Organizational Role | Industry |
|---|---|---|
| Participant A | Training Manager | Financial Services |
| Participant B | Executive Manager: Learning and Development | Retail |
| Participant C | Skills Development Manager | Construction |
| Participant D | Learning and Growth Partner | Retail |
| Participant E | Human Resources Programs Manager | Insurance |
| Participant F | Training and Methodology Manager | Financial Services |
| Participant G | Executive Head of Training | Insurance |
| Participant H | General Manager | Construction |

Data on awareness of serious gaming for each participant shows that there is little awareness of serious gaming among the South African corporate (See Table 2). Since none of the participants had used serious gaming only one of the eight respondents (Participant D) demonstrated a proper understanding of the concept of serious gaming, while two others (Participant A and Participant G) indicated partial awareness of the concept.

**Table 2.** Awareness of serious gaming concepts

| Area of awareness | Participant | | | | | | | | % |
|---|---|---|---|---|---|---|---|---|---|
| | A | B | C | D | E | F | G | H | |
| Concept awareness | No | No | No | Yes | No | No | No | No | 13% |
| Partial concept awareness | Yes | No | No | No | No | No | Yes | No | 25% |
| Benefits awareness | Yes | No | No | Yes | No | No | Yes | No | 38% |
| Partial benefits awareness | No | No | Yes | No | No | No | No | No | 13% |
| Limitations awareness | Yes | Yes | No | Yes | No | Yes | Yes | No | 63% |

Participant D became aware of serious gaming (more specifically DGBL) at a learning conference in 2010 where *"there was an international speaker and he was very, very keen to bring in some kind of digital gaming for learning into Africa"*. The other participants who were partially aware of serious gaming understood it in relation to gamification (Participant G), or generally as *"a way to aid learning by using technology so that learning is more practical, hands on, [and] simulated"* (Participant A). Although there is very little awareness of the concept of serious gaming, there is slightly more aware of the potential benefits that gaming can provide in a corporate context. Four of the eight participants acknowledged the benefits of serious gaming:

> "...you're able to **engage more as a learner**...I think one of the big advantages is you **can learn alone**, you don't always have to rely on group learning. One of the disadvantages of group learning is that you sometimes have to go at the pace of the average learner, so your slower learners need more attention and your quicker learners actually get quite impatient. So when you're able to engage with technology, you **can cater more to individuals**."
> - Participant A

> *"It could even be used in our company which is a construction company and it could be **used in simulation for our [crane] operators** which could be **very beneficial** to the company."*
> - Participant C

> *"If you continuously use gaming I think you are able to learn concepts faster without even realising that you are, you know, by the very repetitive nature of gaming, because if you like something you'll do it over and over again, you would probably be learning much more."*
> - Participant D

> *"...introducing a gaming element provides an experience that people almost learn while they play kind of thing. So I think if you're looking **to drive up knowledge and skill levels, using gaming techniques can help do that in the business context** other than, sort of, traditional training methods."*
> - Participant G

Participants were more aware of the limitations than the benefits or the concept of serious games. Five of the eight participants (63%) identified limitations of gaming in the corporate environment. Although more participants were more aware of the limitations than benefits of serious games, their descriptions of the limitations were less detailed and more abstract than descriptions of the benefits. Limitations include; the impracticality of using games for certain business activities: *"You're not going to be able to convert every kind of organisational functioning into some sort of gaming concept...without losing something in the process"* (Participant G), and target audiences: *"...it probably depends on the target audience... I think it would be very suited for the new generation of trainees or staff"* (Participant F). Participant B highlighted the need for a broader strategic programme to ensure serious games are used appropriately: *"They should be effective within a proper context of a strategy to utilise learning technology to support development of [the] businesses"*.

Positive relationship exists between the participants' level of awareness and their attitude towards serious gaming. As participants' awareness of serious gaming (the concept, benefits and limitations) improve, attitude towards serious gaming became move toward positive. An exception to this rule is Participant G who demonstrated higher than average awareness of serious gaming and was not particularly positive about the prospects of serious gaming. Upon closer review, it became apparent that the lack of positivity shown by Participant G is not directed at serious gaming in general, but specifically at using serious gaming within her particular company:

*"I think there is value [in serious games]...you've got to be careful that you don't try and take the next biggest thing and make it the only thing, especially depending on the kind of business we have... It's not an easy fit for the kind of business we are. We're an insurance business...a more traditional kind of conservative business. The profile of employee and customer we have are probably not your target market for that typically."*

- Participant G

A considerably low level of serious gaming awareness (13%) is a significant result. The observation is even lower than the result of Azadegan et al. (2012) of awareness in the UK (29%). The low level of awareness is likely to affect the results of the subsequent section on "Barriers to Adoption of Serious Gaming" because little is known about the concept of serious gaming itself. Participants correctly identified the potential of serious gaming for education and simulations; however, none identified the potential for collaboration or demonstrations. This could indicate that the participants understand serious gaming in a narrow scope, relating only to training.

Analysis performed is on the barriers to adoption of serious gaming using the framework defined by Azadegan et al. (2012) and the results summarized in Table 3.

**Table 3.** Barriers to adoption

| Type of barrier | Participant | | | | | | | | % |
|---|---|---|---|---|---|---|---|---|---|
| | A | B | C | D | E | F | G | H | |
| Familiarity barriers | Yes | Yes | Yes | Yes | Yes | Yes | Yes | Yes | 100% |
| Financial barriers | No | No | No | Yes | No | No | No | No | 13% |
| Practicality barriers | Yes | No | No | No | No | Yes | Yes | No | 38% |
| IT facilities & support barriers | Yes | No | No | No | No | No | No | No | 13% |

All participants reported that their lack of familiarity with serious gaming was a barrier to its adoption. The prevalence of familiarity barriers is significant, but expected, considering the preceding findings on the low level of serious gaming awareness. Practicality barriers are the second most common reason for not adopting serious gaming, as indicated by three participants (38%). The barriers that participants described least were financial barriers (13%) and the lack of IT facilities and support (13%).

Lack of familiarity is more than telling as a barrier to serious gaming adoption. To analyse the data further, barriers because of familiarity is distinguishable under five related themes. The themes are game perceptions, the lack of promotion of serious gaming, the need for proven cases, unfamiliarity with the technology, and unaware of the concept of serious gaming. Refer to Table 4 distribution of these themes across the various participants.

Half the number of participants, i.e., 50% were unaware of the concept of serious games. These participants were unable to identify other barriers to adopting serious gaming because they were uninformed of this concept, its requirements, and limitations: *"I don't know much about the field...I need to get more information before I can comment"* (Participant C). The other half of the participants had some amount of awareness of the concept of serious games. This informed 50% of the sample; all mentioned the lack of promotion of serious gaming (75%) and/or called for the need for publicizing cases of serious gaming implementations (50%).

**Table 4.**  Breakdown of familiarity barriers

| Theme | Participant | | | | | | | | % |
|---|---|---|---|---|---|---|---|---|---|
| | A | B | C | D | E | F | G | H | |
| Unaware of concept | No | Yes | Yes | No | Yes | No | No | Yes | 50% |
| Lack of promotion | Yes | No | Yes | Yes | No | No | No | No | 38% |
| Need proven cases | No | No | No | Yes | No | No | Yes | No | 26% |
| Unfamiliar with techNology | Yes | No | No | No | No | Yes | Yes | No | 38% |
| Negative perception of games | Yes | No | No | No | No | No | No | No | 13% |

Calls for promotion of serious games in corporate and demand for public cases that had a serious games implementation. Participant G, who was not positive towards serious gaming, hinted at the power of successful case studies:

> *"...if we could get some practical, **tangible case studies and examples** of businesses like ours who are utilising it in certain spheres, [we] **might find that there's more opportunity** than we think. **I might change my mind".**

- Participant G

Three participants mentioned issues relating to a lack of familiarity with the technology involving serious gaming. However, the accuracy of these issues is questionable as the statements were speculative and vague: *"...there's also stuff around tech-savviness, you know..."* (Participant G), *"I'll leave that up to our IT departments who actually do that..."* (Participant F), Participant A was the only participant to suggest that negative perceptions of games, that games are easy and do not add value, among the decision makers would affect the company's adoption of serious gaming.

Only one participant (13%) described financial barriers for adopting serious gaming:

> *"...to set up something like that is always **costly to start** with and then you realise the benefits of the learning but they don't give it quite the chance because most of us **operate on the low cost operating model, so initial setup is always difficult."***

- Participant D

The use of serious gaming was considered impractical firstly because of the nature of the business itself: *"Our environment...doesn't lend itself well to gaming"* (Participant A); and *"It's not an easy fit for the kind of business we are"* (Participant G). Secondly, serious gaming is impractical for the type of people the company employs: *"The profile of employee and customer we have are probably not your target market for that typically"* (Participant G). Thirdly, the absence of the skills needed to implement serious gaming, is why it may consider it as impractical. As explained here *"I think it can be done I just don't know how it can be done"* (Participant F); and *"I think it's a very specialist set of expertise that know how to really utilize the serious gaming or the gamification concepts in the right way. We probably don't have that here"* (Participant G).

Participant A was the only one (13%) to mention the lack of IT facilities and support as a barrier to adoption of serious gaming. This observation conflicts with the finding of Azadegan et al. (2012) who identified that 45% of companies in the United Kingdom experienced barriers related to their IT facilities and support. Given the low level of serious gaming awareness, this inconsistency is likely to be the result of insufficient awareness regarding the IT requirements of serious gaming (as with the case of financial barriers).

Data obtained suggests that there is interest in serious gaming, but possibly not enough interest for companies to embark on serious games. The call for greater promotion of serious gaming and successful case studies reflects an appeal for either a driver of serious gaming – another corporate or a vendor of serious games.

Only one participant (13%) mentioned that the perception of games might have a negative impact on their company. This observation is lower than Azadegan (18%), which is a positive indication for the future of serious gaming in South Africa.

Practicality barriers identified relate to the lack of skills for serious gaming, or the limitations of serious games. Scarcity of serious gaming skills is due to widespread lack of awareness and the adoption. The more companies adopt serious gaming, the more people would acquire the skills necessary to teach and learn the use of serious games. Considering the low level of serious gaming awareness, companies may already possess the skills for using serious gaming that is yet unrecognized by them.

The inability of most participants to identify barriers in terms of finance and IT facilities and support is a further indication of low awareness of serious gaming. South Africa presents numerous relevant IT challenges, such as the high cost of internet bandwidth (Gillwald 2009). Azadegan et al. (2012) found that 45% of companies identified IT facilities and support barriers, compared with 13% in this study. This to mean that participants' inability to identify these barriers indicates a low level of readiness to adopt serious gaming in South Africa.

Analysis carried out on the use of technologies related to serious gaming for each participant. This examination assists in knowing the extent of each participant's technology profile and inclination to use technologies like serious gaming. The technologies of interest are electronic learning, collaborative tools, and simulation tools. For the result of that summarize the analysis, refer to Table 5.

**Table 5.** The use of related technologies

| Technology | Participant | | | | | | | | % |
|---|---|---|---|---|---|---|---|---|---|
| | A | B | C | D | E | F | G | H | |
| E-Learning | Yes | Yes | No | Yes | Yes | Yes | No | No | 63% |
| Collaborative tools | Yes | Yes | Yes | Yes | Yes | Yes | Yes | No | 88% |
| Digital simulations | Yes | Yes | Yes | Yes | Yes | Yes | Yes | No | 88% |
| Physical simulations | No | No | No | No | Yes | Yes | Yes | No | 38% |

Seven participants (88%) reported that they currently use two or more of the related technologies in their corporations. Five participants (63%) currently use all three technologies (E-learning, collaborative tools and digital simulations). Participant H is the only participant that does not use any related technologies.

Digital simulations were used by 88% of participants, and 38% also used physical simulations. The purpose of the simulations was to teach system usage or to simulate a business process as part of training. The extensive use of related technologies by the participants demonstrates their awareness of the technologies and they had the capabilities for implementing them. This implies the participants have the willingness, budget, and skills to implement technologies like serious gaming. The participants with the least use of related technologies are Participant C and Participant H, both of which are in the construction industry. This result may be an indication that the construction industry in general is averse to the related technologies, or that the technologies are impractical in the construction industry. The former is more likely to be true considering the potential of serious gaming for improving construction site safety (Connolly et al. 2012) and visualizing landscapes and architecture (Herrlich 2007).

On the potential for Serious Gaming in South Africa and based on the feedback from participants, there appear to be various opportunities for the use of serious gaming in South Africa. A benefit of serious gaming that is relevant to the participants is its ability to assemble groups of geographically dispersed people. These virtual gatherings are beneficial for corporations because they enable collaboration and training on a large scale without the associated travel and lodging expenses. Data suggests that serious gaming may be useful for dealing with geographically dispersed employees. This observation supports the finding of Ives and Junglas (2008) who identified the benefits by using serious games to connect dispersed people in a virtual world. The data indicates a demand for technology that will improve access to knowledge and reduce operating costs. Connolly et al. (2012) found that serious gaming improves knowledge acquisition, which suggests that the participants will be more inclined to adopt serious gaming if it is not more expensive than their current training methods.

## 5  Conclusion

The researchers show that none of the participating corporations had used serious gaming and only one participant (13%) was aware of the concept. Familiarity barriers were the most common reason for not adopting serious gaming (100%), highlighting the scarcity of serious gaming knowledge. A key finding was the demand for greater promotion of serious gaming and publicised cases of serious gaming implementations. The majority of participating corporations were interested in serious gaming, although previously unaware of it, and sought more information on the topic. This could represent an opportunity for a serious gaming vendor to enter the South African market and drive the adoption of serious gaming. Another key finding to emerge from the data was the widespread use of e-learning, collaborative tools, and simulation tools. By providing an outline of the current state of South African corporations, this study forms the foundation for future research into the adoption and usage of serious games. This research may be of particular interest to South African corporate considering the use of serious gaming, as well as serious games vendors.

# References

Azadegan, A., Riedel, J.C.K.H., Baalsrud Hauge, J.: Serious games adoption in corporate training. In: Ma, M., Oliveira, M.F., Hauge, J.B., Duin, H., Thoben, K.-D. (eds.) SGDA 2012. LNCS, vol. 7528, pp. 74–85. Springer, Heidelberg (2012). https://doi.org/10.1007/978-3-642-33687-4_6

Azadegan, A., Riedel, J.C.K.H.: Serious games integration in companies: a research and application framework. In: IEEE 12th International Conference on Advanced Learning Technologies, pp. 485–487 (2012)

Bergeron, B.: Developing Serious Games. Thompson Delmar Learning, Hingham (2006)

Bozanta, A., Kutlu, B., Nowlan, N., Shirmohammadi, S.: Multi user virtual environments and serious games for team building. Procedia Comput. Sci. **15**, 301–302 (2012)

Breuer, J., Bente, G.: Why so serious? On the relation of serious games and learning. Eludamos J. Comput. Game Cult. **4**(1), 7–24 (2010)

Cohen, D.: OXO aka Noughts and Crosses - The First Video Game. About.com: Classic Video Games (2009)

Connolly, T.M., Boyle, E.A., MacArthur, E., Hainey, T., Boyle, J.M.: A systematic literature review of empirical evidence on computer games and serious games. Comput. Educ. **59**(2), 661–686 (2012)

Cox, T.: Online and multiplayer gaming - an overview. Virtual Reality **5**(4), 215–222 (2000)

Csikszentmihalyi, M.: Flow: The Psychology of Optimal Performance. Harper and Row, New York (1990)

Est, C., Poelman, R., Bidarra, R.: High-level scenario editing for serious games. In: Proceedings of GRAPP, pp. 339–346. Delft University of Technology, Delft (2011)

Fernandes, J., Duarte, D., Ribeiro, C., Farinha, C., Pereira, J.M., Silva, M.M.: iThink: a game-based approach towards improving collaboration and participation in requirement elicitation. Procedia Comput. Sci. **15**, 66–77 (2012)

Gillwald, A.: Between two stools: broadband policy in South Africa. Southern African J. Inf. Commun. **8**, 53–77 (2009)

Graafland, M., Schraagen, J.M., Schijven, M.P.: Systematic review of serious games for medical education and surgical skills training. Br. J. Surg. **99**(10), 1322–1330 (2012)

Grossman, L.: The Army's Killer App. Time **165**, 43–44 (2005)

Halter, E.: From Sun Tzu to Xbox: War and Video Games, pp. 1–364. Thunder Mouth Press, New York (2006)

Harrison Jr., J.: Computer-Aided Information Systems for Gaming. Mclean VA (1964)

Herrlich, M.: A tool for landscape architecture based on computer game technology. In: 17th International Conference on Artificial Reality and Telexistence (ICAT) 2007, pp. 264–268 (2007)

Ives, B., Junglas, I.: APC forum: business implications of virtual worlds and serious gaming. MIS Q. Exec. **7**(3), 151–156 (2008)

Jones, C., Ramanau, R., Cross, S., Healing, G.: Net generation or digital natives: is there a distinct new generation entering university? Comput. Educ. **54**(3), 722–732 (2010)

Levin, M.: 3D internet and enterprise: emergence of virtual worlds and serious games in the workplace. Dev. Learn. Organ. **24**(2), 17–20 (2010)

Loguidice, B., Matt, B.: Vintage Games: An Insider Look at the History of Grand Theft Auto, Super Mario, and the Most Influential Games of All Time, pp. 1–408. Focal Press, Waltham (2009)

MacBeth, T.M.: Psychology of media use. In: Downing, J.D.H., McQuail, D., Schlesinger, P., Wartella, E. (eds.) The SAGE Handbook of Media Studies, pp. 201–225. SAGE Publications Inc., New York (2004)

Michael, D.R., Chen, S.: Serious Games: Games that Educate, Train and Inform, 1st edn. Thomson Course Technology, Boston (2006)

Montfort, N.: Twisty Little Passages: An Approach to Interactive Fiction. The MIT Press, Cambridge (2005)

Moodley, K.: African Renaissance and language policies in comparative perspective. Politikon **27**(1), 103–115 (2000)

Myers, M.D.: Qualitative Research in Business & Management, pp. 1–275. SAGE Publications Inc, London (2009)

Oliveira, V., Coelho, A., Guimarães, R., Rebelo, C.: Serious games in security: a solution for security trainees. Procedia Comput. Sci. **15**, 274–282 (2012)

Piccione, P.A.: In search of the meaning of senet. Archaeology **33**, 55–58 (1980)

Rankin, Y.A., Shute, M.W.: Re-purposing a recreational video game as a serious games for second language acquisition. In: Serious Games Design and Development: Technologies for Training and Learning, pp. 178–180. IGI Global, Hershey (2010)

Saunders, M., Lewis, P., Thornhill, A.: Research Methods for Business Students, 6th edn. Pearson, Harlow (2012)

Serious games Institute: Serious games Institute (SGI) - GaLA Network of excellence in Serious games (2011)

Smith, R.: Game impact theory: the five forces that are driving the adoption of game technologies within multiple established industries. In: The Interservice/Industry Training, Simulation & Education Conference (I/ITSEC), pp. 1–32. National Training Systems Association (2007)

Smith, R.: A History of serious games. In: The Interservice/Industry Training, Simulation & Education Conference (I/ITSEC), pp. 1–81. U.S Army, Orlando (2009)

Spain, J.W., Vega, G.: Sony online entertainment: EverQuest or EverCrack? J. Bus. Ethics **58**(1), 3–6 (2005)

Susi, T., Johannesson, M., Backlund, P.: Serious Games – An Overview, Skövde, pp. 1–21 (2007)

Zyda, M.: From visual simulation to virtual reality to games. IEEE Comput. **38**(9), 25–32 (2005)

# Business Processes

# A Theoretical Framework for IT-Enabled and IT-Enforced Corporate Governance Compliance Utilizing BPMSs

Hendrik Willem Pretorius(iD) and Alta van der Merwe(✉)(iD)

University of Pretoria, Pretoria, South Africa
{Henk.Pretorius, alta.vdm}@up.ac.za

**Abstract.** Corporate governance has been severely condemned, as a result of company failures around the world. Regulatory and legislative measure have been introduced in response to these failures. However, arguments by sceptics advocate that it is time consuming and costly to comply these legislative measures that cause overregulation. These measures further do not always add value to business initiatives and adherence to these measures cannot be enforced or guaranteed. This paper argues for the use of business process management systems (BPMSs) to improve corporate governance. The "dynamics capabilities theory model of IT-enabled organisational performance" [1] is applied in this study as theoretical underpinning. A theoretical framework is proposed for IT-enabled and IT-enforced corporate governance compliance using a BPMS, after collecting data from seven BPMS user companies and a BPMS vendor company in South Africa.

**Keywords:** Fraud · Electronic compliance · Corporate governance · Business process management systems · Automation · Corruption

## 1 Introduction

Corporate governance is defined as the method by which corporations are controlled and directed [2]. Corporate governance in the United States (US), has been condemned because of corporation failures like Tyco, WorldCom, Enron, Global Crossing and Adelphia [3]. Furthermore, industries in the US lose around USD400 billion a year as a result of criminal and unethical behavior [4]. In the US, corporate irresponsibility and managerial negligence carries the blame after the arrest and resignation of top-level corporate US managers. This eroded trust in these corporations, domestically and internationally [5].

Parmalat was one of the biggest corporate failures in Europe [6]. In 2003, Parmalat collapsed showing a hole of 14 billion Euro in its accounts [8]. The Parmalat CEO, Calisto Tanzani, was arrested only hours after the bankruptcy of the corporation. Tanzani was imprisoned for ten years on charges of money laundering and financial fraud. The Parmalat group collapsed and many investors lost their investment money [6]. In the last 10 years, fraud and corruption has doubled in the United Kingdom, while it remained stabled or worsened in other European countries [29].

© IFIP International Federation for Information Processing 2020
Published by Springer Nature Switzerland AG 2020
M. Hattingh et al. (Eds.): I3E 2020, LNCS 12066, pp. 301–312, 2020.
https://doi.org/10.1007/978-3-030-44999-5_25

South Africa, like the US and Europe, experience similar corporate governance problems. In South Africa, particularly in the State Information Technology Agency (SITA), IT vendors are frequently guilty of bribing government employees during tender processes [7]. Around R10-billion was spent on ICT in the 10 years of existence of SITA from 2002 to 2012 [8]. Vendors who want a share in the stake are very attracted to this large amounts of money. The scenario led to numerous forms of fraud and corruption within SITA, at the expense of improving service delivery to citizens of South African [8]. Today, corruption and fraud cases are killing the dreams for a better South Africa for many citizens of South Africa [30, 31]. The various forms of fraud and corruption at SITA include but are not limited to extortion, bribery, nepotism, embezzlement, favouritism, abuse of power, collusion and over-or under-invoicing [8].

In reply to the many failures of corporations around the world, regulatory and legislative changes were developed in numerous countries [3]. The Sarbanes-Oxley Act of 2002 (in the US) was developed to return confidence to capital markets in the US and internationally [3]. Sceptics argue that compliance efforts are costly, timely and cause overregulation [9, 10]. These efforts in many cases lack business value. Adherence to these measures cannot be enforced, are ineffective, unnecessary and at best are seen as an overreaction to the Enron failure [11].

In this article, the authors develop a theoretical framework that utilize electronic, cost-effective means in favor of good corporate governance and business value, asserting that not all corporate governance problems can be resolved with IT or IT automation. Technology increases transparency, information delivery, accountability, promotes efficiency and offers various levels of security [32]. A theoretical framework for effective and improved corporate governance is developed by making use of a BPMS approach that introduces automation, enforced compliance and electronic monitoring to address the issues raised. However, it is unknown what the requirements and components are for a framework like this, therefore the following research question:

What are the requirements and components of a theoretical framework for IT-enabled and IT-enforced corporate governance compliance when using a BPMS approach?

## 2  Business Process Management Systems and Its Architectural Components

A BPMS is defined as a general software information system which is used for the management and automation of organisational processes [12]. A process is defined as a collection of activities that takes various forms of input and generates value for a customer [13]. A BPMS allows for rapid changes in business processes in an organisation in a real-time business environment [14].

A BPMS consists of the *BPM Engine, the Database or Repository, Process modeling, Software integration engine, Business rules* and *Frameworks and Templates,* as illustrated in Fig. 1:

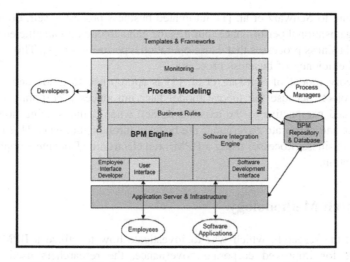

**Fig. 1.** A BPMS and its architectural components [15, 16]

# 3 Theoretical Underpinning

A summary of the "dynamics capabilities theory of IT-enabled organisational performance" by Schwarz et al. [1] is offered in this section. This theory functions as the theoretical underpinning for the research study.

A business process is: "the specific ordering of work activities across time and space (or place), with a beginning and end, and clearly identified inputs and output" [17]. In the context of this study which is focused IT-enforced and IT-enabled business processes through automation, IT-enforced and IT-enabled business processes can be defined as the extent to which IT enforces and enables "the specific ordering of work activities across time and space (or place), with a beginning, an end and clearly identified inputs and outputs" (adapted from Davenport [17]).

Schwarz et al. [1] advocate that IT resources (including business applications) are responsible for the creation of automated or IT-enabled business processes, as depicted in Fig. 2. Automated processes is the degree to which IT allows for the specific ordering of business activities across space and time [1]. These activities have a beginning and an end with recognized inputs and outputs [1].

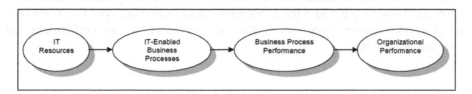

**Fig. 2.** A dynamics capabilities theory model: information technology-enabled organisational performance [1]

According to Schwarz et al. [1] automated business processes self, do not lead to gains in organisational performance, but it is the gains in operational efficiency through automated business processes that cause operational performance [1]. This is called the operational efficiency of business processes.

The theory model of Schwarz et al. [1] is appropriate to guide and inform this research project, because the theory model later introduces a corporate governance dimension and perspective to the existing model, when demonstrating how business performance and corporate governance are bettered through automated IT-enforced and IT-enabled business processes using a BPMS (an electronic IT business application) in the organisation.

## 4  Research Methodology

To conduct the research, which was to investigate how to utilize a BPMSs and its components for improved corporate governance, the researchers used qualitative methods and followed an interpretive research paradigm approach. Case studies of seven South African companies (of varying industry sectors and sizes) that uses BPMS software and one South African BPMS software vendor company were involved. Case study research allows for a wider understanding of the research phenomenon through in-depth analysis and review [18, 19]. Case study research informs the interpretive research stance well and have the potential to improve on practice-based problems [18, 19].

Data was collected thought surveys and interviews at the BPMS vendor company. This involved 12 developers (24%), 8 trainers (16%), 14 business analysts (29%), 12 managers (24%) and 3 other positions (7%). Data at the BPMS user companies, was also collected through surveys and interviews. This involved 17 business analysts (68%), 2 general managers (8%) and 6 IT managers (24%). In all of the case studies, the participants represent different genders, social backgrounds and language groups.

The data was systematically coded into categories and themes as it emerged from the various case studies (thematic analysis), using the constant comparative method [20].

Triangulation between findings of the seven BPMS user case study companies and the BPMS vendor case study company was applied to increase the validity and credibility of the research results, also providing a richer description of the research phenomenon and eliminating research bias [21]. Furthermore, in this study, triangulation assisted to present a more plausible and richer account of a research phenomenon [21].

Finally, the theory of Schwarz et al. [1], namely "dynamics capabilities theory model of IT-enabled organisational performance", was used to synthesize the research results and to provide the base for developing a theoretical framework for IT-enforced and IT-enabled business processes for the improvement of business performance and corporate governance.

## 5  A Framework for IT-Enabled and IT-Enforced Compliance

This section describes a theoretical framework for IT-enabled and IT-enforced corporate governance compliance following a BPMS approach, as depicted in Fig. 3. The theoretical framework was developed from the research findings obtained from seven companies that uses BPMS software and a BPMS vendor company, while the theory of Schwarz et al. [1] was used as underlying theory to synthesize the different stages of the theoretical framework.

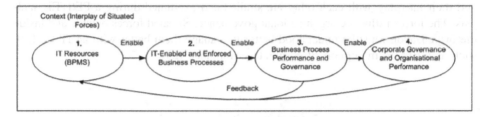

**Fig. 3.** A theoretical framework for IT-enabled and IT-enforced compliance following a BPMS approach

IT resources (see 1 in Fig. 3) consists out of technological artefacts and human agents that develop, configure, design and adapt the technological artefact for a specific purpose in the organisation. In this case, the artefact is a BPMS that is used in the automation of organisational processes. The result is IT-enforced and IT-enabled business processes managed by a BPMS.

IT-enforced and IT-enabled business processes is then used by users (see 2 in Fig. 3), which results in improved process governance and performance (see 3 in Fig. 3). Technological resource support is an essential condition for improved and automated process governance and performance. The efficient enforcement and ordering of work activities cannot be accomplished without these resources.

The control and efficiency gains of automated processes lead to improved governance, compliance, control and operational performance (see 4 in Fig. 3), particularly if aligned strategically to the objectives of the business [1]. These aspects improves organisational competitiveness.

To conclude, to adapt to the changing and flexible environments that businesses face, IT-resources need to adapt tactically to cater for the environmental changes, therefore the feedback loops in the theoretical framework, as indicated in Fig. 3. Furthermore, automated processes on a tactical and strategic level, must be adaptable to handle the dynamic, changing and competitive environments that organisations face for improvements in business compliance, control and performance [1]. The components of the theoretical framework (Fig. 3) are now explained.

## 5.1    Context – Interplay of Situated Forces

There are continuous contextual forces, called situated forces that impact the design and usage of an IT artefact. Therefore, when such an artefact is designed and used for better corporate governance, the contextual forces will also impact the artefact when it is designed and used for the purpose to improve corporate governance.

Various frameworks and checklist have been developed as a way of categorizing possible contextual forces that may impact an organisation. For example, A PEST analysis classifies situated forces as political, economic, social and technological. Two extra forces may be added, namely environmental and legal, to make the analysis a PESTEL analysis, as showed in Fig. 4. The impact of each force on the organization and their interplay with each other are studied and examined during a PESTEL analysis. The forces influence organizational governance. Situated forces outside and inside the organization must be understood better to manage them better with an IT artefact, such as a BPMS, in support of corporate governance [23].

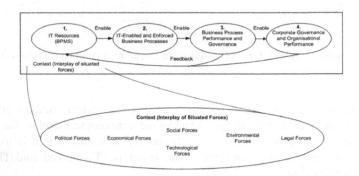

**Fig. 4.**  Context – interplay of situated forces

Furthermore, an IT artefact, such as a BPMS, is embedded in various intersecting social systems [24]. BPMS use within an organisation cause behavioural changes in organisations and therefore, BPMS use may also cause corporate governance supportive or anti-supportive behavioural changes in the intersecting and overlapping social systems of an organization. For example, investors outside an organization may have better trust in an organization, if they know there are good corporate governance supportive measures and practices in place.

## 5.2    Phase 1: IT Resources

As stated before, a generic software system, such as a BPMS can be used to manage, configure design and execute organizational processes. (cf. Sect. 4). Orlikowski and Iacono [22] state, when using an IT artefact such as a BPMS, one must admit that it consist out of several components which may be fragile and fragmentary (cf. Sect. 4). A BPMS consist out of several architectural components namely the Process Modeller, the BPM Engine, the Software Integration Engine, the Business Rule Engine, Monitoring (Reporting Engine) and the Database or BPM Repository.

The technology, in its context, is typically configured by human agents called the designers of the technology [24]. A technology therefore start to exist through human creative action [25]. The technology is further sustained through on-going human adaption and maintenance [25]. The technology designers, even under organizational directive, make use of their situated knowledge and assumptions of the world when configuring the technology for as specific context [24]. In other words, the technology designers, proactively bring forth their own situated organizational realities of "how things are" by using their own interpretive schemes, norms (including corporate governance directives and principles) and organisational facilities, despite the reality of how things really are [24]. Designers are therefore constrained by existing organizational structures, organizational norms, reality and by their own sense making (Fig. 5).

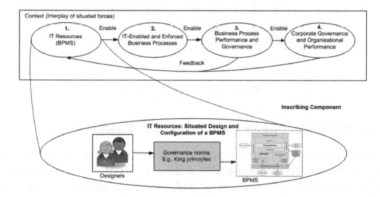

**Fig. 5.** IT resources configure and design the BPMS

However, there are limits when inscribing norms and principles (e.g. King [11, 26, 27]) into a BPMS for better corporate governance. Business rules that are vague, ad-hoc, unstructured and abnormally complex may be difficult to configure or inscribe in a technology such as a BPMS by technology designers or users.

On the other hand, a technological artefact, such as a BPMS may address problems for which solutions are logical, structured and programmable very well during the inscribing or configuration process. Programming involves externalised (not tacit), explicit, structured and logical solutions.

### 5.3 Phase 2: IT-Enabled and IT-Enforced Business Processes

This study investigated how to inscribe norms, such as principles of good corporate governance into the architectural components of a BPMS. Now, when users (human agents) use the system, they draw on the inscribed and configured properties (by designers and users) of the IT artefact [24], as depicted in Fig. 6.

Users also draw on their own experiences, assumptions, power, abilities, skills, training, knowledge and expectations linked to BPMS use [24]. Finally, users, when using the IT artefact, may also draw on the situated facilities within their working and living contexts that is associated with social and cultural conventions [24]. In this manner, situated use of the BPMS, inscribed and configured (in this case also with corporate governance norms), becomes institutionalised in the organisational context, resulting in IT-enforced and automated processes.

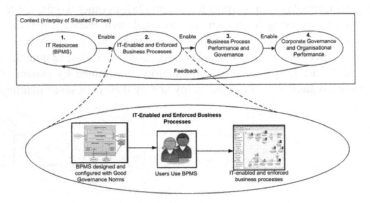

**Fig. 6.** Situated BPMS use

### 5.4    Phase 3: Business Process Governance and Performance

Orlikowski [24] states that the continuous use or enactment of an organizational technology, such as a BPMS, strengthens that technology in the organisation. After a while, the technology becomes routinised and regularised (standard) through repeated and habitual use. The continuous use of the same technology reinforce that technology in the organisation [24]. The technology, in such a way becomes taken for granted within the organization [24]. The technology now dictates behaviour so that it becomes an interpretive template for those that makes use of the IT artefact [24]. With regards to corporate governance, the BPMS acts as a corporate governance behavioural template, as indicated in Fig. 7.

However, when technology designers or users configure or inscribe the technology, the outcome when the technology is used, may be different from that as what was originally anticipated. Then re-design or corrective action need to take place by the designers of the technology, so that the users can use the technology in its anticipated and intended way. In the case of corporate governance, to achieve the anticipated and desired supportive governance behaviours. Corrective intervention is illustrated by a feedback loop in Fig. 7, to accomplish the correct anticipated supportive governance behaviour, going back to the first phase.

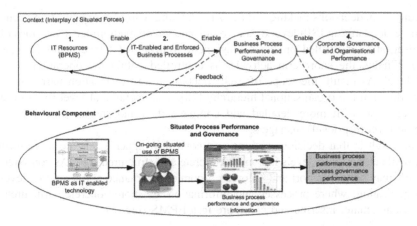

**Fig. 7.** Corporate governance supportive structuration

## 5.5 Phase 4: Improved Corporate Governance and Organisational Performance

The theoretical framework developed from this research caters for continuous change, as the designers and users reconfigure the technology (the BPMS) for organizational improvement [22, 24]. Reconfiguration also occurs when users alter their habits of use or as economic, political and social practices (environmental forces) play out [22, 24]. The findings of the research shows that organisational behaviour, different than expected may occur. As consequence, there may be various iterations of reconfiguration or inscribing to resolve the issues. One can therefore argue that the nature and role of BPMS's towards corporate governance is one of continuous improvement.

Continuous enhancement of IT-enabled (automated) organizational processes cause enforced and improved compliance to corporate governance objectives (acts, rules, legislation, etc.), business strategy and other business initiatives that may have value. Because of improved compliance to standardised processes (all process instances are performed in similar fashion), there may be fewer process exceptions and therefore better risk management.

The research also shows that BPMS use, for improved corporate governance, resulted in behaviour supportive of corporate governance. This may results in contextual best practices for corporate governance.

On the other hand, in manual processes (not automated), there are reduced control,, reduced monitoring, less process compliance, less corporate governance supportive behaviour, poorer risk management, etc., that will end in less best practices for corporate governance.

However, corporate governance initiatives must still be aligned to corporate strategy and business value initiatives for the corporation to perform better. If a corporation performs well in corporate governance and is still not aligned to value initiatives of the business (e.g. alignment to the strategic business objectives), the organisation have a greater risk to fail or perform poorly.

Long-term decisions making and activity planning within an organisation occurs on the strategic planning (SP) level of the organisation. The medium-term activities of the organisation is controlled on the management control (MC) level (middle management). Finally, the short-term activities is controlled within the operational control (OC) level. As result, the scope of each function in an organisation narrows as one moves down in the organisational hierarchy [28]. The operational-level (bottom-level) managers deal with more detailed and complete data and shorter time spans than strategic-level (top-level) managers.

The result is that decisions making and control in upper levels are more unstructured while at the lower levels it is more concrete and structured [28]. As consequence, a BPMS may better support and enforce corporate governance at operational levels of the organisation, where processes and information are more concrete, structured and easier to automate, inscribe and configure in a BPMS (Fig. 8).

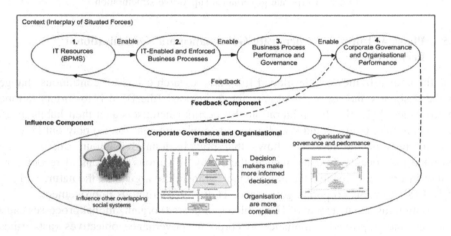

**Fig. 8.** Implications of using a BPMS in support of corporate governance

To conclude, a holistic organisational approach to corporate governance, will contribute to make the theoretical framework for IT-enabled and IT-enforced corporate governance in organisations successful. A holistic approach to corporate governance may include aspects and enablers such as change management, top-management support, leadership, resources to support the process system, a process and process thinking culture and policies.

## 6   Conclusion

This paper proposed a theoretical framework for IT-enabled and IT-enforced corporate governance, by applying a BPMS perspective. In answering the research question: The components of a theoretical framework for IT-enabled and IT-enforced corporate governance compliance when using a BPMS approach consist of an inscribing and automation component (Phases 1 and 2), an organisation performance component (Phases 3 and 4), a feedback component and a contextual influence component (Context), which requires a holistic organisational approach to corporate governance, which may include aspects such as leadership, resources, top-management support and change management to support the process system.

The practical and theoretical contribution of this research lies in explaining the components, insights and facets of a theoretical framework for IT-enabled and IT-enforced corporate governance compliance's drawn from Orlikowski's [24] work to study and address fraud, misconduct, corporate corruption and other corporate governance weaknesses.

# References

1. Schwarz, A., Kalika, M., Kefi, H., Schwarz, C.: A dynamic capabilities approach to understanding the impact of IT-enabled businesses processes and IT-business alignment on the strategic and operational performance of the firm. Commun. Assoc. Inf. Syst. **26**(4) (2010)
2. Bajagai, R.K., Keshari, R.K., Bhetwal, P., Sah, R.S., Jha, R.N.: Impact of ownership structure and corporate governance on capital structure of Nepalese listed companies. In: Rajagopal, B.R. (ed.) Business Governance and Society, pp. 399–419. Palgrave Macmillan, Cham (2019). https://doi.org/10.1007/978-3-319-94613-9_22
3. Hough, J., Thompson, A., Strickland, A., Gamble, J.: Crafting and Executing Strategy (South African Edition). McGraw-Hill, Berkshire (2010)
4. Kreitner, R., Kinicki, A.: Organisational Behaviour. McGraw-Hill, New York (2018)
5. Michell, L.: Corporate Irresponsibility: America's Newest Export. Yale University Press, New Haven (2001)
6. Weeke, S.: Parma's god falls from the sky (2019)
7. Jarvis, K.: IT vendors take rap for corruption. Goverment IT **1**(3), 13 (2009)
8. Mtimunye, M.: SITA lays fraud and corruption ghosts to rest. Goverment IT **1**(3), 15–16 (2009)
9. Kaplan, S., Holmstrom, B.: The state of U.S. Corporate governance: what's right and what's wrong. Nat. Bur. Econ. Res. **15**(3), 8–20 (2003)
10. Park, D.: Overregulation, the final straw for aspiring entrepreneurs. In: Capitalism in the 21st Century Why Global Capitalism Is Broken and How It Can Be Fixed. pp. 107–110. World Scientific Publishing Co. Pte. Ltd. (2019)
11. King III Report: King code of corporate governance in South Africa 2009 and the king report of corporate governance in South Africa. Institute of Directors in Southern Africa, Johannesburg, South Africa (2009)
12. Weske, M., Van der Aalst, W., Berbeek, H.: Advances in business process management. Data Knowl. Eng. **50**, 1–8 (2004)
13. Hammer, M., Champy, J.: Reengineering the Corporation: A Manifesto for Business Revolution. Harper Business, New York (2006)
14. McGoveran, D.: Enterprise integrity. BPMS concepts, Part1-8. EAI J. (2001)
15. Business Process Trends. https://www.bptrends.com/bpt/wp-content/uploads/01-20-14-BPMSEvalART-Miers-Harmon.pdf. Accessed 6 Jan 2020
16. Business Process Trends - The 2007 BPM Suites Report. http://www.bptrends.com/reports_landing.cfm. Accessed 6 Jan 2020

17. Davenport, T.H.: Process Innovation: Reengineering Work Through Information Technology. Harvard Business School Press, Boston (1993)
18. Kwon, T., Zmud, R.: Unifying the fragmented models of information system' implementation. In: Critical Issues in Information Systems Research. Wiley, New York (1987)
19. Schultze, U., Orlikowski, W.J.: A practice perspective on technology-mediated network relations: the use of internet-based self-serve technologies. Inf. Syst. Res. **15**(1), 87–106 (2004)
20. Strauss, A., Corbin, J.: Basics of Qualitative Research: Grounded Theory Procedures and Techniques. SAGE, Newbury Park (2014)
21. Hollard, J.: How to combine multiple research methods: practical triangulation. http://johnnyholland.org/2009/08/practical-triangulation/. Accessed 6 Jan 2020
22. Orlikowski, W., Iacono, C.: Research commentary: desperately seeking the "IT" in IT research - a call to theorizing the IT artifact. Inf. Syst. Res. **12**(2), 121–134 (2001)
23. Pearce, J., Robinson, R.: Strategic Management. McGraw-Hill, New York (2014)
24. Orlikowski, W.J.: Using technology and constituting structures: a practice lens for studying technology in organizations. Organ. Sci. **11**(4), 404–428 (2000)
25. Orlikowski, W.: The duality of technology: rethinking the concept of technology in organisations. Organ. Sci. **3**(3), 298–427 (1992)
26. King I Report: The King Report on Corporate Governance for South Africa. Institute of Directors in Southern Africa, Johannesburg, South Africa (1994)
27. King II Report: The King Report on Corporate Governance for South Africa. Institute of Directors in Southern Africa, Johannesburg, South Africa (2002)
28. Ahituv, N., Neumann, S., Riley, H.: Principles of Information Systems for Management. Wm C Brown Communications, Dubuque (1994)
29. Financier Worldwide: https://www.financierworldwide.com/annual-review-corporate-fraud-corruption-2019#.XhRD1vzRbIU. Accessed 6 Jan 2020
30. GAN - Business Anti-Corruption Portal. https://www.ganintegrity.com/portal/country-profiles/south-africa/. Accessed 6 Jan 2020
31. The University of the Witwatersrand. https://www.wits.ac.za/news/latest-news/opinion/2019/2019-09/why-corruption-killed-dreams-of-a-better-south-africa.html. Accessed 6 Jan 2020
32. Diligent Insights. https://insights.diligent.com/corporate-governance/achieving-strong-corporate-governance-through-technology. Accessed 6 Jan 2020

# The Role of Information Technology in Fintech Innovation: Insights from the New York City Ecosystem

Stanislav Mamonov[(✉)]

Montclair State University, Montclair, NJ 07030, USA
stanislav.mamonov@montclair.edu

**Abstract.** Fintech is an active area of innovation and a rapidly growing sector of the economy, yet relatively little is known about how information technology contributes to innovation in fintech. We draw on the business model canvas framework and we examine the role of information technology in the business models of leading fintech startups in the New York City fintech ecosystem. We find that information technology plays a key role across nearly all components of the business models, orchestrating resources and processes to efficiently deliver personalized financial services to customers. Focusing on the IT-enabled value propositions across the fintech startups in our sample, we find that the startups tend to emphasize low-cost offerings that may pose a threat to incumbent business models in financial services.

**Keywords:** Fintech · Innovation · Business model · Information technology

## 1 Introduction

Disruptive innovations are a common concern for established firms [11]. Disruptive innovations introduce significant changes in the value creation process within established industries by either developing new markets or changing the existing value creation networks [8]. In many cases, such innovations may initially target the less profitable segments of the market, but evolve into dominant business models within the respective industries [38].

Fintech, defined as design and delivery of financial products and services through technology [24], is one of the most active areas of startup innovation. Forecasts for the global fintech market suggest that global fintech revenues will reach $300 billion by 2023 [27]. Despite the practical importance of the fintech market there has been relatively little research on how startups leverage technology in this market and how information technology (IT) may contribute to the disruption of traditional business models in financial services.

To address this gap in research, we draw on the business model canvas literature [29, 30] and we examine the key technology-enabled innovations offered by the leading fintech startups located in New York City. New York City is a global center of finance hosting the headquarters for JPMorgan Chase & Co, Citigroup, Goldman Sachs, Morgan Stanley, AIG, and American Express among other financial institutions,

© IFIP International Federation for Information Processing 2020
Published by Springer Nature Switzerland AG 2020
M. Hattingh et al. (Eds.): I3E 2020, LNCS 12066, pp. 313–324, 2020.
https://doi.org/10.1007/978-3-030-44999-5_26

offering an ideal ecosystem to support fintech development [18]. This study is a part of a broader research stream exploring the role of technology in innovation. Here, we seek to address the following research questions: (1) How does IT contribute to innovation in fintech? and (2) What types of IT-enabled innovations are likely to disrupt existing financial services? To address these questions, we focus on the leading startups in the NYC fintech ecosystem based on the funds raised from investors in the past 5 years and we examine how IT contributes to the value creation within each product or service offering. We also evaluate the likely disruptive impact of the IT-enabled innovations.

Our analysis reveals that information technology is deeply interwoven into nearly all components of the fintech startup business models in our sample. IT plays a dual role of serving as the customer facing artifact in service delivery, but it is also a key coordination mechanism that orchestrates all business processes within the respective companies. Focusing on value propositions offered by the fintech startups in our study, we find that the majority emphasizes low-cost alternatives to traditional financial services, thus posing a potential disruption threat to the incumbent firms in the respective markets.

## 2 Empirical and Theoretical Background

### 2.1 The Role of Technology in Innovation

The connection between technology and innovation is a rich area of research [6, 32, 36] and a full review of this literature is beyond the scope of the current study. Here, we briefly review the key themes that are relevant to our work.

Information technology is broadly acknowledged as an important element of internal process optimization [28, 34], as well as new product and new service development [28]. Whereas much of the earlier work on the impact of IT investments focused on the macro level outcomes, e.g. firm survival and firm revenue [35], more recent research has shown that the effects of IT go beyond increasing operational efficiencies. Mithas et al. [28] have shown the IT investments increase new product and new service introductions, demonstrating that IT investments have a positive effect on innovation within established firms.

Open innovation, i.e. engagement of external parties in the innovation process [5, 13] has emerged as a dominant theme in the discussions on the role of IT in innovation more recently. Open innovation encompasses both supplier-side as well as customer-side innovation. Open source software emerged as a dominant paradigm in supplier-driven innovation [1, 22]. Value co-creation has similarly emerged as an important area in customer-driven product and service innovation [4, 17]. Several scholars suggested that information technologies fundamentally alter the innovation process and they require novel organizing logics designed to capitalize on the core benefits of digital technologies [20, 37].

### 2.2 Fintech

Although a number of competing definitions of fintech have been proposed, we adopt the following definition in our study. Fintech is defined as design and delivery of financial products and services through technology [24]. Financial services encompass a broad range of services that include payments, wealth management, lending, capital markets and insurance among others [23].

An economic analysis of financial services has revealed that despite digitization and adoption of novel technology-supported business services in finance, the industry as a whole has shown little in the way of increasing overall efficiency and the cost of financial intermediation remain stable over time at roughly 2% of GDP [31]. The perceived lack of efficiency in financial services industry has spurred many startups in the fintech domain and their efforts have generally focused on disintermediation and automation [7]. Industry surveys suggest that novel fintech offerings may be particularly appealing to young, high-income, high-value customers [11].

Although the research on fintech is just beginning to emerge, there have been several attempts to develop general taxonomies of fintech innovations. Focusing on the services offered by the companies, Lee and Shin [23] suggested that all fintech startups belong to one of the following categories: payments, wealth management, crowd-funding, lending, capital markets and insurance. Focusing on the technical capabilities, Gai et al. [12] proposed that technical innovations in fintech can be characterized as innovations in authentication and control, risk management, data usage, risk detection, and data storage and processing. Examining innovations in the insurance industry, Szopinski et al. [33] suggested that innovations fall into infrastructure, service or network promotion related categories.

Although prior research contains several fintech taxonomies [12, 23, 33], they do not address the question of *how* information technologies affects fintech business models. In the next section, we discuss the business model canvas framework [2, 39] that provides the theoretical foundation for the examination of the role of IT in fintech business model innovation in our study.

## 2.3  Business Model Canvas and Business Model Disruptions

Business model innovation has been long recognized as an important element of business strategy [2, 39]. Business model canvas emerged as a pragmatic framework focused on defining the key components of a business model with the goal of identifying opportunities for business model innovation [29, 30]. Business model canvas suggests that identification of the (1) key partners, (2) key activities, (3) value proposition, (4) customer relationships, (5) customer segments, (6) key resources and (7) distribution channels can lead to reassessment of the current state and identification of novel options within each of the components that can pave the way to business model innovation.

Disruptive innovation theory emerged from the observation that many dominant firms fell victim to innovations that the firms dismissed at the time of the innovation introduction [8]. For example, IBM famously dismissed the personal computer market opportunity early on [19], and the firm later had to play catchup to the early movers in the market. Christensen's theory of disruptive innovation [8] highlights the fact that ignoring innovative offerings in emergent markets often makes economic sense to the incumbent firms, thus highlighting a fundamental impediment to innovation within the incumbent firms.

The focus of the current study is on understanding how fintech startups leverage IT to produce innovations within the components of the business models and to understand when such innovations may produce disruptions in the incumbent business models. In the next section, we discuss the methodology in our study.

# 3 Methodology

Methodologically, we take on a pragmatic stance that emphasizes the connection to the real world [16]. We follow a multi-case methodology [10] to assess and contrast observations across a theoretically based [15] sample of fintech startups.

## 3.1 Sample Selection

We relied on Crunchbase [9] to identify fintech startups headquartered in New York City. Crunchbase collates information on over 5000 startups across the globe in different sectors of the economy. We filtered Crunchbase listings for "fintech" as the category and "New York" as the headquarters location. We further limited our search to active startups that were founded in the period 2014–2019.

We obtained a list of fintech startups located in New York that includes 224 companies. Many of the startups on the list are in the early stages of development. 95% of the startups had received only a single round of financing and therefore the long-term prospects of these companies are less certain [3]. Historical trends suggest that less than 12% of VC investments lead to successful exits [14]. Because the focus of our analysis is on the effects of IT on business model innovation in fintech, we decided to focus our analysis on the startups that progressed to the second round of raising funding (typically a series B) and raised at least $20 million dollars in total funding. The resultant list contains ten companies that collectively raised over $1.1 billion.

## 3.2 Analytical Methodology

In our analysis on the role of technology in innovation we focused the role of technology in addressing the key components of the business model canvas. We examine the following questions within the analysis of each component [29, 30]:

| | |
|---|---|
| Value proposition | What is the role of IT in the value proposition of each company? |
| Customer segments and distribution channels | How does IT enable the company to address different customer needs? How does IT facilitate/enable different distribution channels? |
| Key activities | How is IT involved in the key activities associated with value delivery? |
| Key resources | How is IT involved in the acquisition/development of key resources associated with value creation/delivery? |
| Key partners | How is IT involved in managing relationships with key partners? |
| Revenue stream | What are the sources of revenue for the company? |

To assess the key value proposition, customer segments and distribution channels, key activities, resources, partners and revenue streams, we reviewed the respective company web sites and news announcements. We used NVivo version 12 software to code the collected documents for the components of the business canvas model as well as the role of IT in the respective components.

# 4 Results

In our sample, we have startups offering a broad spectrum of fintech products and services that offer very different value propositions. Six of ten startups (60%) in our sample are B2C companies offering insurance brokerage, equity trading, retirement planning, online banking, and real estate investment opportunities. One other startup offers consumer purchase financing, but it offers its service via partnerships with retailers, thus operating on a B2B/B2C model. Another startup developed a peer-to-peer (P2P) money transfer services for consumers, but it sells its service to financial institutions that integrate the offering within their digital banking services. This is also an example of hybrid B2B/B2C business model. We find only one pure B2B startup in our sample that offers fraud prevention services to businesses.

The ten startups in our sample have collectively raised $1.175 billion. The mean amount of funding raised is $117.5 million and the median is $97.4 million. Betterment, an online retirement planning service, has raised $275 million putting it in the lead in terms of total fundraising. Venmo, a P2P payment service, raised only $26.2 million.

Focusing on the whether the startup offerings represent low-cost alternatives to existing services or entirely new offerings, we find that nine of ten startups (90%) in our sample are targeting lower price points in the respective markets, whereas only one startup – Cadre - is offering novel services. Cadre is a real estate investment platform that emerged in the wake of the JOBS Act passage that reduced regulator requirements in startup financing reporting and enabled equity crowdfunding as a practice [25]. The company is leveraging the regulatory changes to provide investors with novel investment opportunities that were previously only available to accredited investors [25]. The results are summarized in Table 1 below.

**Table 1.** Startup value proposition, business model type, market focus and funding raised.

| Startup | Value proposition | Market focus | Model type | Funding, $ mil |
|---------|-------------------|--------------|------------|----------------|
| Policygenius | The online service provides an opportunity for insurance seekers to compare policy premiums across several providers and select the best option | L | B2C | 51.1 |
| Stash | The online platform offers low-cost equity trading for individual investors – a basic account costs $1/month | L | B2C | 78.75 |

(continued)

**Table 1.** (*continued*)

| Startup | Value proposition | Market focus | Model type | Funding, $ mil |
|---------|-------------------|--------------|------------|----------------|
| Bread | The IT-based platform enables online retailers to offer purchase financing to their customers | L | B2B/B2C | 140.3 |
| Riskified | The IT-based platform offers fraud prevention services in B2B transactions | L | B2B | 63.7 |
| Betterment | The online service offers low-cost retirement planning for individual investors | L | B2C | 275 |
| N26 | An online bank offers a streamlined list of services to clients | L | B2C | 212.8 |
| TransferWise | An online service that offers lower-cost international wire transfers to individual consumers | L | B2C | 116 |
| Cadre | An online service that provides access to high quality real estate investment opportunities for individual investors | N | B2C | 133 |
| CommonBond | An online service that offers lower interest rates on education loans | L | C2C | 78.6 |
| Venmo | A service that enables P2P payments among individual financial services users | L | B2B/C2C | 26.2 |

L- low cost focus, N – new market focus

In the next step of the analysis, we examined the role of IT in (1) managing relationships with different customer segments, (2) management of distribution channels, (3) support key activities associated with value delivery, (4) provisioning and managing key resources required for product/service delivery, (5) management of relationships with key partners. We also evaluated the key revenue streams for each startup.

## 4.1    IT in Customer Segmentation and Service Delivery

Eight of ten startups in our sample offer online B2C services. It is not surprising then to find that IT plays a key role in service delivery and customer segmentation. IT systems, commonly a combination of web and mobile applications as well as backend services, are the key artifacts that customers interact with. Customer facing systems also facilitate customer segmentation, i.e. identification of customer groups with distinct needs. For example, PolicyGenius assists its customers in finding and evaluating available insurance policies and associated costs in different categories of insurance: home, life, auto, etc. The segmentation based on the insurance needs is seamlessly implemented on the site. Different customer segments navigate the evaluation paths setup to fit the specific insurance needs.

### 4.2    IT Function in Key Activities Associated with Service Delivery

Information technology uniformly plays a key role in automating the key business processes within each startup. For example, the trading platform Stash automates account setup for its customers and it supports efficient workflow on the backend associated with anti-money laundering (AML) and know-your-customer (KYC) regulations. We find similar patterns of front-facing automation and standardization of back-office operations across other B2C platforms in our sample.

The firms operating on the hybrid B2B/B2C models wherein the startups are providing financial services to individual consumers, but service delivery requires integration with business partners, solve the increasing channel complexity with encapsulation of the service-related activities in the IT-systems that are integrated with business partners' systems. Bread, for example, integrates with online retailers to offer purchase financing for consumers. Venmo integrates with financial institutions and provides seamless support for financial transfers among bank account holders who may not even be aware of Venmo's role in the process.

### 4.3    IT in Coordination/Development of Key Resources

Focusing on the role of technology in the development and coordination of key resources, we find that the IT systems themselves become the singular most important resource for each of the startups in our dataset. The IT systems encompass the customer-interfacing digital artifacts for B2C firms. The IT systems also encapsulate the business logic that underpins the operations of all firms in our sample.

### 4.4    IT in Management of Partner Relationships

We find that several of the startups in our sample are critically dependent on their partners for the key resources required for service delivery. For example, an online only bank N26 is critically dependent on its partnership with Mastercard that enables N26 to offer its customers an ATM card that operates across the Mastercard's Maestro platform. N26 leverages IT systems to assure seamless integration of its online banking services with the Maestro network so that its customers can have access to the funds kept at the bank. TransferWise, an online cross-border payment service, is similarly dependent on the Mastercard network in the execution of the international money transfers. TransferWise similarly employs IT systems to assure seamless integration between its web service and the Maestro payment network.

We find several other types of dependencies on IT services for integration with the key partners for service delivery. Riskified, a B2B fraud prevention service is dependent on third-party data in building its risk models. Stash, an online trading platform, is critically dependent on using IT services to connect with exchanges, clearing and settlement partners to assure proper execution and settlement of customer trades.

## 4.5   Revenue Models

We find startups commonly inherit business models from the respective industries in which they operate. For example, PolicyGenius collects referral fees for the insurance policies that customers purchase through the service. Betterment, an investment and retirement planning platform, charges account fees and transaction fees. Riskified offers its service on the software-as-a-service (SaaS) model to business customers and it charges integration and usage fees.

We do find several more aggressive revenue model stances among the startups in our sample. Stash, for example, eschews trading account fees in contrast to many traditional brokers. Similarly, N26, an online bank, offers free accounts and free other-institution ATM use, presumably subsidizing these services from investment revenues. Table 2 summarizes the analysis on the role of IT across the key elements of the business models within the business model canvas framework.

**Table 2.**  The role of IT in customer service delivery, key activities, managing relationships with key partners and revenue stream.

| Startup | Customer segment/distribution | Key activities | Key resources | Key partners | Revenue stream |
|---|---|---|---|---|---|
| Policygenius | The IT platform offers services directly to anyone looking for life, disability, auto and homeowner's insurance | The IT platform supports lead generation and it automates the early stages in the lead screening process | The IT platform supports relationships with insurers and clients | The IT platform manages relationships with life, disability, auto and homeowner's insurance providers | Commissions on purchased insurance policies |
| Stash | The IT platform provides a trading platform to value-conscious traders | The IT platform facilitates all aspects of the online investing services offered by the company | The IT platform provides a full-service trading platform | The IT platform supports relationships with partners that provide account servicing, trade execution and clearing | Trading rebates from exchanges |
| Bread | The IT platform provides integration with online retailers as a conduit to individual consumers | The IT platform enables purchase financing for consumers | The IT platform offers integration, credit scoring and financing management | The IT platform manages relationships with financial partners who are a source of capital | Interest and fees on financed purchases |
| Riskified | The IT platform integrates with enterprise customer workflows | The IT provides a platform for risk assessment in B2B transactions | The IT platform encapsulates proprietary data and risk modeling algorithms | The IT platform is a self-contained offering, however it is dependent on third-party data for service delivery | SaaS licensing |

(*continued*)

**Table 2.** (*continued*)

| Startup | Customer segment/distribution | Key activities | Key resources | Key partners | Revenue stream |
|---|---|---|---|---|---|
| Betterment | The IT platform provides direct access to budget-conscious consumers looking for retirement planning | The IT platform provides retirement planning | The IT platform is the core asset of the company, it provides financial management services for clients | The IT platform streamlines relationships with investment funds that are the key partners to the platform | Account management and trading fees |
| N26 | The IT platform provides direct access to online banking to technology-forward consumers | The IT platform provides online banking services | IT infrastructure is the core asset that supports service delivery to clients | The IT platform integrates with Mastercard to support the service offerings | Investment of customer funds |
| TransferWise | The IT platform provides a lower-cost option for international funds transfer | The IT platform facilitates cross-border financial transfers | The IT platform is the core asset of the company | The IT platform integrates with Mastercard to support the service offerings | Forex fees |
| Cadre | The IT platform provides accredited investors with access to real estate investment opportunities | The IT platform supports the full life cycle of real estate investment management | The IT platform streamlines deal flow acquisition and due diligence | The IT platform integrates with Goldman Sachs. GS provides a source of financing | Fees and interest on investments |
| CommonBond | The IT platform provides students with lower-cost educational loan options | The IT platform supports C2C education lending | The platform that encapsulates loan underwriting is the core asset of the company | The IT platform streamlines relationships with institutional participants on the platform that provide capital | Transaction fees |
| Venmo | The IT platform targets financial institutions and enables P2P payments for individual customers | The IT platform enables P2P payments among individual banking customers | The IT platform and the relationships with financial institutions are the core assets of the company | The IT platform provides integration with the financial institutions that are clients | Transaction fees |

# 5 Discussion

## 5.1 The Contribution of IT to Innovation in Fintech

Our analysis reveals that information technology plays a key role across all components of the business models in fintech firms. IT plays a central role in value proposition formulation across all firms in our sample. IT systems developed by the startups encompass business process logic that underpins the core value creation by the respective companies. This is the case for firms in the B2C and B2B/B2C startups where the IT systems are the focal points of contact with customers. This is also the case in the B2B scenario where the systems deliver value to business partners.

IT systems that are typically developed by startups as layered architectures with web and mobile frontend components, afford a direct channel to end customers. The direct route to end customers is consistent with the general role of technology in the disintermediation trend in fintech innovation that has been noted in prior research [7]. But the IT systems do more than just establish a direct route to end customers, the IT systems also support customer segmentation and personalization. The online insurance, equity trading, wealth management and banking service startups are in a unique position to elicit individual customer preferences and provide service personalization for each individual client through automated segmentation and personalization algorithms.

Across all startups in our sample, the IT systems also perform a key resource and process coordination function. The systems encapsulate and automate business processes, e.g. account application processes, they also provide seamless integration with partner systems where such integration is vital to service delivery, e.g. in the case of online banking and wire transfer services. By the virtue of encapsulating the core business processes and key partner relationships, the IT systems developed by fintech startups become the focal assets that support resource coordination that create value for the customers. In other words, information technology is interwoven into all elements of the fintech business model.

### 5.2    Potential for Disruptive Innovation

In his discussion of disruptive innovations, Christensen noted that disruptive innovations can emerge from low-cost offerings, focus on distinct customer segments, introduction of novel technologies and regulatory changes [8]. In our sample, Cadre exemplifies the case of disruptive innovation brought about by regulatory changes. Cadre offers real estate investment opportunities that were not available to investors prior to the passage of the JOBS Act [26].

We find that all other startups in our dataset focus on cost savings as the primary point of differentiation vis-à-vis traditional financial service providers. For example, the insurance broker PolicyGenius promises savings on the insurance policies. The online bank N26 offers free banking account and no ATM fees. The online trading platform Stash offers free equity trading. These offerings do put pressure on the traditional revenue streams in financial services. For example, *Wall Street Journal* recently reported erosion in the trading commission income across financial institutions offering equity trading that has been driven by online trading platforms offering free equity trading [21].

## 6    Conclusion

Fintech is a rapidly growing area of practice that is expected to reach $300 billion in revenues by 2023 [27], yet relatively little is known about how fintech startups leverage technology for innovation. To address this gap in research, we examined the leading startups in the New York City fintech ecosystem that have collectively raised over $1.1 billion in funding. We drew on the business model canvas framework and we examined how the startups leverage technology across their business model components. We find that technology platforms form the core of the innovative service offerings developed by the startups in our dataset. Further, we find that startups use low-price offering as the dominant strategy for disrupting the existing financial services markets. These observations provide empirical support for the theoretical arguments that call for the reexamination of the organizational logics underlying technology-driven innovation [36].

# References

1. Agerfalk, P., Fitzgerald, B.: Outsourcing to an unknown workforce: exploring opensourcing as a global sourcing strategy. MIS Q. **32**(2), 385–409 (2008)
2. Amit, R., Zott, C.: Creating value through business model innovation. MIT Sloan Manag. Rev. **53**(3), 41 (2012)
3. CB Insights: Venture Capital Funnel Shows Odds of Becoming a Unicorn Are About 1%. CB Research Briefs (2018). https://www.cbinsights.com/research/venture-capital-funnel-2/
4. Chen, L., Marsden, J.R., Zhang, Z.: Theory and analysis of company-sponsored value co-creation. J. Manag. Inf. Syst. **29**(2), 141–172 (2012)
5. Chesbrough, H.: Open Innovation: The New Imperative for Creating and Profiting from Technology. Harvard Business Press, Boston (2006)
6. Chesbrough, H.: Business model innovation: opportunities and barriers. Long Range Plan. **43**(2–3), 354–363 (2010)
7. Chiu, H.: Fintech and disruptive business models in financial products, intermediation and markets- policy implications for financial regulators. J. Technol. Law Policy **21**(1), 55–112 (2016)
8. Christensen, C.M.: The Innovator's Dilemma: When New Technologies Cause Great Firms to Fail. Harvard Business School Press, Boston (1997)
9. Crunchbase: Crunchbase (2019). https://www.crunchbase.com/
10. Eisenhardt, K.M., Graebner, M.E.: Theory building from cases: opportunities and challenges. Acad. Manag. J. **50**(1), 25–32 (2007)
11. Ernst and Young: Who will disrupt the disruptors? J. Financ. Perspect. **3**(3), 1–191 (2015)
12. Gai, K., Qiu, M., Sun, X.: A survey on FinTech. J. Netw. Comput. Appl. **103**, 262–273 (2018)
13. Gassmann, O., Enkel, E., Chesbrough, H.: The future of open innovation. R&D Manag. **40**(3), 213–221 (2010)
14. Giot, P., Schwienbacher, A.: IPOs, trade sales and liquidations: modelling venture capital exits using survival analysis. J. Bank. Finance **31**(3), 679–702 (2007)
15. Glasser, B.G., Strauss, A.L.: Theoretical sampling. In: Denzin, N. (ed.) Sociological Methods: A Sourcebook (Methodological Perspectives), pp. 106–114. Transaction Publishers (2006)
16. Goldkuhl, G.: Pragmatism vs interpretivism in qualitative information systems research. Eur. J. Inf. Syst. **21**(2), 135–146 (2012)
17. Gummesson, E., Mele, C., Polese, F., Galvagno, M., Dalli, D.: Theory of value co-creation: a systematic literature review. Manag. Serv. Qual. **6**, 643–683 (2014)
18. Subrahmanya, M.H.B.: Comparing the entrepreneurial ecosystems for technology startups in Bangalore and Hyderabad, India. Technol. Innov. Manag. Rev. **7**(7), 47–62 (2017)

19. Den Hartigh, E., Ortt, J.R., Van de Kaa, G., Stolwijk, C.C.M.: Platform control during battles for market dominance: the case of Apple versus IBM in the early personal computer industry. Technovation **48**, 4–12 (2016)
20. Henfridsson, O., Lind, M.: Information systems strategizing, organizational sub-communities, and the emergence of a sustainability strategy. J. Strat. Inf. Syst. **23**(1), 11–28 (2014)
21. Intelligent Investor: Your Stock Trades Go Free but Your Cash Is in Chains. Wall Street Journal (2019)
22. Von Krogh, G., Haefliger, S.: Opening up design science: the challenge of designing for reuse and joint development. J. Strat. Inf. Syst. **19**(4), 232–241 (2010)
23. Lee, I., Shin, Y.J.: Fintech: ecosystem, business models, investment decisions, and challenges. Bus. Horiz. **61**(1), 35–46 (2018)
24. Leong, C., Tan, B., Xiao, X., Tan, F.T.C., Sun, Y.: Nurturing a FinTech ecosystem: the case of a youth microloan startup in China. Int. J. Inf. Manag. **37**(2), 92–97 (2017)
25. Mamonov, S., Malaga, R.: Success factors in Title III equity crowdfunding in the United States. Electron. Commer. Res. Appl. **27**, 65–73 (2018)
26. Mamonov, S., Malaga, R.: Success factors in Title II equity crowdfunding in the United States. Venture Cap. **21**(2–3), 223–241 (2019)
27. MarketWatch: Fintech Market: Industry Outlook, Size & Forecast 2018-2023. MarketWatch (2019). https://www.marketwatch.com/press-release/fintech-market-industry-outlook-size-forecast-2018-2023-2019-07-15
28. Mithas, S., Tafti, A., Bardhan, I., Goh, J.M.: Information technology and firm profitability: mechanisms and empirical evidence. MIS Q. **36**(1), 205–224 (2012)
29. Osterwalder, A.: The business model ontology - a proposition in a design science approach. Business Doctor, pp. 1–169 (2004)
30. Osterwalder, A., Pigneur, Y.: Business Model Generation: A Handbook for Visionaries, Game Changers, and Challengers. Wiley, Hoboken (2010)
31. Philippon, T.: The FinTech opportunity. NBR Work. Pap. **3**(1), 1–217 (2016)
32. Rogers, E.M.: Elements of diffusion. In: Diffusion of Innovations, vol. *5*, no. 1.38 (2003)
33. Szopinski, D., Schoormann, T., John, T., Knackstedt, R., Kundisch, D.: Software tools for business model innovation: current state and future challenges. Electron. Markets, 1–26 (2019). https://doi.org/10.1007/s12525-018-0326-1
34. Wade, M.R.: The formation and value of IT-enabled resources: antecedents and consequences of synergistic relationships. MIS Q. **34**(1), 163–183 (2010)
35. Weill, P.: The relationship between investment in information technology and firm performance: a study of the valve manufacturing sector. Inf. Syst. Res. **3**(4), 307–333 (1992)
36. Yoo, Y.: The tables have turned: how can the information systems field contribute to technology and innovation management research? J. Assoc. Inf. Syst. **14**(5), 4 (2012)
37. Yoo, Y., Henfridsson, O., Lyytinen, K.: The new organizing logic of digital innovation: an agenda for information systems research. Inf. Syst. Res. **21**(4), 724–735 (2010)
38. Yu, D., Hang, C.C.: A reflective review of disruptive innovation theory. Int. J. Manag. Rev. **12**(4), 435–452 (2010)
39. Zott, C., Amit, R., Massa, L.: The business model: recent developments and future research. J. Manag. **37**(4), 1019–1042 (2011)

# Governance Challenges Constraining Business Process Management: The Case of a Large South African Financial Services Corporate

Carmen Doyle and Lisa F. Seymour[⊠] [iD]

University of Cape Town, Cape Town, WC, South Africa
lisa.seymour@uct.ac.za

**Abstract.** Obtaining and maintaining a competitive advantage is vital for profit-driven organizations. Business Process Management (BPM) and the governance thereof offer such organizations a framework of management practices within which to achieve this goal. The objectives of this study were to identify and describe the BPM governance challenges that constrain BPM in large South African corporates as BPM in South Africa had not previously received any comprehensive BPM governance focus. Additionally, the BPM and BPM governance bodies of knowledge lack literature on studies focused on BPM governance challenges. Qualitative research methods were utilized to collect useful and descriptive data through secondary document collection and interviews in a single case study. The study confirmed eight of the literature-identified governance challenge themes that constrain BPM and contributed eleven new BPM governance challenge themes to the BPM and BPM governance body of research.

**Keywords:** Business process management governance · Business Process Management · Financial services

## 1 Introduction

Business Process Management (BPM) is a considered, all-encompassing solidification of process practices sharing a common belief that an approach centered on processes leads to significant advancements in system compliance and performance [1, 2]. Increased resource availability, awareness, attention, and formalized responsibility facilitate an increase in BPM success [3]. Though BPM has yielded some success, and despite significant organizational investments in BPM activity, BPM still experiences implementation and expansion challenges [4]. These challenges relate to organizations' inadequate grasp of their methodologies. Additionally, organizations often apply ad-hoc, instead of organization-wide (org-wide), enhancements that yield more effective and longer-term results [4, 5]. It, therefore, is apparent that an understanding of the various aspects that facilitates BPM success remains vital [5, 6]. To this end, BPM provides a governance structure that regulates the modernization of always-transforming businesses and org-wide value chains [2].

© IFIP International Federation for Information Processing 2020
Published by Springer Nature Switzerland AG 2020
M. Hattingh et al. (Eds.): I3E 2020, LNCS 12066, pp. 325–336, 2020.
https://doi.org/10.1007/978-3-030-44999-5_27

BPM governance's impact is far-reaching. It allows organizations to monitor and scrutinize their BPM practices, BP performance, and outcomes. BPM governance, furthermore, helps to rank the importance of BP improvements, increase the organization's capabilities, and manage downstream improvement initiatives [5, 7, 8]. Still, enterprises often struggle to address BPM challenges effectively [9, 10]. The literature is unable to assist as it lacks empirical examination of the business aspects that cause governance-related challenges in BPM. Hence the grand challenge from the BPM 2019 conference that we "take a more empirical angle in our work, trying to identify genuine issues that organizations are facing" [11]. To contribute to this knowledge gap, this study's research question was "What are the governance challenges that constrain BPM in a large South African financial services corporate?" Thus, this paper aimed to describe the corporate's governance-related BPM experiences. The sections that follow provide an overview of the relevant literature, detail of the research method and case description, the results of the findings, followed by research limitations and suggested future research.

## 2 Literature Review

This section summarises the literature on BPM, BPM governance, and governance-related BPM challenges. The study's theoretical framework is then discussed, followed by the literature summary.

BPM interest remains on the rise [7]. Since companies employing BPM practices elevated their levels of interest in the realization of BPM benefits, BPM methodology skills have become sought-after. Benefits realization is achievable when these organizations follow a BPM framework. Frameworks should be well-thought-out to enable BPM understanding as enterprise expertise instead of insulated process improvement initiatives [12]. BPM's comprehensive nature and environment also require a framework construction such that it supports its complexity breakdown [13].

Much research on governance, its meaning, relevance, and benefits are evident in the literature. It is, therefore, no longer perceived as a new concept [14]. BPM governance focuses on process assets as quantifiable assets [14]. This research study adopts the comprehensive view that BPM governance comprises a management framework aimed at guiding all BP-related decision-making and design. Thus, it focusses on the functional, cross-functional, and cross-business unit, org-wide initiatives, and all of its BPM-related practices [1, 9]. Cited BPM governance elements include BP standards, BP roles and responsibility, BP objectives, control methods, assessment methods, governance structures, architecture, and infrastructure [15].

### 2.1 Theoretical Framework

This study examines governance challenges that constrain BPM, to assist Table 1 represents BPM governance challenges derived from the literature which was derived as follows. Firstly elements and their challenges were identified from the literature and then re-categorise into a known BPM governance framework selected to guide the data collection. Secondly, the researcher rationalized the BPM governance categories, themes, and sub-themes identified in the BPM governance frameworks found in the literature. These frameworks are (1) the de Bruin and Rosemann BPM Maturity Model [13]; (2) the Bhat and Fernandez elements of BPM Governance [16], and (3) the Spanyi BPM governance framework checklist [8]. Next, the researcher mapped the six literature-derived BPM governance categories, along with their themes and elements, to the five capability areas contained in the de Bruin and Rosemann BPM Maturity Model's governance factor [13]. The five BPM governance capability areas are (1) Process Management (PM) Decision-making; (2) PM Roles and Responsibilities; (3) PM Metrics and Performance Linkage; (4) PM Standards; and (5) PM Controls. Lastly, the researcher removed the BPM governance elements as they were useful to the framework construction only for categorising the corresponding challenges.

**Table 1.** A summary of the literature-derived BPM governance challenges

| Category | Related challenges | Authors |
| --- | --- | --- |
| PM standards | Lack of standard methods<br>Lack of effective BP's<br>Lack of robust BPMG frameworks<br>Lack of BP enhancement methods | [8, 15–18] |
| | Lack of training, skills definition<br>Lack of adequate incentive schemes<br>Lack of suitable academic programs<br>Lack of BPM definition and shared vision | [8, 15, 17] |
| PM metrics and performance linkage | Lack of management focus:<br>How to strategically align BPs to objectives<br>Essential information systems' strategic alignment | [19] |
| | Lack of attainable & complex maturity models<br>Lack of representation of customer and org-wide<br>Cooperation needs in popular reference models | [8, 18] |
| | Low enterprise integration | [15, 17] |
| | Lack of BP infrastructure integration<br>Lack of internal client infrastructure<br>Difficulties relating to legacy systems | [15–18] |
| PM controls | Difficulty with legislation | [15–18] |
| PM roles and responsibilities | Lack of role definition, BPM skilled roles<br>Loyalty division (admin and process)<br>Resistance to change<br>Traditional BPM governance leadership<br>Slow changing executive thinking | [8, 17, 20] |

Despite BPM governance's significant role within organizations and, particularly in BPM initiatives, it is still an unsuitably addressed enterprise issue. Management commitment remains essential to attain favorable BPM maturity and to transform strategy into realized benefits. Still, as organizations are not able to effortlessly commit, these challenges persist and effective org-wide deployment of these elements' progress remains slow and minimal. The literature review did not surface any studies that have comprehensively examined BPM governance challenges. Thus, the need for the comprehensive examination of BPM governance challenges in all business sectors, industries, and context is substantiated.

## 3   Method and Case Description

The study's research question, research objectives, research strategy and literature guided the data collection. The research objective was to identify and describe governance challenges constraining BPM in large South African financial services corporates. The study embraced a subjective ontological stance and an interpretivist epistemological stance, which promoted understanding the research participants, their interactions, and their impact on the world around them [21]. The purpose of the study was descriptive, and qualitative research methods were employed. By using a case study research strategy, the study described the BPM governance challenges experienced and perceived by the case organization, as well as the complexities that influence these experiences [22, 23]. The single case study organization was known as InvestCo throughout the study to ensure anonymity. At the time, the primary author had been in the case organization's service for many years. Thus, the author had a fair understanding of its strategic objectives and culture. InvestCo was selected for this research study because (1) it is considered one of the largest private sector investment managers in South Africa with an employee count of over 500 and several branches over the breadth of the country; (2) it has not officially adopted BPM; (3) though its maturity level was low, it had established process management practices.

**Table 2.**  Research participants' business roles

| Position | Experience |
|---|---|
| Senior IT manager (3) | 19, 10, 15 years |
| Senior business analyst (2) | 14, 5 years |
| Senior operations manager (1) | 21 years |
| Senior analyst programmer (1) | 6 years |
| Senior compliance officer (1) | 11 years |

The eight participants in Table 2, were purposely sampled. InvestCo's Management-level employees were deemed more likely to contribute to a broader view of the role of BPM governance and its enterprise-wide impact on their organization. InvestCo's organizational permission was secured after the study received university ethical clearance. Useful and descriptive data was obtained through semi-structured interviews with the relevant subject matter experts within the organization. Secondary data (Table 3) was obtained through document collection to achieve triangulation [24].

**Table 3.** Research study-related secondary data

| SDID | Description | SDID | Description |
|------|-------------|------|-------------|
| SDST01-4 | PM standards | STDOTH01-03 | Case description |
| SDST04 | PM metrics and performance linkage | STDOTH02 | Case description |
| SDCT01-6 | PM controls | STDOTH03 | Case description |

The interview protocol ensured that participants were informed of the study's purpose and allowed the flexibility to adjust the interview to suit the outcomes of the individual interviews [25]. After transcribing all interviews, thematic analysis of the data was performed iteratively using Nvivo, and themes were inductively coded as they emerged from the data following Braun and Clarke's method [27]. The analysis took place concurrently with the data collection [24]. The secondary data was analysed in the same wasy as the primary data. The first phase included reading and rereading the data and noting initial ideas. The second phase resulted in initial coding. In the third phase the codes where collated into themes and in the fourth phase the themes were iteratively reviewing by re-reading all text. The final two phases included naming and renaming themes and selecting vivid extracts for cach theme. The literature-derived theoretical framework merely served to guide the study and categorization of themes that emerged from the data. The principle of contextualization acknowledges that contextual differences bring about variances in experiences, perceptions, and under-standing [26].

## 4   Research Findings

This study aimed to describe the BPM governance challenges experienced in the financial services industry. Through thc thcmatic analysis of the reseaich data, the study derived 19 BPM governance-related themes and 31 BPM governance-related sub-themes. A discussion of the themes appearing now follows. The theoretical framework employed in this study served as a lens for the categorization of the themes to render the research findings comparable to the literature.

### 4.1   Lack of PM Controls

The thematic analysis of the data highlighted six *PM controls*-related challenges. Table 4 reflects data excerpts related to the challenges discussed.

**Table 4.** PM-controls-related BPM governance challenges

| Theme | Text reference |
| --- | --- |
| Difficulty with capacity constraints (C1) | *"Technical debt is our biggest problem. We know what we need to fix, but we run lean teams – Lean, as in our teams are too few for how much work needs to be done."* [RP06] |
| Lack of pre-change control rigor (C2) | *"Change Control Forum is to identify ahead of time downstream side effects rather than just before implementation."* [RP08] |
| Impact of external parties on BPs (C3) | *"Regulatory changes take precedence over anything that has an impact on daily trading or client reporting, and after that, the internal processes that aim to improve the existing world."* [RP08] |
| Lack of BPM architecture (C4) | *"Everything is available, and you can find it, it is just that we do not have one, big, process library"* [RP06] |
| Risk around remaining manual BPs (C5) | *"We still have manual BPs, and it brings the risk for errors."* [RP07] |
| Lack of established BP controls and criteria (C6) | *A boutique will have BPs mapped, and their business process is its IP (intellectual property), which is why it stays inside the boutique."* [RP06] |

**Difficulty with Capacity Constraints.** The organization's capacity-related challenges pertained to resourcing difficulty, workforce retention, and the complexities around skilled recruitment. Technical debt was said to include the nice-to-have BP improvement initiatives that, due to strategic priorities, higher priority focuses, and capacity constraints, never reach the top of the list.

**Lack of Pre-change Control Rigor.** Lack of pre-change control rigor challenges comprises a lack of solution design rigor, data governance, and problematic sub-team cultures. Thus, the understanding of BP change requests and implementations need to be adjusted. Adequate data governance is required as data-related updates have a potentially more significant impact on the organization.

**Impact of External Parties on BPs.** The participants mentioned that external parties that often impact the organization's various BPs included their outsourced administrator, data vendors (includes the economic markets), and regulatory bodies. When incidents, originating with the outsourced service provider or data vendors, occur, all business-as-usual activity ceases until the issues are resolved.

**Lack of BPM Architecture.** Although all BP artifacts are available and accessible, awareness is lacking, and storage of these artifacts are not centralized. The lack of dedicated storage resources and policies cause much frustration, particularly when artifacts are stored in multiple locations with various version numbers.

**Risk Around Remaining Manual BPs.** Concerns exist around the organization's few remaining manual BPs. The secondary data suggests the challenge lies somewhere between business-and-IT oversight and prioritization. These issues are possibly brought about by the capacity constraint difficulties mentioned earlier.

**Lack of Established BP Controls and Criteria.** There is the perception that the organization does not have a high-level process management plan. This perception exists as the organizational structure necessitates role-based access and permissions.

## 4.2 Lack of PM Roles and Responsibilities

The thematic analysis highlighted nine *PM roles and responsibilities*-related challenges. Table 5 reflects data excerpts related to the challenges which are now discussed.

**Difficulty Resulting from the Business Unit (BU) Structuring.** Participants shared that the way in which the organization structures its business units and its lean strategic stance of managing income and costs were at the root of the challenges that they are experiencing. The secondary data supported the participants' experiences.

**Lack of Governance Structures.** There was no mention of an officially defined obligation to adhere to BPM or BPM governance. All participants mentioned that their BPM and BPM governance roles were informal. Furthermore, there was a strong sense that cost-saving, and not BPM, had been the strategic goal for the last few years.

**Lack of BPM Roles and Governance Discipline.** No-one is formally driving BPM in the organization. Concerns exist about the organization's perception that documentation of BPs ownership resides in IT. Additionally, concerns exist about the current inability to track BP ownership activity once the BP is handed over to the business.

**Ineffective BP Design Process.** Challenges experienced when the upfront BP design process does not include Information Systems and IT representatives. Often, the business will only discover this oversight when the solution encounters its first exception in a production environment.

**Lack of BPM Principles and Practices.** The challenges that participants mentioned included the fact that no-one was monitoring business activity, or whether they employed BP standards and best practices. Furthermore, no enforcement of best practices was evident in this regard.

**Resistance to Change.** Some of the business units' resistance to change relates to the fear of redundancy. Therefore, they have not been able to embrace the opportunities that automation delivers.

**Division of Loyalty.** Process owners lack authority. Thus complexities, such as capacity constraints, appear to exacerbate the problem. This complexity is particularly true when process managers attempt to manage their BPM initiatives.

**Lack of Catalog Management.** Process catalogs are lacking and would serve as upfront communication around the business' service offerings and process involved with securing those services. In the absence of such a catalog, it is particularly challenging to coordinate building-block BPs.

**Ineffective BP Prioritization.** Various managers review and prioritize work packages. Thus, when the last manager reviews a business units' work package list and, their opinion of priority may differ from another manager's opinion. Such an initiative may then unnoticeably drop of the worklist, or execute without an actual business need.

**Table 5.** PM roles and responsibility-related BPM governance challenges

| Theme | Text reference |
|---|---|
| Difficulty resulting from the BU structuring (C7) | *The main thing they care about is alpha, and not the data integrity, even though data integrity is central to alpha.* [RP08] |
| Lack of governance structures (C8) | *"We do not typically think of BPM as a practice in the everyday world."* [RP04] |
| Lack of BPM roles and governance discipline (C9) | *"I think what the organization lacks in terms of BPM is someone to see that it gets done, that there are standards implemented, tools used, and best practices implemented."* [RP02] |
| Ineffective BP design process (C10) | *"IT is bolted onto the decided upon the business process. Any controls we build are never going to be complete controls."* [RP08] |
| Lack of BPM principles and practices (C11) | *"What is passed on is "Do this," not "Why we are doing this." This lack of context leads to people doing what they are told"* [RP08] |
| Resistance to change (C12) | *"They are only now starting to speak up because someone has left, and now realize that they have an issue."* [RP06] |
| Division of loyalty (C13) | *"So much pressure ... to deal with people that are overworked because of under-resourcing, and I am not the line manager."* [RP03] |
| Lack of catalog management (C14) | *"Every request should have an associated BP - which also speaks to this idea of a service catalog which has come up."* [RP06] |
| Ineffective BP prioritisation (C15) | *Different subject matter experts log or create the work packages; there might be underlying differences in the interpretation of exactly how fair the alignment is with the strategy.* [RP01] |

## 4.3    Lack of PM Standards

The thematic analysis of the data highlighted two PM standards-related challenges. Table 6 reflects data excerpts related to the challenges which are now discussed.

**Lack of BP Documentation Standards.** BP documentation that does not include the process' key risk areas, escalation points, or frequently asked questions is often the result of ineffective BP's. The lack of secondary data supports the participant's views that the organization does not currently enforce any particular BPM standard and very few BPM governance standards.

**Ineffective Employee Assessment.** Unclear links exist between the management of BPs and the organization's incentive reward system. Though the secondary data lightly hinted at his link, the association could easily be overlooked when the staff has a small window to read non-BP related communications. Non-standard requests do not have existing BPs and often result in dissatisfied clients.

**Table 6.** PM standards–related BPM governance challenges

| Theme | Text reference |
|---|---|
| Lack of BP documentation standards (C16) | *"They sometimes miss critical information that would have an impact on the effectiveness of that specific business process."* [RP01] |
| Ineffective employee assessment (C17) | *"Initiatives should be better aligned with our rewards recognition process.* [RP02] *"There is frustration on both sides. But, again, that is an outcome of poor work management on the part of the influencer."* [RP08] |

### 4.4 Lack of PM and Performance Linkage

The thematic analysis of the data highlighted two *PM metrics and performance linkage*-related challenges. Table 7 reflects data excerpts related to the challenges which are now discussed.

**Ineffective Business Unit Monitoring Capabilities.** A concern exists that business units might not all have useful monitoring capabilities. All of the participants felt that the lack of regular BP review was capacity-related.

**Ineffective Performance Review Criteria.** The organization's consideration of the criteria that determined the effectiveness of their BPs' performance is lacking. The missing criteria relate to framework-fit and effective use of staff and teams.

**Table 7.** PM and performance linkage-related BPM governance challenges

| Theme | Text reference |
|---|---|
| Ineffective BU monitoring capabilities (C18) | *"We have not, and I think that might be one of our failings, but the business is now asking 'how can we get that, as well?'"* [RP08] |
| Ineffective performance review criteria (C19) | *"Broader criteria such as 'is this allocated to the most applicable team?' are not part of the conversation."* [RP08] |

## 5 Discussion

The discussion of the research findings was used to answer the research question, "What are the governance challenges that constrain BPM?" Table 8 contains a matrix of the 19 challenges that emerged from the research study, the codes are in Tables 4, 5,

6 and 7. New themes not found in the literature are indicated with an asterisk. While the dominance of certain challenges can't be simplisticly assigned to the number of text references it does give an indication. The interpretation of the findings also supported that the dominant challenge categories were the lack of PM controls (C1-6) with 79 text references and a lack of PM process roles and responsibilities (C7-13) with 45 text references. The dominant challenge was the difficulty with capacity constraints (C1) with 35 text references. No evidence was found to support the PM Decision-Making category within the case organisation. To mitigate potential bias in the grouping of the challenge, interviewees were consulted during the latter part the analysis process. As most of the organization's functions require specialized skills, the recruitment and retention policies require closer scrutiny to assess how they can aid in reducing the challenges experienced in this area. The lack of BP documentation standards challenge is brought about by a lack of organizational policies and results in inconsistent standards applied by individuals. The next steps for the organization are to address influencing policies, prioritize BPM, and embed the much-needed BPM and BPM governance principles, practices, and training.

**Table 8.** Summarised comparison of BPM governance challenge themes with Data sources (DS) and Text references (TR) to the literature.

| # | DS | TR | New*/Existing | # | DS | TR | New*/Existing |
|-----|-----|-----|-----|-----|-----|-----|-----|
| C1 | 8 | 35 | * | C11 | 3 | 6 | |
| C2 | 3 | 13 | * | C12 | 1 | 4 | |
| C3 | 5 | 12 | | C13 | 1 | 2 | |
| C4 | 5 | 10 | | C14 | 1 | 1 | |
| C5 | 3 | 5 | * | C15 | 1 | 1 | * |
| C6 | 3 | 4 | * | C16 | 6 | 17 | |
| C7 | 5 | 11 | * | C17 | 4 | 9 | * |
| C8 | 4 | 9 | * | C18 | 6 | 13 | * |
| C9 | 3 | 6 | | C19 | 2 | 3 | * |
| C10 | 3 | 5 | * | | | | |

# 6   Conclusion

This paper described South African Financial Services governance-related BPM experiences. This study found support for eight of the existing BPM governance challenges identified in the literature. The matching challenges were those that could be generalized across multiple organizations and industries. Additionally, the study has added contextual variation to existing themes, as well as introducing eleven new themes. This empirical study contributes to the BPM and BPM governance body of research in two ways. The study contributes to practice in that its comprehensive BPM governance theoretical framework, together with the literature-derived BPM governance elements framework could hold great value for future top management BPM and

BPM governance-related decision-making in financial services and similar organizations. Not forgetting, though, that any framework should be adjusted to suit the context in which it is used. The study contributes to theory, in that it provides an initial contribution to BPM governance challenges-focused research.

The specific research focus may limit the generalizability of the study's findings. The following research limitations are inherent in the study. Single case studies' research findings and their application may not be generalizable. Instead, this study's findings relate to financial services organizations with informal BPM and BPM governance practices and low BPM maturity levels. Additionally, the collection of more abundant data would have compromised the case organization's competitive and strategic advantage. The main author's proximity to the case organisation introduces potential bias, the possibility exists that the analysis process may have resulted in some inaccuracies. The literature review identified that research gaps remain concerning BPM governance challenges-focused research. South Africa was the deliberate focus as the literature review indicated that a comprehensive examination of the governance challenges constraining BPM had not yet been conducted in the global context, developing context, or the South African context. Therefore, we encourage researchers and practitioners to conduct further empirical studies of the same or similar phenomena, using different research paradigms. Such studies would yield incredibly rich and comprehensive contributions to the BPM and BPM governance bodies of knowledge.

# References

1. Rosemann, M., vom Brocke, J.: The six core elements of business process management. In: vom Brocke, J., Rosemann, M. (eds.) Handbook on Business Process Management 1. IHIS, 2nd edn, pp. 105–122. Springer, Heidelberg (2015). https://doi.org/10.1007/978-3-642-45100-3_5
2. Grela, G.: Measurement of business processes. In: Management, Knowledge and Learning, pp. 1217–1225 (2014)
3. Hernaus, T., Vuksic, V.B., Štemberger, M.I.: How to go from strategy to results? Institutionalising BPM governance within organizations. Bus. Process Manag. J. 22(1), 173–195 (2016)
4. de Bruin, T.: Business process management: theory on progression and maturity. Queensland University of Technology (2009)
5. de Boer, F.G., Müller, C.J., ten Caten, C.S.: Assessment model for organizational business process maturity with a focus on BPM governance practices. Bus. Process Manag. J. 21(4), 908–927 (2015)
6. Kohlbacher, M.: The effects of process orientation: a literature review. Bus. Process Manag. J. 16(1), 135–152 (2010)
7. Syed, R., Bandara, W., French, E., Stewart, G.: Getting it right! Critical success factors of BPM in the public sector: a systematic literature review. Australas. J. Inf. Syst. 22, 1–39 (2018)
8. Spanyi, A.: The governance of business process management. In: vom Brocke, J., Rosemann, M. (eds.) Handbook on Business Process Management 2: Strategic Alignment, Governance, People and Culture. IHIS, 2nd edn, pp. 333–349. Springer, Heidelberg (2015). https://doi.org/10.1007/978-3-642-45103-4_14

9. Markus, M.L., Jacobson, D.D.: Business process governance. In: vom Brocke, J., Rosemann, M. (eds.) Handbook on Business Process Management 2, 1st edn, pp. 201–222. Springer, Heidelberg (2010). https://doi.org/10.1007/978-3-642-01982-1_10

10. Niehaves, B., Plattfaut, R., Budde, M., Becker, J.: Business process governance: theorizing and empirical application. In: Proceedings of the Seventeenth Americas Conference on Information Systems (2011)

11. Recker, J., Reijers, H.A.: The panel discussion at BPM 2019. In: Business Process Management Workshops. BPM 2019. Lecture Notes in Business Information Processing, vol. 362, pp. vii–x (2019)

12. Trkman, P.: The critical success factors of business process management. Int. J. Inf. Manag. 30(2), 125–134 (2010)

13. de Bruin, T., Rosemann, M.: Using the Delphi technique to identify BPM capability areas. In: ACIS 2007 Proceedings, p. 42 (2007)

14. Doebeli, G., Fisher, R., Gapp, R., Sanzogni, L.: Using BPM governance to align systems and practice. Bus. Process Manag. J. 17(2), 184–202 (2011)

15. Santana, A.F.L., Alves, C.F., Santos, H.R.M., Felix, A.L.C.: BPM governance: an exploratory study in public organizations. In: Halpin, T., Nurcan, S., Krogstie, J., Soffer, P., Proper, E., Schmidt, R., Bider, I. (eds.) BPMDS/EMMSAD-2011. LNBIP, vol. 81, pp. 46–60. Springer, Heidelberg (2011). https://doi.org/10.1007/978-3-642-21759-3_4

16. Bhat, J.M., Fernandez, J.: Successful patterns of BPM governance: a case study. In: BPM 2007 Workshop on Business Process Governance, no. September 2007, pp. 16–26 (2007)

17. Valença, G., Alves, C.F., Santana, A.F.L., Oliveira, J., Santos, H.: Understanding the adoption of BPM governance in the Brazilian public sector. In: ECIS, vol. 56, no. 2013, pp. 1–12 (2013)

18. Weerakkody, V., Janssen, M., Dwivedi, Y.K.: Transformational change and business process reengineering (BPR): lessons from the British and Dutch public sector. Gov. Inf. Q. 28(3), 320–328 (2011)

19. Syed, R., Bandara, W., Hidaya, Z.: The role of committed leadership for impactful process reforms in the public sector of developing nations. In: Complete Business Process Handbook, 3rd edn. Morgan Kaufmann Publishers Inc., Burlington (2018)

20. Kettenbohrer, J., Beimborn, D., Kloppenburg, M.: Developing a governance model for successful business process standardization. In: 19th Americas Conference on Information Systems, vol. 2, no. 2, pp. 1–11 (2013)

21. Cussen, N., Cooney, T.: How can local communities use effectuation to increase local economic growth within existing levels of government support? In: 16th European Conference on Research Methods in Business and Management, pp. 392–398 (2017)

22. Myers, M.D.: Critical ethnography in information systems. In: Lee, A.S., Liebenau, J., DeGross, J.I. (eds.) Information Systems and Qualitative Research. ITIFIP, pp. 276–300. Springer, Boston, MA (1997). https://doi.org/10.1007/978-0-387-35309-8_15

23. Bhattacherjee, A.: Social Science Research: Principles, Methods, and Practices, 2nd edn. Global Text Project, Florida (2012)

24. Saunders, M., Lewis, P., Thornhill, A.: Research Methods for Business Research, 7th edn. Pearson Education Limited, Harlow (2016)

25. Birmingham, D., Wilkinson, P.: Using Research Instruments-A Guide For Researchers, no. 1. RoutledgeFalmer, London (2003)

26. Klein, H.K., Myers, M.D.: A set of principles for conducting and evaluating interpretive field studies in information systems. MIS Q. 23(1), 67–94 (1999)

27. Braun, V., Clarke, V.: Using thematic analysis in psychology. Qual. Res. Psychol. 3(2), 77–101 (2006)

# Overcoming the Ivory Tower: A Meta Model for Staged Maturity Models

Katja Bley[(✉)], Hendrik Schön, and Susanne Strahringer

Business Informatics, esp. IS in Trade and Industry,
TU Dresden, Dresden, Germany
{katja.bley, hendrik.schoen,
susanne.strahringer}@tu-dresden.de

**Abstract.** When it comes to the economic and strategic development of companies, maturity models are regarded as silver bullets. However, the existing discrepancy between the large amount of existing, differently developed models and their rare application remains astonishing. We focus on this phenomenon by analyzing the models' interpretability and possible structural and conceptual inconsistencies. By analyzing existing, staged maturity models, we develop a meta model for staged maturity models so different maturity models may share common semantics and syntax. Our meta model can therefore contribute to the conceptual rigor of existing and future maturity models in all domains and can be decisive for the success or failure of a maturity measurement in a company.

**Keywords:** Maturity model development · Meta model · Conceptual modeling

## 1 Introduction

Economic development, the assumption of growth, and the ongoing transformation of processes increase the competitive pressure on enterprises of all sizes. Hence, they search for tools that can help determine their current benchmarking position or assess their subsequent performance compared to a predefined best-practice performance [1]. One famous example of these benchmarking tools is Maturity Models (MMs). Considering their components, two definitions result: 'maturity' as a "state of being complete, perfect or ready" [2] and 'model' as "an abstraction of a (real or language based) system allowing predictions or inferences to be made" [3]. Thus, an MM can be regarded as an abstraction of a system that allows predictions or inferences about a complete or perfect state. Its aim is a structured, systematic elaboration of best practices and processes that are related to the functioning and structure of an organization [4]. The MM is divided into different levels, which are used as benchmarks for the overall maturity of an organization. By application, an object is able to assess its own position in a predefined best-practice approach. An awareness of the maturity level in a particular domain is necessary in order to recognize improvement potentials and stimulate a continuous improvement process [5]. Especially when it comes to emerging phenomena like digitalization or the Industrial Internet, MMs became a favored instrument especially for SMEs in order to determine their own digitalization status and corresponding guidelines for improvement. But it is not only in this area that there has been

M. Hattingh et al. (Eds.): I3E 2020, LNCS 12066, pp. 337–349, 2020.
https://doi.org/10.1007/978-3-030-44999-5_28

an enormous increase in MM publications in recent years. Due to their general applicability, the rather simple development, and the promising competitive advantages many MMs have emerged in both science and practice over the last decade. They differ in the concepts of maturity, the considered domains, the development approach, or the target group [4, 6].

Although there exist several approaches to the rigorous development (i.e. [7–9]), and there are MMs that already follow these guidelines and should be considered as complete and thorough, a plethora of developers still see a need for new and different kinds of MMs. A possible reason for this phenomenon may be that current MMs lack in consistency regarding their semantics, syntax, and concepts. This leads to a situation where many different MMs introduce ontologies that are either conceptually the same but are used for different subjects and in different contexts so researchers do not understand or recognize similar models or they try to differentiate from existing approaches by using different terminology (e.g. level vs. stages, maturity vs. assessment, dimension vs. area). This in turn weakens the benefits of MMs for companies, as they are unable to understand, compare, and apply the models due to different terminology or incomprehensible concepts and relationships. As a consequence, a solution is needed that proposes theoretical and practical solutions for the semantic and syntactical pitfalls and difficulties mentioned.

We address this problem of conceptual divergence by introducing a UML-based meta model of MMs – a formal construct that summarizes the various MM concepts, features, and interdependencies and relates them to each other. We introduce this meta model regarding the different MM concepts, where each MM can be an instance of it as it provides a conceptual template for the rigorous development of new and the evaluation of existing maturity models. We thereby focus on staged MMs, as they have a holistic and cross-organizational structure that is dominant in MM research. Based on the most popular MMs as well as several newly developed MMs, we summarize and discuss already existing MM concepts. We are able to show a valid instantiation of our maturity meta model by classifying different staged MMs in their properties and concepts with our meta model.

## 2 The Anatomy of Maturity Models

### 2.1 Definition and Application of Maturity Models

According to [10], MMs typically consist of: (a) a number of levels (commonly 3–6), (b) a generic description of each level, (c) a number of dimensions or "process areas", (d) a number of elements or activities for each process area, and (e) a description of the performance of each activity or element as it might perform or might be performed at each maturity level. The purpose of MM assessment can vary. Depending on its intended aim, the MM focuses on an assessment of the current state of development (descriptive), the identification of improvement potential (prescriptive), or its application as a benchmarking tool (comparative) for an object under study [11].

MM development has faced an evolution of around 40 years. The early approaches of these models reach back to the late 1970s, when Crosby and Nolan developed the first preliminaries of today's MM: the five-staged Quality Management Maturity Grid and the stage theory on electronic data processing [12, 13]. The concept of these models gained more and more attention, and to date, the Capability Maturity Model Integration (CMMI) [14] represents one of the most well-known and applied MMs.

Although there are different types of MMs, we focus on the dominant form, the staged MM. Its basic assumption is that an organization is constantly evolving, inter- and intra-organizationally, due to learning effects and improvements. This evolution process is represented in a simplified step-by-step approach using a certain number of degrees of maturity (usually 3–6), a combination of key factors that must be given in order to achieve a certain level of maturity. Figure 1 shows a common representation of a staged MM. When using such an MM, the presence of relevant factors is measured via indicators. After conducting this assessment, the results are summarized with corresponding evaluations and a representative maturity level (see Fig. 1).

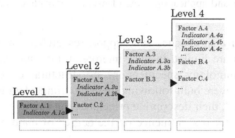

**Fig. 1.** Structure of a staged MM

## 2.2 Development of Maturity Models

Researchers who develop an MM have to decide on a research design for model development (i.e., empirical qualitative/quantitative, conceptual, design-oriented or other), specific research methods to be applied (i.e., case studies, surveys, literature reviews, interviews, conceptual developments or no method at all), and the research content that has to be elaborated and described (i.e., conceptual, descriptive, assessment, comparative, or others) [4]. Considering the long history of MMs, multiple development guidelines evolved over time that focus on these decisive processes and can be regarded as supportive instruments for MM development. [9] present the most established standard for the development of MMs: a six-step generic phase model comprising scope, design, populate, test, deploy, and maintain. A different procedure model is postulated by [8], who strongly focus on a design science research approach. They suggest an eight-phase development approach, focusing on problem definition, comparison of existing MMs, determination of the development strategy, iterative MM development, the conception of transfer and evaluation, implementation of transfer media, evaluation, and rejection of MM. [7] set up general design principles (principles of form and function) for the development of useful MMs. A framework for the characterization of existing MMs is presented by [15]. In order to create sound and widely accepted MMs, he proposes two "maturity model cycles". Based on a development cycle, focusing on a developer's perspective and an application cycle, focusing on a user's perspective, he identifies different decision parameters MM developers should take into account (Fig. 2) [15].

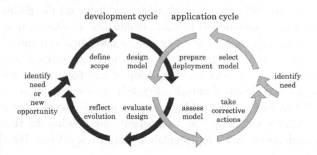

**Fig. 2.** Development and application cycle of maturity models (in accordance with [15])

Summarizing, many approaches can support researchers in creating MMs. However, these guidelines are limited in their interpretability and validity, as they do not provide concrete terminology specifications or structural concept models. Consequently, many models were built following these recommendations, but they still differ in the terminology used, their descriptive principles, the extent of provided information about factors, and the factors' influence on the degree of maturity [7].

### 2.3  Criticism and Inconsistencies of Maturity Models

In spite of their salient popularity, there are also critical voices regarding the scientific implications and the practical applicability of MMs. From a scientific point of view, [7] criticize a lack of empirical research foundation during the development process. This in turn, often leads to a simple copy of existing model structures (i.e., five-staged-MMs) without considering the conceptual suitability for the given context. Furthermore, [16] mention the lack of validation when selecting factors or dimensions for the model as well as the linear course of maturation. Another aspect is the missing operationalization of maturity measurements which impedes replication of an evaluation. Similarly, [17] argue that a simple demonstration of a gap (as done in many MMs) is not enough. Only understanding cause and effect can help to guide action. Otherwise these models might convey the impression of "falsified certainty" to their users [18]. A common promise of MMs is an increase in competitiveness, effectiveness and efficiency in a specific domain or a general improvement of constitution. However, MMs lack a clear description and definition of these concepts in their conceptual grounding, making them theoretical constructs but not applicable models for users (i.e., SMEs).

[19] summarize shortcomings of MMs from a practical perspective. They state that MMs are often inflexible, although a high flexibility is required. Similar to [17], they argue that MMs focus on identifying gaps and raising awareness towards a specific topic, but enterprises are in need of concrete recommendations for action. Furthermore,

these models are disciplinary, impractical, and overwhelming for many enterprises, especially for SMEs where a corresponding executive management level is missing.

However, not only the application and general structure of models is a topic of criticism. Inconsistent terminology of the models' concepts plays a major role in MM research. When developing new MMs, developers tend to invent new titles for common MM approaches in order to stand out from the plethora of already existing MM terms. For instance, designations like "Maturity Model", "Assessment Model", "Roadmap", "Maturity Framework", "Maturity Matrix", "Guide to Maturity", and "Excellence Model" are synonyms for the concept of an MM. Inconsistent terminology used within MMs, indirectly results in an inflation of similar MMs, as these models will not be identified as identical or at least similar approaches. This inconsistent terminology may cause, among other problems, two different semantic-syntax errors between MMs: (a) developers use the same terminology for maturity concepts, but each concept has a different interpretation (e.g., homonyms), and (b) developers address the same concept but label it in a different way (e.g., synonyms). For instance, to describe the field of interest an MM is applied to, MMs use different terms: "domain", "area", or "dimension". But not only the terminology, also the relationships between these concepts remain unclear. There rarely is a standardized definition framework of concepts and relationships. Although there exists a meta model for project management competence models, it is only available in German and focuses on the broader application context, not on the maturity model itself [20]. In conclusion, these inconsistencies represent a research gap as they lead to a situation where a comparison of existing MMs is almost impossible due to a lack of understanding what is actually provided.

## 3  A Meta Model for Staged Maturity Models

A recent study revealed that almost all scientific and many consultancy MMs (in the field of Industrial Internet) are still not being used or are even unknown in business practice, although potential applicants stated a need for and interest in these models in general [21]. As this discrepancy comes as a surprise, we assume a weak point either in the development or application of MMs (Fig. 2); otherwise, the reluctant use in praxis is not explicable. A possible explanation for this phenomenon may be located in the different interpretations of MMs' concepts on both sides of stakeholders. Developers may use concepts and relationships that are interpreted differently by model applicants and by other developers in the same field of research. As a result, possible applicants as well as researchers misinterpret an MM's structure and concepts. In other words, syntax and semantics vary across MMs, which is why, on the one hand, companies (as applicants) do not use or apply the models, as they simply do not understand their structure and effects. On the other hand, researchers tend to develop even more and new MMs, as they do not recognize existing models as similar or comparable MM approaches (i.e., from 2016 to 2018, 18 new MMs had been developed in the domain of Industry 4.0 [21]). What is needed is an overarching, holistic conceptual framework that can unify and standardize the individual objectives and goals. By focusing on the developer's perspective in this paper, the consistency of existing models can be validated, and future models can be developed in a rigorous way, which will then be the foundation for a sound assessment of models later on. A Meta Model, as "a model of models" [22], is an approach that is able to meet the above-mentioned requirements. Originating from software engineering, it can be understood as a model specifying underlying models that are considered instantiations of the meta model. The meta model itself is instantiated from a meta model [23]. In many cases, the meta meta model specifies a subset of the modeling language UML. A meta model typically represents the language (linguistic) and/or structure (ontological) of the underlying (that is, the subordinate) models [24]. It is used as an abstract description of (1) the unification of concepts that are part of the model, (2) the specifications and definition of concepts, and (3) the specifications and definition of concepts. Thus, multiple valid models can be instances from the same meta model. The schematic meta-modeling approach for MMs is shown in Fig. 3. On the top layer (M2), the developed meta model is located. It specifies the underlying MM on M1. Every concept on M1 has to adhere to a type concept specified on M2. Please note that the MM on M1 is, in principle, generally valid for all enterprises. It specifies the ranges and used concepts for a later assessment. The developer creates an MM type on M1 (according to the meta model on M2), which is "instantiated" on M0. On the M0 level, the "instantiated" and applied MM characterizes a concrete enterprise. This can be done by the user (the person who applies a constructed MM onto an enterprise).

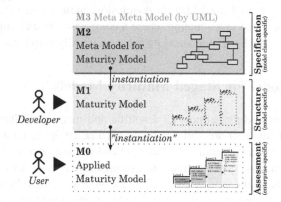

**Fig. 3.** Schematic overview of a meta model for MMs (own illustration)

With a detailed meta model for MMs, different MMs can be regarded as instances of it, leading to common semantics and syntaxes between those models. Only by providing a unified meta model ("specification" in Fig. 3), that reveals concepts, relations and entities, will the developer be able to develop a rigorous and logical MM through instantiation ("structure" in Fig. 3). Our research can therefore contribute fundamentally to the development of future staged MMs in all areas, as its structure on the M1 level and its instantiation on the M0 level are directly interdependent and thus decisive for the success or failure of a maturity measurement in a company.

However, compared to classical meta-modeling, where the M1 model concepts serve as types for M0 level instances, here, the instantiation of M0 from M1 must be interpreted differently. During assessment (the process that creates the M0 instances), only some of the concepts from the M1 level are instantiated with "values" that ultimately (typically by calculation) yield the resulting maturity level for the assessed enterprise.

## 4 Meta Model Development and Concepts

The development of the Meta Model for Maturity Models (*4M*) was based on a study of the most common and representative staged MMs. In order to elaborate sufficient meta model elements that are valid for a broad class of staged MMs, an analysis of different staged MMs, their development and their structure was conducted to summarize and analyze existing concepts, their relationships as well as their multiplicities and instantiations. As a result, universally applicable meta concepts were found and related to each other. For that, we followed an opportunistic approach: we identified the necessary meta model concepts (and their relations) by reduction and selection via decision criteria based on the available content of the investigated MMs. The resulting meta model in Fig. 4 and Table 1 show the M2 level structure as a conceptual and formal description of an MM, whose instances (on M1 level) reflect the actual concepts and interrelations within various staged MMs investigated in our study (see also Sect. 5).

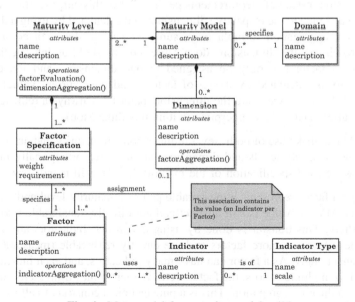

**Fig. 4.** Meta model for maturity models: *4M*

The staged structure of MMs is built on common assumptions, which influenced the meta model's design:

1. A *maturity model* is typically developed within a *domain,* as it represents a path of growth for a specific field of interest.
2. An MM consists of several *maturity levels* (i.e., $L_1$–$L_5$), which have an ascending order and are intended to represent the improvement path of an object's ability.
3. The MM can (but does not have to) be divided into *dimensions* (i.e., $D_1$–$D_5$). These dimensions divide the object of study into fields of interest, mostly depending on the domain in which the model is applied. This subdivision serves the possibility of an incremental measurement of maturity in a certain area.
4. *Factors* are properties of the maturity level and (if available) are grouped in dimensions. There are two possible ways of maturity determination by factors:
    a. In the first approach, the respective maturity level is specified by checking the threshold of certain (related) factors that are applied. Due to the fact that a factor could be used on several levels (however, with different values per level), the *factor specification,* which assigns the concrete expected value of a factor per maturity level, is used between both. Thus, e.g., level $L_1$ could use factor $f$ with the factor specification $f_{L1}$ while level $L_2$ is still able to use $f$ as well (then with its own factor specification $f_{L2}$). This is used to express evolving enterprise maturity via growing requirements per level of the same factor.
    b. Second, there is the possibility that the maturity level can be determined per dimension instead of "requirements per level". For this purpose, the factors need to be assigned to the respective dimensions and calculated by using a dimension-specific aggregation formula (e.g., sum, average, median). In contrast to the approach *(a)*, the dimensions do not use any threshold as intermediate value. Thus, a factor can only be assigned to one dimension, and the dimension maturity is calculated by its set of factors (and their current value). A factor cannot be used twice, and the dimension maturity is always a representation of the current state of the enterprise (within this dimension).

The MM can make use of both, several dimensions of maturity and an overall level maturity since maturity levels and dimensions are modeled orthogonally in the meta model. However, the specification of the maturity level is still mandatory.

5. Although a factor represents a measurable part of a maturity level and a dimension within an MM, its value is still abstract and not directly transferable into an object under study. This transfer is done by using *indicators*. Indicators are measurable properties of one or more factors and are directly retrievable (measurable) for an object under study. As a factor can have many indicators, and each indicator can be relevant for multiple factors, the factors retrieve their values from their indicators by using an indicator aggregation. This is a pure technical construct to allow the shared usage of indicators by different factors. However, the aggregation functions (e.g., sum, average, median) are assigned to the factor to yield its value.
6. The indicator measurement is done on the basis of *indicator types*. This could be, e.g., Likert, ordinal, or cardinal scales, counting or index values.

**Table 1.** Definition of the meta model's concepts

| Concept | Definition |
|---|---|
| Maturity model | Model for the assessment of the relative fulfillment or ability (maturity) of an organizational in a *domain*; can be specified by *dimensions* and consists of several *maturity levels* |
| Domain | Field of interest on which the *maturity model* is developed |
| Dimension | Subdivision of an organizational structure into areas of interest and results from the context of a *maturity model* applied; can aggregate *factors* related to it |
| Factor | Property of the organization, which represents the object/area/process of investigation; used by one or more *maturity level* and can be related to a *dimension* within an organization |
| Factor specification | Technical and foundational requirement construct for determining the *maturity level;* acts as the *maturity level*'s individual expression of a *factor* (needed due to multi-usage of factors) |
| Indicator | Measurable property of one or more *factors* within an organization; uses an *indicator type* for measurement |
| Indicator type | Measuring method for determining of the value of the *indicator* |
| Maturity level | Rank of the organizational maturity that results from factor evaluation by using the *factor specification* (see *4.a*) or aggregation of a dimension's related factors (see *4.b*); subdivides the *maturity model* and represents a relative degree of organizational ability/maturity |

## 5  Meta Model Application and Discussion

The final meta model with its concepts can be used to develop the initial-staged MM. The defined elements (concepts) and their relationships are regarded as best practices in MM development and are practically needed concepts in order to build a functioning staged MM. Although one could decide for several variations, the already discovered concepts in the meta model are the sum of (extracted) expert knowledge from previous MMs. Thus, the non-existence of any part of the meta model in an actual MM is neither considered as an issue in the meta model nor is the MM regarded as incorrect. Rather, the interpretation is that the actual MM lacks a feature that is typically used by other MMs, and it could potentially be improved with such. Further, the relatively small amount of meta concepts is not necessarily a drawback, since the meta model only contains the most powerful concepts found. Despite the few concepts, it provides a strong, defined, and universal framework for a whole class of staged MMs.

Table 2 summarizes an analysis of currently existing and applicable staged MMs regarding the mapping between the developed meta model and the concepts used. The selected MMs represent a sample from different domains, years, and development approaches. The BPMM and CMMI are representatives of the most famous MMs developed [14, 25]. Leyh et al. [26], Gökalp et al. [27], Schumacher et al. [28], and Luftman [29] are representatives of scientific MM approaches from different years.

**Table 2.** Comparison of existing MMs with the meta model concepts (■ concept defined; ◨ concept mentioned; □ concept mentioned implicitly; – concept not available)

| Meta model concept | [25] | [14] | [26] | [27] | [28] | [29] |
|---|---|---|---|---|---|---|
| Maturity model | ■ | ■ | ■ | ■ | ■ | ■ |
| Domain | ■ | ■ | ■ | ■ | ■ | ■ |
| Maturity level | ■ | ■ | ■ | ■ | – | ■ |
| Dimension | – | ■ | ■ | ■ | ■ | ■ |
| Factor | ■ | ■ | □ | ◨ | ■ | ■ |
| Indicator | ■ | ■ | ◨ | – | ◨ | – |
| Indicator type | □ | □ | ◨ | – | ■ | ■ |
| Factor specification | – | – | ■ | □ | ■ | – |

From the analysis of existing MMs, we conclude that very few models have in-depth explanations of all the concepts and relationships used. However, almost every examined model fulfills common concepts like the MM's name, the domain in which it is located, as well as a description of its respective maturity levels (except one). The concepts' names "factor" and "indicator" are not used within the models. Although [27] use the term "indicators", the definition matches the *4M*-concept of a factor. The *4M*-concept of "indicator" is not further described in their model. In general, the low-level concepts (like, e.g., indicator) are rarely specified, possibly due to abstraction from the actual calculation of a maturity level. When it comes to the interpretation of the examined concepts and relationships of factors, indicators, and requirements, no MM can be regarded as an exact instantiation of our meta model, as not every concept is present. There is often a lack of information in the available publications about factors and indicators, which are subject to further calculations, or information on which requirements can be used to derive the maturity level. The mere mentioning of concepts allows conclusions to be drawn about the fact that the authors have basically dealt with the respective concepts, but the relationships between them remain undefined.

Possible, general reasons for this phenomenon could be the length of the publications in which the MMs are presented. Conference papers are often too short to describe a comprehensive presentation of all underlying assumptions. Another reason could be that papers do not describe MMs for application purposes, but rather focus on their contribution. However, we do not consider existing staged MMs that do not match the meta model as incorrect. The meta model, as a conceptual orientation, could help other researchers or developers to understand and interpret the respective intention and improves the developer's cycle of MM development. We claim that this will help these models to overcome their ivory tower. The rather few but strong concepts defined in the meta model are a core skeleton of staged MMs that may lead both the development as well as the understanding of MMs.

Although we have built our meta model on a broad analysis of existing models, our research has limitations. Thus, our meta model approach is only valid for staged models and therefore cannot explain other types of MMs (continuous or focus area MMs). In addition, the meta model initially only considers the development cycle and must be further developed for the application cycle. However, as [15] proposed, both cycles should not be analyzed concurrently anyway, as they differ in their requirements. To this point, we have been able to show with the current approach that the consistency and concepts of existing MMs are often not entirely described in the development cycle. It will be the focus of our future work to concentrate on the application cycle and to compare concepts of assessment with provided concepts in existing MMs.

## 6 Conclusions

In this paper, a meta model for MMs was introduced, which can be used for a standardized and consistent development of MMs. The related concepts, elements, and their relationships were explained and specified in detail. This was done by the analysis of relevant literature that introduces staged MMs and by extracting their core concepts, including their syntax and semantics. Further, the final *4M* was evaluated against several MMs from the research literature showing that the majority of MMs lack in the exact specification of their elements and relationships. This uncertainty and divergence in MM specifications often lead to inconsistent applications and implications derived from their application. The presented *4M* is therefore beneficial regarding consistent MM development and comparison. The *4M*, together with its defined concepts and relationships, is a compact but powerful tool for MM developers for initial development and evaluation of their work, as well as to be consistent with related work and the staged MM semantics in general. However, the *4M* only covers the structural part of an instantiated MM. Consideration of the assessment part as an integrated aspect of the *4M* would be valuable for the MM user. We therefore intend to develop the assessment aspect in the next research step. Also, we do not claim completeness regarding the concepts in the *4M* since we only introduced the concepts that are used by many different MMs. Additional concepts could be introduced; however, we strived for simplicity and usability instead of a complex and over specified meta model. The *4M* is only applicable for staged MMs; thus, a meta model for other MM types (e.g., continuous MMs) has to be constructed separately.

## References

1. Bley, K., Schön, H.: A role-based maturity model for digital relevance. In: Pappas, I.O., Mikalef, P., Dwivedi, Y.K., Jaccheri, L., Krogstie, J., Mäntymäki, M. (eds.) I3E 2019. LNCS, vol. 11701, pp. 738–744. Springer, Cham (2019). https://doi.org/10.1007/978-3-030-29374-1_60
2. Simpson, J.A., Weiner, E.S.C.: The Oxford English Dictionary. Clarendon, Oxford (1989)
3. Kühne, T.: Matters of (meta-) modeling. Softw. Syst. Model. 5, 369–385 (2006)
4. Wendler, R.: The maturity of maturity model research: a systematic mapping study. Inf. Softw. Technol. 54, 1317–1339 (2012)

348 K. Bley et al.

5. Isoherranen, V., Karkkainen, M.K., Kess, P.: Operational excellence driven by process maturity reviews: a case study of the ABB corporation. In: 2015 IEEE International Conference on Industrial Engineering and Engineering Management (IEEM), pp. 1372–1376 (2015)

6. Tarhan, A., Turetken, O., Reijers, H.A.: Business process maturity models: a systematic literature review. Inf. Softw. Technol. **75**, 122–134 (2016)

7. Pöppelbuß, J., Röglinger, M.: What makes a useful maturity model? A framework of general design principles for maturity models and its demonstration in business process management. In: Proceedings of the 19th European Conference on Information Systems (ECIS) (2011)

8. Becker, J., Knackstedt, R., Pöppelbuß, J.: Developing maturity models for IT management. Bus. Inf. Syst. Eng. **1**, 213–222 (2009)

9. De Bruin, T., Freeze, R., Kaulkarni, U., Rosemann, M.: Understanding the main phases of developing a maturity assessment model. In: 16th Australasian Conference on Information Systems (ACIS) (2005)

10. Fraser, P., Moultrie, J., Gregory, M.: The use of maturity models/grids as a tool in assessing product development capability. In: IEEE International Engineering Management Conference, vol. 1, pp. 244–249 (2002)

11. Röglinger, M., Kamprath, N.: Prozessverbesserung mit Reifegradmodellen. Z Betriebswirtsch. **82**, 509–538 (2012). https://doi.org/10.1007/s11573-012-0570-3

12. Crosby, P.B.: Quality is Free: The Art of Making Quality Certain. McGraw-Hill, New York (1979)

13. Nolan, R.L.: Managing crises of data processing. Harvard Bus. Rev. **3**, 115–126 (1979)

14. Software Engineering Institute: CMMI® for Development, Version 1.3 (2010)

15. Mettler, T.: Maturity assessment models: a design science research approach. Int. J. Soc. Syst. Sci. **3**, 81 (2011)

16. Lasrado, L., Vatrapu, R., Andersen, K.: Maturity models development in IS research: a literature review. In: Proceedings of the 38th Information Systems Research Seminar in Scandinavia (IRIS 38), vol. 6 (2015)

17. Pfeffer, J., Sutton, R.I.: Knowing "what" to do is not enough: turning knowledge into action. Calif. Manag. Rev. **42**, 83–108 (1999)

18. Lahrmann, G., Marx, F., Mettler, T., Winter, R., Wortmann, F.: Inductive design of maturity models: applying the rasch algorithm for design science research. In: Jain, H., Sinha, A.P., Vitharana, P. (eds.) DESRIST 2011. LNCS, vol. 6629, pp. 176–191. Springer, Heidelberg (2011). https://doi.org/10.1007/978-3-642-20633-7_13

19. Jugdev, K., Thomas, J.: Project management maturity models: the silver bullets of competitive advantage? Proj. Manag. J. **33**, 4–14 (2002)

20. Ahlemann, F., Schroeder, C., Teuteberg, F.: Kompetenz- und Reifegradmodelle für das Projektmanagement: Grundlagen, Vergleich und Einsatz. Univ., FB Wirtschaftswiss., Organisation u. Wirtschaftsinformatik, Osnabrück (2005)

21. Felch, V., Asdecker, B., Sucky, E.: Maturity models in the age of Industry 4.0 – do the available models correspond to the needs of business practice? In: Proceedings of the 52nd Hawaii International Conference on System Sciences (HICSS), pp. 5165–5174 (2019)

22. Object Management Group: MDA Guide Version 1.0.1 (2003)

23. Object Management Group: UML Infrastructure Specification, Version 2.0 (2003)

24. Strahringer, S.: Metamodellierung als Instrument des Methodenvergleichs: eine Evaluierung am Beispiel objektorientierter Analysemethoden. Shaker, Aachen (1996)

25. Object Management Group: Business Process Maturity Model (BPMM) (2008)

26. Leyh, C., Schäffer, T., Bay, L.: The application of the maturity model SIMMI 4.0 in selected enterprises. In: Proceedings of the 23rd Americas Conference on Information Systems, (AMCIS) (2017)

27. Gökalp, E., Şener, U., Eren, P.E.: Development of an assessment model for Industry 4.0: Industry 4.0-MM. In: Mas, A., Mesquida, A., O'Connor, R.V., Rout, T., Dorling, A. (eds.) SPICE 2017. CCIS, vol. 770, pp. 128–142. Springer, Cham (2017). https://doi.org/10.1007/978-3-319-67383-7_10

28. Schumacher, A., Erol, S., Sihn, W.: A maturity model for assessing Industry 4.0 readiness and maturity of manufacturing enterprises. Procedia CIRP **52**, 161–166 (2016)

29. Luftman, J.: Assessing business-IT alignment maturity. Commun. Assoc. Inf. Syst. **4**, 52 (2000)

# Towards a Strategic Model for Safeguarding the Preservation of Business Value During Human Interactions with Information Systems

Chris D. Grobler and Thomas M. van der Merwe[(✉)] [ID]

School of Computing, University of South Africa, Science Campus,
28 Pioneer Avenue, Florida Park, Roodepoort 1709, South Africa
cdg.postman@outlook.com, vdmertm@unisa.ac.za

**Abstract.** This paper considers the dichotomy inherent in Information Systems where its introduction, for the purposes of creating new or sustaining existing business value, subsequently also inadvertently or deliberately dissipates value. We investigate root people-induced causes, delineated within a rudimentary Conceptual Technology Value Framework. To support a qualitative investigation, the framework is forthwith applied as the basis for a series of interviews within a major South African financial institution operating within the disciplines of information technology, business operations and organisational development. The constructs identified are discussed and find gestalt in an Adjusted Technology Value Model which can be used to safeguard business value against destructive HCI behaviors.

**Keywords:** Information systems · Business value · Value creation · Value Dissipation · Human computer interaction

## 1  Introduction

A topic that has been debated for many years without a clear resolution is the dualistic nature of an information system (IS) impacting on business value, where the adoption and use of an IS in an organisation as an explicit value creator, also brings about the destruction of business value [1]. In adopting a slightly dystopic view, our focus in this paper is seated within the context of the potentially negative impact that end-users have on organisations when discontinuing the use of a particular mandated IS [2], or making misuse of information within an IS that is intended to drive value realisation [3, 4].

Of the numerous studies [e.g. 5, 6] that have placed specific focus on the interactive relationships between humans and computers (HCI) and endeavoured to explain how these relationships contribute positively towards organisational objectives, none have attempted to expressly illuminate the phenomenon where human agents erode information technology enabled benefits through the consumption of IS. Although the primary cause of organisational value erosion was identified by several authors [e.g. 7, 8] to be the human agent, again, none of these authors attempted to articulate the actual IS related behavioural activities or actions executed by the human agent contributing directly to business or organisational value erosion. This is the issue that this paper seeks to investigate.

© IFIP International Federation for Information Processing 2020
Published by Springer Nature Switzerland AG 2020
M. Hattingh et al. (Eds.): I3E 2020, LNCS 12066, pp. 350–357, 2020.
https://doi.org/10.1007/978-3-030-44999-5_29

The primary research question this paper asks is: How can business value be safeguarded against destructive HCI behaviors? The primary purpose is to build a value framework from which an empirically-endorsed model can be constructed, and through which the unintended business value dissipating effects on institutions, as a direct result of end-user's misuse of IS, may be investigated and moderated.

Three secondary objectives that dictate the structure of this paper are pursued: (1) to review key characteristics from several germane models and theories relating to the business impact of HCI that maps to, and refines, a rudimentary Conceptual Technology Value Framework (CTVF), (2) to apply the CTVF as a basis for a qualitative investigation from which an Adjusted Technology Value Model (ATVM) may be derived and contextualized, and (3) to present the ATVM as a first benchmark to identify, investigate, mitigate and minimise or eliminate unintentional value destroying effects.

## 2 Background

In construction of our CTVF, key characteristics from selected germane models and theories relating to the negative business impact of HCI as they relate to our own professional experiences as end-users and IS practitioners were considered. Here it is noted that the relationship between IS use and performance is complex and therefore invites multiple theoretical approaches. Our approach is mainly inductive i.e. the CTVF we propose is not intended to be fully grounded in the literature. We simply chose to follow a bottom-up approach while maintaining a minimum level of theoretical sensitivity. An extensive review of the literature yielded the following three models that contained elements of both HCI and delinquent employee behavior which in turn provided the conceptual constructs framing the CTVF delineated in Fig. 1.

**Task-Technology Fit (TTF):** The model [9] asserts that for technology to have a positive impact on a user's performance, IS user utilisation is required, while an alignment between the characteristics of the task that the user must perform, and the technology needs to exist. In our view, the TTF supports a phenomenon where users may *unintentionally misuse* an IS if some form of misalignment between the user, enabling technology and the task that the user must perform, exists.

**Lazy User Theory (LUT):** The theory [10] moves from the premise that in fulfilling a user need, he will be biased towards those solutions that are perceived as most suitable and usable based on the lowest level of effort. The LUT presents a theoretical situation where a user, partial to a legacy IS, will favour the use of said system above that of a newly introduced system, thereby *passively disusing* the new system, regardless of its utility.

**Agency Theory (AT):** When a self-interested (agent) individual is requested (by a principal) to perform a specific task, he will be motivated by three different conditions: He will perform the task because he is forced to, or he knows he must, or he wants to [11]. AT potentially considers the phenomenon where a self-interested employee will endeavour to *actively abuse* the company's IS for personal gain, and/or, in extreme cases, *intentionally sabotage* the assets of an organisation to achieve some self-interested objective.

From the succinct review of the model/theories it is evident that the benefits realisation of IS usage is fundamentally informed by the actions and behaviours of individuals within the organisational context. Within the context of systems thinking, the structure of a system is constituted by the systemic interrelationships between feedback loops, concluding that said structure constitute the primary driver for a system's behaviour [12]. Within our CTVF, two feedback loops are proposed. The *degree of control* loop attempts to control both quiescent and recalcitrant user behaviour during system usage, while the *degree of influence* loop endeavours to influence user beliefs, attitudes, and intention, towards correct and optimal system use.

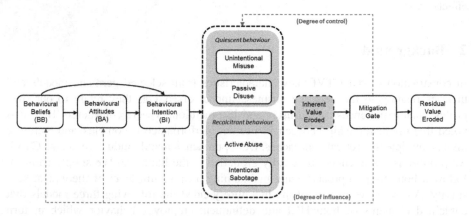

**Fig. 1.** Conceptual technology value framework

In Fig. 1, moving from left to right, the CTVF constructs are described as follows: **behavioural beliefs**, **behavioural attitude** and **behavioural intention** will be applied as in the Wixom and Todd Research Model [13], the latter which ties constructs from the user satisfaction and technology acceptance literature into a single research model. Next, **unintentional misuse** and **passive disuse** are both assumed to possess quiescent qualities. The **unintentional misuse** construct denotes actual behaviour where the user is misapplying the system, either consciously or unconsciously, due to a lack of skill or negligence. In contrast, **passive disuse** can be described as a user's passive-aggressive attitude towards having to use a system, causing the user to avoid interaction with said system. The two recalcitrant value eroding behaviour constructs describe a more sinister scenario. **Active abuse** encompasses situations where a user determinedly employs the system for personal gain or to perform unauthorised transactions. Finally, **intentional sabotage** designates the purposeful disruption or damage to a system by a disgruntled user. The outcomes of each of the actual value eroding behaviour constructs is summated into the **inherent value eroded** determinate which is a precursor to the **mitigation gate**. The latter mediates between the inherent value eroded and the residual value eroded as it attempts to moderate undesirable actioned behaviour through **system controls** and **human influence**. The final construct of **residual value eroded** defines the latent value eroded after measures had been taken to reduce the value erosive effects caused by system users.

## 3 Methodology and Results of Metadata Analysis

The data collection process comprised semi-structured interviews with a convenience sample of 31 professional and experienced employees at a major South African financial institution operating within the disciplines of information technology, business operations and organisational development. Semi-structured interviews required participants to deliberate on the CTVF constructs, their validity, significance, rankings, interrelationship and impact management. A descriptive content analysis method [14] was applied to extract themes and contradictions within the data.

Table 1 presents the results of our metadata analysis. It is evident that, on average, the participants used phrases and terms specific to the four value-eroding behaviours most, followed by the three Behavioural Constructs and the four factors comprising the mitigation of value erosion. The concept of Value Dissipation also scored highly, as did various behavioural relationships. Value Eroding Potential returned mid-range totals. By and large, participants concurred with the statement that the introduction of IS may not only create value for, but likewise inadvertently dissipate value from organisations. Participants also consistently referred to value erosion as a by-product of value creation especially within the areas of unintentional misuse and passive disuse.

**Table 1.** Most mentioned aspects by 31 participants

| KEY TERM | Unintentional Misuse | Active Abuse | Passive Disuse | Intentional Sabotage | Value Dissipation | Degree of Control | Behavioural Relationships | Behavioural Attitudes | Behavioural Beliefs | Behavioural Intention | Value Eroding Potential | Training/ Communicating | Degree of Influence | Monitoring/ Measuring | Value Leadership |
|---|---|---|---|---|---|---|---|---|---|---|---|---|---|---|---|
| TOTALS | 220 | 200 | 197 | 194 | 168 | 164 | 150 | 141 | 130 | 130 | 124 | 99 | 75 | 75 | 75 |
| AVE | 7.1 | 6.5 | 6.4 | 6.3 | 5.4 | 5.3 | 4.8 | 4.5 | 4.2 | 4.2 | 4.0 | 3.2 | 2.4 | 2.4 | 2.4 |

## 4 Findings

### 4.1 Behaviour Constructs Themes

**Unintentional Misuse:** Users may simply not be aware that they are engaging unintentional misuse: "...if you don't know what you're doing is wrong, it means in your mind what you're doing is correct and it's appropriate. So it goes hand in hand with unintentional misuse". (Participant 09). Unintentional misuse was extended to cases where individuals do not make optimal use of a system e.g. front-line completing only mandatory fields, with the role of management in correcting unintentional misuse considered important.

**Passive Disuse:** Passive disuse is perceived to be destroying value: "…that destroys value because, immediately what you have is, you have double work and you also have something that you've paid for that's not being used, so you're effectively wasting a license. So, that is definitely also dissipating value". (Participant 05). A shared consensus prevailed that passive disuse introduced numerous instances of complexity and undesirable noise into the overall IS landscape with time pressure identified as a contributing factor to users returning to familiar legacy systems. Individual passive disuse is also viewed a precursor to team passive disuse, where individuals rationalise improper behaviour and ultimately tend to share *workarounds* with their colleagues. System controls and managerial superintendence were identified as the most effective counter measures.

**Active Abuse:** Except for agreement on the pervasive nature of active abuse, participants did not agree on the extent to which active abuse eroded business value. Active abuse and intentional sabotage were perceived to be reinforcing constructs that: "… feed each other". (Participant 23). Some users may perceive themselves to be self-appointed end-user testers of production systems, and through actions of unsolicited active abuse create awareness of weaknesses and inefficiencies in a particular IS.

**Intentional Sabotage:** No evident pattern emerged. Despite the improbability of intentional sabotage, many agreed that it could possibly cause the greatest harm. One participant noted that a user's deviant belief system developed: "…when people's behavioural beliefs don't align with the values of the organisation". (Participant 27). Two participants highlighted the possibility that some users may be sabotaging systems with good intent, i.e. to draw attention to problems embedded in systems.

**Interrelationship Between the Four Constructs:** While to most participants the relationships between respectively the two quiescent behaviours and the two recalcitrant behaviours were clear, not all agreed on the existence of potential relationships crossing over between quiescent and recalcitrant constructs.

## 4.2    Mitigating Constructs Themes

**Degree of Control:** Participants described control measures as being useful in the prevention, detection and correction of undesirable behaviour, but of little value in addressing individuals' beliefs, attitudes and intentions. Preventative controls were perceived to be more desirous as well as managerial oversight and the examples they set.

**Degree of Influence:** Of paramount importance, executive leadership should positively influence the moral values of employees, to cascade down to every end-user, and which will marginalise individuals with corrupted belief systems, attitudinal problems or malicious intention. "The technology is important but without the users to drive the systems, and effectively leaders to guide the users, the unfortunate outcome would be a failed IS". (Interviewee 10).

## 5   Discussion and Adjusted Technology Value Model

While all the framework constructs were qualitatively endorsed, various arguments exist for, and against relationships, or not. Comparing the CTVF (Fig. 1) to the proposed ATVM (Fig. 2), it is evident that participants were not in agreement as to the flow of the former, the most common view suggesting that while there appears to be a tendency for Behavioural Beliefs and Behavioural Attitudes to display a closer relationship with the quiescent behaviours, and Behavioural Intention, in turn, to display a closer relationship with the recalcitrant behaviours, ultimately, any one may function as a precursor to any one of the four value eroding behaviours. Moving on to the relationships between the four value-eroding behaviours, several participants argued against the existence of any kind of interrelationship between the constructs while others provided unique examples of instances where a specific primary behaviour could trigger a secondary behaviour.

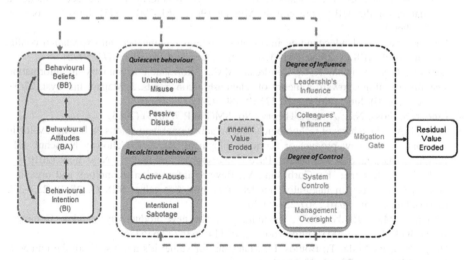

**Fig. 2.** Adjusted technology value model

While all four the mitigating constructs were perceived to be valid, the two Degree of Control constructs, were seen to be more effective in mitigating value eroding behaviour, while the two Degree of Influence constructs were seen to be less effective yet not as costly in the prevention of behaviours that destroyed business value.

The results from the primary research and ensuing ATVM are consistent with the updated DeLone and McLean Model [15] in that both utilization and user attitudes toward technology were shown to be important. The research also supported the *Intention to Use* construct as it further elucidated the behavioural intent of end-users, occasioning IS abuse. The research furthermore confirmed the problem of increased organisational spent on IT with little realisation or insufficient justification on how, why and when IS investments create business value [16, 17]. In a similar vein, the research supported the literature by explicating the continued challenge that exists within organisations to measure and communicate IT value, noting that while many IT metrics measure performance, they do not measure actual value [18]. The investigation also confirmed the contributions made by several authors maintaining that the primary challenges experienced by technology driven organisations lied with the human element [e.g. 7, 8].

In concluding, the ATVF provides a clear articulation of the actual IS related behavioural activities or actions executed by the human agent contributing directly to business or organisational value erosion and offers a model on how business value can be safeguarded against destructive HCI behaviors. Future studies should focus on refining and validating the proposed ATVM.

# References

1. Silver, M.S., Markus, M.L., Beath, C.M.: The information technology interaction model: a foundation for the MBA core course. MIS Q. **19**(3), 361–390 (1995). https://doi.org/10. 2307/249600
2. Bhattacherjee, A.: Understanding information systems continuance: an expectation confirmation model. MIS Q. **25**(3), 351–370 (2001). https://doi.org/10.2307/3250921
3. Dawson, G.S., Watson, R.T., Boudreau, M.C.: Information asymmetry in information systems consulting: toward a theory of relationship constraints. J. Manag. Inf. Syst. **27**(3), 143–178 (2010). https://doi.org/10.2753/MIS0742-1222270306
4. Linder, S., Foss, N.J.: Agency Theory (No. SMG WP 7/2013) (2013)
5. Davis, E.A.: The effects of technological and organizational innovations on business value in the context of a new product or service deployment. (L. J. S. Calloway Namchul, Ed.) ProQuest Dissertations and Theses. Pace University, United States – New York (2010)
6. Melville, N., Kraemer, K., Gurbaxani, V.: Review: information technology and organizational performance: an integrative model of IT business value. MIS Q. **28**(2), 283–322 (2004). https://doi.org/10.2307/25148636
7. Anderson, M.C., Banker, R.D., Ravindran, S.: The new productivity paradox. Commun. ACM **46**(3), 91–94 (2003). https://doi.org/10.1145/636772.636776
8. Haspeslagh, P., Noda, T., Boulos, F.: Managing for value: it's not just about the numbers. Harvard Bus. Rev. **79**, 65–73 (2001)
9. Goodhue, B.D.L., Thompson, R.L.: Task-technology fit and individual performance. MIS Q. **19**(2), 213–236 (1995). https://doi.org/10.2307/249689
10. Tétard, F., Collan, M.: Lazy user theory: a dynamic model to understand user selection of products and services. In: Proceedings of the 42nd Hawaii International Conference on System Sciences (2009)
11. Gurbaxani, V., Whang, S.: The impact of information systems on organizations and markets. Commun. ACM **34**(1), 59–73 (1991). https://doi.org/10.1145/99977.99990
12. Flood, R.L.: The relationship of 'systems thinking' to action research. Syst. Pract. Action Res. **23**(4), 269–284 (2010)

13. Wixom, B.H., Todd, P.A.: A theoretical integration of user satisfaction and technology acceptance. Inf. Syst. Res. **16**(1), 85–102 (2005). https://doi.org/10.1287/isre.1050.0042
14. Oates, B.J.: Researching Information Systems and Computing. Sage Publications, London (2006)
15. Urbach, N., Müller, B.: The updated DeLone and McLean model of information systems success. In: Dwivedi, Y.K., Wade, M.R., Schneberger, S.L. (eds.) Information Systems Theory: Explaining and Predicting Our Digital Society, vol. 28, pp. 1–18. Springer, New York (2012). https://doi.org/10.1007/978-1-4419-6108-2_1
16. Soh, C., Markus, M.: How IT creates business value: a process theory synthesis. In: ICIS (1995)
17. Schryen, G.: Revisiting IS business value research: what we already know, what we still need to know, and how we can get there. Eur. J. Inf. Syst. **22**, 139–169 (2013). https://doi. org/10.1057/ejis.2012.45
18. Mitra, S., Sambamurthy, V., Westerman, G.: Measuring IT performance and communicating value. MIS Q. Exec. **10**(1), 47–60 (2011)

# How to Measure Digitalization? A Critical Evaluation of Digital Maturity Models

Tristan Thordsen[✉], Matthias Murawski, and Markus Bick

ESCP Business School Berlin, Berlin, Germany
{tthordsen,mmurawski,mbick}@escpeurope.eu

**Abstract.** To preserve competitive advantage in a more and more digitalized environment, today's organizations seek to assess their level of digital maturity. Given this particular practical relevance, a plethora of digital maturity models, designed to asses a company's digital status quo, has emerged over the past few years. Largely developed and published by practitioners, the academic value of these models remains obviously unclear. To shed light on their value in a broader sense, in this paper we critically evaluate 17 existing digital maturity models – identified through a systematic literature search (2011–2019) – with regard to their validity of measurement. We base our evaluation on established academic criteria, such as generalizability or theory-based interpretation, that we apply in a qualitative content analysis to these models. Our analysis shows that most of the identified models do not conform to the established evaluation criteria. Based on these insights, we derive a detailed research agenda and suggest respective research questions and strategies.

**Keywords:** Digital maturity models · Measurement · Research agenda

## 1 Introduction

If we believe in the press, consultancies, and the majority of researchers, being 'digital' is paramount for companies to stay competitive in today's business world. The goal is to seize the opportunities of the ongoing digital transformation [1]. To evaluate the status quo of a company's digitalization and to provide guidance for future investments, latest IS literature has established the term digital maturity. Following Chanias and Hess, digital maturity is "the status of a company's digital transformation" – it describes "what a company has already achieved with regard to transformation efforts" [2]. Here, efforts include implemented changes from an operational point of view as well as acquired capabilities regarding the mastering of the transformation process. In this context, given the high practical relevance of the topic, a great variety of so-called digital maturity models (DMMs) has emerged in the past few years. According to Mettler [3] this trend will prevail as the demand for maturity models will further increase.

Largely developed and published by consultancies in a practical setting, DMMs on the one hand aim at measuring the current level of a company's digitalization, on the other hand at providing a model path to digital maturity. However, so far, due to their practical nature and the lack of external quality assessments such as peer reviews, the

© IFIP International Federation for Information Processing 2020
Published by Springer Nature Switzerland AG 2020
M. Hattingh et al. (Eds.): I3E 2020, LNCS 12066, pp. 358–369, 2020.
https://doi.org/10.1007/978-3-030-44999-5_30

generalizability and consistency of DMMs remains largely unclear. The constant publication of new maturity models for similar fields of application suggests a certain arbitrariness and does not contribute to the clarification of this case.

An analysis of corresponding literature of this field shows that the academic community also does not yet provide comprehensive answers to these questions. Although there are scholars attempting to measure digitalization based on more concrete metrics (e.g. [4]), these metrics are however neither comprehensive nor generalizable.

To provide not only practical but also substantial theoretical value, DMMs should conform to several academic requirements such as a common understanding of their underlying concepts. However, although the terms digital and digitalization of a company exist for many years already, they still remain abstract. Related concepts are context-dependent (e.g., society, company, individual) and vary according to the perspectives on the topic (e.g., human, process, technology). This lack of a common and concrete definition leads to a certain ambiguity already when it comes to the basic task of DMMs: measuring a company's level of digitalization. In this context, questions arise such as:

What are relevant variables to measure digitalization? How can they be quantified? How can a certain comparability between companies be ensured? How can we investigate if a certain level of digitalization affects the performance of a company?

Unfortunately, the authors of existing models only rarely reveal their motivation behind the procedures and results of their measurement [5].

Given their high practical relevance and popularity, we have set out to evaluate existing DMMs with regard to their conformity to above mentioned quality standards and thus theoretical value. Determining the status quo of digitalization is the main goal of DMMs. Without such an assessment, DMMs cannot provide a comprehensive path to higher levels of maturity. We thus focus in our analysis on the quality of measurement of a company's digitalization carried out by the single models. While doing so, we follow the request for further scholarly inquiry on digital maturity, in order to contribute to a more profound understanding of the ongoing sociotechnical phenomenon of digital transformation [6]. Furthermore, this work is in line with existing works who are calling for a deeper understanding, analysis and differentiation of IS maturity models and their usefulness for practitioners [7, 8]. With our undertaking we also answer the call to identify and remedy shortcomings of existing maturity models [5]. The research question we have set out to answer is:

*To what extent do DMMs respect quality standards in their measurement of a company's degree of digitalization?*

To answer the research question, we have selected established measurement criteria as basis for the evaluation of the DMMs [9]. In this paper, we will first provide a definition and background information regarding DMMs. Then, we identify quality criteria for the process of measurement and derive a catalogue of requirements from established literature. Based on this catalogue, we will evaluate and compare relevant DMMs identified through a systematic literature search. Finally, after a discussion of this evaluation, we propose a research agenda to remedy shortcomings of existing maturity models and provide guidance for future research.

## 2   Theoretical Background

### 2.1   Digital Maturity Models

The term maturity can be defined as "the ability to respond to the environment in an appropriate manner through management practices" [10]. According to Scott and Bruce maturity with regards to an organization is a "reflection of the appropriateness of its measurement and management practices in the context of its strategic objectives and in response to environmental change" [11]. Rosemann and de Bruin describe maturity more pragmatically as "a measure to evaluate the capabilities of an organization in regard to a certain discipline" [12, p. 2]. Scholars agree that the organization's reaction to its external environment is generally learned rather than instinctive. However, the maturity of an organization does not necessarily relate to its age.

The evaluation of a firm's maturity marks one of the key points in the process of achieving a higher level of organizational performance [11]. Defining and assessing the maturity of different types of organizational resources allows organizations to evaluate their capabilities with respect to different business areas. In this context, for example, the maturity of certain organizational processes, objects or technologies can be the focus of such a reflection. Based on this concept, maturity models are multistage frameworks to describe a typical path in the development of organizational capabilities [12]. Here, the different levels are conceptualized in terms of evolutionary stages [13]. Maturity models can be described as normative reference models. In general, they are applied in organizations in order to assess the current status quo of a set of capabilities, to derive measures for improvement and prioritize them accordingly [1]. Through a set of benchmark variables and indicators for each stage, the matrix frameworks offer a possibility to make the progress of an object of interest towards a desired state tangible [14]. The relationship between maturity and organizational performance is properly understood, e.g. higher maturity leads to higher performance [15].

Given the simplistic character of maturity models and their practical value, several frameworks have emerged over the last decades across all disciplines [8]. Most recently, in the context of digitization, researchers and practitioners have set out to assess the digital maturity of organizations [2].

Despite their relevance and popularity in various management disciplines, the development and application of maturity models still bears a number of shortcomings [16]. The most prominent point of criticism concerns the poor theoretical basis and empirical evidence of maturity models [17]. Furthermore, de Bruin et al. claim that particularly limited documentation on the development of the maturity model may contribute to the lack of validity and rigor [19]. In response, IS researchers have increasingly set out to determine guidelines for the development of maturity models that are intended to bolster more rigorous design processes [18]. However, regarding the measurement procedures of maturity models, existing academic literature does not yet provide specific quality criteria. In the following, we have thus set out to derive a set of requirements for that purpose based on established literature in the field.

## 2.2   Criteria of a Valid Measurement Process

The procedure of measurement can be considered as one of the main components of the research process itself [19]. Ferris provides a comprehensive definition of the term measurement: "It is an empirical process, using an instrument, effecting a rigorous and objective mapping of an observable into a category in a model of the observable that meaningfully distinguishes the manifestation from other possible and distinguishable manifestations [22, p. 101]."

The quality of measurement is determined by its validity. The concept of validity refers to the substance, the proximity to the truth, of inferences made when justifying and interpreting observed scores. The validity of measurement is evaluated through the underlying assertions, building a complex net of arguments to back up the findings. The judgement about validity is thus made based on so-called validity arguments [19]. According to the Standards for Educational and Psychological Testing "validity is the most important consideration in test evaluation" [20]. However, Kane points out that like many virtues, it is more honored than practised [24]. Therefore, Kane et al. have developed a set of requirements designed to warrant a certain level of validity in performance measurement [9].

The five requirements are: (1) Observation, (2) Generalizability, (3) Theory-based Interpretation, (4) Exploration, and (5) Implication [9, 21, 22]. Brühl offers an updated and comprehensive overview of these criteria. After having consulted additional literature in this field, as suggested by Becker et al. [4], we have chosen the five guidelines defined by Kane et al. and Brühl as theoretical foundation and thus as the basis for our argument [19, 25]. The requirements catalogue for a valid measurement process in DMMs is the following:

**Observation:** This argument ensures that the measurement of a single indicator is in line with the predefined measurement procedure [19]. In other words, this requirement makes sure that on the one hand, the appropriate indicator for the subject matter is measured and on the other hand, that it is measured correctly. In this context, the target domain needs to be defined first. The target domain designates the full range of performances actually observed and included in the interpretation. It differs from a wider range of observations that is not subject to interpretation. A target's expected score over all possible performances in the target domain is defined as the target score.To determine the target domain and lay the foundation for the target score, the definition of the subject matter to be interpreted should be as specific as possible [9]. As we have already pointed out, the target domain of interest with regard to a company's digitalization tends to be very broad. Central points of evaluation for the DMMs derived from the argument of observation here are thus:

- Definition of the phenomenon
- Definition of target domain
- Predefined measurement procedure to determine target scores.

**Generalizability:** This requirement constitutes in a statistical generalization. Researchers conclude from the observed target score based on actual performance on all expected scores of similar tasks of the target domain. In this context, it is assumed that observed scores are "based on random or at least representative samples" [9]. It is thus implied that a certain measurement is valid at any point of time; all context-specific factors are abandoned [19]. For this procedure, the measurement needs to involve a sample of performances from the target domain. Generalizability increases as the sample of independent observations increases. Also, standardization of the assessment procedure tends to improve the generalizability of the scores. This argument leads us to a set of two evaluation criteria for the DMMs:

- Measurement approach
- Sample size of independent observations
- Degree of standardization in the measurement procedure.

**Theory-Based Interpretation:** This argument stresses that measurement requires a sound theoretical framework. This means that every single indicator should have a 'theoretical' connection to the overall construct [19]. Assumptions that are made need to be backed up by corresponding theory. Given the practical setting the DMMs largely stem from, we will focus in our evaluation on a single key point:

- Theoretical basis of the model/measurement procedure.

**Extrapolation:** This concept is important for scenarios in which the measured construct is put into relation with other constructs [19]. An example here could be that the level of digital maturity identified by the DMM is put in relation with the performance or competitiveness of a company. In this context, especially the plausibility of inferences is of importance to guarantee the validity of the measurement. With regards to extrapolation we thus focus on:

- Assumed connections between maturity level and other constructs
- Plausibility of inferences to argument for such a relationship.

**Implications:** This criterion is relevant if decisions are to be made based on the measured construct [19]. Here, again the transparency and plausibility of inferences made to justify these decisions are key. A thorough chain of arguments is necessary to back up the path from the initial status quo of digitalization that is measured towards higher levels of digital maturity. For this argument, we thus focus on:

- Justification of steps on the path towards maturity.

With regards to the design of our evaluation and comparison of the DMMs we follow Becker et al.'s established work in the field of IT maturity models [5]. We will take these criteria as the basis for evaluating the DMMs identified through the next step (see Sect. 3.2).

# 3  Research Design

## 3.1  Literature Review for Selecting Digital Maturity Models

Vom Brocke et al. state that the searching process of the literature review "must be comprehensibly described" so that "readers can assess the exhaustiveness of the review and other scholars can more confidently (re)use the results in their own research [23]." In this context, researchers of the IS field suggest a systematic and structured way of identifying and reviewing the literature [24].

We searched through a 8-year period (2011 to 2019) in ten leading IS journals, five major IS conferences and two additional databases (Business Source Premier and Google Scholar). The chosen timeframe appears to be especially relevant as in 2011 the first so called DMM was published by a consultancy. The outlets and databases have been selected based on the experience reported by [12] who have investigated existing IS maturity models.

The search terms used in our systematic review were constructed based on the PICO criteria (Population, Intervention, Comparison and Outcomes). These criteria are usually applied as guidelines in the medical field to frame the research question by identifying keywords and formulating search strings. Kitchenham and Charters deem the PICO criteria as particularly suitable when conducting a systematic review in the academic context of Information Systems [25]. In addition to deriving major search terms through PICO, we identified synonyms and alternative spellings for these keywords by consulting both experts and literature of this field [26]. As a result the following keywords were compiled: "maturity model", "stages of growth model". "stage model", "change model", "transformation model", and "grid". In addition, we framed the literature search using "Information Technology" and "Digital*". Lastly, when constructing the search strings, we used both the Boolean AND and OR to on the one hand link the major terms derived in the first step and on the other hand to incorporate these synonyms and alternative spellings in our systematic literature search. We first applied the search strings to the IS journals and conferences to check for the accuracy of the search terms. As a result, we added "grid" as search term and applied the search string to the electronic databases.

**Table 1.** Identified digital maturity models

| ID | Reference | Name of DMM | Year |
|---|---|---|---|
| 1 | [27] | Industry digitization index | 2011 |
| 2 | [28] | Digital transformation maturity | 2011 |
| 3 | [29] | Digital maturity matrix | 2012 |
| 4 | [30] | Status of digitalization | 2013 |
| 5 | [31] | Digital quotient | 2015 |
| 6 | [32] | Digital transformation index | 2015 |
| 7 | [33] | Digitale reife | 2016 |
| 8 | [6] | Stages in digital business transformation | 2016 |

(*continued*)

**Table 1.** (*continued*)

| ID | Reference | Name of DMM | Year |
|----|-----------|-------------|------|
| 9 | [34] | Digital maturity & transformation report | 2016 |
| 10 | [35] | Digital maturity model 4.0 | 2016 |
| 11 | [36] | Digital maturity model for telecom | 2016 |
| 12 | [37] | Industry 4.0 readiness | 2017 |
| 13 | [1] | Digital maturity in traditional industries | 2017 |
| 14 | [38] | Maturity assessment for industry 4.0 | 2018 |
| 15 | [39] | Digitalisierungsindex mittelstand 2018 | 2018 |
| 16 | [40] | Strategic factors enabling digital maturity | 2019 |
| 17 | [41] | Maturity model of digital transformation | 2019 |

## 3.2   Content Analysis Design

All selected DMMs (see Table 1) were subject to a content analysis. The overarching objective was to identify whether they fulfill the quality criteria defined in Sect. 2.2. We conducted a deductive category assignment in which we considered the corresponding sub-dimensions and assigned one of the following "codes" (see Table 2): A black ('filled') Harvey ball indicates that the respective sub-dimension is completely fulfilled. A black white ('partly filled') Harvey ball means that the sub-dimension is only fulfilled to some extent. A white ('blank') Harvey ball was assigned in case the sub-dimension is not fulfilled at all or not applicable to the model.

For example (see Table 2): DMM 2 has provided a definition for "digital transformation", but not for "digital transformation maturity". Therefore, the subdimension *1(a) Definition of the phenomenon* has only partially been fulfilled and marked with a black white Harvey ball.

Following established criteria of qualitative research, this procedure has been done by two researchers independently. They agreed in 94% of the cases. Remaining cases have been discussed among the authors until consensus was reached.

## 4   Findings

The findings of our analysis are summarized in Table 2. Only three of the 17 analyzed models provide definitions for digital maturity. Five models omit giving any definition of the concept of digital maturity itself or of related concepts such as digital transformation or digitization. However, all of the models offer a number of different dimensions to describe the target domain. Dimensions of the target domain are for example: customer experience, operational processes, business models and digital capabilities. Furthermore, the vast majority of the DMMs have a predefined measurement approach as well as a fairly large sample. A large stake of the models does not provide any information about the degree of standardization in the measurement undertaken. Nine of the analyzed DMMs fail to provide a theoretical basis for their work. In most cases, when assumptions with regards to connections between maturity

**Table 2** Analysis of digital maturity models - overview

| ID | 1. Observation | | | 2. Generalizability | | |
|---|---|---|---|---|---|---|
| | a) Definition of the phenomenon | b) Definition of target domain | c) Predefined measurement procedure | a) Measurement approach | b) Sample size of independent observations | c) Degree of standardization |
| 1 | ◐ | ● | ● | ○ | ● | ● |
| 2 | ◐ | ● | ● | ● | ◐ | ○ |
| 3 | ◐ | ● | ● | ● | ● | ● |
| 4 | ○ | ◐ | ● | ● | ◐ | ● |
| 5 | ○ | ◐ | ● | ○ | ● | ○ |
| 6 | ● | ◐ | ○ | ◐ | ◐ | ○ |
| 7 | ○ | ◐ | ● | ● | ● | ○ |
| 8 | ◐ | ◐ | ● | ● | ● | ● |
| 9 | ◐ | ◐ | ● | ● | ● | ● |
| 10 | ○ | ◐ | ● | ● | ● | ● |
| 11 | ◐ | ◐ | ● | ◐ | ◐ | ○ |
| 12 | ◐ | ◐ | ● | ● | ● | ● |
| 13 | ● | ◐ | ● | ● | ● | ● |
| 14 | ◐ | ● | ● | ● | ◐ | ◐ |
| 15 | ○ | ◐ | ● | ● | ● | ◐ |
| 16 | ● | ● | ● | ● | ● | ◐ |
| 17 | ◐ | ● | ● | ● | ◐ | ◐ |

| ID | 3. Theory-based Interpretation | 4. Extrapolation | | 5. Implications | Peer reviewed |
|---|---|---|---|---|---|
| | a) Theoretical basis of the model | a) Assumed connections between maturity level and other constructs | b) Plausibility of inferences to argument for such relationship | a) Justification of steps on the path towards maturity | published in a journal |
| 1 | ○ | ● | ◐ | ○ | No |
| 2 | ○ | ○ | ○ | ● | No |
| 3 | ○ | ● | ◐ | ● | No |
| 4 | ○ | ○ | ○ | ○ | No |
| 5 | ○ | ● | ◐ | ○ | No |
| 6 | ○ | ● | ◐ | ◐ | No |
| 7 | ● | ● | ◐ | ◐ | No |
| 8 | ◐ | ● | ● | ● | Yes |
| 9 | ◐ | ● | ◐ | ● | No |
| 10 | ○ | ● | ◐ | ◐ | No |
| 11 | ● | ○ | ○ | ● | Yes |
| 12 | ○ | ○ | ○ | ◐ | No |
| 13 | ● | ○ | ○ | ● | Yes |
| 14 | ● | ● | ○ | ● | Yes |
| 15 | ○ | ○ | ○ | ○ | No |
| 16 | ● | ○ | ○ | ● | Yes |
| 17 | ● | ○ | ○ | ● | Yes |

levels and other constructs are made, these were not backed by plausible argumentation. Also, four of the models fail to justify the order of the consecutive steps towards digital maturity. In total, six models are peer reviewed and published in academic outlets.

## 5    Research Agenda

Based on our analysis, we suggest a first draft of a future research agenda for the field of DMMs (see Table 3). The research agenda is the result of the discussion onour findings and corresponding potential avenues for further research.

The main challenge researchers should focus on is developing precise conceptual definitions of DMM-related terms. The current situation with multiple understandings and definitions of the core terms hinders the development of a measurement model [42]. Thus, scholars should put effort in defining digital maturity first. We consider this conceptual work as the most important step for improving the research field around DMMs as it lays the foundation for subsequent tasks. Particularly, definitions form the core of theoretical frameworks [43] that have to be developed to increase the quality of DMM research.

Having discussed required conceptual definitions and theoretical frameworks, we can now take a closer look at the empirical aspects. Most existing DMMs are tested through real data, but the quality of the methods and approaches applied largely differs or cannot be evaluated at all. For example, in most of the analyzed papers, the data collection procedure is not transparently explained. Thus, our first call with regardsto empirical aspects is to increase transparency of both sampling and data collection. Furthermore, depending on the focus of the model, it could be beneficial to concentrate

**Table 3.**  Suggested research agenda

| Category | Selected research problems/questions | Proposed research strategies/methods |
|---|---|---|
| Definitions and measurement procedure | How to define digital maturity? What are the dimensions of DM? | Conceptual research Content validity checks (e.g., interviews) |
| | How to design a measurement procedure for DM? | Construct development |
| Theoretical framework | How to link/position DMM to existing theories? | Conceptual research |
| | Is there a need for a new DMM theory? How could such a theory look like? | Explorative (theory development) Grounded theory |
| Empirical aspects | How to ensure generalizability? | Large data sets, cross-company analysis (multiple case study design) |
| | Evolution of DM over time? | Longitudinal studies |

on specific data groups such as certain company sizes or certain cultures. The second call concerns the methods applied to analyse the data. In most cases, DMMs can be considered as quantitative in nature, which is particularly useful when the goal is for example a comparison between different companies. However, a qualitative approach could contributeto the measurement quality of a company's digital maturity. Qualitative research settings have proven to be especially useful in the process of DMM development [6].

The scope of our suggested research agenda clearly shows that there is a number of significant shortcomings with regards to the measurement validity of existing DMMs. Correspondingly, the overall quality and theoretical value of DMMs is put to the test.

With our research agenda we contributeon atheoretical level by identifying and remedying shortcomings of existing maturity models in the field of IS [5]. On a practical level, we provide managers with a much needed critical evaluation of these popular tools [8]. We acknowledge that due to the practical nature of DMMs, the exhaustiveness of the literature review is questionable. Future research could thus include a systematic literature review of additional practitioners' outlets and search terms to provide a more comprehensive overview. We hope that this research agenda will inspire researchers to further investigate the topic of DMMs which will ultimately lead to a higher practical and theoretical value of these useful models.

# References

1. Remane, G., Hanelt, A., Wiesboeck, F., Kolbe, L.: Digital maturity in traditional industries–an exploratory analysis. In: Proceedings of the 25th European Conference on Information Systems (ECIS) (2017)
2. Chanias, S., Hess, T.: How digital are we? maturity models for the assessment of a company's status in the digital transformation. Manag. Rep./Institut für Wirtschaftsinformatik und Neue Medien 2, 1–14 (2016)
3. Mettler, T.: Thinking in terms of design decisions when developing maturity models. Int. J. Strateg. Decis. Sci. (IJSDS) 1, 76–87 (2010)
4. Kotarba, M.: Measuring digitalization–key metrics. Found. Manag. 9, 123–138 (2017)
5. Becker, J., Knackstedt, R., Pöppelbuß, J.: Developing maturity models for IT management. Bus. Inf. Syst. Eng. 1, 213–222 (2009)
6. Berghaus, S., Back, A.: Stages in digital business transformation: results of an empirical maturity study. In: MCIS, p. 22 (2016)
7. Proença, D., Borbinha, J.: Maturity models for information systems-a state of the art. Procedia Comput. Sci. 100, 1042–1049 (2016)
8. Becker, J., Niehaves, B., Pöppelbuß, J., Simons, A.: Maturity models in IS research. In: 18th European Conference on Information Systems, ECIS2010-0320 (2010)
9. Kane, M., Crooks, T., Cohen, A.: Validating measures of performance. Educ. Meas.: Issues Pract. 18, 5–17 (1999)
10. Bititci, U.S., Garengo, P., Ates, A., Nudurupati, S.S.: Value of maturity models in performance measurement. Int. J. Prod. Res. 53, 3062–3085 (2015)
11. Pedrini, C.N., Frederico, G.F.: Information technology maturity evaluation in a large Brazilian cosmetics industry. Int. J. Bus. Adm. 9, 15 (2018)
12. Poeppelbuss, J., Niehaves, B., Simons, A., Becker, J.: Maturity models in information systems research: literature search and analysis. CAIS 29, 1–15 (2011)

13. Rosemann, M., de Bruin, T.: Towards a business process managment maturity model. In: ECIS 2005 Proceedings, vol. 37 (2005)
14. Lahrmann, G., Marx, F., Winter, R., Wortmann, F.: Business intelligence maturity: development and evaluation of a theoretical model. In: 2011 44th Hawaii International Conference on System Sciences (HICSS), pp. 1–10. IEEE (2011)
15. Dooley, K., Subra, A., Anderson, J.: Maturity and its impact on new product development project performance. Res. Eng. Des. **13**(1), 23–29 (2001). https://doi.org/10.1007/s001630100003
16. Mettler, T., Blondiau, A.: HCMM-a maturity model for measuring and assessing the quality of cooperation between and within hospitals. In: 2012 25th International Symposium on Computer-Based Medical Systems (CBMS), pp. 1–6. IEEE (2012)
17. Carvalho, J.V., Rocha, Á., van de Wetering, R., Abreu, A.: A maturity model for hospital information systems. J. Bus. Res. (2017)
18. Solli-Sæther, H., Gottschalk, P.: The modeling process for stage models. J. Organ. Comput. Electron. Commer. **20**, 279–293 (2010)
19. Brühl, R.: Wie Wissenschaft Wissen schafft – Wissenschaftstheorie für Sozial- und Wirtschaftswissenschaften. UVK Verlagsgesellschaft/Lucius & Lucius, Konstanz (2015)
20. APA, A.: NCME: standards for educational and psychological testing. Washington, DC, American Psychological Association, American Educational Research Association, National Council on Measurement in Education (1985)
21. Kane, M.T.: Validation. Educ. Meas. **4**, 17–64 (2006)
22. Kane, M.T.: An argument-based approach to validity. Psychol. Bull. **112**, 527 (1992)
23. Vom Brocke, J., Simons, A., Niehaves, B., Riemer, K., Plattfaut, R., Cleven, A.: Reconstructing the giant: on the importance of rigour in documenting the literature search process. In: Ecis, vol. 9, pp. 2206–2217 (2009)
24. Bandara, W., Miskon, S., Fielt, E.: A systematic, tool-supported method for conducting literature reviews in information systems. In: Proceedings of the19th European Conference on Information Systems (ECIS 2011) (2011)
25. Kitchenham, B., Charters, S.: Guidelines for performing systematic literature reviews in software engineering (2007)
26. Lasrado, L.A., Vatrapu, R., Andersen, K.N. (eds.): Maturity models development in is research: a literature review (2015)
27. Friedrich, R., Gröne, F., Koster, A., Le Merle, M.: Measuring industry digitization: Leaders and laggards in the digital economy (2011). https://www.strategyand.pwc.com/report/measuring-industry-digitization-leaders-laggards
28. Westerman, G., Calméjane, C., Bonnet, D., Ferraris, P., McAfee, A.: Digital transformation: a roadmap for billion-dollar organizations. MIT Cent. Digital Bus. Capgemini Consult. **1**, 1–68 (2011)
29. Westerman, G., Tannou, M., Bonnet, D., Ferraris, P., McAfee, A.: The digital advantage: how digital leaders outperform their peers in every industry. MITSloan Manag. Capgemini Consult. MA **2**, 2–23 (2012)
30. Becker, W., Ulrich, P., Vogt, M.: Digitalisierung im Mittelstand-Ergebnisbericht einer Online-Umfrage. Univ., Lehrstuhl für Betriebswirtschaftslehre, insbes. Unternehmensführung und Controlling (2013)
31. Catlin, T., Scanlan, J., Willmott, P.: Raising your digital quotient. McKinsey Q. 1–14 (2015)
32. Berger, R.: The digital transformation of industry (2015). www.rolandberger.com/publications/publication_pdf/roland_berger_digital_transformation_of_industry_20150315.pdf

33. Arreola González, A., et al.: Digitale Transformation: Wie Informations-und Kommunikationstechnologie etablierte Branchen grundlegend verändert–Der Reifegrad von Automobilindustrie, Maschinenbau und Logistik im internationalen Vergleich. Abschlussbericht des vom Bundesministerium für Wirtschaft und Technologie geförderten Verbundvorhabens, IKT-Wandel "(Steuerkreis: Grolman von, H., Krcmar, H., Kuhn, K.-J., Picot, A., Schätz, B.) (2016)

34. Berghaus, S., Back, A. Kaltenrieder, B.: Digital maturity & transformation report 2016 (2016). https://crosswalk.ch/dmtr2016-delivery

35. Gill, M., VanBoskirk, S.: Digital Maturity Model 4.0. Benchmarks: Digital Transformation Playbook (2016)

36. Valdez-de-Leon, O.: A digital maturity model for telecommunications service providers. Technol. Innov. Manag. Rev. 6 (2016)

37. Lichtblau, K., et al.: Studie: Industrie 4.0 Readiness. http://www.impuls-stiftung.de/documents/3581372/4875835/Industrie+4.0+Readiness+IMPULS+Studie+Oktober+2015.pdf/447a6187-9759-4f25-b186-b0f5eac69974 (2017)

38. Colli, M., Madsen, O., Berger, U., Møller, C., Wæhrens, B.V., Bockholt, M.: Contextualizing the outcome of a maturity assessment for Industry 4.0. IFAC-PapersOnLine **51**, 1347–1352 (2018)

39. Deutsche Telekom, A.G.: Digitalisierungsindex Mittelstand 2018. Der digitale Status Quo des deutschen Mittelstands, pp. 2–3 (2018)

40. Salviotti, G., Gaur, A., Pennarola, F.: Strategic factors enabling digital maturity: an extended survey (2019)

41. Ifenthaler, D., Egloffstein, M.: Development and implementation of a maturity model of digital transformation. TechTrends **64**, 1–8 (2019). https://doi.org/10.1007/s11528-019-00457-4

42. MacKenzie, S.B., Podsakoff, P.M., Podsakoff, N.P.: Construct measurement and validation procedures in MIS and behavioral research: integrating new and existing techniques. MIS Q. **35**, 293–334 (2011)

43. Whetten, D.A.: What constitutes a theoretical contribution? Acad. Manag. Rev. **14**, 490–495 (1989)

# Business Process Re-engineering and Agile Software Development: Applying the Story-Card Method

Elijah Djan and Marné de Vries[✉]

University of Pretoria, Pretoria, South Africa
djanic327@gmail.com, Marne.devries@up.ac.za

**Abstract.** Enterprise designers need to continuously re-design their enterprise, re-evaluating the technologies that are available to digitize their operations. Although light-weight agile software development approaches are favored by software development service providers, additional requirements elicitation practices should be incorporated when scaling factors apply, since design team members need to have a shared understanding of the operating context and high-level requirements. Research indicated that the organization construction diagram (OCD) could be useful to create a shared context for enterprise operation, linking detailed functional requirements to this shared context during software development. Although the OCD is concise, its associated concepts are abstract and an additional story-card method (SCM) is needed to transform existing enterprise implementations into an OCD. Since additional evaluation of the SCM was required, this study focused on a real-world demonstration of the SCM at a Fintech company where an agile software development approach is applied. The results indicate that the SCM is useful when incorporated within an agile software development approach.

**Keywords:** Enterprise engineering · Story-card method · DEMO · Agile software development

## 1 Introduction

Within a context of volatility, uncertainty, complexity and ambiguity, enterprise designers need to continuously re-design the enterprise, re-evaluating the technologies that are available to digitize their operations. In accordance with the agile paradigm for information system design, enterprises need iterative design approaches to (re-)design their systems incrementally [1]. During information systems design, agile methods and practices may have to be tailored for contexts where *scaling factors apply*, especially regarding the *elicitation and management of requirements* [2, 3].

Since additional *requirements elicitation* practices should be incorporated when *scaling factors apply* [4], the organization construction diagram (OCD), associated with the *design and engineering methodology for organizations* (DEMO), could be used to represent a *blue print* of enterprise operation, creating a foundation for *requirements elicitation* and *tracking* during information systems development [5]. Research indicated that an additional *story-card method* (SCM) was needed to

© IFIP International Federation for Information Processing 2020
Published by Springer Nature Switzerland AG 2020
M. Hattingh et al. (Eds.): I3E 2020, LNCS 12066, pp. 370–382, 2020.
https://doi.org/10.1007/978-3-030-44999-5_31

introduce the abstract OCD concepts to agile development stakeholders [5]. Although previous research experimented with the SCM, the method was applied in isolation, i.e. not within a real-world agile software development context. The main contribution of this study is to demonstrate how the SCM is used within an agile software development approach to solve existing deficiencies at a Fintech company.

Next, we briefly introduce the remaining sections of the article. Section 1 elaborates on the OCD, SCM and other methods and practices that were used at the Fintech company. Section 2 introduces *Framework for Evaluation in Design Science (FEDS)* evaluation design process that guided further evaluation of the SCM within a real-world context. In Sect. 3 we present a demonstration of the SCM and in Sect. 4 we present solution implementation- and evaluation results. Finally, we discuss our findings in Sect. 5 and conclude in Sect. 6.

## 1.1   The SCM to Compile an OCD

The SCM incorporates *collaborative* and *easy-to-use* technologies, i.e. *sticky notes* as *story cards* to facilitate *collaboration* and transformation of existing enterprise implementations (i.e. a *concrete world*) into more *abstract* (and concise) concepts of the OCD [5]. The 5 *inputs* and 10 *method steps* of the SCM is useful to transform a sub-set of implemented processes into a consolidated view of enterprise operations, depicted by the OCD [5]. We briefly introduce the OCD, i.e. the main deliverable of the SCM.

Dietz (in Perinforma [6]) acknowledges that a user's *needs* for information system support starts with an understanding of their day-to-day operations. He presents *four ontological aspect models* that are *coherent, comprehensive, consistent, and concise* and that are useful to represent the *essence of enterprise operation* [7]. The organization construction model (OCM) is the most essential model and consists of three representations, the *organization construction diagram* (OCD) and the *transaction product table* (TPT) and the *bank content table* (BCT) [6, 8].

The OCD provides a graphical representation of actor roles (implemented by human beings) that are involved in a number of transactions. Each transaction is an instance of a particular transaction kind (TK), and every TK incorporates a single production act and multiple coordination acts. Dietz [6, 8] indicates that the coordination acts and production act are arranged according to a pattern, called the *complete transaction pattern*. For every TK, two actor roles are involved, one is the initiating actor role and the other one is the executing actor role. Although the executing actor role is responsible to execute the production act, both actor roles perform several coordination acts.

We explain some of these concepts, referring to the OCD that is depicted in Fig. 1. Every OCD represents some essential operations for a particular scope-of-interest. Figure 1 indicates that the *benefits department* was the scope-of-interest. Furthermore, multiple actor roles may be involved (indicated as rectangles), acting as an initiator (when linked to a solid line) or an executor (when linked to a solid line that ends in a filled diamond). Actor roles interact with one another via several transaction kinds (TKs). Figure 1 includes two TKs, namely T01 (*claim evaluation*) and T02 (*claim payment*). The diamond-disc representation of the TK indicates that every TK consists of a production act/fact (represented by a diamond) and multiple coordination acts/facts (represented by a disc). The actor roles are either classified as elementary or composite. An elementary actor role (indicated by a white rectangle) is the executor of only one TK, as exemplified by the *evaluator* in Fig. 1. A composite actor role, indicated by a grey-shaded rectangle, is the executor of more than one TK. By default, actor roles that are outside the scope-of-interest, are modelled as composite actor roles [6]. Therefore, Fig. 1 indicates that the *broker* and *finance department* are composite actor roles. The actor role within the scope-of-interest (i.e. the *evaluator*) may need to have access to production facts and coordination facts that are produced outside the scope-of-interest. Figure 1 indicates that the *evaluator* needs information access (indicated with a dotted line) to an *in-house software system facts*, i.e. production and coordination facts that are produced outside the scope-of-interest.

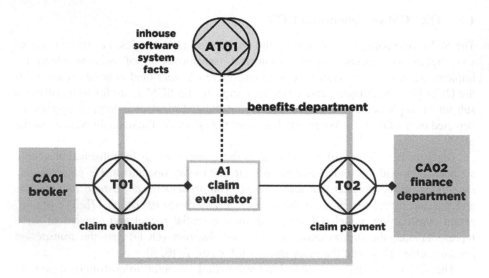

**Fig. 1.** An OCD for the benefits department

The OCD provides a consolidated view of enterprise operation. Every TK on the OCD follows a transaction pattern. Figure 2 depicts the complete pattern of behavior that exists between an initiator and an executor when they perform a TK. Thus, the pattern depicted in Fig. 2 applies to T01 with the initiator being the *broker* and the executor being the *evaluator*. Yet, the same pattern is also followed for T02 where the initiator is the *evaluator* and the executor is the *finance department*.

Perinforma [6] indicates that a TK may be classified according to three categories. A TK is *original* when the associated production act has the intent of creating an *original/new* fact. A TK is classified as *informational* if its associated production act merely recalls/interprets a previously-created original production facts. Lastly, a TK is *documental* when the associated production fact simply transmits/copies/retrieves/destroys the original fact. Usually, the OCD only represents

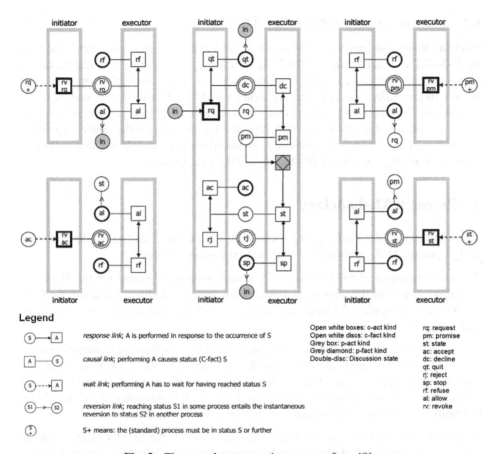

**Fig. 2.** The complete transaction pattern, from [8]

TKs that are of the *original* sort [6], hence extracting only the essence of enterprise operation.

The OCD presented in Fig. 1 is the main deliverable of the SCM. Yet, the SCM starts by identifying existing operational activities that are performed in a particular sequence at an enterprise. Operational activities include TKs of all sorts, i.e. original, informational and documental. The SCM facilitates the process of analyzing the implemented operational activities, re-structuring operational knowledge into a consolidated OCD [5].

Once the SCM has been applied, every operational activity: (1) is traceable to a particular TK on the OCD, and (2) can be considered for semi-automation, transforming the activity into a *user story* [5].

A *user story* is a "general-purpose *agile* substitute for what traditionally has been referred to as *software requirements*" [3]. The next section presents a template to elaborate on the software requirements associated with a *user story*.

## 1.2    User Story Cards and the INSERT Criteria

Patel and Ramachandran [9] provided a *template*, called a *user story card*, that is based on the INSERT validation criteria. The INSERT criteria ensures that every requirement is Independent, Negotiable, Small-enough-to-fit-into-iteration; Estimable, Representative-of-user-functionality and Testable. Applying the INSERT criteria, the analyst has to complete ten fields per story card: (1) story card number, (2) project name, (3) estimation, (4) story name, (5) date, (6) story, (7), acceptance test, (8) note, (9) risk, and (10) points to consider [9]. Later, in Sect. 3.2, we also recommend that another field is added on the *user story card*, tracing each user story back to a TK on the OCD.

## 2    Research Methodology

The study applied the *Framework for Evaluation in Design Science (FEDS)* evaluation design process [10], applying the four-step process as follows:

*Explicate the Goals of the Evaluation:* The main purpose of evaluating the SCM is to determine how well it achieves its expected environmental utility, i.e. using the OCD within an agile system development context within a scaled context to manage and trace requirements.

*Choose the Evaluation Strategy:* In terms of the FEDS evaluation strategies, evaluation of the SCM requires iterative episodes of formative evaluation that follows the naturalistic paradigm, since the major risk of the SCM is social or user oriented. According to [10] naturalistic evaluation explores the performance of a solution technology in its real environment, e.g. within a real-world enterprise.

*Determine the Properties to Evaluate:* As stated in [5], the SCM's utility could be evaluated in terms of ability to address requirements elicitation criteria for agile development within scaled contexts. One of the utility properties, is the *usefulness* of the SCM within a real-world context.

*Design the Individual Evaluation Episode(s):* The *first evaluation episode* involved 21 participants to experiment with the SCM, providing survey feedback in terms of its utility [5]. The positive feedback obtained in [5] gave the impetus to experiment further on the *usefulness* of the SCM within a real-world agile software development context as a *second evaluation episode*. The *second evaluation episode* was conducted and presented in this article. We used user acceptance tests and structured interviews to evaluate the *usefulness* of the SCM and to evaluate the newly-developed software solution and its ability to address some of the deficiencies evident at the enterprise. In addition, the participant-observer, experimenting with the SCM, provided some reflections on using and extending the SCM.

Additional evaluation episodes are needed to experiment with the SCM within different *scaled* agile contexts, as indicated in Sect. 6.

# 3 Story Card Method Demonstration

This section demonstrates the use of the SCM as part of a software development project. Section 3.1 provides background on the company and its problem context. Section 3.2 presents the agile software development approach that incorporated the SCM during the early phases of development, whereas Sect. 3.3 presents an application of the agile software development approach.

## 3.1 The Enterprise Context

A software development project was initiated by one of South Africa's leading Fintech companies of which the *benefits department* interacts with various *brokers* that claim on behalf of claimants. The problem is that the *benefits department* used MS Excel to track claim evaluations. Since employees used the desktop version of Excel, worksheets could not be accessed simultaneously by the employees and the worksheets contained duplicate entry fields. Rapid growth in business created an urgency for digitizing all manual operations, reducing the lead time for claim payments to beneficiaries, and reducing the number of erroneous claim payments. Even though the benefits department used MS Excel, other departments used an in-house system to automate their processes.

## 3.2 The Adapted Agile Approach

One of the core values of *agile software development* indicates a preference for individuals and interactions over processes and tools [11]. Tools and techniques should encourage customer collaboration, enable change, ensure working software and minimize the use of documentation [12]. Yet, minimal documentation often creates problems in tracing requirements to their origin, especially when scaling factors apply [13, 14].

The software development team, working at the Fintech company, already followed an agile software development approach. An opportunity existed to experiment with the SCM, incorporating it within the existing agile development approach, addressing the deficiencies at the *benefits department*. Similar to the iterative and model-based agile software development approach presented by [15], the software development approach started with a scope definition, followed by two stages: (1) a combined problem analysis, requirements analysis and decision analysis; and (2) multiple iterations of design, construction & testing, review and delivery. The next section demonstrates the adapted agile software development approach, elaborating on the first stage, emphasizing the use of the SCM and *user story cards*.

## 3.3 Demonstrating the Adapted Agile Approach

This section elaborates on the *problem analysis*, *requirements analysis* and *decision analysis* of the adapted agile software development approach that was used at the Fintech company.

**Problem Analysis Phase.** Whetherby's [15] PIECES framework was used to extract information-system related deficiencies in terms of Performance, Information (and Data), Economics, Control (and Security) and Efficiencies. Additional problem analysis was also incorporated as part of the next phase.

**Requirements Analysis phase.** Identified deficiencies resulting from the PIECES analysis, were converted into *non-functional solution requirements*. The *functional requirements* were primarily derived via the SCM. The participant-observer applied the 10-step SCM (see [5]) to extract the existing operational activities from enterprise participants. We shortly discuss an application of the 10-step method and also indicate two extensions for *Step 1* and *Step 10*.

- *Step 1: Inquire from a colleague to explain a short process (about 10 to 15 activities) that s/he is involved with.* Figure 3 illustrates the main output of *Step 1*. The participant-observer extended this step, also mapping out the process represented in Fig. 3 to a business process model, using the Business Process Model and Notation (BPMN) specification (see [16]). The extension allowed for critical analysis of the existing process, highlighting inefficient interaction between participants. Problem areas were identified, labelled (e.g. Problem A, Problem B) and described.
- *Step 2: Take a picture (photo) of the process.* See Fig. 3.
- *Step 3: Discuss with your colleague all the actors that are involved and write down composite actors on yellow sticky notes, adding a smiley face, keeping actors aside.* The smiley face sticky notes are illustrated on Fig. 3.
- *Step 4: Explain Dietz's red-green-blue triangle of production acts, also explaining the complete transaction pattern for actor-collaboration regarding production acts.* The participant observer briefly presented the concepts to the participants, only explaining the red-green-blue triangle of production acts. The complete transaction pattern was not explained, since it would be too time-consuming.

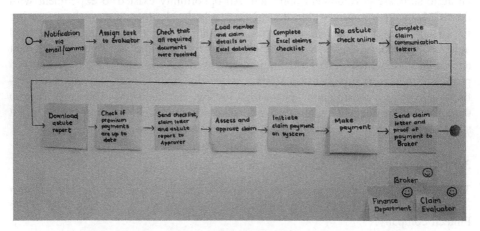

**Fig. 3.** Example of a process to demonstrate method *Step 1* of the SCM

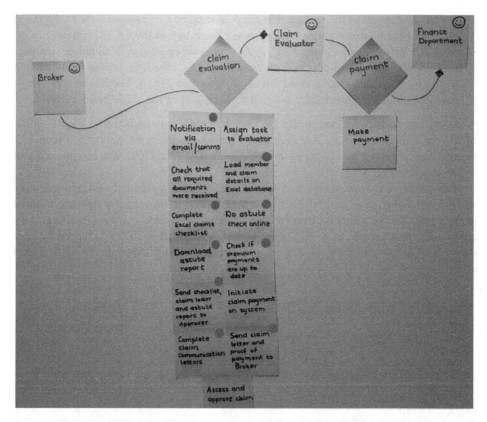

**Fig. 4.** An OCD with composite actor roles is the deliverables of the SCM

- *Step 5: Have a discussion with your colleague as to identify original production acts from his/her process (as mapped out with sticky notes in Step 1).* The discussion and classification followed.
- *Step 6: Classify (in collaboration with your colleague) remaining acts as coordination acts vs. production acts.* Additional classification was performed.
- *Step 7: Remove the original production act notes from the flat surface and phrase appropriate transaction kind descriptions (using adjective + noun) on red sticky notes that are positioned as diamonds on your A1 paper. Collapse initial production act notes underneath re-phrased transaction kind notes.* Figure 4 illustrates the re-structuring of sticky notes according to the OCD-format.
- *Step 8: The remaining activities on your working space should be coordination acts or informational/documental production acts. Remove each of the remaining notes on your working surface and collapse them underneath the appropriate re-phrased transaction kind (red diamond notes) on your A1 paper.* Figure 4 illustrates the re-structuring of sticky notes according to the OCD-format.
- *Step 9: Position the yellow actor role notes on the A1 paper, drawing in (with a black pen) the initiator actors (+initiating links) as well as the executing actors*

*(+executing links) to the transaction kinds, completing a composite OCD.* Figure 4 illustrates the re-structuring of sticky notes according to the OCD-format.

- *Step 10: Validate your composite OCD with your colleague.* Validation was performed. The participant-observer extended this step, identifying those activities that had to be automated, using a red dot as illustrated on Fig. 4. The TK with the most red dots should be prioritized and had to form part of the same build cycle.

According to [5], the composite OCD, such as the one depicted in Fig. 4, needs further tailoring as to ensure that *composite actor roles* that form part of the scope-of-interest are converted into *elementary actor roles*. The final OCD was constructed and is presented in Fig. 1.

Each of the activities, earmarked for automation, was converted into multiple *user story cards*, adhering to the INSERT criteria and the user story card template presented in Sect. 1.2. The participant-observer also added a field called *traceability*. Each story card had to be traceable to a TK on the OCD (represented in Fig. 1). One of the user story cards, depicted in Fig. 5, linked to a *Problem A* and linked to TK T01 (*claim evaluation*) of Fig. 1.

| Story Card 1 | Project Name: Streamlined Front-End Design | Estimation: 1 hour |
|---|---|---|
| **Story Name:**<br>Policy Holder Application Form Upload | **Traceability:**<br>Problem A (T01) | **Date:** 2019/08/29 |
| **Story:**<br>Policy holders should be able to upload their claim forms and required documents online and not via email. | **Acceptance Test:**<br>1. Try to upload nothing<br>2. Try to upload only claim form<br>3. Try to upload only required documents | |
| **Note:**<br>N/A | **Risk:**<br>Low | |
| **Points to be considered:**<br>System should be able to check that the correct documents are indeed uploaded via Optical Character Recognition (OCR) and Artificial Intelligence (AI). | | |

**Fig. 5.** A user story card linked to TK T01

**Decision Analysis Phase.** During this phase, three alternative solutions were identified: (1) Extending the existing in-house software application to replace the existing Excel sheets; (2) Using blockchain technology to create smart contracts to validate and verify the details of the deceased and automate payment; and (3) Creating a web app to replace the existing in-house software application that is currently used by the company. A feasibility analysis matrix, used in accordance with [15], indicated that the urgency of a solution favored the first alternative.

## 4   Results

Since agile software development approaches value *working software* over comprehensive documentation [11], we had to ensure that the adapted agile approach produced *working software*. Section 4.1 reports on the acceptance test results for four implemented story cards. In addition, we wanted to reflect on the story-card-method and its ease-of-use within a real-world project. Section 4.2 provides some reflections on applying the SCM.

## 4.1 Acceptance Tests and Interview Results

As indicated in Sect. 3.2 the software development approach consisted of two stages. The second stage consists of multiple iterations of design, construction & testing, review and delivery. For the first iteration, four out of eight story cards were prioritized and used to construct user interfaces. The newly-developed user-interfaces were evaluated by four participants and acceptance tests were completed with positive results. Participants also had to answer five interview questions in terms of a five-point scale: strongly agree, agree, unsure, disagree and strongly disagree. Participants were encouraged to qualify their response. The results are presented per interview question.

- *Do you believe that the previous process had too many manual steps?* Three participants strongly agreed, while the fourth participant agreed.
- *Has the new solution reduced manual steps by 50%?* Two participants strongly agreed, whereas the other two participants agreed. Participants commented that the consolidation of data capturing on a single system and the use of auto-fill functionality for certain fields drastically decreased the number of manual steps.
- *Do you believe that the new process has reduced processing time of claims?* All participants strongly agreed.
- *Is the new process better than the old process?* Three participants strongly agreed, while the fourth participant agreed. Participants valued the automatic calculation of benefit amounts, replacing the manual entries.
- *Has the use of Microsoft Excel been eradicated?* Three participants strongly agreed, while the fourth participant agreed.

## 4.2 Reflecting on the SCM

The participant-observer facilitated the SCM and provided some reflections in terms of the 10-step method presented in Sect. 3.3:

- *Steps 1 and 2:* This step was easy to perform, since the participant-observer spent ample time at the company to observe the process. A company participant (the claim evaluator) confirmed the validity of the existing process as mapped out with sticky notes.
- *Step 3:* This step was easy to perform and the company participant willingly provided inputs.
- *Steps 4 to 7:* The company participant was not so interested to participate during the classification and re-structuring of activities, but preferred that the facilitator (i.e. the participant-observer) performed these steps. Still, the participant validated the classifications afterwards.
- *Step 8:* The participant-observer valued this step, since it allows for a consolidated view of existing activities and a means to identify areas of improvement.
- *Step 9:* This step was easy to perform.

- *Step 10:* This step and its extension was easy to perform.

Although the participant-observer performed the SCM with ease, the company participants had difficulty in understanding some of the concepts.

The demonstration of the SCM led to two further extensions. *Step 1* was extended representing the rudimentary sticky-note process flow with a process model according to the BPMN specification, using swim lanes and pools to indicate existing work allocation according to enterprise-specific roles. The extension also allowed for critical analysis of the existing process, especially in terms of *inefficient interaction* between company roles. The detailed process model helped to highlight problem areas that were labelled (e.g. Problem A, Problem B) and described.

A second extension was applied in *Step 10*, namely to use red dots to earmark story-cards for automation. The rationale is that story cards that belong to the same TK and earmarked for automation, should also be built during the same build cycle.

## 5 Discussion

Enterprise designers need to continuously re-design their enterprise, re-evaluating the technologies that are available to digitize their operations. Although light-weight agile software development approaches are favored by software development service providers, additional requirements elicitation practices should be incorporated when *scaling factors* apply, since design team members need to have a shared understanding of the operating context and high-level requirements. Research indicated that OCD could be useful to create a shared context for enterprise operation, linking detailed functional requirements to this shared context during software development. Although the OCD is concise, its associated concepts are abstract and an additional SCM is needed to transform existing enterprise implementations into an OCD. Since additional evaluation of the SCM was required, this study provided a real-world demonstration of the SCM within an agile software development context.

The SCM was incorporated within an *agile software development approach.* During its application, the enterprise designer (also the participant-observer) identified the need to further extend *Step 1* and *Step 10* of the SCM.

Two different methods were used for evaluation. First, we evaluated the *agile software development approach*, with the embedded SCM, to assess whether the approach rendered *working software*. User acceptance tests indicated positive results. We also used structured interviews, engaging with relevant participants at the benefits department, to assess whether some of the previous information system deficiencies have been addressed. Positive feedback was obtained.

The second evaluation method entailed some reflection on using the SCM. The participant-observer indicated that the SCM was easy to use. Yet, he fast-tracked some of the steps, reducing some of the explanations about OCD concepts. His reflections emphasized the conditional use of the SCM, i.e. that the facilitator needs sufficient knowledge on the theoretical concepts to provide additional explanations where needed.

# 6   Conclusion and Future Research

The SCM was useful when incorporated within an agile software development approach. Yet, as indicated by the demonstration and participant-observer's feedback, the method may need further adaptation (e.g. extending *Step 1* and *Step 10*) to ensure integration within an existing *agile software development approach*. In addition, the enterprise designer that facilitates the SCM, may need to adapt the theoretical explanations regarding OCD concepts, ensuring that participants will be able to validate the final OCD.

Since the SCM was useful within a real-world context where an agile approach is currently used, *agile at scale* projects, where different scaling factors apply should further validate the usefulness of the SCM within the agile software development context. The main deliverable of the SCM, the OCD, is useful to create a common understanding of the essential operations at an enterprise. The implementation-free OCD becomes the starting point for various different implementation options. Although this study favored further development of the in-house information system, the OCD can also be used as the starting point for implementing blockchain technology.

**Acknowledgements.** This work was demonstrated at a Fintech company. We are grateful for all the assistance and feedback that we received from the company.

# References

1. Beck, K., Beedle, M, Van Bennekum, A., Cockburn, A. et al.: Manifesto for agile software development (2001). www.agilemanifesto.org. Accessed 23 Apr 2018
2. Dikert, K., Paasivaara, M., Lassenius, C.: Challenges and success factors for large-scale agile transformations: a systematic literature review. J. Syst. Softw. **119**, 87–108 (2016)
3. Leffingwell, D.: Agile Software Requirements: Lean Requirements Practices for Teams, Programs, and the Enterprise. Addison-Wesley, New Jersey (2011)
4. Paasivaara, M., Lassenius, C.: Scaling scrum in a large globally distributed organisation: a case study. In: IEEE 11th International Conference on Global Software Engineering. IEEE Computer Society (2016). https://doi.org/10.1109/icgse.2016.34
5. De Vries, M.: DEMO and the story-card method: requirements elicitation for agile software development at scale. In: Buchmann, R.A., Karagiannis, D., Kirikova, M. (eds.) PoEM 2018. LNBIP, vol. 335, pp. 138–153. Springer, Cham (2018). https://doi.org/10.1007/978-3-030-02302-7_9
6. Perinforma, A.P.C.: The Essence of Organisation. 3rd edn. Sapio (2017). www.sapio.nl
7. Dietz, J.L.G.: Enterprise Ontology. Springer, Berlin (2006). https://doi.org/10.1007/3-540-33149-2
8. Dietz, J.L.G., Mulder M.A.T.: DEMOSL-3: DEMO Specification Language Version 3.7. SAPIO (2017)
9. Patel, C., Ramachandran, M.: Story card based agile software development. Int. J. Hybrid Inf. Technol. **2**(2), 125–140 (2009)
10. Venable, J., Pries-Heje, J., Baskerville, R.: FEDS: a framework for evaluation in design science research. Eur. J. Inf. Syst. **25**(1), 77–89 (2016)
11. The Agile Manifesto (n.d.) Manifesto for Agile Software Development. https://www.agilealliance.org/agile101/the-agile-manifesto/. Accessed 11 Nov 2019

12. Strode, D.: Agile methods: a comparative analyis. In: Proceedings of the 19th Annual Conference of the National Advisory Committee on Computing Qualifications (NACCQ) (2006)

13. Inayat, I., Salim, S.S., Marczak, S., Daneva, M., et al.: A systematic literature review on agile requirements engineering practices and challenges. Comput. Hum. Bahav. **51**, 915–929 (2015). https://doi.org/10.1016/j.chb.2014.10.046

14. Heikkilä, VT., Damian, D., Lassenius, C., Paasivaara, M.: A mapping study on requirements engineering in agile software development. In: 2015 41st Euromicro Conference on Software Engineering and Advanced Applications, pp 199–207 (2015). https://doi.org/10.1109/seaa.2015.70

15. Bentley, L.D., Whitten, J.L.: Systems Analysis and Design for the Global Enterprise, 7th edn. McGraw-Hill/Irwin, New York (2007)

16. Object Management Group (n.d.) Business process model & notation. https://www.omg.org/bpmn/. Accessed 30 May 2019

# The Zachman Framework for Enterprise Architecture: An Explanatory IS Theory

Aurona Gerber[1,2](✉) [iD], Pierre le Roux[1], Carike Kearney[1],
and Alta van der Merwe[1] [iD]

[1] Department of Informatics, University of Pretoria, Pretoria, South Africa
aurona.gerber@up.ac.za, pierre.leroux@moyoafrica.com
[2] CAIR, Pretoria, South Africa

**Abstract.** Enterprise Architecture (EA) has had an interesting and often controversial history since its inception in the late 80's by pioneers such as John Zachman. Zachman proposed the Zachman Framework for Enterprise Architecture (ZFEA), a descriptive, holistic representation of an enterprise for the purposes of providing insights and understanding. Some scholars claim that EA is an imperative to ensure successful business structures or business-IT alignment, or more recently with Enterprise Architecture Management (EAM), to manage required organizational transformation. However, EA initiatives within companies are often costly and the expected return on investment is not realized. In fact, Gartner recently indicated in their 2018 Enterprise Architecture Hype Cycle that EA is slowly emerging from the trough of disillusionment after nearly a decade. In this paper we argue that the role and value of EA is often misunderstood, and that EA, specifically the ZFEA for the purpose of this paper, could be considered as a theory given the view of theory within Information Systems (IS). The purpose of IS theories is to analyse, predict, explain and/or prescribe and it could be argued that EA often conform to these purposes. Using the taxonomy of theories as well as the structural components of theory within IS as proposed by Gregor, we motivate that the ZFEA could be regarded as an explanatory theory. Positioning ZFEA as IS explanatory theory provides insight into the role and purpose of the ZFEA (and by extension EA), and could assist researchers and practitioners with mediating the challenges experienced when instituting EA and EAM initiatives within organizations.

**Keywords:** Zachman Framework for Enterprise Architecture · Enterprise Architecture · IS theory · Explanatory IS theory

## 1 Introduction

The initial idea to describe, understand, represent and design different dimensions of the enterprise was developed simultaneously within different disciplines in the late eighties. During this time John Zachman, often hailed as the father of EA, defined EA as a set of descriptive representations relevant to the enterprise where an enterprise is widely defined as any socio-technical organization [1, 2]. He furthermore proposed the Zachman Framework for Enterprise Architecture (ZFEA) that he described as a logical, comprehensive structure "for classifying and organizing the descriptive representations

M. Hattingh et al. (Eds.): I3E 2020, LNCS 12066, pp. 383–396, 2020.
https://doi.org/10.1007/978-3-030-44999-5_32

of an Enterprise that are significant to the management of the Enterprise as well as to the development of the Enterprise's systems, manual systems as well as automated systems" [1].

Since this original establishment of EA in the late 80's, EA has developed as a comprehensive discipline receiving interest from researchers and practitioners. Several frameworks were proposed, refined and implemented in practice [3–9], and scholarly research investigated the nature and impact of EA [10–16]. Recent developments in the broad domain of EA include Enterprise Architecture Management (EAM) that elevates EA as a strategic business function rather than an IT function within organizations, and recent research indicate that EAM may indeed assist with organizational agility and transformation [17–21].

EA in strategic context is directed at the current and future purposes of the organization as well as to assist in reaching organisational goals and objectives, including ensuring that the business with its technologies and resources are aligned [10, 22]. However, enterprises often experience challenges with the implementation of EA initiatives and capabilities [23], resulting in sentiments documented mostly in popular press, for instance stating that *EA is dead* [24, 25]. EA initiatives are often costly and without the expected return on investment. Recent blog posts, for instance, claim that several EA frameworks or tools, specifically the ZFEA, are fake tools without any real value [26]. In their recent 2018 Enterprise Architecture Hype Cycle Gartner found that EA is only now, after more than a decade, emerging from the trough of disillusionment [27].

The authors acknowledge the criticisms, but in this paper we argue that the role and value of EA is often misunderstood, and for the purposes of this paper, we argue that EA, specifically the ZFEA, should be considered as a theory given the perspectives on theory adopted within Information Systems (IS). EA is relevant for the IS domain as IS is the discipline concerned with studying socio-technical systems, and the view of theory within IS is therefore applicable to EA. Some of the views on IS theory include "theory as statements that say how something should be done in practice" or "theory as statements providing a lens for viewing or explaining the world". The purpose of IS theories is to analyse, predict, explain and/or prescribe and it could be argued that the intent of EA often conforms to these purposes.

For this paper we focus on the ZFEA primarily and we support this selection by analysing the foundational aspects of EA. We subsequently adopt the fundamental view about the nature of theories within IS by Gregor. We adopted the taxonomy of theories as well as the structural components of theory within IS as proposed by Gregor [28] to analyse the ZFEA. The main research question answered by this study can be stated as follows: *Given the nature and structure of theories within IS, could the ZFEA be considered as a theory?* Similar to the method used by Gregor to evaluate five types of theory in IS, we evaluate the ZFEA [28]. By establishing whether ZFEA, and by extension, EA in general, could be regarded as IS theories, we believe that insight on what function EA should fulfil, as well as the use and position of EA and its frameworks and tools, specifically given the strategic developments such as EAM, could be enhanced.

The remainder of this paper is structured as follows. In the next sections on related work we provide overviews on EA, the ZFEA and IS theories. We then analyse the foundations of EA and motivate the choice of ZFEA for the purpose of this paper. We subsequently analyse the ZFEA given the nature of IS theories (taxonomy and structure) by Gregor, and we finally conclude.

## 2 Background

Within this background section we provide a short introduction to EA as well as the ZFEA, followed by the background necessary for IS theory as is relevant for this paper.

### 2.1 Enterprise Architecture

EA originally developed from the need to align the business and information technology aspects of the organisation with one another [12], but has since advanced to be viewed from more than one perspective and for more than one application [10]. EA developed from more than one discipline with differing terminology, seeking mostly similar goals such as organisational alignment, integration, and ability to understand and manage complexity and change [16, 29]. Several definitions for EA exist, such as that EA is the continuous practice of describing the essential elements of a socio-technical organization, their relationships to each other and to the environment, in order to understand complexity and manage change [30]. Urbaczewski and Mrdalj defined EA as a description or blueprint that defines the day-to-day operation and structure of an organization [3], and Zachman himself defined EA as a set of descriptive representations relevant to the enterprise [31]. EA is directed at ensuring that the business with its technologies and resources, as well as the current and future purposes of the organization are aligned. Since its inception, several different EA frameworks were developed from different perspectives and disciplines. Due to space limitations, we will mostly focus on the ZFEA, however, several works on the history, evolution, purpose of, and recent developments within EA are included as references [3, 12, 13, 16, 17, 32–38]. In Sect. 4 we analyse the grounding of the EA discipline to motivate the choice of the ZFEA for this paper, and in the next section a short overview of ZFEA is provided.

### 2.2 The Zachman Framework for Enterprise Architecture (ZFEA)

John Zachman is widely acknowledged as the father of EA [16, 39]. Borrowing from the field of engineering, Zachman described how insight into different disciplines and the manufacturing process contributed to the ZFEA [1, 40]. Zachman describes the breakthrough that led to his now well-known ZFEA as the realisation of the existence of different perspectives relevant to a product, which he then applied to an enterprise [39]. The ZFEA was designed after observing that various engineered objects such as computers, buildings and airplanes (the designed artefacts) can be classified according to the fundamental abstractions or interrogatives namely *What? How? Where? Who? When? Why?*, in columns (Table 1), as well as specific audience perspectives and transformations in rows (Table 2) [1]. The ZFEA (Fig. 1), is therefore a 6 × 6 two-dimensional classification schema for designing descriptive representations of the enterprise. The ZFEA is also described as an enterprise ontology with no process or tooling implications [41], or a meta-model of an enterprise represented in a matrix comprised of columns and rows. Each intersection of a column and row provides a unique representation or view of the enterprise [1].

**Fig. 1.** The Zachman Framework for Enterprise Architecture (ZFEA) (reproduced from [1])

**Table 1.** Summary of the ZFEA interrogatives (abstractions) [1].

| Interrogative (Columns) | Description |
| --- | --- |
| What (Data) | What information, business data and objects are involved? |
| How (Function) | How does it work? (process flows) |
| Where (Network) | Where are the components located? (network models/distribution networks) |
| Who (People) | Who are involved? (workflow models or responsibility assignments) |
| When (Time) | When do things happen? (timing cycles) |
| Why (Motivation) | What is the motivation? (business drivers, motivation intensions) |

Table 2. Summary of the ZFEA perspectives [1].

| Perspective (Rows) | Description |
|---|---|
| Executive (Planner) | Contextual View. Defines the limits for all remaining perspectives |
| Business Manager or CEO (Owner) | Conceptual View. This perspective is concerned with the business itself |
| Architect (Designer) | Physical View. The architect or person responsible for narrowing the gap between what is required versus what is physically and technically possible |
| Engineer (Builder) | Represents the perspective of the enterprise engineers interested in 'building' or designing the building blocks identified by the architecture |
| Technician | Represents the perspective of the business technicians such as the database implementers and the workflow system implementers |
| User (Enterprise) | Represents the perspective of the running/functioning enterprise |

## 2.3   Information Systems Theory

In a seminal work on IS theory, Gregor investigated the nature of theory in Information Systems both with regards to theory types and theory components [28]. Gregor emphasized the importance of developing good theory and highlighted the limited discussions regarding the nature of theory as well as the structural components of different types of theories in IS. Theory allows for different perspectives and aims to enhance our understanding of the world by providing explanations, descriptions, predictions and actionable guidance [28]. Gregor's work is foundational for almost all discussions about theory in IS [42–46].

Gregor identified some core aspects for developing and classifying IS theories [28]:

- Causality (cause and effect): Certain circumstances or events will have certain outcomes. It might be required in some instances to determine the cause of an event to provide an explanation. The same is true for predictions, insights into the cause influences the prediction.
- Generalization: An aspect or characteristic can be applied across a range of specific scenarios, places, people, etc. The degree of generalization determines different viewpoints. Generalization applied to a focused area is required for prediction, as without generalizations about the past or the present, a prediction about the future state is difficult to make. Gregor did not use generalization for classifying theory types.
- Prediction: Future occurrences are dependent on preconditions to realise.
- Explanation: Theory aimed at providing understanding on the how, why and when of an occurrence relating to human reasoning and argumentation.

Gregor furthermore proposed a classification scheme or taxonomy of IS theory types. The primary goal of a theory is directly related to a question or a problem that need to be solved. Theories are developed for the purposes of *analysis and description*, *prediction*, *explanation* and *prescription*, and these goals were used to produce a

**Table 3.** A taxonomy of theory types in information systems research (reproduced from [28])

| Theory type | Distinguishing attributes |
|---|---|
| I. Analysis | Says what is: Focuses on analysis and description only. An analysis theory does not include predictions, or indication of causal relationships among occurrences/events/objects |
| II. Explanation | Says what is, how, why, when and where: The main aim is one of explanation and to provide understanding. The theory provides explanations but does not aim to predict with any precision. The theory is not testable |
| III. Prediction | Says what is and what will be: The theory provides predictions and has testable propositions but does not have well-developed justificatory causal explanations |
| IV. Explanation and Prediction (EP) | Says what is, how, why, when, where and what will be: Provides predictions and has both testable propositions and causal explanations |
| V. Design and action | Says how to do something: The theory gives explicit prescriptions (e.g. methods, techniques, principles of form and function) for constructing an artefact or complex object |

**Table 4.** Structural components of theory (reproduced from [28])

| Theory components (Common to all theory) | Definition |
|---|---|
| Means of representation | A physical representation of theory. This might include mathematical terms, symbolic logic, tables, diagrams, graphs, illustrations, models, prototypes |
| Constructs | The focus point or object of the theory. All primary constructs in the theory should be well defined. Many different types of constructs are possible e.g. observational (real) terms, theoretical (nominal) terms and collective terms |
| Statements of relationship | The nature of the relationship among the constructs depends on the purpose of the theory. Types of relationships: associative, conditional, compositional, unidirectional, bidirectional or causal |
| Scope | The scope is specified by the degree of generality of the statements of relationships and statements of boundaries showing the limits of generalization |
| Theory components (Contingent on theory type) | Definition |
| Causal explanations | The theory gives statements of relationships among occurrences/events/objects that show causal reasoning (not covering law or probabilistic reasoning alone) |
| Testable propositions (hypotheses) | Relationships between objects/events (constructs) can be tested by means of observation or experience |
| Prescriptive statements | The theory provides a method or guidance on how to accomplish something in practice e.g. construct a complex object or develop a strategy |

taxonomy of theory types in IS (Table 3) as well as the components of a IS theory (Table 4) [28]. Gregor furthermore classified five different IS theories according to the taxonomy and structural components [28], and for this paper, we adopt the method used by Gregor to evaluate the ZFEA as will be discussed in Sect. 4.

## 3 Motivation for Using the ZFEA

In this section we motivate the selection to use the ZFEA in this paper as representative of EA in general. An understanding of the origins and the thinking underpinning EA has relevance for this paper as it provides the foundation for EA concepts and frameworks, and provides the motivation for using the ZFEA as representative of the structural and ontological aspects of EA in general. Le Roux [47] adopted the approach of Baskerville and Dulipovici [48] to investigate the theoretical grounding of EA, and indicated that the theoretical base for EA emerged from more than one field. The results of this analysis are summarised in Table 5. These results support the legitimacy of the discipline and support the use of EA as a theoretical base. If the ZFEA is a representative of this theoretical underpinning, we could motivate the use of the ZFEA for this paper.

**Table 5.** Summary of works relating to EA origins and their basis of argument

| Author | Basis from which the underlying business problems of alignment, control, efficiency and management of change are addressed |
|---|---|
| Taylor [49] | The business system would have to be placed before the individual, and that scientific management was needed to ensure this is possible. Efficiency through interaction of individuals. Organisation as a holistic entity. Holistic system before the individual |
| Shewhart [50] | From industrial engineering emphasized organizational control to enable adaption. Past experience and process |
| Forrester [51] | Motivate an underlying base to understand the business system as a whole for organizational management. Discuss the elements of the organisation and interactions between elements |
| Drucker [52] | Business management motivation that argue for system as a whole broken into elements, as well as the interactions between elements |
| Blumenthal [53] | Holistic systems planning to adapt to change, focus on IT systems within organisations. Underlying elements and interaction between elements is an enablement factor. Proposed a framework for planning |
| Helfert [54] | Financial management perspective emphasizes resource flows with a holistic platform/system from which to understand flows. The organisation is the complete set of individual resource flows |
| Anthony [55] | A business system consists of diverse individual parts that all contribute to or serve a specific purpose. Framework to understand organisational concepts and their contribution |
| Senge [56] | Emphasizes the system as a whole, with 5 elements of technology that are interdependent, and the interrelationships of system elements. Acknowledged by Zachman |

As indicated in Table 5, systems theory and systems thinking underpin much of the theoretical base of EA. Systems thinking supports a way of thinking about the organisation as a whole while also considering system parts with their interactions [56, 57]. Systems theory provides a theoretical base from which to model the complete organisation as well as elements and interrelationships between elements [16]. The underpinning of systems thinking is furthermore distinguishable in EA in general as published by Lapalme [10], Simon et al. [16] and others [3, 38, 39].

As stated, the ZFEA is one of the original EA frameworks developed by Zachman in the late 80's [2] with origins in engineering, specifically systems thinking and systems theory [10, 16]. Given the theoretical groundings of EA, specifically the adoption of systems theory and systems thinking as established by le Roux [47] in Table 5, we could motivate that the ZFEA, which is fundamentally based on systems thinking, is in general representative of EA for the purpose of the investigation reported on in this paper.

## 4  The ZFEA as IS Theory

For the purposes of this paper, the ZFEA is mapped to Gregor's theory taxonomy as well as the structural components of theory to determine if the framework can serve as an IS theory. The first step is to classify the ZFEA as one of the theory types in the theory taxonomy of Table 3. According to Gregor it is required to look at the primary goals of the theory in order to classify it [28]. The ZFEA is a structural representation or an ontology of an organization and all its elements with their relationships that is descriptive in nature. The ZFEA is directed at providing understanding and insight [58] with no process or tooling specifications [41]. It is depicted as a 6 × 6 two dimensional schema.

In the descriptions of Gregor's theory types taxonomy the last theory type (Type V Theory (design and action)) say *'how to do something'* and the one thing the ZFEA does not do, is to specify a process and modelling approach clearly. This is one of the biggest criticisms against the ZFEA, and the ZFEA is therefore *not* a Type V Theory.

The descriptions of Gregor's first four theory types all specify that the theory specify *'What is'* so in order to be one of the first four theory types, the ZFEA need to conform to this characteristic [28]. Zachman claimed the ZFEA is 'The Enterprise Ontology' or *'a theory of the existence of a structured set of essential components of an object for which explicit expressions is necessary and perhaps even mandatory for creating, operating, and changing the object (the object being an Enterprise, a department, a value chain, a "sliver," a solution, a project, an airplane, a building, a product, a profession or whatever or whatever)'*. According to Zachman, the architecture built using the ZFEA schema would necessarily constitute the total set of descriptive representations that are relevant for describing the enterprise [1, 31]. From these descriptions it can be argued that the ZFEA's intent is clearly one of describing *'What is'*, so it is one of the first four theory types. We now need to determine which one.

The ZFEA does extend beyond 'analysis and description' (Type I Theory) by providing explanations (i.e. *'say what is, how, why when and where'*), but the ZFEA does not aim to predict with precision, which is typical of a Type II Theory. The ZFEA furthermore does not say '*what is and what will be*' and neither does the ZFEA have testable propositions (characteristics of a Type III Theory). The ZFEA aims to support causal explanation but does not pose direct quantitative causal explanations (the nature of Type IV Theories). From the above we could therefore argue that the ZFEA's goal and intent matches that of a Type II or *Explanatory* Theory that '*says what is, how, why, when and where*'. A Type II Theory furthermore '*provides explanation, but does not aim to predict with any precision. There are no testable propositions*'.

According to Gregor's taxonomy descriptions, the ZFEA can be regarded as an explanatory theory since the primary goals of the ZFEA conforms to those of an explanatory theory as discussed above. The next step is to analyse whether it is possible to identify the theory components of an IS theory depicted in Table 4 as is done by Gregor for the classification of theory types [28]. We followed the exact method of Gregor and this analysis is presented in Table 6.

**Table 6.** ZFEA and the theory components of Gregor [28].

| Theory overview | |
|---|---|
| The ZFEA is an ontology, a $6 \times 6$ two-dimensional schema and a structure that is descriptive in nature. The architecture of a specific enterprise that was developed using the ZFEA schema or ontology would necessarily constitute the total set of descriptive representations that are relevant for describing the enterprise | |
| Theory component | Instantiation: ZFEA |
| Means of representation | Conforms: Words, tables, diagrams, the ZFEA is a $6 \times 6$ matrix consisting of a diagram and tables with accompanying descriptions |
| Primary constructs | Conforms: The complex object is the enterprise with its strategy, technology, processes, people, roles, etc. A holistic view is displayed. Objects are viewed from different perspectives and interrogative abstractions |
| Statements of relationship | Conforms: Relationships between the audience perspectives and interrogative abstractions are specified as transformations, and within each cell primitives have predefined relationships. Relationships in the ZFEA (and EA in general) are very comprehensive i.e. dependent, associated, linked, bi-directional or multi-directional, etc. |
| Scope | Conforms: The scope is specified by the degree of generality of the statements of relationships. The ZFEA is a *general* schema that aims to provide a holistic view of any enterprise or engineered (complex) object and a very high level of generality is proposed. Generalization was part of the ZFEA development as the schema is derived from observing many different objects and industries |
| Causal explanations | Conforms: The ZFEA attempts to give statements of relationships among phenomena (represented by the rows and columns in the matrix). The ZFEA aims to support causal explanations |

*(continued)*

**Table 6.** (*continued*)

| Theory component | Instantiation: ZFEA |
|---|---|
| Testable propositions (hypotheses) | Does not conform: Statements of relationships between constructs that are stated in such a form that they can be tested empirically are not present. Zachman states that the model should not be applied deterministically but that it is an ontology that is repeatable and testable (such as the periodic table), however, there is not yet evidence of the ZFEA being implemented in such a way. An explanatory theory typically do not conform to this component |
| Prescriptive statements | Does not conform: Statements in the theory specify how people can accomplish something in practice (e.g., construct an artefact or develop a strategy). This is somewhat supported by the ZFEA as the purpose of the ZFEA is to model an enterprise by using the interrogatives and perspectives, however, detailed process or method is not supported. An explanatory theory typically do not conform to this component |

Given the results of the analyses, the conclusion can be made that the ZFEA could be regarded as an explanatory theory. An explanatory theory aims to provide an understanding on how, when and why an occurrence took place based on causality and argumentation. The ZFEA is aligned as its intent is to provide insights into the how, when and why of an enterprise. The ZFEA is represented in the form of a framework in order to provide a holistic view, but at the same time provides insights given specific perspectives. Each row, column and cell in the architecture is impacted by another e.g. the technology supports the business processes, the business processes the applications and the applications the strategy. Changes in any model will have an effect on the other models. Changes in strategy (cause) for example, will have an impact (effect) on the rest of the enterprise. All components form part of the whole to provide context. The scope is defined by the subset or component being designed. The ZFEA is described as an ontology and a structural schema that aims to be a repeatable and testable description of an enterprise. It can be argued that the main goals of the ZFEA is aligned to the goals of an explanatory theory since both aim to provide insight, understanding and causal explanations, as well as indicate relationships among components.

## 5   Conclusion

In this paper we motivate that the ZFEA could be regarded as an explanatory IS theory given the nature of theory in IS as proposed by Gregor [28]. The paper firstly discussed the need for EA and how the need for a descriptive representation of an enterprise stems from multiple disciplines. Based on the origins of EA, it is clear that EA was initially developed for the purpose of fulfilling the strategic need for a holistic representation of an enterprise that can be used as a common guideline to understand and compare organizations. The paper addressed certain criticisms pertaining to the origins, purpose and functionality of EA. EA, specifically the ZFEA, is often misunderstood, as it is not a methodology and does not provide steps on the implementation of an architecture.

Many different Enterprise Architecture Frameworks (EAF) addressing different business needs are available for use today, but for the purposes of this paper the framework of choice was the ZFEA. The ZFEA is an ontology and a two-dimensional schema aimed at providing a descriptive representation of a complex object [31]. As mentioned, the ZFEA's primary purpose is to provide a holistic understanding, thus supporting the argument of ZFEA serving as an explanatory IS theory.

ZFEA as explanatory theory provides a fresh perspective on how EA can be viewed, not as a methodology, but as a theory providing a lens for viewing or explaining an enterprise. As stated by Gregor, '*theory allows for different perspectives and aims to enhance our understanding of the world by providing explanations, descriptions, predictions and actionable guidance*'. Positioning the ZFEA as IS theory provides insight into the role and purpose of EA and could assist researchers and practitioners with addressing challenges experienced when instituting EA and EAM initiatives within organizations. EA as an explanatory IS theory for organisations also present a new platform, context and therefore perspective, for focussed strategic organisational research. Further research would extend the analysis of EA as IS theory to other frameworks, as well as explore the implications when using EA as theory. We furthermore want to investigate whether the ZFEA as meta-ontology for enterprises, may be considered as a meta-theory for organisational research.

# References

1. Zachman, J.A.: The framework for enterprise architecture: background, description and utility (2016). https://www.zachman.com/resources/ea-articles-reference/327-the-framework-for-enterprise-architecture-background-description-and-utility-by-john-a-zachman
2. Zachman, J.: A framework for information systems architecture. IBM Syst. J. **26**, 276–292 (1987)
3. Urbaczewski, L., Mrdalj, S.: A comparison of enterprise architecture frameworks. Int. J. Manag. Rev. **07**, 18–23 (2006)
4. The Open Group: TOGAF®, an Open Group Standard. http://www.opengroup.org/subjectareas/enterprise/togaf. Accessed 05 Jan 2018
5. Adenuga, O.A., Kekwaletswe, R.M.: Towards a framework for a unified enterprise architecture. IJCIT **03**, 30–33 (2012)
6. OMG: ArchiMate® 3.0.1 Specification. The Open Group (2016). http://pubs.opengroup.org/architecture/archimate3-doc/
7. IFIP-IFAC Task Force: GERAM : Generalised Enterprise Reference Architecture and Methodology, Version 1.6.3. Integration, IFIP–IFAC Task Force on Architectures for Enterprise (1999)
8. Federal Enterprise Architecture Framework. https://web.archive.org/web/20141030032759/http://www.whitehouse.gov/sites/default/files/omb/assets/egov_docs/fea_v2.pdf. Accessed 30 Oct 2019

394     A. Gerber et al.

9. DODAF - DOD Architecture Framework Version 2.02 - DOD Deputy Chief Information Officer. https://dodcio.defense.gov/library/dod-architecture-framework/. Accessed 30 Oct 2019

10. Lapalme, J.: Three schools of thought on enterprise architecture. IT Prof. **14**, 37–43 (2012). https://doi.org/10.1109/MITP.2011.109

11. Lapalme, J., de Guerre, D.: An open socio-technical systems approach to enterprise architecture. In: Gøtze, J., Jensen-Waud, A. (eds.) Beyond Alignment: Applying Systems Thinking to Architecting Enterprises. College Publications, London (2013)

12. Lapalme, J., Gerber, A., van der Merwe, A., de Vries, M., Hinkelmann, K.: Exploring the future of enterprise architecture: a Zachman perspective. Comput. Ind. **79**, 103–113 (2016)

13. de Vries, M., Gerber, A., van der Merwe, A.: The nature of the enterprise engineering discipline. In: Aveiro, D., Tribolet, J., Gouveia, D. (eds.) EEWC 2014. LNBIP, vol. 174, pp. 1–15. Springer, Cham (2014). https://doi.org/10.1007/978-3-319-06505-2_1

14. Rouhani, B.D., Mahrin, M.N., Nikpay, F., Ahmad, R.B., Nikfard, P.: A systematic literature review on enterprise architecture implementation methodologies. Inf. Softw. Technol. **62**, 1–20 (2015). https://doi.org/10.1016/j.infsof.2015.01.012

15. Lankhorst, M. (ed.): Enterprise Architecture At Work: Modelling, Communication, and Analysis. Springer, Heidelberg (2005). https://doi.org/10.1007/3-540-27505-3

16. Simon, D., Fischbach, K.: An exploration of enterprise architecture research. CAIS – Commun. AIS **32** (2013)

17. Aier, S., Gleichauf, B., Winter, R.: Understanding enterprise architecture management design - an empirical analysis (2011)

18. Rahimi, F., Gotze, J., Moller, C.: Enterprise architecture management: toward a taxonomy of applications. Commun. Assoc. Inf. Syst. **40**, 120–166 (2017)

19. Ernst, A.M.: Enterprise architecture management patterns. Presented at the (2008). https://doi.org/10.1145/1753196.1753205

20. Wißotzki, M., Koç, H., Weichert, T., Sandkuhl, K.: Development of an enterprise architecture management capability catalog. In: Kobyliński, A., Sobczak, A. (eds.) BIR 2013. LNBIP, vol. 158, pp. 112–126. Springer, Heidelberg (2013). https://doi.org/10.1007/978-3-642-40823-6_10

21. Matthes, F., Buckl, S., Leitel, J., Schweda, C.M.: Enterprise architecture management tool survey 2008 (2008)

22. Hinkelmann, K., Gerber, A., Karagiannis, D., Thoenssen, B., van der Merwe, A., Woitsch, R.: A new paradigm for the continuous alignment of business and IT: combining enterprise architecture modelling and enterprise ontology. Comput. Ind. **79**, 77–86 (2016). https://doi.org/10.1016/j.compind.2015.07.009

23. Lange, M., Mendling, J., Recker, J.: An empirical analysis of the factors and measures of enterprise architecture management success. Eur. J. Inf. Syst. **26**, 411 (2016). https://doi.org/10.1057/s41303-016-0001-6

24. McLeod, J.: Enterprise architecture is dead. https://medium.com/@JonMcLeodEA/enterprise-architecture-is-dead-33dd0e63cbbf. Accessed 30 Oct 2019

25. Bloomberg, J.: Is enterprise architecture completely broken? https://www.forbes.com/sites/jasonbloomberg/2014/07/11/is-enterprise-architecture-completely-broken/. Accessed 30 Oct 2019

26. Kotusev, S.: Fake and real tools for enterprise architecture. https://www.iqpc.com/events-enterprisearchitecture/blog/fake-and-real-tools-for-enterprise-architecture. Accessed 30 Oct 2019

27. Santos, J., Allega, P.: Hype Cycle for Enterprise Architecture, 2018. Gartner (2018)

28. Gregor, S.: The nature of theory in information systems. MIS Q. **30**, 611–642 (2006). https://doi.org/10.2307/25148742

29. Bernus, P., Nemes, L., Schmidt, G.: Handbook on Enterprise Architecture. Springer, Heidelberg (2003). https://doi.org/10.1007/978-3-540-24744-9
30. van der Merwe, A., Gerber, A., Kotze, P., van der Merwe, P., Mentz, J.: EARF - EA Definition. http://earf.meraka.org.za/earfhome/our-projects-1/completed-projects
31. Zachman, J.A.: The concise definition of the zachman framework (2008). https://www.zachman.com/about-the-zachman-framework
32. Niemi, E., Pekkola, S.: The benefits of enterprise architecture in organizational transformation. Bus. Inf. Syst. Eng. (2019). https://doi.org/10.1007/s12599-019-00605-3
33. Tamm, T., Seddon, P.B., Shanks, G., Reynolds, P.: How does enterprise architecture add value to organisations? Commun. Assoc. Inf. Syst. **28** (2011). https://doi.org/10.17705/1CAIS.02810
34. Hafsi, M., Assar, S.: What enterprise architecture can bring for digital transformation. IEEE (2016)
35. Winter, R., Fischer, R.: Essential layers, artifacts, and dependencies of enterprise architecture. In: 2006 10th IEEE International Enterprise Distributed Object Computing Conference Workshops (EDOCW 2006), p. 30. IEEE, Hong Kong (2006). https://doi.org/10.1109/EDOCW.2006.33
36. Rogers, C.: Proposed enterprise architecture solutions for Industry 4.0 manufacturing simulation information assets based on TOGAF. University of Denver University College (2016)
37. Buckl, S., Ernst, A.M., Matthes, F., Ramacher, R., Schweda, C.M.: Using enterprise architecture management patterns to complement TOGAF. Presented at the September (2009). https://doi.org/10.1109/EDOC.2009.30
38. Aier, S., Kurpjuweit, S., Saat, J., Winter, R.: Enterprise architecture design as an engineering discipline. AIS Trans. Enterp. Syst. **1**, 8 (2009)
39. Lin, F., Dyck, H.: The value of implementing enterprise architecture in organizations. J. Int. Technol. Inf. Manag. **19** (2010)
40. Zachman, J.A.: Enterprise Architecture: Notes on The Zachman Framework (2012). www.zachman.com
41. Kappelman, L.A., Zachman, J.A.: The enterprise and its architecture: ontology and challenges. J. Comput. Inf. Syst. 1–16 (2012)
42. Gregor, S.: Theory – still king but needing a revolution! J. Inf. Technol. **29**, 337–340 (2014). https://doi.org/10.1057/jit.2014.22
43. Urquhart, C., Lehmann, H., Myers, M.D.: Putting the 'theory' back into grounded theory: guidelines for grounded theory studies in information systems: guidelines for grounded theory studies in information systems. Inf. Syst. J. **20**, 357–381 (2009). https://doi.org/10.1111/j.1365-2575.2009.00328.x
44. Iivari, J.: Information systems as a design science. In: Vasilecas, O., Wojtkowski, W., Zupančič, J., Caplinskas, A., Wojtkowski, W.G., Wrycza, S. (eds.) Information Systems Development, pp. 15–27. Springer, Boston (2005). https://doi.org/10.1007/0-387-28809-0_2
45. Andrade, A.D.: Interpretive research aiming at theory building: adopting and adapting the case study design (2009)
46. Dennis, A.: An unhealthy obsession with theory. J. Assoc. Inf. Syst. (2019)
47. le Roux, P.: Enterprise architecture as conceptual support framework for small to medium enterprise growth: a South African study (2019)
48. Baskerville, R., Dulipovici, A.: The theoretical foundations of knowledge management. Knowl. Manag. Res. Pract. **4**, 83–105 (2006). https://doi.org/10.1057/palgrave.kmrp.8500090
49. Taylor, F.W.: The Principles of Scientific Management. Harper, New York (1911)

50. Shewhart, W.A.: Economic Control of Quality of Manufactured Product. Van Nostrand, New York (1931)
51. Forrester, J.W.: Industrial Dynamics. MIT Press, Cambridge (1961)
52. Drucker, P.F.: The Practice of Management. Pan, London (1968)
53. Blumenthal, S.C.: Management Information Systems: A Framework for Planning and Development. Prentice-Hall, Englewood Cliffs (1969)
54. Helfert, E.A.: Techniques of Financial Analysis. Irwin-Dorsey, Georgetown (1972)
55. Anthony, R.N.: Planning and Control Systems: A Framework for Analysis. Harvard University Press, Boston (1979)
56. Senge, P.M.: The Fifth Discipline: The Art and Practice of the Learning Organisation. Random House, London (1990)
57. Checkland, P.: Systems Thinking, Systems Practice. Wiley, Chichester (1981)
58. Zachman, J.: Enterprise architecture: the issue of the century (1996)

# A Scoping Review of the Application of the Task-Technology Fit Theory

Ruan Spies[1]([⊠]) [iD], Sara Grobbelaar[2] [iD], and Adele Botha[3] [iD]

[1] Department of Industrial Engineering, Stellenbosch University, Stellenbosch, South Africa
19008953@sun.ac.za
[2] Department of Industrial Engineering AND DST-NRF CoE in Scientometrics and Science, Technology and Innovation Policy (sciSTIP), Stellenbosch University, Stellenbosch, South Africa
[3] School of Computing, CSIR Meraka & UNISA, Pretoria, South Africa

**Abstract.** The Task-Technology Fit (TTF) theory provides a means of quantifying the effectiveness of technology in a system by assessing the relationship between the technology and the tasks the technology aims to support. The theory is widely recognized and has been applied in various ways, but little work has been done to summarize and synthesize the application of TTF in literature. The aim of this study is to identify and summarize the focus areas of studies that applied TTF, the environment in which it was applied, and the technologies which were considered by conducting a scoping review. It was found that applied studies focused primarily on generating theory or assessing certain real-world phenomena; was applied in a wide range of environments with the majority being in healthcare; and considered various technologies, with an increasing number of studies focusing on mobile technology. The findings of this study contribute to the understanding of TTF applications and assists in framing future research to further analyze TTF studies.

**Keywords:** Task-technology fit · Information technology

## 1 Introduction

Technology has become a fundamental aspect of our society and is embedded into everyday life. The way individuals and organizations work and think continues to be shaped by, and shape, various technologies [1]. In an organization, technology is typically applied to generate value by improving or supporting individual and collective tasks but do require a lot of resources for the acquisition, implementation and usage of the various technologies. Therefore, a common question is how much value the technology creates for an organization [2].

Due to the complexity of the interactions between factors such as the technology, users, systems, tasks and process it is extremely difficult to directly measure the value that technology creates in a system [1, 3]. Alternative measures have therefore been proposed to quantify the impact of technology. One such measure, widely accepted in

© IFIP International Federation for Information Processing 2020
Published by Springer Nature Switzerland AG 2020
M. Hattingh et al. (Eds.): I3E 2020, LNCS 12066, pp. 397–408, 2020.
https://doi.org/10.1007/978-3-030-44999-5_33

Information System (IS) research [4], is the Task-Technology Fit (TTF) theory which has been suggested to be "one of the most important developments in information system theory" [5]. TTF provides a means to quantify the effectiveness of technology in an organizations [6]. In 2012, Furneaux [7] identified the *"notable increase in the use of TTF theory"*. This trend has continued over the years, with both an increase in the yearly number of documents published as well as in the range of environments which the theory is used, as discussed in this paper.

Despite the wide use of the theory, only two publications by Cane and McCarthy [8] and the work by Furneaux [7] was found that summarizes and synthesizes TTF related studies. The article by Cane and McCarthy [8] is limited to a small number of studies, all of which were conducted before 2006, and only considered how the studies defined TTF and its surrounding components. Furneaux [7] considered a much larger sample of studies where TTF was used, all of which were conducted before 2010, to synthesize the conceptualization, methodologies and research contexts. Where both of the former studies focused primarily on *how* TTF was applied, this study is concerned with *why*, *where* and *on what* TTF was applied.

The aim of this paper is to conduct a scoping review (SR) aims to explore the application of the Task-technology fit theory by (1) identifying the scope and range of the available literature that applies the specific components of TTF; and (2) summarizing and disseminating the research findings, specifically, (a) the purpose of applying TTF, (b) the environments where TTF has been applied, (c) the technologies that TTF has been applied on. Based on these objectives, the research questions to be answered in this paper are: (1) What are the intentions for applying TTF? (2) Which environments has TTF been applied in? (3) What technologies has TTF been applied on?

## 2   Conceptualization of Task-Technology Fit

In this section, the TTF model, proposed in the seminal article by Goodhue and Thompson [3], is discussed. Goodhue and Thompson [3] states, *"Models are ways to structure what we know about reality, to clarify understandings, and to communicate those understandings to others. Once articulated and shared, a model can guide thinking in productive ways, but it can also constrain our thinking into channels consistent with the model, blocking us from seeing part of what is happening in the domain we have modeled."*

The basic TTF model, depicted in Fig. 1, therefore provides a lens of technology usage and the value that it creates [3]. In a setting where technology is used by individual's to perform certain tasks, or sets of tasks, the model's premise is that the value/performance of technology is created by the alignment, or fit, of the task requirements and the technology characteristics that allow a user to perform the tasks [6, 9].

Tasks refer to the totality of physical and/or cognitive actions and processes done by individuals in a given environment. Task characteristics are considered specifically in relation to the technology that supports the tasks and are broken down to different levels of detail, depending on the complexity of the tasks performed [3, 10].

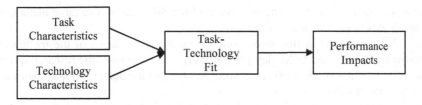

**Fig. 1.** Basic task-technology fit model

Applying the TTF theory in different environments will result in different specific task characteristics. However, in literature, the process followed to identify the task characteristics are similar and typically involve analyzing the tasks performed in an environment and creating various task categories and subcategories that can be related to TTF [4, 6, 11–13].

Technology is defined as the tools that are used by individuals to execute, or assist in executing, their tasks [3, 10, 14]. Similar to the discussion of task characteristics, different technologies will have different characteristics which are defined by the researcher with consideration to the environment which it used in and the tasks it aims to support [15].

TTF is defined as the extent to which a technology assists an individual in performing his or her tasks [3, 10, 14, 16–18] and is consequently affected by the interaction between the characteristics of the task and the functionalities of the technology [4]. Typical dimensions that are considered when measuring fit, as defined by Goodhue and Thompson [3], are data quality, data locatability, authorization to access data, data compatibility, ease of use/training, production timeliness, systems reliability, information system relationship with users.

The purpose of the study by Goodhue and Thompson [3] was to show that a positive impact of technology requires a good TTF. Thus, when technology fits the task characteristics it aims to support, it should result in improved performance [9]. The improved performance is typically due to the smooth execution of the task, reducing the cost of performing the task, or making the task easier to accomplish [4].

## 3 Methodology

In 2005, Arksey and O'Malley [19] published the influential article in which it was discussed that there exists ambiguity in the *"plethora of terminology"* which is used to describe various reviews of literature. The article makes the case that literature review methodologies provide a set of tools which may be used by researchers and that there does not exist an *"ideal type"* of literature review.

The article argues for SRs to be used to develop an overview of domain knowledge. This is achieved by identifying the quantity of literature and analyzing key features of the literature which differs slightly from traditional systematic reviews which aim to comprehensively synthesize literature. The SR does however follow a similar methodological approach as traditional systematic reviews and can also be considered to be replicable and reliable. These features of the SR make it a suitable methodology to answer this study's research questions.

The SR conducted in this study follows the first five stages of the methodology proposed by Arksey and O'Malley [19], namely, to (1) identify the research question; (2) identify relevant studies; (3) select studies; (4) chart the data; (5) collate, summarize and report the results.

The first stage is completed in the Sect. 1 of this study and stages 2–5 are discussed in the following sections and subsections.

### 3.1    Search Strategy

To identify relevant studies that can be used to answer the research questions, a search was conducted on the Scopus research database. Scopus was chosen due to the large number of indexed journals covering a wide range of disciplines. Relevant studies were considered articles published in peer-reviewed journals that *apply* the TTF theory as part of the primary aim of the study and includes any studies that summarizes work done. In literature, it was found that the term *application*, in relation to TTF, is used in a broad manner, extending to the use of smaller concepts, adaptations and findings of TTF as part of the studies. In this paper, *application* (of TTF) is used in a specified manner, to only consider where TTF is used as conceptualized in Sect. 2.

An exploratory search was conducted with the terms "Task-technology fit" OR "technology-to-performance". The titles and abstracts of the top ten cited articles and top ten most recent articles were examined to identify relevant keywords to be included to ensure the comprehensiveness of the search. Variations of the terms evaluate, apply, diagnose and assess were found to be relevant and included in the search. The search was conducted on 04 October 2019 with the search criteria including the terms ("Task-technology fit" OR "technology-to-performance") AND (evaluat* OR appl* OR diagnos* OR assess*), limited to journal articles, which yielded 173 results.

Various measures were taken to ensure that all influential articles were included in the study. Bibliometrix, an R-tool for comprehensive science mapping analysis [20], was used to analyze the most cited articles out of the local 173 results, resulting in one article being added. The tool was also used to determine the top locally cited authors. A further search was done on Scopus and ResearchGate to determine whether any further important studies has been published by these authors, resulting in two articles being added. As a final measure, as full-text articles were screened, a list was compiled of the literature each study used as a theoretical foundation. All of the items on the list were however already included and therefore no further studies were added.

### 3.2    Study Selection

The research questions were used to define the inclusion criteria, and inversely the exclusion criteria, as shown in Table 1. As discussed in the previous section, a large number of studies uses certain concepts of TTF without discussing or applying the theory as conceptualized in Sect. 2, the three exclusion criteria was aimed to specifically eliminate these articles.

The titles and abstracts of the 176 studies were screened and 43 studies were excluded from the review based on EC 1. The online availability of the remaining 133 was checked and 5 were found to be unobtainable. The available full-text studies were downloaded, and the data of the studies was exported from Scopus into MS Excel.

**Table 1.** Inclusion and exclusion criteria

| Inclusion criteria | | Exclusion criteria | |
|---|---|---|---|
| IC 1 | Application of the TTF | EC 1 | No mention of TTF in abstract |
| IC 2 | Thorough discussion of theory | EC 2 | Isolate TTF concepts |
| | | EC 3 | TTF not central to the study |

The criteria were applied to the abstracts and the full-text articles and 91 studies were excluded due to the content being irrelevant to the study, based on EC 2 and EC 3.

The entire process followed in selecting relevant studies, based on the PRISMA statement for reporting systematic reviews [21], is depicted in Fig. 2.

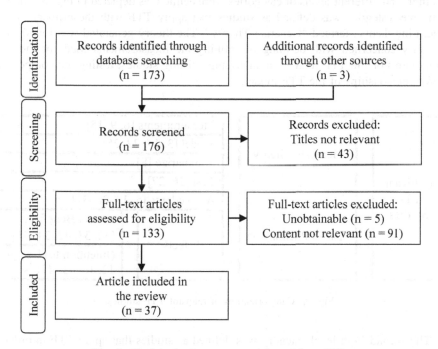

**Fig. 2.** Study selection process. Adapted from [21].

The study selection process resulted in a total of 37 studies, that applies or discusses TTF as conceptualized in Sect. 2, being included in the review. The process followed to identify and extract the data is discussed in the following section.

### 3.3    Charting the Data

The charting phases required the articles included in the review to be re-read thoroughly with the aim of extracting the data relevant to the research questions. A charting form was collectively defined by the researchers to ensure credibility of the data to be extracted. The full-text articles were imported into ATLAS.ti, software used for qualitative data analysis and the charting form was used to define the categories for the coding process. The full-text studies were then read through and coded as applicable.

## 4    Results

In this section, the results obtained from analyzing the studies are discussed to answer the research questions.

### 4.1    Study Categories

The coded data, identified as part of the process discussed in Sect. 3.3, was grouped together, and different levels of categories were defined, as depicted in Fig. 3. The first high-level category was defined as studies that apply TTF with the primary aim of generating theory, termed "Generate Theory". The theory generated was found to be primarily concerned with defining or refining the measurements used for the TTF components or the TTF model; summarizing existing studies; testing the components and/or relationships of the TTF model.

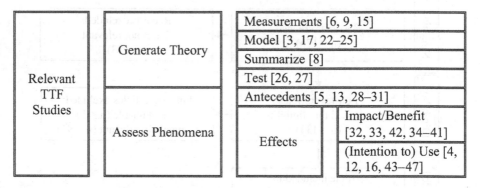

**Fig. 3.**  Categorization of relevant TTF studies.

The second high-level category was defined as studies that apply TTF in order to assess certain real-world phenomena, termed "Assess Phenomena". These applications were concerned with two major aspects – the components, such as the technology characteristics, that are antecedents to TTF and the assessing effects of TTF. These studies concerned with assessing the effects were further broken down into those that assess the impact or benefit of TTF and those that assess factors relating to the use, or intention to use, of the technology based on TTF.

The two high level categories were used to determine the trends in the type of studies published over time. The cumulative number of studies published for the two highest-level categories was calculated over time and depicted in Fig. 4. From the figure, it can be seen that a larger number of studies were initially published that aimed to generate theory and that as time progressed the focus shifted to the application of TTF to assess phenomena.

As the theory gained recognition, different aspects of the theory was refined and the impact of applying the theory for assessing different phenomena was recognized, the focus of studies is expected to shift from predominantly theory based to applying it, as seen in the increasing trend in the figure – eventually exponentially overtaking the theoretical.

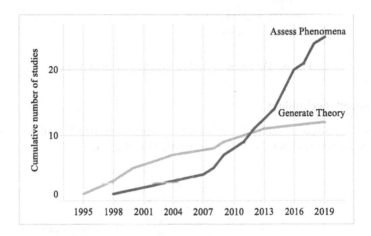

**Fig. 4.** Cumulative number of studies over time for each study category.

The assessment of TTF antecedents was only introduced in 2009, 11 years after the first application of the theory to assess the impact/benefit and is still an emerging area of research which does hold a lot of potential. Since the antecedents have an effect on TTF, applying the theory to assess these factors has shown to be beneficial in identifying improvements that can be made to ultimately improve TTF.

### 4.2   Application Environment

For each of the relevant studies, the specific environment in which the TTF was applied was identified, collectively categorized by the researchers and is summarized in Fig. 5.

The majority of the studies were applied in either a healthcare setting or in various different, but not explicitly identified, environments. Although the tasks performed in these different environments will vary greatly, the wide range of application environments provides evidence that the TTF can applied in diverse settings. Furthermore, the diverse environments create the opportunity for interesting future research to be done in the similarities and differences in the way in which TTF is applied.

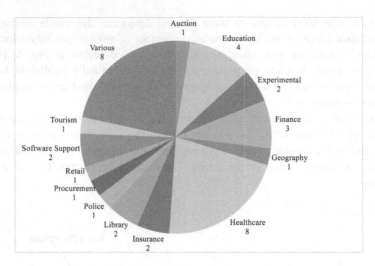

**Fig. 5.** Divisions of TTF application environments.

### 4.3   Assessed Technology

The technology used in each of the relevant studies was also identified, collectively categorized by the researchers and is summarized in Fig. 6.

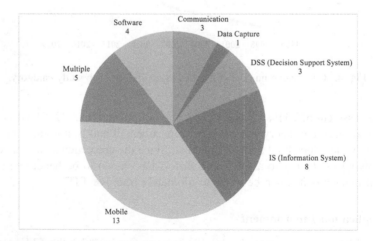

**Fig. 6.** Divisions of the technology assessed in the relevant studies.

Since the TTF theory is mainly part of IS research, it was expected that the application of TTF would primarily be concerned with IS. An interesting observation was the growing research interest in mobile technology. The first two relevant studies applying TTF to mobile technology [15, 36] was published in 2004 after which the majority of future published articles included in this study (40.7%) was focused on mobile technology. This finding makes sense in considering the rapid uptake, improved capabilities and gradual dependence on smartphone technology since 2004.

## 5 Conclusion

The TTF theory has been an important development in IS research and has been widely applied in various environments and on a range of technologies. This study aimed to identify and analyze relevant literature that applies the specific components of TTF to answer three research questions concerned with *why, where* and *on what* TTF was applied.

As part of the chosen SR methodology, a structured search and screening approach was followed to identify relevant studies, the detailed discussion on the process followed ensuring the reliability and replicability thereof. These studies were then analyzed, the data extracted, and the findings synthesized to answer the research questions. The implementation and discussion of the methodology ensured the validity and reliability of the study.

The first research question is answered in the analysis and synthesis of the intentions for applying TTF where various levels of categories were defined for the intentions. The categories were further used to determine specific trends over time, revealing how the focus of studies shifted from predominantly theory based to the application of TTF to assess various phenomena.

The analysis and synthesis of the application environment and assessed technology revealed the wide range of environments and technologies associated with the application of TTF, consequently answering both the second and final research questions. These findings reveal the wide range of applicability of the TTF theory and also the potential that it holds for both industry and academia in applying TTF in different environments and with new technologies.

The results of the scoping review are dependent on the studies included for analysis. The initial search for relevant articles is limited in that only one database was used to search for relevant articles. This may have resulted in further relevant works being excluded from this study. Various measures were however taken to ensure that all influential studies potentially missed in the search were included in this study. Although the intention was to define screening criteria in a manner that would ensure reliability and replicability of the screening process, the authors acknowledge that

Despite the limitations of the study, the findings of this study are valuable and further assists in framing future research on the application of TTF. The different studies which apply TTF may be further analyzed to determine trends in the methodologies followed within and/or across the different application categories, environments and technologies. This in turn may be used to provide guidelines in the quantitative measurement of different TTF constructs, given a specific intention for, and context of, use. The suggested future research may assist in the classic pursuit to better understand, account for and explain the impact of technologies within a system.

# References

1. Orlikowski, W.J.: Using technology and constituting structures: a practice lens for studying technology in organizations. Organ. Sci. **11**, 404–428 (2000). https://doi.org/10.1287/orsc.11.4.404.14600
2. Melville, B.N., Kraemer, K.: Review: information technology and organizational performance. MIS Q. **28**, 283–322 (2004)
3. Goodhue, D.L., Thompson, R.L.: Task-technology fit and individual performance. MIS Q. Manag. Inf. Syst. **19**, 213–233 (1995)
4. Lee, C.C., Cheng, H.K.H.H.: An empirical study of mobile commerce in insurance industry: task-technology fit and individual differences. Decis. Support Syst. **43**, 95–110 (2007). https://doi.org/10.1016/j.dss.2005.05.008
5. Melchor-Ferrer, E., Buendía-Carrillo, D.: Financial information management for university departments, using open-source software. Int. J. Inf. Manag. **34**, 191–199 (2014). https://doi.org/10.1016/j.ijinfomgt.2013.12.009
6. Goodhue, D.L.: Development and measurement validity of a task-technology fit instrument for user evaluations of information system. Decis. Sci. **29**, 105–138 (1998). https://doi.org/10.1111/j.1540-5915.1998.tb01346.x
7. Furneaux, B.: Task-technology fit theory - a survey and synopsis of the literature.pdf. In: Information Systems Theory Integrated Series in Information Systems, pp. 87–106 (2012)
8. Cane, S., McCarthy, R.: Analyzing the factors that affect information systems use: a task-technology fit meta-analysis. J. Comput. Inf. Syst. **50**, 108–123 (2009)
9. Goodhue, D.L., Klein, B.D., March, S.T.: User evaluations of IS as surrogates for objective performance. Inf. Manag. **38**, 87–101 (2000). https://doi.org/10.1016/S0378-7206(00)00057-4
10. Ammenwerth, E., Iller, C., Mahler, C.: IT-adoption and the interaction of task, technology and individuals: a fit framework and a case study. BMC Med. Inform. Decis. Mak. **6**, 1–13 (2006). https://doi.org/10.1186/1472-6947-6-3
11. Barki, H., Titah, R., Boffo, C.: System use-related activity: an behavioral conceptualization of expanded information system use. Inf. Syst. Res. **18**, 173–192 (2007). https://doi.org/10.1287/isre.l070.0122
12. Wang, S.L., Lin, H.I.: Integrating TTF and IDT to evaluate user intention of big data analytics in mobile cloud healthcare system. Behav. Inf. Technol. **3001**, 974–985 (2019). https://doi.org/10.1080/0144929X.2019.1626486
13. Ali, S.B., Romero, J., Morrison, K., Hafeez, B., Ancker, J.S.: Focus section health IT usability: applying a task-technology fit model to adapt an electronic patient portal for patient work. Appl. Clin. Inform. **9**, 174–184 (2018). https://doi.org/10.1055/s-0038-1632396
14. Yang, L., Yang, S.H., Plotnick, L.: How the internet of things technology enhances emergency response operations. Technol. Forecast. Soc. Change **80**, 1854–1867 (2013). https://doi.org/10.1016/j.techfore.2012.07.011
15. Gebauer, J., Shaw, M.J.: Success factors and impacts of mobile business applications: results from a mobile e-procurement study. Int. J. Electron. Commer. **8**, 19–41 (2004). https://doi.org/10.1080/10864415.2004.11044304
16. Dishaw, M.T., Strong, D.M.: Assessing software maintenance tool utilization using task-technology fit and fitness-for-use models. J. Softw. Maint. Evol. **10**, 151–179 (1998)
17. Howard, M.C., Rose, J.C.: Refining and extending task–technology fit theory: creation of two task–technology fit scales and empirical clarification of the construct. Inf. Manag. **56**, 103134 (2018). https://doi.org/10.1016/j.im.2018.12.002

18. Fuller, R.M., Dennis, A.R.: Does fit matter? The impact of task-technology fit and appropriation on team performance in repeated tasks. Inf. Syst. Res. **20**, 2–17 (2009). https://doi.org/10.1287/isre.1070.0167

19. Arksey, H., O'Malley, L.: Scoping studies: towards a methodological framework. Int. J. Soc. Res. Methodol. **8**, 19–32 (2005). https://doi.org/10.1017/s0922156508005621

20. Aria, M., Cuccurullo, C.: bibliometrix: an R-tool for comprehensive science mapping analysis. J. Informetr. **11**, 959–975 (2017)

21. Moher, D., Liberati, A., Tetzlaff, J., Altman, D.G., PRISMA Group: Preferred reporting items for systematic reviews and meta-analyses: the PRISMA statement. PLOS Med. **6**, 1–6 (2009). https://doi.org/10.1371/journal.pmed.1000097

22. Dishaw, M.T., Strong, D.M.: Supporting software maintenance with software engineering tools: a computed task-technology fit analysis. J. Syst. Softw. **44**, 107–120 (1998). https://doi.org/10.1016/S0164-1212(98)10048-1

23. Gebauer, J., Tang, Y.: Applying the theory of task-technology fit to mobile technology: the role of user mobility. Int. J. Mob. Commun. **6**, 321–344 (2008). https://doi.org/10.1504/IJMC.2008.017514

24. Liu, Y., Lee, Y., Chen, A.N.K.: Evaluating the effects of task-individual-technology fit in multi-DSS models context: a two-phase view. Decis. Support Syst. **51**, 688–700 (2011). https://doi.org/10.1016/j.dss.2011.03.009

25. Yang, H.D., Kang, S., Oh, W., Kim, M.S.: Are all fits created equal? A nonlinear perspective on task-technology fit. J. Assoc. Inf. Syst. **14**, 694–721 (2013)

26. Staples, D.S., Seddon, P.B.: Testing the technology-to-performance chain model. Adv. Top. End User Comput. **4**, 42–64 (2005). https://doi.org/10.4018/978-1-59140-474-3.ch003

27. Zigurs, I., Buckland, B.K., Connolly, J.R., Vance Wilson, E.: A test of task-technology fit theory for group support systems. Data Base Adv. Inf. Syst. **30**, 34–50 (1999). https://doi.org/10.1145/344241.344244

28. Gebauer, J., Ginsburg, M.: Exploring the black box of task-technology fit. Commun. ACM **52**, 130–135 (2009). https://doi.org/10.1145/1435417.1435447

29. Hsiao, J., Chen, R.-F.: An investigation on fit of mobile nursing information systems for nursing performance. CIN - Comput. Inform. Nurs. **30**, 265–273 (2012). https://doi.org/10.1097/NCN.0b013e31823eb82c

30. Pelzer, P., Arciniegas, G., Geertman, S., Lenferink, S.: Planning support systems and task-technology fit: a comparative case study. Appl. Spat. Anal. Policy **8**, 155–175 (2015). https://doi.org/10.1007/s12061-015-9135-5

31. Rivera, M., Croes, R., Zhong, Y.S.: Developing mobile services: a look at first-time and repeat visitors in a small island destination. Int. J. Contemp. Hosp. Manag. **28**, 2721–2747 (2016). https://doi.org/10.1108/IJCHM-02-2015-0052

32. Bere, A.: Applying an extended task-technology fit for establishing determinants of mobile learning: an instant messaging initiative. J. Inf. Syst. Educ. **29**, 239–252 (2018)

33. Cady, R.G., Finkelstein, S.M.: Task-technology fit of video telehealth for nurses in an outpatient clinic setting. Telemed. e-Health **20**, 633–639 (2014). https://doi.org/10.1089/tmj.2013.0242

34. Chen, P., Yu, C., Chen, G.Y.: Applying task-technology fit model to the healthcare sector: a case study of hospitals' computed tomography patient-referral mechanism. J. Med. Syst. **39** (2015). https://doi.org/10.1007/s10916-015-0264-9

35. Glowalla, P., Sunyaev, A.: ERP system fit – an explorative task and data quality perspective. J. Enterp. Inf. Manag. **27**, 668–686 (2014). https://doi.org/10.1108/JEIM-08-2013-0062

36. Ioimo, R.E., Aronson, J.E.: Police field mobile computing: applying the theory of task-technology fit. Police Q. **7**, 403–428 (2004). https://doi.org/10.1177/1098611103251113

37. Kim, D.-Y., Han, S.-M., Youngblood Jr., M.: Sequential patient recruitment monitoring in multi-center clinical trials. Commun. Stat. Appl. Methods **25**, 501–512 (2018). https://doi.org/10.29220/CSAM.2018.25.5.501

38. McGill, T.J., Klobas, J.E.: A task-technology fit view of learning management system impact. Comput. Educ. **52**, 496–508 (2009). https://doi.org/10.1016/j.compedu.2008.10.002

39. Raven, A., Le, E., Park, C.: Digital video presentation and student performance: a task technology fit perspective. Int. J. Inf. Commun. Technol. Educ. **6**, 17–29 (2010). https://doi.org/10.4018/jicte.2010091102

40. Tam, C., Oliveira, T.: Understanding the impact of m-banking on individual performance: DeLone & McLean and TTF perspective. Comput. Human Behav. **61**, 233–244 (2016). https://doi.org/10.1016/j.chb.2016.03.016

41. Yi, Y.J., You, S., Bae, B.J.: The influence of smartphones on academic performance: the development of the technology-to-performance chain model. Libr. Hi Tech **34**, 480–499 (2016). https://doi.org/10.1108/LHT-04-2016-0038

42. Lepanto, L., Sicotte, C., Lehoux, P.: Assessing task-technology fit in a PACS upgrade: do users' and developers' appraisals converge? J. Digit. Imaging **24**, 951–958 (2011). https://doi.org/10.1007/s10278-011-9378-x

43. Vongjaturapat, S.: Application of the task-technology fit model to structure and evaluation of the adoption of smartphones for online library systems. Sci. Technol. Asia **23**, 39–56 (2018). https://doi.org/10.14456/scitechasia.2018.6

44. Chang, H.H.: Intelligent agent's technology characteristics applied to online auctions' task: a combined model of TTF and TAM. Technovation **28**, 564–577 (2008). https://doi.org/10.1016/j.technovation.2008.03.006

45. Huang, L., Shiau, W.-L.W., Lin, Y.: What factors satisfy e-book store customers? Development of a model to evaluate e-book user behavior and satisfaction. Internet Res. **27**, 563–585 (2017). https://doi.org/10.1108/IntR-05-2016-0142

46. Pendharkar, P.C., Khosrowpour, M., Rodger, J.A.: Development and testing of an instrument for measuring the user evaluations of information technology in health care. J. Comput. Inf. Syst. **41**, 84–89 (2001)

47. Sheehan, B., Lee, Y., Rodriguez, M., Tiase, V., Schnall, R.: A comparison of usability factors of four mobile devices for accessing healthcare information by adolescents. Appl. Clin. Inform. **3**, 356–366 (2012). https://doi.org/10.4338/ACI-2012-06-RA-0021

# A Broker-Based Framework
# for the Recommendation of Cloud Services:
# A Research Proposal

Raoul Hentschel[(✉)] and Susanne Strahringer

Business Informatics, esp. IS in Trade and Industry,
TU Dresden, Dresden, Germany
{raoul.hentschel,susanne.strahringer}@tu-dresden.de

**Abstract.** Finding and comparing appropriate cloud services that best fit cloud service consumer requirements can be a complex, time-consuming and cost-intensive process, especially for small and medium-sized enterprises. Since there is no "one-fits-all" cloud service provider, companies face the challenge of selecting and combining services from different vendors to meet all their requirements. Therefore, this paper calls for the design of a cloud brokering framework that would enable faster and easier selection of cloud services by recommending appropriate services through a matchmaking system. Drawing on previously conducted studies and considering current issues and practical experiences both from provider and user perspectives, we propose a framework that would identify, rank and recommend cloud services from multiple modules and components to individual consumers. Furthermore, we contribute an early-stage design of a cloud broker framework that considers cloud-service consumers' sourcing preferences while making new cloud-sourcing decisions and that can be used in the selection and adoption phase of implementing cloud services and/or as part of a multicloud strategy.

**Keywords:** Cloud computing · Cloud brokering · Guidance support system · Multi-sided platform · Matchmaking platform

## 1 Introduction

Cloud computing (CC) is a driving force in the current digitization debate that offers companies of all sizes new benefits such as consuming computing resources (e.g., networks, servers, storage, applications, and services) with low/minimal entry costs, pay-per-use options, great flexibility, and scalability. Due to the recent proliferation of CC, the number of cloud services on the market is increasing rapidly. Therefore, the selection and implementation of suitable cloud services is a challenging, knowledge-intensive process that requires widespread participation and ownership among heterogeneous stakeholder groups (e.g., business managers, IT units, etc.) [1]. The variety of available services is further complicated by a lack of informational transparency concerning product characteristics, technology, QoS, pricing and their inter-correlations (e.g., price/quality trade-offs). This makes it difficult to compare cloud services and select the option that best fits the cloud service consumers'

© IFIP International Federation for Information Processing 2020
Published by Springer Nature Switzerland AG 2020
M. Hattingh et al. (Eds.): I3E 2020, LNCS 12066, pp. 409–415, 2020.
https://doi.org/10.1007/978-3-030-44999-5_34

(CSC) requirements. Finding a suitable cloud service provider (CSP) that matches all the CSC's requirements is a complex, time-consuming and cost-intensive process that can prevent the adoption of CC especially in small and medium-sized enterprises (SME) [2]. The reasons for this are manifold: a lack of universal definitions and standards for cloud services [3], the challenge of comparing the characteristics and performance metrics of cloud services over different maturity levels and quality standards, and different naming conventions for the same services, an understanding of which requires domain-specific knowledge of CSCs [4, 5].

As a result, CSCs increasingly need guidance support systems [6] that enable faster, easier and more reliable cloud services selection by helping SMEs choose (the best) services from a wealth of alternatives. We define these alternatives as service configuration options (SCO). To the best of our knowledge, there is currently no approach available that specifically supports the (semi-)automated identification and recommendation of cloud service alternatives for SMEs using a cloud brokering and matchmaking system. In order to address this problem, we propose a cloud service broker framework called "ViBROS" as a starting point for supporting CSCs in their decision-making process by recommending appropriate cloud services based on CSC requirements using dynamic and extensible matching methods. Thus, our research question (RQ) is: How should a cloud-service brokering framework be designed to support cloud service consumers in SMEs in the selection and adoption phase of implementing cloud services? In order to answer this RQ, the remainder of the paper is organized as follows: the introduction and definition of the problem included above (Sect. 1) are followed by the theoretical background (Sect. 2) and the proposal of a new framework (Sect. 3). The paper ends with the conclusion and future recommendations (Sect. 4).

## 2 Theoretical Background

### 2.1 Cloud Computing

CC is an alternative approach to IT sourcing that enables companies to access a shared pool of managed and scalable IT resources (e.g., networks, servers, storage, applications, and services) that are accessible via the internet on a pay-per-use basis without necessitating long-term investments [2]. CC services are typically classified by the type of service differentiated by a given resource (e.g., application (SaaS), platform (PaaS) and infrastructure (IaaS) level) [7]. In addition to the more technical characteristics, more business-oriented classifications have also emerged to differentiate these services from one another. Böhm et al. [8] identified eight common market actors that interact in a cloud value network. Additionally, the NIST defines five major actors: *cloud consumer, cloud provider, cloud auditor, cloud broker,* and *cloud carrier* where each entity (a person or organization) performs tasks in CC [9].

## 2.2 Cloud Brokering and Two-Sided Platforms

A cloud broker (CB) is an entity who acts as an intermediary between the CSP and the CSC and performs tasks that involve the selection, integration, or delivery of cloud services. Additionally, CBs also fulfill functions such as aggregating information concerning goods and fostering trust between cloud providers and cloud consumers [9]. There are many examples of markets in which two or more groups interact via intermediaries or platforms to benefit each other and potentially create cross-platform network effects (e.g., Airbnb, Uber, etc.) [10, 11]. All these so-called multi-sided platforms (MSP) have one thing in common: they can only be successful when the "chicken-and-egg problem" can be solved by convincing both sides of the market to engage their services [12]. Matchmaking platforms, such as cloud brokering platforms, can also be seen as two-sided in the sense that the matching "platform" is more attractive when more participants on the other end of the market participate [13–15]; hence, a successful CB will be of value for both consumers and vendors [16]. Two of the main benefits of CBs from a consumer's point of view are its ability to minimize search time, thereby saving costs, and its providing an opportunity to interact with an expert instead of working with numerous CSPs [17]. Consumers also benefit from the support provided for activities such as the selection, implementation and management of cloud services and can thereby avoid being "locked-in" to a single provider. For CSPs, cooperation with a CB may enhance market visibility and result in a higher rate of revenue growth [18].

The need for brokering mechanisms for cloud services first arises when using cloud federation architectures, such as Intercloud [19] or Stratos [20]. There are various concepts about and frameworks for cloud brokering that have been discussed in prior research [21], including those dealing with service intermediation between CSPs and CSCs [19, 22]. However, most of the literature focuses on building cloud brokerage systems where users either provide low-level specifications (e.g. resource requirements for applications or QoS requirements for applications) that are measurable and comparable functional requirements [23] or are limited to technical issues that can be solved using multiple-criteria decision-making (MCDM) methods [24]. However, the literature does not consider organizational or environmental aspects. Additionally, we were unable to find any approaches specific to the needs of SMEs [25]. We argue that start-ups and SMEs need cloud brokering systems that are not only designed for large cloud implementation projects but are also better aligned with the nature of cloud services (e.g. flexible, automated) in terms of type and cost. Also, the selection and integration of new services is a very dynamic process that will affect daily business operations.

## 3  Proposal of a New Cloud Brokering Framework

The goal of our research is to address the gap in the literature and, as a first step, to propose a framework that considers the functional and non-functional requirements of cloud consumers on the technical, organizational and environmental levels. This will enable SMEs to make a reasonable decision about CSPs, even without domain-specific knowledge, while achieving lower costs and saving time in comparison to traditional consultants and cloud brokers. Second, we propose a prototype that enables a (semi-) automated selection of cloud services as part of a recommendation system. To do so, we follow a design science research (DSR) approach. DSR is an important paradigm in IS research as it serves as a guideline for the process of constructing socio-technical artifacts in the IS domain [26]. We follow the process of Peffers et al. [27] for creating design science artifacts and then map these artifacts onto the digital innovation roles in DSR, as proposed by [28]. In order to adequately consider current issues and practical experiences, the requirements of SMEs for such a framework were analyzed from both the provider and user perspectives in a previous work [25, 29]. Based on the findings of that piece and an extensive literature review on existing frameworks, we have iteratively developed the first version of our *Virtual Broker as a Service Framework*, called *ViBROS*, as part of our design-oriented approach (see Fig. 1). *ViBROS* discovers and ranks cloud services for CSCs based on one or more *Decision Components* and filters the results to finally make a recommendation at the user's request.

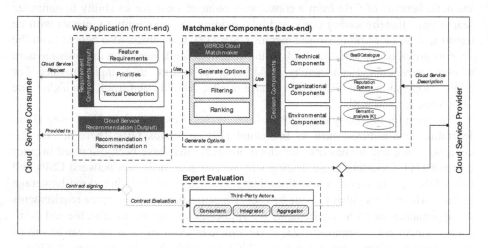

**Fig. 1.** Virtual Broker as a Service Framework (ViBROS)

Inputs are (feature) requirements and a textual description in natural language of the desired features of the cloud service. These provided inputs (*Requirements Components*) can then be prioritized and processed by a discovery service called *ViBROS Cloud Matchmaker* that uses the back-end *Decision Components* for the subsequent matchmaking. The *Decision Components* are defined by the platform owner and can be dynamically added and/or removed and are accessible via API (e.g., RESTful Web services). Each component can be addressed and enriched with information provided by CSPs.

Finally, the *ViBROS Cloud Matchmaker* generates options determined by users' preferences, makes a pairwise comparison of every SCO using the AHP method, and recommends those that are suitable. It thus finds a match between the appropriate cloud services and the SME looking for one. Since not every CSC is willing or able to sign a contract with a CSP immediately, the CSC can also evaluate the cloud SCOs proposed by a neutral expert (i.e., consultants, integrators, etc.). Thus, the expert has the option to support the consumer in steps that go beyond the selection of a CSP (e.g. in the implementation of services) and thereby generates more business. As a result, the CSC receives a bundle of suitable cloud services, ranked according to their specific suitability with the option of having them evaluated by an expert, before finally selecting one or more cloud services to implement.

# 4 Conclusion and Future Work

The current state of our research shows that many existing frameworks only provide partial guidance in the selection phase of cloud services. This research-in-progress article addresses this gap and proposes a new framework called *ViBROS* as a starting point for providing a more reliable and cost-efficient approach for SMEs to use while selecting appropriate cloud services. Since there is no "one-fits-all" CSP, CSCs can benefit from receiving recommendations for cloud SCOs, which will therefore reduce search costs while taking sourcing preferences (e.g., requirements, priorities, etc.) into consideration in the selection and adoption phases. Researchers can use key components of the framework to support their own cloud brokering problems. In future work, the back-end *Decision Components* and *Cloud Matchmaker* algorithms of the framework must be designed in more detail in order to instantiate a prototype of *ViBROS*. Also, the handling of the heterogeneity of cloud services must be addressed in more detail. Currently, the framework is not limited to a particular CC service type (SaaS, PaaS, IaaS). However, an initial focus on one of these types in order to limit the number of SCOs could be beneficial for a first prototypical implementation.

# References

1. Winkler, T.J., Brown, C.V.: Horizontal allocation of decision rights for on-premise applications and software-as-a-service. J. Manag. Inf. Syst. **30**, 13–48 (2014). https://doi.org/10.2753/MIS0742-1222300302
2. Yang, H., Tate, M.: A descriptive literature review and classification of cloud computing research. Commun. Assoc. Inf. Syst. **31**, 35–60 (2012). https://doi.org/10.17705/1CAIS.03102
3. Höfer, C.N., Karagiannis, G.: Cloud computing services: taxonomy and comparison. J. Internet Serv. Appl. **2**, 81–94 (2011). https://doi.org/10.1007/s13174-011-0027-x
4. de Vaulx, F., Simmon, E., Bohn, R.: Cloud computing service metrics description. Special Publication (NIST SP) - 500-307 (2017). https://doi.org/10.6028/NIST.SP.500-307
5. Slawik, M., Küpper, A.: A domain specific language and a pertinent business vocabulary for cloud service selection. In: Altmann, J., Vanmechelen, K., Rana, O.F. (eds.) GECON 2014. LNCS, vol. 8914, pp. 172–185. Springer, Cham (2014). https://doi.org/10.1007/978-3-319-14609-6_12
6. Morana, S., Schacht, S., Scherp, A., Maedche, A.: A review of the nature and effects of guidance design features. Decis. Support Syst. **97**, 31–42 (2017). https://doi.org/10.1016/j.dss.2017.03.003

7. Mell, P., Grance, T.: The NIST definition of cloud computing. Special Publication (NIST SP) - 800-145 (2011). https://doi.org/10.6028/NIST.SP.800-145

8. Böhm, M., Koleva, G., Leimeister, S., Riedl, C., Krcmar, H.: Towards a generic value network for cloud computing. In: Altmann, J., Rana, O.F. (eds.) GECON 2010. LNCS, vol. 6296, pp. 129–140. Springer, Heidelberg (2010). https://doi.org/10.1007/978-3-642-15681-6_10

9. Hogan, M.D., Liu, F., Sokol, A.W., Jin, T.: NIST cloud computing standards roadmap. Special Publication (NIST SP) - 500-291 (2011)

10. Armstrong, M.: Competition in two-sided markets. RAND J. Econ. **37**, 668–691 (2006). https://doi.org/10.1111/j.1756-2171.2006.tb00037.x

11. Boudreau, K.J.: Let a thousand flowers bloom? An early look at large numbers of software app developers and patterns of innovation. Organ. Sci. **23**, 1409–1427 (2012). https://doi.org/10.1287/orsc.1110.0678

12. Rochet, J.-C., Tirole, J.: Platform competition in two-sided markets. J. Eur. Econ. Assoc. **1**, 990–1029 (2003). https://doi.org/10.1162/154247603322493212

13. Rysman, M.: The economics of two-sided markets. J. Econ. Perspect. **23**, 125–143 (2009)

14. Caillaud, B., Jullien, B.: Chicken & egg: competition among intermediation service providers. RAND J. Econ. **34**, 309 (2003). https://doi.org/10.2307/1593720

15. Damiano, E., Hao, L.: Competing matchmaking. J. Eur. Econ. Assoc. **6**, 789–818 (2008). https://doi.org/10.1162/JEEA.2008.6.4.789

16. Rask, M., Kragh, H.: Motives for e-marketplace participation: differences and similarities between buyers and suppliers. Electron. Mark. **14**, 270–283 (2007)

17. Bakos, J.Y.: A strategic analysis of electronic marketplaces. MIS Q. **15**, 295–310 (1991). https://doi.org/10.2307/249641

18. Evans, D.S.: Some empirical aspects of multi-sided platform industries. Rev. Netw. Econ. **2**, 1–19 (2003). https://doi.org/10.2202/1446-9022.1026

19. Hsu, C.-H., Yang, L.T., Park, J.H., Yeo, S.-S. (eds.): Algorithms and Architectures for Parallel Processing. LNCS, vol. 6081. Springer, Heidelberg (2010). https://doi.org/10.1007/978-3-642-13119-6

20. Pawluk, P., Simmons, B., Smit, M., Litoiu, M., Mankovski, S.: Introducing STRATOS: a cloud broker service. In: 2012 Proceedings of the IEEE 5th International Conference on Cloud Computing (CLOUD 2012), pp. 891–898 (2012). https://doi.org/10.1109/CLOUD.2012.24

21. Demchenko, Y., et al.: Intercloud architecture framework for heterogeneous cloud based infrastructure services provisioning on-demand. In: 2013 27th International Conference on Advanced Information Networking and Applications Workshops, pp. 777–784 (2013). https://doi.org/10.1109/WAINA.2013.237

22. Nair, S.K., et al.: Towards secure cloud bursting, brokerage and aggregation. In: 2010 Eighth IEEE European Conference on Web Services, pp. 189–196. IEEE, Washington, DC (2010). https://doi.org/10.1109/ECOWS.2010.33

23. Anastasi, G.F., Carlini, E., Coppola, M., Dazzi, P.: QBROKAGE: a genetic approach for QoS cloud brokering. In: IEEE International Conference on Cloud Computing (CLOUD), pp. 304–311 (2014)

24. Cochrane, J., Zeleny, M.: Multiple Criteria Decision Making. University of South Carolina Press, Columbia (1973)

25. Hentschel, R., Leyh, C., Baumhauer, T.: Critical success factors for the implementation and adoption of cloud services in SMEs. In: Proceedings of the 52nd Hawaii International Conference on System Sciences (2019). https://doi.org/10.24251/hicss.2019.882

26. Gregor, S., Hevner, A.R.: Positioning and presenting design science research for maximum impact. MIS Q. **37**, 337–355 (2013)

27. Peffers, K., Tuunanen, T., Rothenberger, M.A., Chatterjee, S.: A design science research methodology for information systems research. J. Manag. Inf. Syst. **24**, 45–77 (2007). https://doi.org/10.2753/MIS0742-1222240302
28. Hevner, A., vom Brocke, J., Maedche, A.: Roles of digital innovation in design science research. Bus. Inf. Syst. Eng. **61**, 3–8 (2019). https://doi.org/10.1007/s12599-018-0571-z
29. Hentschel, R., Leyh, C., Petznick, A.: Current cloud challenges in Germany: the perspective of cloud service providers. J. Cloud Comput. (2018). https://doi.org/10.1186/s13677-018-0107-6

# Big Data and Machine Learning

# Unsupervised Anomaly Detection of Healthcare Providers Using Generative Adversarial Networks

Krishnan Naidoo[1](✉)(iD) and Vukosi Marivate[1,2](✉)(iD)

[1] University of Pretoria, Pretoria, South Africa
marionaidoo@gmail.com, vukosi.marivate@cs.up.ac.za
[2] Council for Scientific and Industrial Research, Pretoria, South Africa

**Abstract.** Healthcare fraud is considered a challenge for many societies. Health care funding that could be spent on medicine, care for the elderly or emergency room visits are instead lost to fraudulent activities by materialistic practitioners or patients. With rising healthcare costs, healthcare fraud is a major contributor to these increasing healthcare costs. This study evaluates previous anomaly detection machine learning models and proposes an unsupervised framework to identify anomalies using a Generative Adversarial Network (GANs) model. The GANs anomaly detection (GAN-AD) model was applied on two different healthcare provider data sets. The anomalous healthcare providers were further analysed through the application of classification models with the logistic regression and extreme gradient boosting models showing good performance. Results from the SHapley Additive exPlanation (SHAP) also signifies that the predictors used explain the anomalous healthcare providers.

**Keywords:** Generative Adversarial Networks · Anomaly detection · Healthcare providers · Machine learning · Deep learning

## 1 Introduction

In 2016, the global spend on health was US\$ 7.5 trillion, representing close to 10% of global GDP [27]. Studies across Europe estimate around 30% have been lost to wasteful spending [14]. A study in 2016 by [25] confirms the financial value of fraud cases in Europe, with France leading the way with (€ 46.3M) of which 37% was committed by healthcare practitioners, 27% by health facilities and less than 20% by insured persons. Netherlands (€ 18.7M) fraudulent activity was mostly relating to wrongful billings, followed closely by UK (€ 11.9M) relating to fraud, bribery and corruption. In the United States healthcare fraud ranges from \$80 billion to \$200 billion [19] with some of reasons relating to improper coding, phantom billing, kickback schemes and wrong diagnosis.

In Africa, challenges like the lack of strong financial, processes and systems are some of the reasons contributing to healthcare fraud [20]. Reports suggests

© IFIP International Federation for Information Processing 2020
Published by Springer Nature Switzerland AG 2020
M. Hattingh et al. (Eds.): I3E 2020, LNCS 12066, pp. 419–430, 2020.
https://doi.org/10.1007/978-3-030-44999-5_35

that approximately 3–4% of the R160 billion medical industry relates to fraudulent claims and abusive or wasteful healthcare costs in South Africa [4,15]. Despite numerous efforts to solve for healthcare fraud, detection of these fraudulent activities within the healthcare sector is still a challenge due to poor data quality or lack of data [17,24].

Due to the lack of confirmed fraud cases of healthcare providers, it is necessary to mention that GANs is a remarkable deep learning model in unsupervised and semi-supervised learning. Not only does the GANs model detect fraudulent activities and malicious users on online social platforms [7], they have been used to augment minority class that solve classification between fraudulent and normal samples [26]. Previous studies used traditional machine learning approaches to solve anomaly/fraud detection problems [2,5,23,24], there has also been an increase in deep learning approaches to solve similar problems. These solutions have been predominately focusing on image problems and there is an opportunity for deep learning models to be applied within the health care domain to classify anomalies [12,23,26].

The objective was to build a single model across the various healthcare provider types to predict if a provider is fraudulent or not. This study uses a public data set from *Medicare Provider Utilization and Payment Data: Physician and Other Supplier* [4] and another private dataset from a *South African claim administration organisation*.

The remaining parts of this paper are structured as follows, Sect. 2 introduces the previous literature on healthcare provider cost abuse, discusses the various anomaly detection techniques and anomaly score. Section 3 presents our proposed methodology highlighting the GANS architecture, anomaly score function, algorithms, data sets used, data pre-processing and performance metrics. Section 4 discusses the results and implications. Finally Sect. 5 summarises the paper and proposes possible future work.

## 2    Literature Review

This section covers previous literature regarding the constructs, cost abuse and wastage, and anomaly detection models within the healthcare domain. Further to this, the literature was reviewed in the context of how machine learning has assisted in anomaly detection within the insurance and healthcare industry.

### 2.1    Healthcare Cost Abuse and Wastage

Healthcare fraud is an intentional deception to obtain unauthorised benefits. Research by [10] describes healthcare provider abuse as, a healthcare provider who practices, either directly or indirectly, in a manner that results in unnecessary costs to the provider. Abuse also relates to any healthcare provider that is not consistent in providing patients with medical services that are necessary, inconsistent adherence to professionally recognised standards and are not fairly priced [4,24].

Recently a model proposed by [3] identified potentially fraudulent hospitals in the Brazilian public healthcare system. The methodology was based on analysing various procedures carried out across different hospitals in each city. The model makes use of a 2 step approach using the consumer anomaly detection using a K-nearest neighbours (kNN) algorithm and thereafter a consumer-provider transfer score showing the relationship between consumer and provider. In contrast, the kNN model was not effective with either very small or very big cities. Further challenges were experienced when the procedures were distributed across several cities.

Literature by [24] discusses how fraud detection could help combat healthcare provider cost abuse by securing the claim input process, checking on irregularities and analysing claim data sets to identify behavioural indicators of fraud. Anomaly detection can be used to identify potentially fraudulent behaviour which we discuss next.

## 2.2  Anomaly Detection

Anomalies are defined as patterns in data that do not conform to expected or normal behaviour [11]. The finding of such patterns is often referred to as anomaly detection [11,29,31]. Different anomaly detection techniques may be applied depending on the nature of the data. Usually if fully labelled data is available, supervised anomaly detection may be adopted. Data sets are considered as labelled if both the normal and anomalous data points have been recorded [29,31]. When labels are not recorded or available, the only option is an unsupervised anomaly detection approach [31].

Research by [2] looked at supervised machine learning methods to detect fraudulent medicare providers across various states across America. The study evaluated three machine learning models indicating the decision tree and logistic regression as good performing models. The lack of fraud labels contributed to the imbalance of data and a random under-sampling strategy was employed to create the different class distributions. Sparsity of medical claim data and the availability of labelled fraudulent cases highlighted in [2,10,16,23,24] is a common challenge when solving for anomaly detection problems.

Canadian researchers [16] experimented on detecting anomalies using an unsupervised spectral ranking approach (SRA). The problem was approached as unsupervised learning which did not use labels when generating anomaly ranking using SRA. The study focused on detecting anomaly in the feature dependence using similarity kernels [16]. In addition, outcomes from the research highlighted the most important features to classify fraudulent claims are policy features, car types and cause of accident features.

The work of [5] includes a comparative survey over the last 20 years of outlier detection relating to fraud detection machine learning algorithms. The study indicates that Isolation Forest is a suitable model for efficiently identifying anomalies with good potential on scalability along with optimized memory utilisation when using large data sets. In contrast, One Class Single Vector Machines (OCSVM) is considered to be another good model for anomaly detection but does not perform well on large data sets and also can be challenging in tuning the input parameters [16].

Popular research across the healthcare and machine learning domains are either based on supervised learning [2], predefined medical rules [9], application of anomaly detection on medical images [21] or non healthcare data [28]. Further to this, research like [2,3] also highlighted challenges like availability of data relating to healthcare providers, even if it is available there is not enough data or the data is not reliable since the providers themselves generate it [3].

Given the above, our methodology is a two step approach for anomaly detection. First, a GAN based approach was applied to identify the *anomaly* or *normal* labels. Second, the results from the deep learning model served as labels into identifying the features that contribute to the anomalous data points.

## 3   Methodology

Figure 1 illustrates the two step modelling approaches used describing the proposed methodology carried out. The first modelling step is a GANs model designed to identify the anomalous healthcare providers based on the reconstruction error. The second modelling step uses the anomaly labels in the supervised classification models and SHAP (SHapley Additive exPlanation) to explain the features contributing to the anomaly.

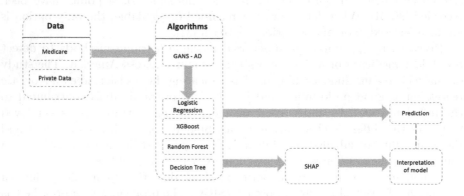

**Fig. 1.** Proposed methodology approach

### 3.1   Data Collection and Pre-processing

To evaluate our anomaly detection approach, we describe the datasets and pre-processing in detail.

**Medicare Dataset:** The data for the current study is a public data set from the Centers for Medicare and Medicaid Services (CMS) for the 2016 calendar year only [4]. The *Medicare Provider Utilization and Payment Data: Physician and Other Supplier* contains payment and claims data with information on services and procedures provided to claimants and beneficiaries. The medicare dataset is aggregated containing 1,053,958 samples with 70 features. As part of the data pre-processing phase, a one-hot encoding representation was applied on categorical features. Thereafter, standardised scaling was applied and highly correlated features was removed. The final output from the pre-processing step that was used in the GANs model contained 91 features with a combination of categorical features representing the practitioner type, type of injury and continuous features representing payment across beneficiaries and injury types.

**Private Dataset:** The research also used data from an organization for which access has been granted to carry out the research. The required data was obtained from a South African company that performs the administration of claims occupational injuries and diseases according to the South African Compensation for Occupational Injuries and Diseases Act (COIDA). The data was aggregated to healthcare provider level with features created to represent financial and injury information. Thereafter the similar pre-processing step applied on the Medicare data set was also applied on the private data set. The final output from the pre-processing step was used in the GANs model contained 95 features.

We applied our modelling approach to both data sets. The data has been modified to mask the healthcare providers details in the results, and examples shown in this paper due to ethical and privacy issues.

## 3.2 Algorithms

Both data sets described in Sect. 3 does not contain any labels. Unlike other machine learning algorithms, that requires a vast amount of labelled data in order to generalize well, GANs can be trained with missing data [1, 21] and can also improve the performance of classifiers when limited data is available. The labels were defined by the application of a GANs with a "feature-matching" anomaly score. Thereafter several classification models (Random Forest, Decision Trees, Logistic Regression and Extreme Gradient Boosting) were applied to get a deeper understanding of how the features contribute to the anomalous labels.

**Generative Adversarial Networks (GANs)** algorithm consists of two adversarial networks, a generator $G$ and a discriminator $D$ [8]. In the context of anomaly detection, the first term in Eq. 1 ($[\log D(\mathbf{x})]$) is the real distribution of data that passes through the discriminator (normal data). The discriminator tries to maximize these data samples to 1. The second term in Eq. 1 ($[\log(1 - D(G(\mathbf{z})))]$) represent data from random input that passes through the generator, which then generates fake samples which is then passed through the discriminator to identify the anomaly. In this term, discriminator tries to maximize it to 0. So overall, the discriminator tries to maximize the function V. Similarly, the task of generator is exactly opposite, it tries to minimize the function V so that the differentiation between normal and anomalous data is at a minimum.

$$\min_{G}\max_{D} V(D.G) = \mathbb{E}_{\mathbf{x}\sim p_{data}(x)}\left[\log D(\mathbf{x})\right] + \mathbb{E}_{\mathbf{z}\sim p_{\mathbf{z}}(z)}\left[\log(1 - D(G(\mathbf{z})))\right] \quad (1)$$

**Detection of an Anomaly:** The GANs algorithm labelled data as normal or anomalous through the use of a loss function called the *anomaly score*. The *anomaly score* is calculated for every evaluation between normal and generated samples in the training process [21, 28]. The *anomaly score* is represented by the following equation:

$$A(x) = (1 - \lambda) \cdot \mathbf{G}(x) + \lambda \cdot \mathbf{D}(x) \qquad (2)$$

In Eq. 2 the generator score $\mathbf{G}(x)$ and the discrimination score $\mathbf{D}(\mathbf{x})$ are defined by the *generator loss* $\mathcal{L}_G$ and the discrimination loss $\mathcal{L}_D$ respectively. For a given data sample $x$, a high anomaly score of $A(x)$ indicates possible anomalies within the sample. The evaluation criteria for this is to a threshold ($\phi$) the score, where $A(x) > \phi$ indicates anomaly. In the current study the threshold is set to 90%.

**Classification Algorithms:** Four binary classification algorithms were applied in the second part of the study to give interpretability to the anomalies. The algorithms applied include the logistic regression (LR), extreme gradient boosting (XGB), random forest (RF) and decision tree (DT) [22]. These algorithms are summarised highlighting their core capability.

*Logistic Regression (LR)* is a classification algorithm that is used to predict the probability of a binary dependent variable. In the current context, the dependent variable contains data coded as 1 (anomaly) or 0 (normal). *Extreme Gradient Boosting (XGB)* is a powerful machine learning technique for classification, regression and ranking problems [18] which produces a prediction model in the form of an ensemble decision tree [18]. The XGB model is built in a multi step approach where each step, introduces a new weak learner to compensate the shortcomings of the existing weak learners [18]. *Random Forest (RF)* is a tree constructed algorithm from a set of possible trees with random features at each node. Random forest can be generated efficiently and the combination of large sets of random trees generally leads to accurate models to detect anomalies [22]. Moreover, the random forest algorithm has been used in this study due to its versatility in being applied to large data sets and feature importance [6]. *Decision Tree (DT)* is a simple and intuitive algorithm that utilizes a top-down approach in which the root node creates binary splits until a certain criteria is met [6]. In the current context of anomaly classification, the decision tree model outputs a predicted target class (anomaly or normal) for each terminal node produced. Decision Trees automatically reduce complexity, selection of features and the predictive analysis structure is understandable and interpretable [22].

The LR, XGB, RF and DT algorithms are successful in detecting anomalies [6, 18, 22] however their main use in the current study is their ability to generalize, feature selection, interpretability [6, 18, 22, 30] and further explain how the features contribute to the anomalous healthcare providers. This explanation was further achieved through the use of SHapley Additive exPlanation (SHAP)[13].

**SHAP (SHapley Additive exPlanation)** objective is to explain the prediction of anomalous healthcare providers by computing the contribution of the features to the prediction. The explanation method within SHAP computes

Shapley values from game theory [13] which indicates how the distribution of the anomaly label (the prediction) among the predictors (features). In the context of the current study, SHAP provided a unified approach for the interpretability of the features in detecting anomalies across healthcare providers. The SHAP framework was applied to assist in explaining the accuracy, consistency, stability, certainty, feature importance and representation of the features.

## 4    Results and Analysis

In this section, we discuss the predication results of our proposed methodology on the two data sets. First, we discuss the generative capability of the GANs and the appropriateness of the data generation and scoring approach for anomaly detection. Thereafter, we discuss the four classification models and SHAP results.

### 4.1    Unsupervised Label Generation

**Generation of Realistic Data:** The challenge in the study is the lack of fraud labels across the data sets which plays an important role in measuring model performance and accuracy in machine learning models. This simplify the current study to adopt a GANs approach to generate fraud labels that is used as the ground truth. The trained GANs model generates realistic data across the different features. The generated data is conditioned by sampling from latent representations $z$ discussed in Sect. 3. The data distribution for the generated data and real data is represented for one feature across the two data sets (see Fig. 2). The distribution of the generated data show some similarities to the real data and also points that is vastly different from the normal data points.

**Detection of Fraud Labels:** Figure 4 shows the anomaly detection based on the anomaly score from the GANs algorithm (Eq. 2). The distributions of the anomaly score (Figs. 3 and 4) show that both components of the proposed adversarial score are suitable for the classification of normal and anomalous samples.

### 4.2    Model Interpretation

In the following subsection, the results are based on the model performance from the Logistic Regression, Random Forest, Decision Tree and Extreme Gradient Boosting algorithms. The supervised modelling process used 60% of instances for training and the remainder in test (20%). Due to the imbalance of data between normal and anomalous labels under sampling was applied during the training process. Table 1 highlight the results from the supervised classification-based models.

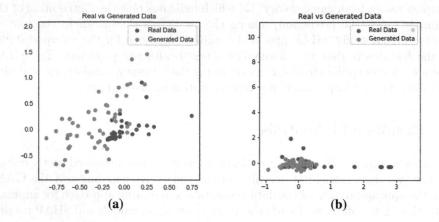

**Fig. 2.** Real vs Generated data across (a) Medicare and (b) private data set

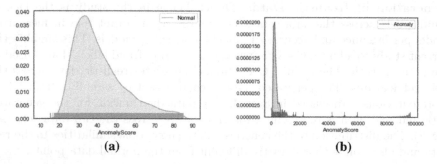

**Fig. 3.** The anomaly scores on Medicare data set for (a) normal healthcare providers is at the lower end (below 100) whereas (b) anomalous healthcare providers is spread across low and high anomaly scores

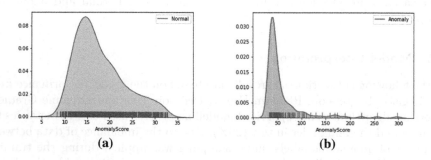

**Fig. 4.** The anomaly scores on private data set for (a) normal healthcare providers is at the lower end (below 100) whereas (b) anomalous healthcare providers have higher anomaly scores

The performance across all the models exceeds 90% on the private data set with the two high performing models based on Area Under Curve (AUC) was LR (97.4%) and XGB (90.3%) respectively. On the Medicare data set the performing model based on AUC was the LR (75.7%) followed by the XGB (74.7%). Table 1 shows the LR results on both data sets with regards to AUC, 75.7% and 97.4% respectively. With sensitivity and specificity rates of 81.3% and 70.1% for the Medicare dataset, and 99.6% and 95.2% for the private dataset. The high sensitivity rate across the two data sets indicates the LR model does well in classifying the anomalous labels identified by the GANs model.

In the context of the current classification problem, a higher sensitivity value would be preferred in identifying anomalous healthcare providers. The second part of the study was aimed to identify the key features contributing to the anomalies so the necessary controls can be in place. Further to this, the results indicates that the supervised classification algorithms performed well across the private data however the results on the Medicare dataset is lower. This can be attributed to the imbalance of labels in the dataset.

**Table 1.** Model results across the Medicare and private dataset

| Model | Medicare | | | | Private | | | |
|---|---|---|---|---|---|---|---|---|
| | Accuracy | Sensitivity | Specificity | AUC | Accuracy | Sensitivity | Specificity | AUC |
| **LR** | **0.802** | **0.813** | 0.701 | **0.757** | **0.992** | **0.996** | **0.952** | **0.974** |
| CART | 0.7 | 0.702 | 0.688 | 0.695 | 0.972 | 0.99 | 0.812 | 0.901 |
| XGB | 0.759 | 0.762 | **0.731** | 0.747 | 0.976 | 0.994 | 0.812 | 0.903 |
| RF | 0.787 | 0.797 | 0.689 | 0.743 | 0.972 | 0.993 | 0.783 | 0.888 |

## 4.3   SHAP

SHAP analysis was conducted and shows the features which push the base value to the model output. Figures 5 and 6 shows features pushing the prediction higher (in red) and those pushing the prediction lower (in blue).

Figure 5 shows the features in Medicare containing high values for total unique beneficiaries, number of HCPCS and beneficiaries between 65 and 74 indicating major impact on increasing the prediction. In addition, low feature values for total unique beneficiaries, number of HCPCS, beneficiaries between 65 and 74 indicate these features decreases the prediction value.

Figure 6 shows the features in the private dataset containing high values for reporting lag, days to end of month and payment have a major impact on increasing the prediction, while low feature value for reporting lag decreases the prediction. Overall features like reporting lag, value of payments and number of injuries for a specific injury group are important features in determining if a healthcare provider is fraudulent or not.

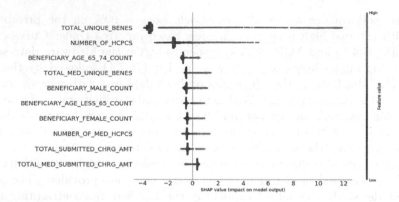

**Fig. 5.** SHAP feature summary - Medicare (Color figure online)

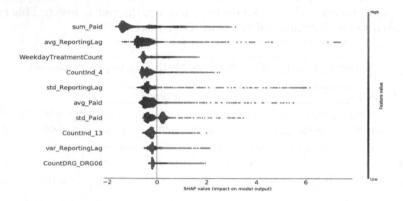

**Fig. 6.** SHAP feature summary - Private (Color figure online)

## 5   Conclusion

The study proposed an anomaly detection model based on generative adversarial networks. By training a generator and discriminator model, anomalies were identified from unseen data based on unsupervised training of a model. The labels generated from the GANs model was used as the ground truth in the supervised classification models to gain further insight on the features contributing to the anomalous healthcare providers. Across the four supervised models evaluated, the logistic regression was the best performing classifier across the two data sets. This methodology applied on similar data sets can offer subject matter experts the ability to detect anomalous healthcare providers with a high degree of accuracy.

Results showed the GANs model identified anomalous healthcare providers and the use of SHAP explained predictors. This approach can be beneficial to future researchers where availability of fraud labels is a challenge. Future studies could solve some of the limitations in the evaluation of the model. The evaluation of label generation in unsupervised models is a challenge and solving this problem would give researchers the opportunity of evaluating the labelling method more precisely. Furthermore explore the use of SHAP directly on deep learning models to better explain feature importance and interpretability.

# References

1. Akcay, S., Atapour-Abarghouei, A., Breckon, T.P.: GANomaly: semi-supervised anomaly detection via adversarial training. Ph.D. thesis (2018)
2. Bauder, R.A., Khoshgoftaar, T.M.: The detection of Medicare fraud using machine learning methods with excluded provider labels. In: The Thirty-First International Florida Artificial Intelligence Research Society Conference, pp. 404–409 (2017)
3. Carvalho, L.F., Teixeira, C.H., Meira, W., Ester, M., Carvalho, O., Brandao, M.H.: Provider-consumer anomaly detection for healthcare systems. In: Proceedings of the 2017 IEEE International Conference on Healthcare Informatics (ICHI 2017), pp. 229–238 (2017)
4. CMS: Research, Statistics, Data and Systems (2014). https://www.cms.gov/research-statistics-data-and-systems/research-statistics-data-and-systems.html
5. Domingues, R., Filippone, M., Michiardi, P., Zouaoui, J.: A comparative evaluation of outlier detection algorithms: experiments and analyses. Pattern Recogn. **74**, 406–421 (2018)
6. Dora, P., Sekharan, G.H.: Healthcare insurance fraud detection leveraging big data analytics. Int. J. Sci. Res. **4**, 2073–2076 (2015)
7. Goix, N.: Machine Learning and Extremes for Anomaly Detection-Apprentissage Automatique et Extrêmes pour la Détection d'Anomalies Spécialité "Signal et Images" présentée et soutenue publiquement par (2016)
8. Goodfellow, I.J., et al.: Generative adversarial networks. In: Advances in Neural Information Processing Systems, pp. 1–9 (2014)
9. Herland, M., Bauder, R.A., Khoshgoftaar, T.M.: The effects of class rarity on the evaluation of supervised healthcare fraud detection models. J. Big Data **6**(1), 1–33 (2019). https://doi.org/10.1186/s40537-019-0181-8
10. Joudaki, H., et al.: Using data mining to detect health care fraud and abuse: a review of literature. Glob. J. Health Sci. **7**, 194–202 (2014)
11. Lazarevic, A., Ertoz, L., Kumar, V., Ozgur, A., Srivastava, J.: A comparative study of anomaly detection schemes in network intrusion detection, pp. 25–36. Army High Performance Computing Research (2013)
12. Liu, E., et al.: Automatic Detection of Excess Healthcare Spending and Cost Variation in ACOs. SIAM (2018)
13. Lundberg, S.M., Lee, S.I.: A unified approach to interpreting model predictions. In: Neural Information Processing Systems Conference, pp. 426–430 (2012)
14. McDaid, D., Merkur, S., Maresso, A.: EuroHealth Report. European Observatory on Health Systems and Policies, pp. 1–44 (2011)
15. Molefe, P.: CMS news the council for medical schemes. Technical report (2018)
16. Nian, K., Zhang, H., Tayal, A., Coleman, T., Li, Y.: Auto insurance fraud detection using unsupervised spectral ranking for anomaly. J. Finance Data Sci. **2**, 58–75 (2016)
17. Nicolaides, A., De Beer, F.: Practitioner ethics, medical schemes and fraud in the South African private healthcare sector. Med. Technol. SA **31**, 1–11 (2017)

18. Niu, X., Wang, L., Yang, X.: A comparison study of credit card fraud detection: supervised versus unsupervised. Association for the Advancement of Artificial Intelligence (2019)
19. OECD Publishling: Health at a Glance: Europe 2018: State of Health in the EU Cycle (2018)
20. World Health Organization: Prevention not cure in tackling health-care fraud. Bull. World Health Organ. **89**, 853–892 (2011). https://www.who.int/bulletin/volumes/89/12/11-021211/en/
21. Schlegl, T., Seeböck, P., Waldstein, S.M., Schmidt-Erfurth, U., Langs, G.: Unsupervised anomaly detection with generative adversarial networks to guide marker discovery. In: Niethammer, M., et al. (eds.) IPMI 2017. LNCS, vol. 10265, pp. 146–157. Springer, Cham (2017). https://doi.org/10.1007/978-3-319-59050-9_12
22. Sekhar, C.R., Minal, Madhu, E.: Mode choice analysis using random forrest decision trees. Transp. Res. Procedia **17**, 644–652 (2016)
23. Shi, Y., Sun, C., Li, Q., Cui, L., Yu, H., Miao, C.: A fraud resilient medical insurance claim system. In: Proceedings of the 30th Conference on Artificial Intelligence (AAAI 2016), pp. 4393–4394 (2016)
24. Thornton, D., Brinkhuis, M., Amrit, C., Aly, R.: Categorizing and describing the types of fraud in healthcare. Procedia Comput. Sci. **64**, 713–720 (2015)
25. Vincke, P.: Fighting fraud & corruption in healthcare in Europe: a work in progress. Technical report (2016)
26. Wang, Y., Xu, W.: Leveraging deep learning with LDA-based text analytics to detect automobile insurance fraud. Decis. Support Syst. **105**, 87–95 (2018)
27. Xu, K., et al.: Public spending on health: a closer look at global trends. Technical report (2018)
28. Zenati, H., Foo, C.S., Lecouat, B., Manek, G., Chandrasekhar, V.R.: Efficient GAN-based anomaly detection. In: ICLR, pp. 1–7 (2018)
29. Zhang, C., et al.: A deep neural network for unsupervised anomaly detection and diagnosis in multivariate time series data. Association for the Advancement of Artificial Intelligence (2018)
30. Zhou, X., et al.: A state of the art survey of data mining-based fraud detection and credit scoring. In: MATEC Web of Conferences (2018)
31. Zoppi, T., Ceccarelli, A., Bondavalli, A.: On algorithms selection for unsupervised anomaly detection. In: Proceedings of IEEE Pacific Rim International Symposium on Dependable Computing (PRDC), pp. 279–288 (2019)

# Data Governance as Success Factor for Data Science

Paul Brous[1]([⊠]) [iD], Marijn Janssen[1] [iD], and Rutger Krans[2]

[1] Delft University of Technology, Delft, The Netherlands
{P. A. Brous, M. F. W. H. A. Janssen}@tudelft.nl
[2] Rijkswaterstaat, Utrecht, The Netherlands
Rutger.Krans@rws.nl

**Abstract.** More and more, asset management organizations are introducing data science initiatives to support predictive maintenance and anomaly detection. Asset management organizations are by nature data intensive to manage their assets like bridges, dykes, railways and roads. For this, they often implement data lakes using a variety of architectures and technologies to store big data and facilitate data science initiatives. However, the decision-outcomes of data science models are often highly reliant on the quality of the data. The data in the data lake therefore has to be of sufficient quality to develop trust by decision-makers. Not surprisingly, organizations are increasingly adopting data governance as a means to ensure that the quality of data entering the data lake is and remains of sufficient quality, and to ensure the organization remains legally compliant. The objective of the case study is to understand the role of data governance as success factor for data science. For this, a case study regarding the governance of data in a data lake in the asset management domain is analyzed to test three propositions contributing to the success of using data science. The results show that unambiguous ownership of the data, monitoring the quality of the data entering the data lake, and a controlled overview of standard and specific compliance requirements are important factors for maintaining data quality and compliance and building trust in data science products.

**Keywords:** Data lake · Data governance · Data quality · Big data · Digital transformation · Data science · Asset management

## 1 Introduction

More and more, asset management organizations are introducing data science initiatives to support the digital transformation of their business processes [1]. However, in order for data science to be successful, it is vital that asset management organizations are able to trust the integrity of the digital environment [2, 3]. Managers have, in the past, found it difficult to trust data science products as, for example, the data is often found to be lacking the required quality [4–7]. Furthermore, as suggested by Wallis et al. [7], data collections are only as valuable as the data they contain, and users need to be able to trust the data based on the integrity of the data systems and the intrinsic quality of the data. Managers need to be able to trust data science products before they

M. Hattingh et al. (Eds.): I3E 2020, LNCS 12066, pp. 431–442, 2020.
https://doi.org/10.1007/978-3-030-44999-5_36

are confident enough to use these products to support their business processes to make crucial decisions [6]. Examples of these decisions in the asset management domain are maintaining dykes or replacing a bridge. Decisions in these scenarios have long term implications and wrong decisions can be expensive and risky. A lack of trust in data science projects can often be attributed to the lack of data quality, and the success of data science projects is often highly reliant on the quality of the data being used [8–10]. There is no single factor defining the successful outcomes of a data science project [11, 12], but recently data governance has gained traction by many organizations as being important for ensuring quality and compliance in data science outcomes [11, 13]. However, it remains unclear how data governance contributes to the success of data science outcomes, leading to calls for more research in this area [11, 14, 15].

Data Governance can be defined as *"the exercise of authority and control (planning, monitoring and enforcement) over the management of data assets"* [16] (p. 67), and can provide direct and indirect benefits [17]. For example, Brous et al. [14] showed that adoption of data governance can improve operational efficiency, increase revenue, reduce risk (for example with regards to privacy violations), reduce costs, improve perception of how information initiatives perform, improve acceptance of spending on information management projects, and improve trust in information products.

The main objective of the paper is to understand the role of data governance as a factor for successful data science outcomes. Our main research question therefore asks how does data governance contribute to more successful data science outcomes? This paper analyses a case study in the asset management domain with specific regard for the role of data governance as success factor for data science outcomes. The case under study is managed by Rijkswaterstaat in the Netherlands. Rijkswaterstaat is part of the Dutch Ministry of Infrastructure and Water Management and is responsible for the design, construction, management and maintenance of the main infrastructure facilities in the Netherlands. The paper reads as follows. Section 2 presents the background of literature regarding the relationship between data governance, trust and the digital environment. In Sect. 3 the methodology of the research is described. Section 4 describes the findings of the case study. Section 5 discusses the findings of the case study and Sect. 6 presents the conclusions.

## 2   Literature Background

Although more attention has been paid to data governance in the literature in recent years, there have been several calls within the scientific community for more systematic research into data governance and its impact on the business capabilities of organizations [18–20]. Little evidence has been produced so far indicating what actually has to be organized by data governance and what data governance processes may entail [20, 21], and many organizations find data governance difficult to implement [22, 23]. There appears to be no "one-size-fits-all" approach to data governance [24] and the nuances attached to various domains and organizational types have not yet been extensively described [25, 26]. Furthermore, evidence is scant as to the role data governance plays in ensuring the successful outcomes of data science initiatives [18, 19].

Recent years have witnessed more and more asset management organizations adopting data science initiatives in order to support the digital transformation of their business processes [27, 28], and Van der Aalst [29] go so far as to suggest that organizations without a data science capability may not survive. According to Provost and Fawcett [1] (p. 52), data science is *"a set of fundamental principles that support and guide the principled extraction of information and knowledge from data"*. From this perspective, data science encompasses a broad range of knowledge and capabilities such as data-mining and machine learning, which are designed to extract knowledge from data and are important for creating value and moderating risk in data science initiatives. As such, data governance can help organizations make use of data as a competitive asset [21, 23]. Data governance aims at maximizing the value of data assets in enterprises [1, 37]. For example, capturing electric- and gas-usage data every few minutes benefits the consumer as well as the provider of energy. With active governance of big data, isolation of faults and quick fixing of issues can prevent systemic energy grid collapse [38].

Data science can improve asset management decision-making which is needed to facilitate more efficient and secure asset management operations, as well the need for better situational awareness about network disturbances [10, 27]. Data science initiatives such as predictive maintenance modelling generally require big data [10, 30, 31]. Asset management organizations often choose to implement data lakes using a variety of architectures and technologies to store big data and to make this data available for use. A data lake is *"a central repository system for storage, processing, and analysis of raw data, in which the data is kept in its original format and is processed to be queried only when needed"* [32] (p. 456). Data lakes are different to traditional data warehouses which often have their own native formats and structures as data is stored in its original, raw, format [33, 34]. Often, the data processing systems which are required to allow the data to be ingested without compromising the data structure are also included in the definition [32, 34]. The data in the data lake is generally immediately accessible, allowing users to utilize dynamic analytical applications [34, 35]. This immediate accessibility, as well as the retaining of data in its original format presents a number of challenges regarding management of the data lake, including data quality management, data security and access control [33, 36], as well as in maintaining compliance with regards to privacy [21, 36]. As such, data governance has increasingly gained popularity as a means of ensuring data quality and maintaining compliance.

Managing data quality is considered by many researchers to be an important reason for adopting data governance (e.g. [24, 37, 39]). However, big data can provide asset management organizations with complex challenges in the management of data quality. According to Saha and Srivastava [40], the massive volumes, high velocity and large variety of automatically generated data can lead to serious data quality management issues which can be difficult to manage in a timely manner [41]. For example, IoT sensors calibrated to measure the salinity of water may, over time, begin to provide incorrect values due to biofouling. Data science information products often rely on near real-time data to provide timely alerts, and, as such, problems may arise if these data quality issues are not timely detected and corrected.

As well as establishing data management processes which manage data quality, data governance should also ensure that the organization's data management processes are compliant with laws, directives, policies and procedures [42]. For example, Panian [43] states that establishing and enforcing policies and processes around the management of data should be the foundation of effective data governance practice as using big data for data science often raises ethical concerns. Automatic data collection may cause privacy infringements [44, 45] such as cameras used to track traffic on highways which often record personally identifiable data such as number plates or faces of persons in the vehicles. Data governance processes should ensure that these personally identifiable features are removed before data is shared or used for purposes other than legally allowed. Data governance should therefore establish what specific data privacy policies are appropriate [39] and applicable across the organization [38]. For example, Tallon [46] states that organizations have a social and legal responsibility to safeguard personal data, whilst Power and Trope [47] suggest that risks and threats to data and privacy require diligent attention from organizations.

In summary, asset management organizations often choose to implement data science initiatives such as predictive maintenance and anomaly detection, using methods such as data-mining and machine learning, in order to support the digital transformation of their business processes. Many modern data science methods require big data which is often stored and made available through data lakes. However, asset management organizations are increasingly being faced with challenges which impact the success of data science outcomes, often related to: 1. a lack of trust in the quality of data [40, 41], 2. whether or not the data is being used in an ethical way [46], and 3. whether or not the management and use of the data is compliant with relevant legislation and internal policies [47]. In order to tackle these challenges, data governance assigns responsibilities for decision-making [24], defines processes for monitoring an managing data quality [41], and defines policies for monitoring and maintaining compliance with relevant legislation [47].

The propositions of the research are based on the results of the background literature review as well as on existing theory regarding the principles of data governance in asset management organizations and the reasons why asset management organizations choose to implement data governance [13, 14, 48]. The propositions of the research therefore read as follows:

1. Defining clear roles and responsibilities for data management will result in easier generation of business value from data science efforts.
2. Monitoring and managing data quality will result in more useful outcomes from data science efforts.
3. Compliance monitoring and control is a required condition for data science.

As discussed above, the literature shows that many organizations have implemented data governance in an attempt to improve trust in data science efforts through the improved management of data quality and compliance to relevant legislation.

# 3   Methodology

This paper describes a single case study using a multi-method approach to investigate the role of data governance as success factor for data science. Case study is a widely adopted method for examining contemporary phenomenon such as the adoption of data governance [49, 50]. In this research we analyze a single case, following the design of an explanatory case study research proposed by Yin [51], including the research question, the propositions for research, the unit of analysis, and the logic linking the data to the propositions. Single case study was selected as being appropriate for this research as there is a need to investigate data governance as success factor for data science in greater detail. In this regard, single case studies may be more appropriate than multiple case studies, as a single case study provides the opportunity to have a deeper understanding of data governance in a specific context [51, 52], in this case, data science efforts in the asset management domain. As suggested by Eisenhardt [50], the research was contextualized by a review of background literature, identifying the generally accepted roles of data governance in a data science context. The literature background reveals data science initiatives often face a number of challenges, and not all efforts lead to successful outcomes [15, 48, 53]. Facing these challenges has led many organizations to adopt data governance as a means of improving the outcomes of data science efforts [13]. However, data governance remains a poorly understood concept [22, 36] and its contribution to the success of data science has not been widely researched [36]. As discussed above, our main research question therefore asks *how does data governance contribute to more successful data science outcomes?*

Following Ketokivi and Choi [54], deduction type reasoning augmented by contextual considerations provided the basic logic for the propositions to be tested in a particular context, namely data science in an asset management domain. The data analysis in this research utilizes "within case analysis" [55]. Within case analysis helped us to examine the impact of data governance on the success of data science in a single context. In this case, the unit of analysis was a single data science project in the asset management domain. The case selected was managed and implemented by Rijkswaterstaat, often abbreviated to RWS and referred to as such in this paper. RWS is the Directorate-General for Public Works and Water Management and an operational agency of the Ministry of Infrastructure and Water Management of the Netherlands. RWS is charged with the management and maintenance of the major highways, waterways and shipping lanes in the Netherlands. In order to prepare the organization for the case study research project, RWS was provided with information material outlining the objectives of the project.

Following the suggestions of Yin [51], the case study was conducted using a multi-method approach and multiple data sources were used. Methods used are document analysis and face-to-face interviews. The interviews were conducted during 2019 taking the form of one-on-one, face-to-face interviews. The interviewees were mainly selected from RWS staff members directly involved in the data science project in various roles, but also included other staff members involved in the governance and management of the data and the monitoring of the data in order to ensure saturation. Secondary data sources included relevant internal documentation, including project reports, data governance workshop reports, and data and information technology strategy documents. Company websites which included relevant data governance information and reports on the data science case were also included. Triangulation of aspects of data governance which contribute to the successful outcome of the data science case was made by listing aspects of data governance found in internal documentation and testing these in the one-on-one interviews. In the interviews the interviewees were asked as to the contribution of these aspects of data governance towards the successful outcome of the project. In the interviews the interviewees were also asked to name other aspects of data governance that may have had a significant contribution to the successful outcome of the data science project but which may have been overlooked.

## 4   Case Study Description

RWS is tasked with the management and maintenance of the national public infrastructure including the construction and maintenance of shipping lanes, major waterways (including flood prevention) and national roads and highways. RWS has a spend of approximately €200 million per annum on asphalt maintenance, with operational parameters traditionally focused on traffic safety. In the past this has led to increasing overspend due either to premature maintenance, or to expensive emergency repairs. The prediction of asphalt lifetime based on traditional parameters has been shown to be correct one third of the time. RWS is seeking to reduce these costs by extending the lifespan of asphalt where possible whilst reducing the number of emergency repairs made by adopting data science techniques for the purpose of predictive, "just-in-time" maintenance. Using available big data in a more detailed manner, such as raveling data collected by a Laser Crack Measurement System combined with Weigh-in-Motion data has doubled the prediction consistency. According to RWS officials, improving the accuracy of asphalt lifetime prediction has enabled better maintenance planning which has significantly reduced premature maintenance, improving road safety and cost savings, and reducing the environmental impact due to reduced traffic congestion and a reduction in $CO_2$ emissions. The data science model uses data related to traditional inspections, historical data generated during the laying of the asphalt, road attribute data and planning data, as well automatically generated, streaming data such as weather data, traffic data, and IoT sensor data. The current model takes about 400 parameters into consideration. According to an RWS official, "this number will only grow, as the *(project partners)* continue to supply new data". According to RWS, the ultimate goal is a model that can accurately predict the lifespan of a highway.

With regards to defining *roles and responsibilities* RWS has asked the data managers of each of the datasets used in the data science project to each appoint an executive sponsor or data owner. The data owner is a business sponsor. Once ownership is established, the current and desired future situations are assessed in terms of production and delivery. A roadmap is then established which was translated into concrete actions and a delivery agreement is reached. RWS also uses "open" data from external sources. Due to its many open data partnerships, RWS has implemented a policy of providing knowledge, tools and a government-wide contact network in which best practices are shared with other government organizations. These best practices refer to organization of data management, data exchange with third parties, data processing methods and individual training. According to staff members, RWS has implemented data governance for their big data in order to remain "future-proof, agile and to improve digital interaction with citizens and partners". According to an RWS executive manager, "RWS wants to be careful, open and transparent about the way in which it handles big and open data and how it organizes itself". Furthermore, RWS has introduced the policy of assessing and publishing the monetary cost of data assets in order to raise awareness of the importance of data quality management. This means that every RWS process and every RWS organizational unit is encouraged to be aware of its data needs and the incurred costs.

With regards to *data quality*, RWS has implemented a data quality framework to improve their control of data quality. RWS staff believe that "the return (of the investment) stands or falls with the quality of data and information". As such, according to RWS staff, the underlying quality of the data and information is of great importance to work in an information-driven way. RWS staff members have suggested that, in the past, a significant amount of production time has often been lost due to inadequate data quality. The RWS data quality management process follows an eight step process which begins by identifying: 1. the data to be produced, 2. the value of the data for the RWS primary processes, and 3. a data owner. RWS has developed an automatic auditing tool (AAT) in combination with a Manual Auditing Tool (MAT) to monitor the quality of the data as a product in order to further improve its grip on data quality. According to RWS staff, the AAT and the MAT ensured that quality measurements were mutually comparable, provided tools for more focused management, and caused a change in the conscious use of data as a strategic asset. Alongside with the AAT, the MAT is considered important as it is not yet possible to automate the monitoring of all data quality dimensions. Data quality measuring is centralized at RWS, the goal being to ensure a standardized working method. However, RWS maintained the policy that every data owner is responsible for improvements to the data management process and the data itself. The RWS data quality framework was based on fitness for use and data quality measurement was maintained according to 8 main dimensions and 47 subdimensions.

With regards to *compliance*, RWS has translated their data policies and principles into a data agenda in which the opportunities, risks and dilemmas of their data policies and ambitions are identified in advance and are made measurable and practicable. Terms and definitions have been coordinated with the Dutch legal framework related to the environment to ensure compliance. Responsibilities relating to compliance to privacy laws are centralized and RWS has assigned privacy officers to this role. The CIO has the final responsibility for ensuring that privacy and security are managed and maintained, however, business data owners are held accountable for ensuring compliance to dataset specific policy and regulations.

# 5  Discussion

Case study methodology was used in this research to identify the role that data governance plays as success factor for data science. The choice for an in-depth, single case study was based on the contemporary nature of both data science and data governance and the need to study data governance as success factor for data science in greater depth. The study was conducted as a single case study and the results should be regarded in this light. Single case study has been criticized in the past due to the difficulty of providing a generalizing conclusion [51, 56]. In order to overcome this, the data collection made use of multiple sources including reports, presentations and face-to-face interviews. More research is recommended in this area to test the applicability of the propositions in other domains and organizational types. The study was conducted in the asset management domain as asset management organizations by nature are often data rich due to the need to monitor the state of the infrastructure assets. This may limit the applicability of the study for domains which are less data intensive, however the essence of generating value from data is likely to be the same in other domains.

## 5.1  Proposition 1: Defining Clear Roles and Responsibilities for Data Management Will Result in Easier Generation of Business Value from Data Science Efforts

Proposition 1 proposes that data science is likely to generate more business value if responsibilities for data management are clearly defined. RWS has many various open data partners, as well as a large variety of sources from which the data is collected. As a result RWS has experienced difficulties in managing responsibilities for data quality and data management processes. RWS has therefore assumed a leadership role in maintaining a government-wide contact network in which knowledge, tooling and best practices with regards to data management and data sharing are shared with other government organizations. Internally, RWS has assigned business sponsors to assume ownership of datasets so that roles and responsibilities of data management are clearly defined. In order to ensure that sufficient resources are made available for data quality management, RWS has also defined a "price" for each dataset so that business owners are aware of the value of each dataset. This allows the organization to treat the data as a business asset, promoting the need to maintain the expected quality of each dataset.

## 5.2  Proposition 2: Monitoring and Managing Data Quality Will Result in More Useful Outcomes from Data Science Efforts

Proposition 2 proposes that data science is more likely to result in useful outcomes if data quality is monitored and controlled. RWS actively monitors their data inputs by means of an "automatic audit tool". RWS has assembled a library of business rules which form the input for the calculation of the data quality. The results of the calculations are displayed in the form of a dashboard which indicates whether the calculated values fall within acceptable limits or not. The acceptable limits are described in the RWS data quality framework which has standardized the calculation and description of data quality throughout RWS. The results of the data quality monitor are used to define which interventions need to be taken in order to achieve the desired levels of quality and also to monitor the effects of the interventions on the data quality. Traditionally, data quality projects at RWS were based on "hearsay" from staff whereby the general feeling was that the quality was below requirements. The AAT has allowed RWS to be more data driven with regards to their data management processes. According to RWS staff, the active monitoring of data quality has led to "identification of gaps in data governance, harmonization of processes across organizational departments, increased awareness and cost savings".

### 5.3 Proposition 3: Compliance Monitoring and Control Is a Required Condition for Data Science

Proposition 3 proposes that compliance with relevant legislation is a necessary and required condition for data science. RWS has had a central, IT-centered approach to data privacy to ensure that legal requirements and guidelines regarding the European General Data Protection Regulation (GDPR) are standardized and consistent throughout the organization. RWS has published a transparent list of systems in which personal data is collected, and has published detailed instructions as to how personal data may be viewed and, where necessary, deleted. RWS has appointed privacy and compliance officers to assume this responsibility and has appointed the CIO has the responsible executive sponsor. The monitoring of other compliance related activities is done using the AAT or the MAT. Responsibility for the actions flowing from the results of the AAT or the MAT lies with the data managers and ownership lies with the data sponsor. This hybrid approach allows RWS to standardize compliance processes where possible, whilst also being able to tailor customized solutions for particular data issues. Currently the feasibility of a nationwide data platform for asphalt pavement data is being explored in which easy data accessibility, authorization, storage, scalability, architecture, plateau planning, solution directions and cost estimations are addressed.

## 6 Conclusions

In this research paper we analyzed a case study regarding the governance of data in a data lake in the asset management domain to identify factors contributing to the success of using data science. The objective of the case study is to understand the role of data governance as success factor for data science. The case under study is a data science project which predicts the maintenance requirements of asphalt on national highways over time. Three propositions were defined on the basis of existing theory on data governance, namely: 1. defining clear roles and responsibilities for data management will result in easier generation of business value from data science efforts, 2. monitoring and managing data quality will result in more useful outcomes from data science efforts, and 3. compliance monitoring and control is a required condition for data science. These propositions were derived from the literature and confirmed in the case study, suggesting that data governance should be regarded as an important success factor for data science outcomes. The results show that clearly defined ownership of the data, monitoring the quality of the data entering the data lake, and a controlled overview of compliance requirements are important factors for successful data science outcomes. The results also show that efficient management of compliance may be performed by developing centrally managed, standardized solutions for privacy and security requirements. However, system-specific compliance requirements need to be developed by data managers and these requirements should be owned by a business sponsor who assumes responsibility for these requirements. As such, the results show the data governance is an important success factor for data science outcomes as it ensures that data quality and compliance are effectively managed.

# References

1. Provost, F., Fawcett, T.: Data science and its relationship to Big Data and data-driven decision making. Big Data 1(1), 51–59 (2013)
2. Council on Library and Information Resources (eds.): Authenticity in a Digital Environment. Council on Library and Information Resources, Washington, D.C (2000)
3. Randall, R., Peppers, D., Rogers, M.: Extreme trust: the new competitive advantage. Strategy Leadersh. 41, 31–34 (2013)
4. Lin, S., Gao, J., Koronios, A.: The need for a data quality framework in asset management. Presented at the Australian Workshop on Information Quality, Adelaide, Australia, vol. 1 (2006)
5. Symons, J., Alvarado, R.: Can we trust Big Data? Applying philosophy of science to software. Big Data Soc. 3(2), 205395171666474 (2016)
6. Passi, S., Jackson, S.J.: Trust in data science: collaboration, translation, and accountability in corporate data science projects. In: Proceedings of the ACM Human-Computer Interaction, vol. 2, no. CSCW, pp. 1–28, November 2018
7. Wallis, J.C., Borgman, C.L., Mayernik, M.S., Pepe, A., Ramanathan, N., Hansen, M.: Know thy sensor: trust, data quality, and data integrity in scientific digital libraries. In: Kovács, L., Fuhr, N., Meghini, C. (eds.) ECDL 2007. LNCS, vol. 4675, pp. 380–391. Springer, Heidelberg (2007). https://doi.org/10.1007/978-3-540-74851-9_32
8. Manco, G., et al.: Fault detection and explanation through Big Data analysis on sensor streams. Expert Syst. Appl. 87, 141–156 (2017)
9. Lee, D., Pan, R.: Predictive maintenance of complex system with multi-level reliability structure. Int. J. Prod. Res. 55(16), 4785–4801 (2017)
10. Kezunovic, M., Xie, L., Grijalva, S.: The role of Big Data in improving power system operation and protection. In: Bulk Power System Dynamics and Control - IX Optimization, Security and Control of the Emerging Power Grid (IREP), 2013 IREP Symposium, pp. 1–9 (2013)
11. Saltz, J.S., Shamshurin, I.: Big Data team process methodologies: a literature review and the identification of key factors for a project's success. In: 2016 IEEE International Conference on Big Data (Big Data), Washington DC, USA, pp. 2872–2879 (2016)
12. Cato, P., Golzer, P., Demmelhuber, W.: An investigation into the implementation factors affecting the success of Big Data systems. In: 2015 11th International Conference on Innovations in Information Technology (IIT), Dubai, United Arab Emirates, pp. 134–139 (2015)
13. Brous, P., Herder, P., Janssen, M.: Governing asset management data infrastructures. Procedia Comput. Sci. 95, 303–310 (2016)

14. Brous, P., Janssen, M., Vilminko-Heikkinen, R.: Coordinating decision-making in data management activities: a systematic review of data governance principles. In: Scholl, H.J., et al. (eds.) EGOVIS 2016. LNCS, vol. 9820, pp. 115–125. Springer, Cham (2016). https://doi.org/10.1007/978-3-319-44421-5_9

15. Yoon, A.: Data reusers' trust development. J. Assoc. Inf. Sci. Technol. **68**(4), 946–956 (2017)

16. DAMA International: DAMA-DMBOK: Data Management Body of Knowledge. Technics Publications (2017)

17. Ladley, J.: Data Governance: How to Design, Deploy and Sustain an Effective Data Governance Program. Newnes (2012)

18. Fruehauf, J., Al-Khalifa, F., Coniker, J., Grant Thornton, L.L.P.: Using the Bolman and deal's four frames in developing a data governance strategy. Issues Inf. Syst. **16**(2), 161–167 (2015)

19. Hashem, I.A.T., Yaqoob, I., Anuar, N.B., Mokhtar, S., Gani, A., Khan, S.U.: The rise of 'big data' on cloud computing: review and open research issues. Inf. Syst. **47**, 98–115 (2015)

20. Otto, B.: A morphology of the organisation of data governance. In: ECIS, vol. 20, p. 1 (2011)

21. Morabito, V.: Big Data governance. In: Morabito, V. (ed.) Big Data and Analytics, pp. 83–104. Springer, Cham (2015). https://doi.org/10.1007/978-3-319-10665-6_5

22. Mathes, C.A.: Big Data has unique needs for information governance and data quality. J. Manag. Sci. Bus. Intell. **1**(1), 12–20 (2016)

23. Thompson, N., Ravindran, R., Nicosia, S.: Government data does not mean data governance: Lessons learned from a public sector application audit. Gov. Inf. Q. **32**(3), 316–322 (2015)

24. Wende, K., Otto, B.: A contingency approach to data governance. Presented at the International Conference on Information Quality, Cambridge, USA (2007)

25. Wang, C.-S., Lin, S.-L., Chou, T.-H., Li, B.-Y.: An integrated data analytics process to optimize data governance of non-profit organization. Comput. Hum. Behav. **101**, 495–505 (2019)

26. Abraham, R., Schneider, J., vom Brocke, J.: Data governance: a conceptual framework, structured review, and research agenda. Int. J. Inf. Manag. **49**, 424–438 (2019)

27. Waller, M.A., Fawcett, S.E.: Data science, predictive analytics, and big data: a revolution that will transform supply chain design and management. J. Bus. Logist. **34**(2), 77–84 (2013)

28. Berman, S.J.: Digital transformation: opportunities to create new business models. Strategy Leadersh. **40**(2), 16–24 (2012)

29. van der Aalst, W.: Data Science in Action. In: Mining, P. (ed.) van der Aalst W, pp. 3–23. Springer, Berlin (2016). https://doi.org/10.1007/978-3-662-49851-4_1

30. Chen, H., Chiang, R.H., Storey, V.C.: Business intelligence and analytics: from Big Data to big impact. MIS Q. **36**, 1165–1188 (2012). (Special Issue: Business Intelligence Research) (Essay)

31. Fosso Wamba, S., Akter, S., Edwards, A., Chopin, G., Gnanzou, D.: How 'big data' can make big impact: findings from a systematic review and a longitudinal case study. Int. J. Prod. Econ. **165**, 234–246 (2015)

32. Couto, J., Borges, O., Ruiz, D., Marczak, S., Prikladnicki, R.: A mapping study about data lakes: an improved definition and possible architectures. Presented at the Proceedings of the International Conference on Software Engineering and Knowledge Engineering (SEKE), vol. 2019, July, pp. 453–458 (2019)

33. Madera, C., Laurent, A.: The next information architecture evolution: the data lake wave. Presented at the 8th International Conference on Management of Digital EcoSystems (MEDES 2016), pp. 174–180 (2016)

34. Miloslavskaya, N., Tolstoy, A.: Big Data, fast data and data lake concepts. Procedia Comput. Sci. **88**, 300–305 (2016)

35. Ullah, S., Awan, M.D., Sikander Hayat Khiyal, M.: Big Data in cloud computing: a resource management perspective. Sci. Program. (2018). https://www.hindawi.com/journals/sp/2018/5418679/. Accessed 18 Oct 2019

36. Kroll, J.A.: Data science data governance [AI ethics]. IEEE Secur. Priv. **16**(6), 61–70 (2018)

37. Otto, D.B.: Data governance. Bus. Inf. Syst. Eng. **3**(4), 241–244 (2011)

38. Malik, P.: Governing big data: principles and practices. IBM J. Res. Dev. **57**(3–4), 1 (2013)

39. Khatri, V., Brown, C.V.: Designing data governance. Commun. ACM **53**(1), 148–152 (2010)

40. Saha, B., Srivastava, D.: Data quality: the other face of big data. In: 2014 IEEE 30th International Conference on Data Engineering, pp. 1294–1297 (2014)

41. Hazen, B.T., Boone, C.A., Ezell, J.D., Jones-Farmer, L.A.: Data quality for data science, predictive analytics, and Big Data in supply chain management: an introduction to the problem and suggestions for research and applications. Int. J. Prod. Econ. **154**, 72–80 (2014)

42. Wilbanks, D., Lehman, K.: Data governance for SoS. Int. J. Syst. Syst. Eng. **3**(3–4), 337–346 (2012)

43. Panian, Z.: Some practical experiences in data governance. World Acad. Sci. Eng. Technol. **38**, 150–157 (2010)

44. Cecere, G., Le Guel, F., Soulié, N.: Perceived internet privacy concerns on social networks in Europe. Technol. Forecast. Soc. Change **96**, 277–287 (2015)

45. van den Broek, T., van Veenstra, A.F.: Governance of big data collaborations: how to balance regulatory compliance and disruptive innovation. Technol. Forecast. Soc. Change **129**, 330–338 (2018)

46. Tallon, P.P.: Corporate governance of big data: perspectives on value, risk, and cost. Computer **46**(6), 32–38 (2013)

47. Power, E.M., Trope, R.L.: The 2006 survey of legal developments in data management, privacy, and information security: the continuing evolution of data governance. Bus. Lawyer **62**(1), 251–294 (2006)

48. Brous, P., Janssen, M., Schraven, D., Spiegeler, J., Duzgun, B.C.: Factors influencing adoption of IoT for data-driven decision making in asset management organizations. Presented at the 2nd International Conference on Internet of Things, Big Data and Security, pp. 70–79 (2017)

49. Choudrie, J., Dwivedi, Y.K.: Investigating the research approaches for examining technology adoption issues. J. Res. Pract. **1**(1), 1 (2005)

50. Eisenhardt, K.M.: Building theories from case study research. Acad. Manag. Rev. **14**(4), 532–550 (1989)

51. Yin, R.K.: Case Study Research: Design and Methods. Sage, Thousand oaks (2009)

52. Gustafsson, J.: Single case studies vs. multiple case studies: a comparative study. Engineering and Science, Halmstad University, Halmstad, Sweden, pp. 1–15 (2017)

53. Cao, Q.H., Khan, I., Farahbakhsh, R., Madhusudan, G., Lee, G.M., Crespi, N.: A trust model for data sharing in smart cities. Presented at the IEEE International Conference on Communications 2016 (ICC 2016) (2016)

54. Ketokivi, M., Choi, T.: Renaissance of case research as a scientific method. J. Oper. Manag. **32**(5), 232–240 (2014)

55. Miles, M.B., Huberman, A.M.: Qualitative Data Analysis: An Expanded Sourcebook. Sage, Thousand Oaks (1994)

56. Zainal, Z.: Case study as a research method. Jurnal Kemanusiaan **5**(1), 2–6 (2017)

# Happiness and Big Data – Theoretical Foundation and Empirical Insights for Africa

Anke Joubert, Matthias Murawski[✉], Julian Bühler,
and Markus Bick

ESCP Business School Berlin, Berlin, Germany
anke.joubert@edu.escpeurope.eu,
{mmurawski,jbuehler,mbick}@escpeurope.eu

**Abstract.** Big data has gained academic relevance over the last decade and is also of interest to other role-players such as governments, businesses and the general public. Based on our previous work on the Big Data Readiness Index (BDRI) we place the focus on one under-investigated aspect of big data: the linkage to happiness. The BDRI, applied on Africa, includes the topic of happiness within the digital wellbeing driver, but the link between the two topics requires further investigation. Thus, two underlying questions emerge: what is the relation between happiness and big data? And how does Africa perform in digital wellbeing? This paper includes a structured literature review highlighting five key clusters indicating this link. Furthermore, we present some first empirical insights using the BDRI focusing on Africa. Overall, the African continent performs best in the social inclusion cluster of happiness, with the most room for improvement in the job creation cluster.

**Keywords:** Africa · Big data · Digital wellbeing · Happiness

## 1 Introduction

Big data analytics is a research field that has gained academic relevance over the past 12 years. Big data is not only of interest for academics, but also for governments, businesses and society. This is due to its ability to use existing data for improved operational efficiency, better decision making, facilitation of innovation and delivery of solutions with a social and developmental impact, amongst other things [1, 2].

In this paper, we place the focus on an under-investigated aspect of big data: the linkage to the topic of happiness. As shown by Wang et al., this linkage has been addressed in only a few studies, with this focus becoming increasingly important [3]. Aside from concrete economic measures, happiness is more and more considered an important aspect of country indices and rankings, indicated, for instance, by the United Nations (UN)-published World Happiness Report or the emergence of the concept of Gross National Happiness (GNH) [4]. Happiness research stretches across domains, playing a large role in philosophy, psychology, religion, environmental studies, healthcare, politics and economics [5]. Throughout history, large events have affected how people define happiness. The age of big data is expected to also have an impact on human happiness.

© IFIP International Federation for Information Processing 2020
Published by Springer Nature Switzerland AG 2020
M. Hattingh et al. (Eds.): I3E 2020, LNCS 12066, pp. 443–455, 2020.
https://doi.org/10.1007/978-3-030-44999-5_37

In a previous paper [6], we have suggested the Big Data Readiness Index (BDRI), which can be used to compare big data readiness on a country level. The BDRI, which is built on the five prominent v's: volume, variety, velocity, veracity and value, includes the topic of happiness under veracity, more detailed under the driver *digital wellbeing*[1]. There is a need for deeper research into the relation between happiness and big data focusing on a stronger theoretical foundation. Based on this, we formulate the following research question that will be answered by conducting a structured literature review:

*RQ1: What is the relation between happiness and big data?*

The second objective of this paper is to present some empirical insights on big data and happiness. Therefore, we apply the BDRI driver digital wellbeing using open data focused on the African continent. Our interest in Africa is grounded in a massive under-representation of this continent in big data research, resulting in a research gap. Furthermore, our BDRI has been developed in the context of the particular aspects of Africa [6]. Thus, the second research question is:

*RQ2: How do African countries perform in terms of digital wellbeing?*

The remainder of this paper is organized as follows: We begin with a general introduction of the topics of happiness and big data, as well as our research focus on Africa in Sect. 2. We present our literature review in Sect. 3, before the research questions are answered in Sect. 4, based on our findings. We conclude the paper in Sect. 5.

## 2    Theoretical Background

### 2.1    Introduction to Happiness

Constantinescu [7] explains how the concept of happiness has always been present and is constantly being reshaped. Definitions of happiness place the focus on different aspects, for instance: *a virtue that could be obtained through values accepted by society that represented the good, true and beautiful* [8], *balance between nature and the world's will* [7] or *long life, riches, health, love of virtue, and a natural death* [9].

The industrial revolution moved the definition of happiness to include consumerism through the increased aspiration to own material goods [7]. Twentieth century media spread this conception of success through owning. The financial crisis questioned the absence of morals within happiness through consumerism [8], consequently literature on the failure of consumerism to create happiness emerged. Seeing how happiness has always played a role in society and changed according to civilization's circumstances make it evident that the age of analytics will also have an impact on human happiness.

Criticism of happiness research points at the fact that it is a highly individual trait and thus aggregating happiness to a people can be misleading [7]. Taking this into

---

[1] *Wellbeing* is commonly used to relate to the level of happiness for a group of citizens or nations [4]. Happiness and wellbeing are used interchangeably by many researchers as well as in this paper.

consideration, indexes should carefully consider how different individuals would experience different circumstances and weight and collect indicators accordingly. Therefore, a Human Wellbeing Index (HWI) together with an Ecosystem Wellbeing Index (EWI) have been developed, striving to find a balance between good human and good ecosystem conditions. The HWI was built on five categories of wellbeing: health and population, wealth, knowledge and culture, community and equity [9].

In July 2011, the UN General Assembly invited member states to measure the level of happiness of their citizens and use this as a guide for developing public policies, followed by the first UN summit on happiness and wellbeing in early 2012. From this year onwards, the UN published an annual World Happiness Report. The World Happiness Report takes variables such as GDP per capita, social support, life expectancy at birth, freedom to make life choices and the level of corruption into account [7].

In this study we understand happiness as an individual attribute that can be defined differently among societies and individuals. It points towards the positive personal or societal experience or value, driven through different factors referring to life quality and purpose, societal equality, social interaction, human rights, and the surrounding environment. While measuring development and setting up policies or rules, it is necessary to consider happiness.

## 2.2  Introduction to Big Data

There is no globally accepted definition for the term 'big data'. The complexity of defining this term increased due to a shared origin and usage between academia, industry, media together with wide public interest.

According to Ward and Baker [10], large international IT role-players also provide conflicting definitions of big data, including: a process of applying serious computing power, including techniques such as machine learning and artificial intelligence (Microsoft) or the derivation of value from traditional relational databases by augmenting it with new sources of unstructured data (Oracle). Fosso-Wamba et al. [11] summarize some descriptions of the impact of big data in previous literature as the next big thing in innovation; the fourth paradigm of science; the next frontier for innovation, competition, and productivity and that big data is bringing a revolution in science and technology. Various stakeholders providing diverse definitions lead to the emergence of literature that attempt to establish a common definition.

The first academic concepts associated with big data describe big data using the three v's: volume, velocity, and variety. This approach has been reiterated in various studies [12–14]. Volume refers to the size and magnitude of data, whereas velocity refers to the speed and frequency of generating data. Variety highlights the fact that big data is generated from a large number of sources, formats and types that include structured and unstructured data [14]. A fourth v for value and a fifth for veracity was subsequently suggested, sometimes referred to as verification. Value emphasizes the importance of extracting economic benefits from data [15, 16]. Veracity stresses the importance of data quality and includes security measures and techniques to assure trustworthy big data analysis results [17, 18]. This paper considers big data as the overarching approach of collecting, managing, processing and gaining value from the 5

Vs (volume, variety, velocity, veracity and value). The BDRI bases an index on measuring big data readiness with these five v's as core components.

### 2.3 Research Focus: Africa

Data related analysis and academic studies focusing on the African continent are scarce due to limited data availability, old and inaccurate data, limited coverage of the available data and a small reference research pool [6]. Due to these challenges, Africa has often been referred to as the continent of missing data. Duermeijer et al. [19] confirms that Africa produces less than 1% of the world's research even though 12,5% of the world's population is from Africa. With regard to published big data related literature up to 2015, most authors are from China, the USA, Australia, the UK and Korea [20]. This unequal geographic coverage raises the question whether this is due to a global big data divide or lack of essential knowledge to undertake big data studies [6]. If big data implementation excludes the developing world, it can lead to greater inequalities. Additional challenges such as data availability and infrastructure hinder easy implementation of big data analytics, but the implementation of big data itself can have large positive effects to alleviate these initial shortcomings [21].

With the spreading of smart mobile devices in developing countries enabling the collection of multiple data inputs for possible big data solutions, big data research does no longer have to be restricted to the developed world. Bifet [22] estimate that 80% of mobile phones are located in developing countries. These developments will increase data availability in Africa and allow new sources of collected data to emerge. Furthermore, Africa has a population of 1.2 billion people of whom around 60% are under 25 years old [23]. This growing number of future digital natives, who will be generating data increasingly, shows the research potential in previously unconnected countries.

Our focus on Africa will attempt to fill this geographical research gap and increase the research pool in order to encourage other authors to focus on this high potential region. We will make use of open data in order to make a country-based comparison, using the BDRI [6] and specifically focusing on the digital wellbeing driver within the velocity component to see how happiness and big data are connected to answer RQ2.

## 3   Structured Literature Review

A core step which links the theoretical foundation with the empirical analysis in our paper is a structured literature review on the two leading terms, "happiness" and "big data". Vital discussions among information system (IS) researchers exist about how to approach a literature review. Some authors argue for a comprehensible approach by covering all articles somehow related to the review topic [e.g., 24], others such as vom Brocke et al. [25] actively claim the exclusion of articles while being as transparent as possible. For this review, we apply a hybrid approach of systematicity [26], because we are particularly interested in the combination of the two terms "happiness" and "big data". Thus, we exclude articles that can be associated with only one of the key terms to achieve a holistic review of all scientific articles that combine both terms. In the following phase, we use three exclusion criteria to filter the articles in a funneling process. The final search string for the queries consequently is:

happiness AND 'big data'

Following the guideline by Webster and Watson [27], we screened three major databases for scientific publications, *EBSCO*, *JSTOR*, and *Web of Science*. This guarantees a good coverage of articles positioned beyond the boundaries of IS, which is in line with the authors' advice for a literature review in an interdisciplinary and connected field, such as IS [27]. The results that cover all available fields in the databases' advance search options (e.g., title, keywords, abstract) are presented in the following section.

Search results for "happiness" solely, which we initially applied for crosschecks on our combined search string, revealed a huge number of more than 20.000 articles. Combined with the second term "big data", the queries applied to the three databases listed a total number of 154 peer-reviewed journal articles. We applied a set of three major criteria to limit the number of articles to a reasonable and suitable number for our purposes. First, we downloaded and screened the title, keywords and abstracts of all articles and used this as first methodological screening criteria [26]. In this step duplicated articles, non-English articles and certain types of articles such as short editor's notes as a preface or front and back matters were eliminated (A). Furthermore, we eliminated articles that are directly related to the medical or health sector: they use *happiness* in the context of wellbeing after medical treatment, which is out of scope for this study (B). In a final step, we conducted an individual screening of all the articles and applied final content-related criteria. All articles were removed which refer only once to either of the two core terms. These articles appear correctly as search results but provide a very vague connection between the two terms at most. Additionally, we eliminated articles that are out of scope (C). In total, 20 articles with a strong relation between the terms "happiness" and "big data" remained after the three elimination steps. The initial pool of articles, those excluded at each step, as well as those that remained and form our final sample are summarized in Table 1:

**Table 1.** Overview of literature review statistics

| Database | Articles | Exclusion criteria | Articles |
|---|---|---|---|
| EBSCO | n = 12 | A) duplicates, defined types and non-English | n = 32 |
| JSTOR | n = 114 | B) medical or health sector related | n = 8 |
| Web of Science | n = 28 | C) content | n = 94 |
| **Raw sample** | **Σ = 154** | **Final sample (n raw sample – n excluded)** | **Σ = 20** |

## 4 Findings and Discussion

### 4.1 Relation of Happiness and Big Data

Based on the literature review results (cf. Table 1), we extracted a total of 20 peer-reviewed articles, which we then clustered regarding potential linkages between happiness and big data. We screened the articles and aggregated them according to central themes, research areas and methodology. These clusters from the BDRI will be explained in this section, specifically indicating how big data could affect mentioned clusters and how this in turn effects happiness, thereby establishing the general relation between big data and happiness.

A first cluster we could identify can be associated with jobs, specifically *job creation* and increased productivity. According to one paper we associated with this cluster, Frey and Stutzer [28], unemployment has a strong negative effect on the individual as well as an entire society. Consequently, lowering unemployment potentially leads to greater levels of happiness, greater bonds towards a community, and life satisfaction [29]. This effect is even stronger for younger adults [30]. The implementation of big data concepts can support the process of job creation in general, but it is diverse with regard to different target groups within a society. New jobs will predominantly increase happiness of a minority, which due to a reasonable level of education, has the option to work in big data fields. To address *job creation* coherently, we put our focus on big data concepts that also impact existing jobs. Heeks [31] uses Bhutan as an example where e-agriculture can assist farmers who represent the majority of the population. In this example, big data concepts support agricultural extension, better planting, cropping, animal husbandry, and monitoring market prices for better market revenue. Implementation of big data analytics can not only improve productivity within existing jobs but also lead to creation of new jobs. Evidently, a meaningful source of income and higher productivity has positive impacts on the level of happiness in society, explaining how through this cluster *job creation* and productivity big data can contribute to happiness.

Big data can also be used to reduce *socio-economic inequalities*, our second cluster. Investments in new technologies can have a reasonable positive impact on multiple users simultaneously. They can benefit from one investment, such as a shared computer in a school. In return, research results indicate that countries with poorer socio-economic conditions, e.g., less or no investments, also perform worse in happiness studies [8]. Other meta studies in the review addressed *socio-economic equality* using big data concepts to investigate links between various factors that consolidate a society, such as religiousness [32] or a predominant mindset [33]. This cluster links big data to happiness through the potential impact of big data on reducing socio economic inequalities, which creates a happiness surplus though having a more equal society.

Furthermore, the literature review revealed a third cluster referring to *social inclusion*, which covers closer relationships with others including friends and family that ultimately increase happiness. Communication networks such as social media play a key role in this cluster. This has been analyzed by researchers with the help of big data concepts. For example, Dodds et al. [34] used large-scaled text and word analyses to measure what they call 'societal happiness' on Twitter. Kosinski et al. [35] predicted 'sensitive personal attributes' including happiness based on nearly 60,000 digital Facebook records. Similarly, helping others or the Good Samaritan effect is shown to increase happiness of the helper as well as of the one being helped [36]. However, lack of emotional expressions communicated by others via social media services tend to lower an individual user's level of happiness [37]. As big data has the potential to provide the opportunity of higher connectivity, this cluster improves societal happiness of those experiencing a higher degree of social inclusion.

A fourth cluster called *good governance* comprises governmental aspects such as political participation and the trust in the government's policies and performance [38], where big data can help increase the level of transparency towards citizens [39]. Democracy itself increases happiness as the majority of citizens have voted to get their preferential policies in place [28]. The government can use big data technologies for improved decision making and implementing policies more effectively. Two real-life examples include the use of mobile phone data and airtime credit purchases to estimate food security in East Africa or using mining citizen feedback data in order to gain input for government decision making in Indonesia [40, 41]. This reveals that big data can lead to better governance, which in turn will impact overall happiness, as shown by happiness-studies. In addition, our literature review revealed other than politically driven contexts of happiness, through life satisfaction of people influenced by their residential status. Jokela et al. [42] used big data techniques to analyze more than 56,000 records. This study found a strong link between "life satisfaction" and "neighborhood characteristics", which were set up by public authorities.

The final cluster *healthy environment* has some connections with *good governance* but with a stronger focus on environmental aspects. As people, we are highly dependent on our environment for daily living, especially in developing regions such as Africa where agriculture is still the largest sector in more than half of the countries [5]. Particularly big data concepts that address superordinate living conditions are relevant. One example from our literature review is a study by Zhao et al. [43] linking wellbeing, amongst other things, with economic growth and green space in larger Chinese cities. Results reveal a significant positive relationship between wellbeing and a high percentage of green space in a city. A healthy environment includes low levels of pollution, good water quality as well as the concept of sustainability that is gaining popularity especially among millennials [44]. Cloutier et al. [45] show how well individual cities and communities embrace sustainable practices and how these practices translate to opportunities for residents to pursue happiness. Applying big data to have smart cities, will lead to a more sustainable and effective society, and by doing so the healthier environment cluster is the fifth identified cluster through which big data relates to higher levels of happiness.

Before discussing our specific empirical findings for Africa in the next section, we would like to address the initially raised research question RQ1 by summarizing that the relation between happiness and big data can be constituted by the five extracted clusters that are found in the BDRI: *job creation*, *socio economic equality*, *social inclusion*, *good governance*, and *healthy environment*.

### 4.2 Empirical Findings for Africa

We use the BDRI, to zoom into digital wellbeing. The BDRI was developed using the five v's: volume, variety, velocity, veracity and value as components, with sub-drivers. Digital wellbeing is a driver under veracity, including indicators for the five previously extracted clusters *job creation* including improved productivity, *social-economic equality*, *social inclusion*, *good governance* and a *healthy environment*.

The digital wellbeing driver is based on happiness research. Heeks [31] suggests a model that looks at substrates of happiness and unhappiness to link ICT to happiness. This has been adapted in the BDRI to incorporate possible links of big data as a technological priority to happiness. Other BRDI components such as trust and security deal with eliminating unhappiness caused by implementing big data technologies, thus digital wellbeing focusses on five clusters contributing to societal happiness.

**Fig. 1.** Digital wellbeing across Africa

Indicators used to measure these five happiness clusters include, amongst others, the unemployment rate to indicate the opportunity of *job creation* and improved productivity through big data innovation [46]. The human development index score that takes three characteristics into account including a long and healthy life, access to knowledge and a decent standard of living to show *socio economic equality* [47]. Policies for *social inclusion* and equity including gender equality policies, equity of public resource use, social protection policies and policies for institutional sustainability are included in the social inclusion measure [48]. Political participation, political rights, legitimacy of policy, electoral process, power to govern workers' rights, the right to collective bargaining, freedom of -expression, -association and, -press and electoral self-determination are included as measures for *good governance* [49]. The indicator for a *healthy environment* measures sustainability through considering the share of renewable electricity to total electricity generated by all types of plants, and other factors [50]. Isolating and aggregating these indicators of the BDRI digital wellbeing driver, shows how Africa performs in terms of the big data related happiness clusters (cf. Fig. 1).

All countries in the upper quintile, with the exception of Cameroon, lie in the Southern Hemisphere, of which Sao Tome & Principe, Gabon and Kenya lie on the equator. Looking at the different regions: North Africa, East Africa, Southern Africa,

West Africa and Central Africa, it is clear that Southern Africa outperforms other regions including 6 of the top 10, also Namibia, South Africa and Mauritius.

Southern Africa is also the top performing region in the overall BDRI. Thus, it is interesting to have a look at the top 10 BDRI performers and look at differences in terms of digital wellbeing. The BDRI top ten includes mostly coastal and island nations, with Rwanda as the only landlocked exception [6]. Even though this group of 10 countries outperforms their peers in terms of big data readiness, there is a large gap in terms of their performance in digital wellbeing. Missing data allows limited comparison in two of the five happiness clusters: *job creation* and *social inclusion*.

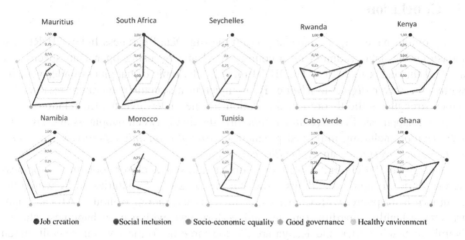

Fig. 2. BDRI top 10 - Digital wellbeing

Using various indicators to aggregate the five clusters of digital wellbeing in the BDRI gives some insights on the performance of African countries, not only within big data readiness, but also within the specific digital wellbeing driver. These indicators was selected following the Design Science Research approach [15].

Namibia, ranking sixth in the overall BDRI (cf. Fig. 2), performs best in the digital wellbeing driver. This desert nation performs well in available fields, showing highest performance in the *healthy environment* cluster. Amongst many factors included in the BDRI digital wellbeing driver, Namibia's well managed mineral wealth from a political and legal perspective, has allowed it to avoid the 'resource curse' seen across Africa - where countries rich in resources have low growth [51]. South Africa, in second position in both the overall BDRI and the digital wellbeing driver, performs well compared to its African peers in all clusters, except *healthy environment*. This field includes sustainability through the proxy of the share of renewable electricity to total electricity. South Africa derives 70% of total primary energy supply from coal, making this economy a large producer of greenhouse gases [52]. Kenya is the third-best performer in digital wellbeing from the BDRI top 10, followed by island nations Seychelles and Mauritius in fourth and fifth place. Of the BDRI top ten, Morocco ranks lowest in digital wellbeing, with a low comparative score in most digital wellbeing clusters. Amongst other clusters, the indicators aggregated to proxy *job creation* shows

Morocco to have high labor market inefficiency, with high minimum wages and labor taxes being the main points of concern [46].

To answer research question RQ2 it is clear that a major difference exists between digital wellbeing across the 54 African countries. An overall view on digital wellbeing in Africa shows that on average the continent performs best in the cluster of *social inclusion*. Overall, the countries struggle most with *socio-economic equality* and *job creation*. This calls for policy intervention to focus on decreasing socio-economic inequality and reducing unemployment.

## 5   Conclusion

In a previous paper [6], we have suggested the Big Data Readiness Index (BDRI) that measures big data readiness on a country level and by using open data specifically applied this index to Africa. The BDRI includes the topic of happiness under veracity within the driver *digital wellbeing*. By completing a structured literature review, this paper strengthens the theoretical foundation for the under-investigated relation of big data and happiness. Five overall clusters form the link between happiness and big data: *job creation* including improved productivity, *social-economic equality, social inclusion, good governance* and a *healthy environment*.

Using the BDRI digital wellbeing driver allowed a closer look into happiness across Africa. Empirical findings show that the top 20% of countries all lie within the Southern hemisphere, with Cameroon as the only exception. Although African countries vary highly regarding ranking and performance within each happiness cluster, Namibia, South Africa and Kenya are the top three performers within overall digital wellbeing from the countries in the BDRI top 10.

Our study also has limitations which can be used as avenues for future studies based on the BDRI. It could be beneficial in terms of the model design to investigate causality and the direction of effects between happiness and big data. Regarding the country-specific analysis, we focused on Africa in its entirety and highlighted specific countries, which revealed significant results (cf. Fig. 2). Future studies could distinctively focus on the integration of cultural studies though, such as GLOBE or Hofstede, and compare the cultural clusters within Africa with other cultural clusters outside Africa. This would also help overcome the issue of scarce data availability for many countries in Africa, which makes empirical research in this area more difficult. A larger data pool would also be beneficial for consolidating the BDRI results.

## References

1. Grover, V., Chiang, R.H.L., Liang, T.-P., Zhang, D.: Creating strategic business value from big data analytics: a research framework. J. Manage. Inf. Syst. **35**, 388–423 (2018)
2. Keller, S.A., Koonin, S.E., Shipp, S.: Big data and city living - what can it do for us? Significance **9**, 4–7 (2012)
3. Wang, H., Xu, Z., Fujita, H., Liu, S.: Towards felicitous decision making: an overview on challenges and trends of Big Data. Inf. Sci. **367**, 747–765 (2016)

4. Durahim, A.O., Coskun, M.: #iamhappybecause: Gross National Happiness through Twitter analysis and big data. Stochastic Process. Appl. **99**, 92–105 (2015)
5. Leith, B., Krugel, L., Viljoen, C., Kirsten, N., Joubert, A.: How good is life in Africa? Digging deeper than GDP. KPMG Good Life Index (2016)
6. Joubert, A., Murawski, M., Bick, M.: Big data readiness index – Africa in the age of analytics. In: Pappas, I.O., Mikalef, P., Dwivedi, Y.K., Jaccheri, L., Krogstie, J., Mäntymäki, M. (eds.) I3E 2019. LNCS, vol. 11701, pp. 101–112. Springer, Cham (2019). https://doi.org/10.1007/978-3-030-29374-1_9
7. Constantinescu, E.M.: A new design of happiness in the context modern world. Soc. Econ. Debates **6**(2), 6 (2017)
8. Helliwell, J.F., Layard, R., Sachs, J.D.: World Happiness Report 2013. Sustainable Development Solutions Network, New York (2013)
9. Prescott-Allen, R.: The Wellbeing of Nations. A Country-by-Country Index of Quality of Life and the Environment. Island Press, Washington D.C. (2001)
10. Ward, J.S., Barker, A.: Undefined By Data: A Survey of Big Data Definitions. University ofSt Andrews, UK (2013). https://arxiv.org/pdf/1309.5821.pdf
11. Fosso Wamba, S., Akter, S., Edwards, A., Chopin, G., Gnanzou, D.: How 'big data' can make big impact: Findings from a systematic review and a longitudinal case study. Int. J. Prod. Econ. **165**, 234–246 (2015)
12. Kwon, O., Sim, J.M.: Effects of data set features on the performances of classification algorithms. Expert Syst. Appl. **40**, 1847–1857 (2013)
13. McAfee, A., Brynjolfsson, E.: Big data: the management revolution. Harvard Bus. Rev. **90**, 60–6, 68, 128 (2012)
14. Russom, P.: Big data analytics. TDWI Best Pract. Rep. **19**, 1–34 (2011). Fourth Quarter
15. Hevner, A.R., March, S.T., Park, J., Ram, S.: Design science in information systems research. MIS Q. **28**, 75–105 (2004)
16. Chen, H., Chiang, R.H.L., Storey, V.C.: Business intelligence and analytics: from big data to big impact. MIS Quart. **36**, 1165 (2012)
17. White, M.: Digital workplaces. Bus. Inf. Rev. **29**, 205–214 (2012)
18. Opresnik, D., Taisch, M.: The value of Big Data in servitization. Int. J. Prod. Econ. **165**, 174–184 (2015)
19. Duermeijer, C., Amir, M., Schoombee, L.: Africa generates less than 1% of the world's research; data analytics can change that. An in-depth analysis of the continent's research reveals promising developments – and strategies for continued improvement (2018)
20. Sivarajah, U., Kamal, M.M., Irani, Z., Weerakkody, V.: Critical analysis of Big Data challenges and analytical methods. J. Bus. Res. **70**, 263–286 (2017)
21. Loebbecke, C., Picot, A.: Reflections on societal and business model transformation arising from digitization and big data analytics: a research agenda. J. Strateg. Inf. Syst. **24**, 149–157 (2015)
22. Bifet, A.: Mining big data in real time. Informatica (Slovenia) **37**, 15–20 (2013)
23. Chakravorti, B., Chaturvedi, R.S.: Digital planet: how competitiveness and trust in digital economies vary across the world. https://sites.tufts.edu/digitalplanet/files/2017/05/Digital_Planet_2017_FINAL.pdf. Accessed 23 Oct 2019
24. Schwarz, A., Mehta, M., Johnson, N., Chin, W.W.: Understanding frameworks and reviews. In: SIGMIS Database, vol. 38, p. 29 (2007)
25. vom Brocke, J., Simons, A., Niehaves, B., Riemer, K., Plattfaut, R., Cleven, A.: Reconstructing the giant: on the importance of rigour in documenting the literature search process. In: Proceedings of the European Conference on Information Systems. Verona (2009)

26. Rowe, F.: What literature review is not: diversity, boundaries and recommendations. Eur. J. Inf. Syst. **23**, 241–255 (2014)
27. Webster, J., Watson, R.T.: Analyzing the past to prepare for the future: writing a literature review. MIS Q. **26**, xiii–xxiii (2002)
28. Frey, B.S., Stutzer, A.: What can economists learn from happiness research? J. Econ. Lit. **40**, 402–435 (2002)
29. Yeniaras, V., Akkemik, K.A., Yucel, E.: Re-considering the linkage between the antecedents and consequences of happiness. J. Econ. Psychol. **56**, 176–191 (2016)
30. Blanchflower, D.G., Oswald, A.: The rising well-being of the young. In: Blanchflower, D.G., Freeman, R.B. (eds.) Youth Employment and Joblessness in Advanced Countries. University of Chicago Press, Chicago (2000)
31. Heeks, R.: Information technology and gross national happiness. Commun. ACM **55**, 24 (2012)
32. Yu, C.H., Trier, H., Slama, M.: A data mining and data visualization approach to examine the interrelationships between life satisfaction, secularization and religiosity. J. Relig. Health **58**, 271–288 (2019)
33. Yoo, H., Chung, K.: Mining-based lifecare recommendation using peer-to-peer dataset and adaptive decision feedback. Peer-To-Peer Network. Appl. **11**, 1309–1320 (2018)
34. Dodds, P.S., Harris, K.D., Kloumann, I.M., Bliss, C.A., Danforth, C.M.: Temporal patterns of happiness and information in a global social network: hedonometrics and Twitter. PLoS ONE **6**, e26752 (2011)
35. Kosinski, M., Stillwell, D., Graepel, T.: Private traits and attributes are predictable from digital records of human behavior. Proc. Natl. Acad. Sci. U.S.A. **110**, 5802–5805 (2013)
36. van de Sande, C., Leinhardt, G.: The good Samaritan effect: a lens for understanding patterns of participation. In: Proceedings of the 8th International Conference for the Learning Sciences (ICLS). Utrecht, The Netherlands (2008)
37. Kramer, A.D.I., Guillory, J.E., Hancock, J.T.: Experimental evidence of massive-scale emotional contagion through social networks. Proc. Natl. Acad. Sci. U.S.A. **111**, 8788–8790 (2014)
38. Lepenies, P.: Transforming by metrics that matter – progress, participation, and the national initiatives of fixing well-being indicators. Hist. Soc. Res./Historische Sozialforschung **44**, 288–312 (2019)
39. Manyika, J., et al.: Big data: the next frontier for innovation, competition, and productivity (2011)
40. Decuyper, A., et al.: Estimating Food Consumption and Poverty Indices with Mobile Phone Data. Preprint arXiv:1412.2595 (2014). https://arxiv.org/abs/1412.2595
41. UN Global Pulse: Mining Citizen Feedback Data for Enhanced Local Government Decision-Making. Global Pulse Project Series 16 (2015)
42. Jokela, M., Bleidorn, W., Lamb, M.E., Gosling, S.D., Rentfrow, P.J.: Geographically varying associations between personality and life satisfaction in the London metropolitan area. Proc. Natl. Acad. Sci. U.S.A. **112**, 725–730 (2015)
43. Zhao, Y., Yu, F., Jing, B., Hu, X., Luo, A., Peng, K.: An analysis of well-being determinants at the City Level in China using big data. Soc. Indic. Res. **143**, 973–994 (2019)
44. Hanks, K., Odom, W., Roedl, D., Blevis, E.: Sustainable millennials. In: Czerwinski, M. (ed.) Proceedings of the SIGCHI Conference on Human Factors in Computing Systems, p. 333. ACM, New York (2008)
45. Cloutier, S., Jambeck, J., Scott, N.: The Sustainable Neighborhoods for Happiness Index (SNHI): a metric for assessing a community's sustainability and potential influence on happiness. Ecol. Ind. **40**, 147–152 (2014)
46. ILOSTAT database: unemployment statistics. https://ilostat.ilo.org/. Accessed 30 Oct 2019

47. United Nations Development Programme: Human Development Data. http://hdr.undp.org/en/data. Accessed 29 Oct 2019
48. World Bank Group: CPIA database - policies for social inclusion/equity cluster average (1 = low to 6 = high). https://data.worldbank.org/indicator/IQ.CPA.SOCI.XQ?view=chart. Accessed 30 Oct 2019
49. Delapalme, N., et al.: Political participation. http://mo.ibrahim.foundation/iiag. Accessed 30 Oct 2019
50. International Energy Agency: For healthy environment. http://www.iea.org/stats/index.asp. Accessed 27 Oct 2019
51. Mehlum, H., Moene, K., Torvik, R.: Institutions and the resource curse. Econ. J. **116**, 1–20 (2006)
52. Winkler, H.: Energy policies for sustainable development in South Africa. Energy. Sustain. Dev. **11**, 26–34 (2007)

# Predicting Information Diffusion on Twitter a Deep Learning Neural Network Model Using Custom Weighted Word Features

Amit Kumar Kushwaha[✉], Arpan Kumar Kar,
and P. Vigneswara Ilavarasan

Department of Management Studies, Indian Institute of Technology,
Delhi, New Delhi 110016, India
Kushwaha.amitkumar@gmail.com, arpan_kar@yahoo.co.in,
vignes@iitd.ac.in

**Abstract.** Researchers have been experimenting with various drivers of the diffusion rate like sentiment analysis which only considers the presence of certain words in a tweet. We theorize that the diffusion of particular content on Twitter can be driven by a sequence of nouns, adjectives, adverbs forming a sentence. We exhibit that the proposed approach is coherent with the intrinsic disposition of tweets to a common choice of words while constructing a sentence to express an opinion or sentiment. Through this paper, we propose a Custom Weighted Word Embedding (CWWE) to study the degree of diffusion of content (retweet on Twitter). Our framework first extracts the words, create a matrix of these words using the sequences in the tweet text. To this sequence matrix we further multiply custom weights basis the presence index in a sentence wherein higher weights are given if the impactful class of tokens/words like nouns, adjectives are used at the beginning of the sentence than at last. We then try to predict the possibility of diffusion of information using Long-Short Term Memory Deep Neural Network architecture, which in turn is further optimized on the accuracy and training execution time by a Convolutional Neural Network architecture. The results of the proposed CWWE are compared to a pre-trained glove word embedding. For experimentation, we created a corpus of size 230,000 tweets posted by more than 45,000 users in 6 months. Research experimentations reveal that using the proposed framework of Custom Weighted Word Embedding (CWWE) from the tweet there is a significant improvement in the overall accuracy of Deep Learning framework model in predicting information diffusion through tweets.

**Keywords:** Information diffusion · Twitter analytics · Deep learning · Convolutional neural network · Linguistic

## 1 Introduction

Microblogging website Twitter has emerged as one of the primary online social media platforms across the globe for sharing opinions, interests, and points of view on events and issues varying from education, sports, online content to politics. Users on Twitter

© IFIP International Federation for Information Processing 2020
Published by Springer Nature Switzerland AG 2020
M. Hattingh et al. (Eds.): I3E 2020, LNCS 12066, pp. 456–468, 2020.
https://doi.org/10.1007/978-3-030-44999-5_38

can associate their share of opinions related to a subject matter by writing a simple tweet and posting it in real-time. The selection of right expletives and positioning the same in a tweet sentence plays a critical role in attracting the attention of right receivers (users of Twitter) of this tweet with similar interests inside the Twitter platform. Sharples [1] has claimed that readers on any platform of communication should treat writing as a creative act of writers using which they deliberately select phrases and position them to impose a certain interpretation through lexical and linguistic preferences. This hypothesis was first developed by Maun [2], showing how diverse set of writers from various backgrounds, are extremely cognizant of articulated aspects of writing, positioning the expletives with opinions that we should hypothesize as writing practice and as an act of thoughts representation. The idea of sentence writing includes the design of the factual or non-factual information of a topic, person, event or domain, followed by opinion generation through experience or knowledge expressed in words, within a framework requiring the expertise of linguistics as well as the nature of genres and domains in which the communication is taking place. The sentence then reaches the receiver (also referred to diffusion in modern world) to whom the original writer/sender was planning to convey the message to. The receiver in turn again uses the knowledge of linguistics to interpret the meaning which original sender was trying to convey. Hence linguistic competence is central to understand the degree of diffusion of information in any communication channel.

Social media application Twitter bring users with similar opinion across the globe on the same platform to communicated, cascade the information to a wider set of users beyond their group referred to as information diffusion (also referred to as retweet on Twitter) in a real-time basis. This, in turn, creates mass information on Twitter. The ability of Twitter to elevate the exposure of any information through a simple tweet is contained in various aspects of the same tweet. Like the number of users connected to the account from which the tweet got generated, how active the user has been in the past, how active the followers in the network of the user are on Twitter.

To achieve effective diffusion of information, other than the previously listed factors, one more aspect that plays a key role is: the sentence used in a tweet should be conveying the appropriate information with a factual point of view. Prior research appears a little apprehensive about the accurate enriching relationship between the selection of words, placing in a certain order, and about how the thoughts get reconstructed when we alter the sequence of words. The area of linguistics has well-described literature on how a well-formed sentence structure can guide the communication of inference and opinion expressed and at the same time increase the penetration of the sentence at the user level. Aligning the sentences for an appropriate theme and rheme and the idea of linearization of the words in which 'what an author places first will drive the interpretation and penetration of rest that has to follow' [3] are known ideas to linguist researchers. Also is the goal of concluding remarks in a sentence [4]: because the initial vocable or noun in a phrase gains more importance, and professional writers will change the order of the words to engage the reader's attention to the factual information using the active mode of writing a sentence. These are design alternatives which the writer of a sentence or a tweet on Twitter has to learn and there are options within this learning that require attention, be it direct or indirect, that a verbally spoken sentence is not the same as a written one. Using the linguistic aspect of feature formation is not entirely explored in the area of research of feature extraction from verbatim of tweet [5–8].

Through this paper, we are presenting and contribute to the literature an original and creative approach combined with the deep learning neural network architecture and the branch of linguistics for feature extraction. We assign custom weights to the word vector matrix calculated by the index of these words in the neighborhood of the sequence of the rest of the words in the same sentence. We are further defining this feature engineering framework as Custom Weighted Word Embedding (CWWE). We then try to combine this feature engineering framework with the state of the art Long Short Term Memory (LSTM) to train an initial model that is further optimized by adding convolutional layer 1D on top of embedding to make it more time-efficient while training and improve the accuracy as well. For benchmarking the results of classification using the proposed architecture, we compare the overall accuracy with a CNN model running on the same architecture using a pre-trained glove word embedding instead of the experimented Custom Weighted Word Embedding (CWWE). In the scope of current research, we hypothesize that the proposed framework works better in classifying a tweet as re-tweetable or not if we take into consideration the linguistic art of sentence formation. The ideology behind the research in the current paper is to create the features in such a way that these are not only geography independent but also independent of any theme of any event which makes the proposed framework easily generalizable in any situation.

The rest of the research paper is structured as: in Sect. 2, prior literature is discussed for defining information diffusion, social media analytics and deep leaning architecture, in Sect. 3, we describe the proposed CWWE (Custom Weight Word Embedding). To begin the experimentation phase, we first train a base LSTM model, record the results and define as "baseline results1". We then introduce our novel framework with Convolutional Neural Network and record the results as "proposed framework results". With the same CNN architecture used to test the proposed features but predict the results using a pre-trained glove model of 10,000-word embedding instead of CWWE and define the results as "baseline results2". Finally, we discuss the findings by comparing "baseline results1" vs. "baseline results2" vs. "proposed framework results" and conclude with proposing future scope of research in Sect. 4.

## 2   Prior Literature

The literature review has been designed to follow the following flow: we start with defining the information diffusion, how social media analytics has helped the researchers' community to gain insights about the domain, followed by discussing the established vectorization process as one of the techniques from the social media analytics toolkit and concluding with deep learning architectures used for unstructured data like tweet text.

## 2.1    Information Diffusion and Social Media Analytics

With the internet opening the barriers of communication among people across the globe, there is a need to perform research on effective ways of communication. When there is more communication there is more information diffusion too [9–11]. We define information diffusion as the travel process of a piece of knowledge having factual or non-factual details about a person, event, domain or place getting initiated from a sender and reaching a set of receivers through a channel or carrier. In the case of Twitter [12, 13], the carrier is the tweet posted on the channel Twitter, the sender is the user posting the tweet and receivers are followers of the user posting the tweet. There are three aspects of information diffusion: innovation in communication practice, factual information and right audience (user-network) which plays an important role in predicting the degree of information diffusion.

With the increase of internet penetration, social media platforms have started to gain importance as a channel for message penetration and propagation. Twitter is constantly explored by organizations and individuals for multiple communications which creates an abundance of information and hence researchers have started exploring various analysis frameworks to gain insights and one such framework is Social Media Analytics (SMA). SMA as an evolving cross-domain research area for gaining insights through social media has made the usage of Twitter for information communication and diffusion across multiple domains possible. Many researchers from their work have proved the potential of SMA across different academic disciplines and business domains. Prior work strongly shows that SMA can provide important insights around disciplines such as marketing [14], in deliberation on political [15] and social concerns [16], in emergency [17], for building public relation [18] or even ruling out possibility of polarization of any major event [19]. Social media platforms like Twitter can also help us to gain insights into any specific domain [20] or technology [21]. However, in the domain of social media, penetration and diffusion of communication has three strong pillars, firstly managing and controlling misinformation [22], secondly use machine learning to automatically predicting the information (tweet) diffusion speed, scale, range and trend [23] and thirdly use frameworks to evaluate the credibility of a tweet, i.e. whether to trust the tweet and the person writing the tweet.

## 2.2    Word Features and Deep Learning Architecture

The most popular model in SMA for predicting the information diffusion (retweet on Twitter) is to convert sentences to words and then to vectors and finally use these vectors as features in classifiers to predict the probability of reweet. Most of the prior experimentation performed in the retweet prediction is based on the opinion similarity analysis of the words used in the tweet or at the user account and network level. Xu and Yang [24] have proposed term frequency-inverse document frequency hinged BOW (bag of words) for every tweet in a content-based model for retweet prediction. The research by [25] presented the work of information-sharing approach and trend of users on social media platforms. The assessment of the importance of these variables in the same research presented that the term frequency–inverse document frequency weighted BOW homogeneity of retweeted tweets performing as the highest significant variable in predicting user retweet trend. Brief research also exists around computational linguistic research [26] to predict the impact of any information, but there certainly exist a gap for thorough research which has motivated us to take up this research.

Many people try to reword the original sentence in their own words with the intent of communicating the original message in a much better way. However, as such, any literature or verbatim synopsis is already abstractive in nature and has very little possibility of reproduction of the original sentence. With all deep learning architectures getting noticed by researchers in the field of unstructured data, it has become a more practical option for any NLP analysis, researchers have begun to consider these frameworks as a fully data-driven alternative to abstractive text summarization. The possibility of storing the meaning of a sentence with abstract features extracted is not completely explored. In the latest research, Lopyrev [27] relates an application of an encoder-decoder RNN (recurrent neural network) with LSTM units and notices that the framework starts creating headlines from the actual text of news articles. In a slightly different but related work, Rush [28] presented a fully data-driven framework for sentence summarization. His approach makes use of an attention driven algorithm that creates each word from the input sentence as summary transformed. Chopra [29] proposes a constraint-based RNN (recurrent neural network) which can easily create an abstract of any input phrase. The transformation has been done by a unique approach in which a convolutional encoder is implemented to make sure that the corresponding decoder centers around the proper input words at each phase of generation. In an alternate paper that sharply resonates with our proposed framework, Ramesh Nallapati [30] has proposed a summary-based text abstraction using Attentional Encoder-Decoder RNN (Recurrent Neural Network), and show that these models achieve state-of-the-art performance on two different corpora [31–33]. Our work starts with a similar-looking framework but with the focus of extracting and storing the original sense of a sentence (tweets on Twitter) in very abstract features (CWWE) and assigning custom weights which will be further used to predict the diffusion (retweet) of the same sentences (tweets on Twitter).

# 3   CWWE-Based LSTM-CNN Model Experimentation

## 3.1   Data Collection

The first step in developing a classifier is to create a training corpus. In our study, we are focusing on collecting data from Twitter. The reason behind selecting Twitter is its flexible architecture that allows one-to-many communication and is less restricted when compared to other social networking sites like Facebook.

We specifically targeted to collect tweets for "Game of Thrones season8" because there will not be any sponsored posts and this series (particularly season8) was liked, watched and hated by viewers across the globe from different ethnicity. Hence the process of data extraction, gave us tweets originated at different parts of the world with varied writing styles. To achieve this, we used the following tags: [#GOTS08, #Game of Thrones Season8, #Game of Thrones Final Season, #Game of Thrones Last Season, #GOT Season8]. Through streaming API of Twitter, we can scrap (free) one percent of tweets posted every day. Using Python as a tool, we used streaming API to collect tweets during the period: [April 14 to May 19, 2019]. This helped us to create a corpus of 300,000 tweets relevant to our analysis. Out of 300,000 tweets, a corpus of 234,884 tweets was created after data cleaning and removing the tweets which were posted by major official accounts. Finally, 234,884 tweets were labeled as "Viral" vs "Non-Viral" basis if the number of retweets of the tweet was greater than '10' referred to as "Viral" and the tweets for which the retweets was less than '10' was referred to as "Non-Viral" tweets. Table 1 below represents the exploratory description of the tweet corpus.

**Table 1.** Descriptive statistics of data set

| | Tweet corpus size | Distinct users | Viral tweets | Non-Viral tweets | Average age of the twitter account in the corpus | Average number of tweets per user per day | Average number of followers per user |
|---|---|---|---|---|---|---|---|
| # | 234,884 | 46,302 | 56,936 | 177,948 | 6 years | 9 | 7200 |

### 3.2  Data Cleaning

The pretreatment of the tweet text is a mandated step as it cleans and converts the actual tweet to structured features matrix, ready for analysis, i.e., it becomes easier to extract rich and factual information from the tweet and apply machine learning algorithms to it. If we bypass this data preparation step, then there is a highly likely a chance that we are dealing with noisy and incompatible data. The goal of this data cleaning exercise is to not only smoothen out the noise, the ones that are much less relevant to uncover the sentiment of tweets together with punctuation, special characters, numbers, and phrases that do not convey a lot of weight in context to the text. In the next steps of data cleaning, we are converting unstructured data of text to more structured data by generating the matrix of words extracted from the original tweet. If the initial data cleansing of tweets is done diligently, then the resulting feature space will also be of good quality.

Initial data cleaning makes every tweet to go through the following phases: Firstly, we know that owing to security concerns, Twitter never reveals the actual Twitter handle posting the tweet. Hence as part of the data cleaning process, we clear the special character sign of "@" which masks the Twitter handle. Secondly, we also know from the linguistic literature that special characters, alphanumeric, numeric and lingos do not convey any specific factual information hence, we cleaned any other special characters, alphanumeric, numeric and lingos from the actual tweets. Thirdly we have replaced most of the shorter words with the root words like: "haven't": "have not", "doesn't": "does not". Once every tweet loops through the above 3 steps we extract words from all the tweets and create a matrix with all the words from the corpus as columns. However, we have a huge corpus of tweets and hence the size of the matrix of words also becomes large. To reduce the dimension, we reduced same versions of the words to its original root word, like: {like, likable}: {like}.

### 3.3   Build a Preliminary LSTM Model with Standard Word Embedding

For simplicity, we start with the retweet column which represents how many retweets a tweet has received. Tweets that have more than ten ('10') as the retweet value are considered as the tweets which got diffused easily and strongly and will be labeled as "Retweeted" tweets for our research. The tweets for which the retweet column has less than ten ('10') as value will be labelled as the tweets which were not able to diffuse (were not retweeted) on twitter. We define this new column as "Retweet Identifier" which will have binary values and will be treated as the class label in our research analysis. Because we have a class label classifier (retweet identifier) to label each tweet, the research problem can now be defined as supervised learning and the theories of any classifier algorithm can be implemented to train, validate and test our model. We start our feature engineering with first tokenizing the text and convert them to word vectors. For feature dimension control and reduction, we are placing a constraint of 50 words on each tweet. This means that tweets having texts shorter than 50 words are padded with zeros, and longer texts are truncated. We now start with the model training.

The architecture of the neural network starts with an embedding layer wherein each word from a lower dimension is projected to a higher dimension, which in turn helps the network to learn every word vector in a more descriptive manner. The layer takes 20000 as the first argument, which is the size of our vocabulary, and 100 as the second input parameter, which is the dimension of the embedding. The third parameter has been constrained at 50 for the maximum size of every tweet sentence. We have also divided the entire tweet corpus into three sections: training (on which we let the model to train and optimize the parameters by minimizing the loss function), validation (on which the model validates the new parameters selected after every iteration) and test data (on which the trained model is tested for its performance on an unseen data). Model results at the end of training at this step are recorded and represented in Table 2.

**Table 2.**   Model results for a preliminary LSTM model

| Test data set accuracy | | | |
|---|---|---|---|
| LSTM | 0.52 | | |
| Confusion matrix | | | |
| Model | | Retweet | |
| | | Yes | No |
| | Yes | 10482 | 15539 |
| | No | 2561 | 9000 |

Precision = 0.8
Recall = 0.4

### 3.4   Build a Custom Weight Word Embedding Matrix

With the hypothesis of establishing information diffusion as a function of the weights derived from position based linguistic features [16], we pursue with the first step of our proposed CWWE framework. To establish the relative position index, we extract each word of a tweet as an independent feature and locate the relative presence of this word feature in the presence of other words in the respective tweet. We also try to see the context in which the word is used in the tweet while conveying a message. We try to explain the above concept with a basic illustration below:

James played **brilliantly** [manner] in the **match** [place] on **Saturday** [time] evening.

vs.

The **match** [place] played on **Saturday** [time], James performed comparatively good from his last game **good** [manner].

In the first sentence, the writer gives more emphasis by using the word **brilliantly** at the beginning of the sentence and the reader might not read the entire sentence to interpret that James performed brilliantly in the match. On the contrary in the second sentence, how the player played is being placed at last, which might leave less emphasis on the player James and some of the readers might even skip that part. Considering the tweet was about player James, we hypothesize that if the word **brilliantly** is used at the beginning there is highly likely chance that this tweet will diffuse (will be retweeted) in the Twitter network faster as compared to the second sentence. With this hypothesis, we will be testing the proposed framework by assigning the custom weights depending upon the relative position of the words. The details of the framework are explained in the following steps below.

Step 1: After the cleaning the tweet text, performing the text to Word2Vector matrix (Table 3).

**Table 3.** Step1 of building a custom weight word embedding matrix

| Tweet text | James | played | brilliantly | match | Saturday | good |
|---|---|---|---|---|---|---|
| James played brilliantly in the match on Saturday evening | 1 | 1 | 1 | 1 | 1 | 0 |
| The match played on Saturday, James performed comparatively good from his last game | 1 | 1 | 0 | 1 | 1 | 1 |

Step 2: After generating the Word2Vector matrix, we now try to find the length of each tweet text, mid-point index, first quartile and third quartile basis the length of text (Table 4).

**Table 4.** Step2 of building a custom weight word embedding matrix

| Tweet text | Length | Mid-point index | First quartile | Third quartile |
|---|---|---|---|---|
| James played brilliantly in the match on Saturday evening | 9 | 5 | 3 | 6 |
| The match played on Saturday, James performed comparatively good from his last game | 13 | 7 | 4 | 9 |

Step 3: We now look at the position index of each word from the Word2Vector matrix in the tweet text and check if the index falls in the first quartile, close to mid-point, in the third quartile or beyond the third quartile (Table 5).

**Table 5.** Step3 of building a custom weight word embedding matrix

| Tweet text | James | played | brilliantly | match | Saturday | good |
|---|---|---|---|---|---|---|
| James played brilliantly in the match on Saturday evening | First | First | Third | Third | Third | 0 |
| The match played on Saturday, James performed comparatively good from his last game | Mid | First | 0 | First | First | Third |

Step 4: In the last step we assign a weight of 0.75 to the word which appears close to the first quartile, nothing to the words which are close to the middle part of the sentence and 0.25 to the words which are close to the third quartile of the tweet text. We further multiply these weights for the respective words in the respective tweets to the matrix from step1. The resulting matrix for the illustration looks like below (Table 6).

**Table 6.** Final step of building a custom weight word embedding matrix

| Tweet text | James | played | brilliantly | match | Saturday | good |
|---|---|---|---|---|---|---|
| James played brilliantly in the match on Saturday evening | 0.75 | 0.75 | 0.75 | 0.25 | 0.25 | 0 |
| The match played on Saturday, James performed comparatively good from his last game | 0 | 0.75 | 0 | 0.75 | 0.75 | 0.25 |

### 3.5  Build a CNN Model with CWWE

The LSTM model worked well with the initial Word2Vec matrix. However, it took forever to train one epoch. CNN is known to work well in image processing domains but the potential usage of CNN architecture in unstructured data like tweet analysis is still a fairly new area for research. Literature suggests that to increase the response time of the models while training on the data, we can add a convolutional layer, by doing so, uses a "filter" over the input feature matrix and calculates a higher-level representation. We then perform max pooling through a kernel of the input dimensions which in turn reduces the parameters required and this, in turn, reduces the training time. While doing

**Table 7.** Model results for the CNN model with CWWE

| Test data set accuracy | | | |
|---|---|---|---|
| CNN | 0.80 | | |
| Confusion matrix | | | |
| Model | | Retweet | |
| | | Yes | No |
| | Yes | 19798 | 6223 |
| | No | 1603 | 9958 |
| Precision = 0.9 | | | |
| Recall = 0.76 | | | |

the same we also introduce the model to the new CWWE features to test if the new derived features help to increase the accuracy of the classification. Model results at the end of training at this step are captured and represented in Table 7.

### 3.6   Build a CNN Model with a Pre-trained Glove Word Embedding

In this step, we use the same network architecture from *3.5* above, but instead of using CWWE, we now use the pre-trained glove 100-dimension word embedding as input features and consider the results as a benchmark to compare against the results recorded from step *3.5*. If the results from step *3.5*, outperform the results of the current step then our original hypothesis is correct. The glove model used in this sub-section is pre-trained on four hundred thousand (400,000) words over a billion tokens. The glove has embedding vector sizes, including 50, 100, 200 and 300 dimensions. We chose the 100-dimensional version. We also want to see the model behavior in case the learned word weights do not get updated. We, therefore, set the trainable attribute for the model to be False. The results of this step are recorded and represented in Table 8 below.

**Table 8.** Model accuracy

| Test data set accuracy | | | |
|---|---|---|---|
| CNN + Glove | 0.70 | | |
| Confusion matrix | | | |
| Model | | Retweet | |
| | | Yes | No |
| | Yes | 17004 | 9017 |
| | No | 2665 | 8896 |
| Precision = 0.8 | | | |
| Recall = 0.65 | | | |

### 3.7   Summarization of the Results

A summarization of the results reveal that using the proposed framework of Custom Weighted Word Embedding (CWWE), if the word features extracted from the tweet are assigned custom weights basis the relative position of these words in the sentence, we record a significant improvement in the overall accuracy of CNN model from 53% to 80%. We also see that precision and recall of the model with the proposed framework outperforms the preliminary model at 0.90 and 0.76 as compared to 0.80 and 0.40 respectively for the concerned class which is - will a tweet retweet (retweet > 10). The CNN model with the proposed framework has also outperformed pre-trained established glove word-based CNN model experimentation with the same architecture with the latter's values as (accuracy: 0.70, precision: 0.8, recall: 0.65). Hence we can state that our initial hypothesis of a writer's deliberate choice of placing the more influential words (like nouns, adjectives) at the first half of the tweet puts more emphasis on the intent interpretation by the readers and helps to cascade the same at a faster rate on social media platform as compared to sentences/tweets where these words are used at the latter half is correct.

## 4  Discussion

The primary contribution of our research paper is CWWE with a combination of CNN in using the linguistic features. With the outcome of our experimentation set-up we confirm our hypothesis that degree and rate of any information diffusion on twitter (tweet getting retweeted) can be established as a function of how a user has designed the sentence with the constraint limitation of the size of the tweet (140 characters). Intentionally placing more impactful words related to the context of discussion can increase of potential retweet faster and hence for it is important to also understand the linguistic aspect of writing English literature. We were also able to bring down the training time of the model knowing that unstructured data will have higher dimension of features set as compared to other regular analysis. We have proved through our experimentation and research that the proposed CWWE can outperform any other established word-embedding framework.

## 5  Conclusion

Every tweet contains both micro and macro-level information about the information conveyed that can be extracted and then can be further used to represent a tweet. With this motivation we chose the semantics which represents the micro level information of a tweet and developed a framework of embedding matrix representing a writer's habit of placing the part of speech (Nouns and adjectives). We further used the rules of semantic information with the help of deep neural network framework to predict if a tweet will be retweeted on not. We proved that the diffusion of a particular content on Twitter can be driven by a sequence of nouns, adjectives, adverbs forming a sentence. We exhibited that the proposed approach in this paper is coherent with the intrinsic disposition of tweets to a common choice of words while constructing a sentence to express an opinion or sentiment. With this experimentation we have established that if a writer uses an adjective or a noun at the beginning of the sentence, there is highly likely a chance that the sentence/text/information is going to diffuse at a faster rate.

Motivated by the positive results of the current experiment, as next steps for future research work, we plan to extend the CWWE along with the other features like size of the network structure, the user is part of and understand the relation with social influence on social media platform Twitter. The framework should be able to predict the exact social influence in terms of number of retweets any user will get while posting any tweet.

## References

1. Sharples, M.: How We Write: Writing as Creative Design. Routledge, London (2016)
2. Maun, I., Myhill, D.: Text as design, writers as designers. Engl. Educ. **39**(2), 5–21 (2005)
3. Brown, G., Yule, G.: Discourse Analysis. Cambridge University Press, Cambridge (1983)
4. Leech, G.N., Svartvik, J.: A Communicative Grammar of English. Longman, London (1975)

5. Danyluk, A.P., Bottou, L., Littman, M.L. (eds.): ICML, ACM International Conference Proceeding Series, vol. 382, p. 140. ACM (2009)
6. Shi, Q., Petterson, J., Dror, G., Langford, J., Smola, A., Vishwanathan, S.: Hash kernels for structured data. J. Mach. Learn. Res. **10**, 2615–2637 (2016)
7. Ganchev, K., Dredze, M.: Small statistical models by random feature mixing. In: Proceedings of the ACL 2008, Workshop on Mobile Language Processing. Association for Computational Linguistics (2008)
8. Colmenares, C.A., Litvak, M., Mantrach, A.: HEADS: headline generation as sequence prediction using an abstract feature-rich space. In: HLT-NAACL, pp. 133–142 (2015)
9. Goel, S., Anderson, A., Hofman, J., Watts, D.J.: The structural virality of online diffusion. Manage. Sci. **62**, 180–196 (2016)
10. Myers, S.A., Leskovec, J.: Clash of the contagions: cooperation and competition in information diffusion. In: Proceedings of the IEEE 12th International Conference on Data Mining, 2012, pp. 539–548. IEEE, Brussels (2012)
11. Romero, D.M., Meeder, B., Kleinberg, J.: Differences in the mechanics of information diffusion across topics: idioms, political hashtags, and complex contagion on Twitter. In: Proceedings of the 20th International Conference on World Wide Web, pp. 695–704. Association for Computing Machinery, New York (2011)
12. Stieglitz, S., Dang-Xuan, L.: Emotions and information diffusion in social media sentiment of microblogs and sharing behavior. J. Manage. Inf. Syst. **29**(4), 217–248 (2013)
13. Yoo, E., Rand, W., Eftekhar, M., Rabinovich, E.: Evaluating information diffusion speed and its determinants in social media networks during humanitarian crises. J. Oper. Manage. **45**, 123–133 (2016)
14. Aswani, R., Kar, A.K., Ilavarasan, P.V., Dwivedi, Y.: Search engine marketing is not all gold: insights from Twitter and SEOClerk. Int. J. Inf. Manage. **38**(1), 107–116 (2018)
15. Grover, P., Kar, A.K., Dwivedi, Y.K., Janssen, M.: The untold story of USA presidential elections in 2016 - insights from Twitter analytics. In: Kar, A.K., et al. (eds.) I3E 2017. LNCS, vol. 10595, pp. 339–350. Springer, Cham (2017). https://doi.org/10.1007/978-3-319-68557-1_30
16. Mohan, R., Kar, A.K.: #Demonetization and its impact on the Indian economy – insights from social media analytics. In: Kar, A.K., et al. (eds.) I3E 2017. LNCS, vol. 10595, pp. 363–374. Springer, Cham (2017). https://doi.org/10.1007/978-3-319-68557-1_32
17. Starbird, K., Palen, L.: Pass it on? Retweeting in mass emergency. In: Proceedings of the 7th International Conference of Information Systems for Crisis Response and Management, pp. 1–10 (2010)
18. Grover, P., Kar, A.K., Ilavarasan, P.V.: Impact of corporate social responsibility on reputation – insights from tweets on sustainable development goals by CEOs. Int. J. Inf. Manage. **48**, 39–52 (2019)
19. Grover, P., Kar, A.K., Dwivedi, Y.K., Janssen, M.: Polarization and acculturation in US Election 2016 outcomes – can Twitter analytics predict changes in voting preferences? Technol. Forecast. Soc. Change **145**, 438–460 (2018)
20. Grover, P., Kar, A.K., Davies, G.H.: "Technology enabled Health" – insights from Twitter analytics with a socio-technical perspective. Int. J. Inf. Manage. **43**, 1–13 (2018)
21. Grover, P., Kar, A.K., Janssen, M., Ilavarasan, P.V.: Perceived usefulness, ease of use and user acceptance of blockchain technology for digital transactions – insights from user-generated content on Twitter. Enterp. Inf. Syst. **13**(6), 1–30 (2019)
22. Aswani, R., Kar, A.K., Ilavarasan, P.V.: Experience: managing misinformation in social media – insights for policy makers from the Twitter analytics. J. Data Inf. Qual. Article No. 6 (2019)

23. Yang, J., Counts, S.: Predicting the speed, scale, and range of information diffusion in Twitter. In: Proceedings of the Fourth International AAAI Conference on Weblogs and Social Media (2010)
24. Xu, Z., Yang, Q.: Analyzing user retweet behavior on Twitter. In: IEEE/ACM International Conference on Advances in Social Networks Analysis and Mining (ASONAM), pp. 46–50. IEEE (2016)
25. Nguyen, D.A., Tan, S., Ramanathan, R., Yan, X.: Analyzing information sharing strategies of users in online social networks. In: Proceedings of the IEEE/ACM International Conference on Advances in Social Networks Analysis and Mining, pp. 247–254. IEEE Press (2016)
26. Lerman, K., Gilder, A., Dredze, M., Pereira, F.: Reading the markets: forecasting public opinion of political candidates by news analysis. In: Proceedings of the 22nd International Conference on Computational Linguistics, vol. 1, pp. 473–480 (2008)
27. Riedhammer, K., Favre, B., Hakkani-Tür, D.: Long story short–global unsupervised models for key phrase based meeting summarization. Speech Commun. 52(10), 801–815 (2010)
28. Zhang, Y., Shen, D., Wang, G., et al.: Deconvolutional paragraph representation learning. In: Advances in Neural Information Processing Systems, pp. 4172–4182 (2017)
29. Li, J., Luong, M.T., Jurafsky, D.: A hierarchical neural auto encoder for paragraphs and documents. arXiv preprint arXiv:1506.01057 (2015)
30. Rush, A.M., Chopra, S., Weston, J.: A neural attention model for abstractive sentence summarization. arXiv preprint arXiv:1509.00685 (2015)
31. Gu, J., Lu, Z., Li, H., et al.: Incorporating copying mechanism in sequence-to-sequence learning. arXivpreprint arXiv:1603.06393 (2016)
32. Zhong, B., Xing, X., Love, P., Wang, X., Luo, H.: Convolutional neural network: deep learning-based classification of building quality problems. In: Advanced Engineering Informatics, ScienceDirect, pp. 46–57, vol. 40, April 2019. Elsevier (2019)
33. Yu, M., Huang, Q., Qin, H., Scheele, C., Yang, C.: Deep learning for real-time social media text classification for situation awareness – using Hurricanes Sandy, Harvey, and Irma as case studies. Soc. Sens. Big Data Comput. Disaster Manage. 12(11), 1230–1247 (2019). International Journal of Digital Earth

# Requirements of Data Visualisation Tools to Analyse Big Data: A Structured Literature Review

Joy Lowe[✉] and Machdel Matthee

Department of Informatics, University of Pretoria, Pretoria, South Africa
u16331878@tuks.co.za, machdel.matthee@up.ac.za

**Abstract.** The continual growth of big data necessitates efficient ways of analysing these large datasets. Data visualisation and visual analytics has been identified as a key tool in big data analysis because they draw on the human visual and cognitive capabilities to analyse data quickly, intuitively and interactively. However, current visualisation tools and visual analytical systems fall short of providing a seamless user experience and several improvements could be made to current commercially available visualisation tools. By conducting a systematic literature review, requirements of visualisation tools were identified and categorised into six groups: dimensionality reduction, data reduction, scalability and readability, interactivity, fast retrieval of results, and user assistance. The most common themes found in the literature were dimensionality reduction and interactive data exploration.

**Keywords:** Big data visualisation · Visualisation tools · Visual analytics

## 1 Introduction

Big data is growing at an exponential rate due to unprecedented data capture from smart devices, the internet of things, measurement and sensor technology, transaction data, metadata, and social media (Ali et al. 2016; Gisbrecht 2013; Resnyansky 2019). With an estimated 3.7 billion internet users globally (Marr 2018) the internet is a significant factor in the generation of data. Google, the most popular search engine, receives at least 5.5 billion search queries per day (Sullivan 2016) and processes 24 petabytes of data per day (Ali et al. 2016). User generated social media data is another significant contributor to big data, with Facebook reporting 2.32 billion active monthly users (Noyes 2019a) and Twitter reporting 321 million active monthly users with 500 million tweets posted daily (Noyes 2019b)

Big data is defined as large, complex, high velocity data sets (Seokyeon et al. 2015). Big data is characterised by volume, velocity, value, variety, variability, and complexity (Katal et al. 2013). Due to the nature of these large, heterogeneous data sets, interpretation and comprehension of the data is often difficult, and current data storage and analysis technologies are no longer able to effectively store and analyse such large datasets (Genender-Feltheimer 2018). However, using big data brings new opportunities for research and new insights across a wide variety of fields (Resnyansky

M. Hattingh et al. (Eds.): I3E 2020, LNCS 12066, pp. 469–480, 2020.
https://doi.org/10.1007/978-3-030-44999-5_39

2019) and by visually exploring and analysing the data, unexpected discoveries can be found.

Data visualisation is a solution to aid meaningful analysis, accessibility and interpretation of big data as it relies on human cognitive capabilities to process visual information (Gisbrecht 2013). Visualising data creates an image that the user is able to parse in three subtasks: perceptual grouping, image segmentation and object recognition (Zhu 2003). Image parsing is an efficient means of comprehending large datasets because grouping or clustering of data points, as well as outliers, become apparent. Further, the inclusion of interactive technology and visual analytics allows users to gain more information about specific data points and areas of interest through visual exploration, which facilitates the formation, testing and validation of hypotheses (Elmqvist and Fekete 2010).

Increasingly complex and sophisticated data analytics and visualisation algorithms are required in response to the increasing significance of big data (Gisbrecht 2013). The velocity at which the data is generated produces the need for real time analysis. This paper will explore and compare various techniques which have been developed in response to these requirements to effectively visualise and comprehend big data.

## 2  Literature Background

### 2.1  The Growth of Big Data

Big data has been hailed as one of the greatest challenges of the 21st century due to the volume of data, the speed at which the data is being generated, as well as the inconsistency of the data (Katal et al. 2013). A number of factors contribute to the growth and complexity of big data including the internet of things (IOT), click stream data, and social media data. Big data has become an integral part of business, social media, scientific research and several other fields (Olshannikova et al. 2015) and the data is predicted to grow even further, at faster rates.

### 2.2  The Need for Visualisations to Comprehend Big Data

Big data is now beyond human comprehension through simple exploration and investigation of the data (Long and Linsen 2011). People are able to comprehend the world more quickly and easily through visual cues, and this extends to visualising data. Vision is the most valuable human sense and most people prefer visual representations to other sensory information.

In order to capitalise on the big data revolution and gain as much insight as possible, it is imperative that the data is analysed efficiently and accurately, and thereafter visualised to allow for the fast interpretation of the data, much of which is generated in real time.

Furthermore, visualisations of data make trends and patterns in the data much more apparent such as clustering, the distribution of the data, and correlation within the data (Long and Linsen 2011). The goal of many businesses regarding data analysis is to recognise such patterns, emphasizing the need for data visualisation to achieve strategic objectives.

Visualising data is a means of "uniting the abstract world of data with the physical world through visual representation" (Olshannikova et al. 2015). Visualisations can be likened to the front end of big data (Wang et al. 2015) and can be used to access and interpret the data, making the insights and trends more apparent.

## 2.3 The Need for Awareness of Data Visualisation Techniques Among Professionals

Many business professionals now need to be educated in data related information and become "data literate" in order to generate business reports as well as interpret reports and business intelligence executive dashboards. These business professionals must be made aware of the features and limitations of each visualisation technique and visualization software or tool, particularly with interactive dashboards becoming more popular. In this paper some visualization tools and techniques will be discussed.

## 2.4 Commercially Available Business Intelligence and Visualisation Tools

There are a number of currently available commercial Business Intelligence tools that include the ability to create visualisations, which can be utilized by professionals in a number of different fields and industries. Figure 1 below shows the Magic Quadrant for Analytics and Business Intelligence Platforms published by Gartner in February 2019. This quadrant displays the 'leaders', 'visionaries', 'challengers', and 'niche players' of business intelligence platforms and provides a good overview of the landscape of the industry at present.

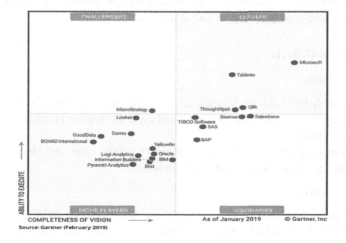

**Fig. 1.** Gartner magic quadrant for analytics and business intelligence platforms (Orad 2019)

## 3   Research Method

A systematic literature review was carried out during the course of this research. The following eight steps are suggested when conducting a systematic review of Information Systems research (Okoli and Schabram, n.d.):

1. Identifying the purpose and intended goals of the literature review
2. Outlining the protocol and detailed procedure to be followed
3. Searching for the literature
4. Practical screening/screening for inclusion
5. Quality appraisal/screening for exclusion
6. Data extraction
7. Synthesis/analysis of studies
8. Writing the review.

### 3.1   Research Question

What are the requirements of data visualisation tools used to analyse big data?

### 3.2   Search Terms

Title (data) AND title (visual*) AND abstract (big data).

The wild card search term "visual*" was used to cater for all variations of the words that derive from the common stem 'visual' including visualise, visualising, visualisation, visualisations, as well as being inclusive of both variations of spelling for each of these words: the American spelling which includes a 'z' and the English spelling which contains an 's'. In the case where a search engine did not support wild cards, all possible variations of the word were specified using OR Boolean clauses so that any of the spellings would be included in the search results.

### 3.3   Selection Criteria

**Inclusion Criteria**

- Articles published between January 2014 and October 2019 were included to ensure the most up to date research was evaluated since the field of big data visualisation is changing rapidly.
- Peer reviewed journal articles and conference papers were included.
- Only articles written in English were included.

**Exclusion Criteria**

- Articles published prior to January 2014 and after October 2019 were excluded.
- The following document types were excluded: periodicals, editorials, books, and book chapters.

### 3.4   Source Selection

The following sources and databases were consulted during the course of this research:

- ABI/Inform
- ACM Digital Library
- EBSCOhost
- ScienceDirect

The Prisma flow chart below shows the number of articles identified through each database and the process of exclusion that was followed to reach the final 31 articles that were included in the literature review (Fig. 2).

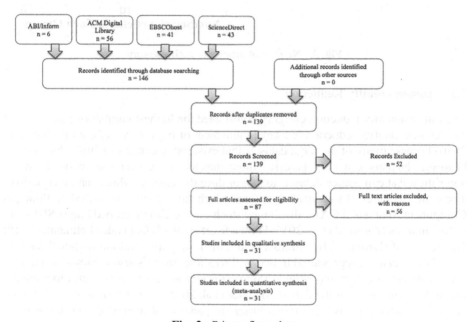

**Fig. 2.**  Prisma flow chart

## 4   Analysis of Findings

After reviewing the literature, many authors are in agreement that data visualisation will become increasingly important as big data becomes more prevalent in more organisations and in order to interpret the data, effective visualisation techniques will be required (Wang and Li 2019). There has also been a call to improve current visualisation techniques (Li et al. 2016; Olshannikova et al. 2015) in order to handle the challenges of visualising big data.

A combined list of requirements of data visualisation tools to interpret big data found in the literature are shown in Fig. 3 below. The bar graph shows the number of papers included in the literature which fall into each category. Note that some articles address more than one category, thus the total of the values of the bars in Fig. 3 is greater than the total number of articles included in the literature review.

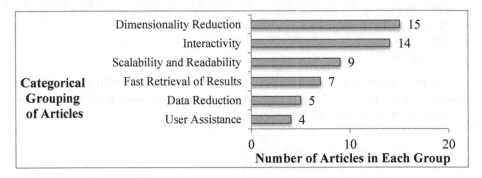

Fig. 3. Number of articles in each category

## 4.1  Dimensionality Reduction

The dimensionality reduction category contributed the highest number of papers (15 of 31). Dimensionality reduction is a key requirement of big data visualisation (Zou et al. 2016) because many of the large datasets that exist today contain multiple dimensions, however, humans can only perceive three dimensions, giving rise to the need for algorithms that can reduce datasets to two or three dimensions which can be visualised. There are a number of statistical algorithms which can achieve this including Principal Component Analysis (PCA), t-distributed stochastic neighbour embedding (t-SNE) and diffusion maps (Agrawal et al. 2015; Fernandez et al. 2015; Genender-Feltheimer 2018; Gisbrecht and Hammer 2015; Shirota et al. 2017). Mapping multidimensional datasets into clusters that are represented in two or three dimensions is also common and allows the partitioning of data into similar groups (Keck et al. 2017). It is useful to maintain the original structures of the data (Fernandez et al. 2015) so that further analysis can be carried out after identifying certain clusters or patterns of interest during the two- or three-dimensional exploration of the data (Keck et al. 2017; Xie et al. 2016). Advantages of dimensional reduction include easily understood visualisations, reduced data quality challenges, and improved computational efficiency (Genender-Feltheimer 2018).

Dimensionality reducing algorithms are either linear, or non-linear. Linear algorithms are only able to learn linear underlying topological spaces, while non-linear algorithms are able to learn complex underlying topological spaces and focus on preserving neighbourhood geometry (Genender-Feltheimer 2018). Dimensionality reduction algorithms can also be grouped into supervised and unsupervised algorithms. Supervised algorithms require a 'training' data set to 'learn' from, and subsequently the model is applied to a second 'scoring' data set. Unsupervised algorithms do not require a training dataset, but rather, are able to detect patterns in the data (Mwangi et al. 2014). Examples of supervised algorithms include Linear Discriminant Analysis and Linear Regression; and examples of unsupervised algorithms include neural networks and other deep learning methods. Supervised algorithms have the potential to be tainted with human bias, as the training dataset contains user defined target labels (Mwangi et al. 2014).

## 4.2 Interactivity

By providing a visual interface which the user can interact with, the user is able to intuitively comprehend the data, perceive the underlying patterns (Lugmayr et al. 2017) and query the data visually, without the need for programming knowledge. The ability for a user to interact with a visualisation makes visual exploration of the dataset possible and this has the major advantage of combining both human and machine intelligence (Chen et al. 2019) to uncover unexpected and interesting phenomena within the dataset (Cho et al. 2014). The benefits of visual analytics are "visual perception, interactive exploration, improved understanding, informed steering and intuitive interpretation" (Liu 2019). This has the potential to uncover patterns in the data using a bottom-up approach (Ruan and Zhang 2017) or to test theories and search for evidence within the data using a top-down approach (Genender-Feltheimer 2018; Mwangi et al. 2014). Visualisation tools should enable the user to drill down into areas of interest within the data (Zhao et al. 2017) to aid in the visual analysis.

Several authors write about the need to keep the user informed at each step of the visual analytics process. This gives the user situational awareness and keeps the user informed about the underlying processes being run in order to render the data or return results (Zhao et al. 2017). Currently, many visualisation tools are a "Black Box" and do not give enough feedback to the user. Results are produced without a description of how the results were calculated, and in some visualisation systems, the user is not given the option to select a statistical method of their choice (Seokyeon et al. 2015).

## 4.3 Scalability and Readability

The displays on which the visualisations are rendered have a limited number of pixels, thus the lowest granularity possible is to plot one data point onto one pixel (Molina-Solana et al. 2017; Olshannikova et al. 2015; Yang et al. 2015). Visualisation tools are required to "squeeze a billion records into a million pixels" (Bikakis 2018) emphasizing the need for summarisation of data, particularly when creating visualisations. If the dataset is not sufficiently summarised, or if every data point is plotted, this may result in 'over plotting' which is inefficient and it can be difficult to discern the patterns and trends within the data (Li et al. 2016). The number of pixels is even lower on mobile device screens, thus the scalability of visualisations for mobile devices are even more important (Li et al. 2016; Molina-Solana et al. 2017). Furthermore, attempting to plot all data points overloads the users' cognitive capabilities, thus it is important to ensure readability and scalability across all screen sizes and in all contexts (Eldawy et al. 2015). In order to achieve this, visualisation tools should include zooming; overview and detail; and brushing of the visualisation (Li et al. 2016). The visualisation tools should also use the approach of providing a high level overview of the data initially, and subsequently load more detailed data as the user queries and drills down into areas of interest (Agrawal et al. 2015).

## 4.4  Fast Retrieval of Results

It is imperative that data visualisation and visual analytics systems retrieve data fast enough so that the user does not lose their focus and momentum when visually analysing a dataset. The intention is to hold the users concentration, enabling them to problem solve at a high level and creatively formulate queries to investigate further (Liu 2019). Several authors agree that the result should be returned within one second, while some authors specify not more than ten seconds (Li et al. 2016).

One approach to address this is called approximate query processing, whereby an approximation of the data is returned quickly and the exact results are continuously processed in the background while the user moves onto other queries (Zhao et al. 2017). When the query has finished processing, which may take up to ten minutes, the user is informed and the discrepancies between the original estimate and the final results are displayed to the user (Moritz et al. 2017). Generally, it is more important to get a broad overview of the data, rather than exact figures, and in this regard, the approximate processing approach works well. Displaying the confidence interval of the estimate during the initial load of the data gives further benefit to this method, as the user is given an estimate and an indication of how accurate the estimate is. This is particularly useful when the results of simple queries are needed urgently (Masiane 2019; Zhao et al. 2017).

Other approaches which may speed up data retrieval include catching or prefetching the results of frequent queries. It may also be advantageous to divide the data processing across several computers. Online Analytical Processing (OLAP) is another method which speeds up query processing (Moritz et al. 2017). Where possible, it can be useful to parallelise data processing and rendering so that they are performed simultaneously rather than sequentially (Hassan and Pernul 2014).

## 4.5  Data Reduction

As mentioned in Sect. 4.3, computer screens have a limited number of pixels onto which data points can be rendered. A possible solution is to make use of data reduction techniques to utilise the "screen real estate" efficiently (Yang et al. 2015). There are a number of ways to reduce the data, including filtering, clustering, and sampling techniques (Masiane 2019). Examples of sampling techniques that could be used to reduce the dataset include stratified random sampling, systematic random sampling, and quota sampling. Probability sampling techniques select the data in such a way that each data point has an equal probability of being selected. In contrast, non-probability sampling techniques are useful in some cases for the purposes of including at least one data point within each group or category that may be present in the data, meaning that data points which fall into a smaller group or category have a higher chance of being selected than data points which fall into larger categories or groups. This ensures each group is represented in the sample by the inclusion of at least one data point from each group or category (Genender-Feltheimer 2018).

An inevitable disadvantage of data reduction is information loss (Abidi et al. 2018) resulting in the inability to identify nuances such as outliers as well as the true patterns and trends in the data (Keck et al. 2017).

### 4.6 User Assistance

Currently, the majority of visual analytics is carried out by domain experts, or mathematicians and statisticians with the appropriate analytical software and resources (Ko and Chang 2018). However, with increasingly user friendly web-based visualisation tools, many more novice users or laymen could conduct data analysis in future (Seokyeon et al. 2015). According to Behrisch et al., however, the visualisation tools that are commercially available currently still require much improvement in order to provide users with appropriate assistance (Behrisch et al. 2019). Examples of methods to provide the user with assistance include recommending which visualisation techniques are most suitable, given a particular dataset as input (Seokyeon et al. 2015). Behrisch et al. (2019) recommend calculating statistics as soon as the input data is loaded and displaying the results to the user immediately. The visualisation tool could further assist the user by predicting user queries based on use case, user profile, and the relevant information could be displayed based on these parameters.

Human Computer Interaction (HCI) principles are highly relevant in this domain and the user experience could be enhanced by incorporating principles such as gestault laws of grouping, and providing frequent and appropriate feedback (Seokyeon et al. 2015). Similarly, the use of colours is a simple way to highlight similarities or differences in the data (Elaiza et al. 2014). As mentioned in Sect. 4.2, visualisation tools must keep the user informed at each stage of the analysis to give the user situational awareness, inform the user of the progress of the query, and to give the user more control over the analysis (Behrisch et al. 2019; Zhao et al. 2017). Zhao et al. (2017) argue that most visual analytic systems are designed too specifically, thus they are only suitable for a limited range of situations as they restrict data types and data structures. A potential solution to make visualisation systems more dynamic and flexible is through customisation and the use of plug-ins and dynamically linked libraries (Liu 2019).

## 5 Conclusion

Big data and the visualisation of large datasets brings many promising opportunities for discoveries of patterns within the data. However, to fully capitalise on these opportunities, visualisation tools must be able to: perform dimensional reduction of multidimensional datasets; perform data reduction as it is not feasible to render each data point; ensure scalability and readability of visualisations; allow the user to interact with the data and visually analyse the data; retrieve results quickly so that the user does not lose their focus; and provide user assistance. Visualisation tools are currently too narrowly focused, and must be more flexible in terms of the data types they are able to process and the functions they are able to perform. As big data continually grows, data visualisation tools must improve rapidly to enable the exploration and analysis of the masses of data that are produced. Data visualization tools must improve at an equally rapid pace.

# References

Abidi, F., Polys, N., Rajamohan, S., Arsenault, L.: Remote high performance visualization of big data for immersive science (2018)

Agrawal, R., Dai, X., Andres, F.: Challenges and opportunities with big data visualization (2015)

Ali, A., Qadir, J., ur Rasool, R., Sathiaseelan, A., Zwitter, A.: Big data for development: applications and techniques. Big Data Anal. **1**, 2 (2016). https://doi.org/10.1186/s41044-016-0002-4

Behrisch, M., et al.: Commercial visual analytics systems – advances in the big data analytics field. IEEE Trans. Vis. Comput. Graph. **25**(10), 3011–3031 (2019). https://doi.org/10.1109/TVCG.2018.2859973

Bikakis, N.: Big data visualization tools, pp. 1–11 (2018)

Chen, Y., Guan, Z., Zhang, R., Du, X., Wang, Y.: A survey on visualization approaches for exploring association relationships in graph data. J. Vis. **22**(3), 625–639 (2019). https://doi.org/10.1007/s12650-019-00551-y

Cho, W., Lee, H., Varma, M. K., Lee, M.: Big data analysis with interactive visualization using R packages (2014)

Elaiza, N., Khalid, A., Yusoff, M., Kamaru-zaman, E.A., Izzati, I.: Multidimensional data medical dataset using interactive visualization star coordinate technique. Proc. – Proc. Comput. Sci. **42**, 247–254 (2014). https://doi.org/10.1016/j.procs.2014.11.059

Eldawy, A., Mokbel, M.F., Jonathan, C.: A demonstration of HadoopViz - an extensible MapReduce system for visualizing big spatial data, p 1896 (2015)

Elmqvist, N., Fekete, J.D.: Hierarchical aggregation for information visualization: overview, techniques, and design guidelines. IEEE Trans. Vis. Comput. Graph. **16**(3), 439–454 (2010). https://doi.org/10.1109/TVCG.2009.84

Fernandez, A., Gonzalez, A., Diaz, J., Dorronsoro, J.: Diffusion maps for dimensionality reduction and visualization of meteorological data. Neurocomputing **163**, 25–37 (2015)

Genender-Feltheimer, A.: Visualizing high dimensional and big data. In: Complex Adaptive Systems Conference with Theme: Cyber Physical Systems and Deep Learning. Chicago, Illinois, USA (2018)

Gisbrecht, A.: Advances in dissimilarity-based data visualisation. Bielefeld University (2013)

Gisbrecht, A., Hammer, B.: Data visualization by nonlinear dimensionality reduction. Wiley Interdisc. Rev.: Data Min. Knowl. Discov. **5**(April), 51–74 (2015). https://doi.org/10.1002/widm.1147

Hassan, S., Pernul, G.: Efficiently managing the security and costs of big data storage using visual analytics categories and subject descriptors (2014)

Katal, A., Wazid, M., Goudar, R.H.: Big data: issues, challenges, tools and Good practices. In: 2013 6th International Conference on Contemporary Computing, IC3 2013, pp. 404–409 (2013). https://doi.org/10.1109/IC3.2013.6612229

Keck, M., et al.: Towards glyph-based visualizations for big data clustering. In: Proceedings of VINCI 2017, Bangkok, Thailand, 14–16 August 2017, p. 129 (2017)

Ko, I., Chang, H.: Interactive data visualization based on conventional statistical findings for antihypertensive prescriptions using national health insurance claims data. Int. J. Med. Inform. **116**(May), 1–8 (2018). https://doi.org/10.1016/j.ijmedinf.2018.05.003

Li, X., Kuroda, A., Matsuzaki, H.: Polyspector$^{TM}$: an interactive visualization platform optimized for visual analysis of big data, pp. 109–111 (2016)

Liu, Z.: Advances in engineering software a prototype framework for parallel visualization of large flow data. Adv. Eng. Softw. **130**(December 2018), 14–23 (2019). https://doi.org/10.1016/j.advengsoft.2019.02.004

Van Long, T., Linsen, L.: Visualizing high density clusters in multidimensional data using optimized star coordinates. Comput. Stat. **26**, 655–678 (2011). https://doi.org/10.1007/s00180-011-0271-3

Lugmayr, A., Greenfeld, A., Zhang, D.J.: Selected advanced data visualizations : "the UX-machine", cultural visualisation, cognitive big data, and communication of health and wellness data, pp. 247–251 (2017)

Marr, B.: How much data do we create every day? The mind-blowing stats everyone should read (2018). https://www.forbes.com/sites/bernardmarr/2018/05/21/how-much-data-do-we-create-every-day-the-mind-blowing-stats-everyone-should-read/#5d18565f60ba%0Ahttps://www.forbes.com/sites/bernardmarr/2018/05/21/how-much-data-do-we-create-every-day-the-mind-blowing-st. Accessed 31 Mar 2019

Masiane, M.: Towards insight driven sampling for big data visualisation (2019)

Molina-solana, M., Birch, D., Guo, Y.: Improving data exploration in graphs with fuzzy logic and large-scale visualisation. Appl. Soft Comput. J. **53**, 227–235 (2017). https://doi.org/10.1016/j.asoc.2016.12.044

Moritz, D., Fisher, D., Ding, B., Wang, C.: Trust but verify: optimistic visualizations of approximate queries for exploring big data, p. 2904 (2017)

Mwangi, B., Soares, J.C., Hasan, K.M.: Visualization and unsupervised predictive clustering of high-dimensional multimodal neuroimaging data. J. Neurosci. Methods **236**, 1–7 (2014)

Noyes, D.: The top 20 valuable Facebook statistics – updated December 2015 (2019a).https://zephoria.com/top-15-valuable-facebook-statistics/. Accessed 31 Mar 2019

Noyes, D.:. Top 10 Twitter Statistics – Updated March 2019 (2019b). https://zephoria.com/twitter-statistics-top-ten/. Accessed 31 Mar 2019

Okoli, C., Schabram, K.: A guide to conducting a systematic literature review of information systems research. **10**(2010) (n.d.)

Olshannikova, E., Ometov, A., Koucheryavy, Y., Olsson, T.: Visualizing big data with augmented and virtual reality: challenges and research agenda. J. Big Data 1–27 (2015). https://doi.org/10.1186/s40537-015-0031-2

Orad, A.: 2019 Gartner Magic Quadrant (2019). https://www.sisense.com/gartner-magic-quadrant-business-intelligence/. Accessed 6 Jan 2020

Resnyansky, L.: Conceptual frameworks for social and cultural big data analytics: answering the epistemological challenge. Big Data Soc. **6**(1), 205395171882381 (2019). https://doi.org/10.1177/2053951718823815

Ruan, G., Zhang, H.: Closed-loop big data analysis with visualization and scalable. Big Data Res. **8**, 12–26 (2017). https://doi.org/10.1016/j.bdr.2017.01.002

Seokyeon, K., et al.: Big data visual analytics system for disease pattern analysis, p 175 (2015)

Shirota, Y., Hashimoto, T., Basabi, C.: Visualization challenge on time series statistical data, p. 12 (2017)

Sullivan, D.: Google now handles at least 2 trillion searches per year (2016). http://searchengineland.com/google-now-handles-2-999-trillion-searches-per-year-250247. Accessed 31 Mar 2019

Wang, L., Wang, G., Alexander, C.A.: Big data and visualization: methods, challenges and technology progress. Digit. Technol. **1**(1), 33–38 (2015). https://doi.org/10.12691/dt-1-1-7

Wang, S., Li, W.: Computers, environment and urban systems capturing the dance of the earth: polarglobe: real-time scientific visualization of vector field data to support climate science. Comput. Environ. Urban Syst. **77**(June), 101352 (2019). https://doi.org/10.1016/j.compenvurbsys.2019.101352

Xie, Y., Chenna, P., Le, L., Planteen, J.: Visualization of big high dimensional data in three dimensional space. In: 3rd International Conference on Big Data Computing, Applications and Technologies (2016)

Yang, Y., Zhang, K., Wang, J., Nguyen, Q.V.: Cabinet tree: an orthogonal enclosure approach to visualizing and exploring big data. J. Big Data **2**, 15 (2015). https://doi.org/10.1186/s40537-015-0022-3

Zhao, H., Zhang, H., Liu, Y., Zhang, Y., Luke, X.: Pattern discovery: a progressive visual analytic design to support categorical data analysis. J. Vis. Lang. Comput. **43**, 42–49 (2017). https://doi.org/10.1016/j.jvlc.2017.05.004

Zhu, S.-C.: Statistical modeling and conceptualization of visual patterns. IEEE Trans. Pattern Anal. Mach. Intell. **25**(6), 691–712 (2003). https://doi.org/10.1109/tpami.2003.1201820

Zou, Q., Zeng, J., Cao, L., Ji, R.: A novel features ranking metric with application to scalable visual and bioinformatics data classification. Neurocomputing **173**, 346–354 (2016). https://doi.org/10.1016/j.neucom.2014.12.123

# Implementation Considerations for Big Data Analytics (BDA): A Benefit Dependency Network Approach

Juane Maritz⬤, Sunet Eybers(⊠)⬤, and Marie Hattingh⬤

University of Pretoria, Private Bag X20, Pretoria 0028, South Africa
maritzjuane@gmail.com,
{sunet.eybers,marie.hattingh}@up.ac.za

**Abstract.** The benefits of Big Data Analytics (BDA) are substantial in instances where organisations manage to successfully implement analytical capabilities. These benefits include improved, data driven decision-making, which can lead to deeper insight into business operations and as a result better performing organisations. Not surprisingly, an increased number of organisations are researching best implementation practices for BDA projects.

Similar to software projects, research has shown that many BDA projects fail or do not deliver the business value as promised. To address this issue, the main objective of this research is to identify BDA implementation considerations for new BDA endeavors that will help organisations to align their BDA efforts with their overall business strategy to maximize business value.

Based on a Benefit Dependency Network (BDN) model as main theoretical underpinning, a structured literature review was conducted focusing on investment objectives, business benefits, enabling changes and IT enablers when implementing BDA. A BDA implementation requires a holistic approach by considering aspects such as the skills of people which will have an impact on the structure of the organisation, business processes and technology changes to deliver benefits and investment objectives. Each of the domains of the BDN should be considered prior to BDA implementations.

The research offers a guideline to organisations implementing BDA, based on the foundation of BDN.

**Keywords:** Big Data Analytics · Structured literature review · Benefit Dependency Network (BDN)

## 1 Introduction

Data is continuously being created and shared by people, tools and machines [1]. Huge data sets can be attributed to the introduction, evolvement, and advancement of new sharing technologies, the connectivity of devices and number of data generating devices/platforms like Facebook, internet connected cars, wearable devices and cell phones [3]. Big datasets often contain untapped, hidden value. To realise the value of big data, organisations need to apply sophisticated analytical methods to extract actionable

© IFIP International Federation for Information Processing 2020
Published by Springer Nature Switzerland AG 2020
M. Hattingh et al. (Eds.): I3E 2020, LNCS 12066, pp. 481–492, 2020.
https://doi.org/10.1007/978-3-030-44999-5_40

insight from these datasets. As a result, organisations acknowledge the need for Big Data Analytics (BDA) to help drive decisions making within the organisations [4].

Despite the obvious financial benefits of big data analytics, organisation still face challenges implementing BDA projects [6]. One of the suggestions is that BDA can only be implemented successfully where organisation understand the organisational changes that needs to be considered before embarking to such implementations, and, similar to IT implementations, fully understand the requirements [7].

The need for a holistic BDA implementation guideline lays the foundation for this research. It is argued, for an organisation to successfully implement BDA, the organisation and technical IT teams must work together to successfully implement BDA [8]. An all-encompassing approach is therefore required considering multiple facets within the organisation [9]. The research question of this study is *'What are the changes that an organisation need to make to successfully implement big data analytics?'*. The research is therefore conducted through the lens of organisational improvement.

The research paper starts with evaluating the meaning of BDA and subsequently identify the challenges associated with the implementation and realization of business value. The Benefit Dependency Diagram (BDN) is explained followed by the research approach. As part of the discussion of findings, a preliminary BDN summarizes findings using the different domains of the BDN where after the research is concluded.

## 2    Big Data Analytics (BDA)

Big data analytics (BDA) incorporates techniques and technologies that are used to capture, store, transfer, analyse and visualize enormous amounts of structured and unstructured data [10]. A good descriptive definition of BDA was proposed by the Operations Research and Management Science stating that BDA is a process of transforming data into insight that will guide business decision making and organisational strategic direction based on insight derived from data to predict the future [11]. BDA therefore includes skills, technologies, methodologies, and practices to analyze data, enabling organisations to better understand their customers, their markets and to help drive future decision making [12].

According to the Chartered Global Management Accountant (CGMA), (a governing body focusing on governing accountants), BDA constitutes four levels namely reporting, analysis, monitoring and prediction [13]. Reporting visualizes data and can explain past events within the organisation. Analysis refers to the deep understanding of possible reasons for past events. Monitoring enables the organisation to understand what is currently happening within the organisation. Prediction is the action of using data and determining what could happen in future within the organisation, i.e. predict future events [13]. Although BDA can assist with providing insight on all four levels, the strength of BDA lies in the ability to predict and anticipate events based on current data. As a result, BDA can assist decision makings to create appropriate business strategies, providing them with the right knowledge to the correct people at the right time and in the right format [14]. Only after performing data analytics tasks can the organisation gain insight from big data. Insight is an actionable piece of knowledge that can drive decision making, strategic decision making and improve productivity and efficiency [2].

## 2.1 BDA Implementation Challenges

Although BDA promise a lot of advantages to the business, research has indicated that managers and organisations struggle with the successful implementation of Big Data Analytics strategies, in particular aligning data analytics projects with current business strategy [13, 15]. Furthermore, research has indicated that management does not comprehend how to identify business benefits from BDA implementations [16].

The reason why organisations struggle to realise business value from BDA can be grouped into three main categories, namely technical related challenges, managerial challenges as well as organisational challenges. Technical challenges include data related issues (challenges consolidating data from different sources and data quality); challenges with the presentation of findings (intelligent visualization and presentation of data) and making the appropriate technology choices [4, 13]. Managerial challenges include the inability of managers to gain insight from data analytics results, and subsequently linking the insight to actual business problems with the objective of increasing revenue [13]. Organisational related challenges include changes in decision making and leadership, organisation culture changes, adoption of a data-driven decision-making culture and clear direction of initiatives [10].

## 2.2 Realising the Value of BDA

The challenge to implement new IT technologies, such as BDA, has been ongoing for many years. An astonishing 70% of most IT projects fail or deliver the actual benefit promised when implementing the new technology [17]. Research has shown that IT projects fails due to numerous reasons, of which change management, both on organisation as well as process level, are the most prevalent [18]. According to Peppard [17], benefits from IT investments don't just "happen" - it needs a firm commitment from organisations to drive the investment through organisational change [17].

Multiple proprietary tools have been developed to assist the organisation in making IT investment decisions. Examples include a SWOT analysis [19], Balanced Scorecard [20] and the Benefit Dependency Network (BDN) diagram [17] (to name a few). These tools consider possible intangible benefits of investments and can, when used properly, assist management to maximize the benefits of their IT investment by conducting a proper evaluation of the planned investment. These tools are also designed to assist organisations in the alignment of their IT investments to the overall business strategy.

The BDN was selected as main theoretical foundation for this study. The tool was selected due to the powerful visual ability to graphically highlight change requirements, both on a holistic (enterprise) and functional level, that managers can use as a guide to evaluate the extent of changes required prior to embarking on new IT investments, in this instance the adoption of BDA [17]. It furthermore considers the relationship between people, processes, and technology assisting managers to understand how the expected benefits will be delivered through the combination of technology and business changes. From an organisational perspective the one-page graphical model assists with the alignment of IT investments with the business strategy and highlights the fact that IT investments should not be driven by technology but rather by clear business objectives.

The BDN is not a widely adopted and researched tool and does not consider the strengths, weaknesses, constraints and challenges that organisations might face when adopting new technologies. Although critics feel that the model lacks strong empirical evidence, the tool seemed appropriate for this level of initial investigation into the identification of organisational adjustments required prior to implementing BDA. Furthermore, it was only used as a lens to analyse data and guide the discussion.

## 3 Research Approach

The main purpose of this research was to identify strategic level implementation considerations prior to the implementation of BDA. As a result, the research aimed to identify how the maximum value can be achieved from BDA implementations.

A structured literature review was conducted, using keywords such as big data implementation, big data analytics implementation, data analytics implementation, analytics implementation model, business intelligence and implementation. Business Intelligence (BI) was included as a search term because BI was perceived as part of a BDA implementation. Peer reviewed articles were only considered when written in English, for the period 2015 to 2019, on the following databases: ABI/Inform collection, EBSCOhost and Emerald Insight. Both the Forbes and Harvard Business Review online sources were consulted. There was no restriction placed on the discipline on which the article focused as IT is perceived as a multidisciplinary field.

The initial, preliminary number of articles returned after the search process was 2453. Following the application of the inclusion criteria it was reduced to 300. This preliminary pool of 300 articles were further evaluated for applicability by considering the abstract section of each article using the proposed quality assurance criteria by Kitchenham and Charters [21]. The criteria allowed a score rating of 0, 0.5 or 1 to be allocated to each article based on a clear description of the research process, identification of clear research limitations and finally the extent to which the research was applied in practice. The final article pool consisted of 15 articles.

Each of the 15 top articles were evaluated and classified by means of thematic content analysis using each of the 'domains' of the BDN tool (namely the investment objectives, business benefits, business changes, enabling changes and IT enablers, as described in Sect. 2.2). A matrix was created listing the each of the domains horizontally with a specific measurement identified in literature supporting the domain. For example, articles indicating a clear statement of what the BDA implementation should achieve was included in the investment objective; advantages and benefits achieved as part of a BDA implementation was included under the business benefits section; permanent business changes such as business processes as part of the business changes heading; enabling changes referring to non-permanent, short term changes in the organisation; and IT enablers refers to any technology related requirements for BDA. Table 1 contains an example of the matrix used. The authors of the various articles were listed on each table row. Where research focused on a particular concept, an X was used in the table to indicate research applicability.

**Table 1.** Concept mapping matrix

| Concept | | | | | |
|---------|-----------------------------------|--------------------------------------------|------------------------------------------------|-------------------------------------------------|--------------------------|
|         | Investment objectives             | Business benefits                          | Business changes                               | Enabling changes                                | IT enablers              |
|         | What BDA implementation objectives | Organisational advantage and benefits      | Permanent, long term organisational change     | Non-permanent, short term organisational change | Technology requirements  |
| Author  |                                   |                                            |                                                |                                                 |                          |

## 4   Discussion of Findings

The discussion of findings is based on the summary of the final pool of 15 articles (available on request). As mentioned previously the analysis was conducted per domain, starting with the investment objectives, business benefits, business changes enabling changes and IT enablers (read from right to left on the BDN). The order of the domains is of extreme importance to ensure that technology support the overall investment and align with the business strategy. Arrows on the diagram indicate a relationship or inter-domain dependency between. A change in one of the items can influence another domain and can therefore assist in the identification of change to be consider imperative to realising benefits (see Fig. 1).

Any benefits management intervention starts with a clear need to change, in this instance referred to as the "driver". Drivers are elements that top management regard as the main driving force behind the need for the business to change [22, 23], and can be both internal and/or external to the organisation. In this instance, the organisation wants to adopt BDA due to the need to analyze huge amounts of data. For example, they need to replace existing BI systems and move towards the implementation of BDA which will lead to improved sales and customer service. BDA is therefore the driver or reason behind the planned intervention [22].

### 4.1   Investment Objectives

Investment objectives are specific to the project and focuses on the outcome of the project, i.e. what the project will achieve if successful [22]. It is set for a particular period (linked to the project duration) and are specific, measurable, achievable [24].

Fourteen (out of fifteen) articles evaluated indicated that they identified reasons for investing in BDA prior to the actual investments made (for example [8, 12, 29]). Ten articles agreed that organisations invest in BDA with the main objective to achieve business transformation (for example [8]). Multiple definitions existed for business transformation, but the trend was clear that business transformation happens through the identification of new business models, products and services that are identified through BDA activities. BDA leads to fundamentally changing processes, people, technology and organisational structure across the organisation that lead to business transformation. No clear consensus was reached on what business transformation is, but all agreed it can be achieved through the introduction of new/refined products, services and new technology through BDA activities.

Organisations also invest in BDA to improve decision making. Nine articles indicated that most organisations base their decisions on the intuition and experience of employees within the organisation [12, 29]. This is a flawed process as optimal decision making can only be made based on timeous information [25, 26]. Big Data Analytics enables organisation to integrate various data sources and make various data sources available to the employees for improved decision making [8, 29]. Unfortunately, employees could therefore only improve decision making if they have access to BDA. Therefore, a clear dependency exists between data driven decision making and big data analytics system availability and adoption.

An analysis of the articles further indicated that BDA had the potential of identifying flaws in business processes. BDA can also be used as a risk mitigation tool by means of the following: identifying data leakage, poor performance in business processes, lack of adhering to processes, and gaps in processes [27]. As a result, BDA can assist organisations in the implementation of better business processes by removing flawed business processes to increase efficiency. More efficient processes reduce risks and can assist in achieving the organisational objective of fraud prevention [2].

The overarching trends identified as the main reasons for investing in BDA was to gain competitive advantage through the attraction of more customers, increasing organisation performance, timeous and improved decision making and decreased product time to market.

Only one article explicitly stated the need to increase revenue as an important investment objective of BDA [27]. The results of the remainder of the articles indicated an indirect relationship to increases revenue. An interdependency therefore exists between the need to increase revenue and all other investment objectives. For example, when improving process efficiency revenue will increase by reducing wasted cost. The need for increased revenue is therefore an important investment objective to create business value.

## 4.2   Benefits

Benefits are advantages that is incurred as a result of the project and can be financially related. The investment objectives can only be achieved if some business benefits are incurred [22]. When these benefits are delivered, they will lead to achieving the investment objectives. Thus, to achieve objectives benefits must be delivered. The identified business benefits can serve as Key Performance Indicators (KPI's) by top management to ensure that progress of the projects. This is also used to determine if BDA projects are still aligning to project roadmap [24].

Many overarching business benefits were identified through the analysis of the articles. As a result, it is anticipated that the investment in BDA will result in multiple business benefits. Some of these business benefits are discussed below.

BDA will enable organisations to have a deeper understanding of their customer's needs and behavior, assisting the organisation to reduce their product time to market. This will also enable the organisation to refine their products, services and business processes based on trends identified in the data. By addressing the needs of the customers, it should be easier to retain customers [24].

Another benefit of investing in BDA is the access to refined, processed data that will improve decision making [2, 7]. BDA implementations often provide users with a consolidated view of data from multiple data sources [29]. In some instances, these data sources are available to end users for the first time ever. Employees, on multiple levels of the organisation, are given access to the data, on which decisions could be made.

Based on business process related data and the subsequent analysis thereof, flaws can be identified in processes and improved, contributing to more efficient organisations and increased organisational performance. It is also an important component in the proactive identification of fraud [2].

Organisations will be able to monitor business processes internally as well as external to the organisation. This assist the organisation in the monitoring of competitor markets and competitor trends. Evidence based decision making can be applied to identify new business models based on these trends [2].

BDA furthermore assist organisations in becoming a learning organisation. A learning organisation imply the ability of the organisation to use analyzed data to transform, adapt and improve the way they function [9].

### 4.3   Business Changes

Business changes are required for an organisation to achieve benefits. It refers to permanent changes to practices, processes and relationships within the organisation to deliver business benefits [28]. These changes cannot normally be implemented until all the enabling changes have been realised. An example of a business change is a an organisational culture change [12].

On a high level, organisational changes focus on data related adjustments as well as organisational environmental changes implemented through proper change management procedures (such as organisation structure, culture and risk management) [8, 9].

Organisational structure refers to structural changes an organisation needs to implement prior to BDA. One main theme that was prevalent was multiple aspects of *data related adjustments* [8, 29]. For example, structural changes in the way they deal with data needs to be considered. Data is considered to be one of the most valuable assets within organisations. Not surprisingly many business changes evolve around data.

The majority of the articles focused on the need for organisations to implement structural organisation changes ensuring that the data used for BDA is of good quality. The need to have good quality data was not classified as part of the IT enabling domain as it focused on the business process of gathering data (and not on the technology used to gather and store data). Examples include data quality procedures, data access procedures and data security procedures [29].

Good quality data is characterized by integrity (the data is what it says it is), confidentiality (not widely available), reliability (reputable source of data), timeliness (recent data), accessibility (controlled access to data), accuracy (level of correctness of data) and completeness (having all sources). Data quality was supported by almost all articles and is also highlighted as the most important business change (for example see [29]).

Another business change that was identified was the relationship between the quality of data and BDA end user utilization [8, 12, 29]. BDA systems will only be used when end users trust the data. End user utilisation is a critical success factor for BDA.

Setting up governance procedures for BDA will create trusted environments for data processing and storage [8, 29]. Trusted environments are environments that has high quality data with high availability. If the systems fail and lose data the organisation loses assets. When losing assets, the organisation lose business value.

Finally, data as an organisational asset needs to be protected. Clear data access processes, rules and access procedures are required specifying user access [29].

BDA requires new skills and new employees therefore require organisational structural changes to the organisational outline such as the *hierarchy* [8, 12, 29]. For example, new positions will have to be created after the required skills were identified. This will trigger recruitment drives as well as educational and training programs to reskills employees. New risk management procedures will have to be considered to cater for the new organisational outline to protect information and intellectual property. It is important for organisations to implement an effective change management process to assist employees in transitioning into a new organisational structure [8, 9, 18].

Another major trend that was recognized is the importance of business involvement (i.e. the correct people) in new BDA implementations [27]. Business involvement can be increased by, (a) setting up effective communication channels with decision makers; (b) training of decision makers in the concept of data driven decision making; (c) easy to use systems; (d) linking current business problems to the analysis of data; (e) integration of BDA into daily operations.

## 4.4   Enabling Changes

Enabling changes are adjustments or changes that needs to be implemented for business changes to take place [28]. Examples of enabling changes include defining and agreeing to new work practices, redesigning processes, agreeing on changes to job roles or introducing new job roles and responsibilities, introducing new performance management systems and training and education (for example see [8]). These types of changes can be made before the implementation of the new system.

Similar to the business changes required, data related themes have been identified and considered to be of importance. Other themes identified include human resources related changes, business processes and organisational environmental adjustments [18].

To implement BDA successfully the organisation will have to setup training programs to re-skill existing human resources. A once off, organisation readiness assessment can identify specific skills required prior to the BDA implementation [27]. For example, an organisational readiness assessment can identify new roles such as data scientist and developers with specific analytical skills. The organisation have to make provision for these roles in the organisational structure and these roles needs to be defined. A skills matrix can further assist the organisation in establishing the current level of competency of human resources.

The organisation will have to define a number of new processes within the organisation for example support and data related process [8, 29]. The first new process that will have to be established is a data governance process. Data governance processes help to promote data quality and data safety and should be aligned to legislation. It is important that data access roles (i.e. who will be able to view/edit data) is established and included in the data governance procedures. New data security policies and procedures will ensure the safety of data. Support processes will focus on the level of support end users and technical staff members can expect from the business owners. Therefore, new communication channels will be established.

New risk management processes and procedures needs to be implemented to ensure that the data is not compromised [8, 9]. Data is one of the organisations most valuable assets as well as the data analysis techniques and findings. The organisation needs to implement procedures to prevent the data assets to be compromised. At this stage, different technological options might be considered.

### 4.5  IT Enablers

IT Enablers are the IT tools that must be implemented as well as IT considerations to be evaluated before introducing a new technology. These items enable organisational change. The majority of articles indicated that Big Data technologies such as Apache Hadoop, NoSQL Data bases such as MongoDB, Apache Cassandra, Apache Mahout, Spark and Storm, are considered [3, 5, 8, 12].

BDA requires data to be consolidated from various data sources. The organisation needs to identify which sources they want to use for their BDA projects and how these will be integrated. Big Data Sources identified in the articles were internal and external databases, clickstream, social media as well as user-generated data [8, 29].

Information needs to be extracted from the identified data sources, for which data extraction procedures will have to be compiled as well as the appropriate technological tool selected [2, 9]. Analytical tools will also be considered at this stage as the extraction and analytical tool is often bundled together.

Big Data requires scalable storage solutions to enable large amounts of data processing. The organisation also need to keep in mind that massive amounts of data will be entering the organisation. The organisation need to look at their network infrastructure to ensure that the infrastructure will support increased data volumes [8].

The organisation need to consider various visualization tools and platforms to display data analytics [3]. These tools should be user friendly with high availability and acceptable response times [8] as this can increase the adoption rate of BDA.

Rapid scaling cloud platforms are available for organisations to deploy their BDA solutions. This means that organisations can outsource their BDA solutions and therefore do not need to take responsibility for the maintenance of servers and high amounts of data flowing into their solutions. The organisation should, however, consider regulations when storing information on cloud platforms and make use of reputable service providers [8, 29].

## 4.6    Proposed BDN Model for BDA

Based on the discussion of findings in Sects. 4.1 to 4.5 above, a preliminary BDN model for BDN were created. It provides the reader with a summary of the sections for each of the domains and displays the interrelationships between items, a distinguishing factor offered by the BDN approach.

A typical example of how the BDN could be used: the first identified Investment Objective was to reduce response time to market changes. A clear business benefit of this overall objective will be that emerging customer trends will be identified. This can only be achieved if (new) data sources, containing relevant data, is available to decision makers when required. For this reason, the relationship between system performance ("review system performance", enabling changes domain) are of vital importance and should be considered when selecting data sources. This can only be achieved through the implementation of rapid scaling technology (IT enablers' domain).

During the analysis of the findings, similar elements were consolidated and combined. Data quality was combined with data integrity, confidentiality and accountability [29]. Data integrity, confidentiality and accountability are considered to be characteristics of quality data. Trustworthiness of data and the completeness of data [8, 12, 29], forms part of the characteristics of good quality data and were included as such.

Below is the proposed BDN model constructed from the articles.

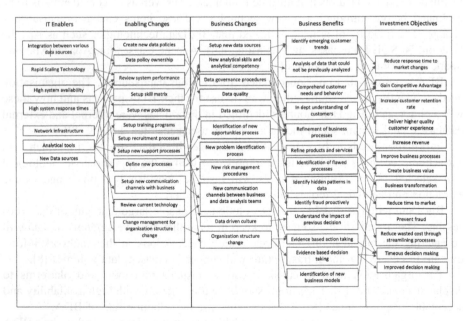

**Fig. 1.** The BDN analysis of literature

# 5   Conclusion

The main research question was *'What are the changes an organisation need to consider to successfully implement big data analytics?'*. After a systematic structured literature review, a preliminary BDN model was constructed considering the various aspects of the BDN network, namely investment objectives, business benefits, business and enabling changes as well as IT enablers. The model furthermore identified specific relationships between components and the alignment to overall business strategy.

From the results it is clear that BDA implementations should focus on more than just technology. Organisations will have to take a holistic approach when implementing BDA. Considerations should include important decisions with regards to the skills of people, which will have an impact on the structure of the organisation, business processes and technology changes to deliver benefits and investment objectives. Each of the domains of the BDN should be considered prior to BDA implementations.

Finally, BDA is a disruptive technology. Organisations will therefore have to find new ways to implement new technology without completely relying on existing technology. A BDN model approach can assist in identify organisational technology considerations. Further research is proposed to refine the findings of this work.

# References

1. Ernst and Young: Big data - Changing the way businesses compete and operate. EY (2014)
2. McKinsey & Company: Big Data: The Next Frontier for Innovation. Competition and Productivity. McKinsey Global Institute, New York (2011)
3. Comuzzi, M., Patel, A.: How organisations leverage big data: a maturity model. Ind. Manage. Data Syst. **116**(8), 1468–1492 (2016)
4. McAfee, A., Brynjolfsson, E.: Big data: the management revolution. Harv. Bus. Rev. **90**(10), 60–68 (2012)
5. Chen, H., Chiang, R.H., Storey, V.C.: Business intelligence and analytics: from big data to big impact. MIS Q. **36**(4), 1165–1188 (2012)
6. Chen, M., Mao, S., Liu, Y.: Big data: a survey. Mob. Netw. Appl. **19**(2), 171–209 (2014)
7. Court, D., Perry, J., McGuire, T., Gordon, J., Spillecke, D.: Smart Analytics: How Marketing Drives Short-Term and Long-Term Growth. McKinsey & Company, New York (2015)
8. Wadhwani, K., Wang, D.Y.: Big data challenges and solutions. Technical report (2017). https://doi.org/10.13140/rg.2.2.16548.88961
9. Kholkar, D., Tierney, M.: When data isn't enough: how change management can predict the success or failure of your big data implementation, big data quarterly online (2018)
10. Hopkins, M.S., Krusschwitz, N., LaValle, S., Lesser, E., Schockley, R.: Big data, analytics and the patch from insights to value. MIT Sloan Manage. Rev. **52**(2), 21–31 (2011)
11. Saltz, J.S.: The need for new processes, methodologies and tools to support big data teams and improve big data project effectiveness, Santa Clara, CA, USA (2015)
12. Verma, S., Bhattacharyya, S.S., Kumar, S.: An extension of the technology acceptance model in the big data analytics system implementation environment. Inf. Process. Manage. **54**(1), 791–806 (2018)
13. Espinosa, A.J., Armour, F.: The big data analytics gold rush: a research framework for coordination and governance. In: 49th Hawaii International Conference, Hawaii (2016)

14. CGMA: From insight to impact - unlocking opportunities in big data. CGMA, New York (2013)
15. Dehinbo, J.: Theoretical base for developing a holistic knowledge management strategy for effective learning in organisations, Pretoria (2012)
16. Segarra, L., et al.: A framework for boosting revenue incorporating big data. J. Innov. Manage. 4(1), 39–68 (2016)
17. LaValle, S., Lesser, E., Shockley, R., Hopkins, M., Kruschwitz, N.: Big data, analytics and the path from insights to value. MIT Sloan Manage. Rev. 52(2), 21–32 (2011)
18. Peppard, J.: A tool to map your next digital initiative. Harvard Business Review, Berlin (2016)
19. Daniel, E., Peppard, J., Ward, J.: Managing the realization of business benefits from IT investments. MIS Q. Exec. 6(1), 1–11 (2007)
20. Humphrey, A.: SWOT analysis for management consulting. SRI Alumni Newsl. 1, 7–8 (2005)
21. Kaplan, R.S., Norton, D.P.: The balanced scorecard: translating strategy into action, Massachusetts (1996)
22. Schwalbe, K.: Information Technology Project Management, 7th edn. Cengage Technology Cengage Learning, Boston (2014)
23. Ward, J., Taylor, P., Bond, P.: Evaluation and realization of IS/IT benefits: an empirical study of current practice. Eur. J. Inf. Syst. 4(1), 214–225 (1996)
24. Wilson, H., Clark, M., Smith, B.: Justifying CRM projects in a business-to-business context: the potential of the benefits dependency network. Ind. Mark. Manage. 36(1), 770–783 (2007)
25. Ward, J., Daniel, E.: The strategic performance management cycle. Performance Measurement Association (2006)
26. Peppard, J., Ward, J., Daniel, E.: Managing the realization of business benefits from IT investments. MIS Q. Exec. 6(1), Article 3 (2008). https://aisel.aisnet.org/misqe/vol6/iss1/3
27. Ashraf, T.: Organisational development and big data: factors that impact successful big data implementations. ProQuest, Lisle (2017)
28. Leavitt, H., Bahrami, H.: Managerial Psychology: Managing Behavior in Organisations, 5th edn. University of Chicago, Chicago (1988)
29. Halaweh, M., Massry, A.E.: Conceptual model for successful implementation of big data in organisations. J. Int. Technol. Inform. Manage. 24(2), 21–34 (2015)

# A Model for Evaluating Big Data Analytics Tools for Organisation Purposes

Phaphama Kangelani and Tiko Iyamu[(⌧)]

Cape Peninsula University of Technology, Cape Town, South Africa
phaphama3@gmail.com, iyamut@cput.ac.za

**Abstract.** Big data analytics tools have many functions that are common or similar to one another. This is a problem for many organisations that are either interested or have deployed some of the tools. The problem arises because there is no mechanism on how to determine appropriateness of the tools within context in an environment. Some of the implications of the problem are that it is difficult to assess appropriateness of the tools in an environment, which sometimes result to duplication; and the value of the tools. The aim of this project was to propose a solution through a model that can be used to evaluate big data analytics tools for organisations' benefits. The qualitative method, case study approach and semi-structured interview technique were applied in the study. From the analysis, the role of criteria, business and IT alignment, governance, and skill-sets were revealed as critical factors. Based on the factors, a model was developed, which can be used as a building block through which evaluation of big data analytics tools in an organisation is carried out.

**Keywords:** Big data analytics · Evaluation · Criteria

## 1 Introduction

Big data is not about the size of data, but characterised by three dimensions: variety, volume and velocity [1]. Big data is processed by computerised software or applications, which is referred to as big data analytics [2]. Some of the big data analytics (BDA) tools include Hadoop, MapReduce [3]. There is increasing interest in the use of BDA from both academia and industry [4, 5], which can be attributed to the premise that the concept brings positive change to an environment that deploys it [6].

Organisations adopt big data concept to get some insights into the data to predict the future. Many organisations employ big data with the intention of improving activities and events such as sales, advertising, and future predictions [7]. In the process of optimising the benefits of BDA, some organisations divide it into two sections: management, which is the extraction, retrieval and storage of datasets for transformation and decision-making purposes; and as the technology tool for analysing big data [8].

Despite the benefits that BDA seem to present, there are challenges with the concept, which include violation of privacy, security, data quality, slowness in query processing, scalability problems, integration complexities, and scarcity of big data skills [1, 9, 10]. Some of the challenges persist because there has been slow or lack of

M. Hattingh et al. (Eds.): I3E 2020, LNCS 12066, pp. 493–504, 2020.
https://doi.org/10.1007/978-3-030-44999-5_41

research, theoretical constructs, and academic rigor from management and perspective, in the areas of big data and BDA [11]. At large, there has also been a lack of research studies that comprehensively addresses the key challenges of BDA, or which investigates opportunities for new theories or emerging practices. This includes evaluation of big data analytics tools [12].

The main challenge is that there are no evaluation models or methods that can be used to assess BDA tools, and research have not focused on this aspect. Because of the variation of the big data analysis tools, some organisations have a challenge in selecting the most appropriate application for analysis [13]. There are some models, but they only focus on the evaluation of [14, 15]. As at the time of this research, the only study that focuses on evaluation of BDA tools, Hadoop, Spark, and Flink is from performance perspective [16]. This means that the gap remains, which this study aimed to address. Thus, the aim of this study was to propose a solution through a model that can be used to evaluate BDA tools in selecting the most appropriate for organisations' purposes. Thus, the objectives of this study were: (1) To determine the factors (technical and business) that influence the selection of big data analytics in organisations; and (2) To establish criteria for appropriateness of big data analytics tools in an organisation.

## 2   Literature Review

This review of literature was split into three areas in order to gain more insight on the specific areas, which are big data analytics, value of big data in organisations, and evaluation technique.

### 2.1   Big Data Analytics

The BDA approaches include predictive, descriptive and prescriptive [17]. The approaches focus on analysing unstructured, semi-structured and structured datasets, which can be images, audio or text [1]. The analysis of big data involves machine learning applications or software like Hadoop, MapReduce, Apache and many more [3].

The predictive analytics tools focuses on historical data to predict the future. The analysis makes use of machine learning algorithms and statistical models to assess historical datasets for future predictions [18]. The descriptive analytics focuses on current state, present datasets [19]. It uses historical datasets to identify patterns that can be reported or compared to current trend. The prescriptive analytics as an assessment of current situation to make decision [1]. It combines both the descriptive and predictive analytics in finding new ways to achieve positive outcomes for organisations.

The efficiency of BDA is one of the reasons that organisation adopt and use the concept as a solution to decision making [20]. Competitiveness is one of organisation's purposes in the use of BDA for predicting the future outcomes [18]. It is argued that the BDA are used to deliver predictive insights in operations, drive real-time in decision making, and redesigning of business processes, in achieving results for organisational goals and objectives [21]. Despite the consistent argument that the BDA has a lot to offer to organisations, many challenges have been identified in the use of the concept [3], which include data validation, data cleansing, scalability of algorithms, and parallel data processing [22].

## 2.2 Value of Big Data Analytics in Organisations

In recent years, there has been increase in the use of BDA tools, which can be attributed to the values that are associated to the concept [7]. Grover et al. suggest that the concept of BDA can be used to promote productiveness and decision-making, which brings forth to organisations [23]. Two socio-technical features, convenience and interconnectivity are identified as the factors that influence the value of BDA in organisations [24]. Some organisations are fascinated with the capabilities of the BDA in that it enable integration of data types, from different perspectives such size and variety [23].

In organisations, the value of BDA is viewed from different perspectives. One viewpoint, the value of BDA for an organisation is the process of collecting, storing and gaining insights to enhance organisation's performance [25]. From another angle, the ability to integrate, accessibility, response time are the value of the BDA in some organisations [26]. However, the BDA tools do not operate themselves, which is another challenge that is associated to the concept, and influence the type of value that is obtained. The emerging nature of the BDA makes skillsets scarce [27, 28].

## 2.3 Evaluation Models and Techniques

In the field of IS, evaluation of software is critical, due to increasing reliance on it as solution in organisations. Another rationale for evaluating software is to ensure awareness and detect deficiency [29]. Thus, many computer systems undergo evaluation process [15]. Within the computing environment, there are various models and techniques for conducting evaluation of software and approaches. One of the techniques is that the evaluation begins with measuring technology functionalities, to align with the business requirements and needs [30].

There are numerous types of evaluation models and techniques. One of the evaluation technique is a Holistic Framework on IS evaluation which consists of five evaluation factors: Strategic value, Profitability, Risk, Successful Development and Procurement, and Successful Use and Operations [31]. Another rationale for evaluation in IS field is to mitigate against risk in projects and assess effectiveness of systems in an organisation. Also, there is no limit to evaluation is that there will always be new factors to evaluate [32].

# 3   Research Methodology

Based on the objective of the study, which was to examine and understand the factors that influence big data analytics and its appropriateness, the qualitative method, case study approach were employed in the study. This means that individuals and groups opinions and views was sought, which the qualitative method allows. The qualitative research is mostly employed in a scientific research to collect data, find answers to questions and draw conclusion from the findings produced [33]. The focus of the qualitative method is not about numbers or statistics, it rather on human reactions such as feelings, emotions, and experiences in their real world [34]. The qualitative approach is mostly associated with subjectivism [35].

The case study approach was employed mainly because it focuses on the in-depth of the phenomenon being studied. Yin defines case study as an adaptable and open-minded technique of information gathering [36]. The approach is broad, meaning a case can be an individual, an organisation, a community, a group, or an event [37]. The Plan Investments organisation was used as a case in the study. The organisation is a financial institution situated in Cape Town. It has over 150 employees at the time of this study.

Based on the level of the study, a criterion was used for a selection of participants. The criterion included the following: (1) organisation that employ big data analytics tools, and grants permission for the study; (2) participants should have be with the organisation for at least a year. Within the case study, data was collected. Participants that were interviewed included IT manager and Architects.

The semi-structured interview technique was used to collect data. This was to ensure flexibility during the process, in asking questions, which ultimately increases the chances of collecting rich data. The interviews was conducted with interviewees on one-on-one basis. The venue of the interviews was decided by the interviewees, to ensure their comfort. The interviews was tape recorded on the permission of the interviewees. In addition, notes were taken during the interviews, to increase comprehensiveness of the data collected.

The hermeneutics approach was applied in the analysis of the data, from the perspective of the interpretivist approach [38]. The hermeneutics approach proposes a method for understanding textual data [39]. The approach helps to clarify and guide an understanding of objects and subjects in an interpretive manner [40]. Interpretivist approach is about understanding phenomenon from individuals' viewpoints by exploring interaction among people [41]. The hermeneutics approach was used from two main angles in the analysis: (1) the relationships that exist between humans and big data in an organisation; and (2) the interactions that happen between humans in one hand, and on another between humans and big data. Through understanding of the relationships and interactions that happen between: human-to-human; and human-to-big data, the objectives of the study was achieved.

# 4   Case Study: Data Analysis

Based on the objectives of the study as stated in section above, data was collected as discussed in the section above. The participants in the study were coded, for the following reasons: (1) To adhere to research ethics of the university (CPUT); (2) To preserve the identity of the participants; and (3) To respect the policy of the organisation that was used a case in the study. Thus, the code is as follow: participantcodename, page#: line#. PuInter01, Pg2: 3–5 – this means: participant 1, page 2, line 3 to 5 of the interview transcript.

The data was analysed following the hermeneutics approach from the interpretivist perspective. The hermeneutics approach was used in the analysis from the interpretivist perspective. The analysis focuses on two main areas: (1) The relationships that exist between humans and big data in an organisation; and (2) The interactions that happen between humans in one hand, and on another between humans and big data. This was to gain better understanding of the relationships and interactions that happen between: human-to-human; human-to-big data; and big data-to-big data, in achieving the objectives of the study. The analysis was conducted according to the objectives of the study, which were (1) to determine the factors that influence the selection of BDA in organisations; and (2) to establish criteria for appropriateness of BDA tools in an organisation.

## 4.1 The Factors that Influence the Selection of Big Data Analytics in Organisations

Big data is not all about volume, but defined by its characteristics, which include the Vs, volume, velocity, veracity, variety, and value [1]. The tools that are employed in the analyses of big data are referred to as analytics tools. Some BDA tools/software have the capabilities to process datasets which are employed by organisations for various purposes. There are different types of big data analytics tools, which include diagnostic, descriptive, predictive, and prescriptive [17]. Through the use of big data analytics tools organisations make effective and appropriate strategic decisions.

Big data analytics is on one hand sophisticated. On another hand, the same sophistication makes it complex. Thus, many people including organisation are sometimes confused about the purposes as well as the types of big data analytics. According to the senior manager in the organisation:

> We are using Pentaho data integrator and Pentaho business analytics for the analysis of our big data (PuInter01, Pg1: 32–34).

The BDA topic appears to be an overwhelming subject in the organisation, as it focuses on the bigger picture in terms of the terminology that comes with the tools. In the organisation there was a process that was followed in the selection of BDA tools. The process was sequential, meaning one step after the other. The primary components of the process include an understanding and formulation of organisational needs, exploration of available analytics tools, and evaluation of the tools within the context of the organisation. In the evaluation, the components were viewed from the aspects of technical and non-technical factors.

An organisation's goals and mission are a guide to choosing tools that suit its business needs. The selection of analytics tools does not only depend on the business goal, humans' involvement was critical, particularly in the decision-making as well as consideration of the users. Individuals such as business mangers seem to influences the decision in the selection of BDA tools. Nonetheless in the organisation it appears to be person leading the IT unit that agrees and takes ownership of the selecting the tools employed, however the tool that is selected has to be aligned with the business objectives. According to one of the participants, a senior architect in the organisation:

> The organisation's requirements determine the selection of the tool. The challenge is mostly in formulating requirements, which include processes and events (PuInter02, Pg6: 20–23).

In the organisation the input of other employees that are using these tools influences the selection of the tools being employed in the organisation. Despite the requirements from the business the staff consider and evaluate the technical and non-technical factors of the tools because they are equipped with knowledge of how the tools work. According to an IT senior manager in the organisation:

> This is not a visualization tool it is more of a data analytics tool. It sometimes get restricted by the ability of the user. Whereas some other tools basically aid the users towards achieving their objectives (PuInter01, Pg3: 1–3).

Despite the existence of numerous number of big data analytics tools, the organisation did choose few that were suitable for its business processes, activities and events. In the organisation the evaluation phase covers a lot of aspects. The aim of the organisation is to have a tool that can put the organisation on the direction of success. It is also to get big data analytics tools that are flexible and scalable. They seem to look at the knowledge they have on the tool itself. There seem to be a lot that the organisation covers in terms of creating an environment that the employees are familiar with.

## 4.2 Criteria for Appropriateness of Big Data Analytics Tools in an Organisation

Criteria is a set of standards and principles purposely for guide decision-making, and measuring scope and boundaries of actions in an activity or environment, the standards and principles are embedded with factors [42]. In the organisation, criteria was formulated, and used in the selection of BDA tools. The criteria consisted of factors, such as cost, supportability, features, and skills required to use and support the tools. Despite a set of criteria, familiarity with a tool was most important. According to one of the participants:

> Cost, knowledge of skills are some of the factors that are required in the evaluation of the tools. We have got to understand our future direction in line with the tool (PuInter01, Pg2: 5–7).

In the organisation the criteria was used as guidelines in selecting a tool that was intended to benefit the organisation from return on investment point of view. This means that the also act as principle, which guided the employees in their focus and actions, and did not allow easy move from one tool to another. According to a senior architect in the organisation:

> Some of the tools are very well marketed by the owners and vendors. As a result, without requirements, there is a high possibility of selecting inappropriate tools (PuInter02, Pg3: 14–16).

There were requirements two, business and IT units that formed the criteria, which was enabled by communication. Through the communication between the units including management team, the criteria was defined. The management of both IT and business units of the organisation were involved in gathering of the requirement that were used to formulate the criteria. This was primarily because they knew better knowledge about the current and future states of the organisation. Although there was no particular explanations why certain big data analytics tool was selected from the employees that were involved. This is attributed to the fact that the management of the organisation takes ownership of the process and the tool that was selected.

Despite the strengths of the tools that were employed in the organisation that has been used as a case in the study, there are challenges that have been highlighted. The main challenges that the organisation seem to be facing with the tools that were currently employed is about scarcity of skilled personnel, to use and provide technical support. In achieving the organisation' objectives, the current tools requires special skills, a person with an understanding of the functionalities and operations of the tools. One of the participants explains:

> Our current tool is focuses more on data specialisation. It is therefore unrestricted to data analysis and management (PuInter01, Pg2: 35–37).

Looking for a tool that would cater for everything is almost impossible. The organisation highlighted a challenge while selecting the appropriate tool from the limitless tools/applications that are available in the market. Without a properly defined requirements and formulation of criteria, there will always be challenges in selecting BDA tools. Also, organisation would change the tools frequently as they get influenced by excitable new functions that the some of the tools present.

Changing the tools from one BDA tools to another takes a lot effort and can be costly. The organisation seem to have a strategy, which can accommodate such situation. In the organisation the change is accepted only when there is a tool that offers better features than the one that is currently in use. Also, the organisational change leans towards goals and objectives.

## 5  Findings and Discussion

Based on the analysis as presented above, four factors were found to be critical in shaping and influencing the selection of BDA tools in an organisation. The factors were revealed based on the understanding of the analysis, which come from subjective reasoning. As shown in Fig. 1, the factors are criteria, business/IT alignment, governance, and skill-sets. The factors are based on organisational vision. The factors are therefore a set of building block, as discussed below.

### 5.1  The Role of Criteria

Criteria is a set of guidelines that are built on principles and standards that can be used to evaluate the BDA tools for organisations [43]. In this study, criteria consist of two main components, which are the business requirements and IT requirements. Business requirements is mostly connected with the goals, mission and objective, which come from the organisation vision. Business requirements work toward paving and setting what the business seeks to achieve. The IT requirements are based on attributes such as

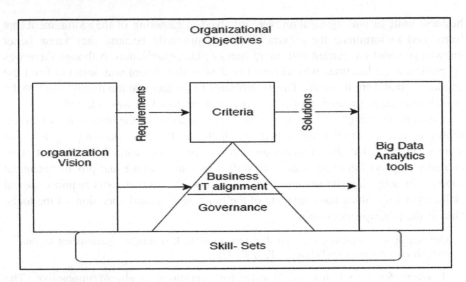

**Fig. 1.** Building blocks

technology types, co-existence and compatibility, capacity, and flexibility of technologies. The IT requirements seek to enable and support the business requirements toward achieving the objectives of the organisation. This also means IT can be a constraint in that deficiency within the IT will have negative impact on the business requirements.

Based on both business and IT requirements, the set of criteria can be used as a control mechanism for selecting the most appropriate big data analytics tools for organisational purposes. The vital role of the criteria is that the organisation have rich understanding in what they want to do and what will fit the organisation needs. This also means that there is an evaluation process undertaken in the selection of the tools. Another significance factor in creating criteria is that it minimizes the chances of duplicating analytics tools for the same or similar purpose, and it mitigates against risks.

## 5.2  Business and IT Alignment

The concept of Business and IT alignment is not new, it has been explored or applied in various ways. Also, it has been expressed in several terms such as, linkage, integration, and agreement. However, alignment does not refer to being aligned or not aligned, rather it how the relationship needs to be adjusted based on business unforeseen event [44]. Some of the most important and crucial contributors identified in the alignment between business/IT in the selection of BDA tools are communication and uniformity. Communication plays a significance role between the business and IT units in decision making. In addition, the uniformity of how things are done, following processes and policies of an organisation is important.

Lack of alignments between the business and IT units can cause chaos in selecting BDA tools. As a result, working environment can become unstable, and leads to deploying applications that cannot serve the organisational purpose. It is clear that lack of alignment between business and IT units have huge implications, such as cost prohibitive, and technology compatibility risks for an organisation in selecting BDA tools.

### 5.3 Governance

Governance consists of standards, principles, and policies [45]. It gives a structural guide to specialists and managers in decision-making. It is also procedural, which gives power to relevant authority to make decisions [46]. Thus, governance can be used to guide the selection of appropriate BDA tools in an organisation. There is means that the selected BDA tools adhere to standards and principles of the organisation.

Selection of the analytics tools is one thing, and its use is another thing. The use of the BDA tools is as critical as the selection, which therefore also require guidance. Governance can be used to guide the use and management of the tools, to avoid technology conflicts and abnormalities. Lack of governance principles in organisation promote poor product quality. Also, it allows employees to avoid or shift accountability and responsibility as they deemed.

### 5.4 Skill-Set

Big data analytics is an emerging concept, particularly in developing countries such as South Africa. As a result, there is scarcity of skill-set in the area of BDA, which affects the slow deployment of the concept in South African organisations. The skill-set play a very critical role in the deployment and use of BDA [47]. The noticeable reasons of the complexity of BDA require data scientist to perform. The machine learning applications designed to analyse big data requires skills of data scientist.

Although it is crucial to have the skill-set, what is even more important is retention of the personnel. Retention allows an organisation to keep their trained and skilled personnel as long as possible. This saves cost of upskilling, which can be very prohibitive, and affect return on investment. Lack of skills lead to incorrectness of data and operations falling apart, which influence decision-making, and ultimately affect business goal negatively.

## 6   Conclusion

This study that was conducted is proposed to assist organisation that wish to deploy and those that have already deployed BDA tools by doing an evaluation of the tools to seek for the tools that suit the organisations goal. In this study organisations will get a better understanding of the process of selecting an appropriate tools using criteria as guide. This study can be of usefulness in organisation that seek to understand the value of having a criteria to evaluate the BDA tool in the market. The research was limited to evaluation of BDA tools. This means that it excludes other activities such as deployment and readiness, as well as the application that are connected to BDA tools.

# References

1. Gandomi, A., Haider, M.: Beyond the hype: big data concepts, methods, and analytics. Int. J. Inf. Manage. **35**(2), 137–144 (2015)
2. Cukier, K., Mayer-Schönberger, V.: Big Data: A Revolution That Will Transform How We Live, Work, and Think. Houghton Mifflin Harcourt, Boston (2013)
3. Katal, A., Wazid, M., Goudar, R.H.: Big data: issues, challenges, tools and good practices. In: 2013 Sixth International Conference on Contemporary Computing (IC3), pp. 404–409. IEEE, August 2013
4. Hofacker, C.F., Malthouse, E.C., Sultan, F.: Big data and consumer behavior: imminent opportunities. J. Consum. Mark. **33**(2), 89–97 (2016)
5. Ghazal, A., et al.: BigBench: towards an industry standard benchmark for big data analytics. In: Proceedings of the 2013 ACM SIGMOD International Conference on Management of Data, pp. 1197–1208. ACM, June 2013
6. Demchenko, Y., De Laat, C., Membrey, P.: Defining architecture components of the Big Data Ecosystem. In: 2014 International Conference on Collaboration Technologies and Systems (CTS), pp. 104–112. IEEE (2014)
7. Mgudlwa, S., Iyamu, T.: Integration of social media with healthcare big data for improved service delivery. S. Afr. J. Inf. Manag. **20**(1), 1–8 (2018)
8. De Mauro, A., Greco, M., Grimaldi, M.: What is big data? A consensual definition and a review of key research topics. In: AIP Conference Proceedings, vol. 1644, no. 1, pp. 97–104, February 2015
9. Veiga, J., Expósito, R.R., Pardo, X.C., Taboada, G.L., Tourifio, J.: Performance evaluation of big data frameworks for large-scale data analytics. In: 2016 IEEE International Conference on Big Data (Big Data), pp. 424–431. IEEE, December 2016
10. Suthaharan, S.: Big data classification: problems and challenges in network intrusion prediction with machine learning. Perform. Eval. Rev. **41**(4), 70–73 (2014)
11. Sivarajah, U., Kamal, M.M., Irani, Z., Weerakkody, V.: Critical analysis of Big Data challenges and analytical methods. J. Bus. Res. **70**, 263–286 (2017)
12. George, G., Haas, M.R., Pentland, A.: Big data and management. Acad. Manag. J. **57**(2), 321–326 (2014)
13. Barton, D., Court, D.: Making advanced analytics work for you. Harvard Bus. Rev. **90**(10), 78–83 (2012)
14. Delone, W.H., McLean, E.R.: The DeLone and McLean model of information systems success: a ten-year update. J. Manage. Inf. Syst. **19**(4), 9–30 (2003)
15. Andargoli, A.E., Scheepers, H., Rajendran, D., Sohal, A.: Health information systems evaluation frameworks: a systematic review. Int. J. Med. Informatics **97**, 195–209 (2017)
16. Agostinho, C., et al.: Towards a sustainable interoperability in networked enterprise information systems: trends of knowledge and model-driven technology. Comput. Ind. **79**, 64–76 (2016)
17. Iyamu, T.: A multilevel approach to big data analysis using analytic tools and actor network theory. S. Afr. J. Inf. Manag. **20**(1), 1–9 (2018)
18. Davenport, T.H., Dyché, J.: Big data in big companies. International Institute for Analytics, no. 3 (2013)
19. Daniel, B.: Big Data and analytics in higher education: opportunities and challenges. Br. J. Educ. Technol. **46**(5), 904–920 (2015)
20. Wamba, S.F., Akter, S., Edwards, A., Chopin, G., Gnanzou, D.: How 'big data' can make big impact: findings from a systematic review and a longitudinal case study. Int. J. Prod. Econ. **165**, 234–246 (2015)

21. Wolfert, S., Ge, L., Verdouw, C., Bogaardt, M.J.: Big data in smart farming–a review. Agric. Syst. **153**, 69–80 (2017)
22. Najafabadi, M.M., Villanustre, F., Khoshgoftaar, T.M., Seliya, N., Wald, R., Muharemagic, E.: Deep learning applications and challenges in big data analytics. J. Big Data **2**(1), 1 (2015). https://doi.org/10.1186/s40537-014-0007-7
23. Grover, V., Chiang, R.H., Liang, T.P., Zhang, D.: Creating strategic business value from big data analytics: a research framework. J. Manage. Inf. Syst. **35**(2), 388–423 (2018)
24. Günther, W.A., Mehrizi, M.H.R., Huysman, M., Feldberg, F.: Debating big data: a literature review on realizing value from big data. J. Strateg. Inf. Syst. **26**(3), 191–209 (2017)
25. Erevelles, S., Fukawa, N., Swayne, L.: Big Data consumer analytics and the transformation of marketing. J. Bus. Res. **69**(2), 897–904 (2016)
26. Ji-fan Ren, S., Fosso Wamba, S., Akter, S., Dubey, R., Childe, S.J.: Modelling quality dynamics, business value and firm performance in a big data analytics environment. Int. J. Prod. Res. **55**(17), 5011–5026 (2017)
27. Wang, Y., Kung, L., Byrd, T.A.: Big data analytics: understanding its capabilities and potential benefits for healthcare organisations. Technol. Forecast. Soc. Chang. **126**, 3–13 (2018)
28. Alharthi, A., Krotov, V., Bowman, M.: Addressing barriers to big data. Bus. Horiz. **60**(3), 285–292 (2017)
29. Pearlson, K.E., Saunders, C.S., Galletta, D.F.: Managing and Using Information Systems, Binder Ready Version: A Strategic Approach. Wiley, Hoboken (2016)
30. Laudon, K.C., Laudon, J.P.: Management Information System. Pearson Education India, New York (2016)
31. Hallikainen, P., Chen, L.: A holistic framework on information systems evaluation with a case analysis. Lead. Issues ICT Eval. **9**, 57–64 (2006)
32. Irani, Z., Love, P.E.: Developing a frame of reference for ex-ante IT/IS investment evaluation. Eur. J. Inf. Syst. **11**(1), 74–82 (2002)
33. Iyamu, T.: Collecting qualitative data for information systems studies: the reality in practice. Educ. Inf. Technol. **23**, 2249–2264 (2018). https://doi.org/10.1007/s10639-018-9718-2
34. Kumar, R.: Research Methodology: A Step-by-Step Guide for Beginners. Sage Publications Limited, Thousand Oaks (2019)
35. Walliman, N.: Research Methods: The Basics. Routledge, New York (2017)
36. Yin, R.K.: Case Study Research and Applications: Design and Methods. Sage Press, Los Angeles (2017)
37. Neuman, W.L.: Social Research Methods: Qualitative and Qualitative Approaches. Allyn and Bocon, Boston (2000)
38. Butler, T.: Towards a hermeneutic method for interpretive research in information systems. J. Inf. Technol. **13**(4), 285–300 (1998). https://doi.org/10.1057/jit.1998.7
39. Boell, S.K., Cecez-Kecmanovic, D.: Literature reviews and the hermeneutic circle. Aust. Acad. Res. Libr. **41**(2), 129–144 (2010)
40. Myers, M.D., Avison, D.: An introduction to qualitative research in information systems. Qual. Res. Inf. Syst. **4**, 3–12 (2002)
41. Scotland, J.: Exploring the philosophical underpinnings of research: relating ontology and epistemology to the methodology and methods of the scientific, interpretive, and critical research paradigms. Engl. Lang. Teach. **5**(9), 9–16 (2012)
42. Etzioni, A.: Mixed-scanning: a "third" approach to decision-making. Public Adm. Rev. **27**, 385–392 (1967)
43. Cai, L., Zhu, Y.: The challenges of data quality and data quality assessment in the big data era. Data Sci. J. **14**, 2 (2015)

44. Luftman, J., Lyytinen, K., Zvi, T.B.: Enhancing the measurement of information technology (IT) business alignment and its influence on company performance. J. Inf. Technol. **32**(1), 26–46 (2017)
45. Shaanika, I., Iyamu, T.: Developing the enterprise architecture for the Namibian government. Electron. J. Inf. Syst. Dev. Ctries. **84**(3), e12028 (2018)
46. Bennett, B., Bradbury, M., Prangnell, H.: Rules, principles and judgments in accounting standards. Abacus **42**(2), 189–204 (2006)
47. Ahmed, E., et al.: The role of big data analytics in Internet of Things. Comput. Netw. **129**(2), 459–471 (2017)

# ICT and Education

ICT and Education

# Development of a Quantitative Instrument to Measure Mobile Collaborative Learning (MCL) Using WhatsApp: The Conceptual Steps

Bangisisi Zamuxolo Mathews Nyembe and Grant Royd Howard[✉] (iD)

University of South Africa (Unisa), Florida, South Africa
54830222@mylife.unisa.ac.za, howargr@unisa.ac.za

**Abstract.** It has been reported that WhatsApp, a social media application, had approximately 1.6 billion active users globally as of July 2019, almost one-fifth of the total world's population. Thus, research about WhatsApp's influence in general and especially its influence in education was relevant and significant. While there was much research involving WhatsApp and learning, it was not conclusive about the effects of WhatsApp on student learning. Specifically, research focusing on collaborative learning using WhatsApp was lacking, including research instruments for measuring collaboration on WhatsApp. Consequently, the paper's research problem was the lack of research instruments for measuring collaboration on WhatsApp in relation to academic achievement. To address the research problem, the study followed the important initial and conceptual steps of the instrument development process to develop a research instrument to measure collaboration on WhatsApp in relation to academic achievement. The result of the paper was a developed instrument that provides researchers with a basis to measure the explanatory constructs involved in mobile collaborative learning (MCL) processes on WhatsApp and potentially other social media platforms. Therefore, the paper made an appropriately theoretical contribution, which was grounded in the scientific literature. The study facilitated positivistic research and epistemology for acquiring objective and precise scientific knowledge. Such deductive research promotes theory testing and development and presents educators and students with scientific evidence about learning with MCL applications such as WhatsApp from which both curriculum and learning design can be informed and benefited. In the age of connected mobility this is a necessity.

**Keywords:** Information Systems (IS) · Information Technology (IT) · Mobile collaborative learning (MCL) · Mobile learning (M-learning) · Quantitative instrument development · Social media · WhatsApp

## 1 Introduction

Mobile digital technologies and social media continue to pervade many facets of our daily lives and enable communication, collaboration and content creation. Within the broad scope of mobile digital technologies and social media, the social media

M. Hattingh et al. (Eds.): I3E 2020, LNCS 12066, pp. 507–519, 2020.
https://doi.org/10.1007/978-3-030-44999-5_42

application called 'WhatsApp' has become particularly prevalent. WhatsApp is technically an internet-based cross-platform instant messaging and voice over Internet Protocol (VoIP) service for mobile devices [1].

As of July 2019, it was reported that WhatsApp had approximately 1.6 billion active users globally [2], which is almost one-fifth of the total world's population at that time. In the context of other popular worldwide social media applications, WhatsApp is placed behind Facebook and YouTube only as the most popular social media application. WhatsApp's user base is significant, which warrants scientific evidence of its effects in our lives.

WhatsApp's user base includes students and while there is active research involving WhatsApp and learning, the research is not conclusive about the effects of WhatsApp on student learning. For example, one study reported that WhatsApp improved learning [7] and another reported that WhatsApp did not [8]. Furthermore, in a recent study, the reviewed literature showed research about WhatsApp and teaching and learning from various viewpoints, but none measured collaboration on WhatsApp in relation to academic achievement [9], including there being a lack of instruments for measuring collaboration on WhatsApp. This was the research problem.

Subsequently, the research question was what constructs and instrument were appropriate for measuring collaboration on WhatsApp in relation to academic achievement? The research objective was to develop a quantitative instrument to answer the research question. The study focused on the important conceptual steps of the instrument development process rather than the empirical steps. Thus, the study made an appropriately theoretical contribution, which was grounded in the scientific literature.

Answering the research question has significant value for researchers in the domain. It allows them the quantify the effects of collaboration on social media and similar applications in relation to academic achievement and it facilitates theory development. This provides significant value to educators and students about how to incorporate social media, mobile collaborative learning (MCL) and WhatsApp into their teaching and learning. The paper facilitates a positivistic epistemology based on the scientific method for objectivity and precision. Hence, the study provides an original contribution to the scientific body of knowledge in the broad domains of MCL and m-learning. Furthermore, the study contributes to knowledge generation in Africa, since less than a fifth of the articles reviewed related to studies in Africa [9].

The paper consists of four sections. The first section introduced the study's context and explained the research problem, question and objective. The next section reviewed m-learning and WhatsApp and learning. Section 3 provided the instrument development process, which enabled the study to answer the research question. Section 4 concludes the paper and explains its contribution, limitations and opportunities for future research.

## 2  Literature Review

### 2.1  Mobile Learning (M-learning)

Mobile and social media technologies are a relatively recent development, but human learning is a natural human process and many theories to explain how human learning occurs have been developed since the time of the Ancient Greek philosophers [9]. However, Collaborative Learning, Communities of Practice, Connectivism, Conversation Theory and Social Learning Theory appear to relate especially well to learning with mobile and social media technologies. Nevertheless, researchers continued with a new learning theory to explain specifically learning with mobile technologies, namely M-learning Theory [10].

M-learning Theory has attracted the attention of many researchers who acknowledge the potential of applying mobile and social media technologies to improve learning [11, 12]. M-learning Theory does not replace traditional learning theories; instead it complements them by emphasizing the mobility of learning, including how learning is acquired across various contexts, while on the move and across the transitions of life. M-learning Theory also takes into consideration learning that happens at home, work, outdoors, places of leisure, places of worship, cafes, stores and while travelling. M-learning Theory continues to be researched, defined and evolved together with the evolution of mobile hardware, software and social media technologies.

Three key aspects of M-learning Theory have been identified, namely personalization, authenticity and collaboration, which occur outside of the traditional learning time and space constraints [13]. Personalization is based in Socio-cultural Theory and Motivational Theory and involves learner choice, agency, self-regulation and customization. Authenticity refers to the real-world relevance, practices and personal meaning in everyday life situations. Collaboration involves participating in rich learning interactions with other people, which is the m-learning aspect that the study focused on together with the social media application called 'WhatsApp'.

### 2.2  WhatsApp and Learning

WhatsApp has evolved into a promising educational tool that has the potential to promote interaction and participation during student learning activities [14–17]. WhatsApp enables anonymous, asynchronous collaborative learning, which is reported to improve and increase the productivity and participation of less confident learners [18]. WhatsApp helps to create immediacy and connection in informal learning, formal blended learning, open distance learning and learning outside of the classroom [15, 19].

However, despite the documented benefits, challenges have been reported, including extra workload, distraction from learning, less commitment to participate, exposure to unregulated messages, false information, addictive behavior and increased expenses [17, 20]. In addition, WhatsApp use may result in stress, lack of privacy and difficulties managing responsibilities, especially for more mature students [15]. Married students have also found WhatsApp disruptive because its use collided with their family time [18]. In contrast, there is research indicating that students have found learning on WhatsApp interesting, convenient and motivating [21]. It can be argued that WhatsApp is affordable to use and increases the chances of learners participating in learning activities [22].

Several learning theories have been applied in WhatsApp studies. Socio-cultural Theory was involved in a study where WhatsApp was used for learning English as a second language [16]. Activity Theory was used to analyze learner interactions on WhatsApp for improving critique writing skills of English as a foreign language [23] and in a WhatsApp study to identify factors that influence students' participation in mobile learning activities and online discussions [19]. Activity Theory, Situated Learning Theory and Communities of Practice were applied in a study to understand how WhatsApp could support teaching and learning in higher education [15]. Experiential Learning Theory was applied in a study where WhatsApp was used to improve the standard of primary health care education [24]. Thus, several of the prominent learning theories have been applied in various ways to study WhatsApp. However, the important concept of collaboration had not been explicitly measured to expose its effect on learning anywhere and anytime with WhatsApp.

## 3  Instrument Development

### 3.1  MacKenzie et al.'s (2011) Framework

MacKenzie et al.'s (2011) framework for instrument development was used to guide the development of the quantitative instrument for measuring collaboration using WhatsApp [25]. This framework was selected because it was published in an extensive study updating important prior research on Information Systems (IS) instrument development and published in arguably the top journal in the IS field, namely MIS Quarterly. In addition, it is a fairly recent publication and has been cited by 1793 according to Google Scholar as of 22 December 2019. The framework provides a 10-step procedure for instrument development starting with construct conceptualization or reconceptualization and ending in the development of norms [26]. Nonetheless, since the scope of the study was limited to the important conceptual steps only, the first four conceptual steps of the framework were applied.

### 3.2  Step 1: Conceptualization

Constructs are abstract concepts developed for research or scientific purposes [25]. Construct conceptualization involves defining the conceptual domain of each construct. Each construct should be defined unambiguously and consistently with prior research. Thus, instruments that related to the measurement of collaboration from various fields were reviewed and evaluated based on their appropriateness and construct validity and reliability measures [27, 28]. Only those that had applicability, established construct validity and high reliability measures were included as inputs into the instrument development process.

The instruments were the Thomson, Perry and Miller Collaboration Instrument [29], the Thomson, Perry and Miller (2007) Collaboration Instrument in the South

African Context [30], the Collaboration with Medical Staff Scale of the Nurses Opinion Questionnaire (CMSS-NOQ) [31], the Collaboration and Trust in an Education Context [32], the Wilder Collaboration Factors Inventory [33], the Collaboration Index [34], the Collaborative Culture Scale [35], the Assessment of Inter-professional Team Collaboration Scale [36], the Collaboration Assessment Tool (CAT) [37], the Transdisciplinary Tobacco Use Research Centers (TTURC) Researcher Survey [38], the Index of Interprofessional Team Collaboration for Expanded School Mental Health (IITC-ESMH) [39], the Teacher Collaboration Assessment Survey (TCAS) [40], the Distance Education Learning Environment Survey (DELES) [41], the Index of Interdisciplinary Collaboration (IIC) [42], the Expanded School Mental Health Collaboration Instrument [School Version] [43] and the Collaborative Practice Assessment Tool (CPAT) [44].

For each instrument, all its specified factors/constructs were evaluated by the authors. The evaluation was directed by importance to the research problem and parsimony. The selected and adapted constructs were Interaction (IA), Support (S), Information Exchange (IE), Sense of Community (SC), Interdependence (ID), Trust (T), Active Learning (AL), Formality (F) and Collaboration (C). In addition, the construct Academic Achievement (AA) was included since it was essential for addressing the research problem. All the constructs would apply to students/learners who use WhatsApp for academic learning.

Interaction (IA) was defined as the amount of reciprocal action and engagement, such as discussing, sharing, chatting and meeting, between two or more learners using WhatsApp for academic learning. Support (S) was defined as the amount of help and assistance that is provided to a learner, who is experiencing learning difficulties, by other learners using WhatsApp for academic learning. Information Exchange (IE) was defined as the amount of information exchanged as part of the learning processes using WhatsApp for academic learning. Sense of Community (SC) was defined as a learner's feeling of belonging to a group with shared interests, goals and needs, using WhatsApp for academic learning. Interdependence (ID) was defined as the contingency or condition that other learners are part of a learner's learning process, using WhatsApp for academic learning. Trust (T) was defined as the level of confidence that a learner has in other learners using WhatsApp for academic learning. Active Learning (AL) was defined as being opposite to passive learning and comprises meaningful learning activities and applied learning on WhatsApp for academic learning. Formality (F) was defined as how casual and relaxed or academically correct and serious the engagement is between a learner and the other learners by virtue of the language they use, using WhatsApp for academic learning. Collaboration (C) was defined as the amount of working and contributing together that takes place in a group of learners to achieve the common goal of learning using WhatsApp.

In addition, it is necessary to measure a student's academic achievement in an acceptable way to address the research problem. Actual student grades are variables that measure academic achievement. However, the eventual instrument users may not have access to respondents' grades, thus, a construct called Academic Achievement (AA) was defined as a learner's self-reported academic achievement.

## 3.3  Step 2: Generate Items to Represent the Constructs

Following the conceptual definitions of the selected constructs, a set of items to represent the conceptual domain of each construct was generated [25]. The items generated were adapted from the instruments reviewed and are provided in Table 1. Six items per construct were generated to balance adequate domain sampling and parsimony for construct and content validity and response bias and fatigue [45]. Each item is measured using a five-point Likert measurement scale from 1 to 5, where 1 = "strongly disagree", 2 = "disagree", 3 = "neither disagree nor agree", 4 = "agree" and 5 = "strongly agree" [46]. The higher the aggregate value for each item the more of that construct is evident on WhatsApp for academic learning.

In addition to the items in Table 1, a participant would be asked several initial questions that would provide useful information and analyses about their characteristics. These questions include gender, home language, age range, study major, study qualification level, year level of qualification, do you use WhatsApp with other students for learning (if you mark "No", then please indicate your reasons for not using WhatsApp for learning and then there are no further questions for you to answer, thank you for participating)? How many hours do you estimate that you spend on WhatsApp every week with other students for learning? What devices do you use when learning with other students on WhatsApp? Where, what places, do you use WhatsApp for learning with other students? Is there anything that prevents you from using WhatsApp more often or in more places for learning with other students?

**Table 1.**  Measurement items for each construct.

| # | Construct | Measurement items |
|---|---|---|
| 1 | Interaction (IA) | ***When I am on WhatsApp with other students:*** |
| | | 1. We have discussions to learn from each other |
| | | 2. We participate with each other to learn |
| | | 3. We have chats to learn from each other |
| | | 4. We share with each other to learn |
| | | 5. We have meetings with each other to learn |
| | | 6. We communicate with each other to learn |
| 2 | Support (S) | ***When I am on WhatsApp with other students:*** |
| | | 1. They help me on my courses/modules |
| | | 2. They reduce the stress from my courses/modules |
| | | 3. They assist with difficult parts of my courses/modules |
| | | 4. They aid me when I am stuck on my courses/modules |
| | | 5. They lend a hand so I can figure out my courses/modules |
| | | 6. They encourage me to keep going on my courses/modules |

(*continued*)

**Table 1.** (*continued*)

| # | Construct | Measurement items |
|---|-----------|-------------------|
| 3 | Information Exchange (IE) | *When I am on WhatsApp with other students:* |
| | | 1. We send and receive course/module information |
| | | 2. Course/module material gets passed around |
| | | 3. We swap course/module information |
| | | 4. Course/module material is spread around |
| | | 5. We distribute course/module information |
| | | 6. Course/module knowledge is circulated |
| 4 | Sense of Community (SC) | *When I am on WhatsApp with other students:* |
| | | 1. I feel that I belong to a learning group |
| | | 2. I matter to my learning group |
| | | 3. My learning group matters to me |
| | | 4. My learning group benefits our learning |
| | | 5. My learning group has shared interests in learning |
| | | 6. My learning group has similar academic goals |
| 5 | Interdependence (ID) | *When I am on WhatsApp with other students:* |
| | | 1. I rely on other students to learn |
| | | 2. Other students rely on me to learn |
| | | 3. My learning requires other students |
| | | 4. I need other students to learn |
| | | 5. Other students need me to learn |
| | | 6. My learning is conditional on other students |
| 6 | Trust (T) | *When I am on WhatsApp with other students:* |
| | | 1. Other students provide honest course/module advice |
| | | 2. I believe in what other students say to me about courses/modules |
| | | 3. I have faith in the course/module communication from other students |
| | | 4. The course/module discussions with other students are sincere |
| | | 5. The course/module conversations with other students are genuine |
| | | 6. I am certain that other students provide truthful information |
| 7 | Active Learning (AL) | *When I am on WhatsApp with other students:* |
| | | 1. I learn by having debates with other students |
| | | 2. I learn by working on questions with other students |
| | | 3. I learn by doing activities with other students |
| | | 4. I learn by solving study problems with other students |
| | | 5. I teach other students learning material |
| | | 6. I show other students how to figure out their courses/modules |

(*continued*)

**Table 1.**  (*continued*)

| # | Construct | Measurement items |
|---|-----------|-------------------|
| 8 | Formality (F) | ***When I am on WhatsApp with other students:*** |
|   |   | 1. We use academic language only when talking about courses/modules |
|   |   | 2. Messages about courses/modules contain academic content only |
|   |   | 3. When learning, we use correct wording only |
|   |   | 4. When learning, we discuss academic content only |
|   |   | 5. During course/module communication, we use scientific language only |
|   |   | 6. We use textbook wording only when chatting about courses/modules |
| 9 | Collaboration (C) | ***When I am on WhatsApp with other students:*** |
|   |   | 1. We work together to understand our courses/modules |
|   |   | 2. We learn collectively to solve course/module problems |
|   |   | 3. We contribute jointly to learn our courses/modules |
|   |   | 4. When preparing for tests or exams we learn together |
|   |   | 5. We study as a group |
|   |   | 6. We learn our courses/modules together |
| 10 | Academic Achievement (AA) | ***Since I started using WhatsApp for learning:*** |
|   |   | 1. My courses'/modules' marks have improved |
|   |   | 2. I do better in tests and exams |
|   |   | 3. I am able to achieve better success in my assignments |
|   |   | 4. I have had more success in my courses/modules |
|   |   | 5. I understand my courses/modules better |
|   |   | 6. My courses/modules are easier to do |

## 3.4    Step 3: Assess the Content Validity of the Items

After the items were generated for each construct, they were assessed for their content validity, which relates to how well a construct's items represent all aspects of that construct [25]. Raters are recommended for doing this assessment and university educated students are considered adequately representative of the intended generalized population [25]. Given the conceptual focus of the study, the study's supervisor performed the initial item generation and adaptation and the study's second researcher, a postgraduate university educated student conducted the assessment. Although it is recommended to use one-way repeated measures ANOVA to determine if an item's mean rating on one construct differs from its ratings on the other constructs, it requires more than two raters [47], so instead a qualitative assessment was conducted by the second researcher. The second researcher was requested, for each item, to assess whether the item represented the content of the construct that it was assigned to measure, and for each construct, whether all the items assigned to measure that construct represented the entire content of that construct. After three iterations and changes, the final items are presented in Table 1.

## 3.5    Step 4: Formally Specify the Measurement Model

Step 4 involves specifying the measurement model, including how the items relate to the constructs. Figure 1 provides the initial measurement model which depicts all constructs with reflective indicators. The paper specifies all of the constructs as uni-dimensional or reflective constructs and there are no sub-dimensions or conceptually distinguishable facets [48].

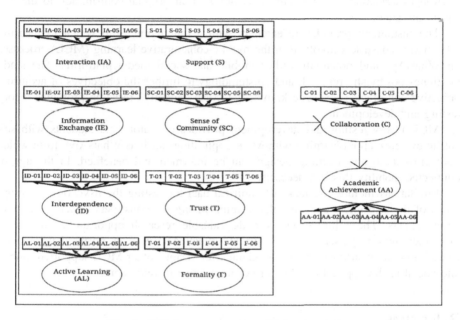

**Fig. 1.** Initial measurement model for the study.

At this conceptual stage it is not known how each of the constructs IA, S, IE, SC, ID, T, AL and F interrelate. However, based on the reviewed instruments and literature it is evident that they are important when measuring and influence C. Thus, only a general relationship is specified between all those constructs and C. Also, the relationship from C to AA is specified since it is the central focus of the study. These relationships can be specified as the following alternate hypotheses (HA1-n): IA positively influences C, S positively influences C, IE positively influences C, SC positively influences C, ID positively influences C, T positively influences C, AL positively influences C, F negatively or positively influences C and C positively influences AA. The corresponding null hypotheses (H01-n) specify that there are no associations among each set of constructs.

## 4 Conclusion

The study has addressed the research problem, being the lack of research instruments measuring collaboration on WhatsApp in relation to academic achievement, by completing the conceptual steps to develop an appropriate measurement instrument. The developed measurement instrument answers the research question by demonstrating appropriate constructs and an instrument for measuring collaboration on WhatsApp in relation to academic achievement. This provides an original contribution to the scientific literature.

The instrument provides researchers with a foundation from which to measure informative constructs involved in the mobile collaborative learning (MCL) processes on WhatsApp and potentially other mobile and social media platforms. The study facilitates positivistic research and epistemology to further the objectives of acquiring objective and precise scientific knowledge. Such deductive research promotes theory testing and development.

MCL theory testing and development provides educators and students with scientific evidence about learning with MCL applications such as WhatsApp, from which both curriculum and learning design can be informed and benefited. In the age of connected mobility this is a necessity.

Limitations include the lack of empirical data for testing the psychometric properties of the instrument and the relationships among the constructs in actual learning environments. These limitations provide valuable research opportunities involving instrument pilot tests, scale purification and refinement and even norms development. In addition, the instrument could be adapted for various other MCL supported mobile and social media applications for further knowledge development.

## References

1. WhatsApp: WhatsApp.com. https://www.whatsapp.com. Accessed 04 Nov 2019
2. Statista.com: Global-social-networks-ranked-by-number-of-users. https://www.statista.com/statistics/272014/global-social-networks-ranked-by-number-of-users/. Accessed 4 Nov 2019
3. Gikas, J., Grant, M.M.: Mobile computing devices in higher education: student perspectives on learning with cellphones, smartphones & social media. Internet High. Educ. **19**, 18–26 (2013). https://doi.org/10.1016/j.iheduc.2013.06.002
4. Jeng, Y.-L., Wu, T.-T., Huang, Y.-M., Tan, Q., Yang, S.J.H.: The add-on impact of mobile applications in learning strategies: a review study. J. Educ. Technol. Soc. **13**, 3–11 (2010). https://www.jstor.org/stable/jeductechsoci.13.3.3
5. Garcia-Cabot, A., De-Marcos, L., Garcia-Lopez, E.: An empirical study on m-learning adaptation: learning performance and learning contexts. Comput. Educ. **82**, 450–459 (2015). https://doi.org/10.1016/j.compedu.2014.12.007
6. Caballé, S., Xhafa, F., Barolli, L.: Using mobile devices to support online collaborative learning. Mob. Inf. Syst. **6**, 27–47 (2010). http://dx.doi.org/10.3233/MIS-2010-0091
7. Pimmer, C., Brühlmann, F., Odetola, T.D., Oluwasola, D.O., Dipeolu, O., Ajuwon, A.J.: Facilitating professional mobile learning communities with instant messaging. Comput. Educ. **128**, 102–112 (2019). https://doi.org/10.1016/j.compedu.2018.09.005

8. Alkhalaf, A.M., Tekian, A., Park, Y.S.: The impact of WhatsApp use on academic achievement among Saudi medical students. Med. Teach. **40**, S10–S14 (2018). https://doi.org/10.1080/0142159X.2018.1464652

9. Nyembe, B.Z.M., Howard, G.R.: The utilities of prominent learning theories for mobile collaborative learning (MCL) with reference to WhatsApp and m-learning. In: Maharaj, M., Singh, U.G. (eds.) The 2nd International Conference on Advances in Big Data, Computing and Data Communication Systems (icABCD), Winterton, South Africa, pp. 227–232. IEEE (2019). https://doi.org/10.1109/ICABCD.2019.8851042

10. Parsons, D.: A mobile learning overview by timeline and mind map. Int. J. Mob. Blended Learn. **6**, 1–21 (2014). https://doi.org/10.4018/ijmbl.2014100101

11. Sharples, M., Taylor, J., Vavoula, G.: Towards a theory of mobile learning. In: The 4th World Conference on Mobile Learning (mLearn 2005), Cape Town, South Africa, pp. 1–9 (2005)

12. Vavoula, G., Sharples, M.: Meeting the challenges in evaluating mobile learning: a 3-level evaluation framework. Int. J. Mob. Blended Learn. **1**, 54–75 (2009). https://doi.org/10.4018/jmbl.2009040104

13. Kearney, M., Schuck, S., Burden, K., Aubusson, P.: Viewing mobile learning from a pedagogical perspective. Res. Learn. Technol. **20**, 1–17 (2012). https://doi.org/10.3402/rlt.v20i0.14406

14. Bouhnik, D., Deshen, M.: WhatsApp goes to school: mobile instant messaging between teachers and students. J. Inf. Technol. Educ. **13**, 217–231 (2014). https://0-doi-org.oasis.unisa.ac.za/10.28945/2051

15. Gachago, D., Strydom, S., Hanekom, P., Simons, S., Walters, S.: Crossing boundaries: lectures' perspectives on the use of WhatsApp to support teaching and learning in higher education. Progressio **37**, 172–187 (2015). https://0-hdl-handle-net.oasis.unisa.ac.za/10520/EJC180393

16. Andujar, A.: Benefits of mobile instant messaging to develop ESL writing. System **62**, 63–76 (2016). https://0-doi-org.oasis.unisa.ac.za/10.1016/j.system.2016.07.004

17. Aburezeq, I.M., Ishtaiwa, F.F.: The impact of WhatsApp on interaction in an Arabic language teaching course. Int. J. Arts Sci. **6**, 165–180 (2013). https://0-search-proquest-com.oasis.unisa.ac.za/docview/1496695544?accountid=14648

18. Rambe, P., Bere, A.: Using mobile instant messaging to leverage learner participation and transform pedagogy at a South African University of Technology. Br. J. Educ. Technol. **44**, 544–561 (2013). https://doi.org/10.1111/bjet.12057

19. Barhoumi, C.: The effectiveness of WhatsApp mobile learning activities guided by activity theory on students' knowledge management. Contemp. Educ. Technol. **6**, 221–238 (2015). https://search.proquest.com/docview/2135157613?accountid=14648

20. Ahad, A.D., Lim, S.M.A.: Convenience or nuisance?: The 'WhatsApp' dilemma. Procedia Soc. Behav. Sci. **155**, 189–196 (2014). https://0-doi-org.oasis.unisa.ac.za/10.1016/j.sbspro.2014.10.278

21. So, S.: Mobile instant messaging support for teaching and learning in higher education. Internet High. Educ. **31**, 32–42 (2016). https://0-doi-org.oasis.unisa.ac.za/10.1016/j.iheduc.2016.06.001

22. Bere, A., Rambe, P.: An empirical analysis of the determinants of mobile instant messaging appropriation in university learning. J. Comput. High. Educ. **28**, 172–198 (2016). https://0-doi-org.oasis.unisa.ac.za/10.1007/s12528-016-9112-2

23. Awada, G.: Effect of WhatsApp on critique writing proficiency and perceptions toward learning. Cogent. Educ. **3**, 1–25 (2016). https://doi.org/10.1080/2331186X.2016.1264173

24. Willemse, J.J.: Undergraduate nurses reflections on Whatsapp use in improving primary health care education. Curationis **38**, 1–7 (2015). https://doi.org/10.4102/curationis.v38i2. 1512

25. MacKenzie, S.B., Podsakoff, P.M., Podsakoff, N.P.: Construct measurement and validation procedures in MIS and behavioral research: integrating new and existing techniques. MIS Q. **35**, 293–334 (2011). https://doi.org/10.2307/23044045

26. Hoehle, H., Venkatesh, V.: Mobile application usability: conceptualization and instrument development. MIS Q. **39**, 435–472 (2015). https://pdfs.semanticscholar.org/8171/405b2c1538c6b2eff0eb7fb87b7b2c68eeba.pdf

27. Ariola, M.M.: Principles and Methods of Research. Rex Book Store Inc., Manilla (2006)

28. Straub, D.W.: Validating instruments in MIS research. MIS Q. **13**, 147–169 (1989). https://doi.org/10.2307/248922

29. Thomson, A.M., Perry, J.L., Miller, T.K.: Conceptualizing and measuring collaboration. J. Public Adm. Res. Theory. **19**, 23–56 (2009). https://0-doi-org.oasis.unisa.ac.za/10.1093/jopart/mum036

30. Roberts, D., Van Wyk, R., Dhanpat, N.: Validation of the Thomson, Perry and Miller (2007) collaboration instrument in the South African context. SA J. Hum. Resour. Manag. **15**, 1–11 (2017). https://dx.doi.org/10.4102/sajhrm.v15i0.793

31. Dougherty, M.B., Larson, E.: A review of instruments measuring nurse-physician collaboration. JONA J. Nurs. Adm. **35**, 244–253 (2005). https://journals.lww.com/jona journal/Abstract/2005/05000/A_Review_of_Instruments_Measuring_Nurse_Physician.8. aspx

32. Hoy, W.K., Tschannen-Moran, M.: Five faces of trust: an empirical confirmation in urban elementary schools. J. Sch. Leadersh. **9**, 184–208 (1999). https://doi.org/10.1177/10526846 9900900301

33. Townsend, A., Shelley, K.: Validating an instrument for assessing workforce collaboration. Community Coll. J. Res. Pract. **32**, 101–112 (2008). https://doi.org/10.1080/1066892070 1707813

34. Simatupang, T., Sridharan, R.: The collaboration index: a measure for supply chain collaboration. Int. J. Phys. Distrib. Logist. Manag. **35**, 44–62 (2005). https://doi.org/10.1108/09600030510577421

35. López, S.P., Peón, J.M.M., Ordás, C.J.V.: Managing knowledge: the link between culture and organizational learning. J. Knowl. Manag. **8**, 93–104 (2004). https://0-doi-org.oasis. unisa.ac.za/10.1108/13673270410567657

36. Orchard, C.A., King, G.A., Khalili, H., Bezzina, M.B.: Assessment of interprofessional team collaboration scale (AITCS): development and testing of the instrument. J. Contin. Educ. Health Prof. **32**, 58–67 (2012). https://doi.org/10.1002/chp.21123

37. Marek, L., Brock, D., Savla, J.: Evaluating collaboration for effectiveness: conceptualization and measurement. Am. J. Eval. **36**, 67–85 (2015). https://doi.org/10.1177/109821401453 1068

38. Mâsse, L.C., et al.: Measuring collaboration and transdisciplinary integration in team science. Am. J. Prev. Med. **35**, S151–S160 (2008). https://doi.org/10.1016/j.amepre.2008. 05.020

39. Mellin, E.A., Bronstein, L., Anderson-Butcher, D., Amorose, A.J., Ball, A., Green, J.: Measuring interprofessional team collaboration in expanded school mental health: model refinement and scale development. J. Interprof. Care **24**, 514–523 (2010). https://doi.org/10. 3109/13561821003624622

40. Woodland, R., Lee, M.K., Randall, J.: A validation study of the teacher collaboration assessment survey. Educ. Res. Eval. **19**, 442–460 (2013). https://doi.org/10.1080/13803611. 2013.795118

41. Walker, S.L., Fraser, B.J.: Development and validation of an instrument for assessing distance education learning environments in higher education: the Distance Education Learning Environments Survey (DELES). Learn. Environ. Res. **8**, 289–308 (2005). https://0-doi-org.oasis.unisa.ac.za/10.1007/s10984-005-1568-3

42. Bronstein, L.R.: Index of interdisciplinary collaboration (Instrument Development). Soc. Work Res. **26**, 113–127 (2002). https://link.gale.com/apps/doc/A89491142/AONE?u=usa_itw&sid=AONE&xid=0d0d968c

43. Mellin, E.A., Taylor, L., Weist, M.D.: The expanded school mental health collaboration instrument [school version]: development and initial psychometrics. School Ment. Health **6**, 151–162 (2014). https://doi.org/10.1007/s12310-013-9112-6

44. Schroder, C., et al.: Development and pilot testing of the collaborative practice assessment tool. J. Interprof. Care **25**, 189–195 (2011). https://doi.org/10.3109/13561820.2010.532620

45. Hinkin, T.R.: A review of scale development practices in the study of organizations. J. Manage. **21**, 967–988 (1995). https://doi.org/10.1177/014920639502100509

46. Sekaran, U., Bougie, R.: Research Methods for Business: A Skill Building Approach. Wiley, Chichester (2013)

47. Tredoux, C., Durrheim, K. (eds.): Numbers, Hypotheses & Conclusions: A Course in Statistics for the Social Sciences. UCT Press, Cape Town (2005)

48. Petter, S., Straub, D.W., Rai, A.: Specifying formative constructs in information systems research. MIS Q. **31**, 623–656 (2007). https://doi.org/10.2307/25148814

# Understanding Rural Parents' Behavioral Intention to Allow Their Children to Use Mobile Learning

David Mutambara and Anass Bayaga(✉)

University of Zululand, KwaDlangezwa, Empangeni, South Africa
vadmutambara@gmail.com, bayagaa@unizulu.ac.za

**Abstract.** Faced with many challenges resulting in learners' poor performance at the matriculation level, emphasis on Science, Technology, Engineering and Mathematics (STEM) education is in its infancy in South African's high schools. However, studies have shown that mobile learning (m-learning) can be used to mitigate the challenges of STEM education. Despite, the benefits of mobile learning to rural STEM learners, its full potential has not been realized because the adoption of m-learning depends on users' acceptance. Prior studies focused on teachers' and learners' acceptance of mobile learning. However, little is known about parents' acceptance of m-learning, especially in rural areas. This study explores the acceptance of m-learning by parents of rural high school STEM learners. The study proposes the parents' acceptance of m-learning model, which extends the technology acceptance model by introducing perceived social influence and perceived resources. Stratified random sampling was used to select 200 parents in the survey. Partial least squares structural equation modeling (PSL-SEM) was used to analyze data from 129 valid questionnaires. The proposed model explained 41% of the variance in parents' acceptance of mobile learning. Attitude towards the use was found to be the best predictor and the only factor that have a direct effect on behavioral intention to use mobile learning. However, all other factors have an indirect influence on behavioral intention. The findings revealed that for mobile learning to be successfully implemented in rural areas, resources need to be provided.

**Keywords:** Technology acceptance model · Perceived social influence · Perceived resources · STEM · Perceived usefulness · Perceived ease of use

## 1 Introduction

The integration of Science, Technology, Engineering and Mathematics (STEM) education is a growing area in both developed and developing countries [1]. Despite, STEM's fast growth, there is a lack of a universally accepted definition of STEM education [2]. In the study [3], STEM education was defined as "…fostering sustained engagement with the STEM disciplines where students can become competent contributors and critical participants in a range of STEM-related activities." What can be drawn from this definition is that STEM education aims at shifting teaching practices from teacher-centered into learner-centered and problem-based learning.

© IFIP International Federation for Information Processing 2020
Published by Springer Nature Switzerland AG 2020
M. Hattingh et al. (Eds.): I3E 2020, LNCS 12066, pp. 520–531, 2020.
https://doi.org/10.1007/978-3-030-44999-5_43

As STEM education is in its infancy in South African's high schools, it is faced with many challenges resulting in learners' poor performance at the matriculation level [4, 8], especially in rural areas. Makgato [6] attributed this poor performance in STEM-related subjects in rural areas to lack of learning materials, science laboratory and equipment to promote effective teaching and learning. Lack of parental involvement in their children's education also contributes to learners' poor performance in STEM-related subjects [5]. All the challenges that rural high school STEM learners face lead to demotivation when learning STEM-related subjects [4]. Based on these studies [4, 5], one can conclude that there is no effective STEM teaching and learning in rural high schools.

Studies have shown that m-learning can be used to mitigate the challenges of STEM education [7–9]. M-learning enables the use of visualized science experiments. This can positively influence learners' knowledge of science, which can enable them to give complete descriptions of scientific concepts [9]. Furthermore, m-learning makes studying materials available to learners anytime anywhere [7]. One can conclude that even though there are challenges in rural high schools, learners can still benefit from m-learning as they have access to learning materials and to visualize experiments using their mobile devices [7, 9]. According to Kong [8], m-learning improves parents' involvement in their children's learning, which in turn improves learners' motivation and performance in STEM-related subjects.

However, despite the positive effects m-learning can bring to rural STEM learners and the ubiquity of mobile devices, its adoption into the classroom is far below the expected rate [10]. Davis [11] stated that the successful adoption of any information system contingent on the user's acceptance. As a consequence of Davis' [11] assessment, it could be argued that successful implementation of m-learning in high schools of developing countries requires investigation of all stakeholders' attitudes. A plethora of studies has been conducted to identify factors that affect the acceptance of mobile learning [12–15]. However, a key issue is whether academics have adopted an adequately broad approach when investigating the attitudes of the main players in a high school instructional setting [16]. Most of these m-learning acceptance studies have concentrated on teachers [14, 17] and learners [13, 17]. Little is known about the parents' attitude towards m-learning, especially in rural areas of developing countries. Teacher and learner preferences aside, parents have the last decision on whether to use m-learning. Parents' roles in m-learning include; financial support, encouragement, purchasing of the mobile device and data, monitoring that the devices are used in a meaningful way that enhances learning [8]. In spite of parents playing an important role in the adoption of m-learning, their attitude towards mobile learning has not been given the attention it deserves [19]. Ford [18] stressed the need to carry out studies on the acceptance of m-learning in the South African context and not to blindly follow examples in developed countries. On the basis of the argument thus far, the current research sought to examine the perceptions of parents of rural high school STEM learners towards m-learning.

Identifying and understanding these factors is important for the successful implementation of m-learning. Hence, this study used the technology acceptance model (TAM) to investigate the factors that predict rural high school STEM learners' parents' attitudes towards m-learning. Specifically, the study seeks to answers the following research questions:

RQ 1: What is the effect of parents' perceived usefulness, perceived ease of use, attitude towards the use, perceived resources and perceived social influence on their behavioral intention to use m-learning?

RQ2: What is the relative importance of each of these factors in explaining parents' behavioral intention to use m-learning?

The findings of this study may provide more insight on m-learning acceptance in developing counties, and help policymakers and all other stakeholders in education on how to successfully implement m-learning in rural areas.

# 2   Literature Review and Model Development

## 2.1   Literature Review

Traditionally, the integration of m-learning has considered the home environment as the basis for extending formal learning beyond the wall of the classroom [16]. However, there is a big difference between what teachers hoped for and what mobile devices are actually being used for at home. At home mobile devices are mostly used for communication and playing games [39]. The most effective way of integrating m-learning into schools is through involving parents [8]. Parents' beliefs about m-learning influence their children's use [19]. Studies have shown that parents have contradictory attitudes towards the integration of m-learning in children's education [16, 19, 39]. In a study carried out by Genc [39] on the perception of parents towards mobile learning, the results show that about 46.88% of parents were having negative perceptions, while 26.88% were neutral while 26.56% were having positive perceptions towards mobile learning. Genc's [39] results were congruent to Bourgonjon et al's [16] findings, who stated that some parents expressed negative perception towards the use of mobile digital games-based learning. In both studies [16, 39], parents who had positive perceptions towards the integrating technology cited the usefulness of it in their children's education. However, parents were concerned about the health and social issues associated with overexposure to technology [16]. A plethora of studies has shown that parents' PEOU has a positive effect on their ATT and PU [10, 16, 17, 19, 29, 39]. However, there is some inconsistency when it comes to the relationship between parents' PEOU and their BI to allow their children to use m-learning. Studies [10] and [16] found that PEOU does not necessarily have a direct effect on BI. On the contrary, Alshmrany et al. [17] reported that PEOU has a positive direct effect on BI. Tsuei [19] studied the effect of parents' PSI on their PU and PEOU. The results showed that parent-teacher communication positively influenced both PU and PEOU. However, the communication between children and their parents only influenced parents' PU but not PEOU [19]. These results show that social influence plays an important role in parents' acceptance of information and communication technology (ICT) learning. Tsuei [19] highlighted the need to build partnerships between schools and parents for the successful integration of ICT learning.

## 2.2   Technology Acceptance Model (TAM) Variables

TAM and the Unified Technology of Acceptance and Use Theory (UTAUT) are the commonly used models to study factors that affect the acceptance of m-learning. In this study, TAM was selected because it is considered to be robust and it is mostly used model for the study of the adoption of technology in educational contexts [23, 24].

TAM expounded upon the ideas of the Theory of Reasoned Action [20]. Perceived usefulness and perceived ease of use are the two pillars of TAM. These two pillars predict users' attitudes toward the use, which, in turn, affect behavioral intention to use an information system [11]. Venkatesh [21] suggested that more variables that are context-related can be added to TAM to improve its explanatory power of the acceptance of the technology in question as further explained [13].

### Behavioral Intention to use (BI)
BI was defined by Fang [25] as," ... the cognitive representation of a person's readiness to perform a given behavior", and it is considered to be the best antecedent of behavior." Thus, TAM assumes that parents' adoption is determined by their BI to use m-learning [16].

### Attitude Towards the Use (ATT)
Attitude toward a behavior is defined as, "... the degree to which a person has a favorable or unfavorable evaluation or appraisal of the behavior studied" [26]. That is beliefs and attitudes play an important role in rejecting or accepting m-learning [28]. Parents' attitudes towards m-learning positively affect their behavioral intention to use [19]. This finding is congruent to the finding of Davis [11] and Dutota et al. [26]. Therefore, the hypothesis:

H1: Attitude toward use has a positive effect on behavioral intention.

### Perceive Usefulness (PU)
In the m-learning context, PU is explained as a person's perception that using m-learning will improve his or her teaching and learning [27]. One of the main factors behind parents' adoption of m-learning is the perception that m-learning is going to improve the performance of their children [16, 19]. Bourgonjon [16] studied the factors that make parents accept digital game-based learning and found that learning opportunities were the single best predictor of parents' preference for video games. If parents perceive advantages in using m-learning, their attitude towards the use of these technologies will be more positive. Therefore, the hypotheses:

H2: Perceived Usefulness has a positive effect on perceived attitude towards the use.
H3: Perceived Usefulness has a positive effect on behavioral intention to use.

### Perceived Ease of Use (PEOU)
In the m-learning context, PEOU can be defined as the extent to which users believe that adopting m-learning would be free from effort. When parents perceive that their children can use m-learning for learning STEM-related subject with minimum effort, they will have a positive attitude towards it, will realize its utility and adopt it. Thus, the hypotheses:

H4: Perceived ease of use has a positive effect on perceived usefulness.
H5: Perceived ease of use has a positive effect on behavioral intention to use.
H6: Perceived ease of use has a positive effect on attitude towards the use.

## Perceived Resources (PR)

PR is defined as "… the extent to which an individual believes that he or she has the personal and organizational resources needed to use an information system" [30]. Perceived resources was found to have a positive effect on PU, PEOU and ATT [31–33]. In the studies [31–33], researchers investigated the effects of the availability of resources on teachers' acceptance of ICT into the classroom. They found that lack of laptops, computer technical support from peers negatively affected the integration of ICT into the classroom. Mboweni [34] found that most of the rural parents rely on social grants and have financial problems. M-learning requires money for purchasing of devices and data. Basing on the results of Lim [31] and Mboweni [34], one can learn that rural parents' perceived resources will affect their PU and PEOU towards the use of m-learning. Therefore, the hypotheses:

H7: Perceived resources has a positive effect on perceived usefulness

H8: Perceived resources has a positive effect on perceived ease of use.

## Perceived Social Influence (PSI)

PSI is similar to the theory of reasoned action's subjective norm [20], which was defined as "… a person's perception that most people who are important to him think he should or should not perform the behavior in question". In this study, PSI is when parents of high school STEM learners consider the view of those who are important to them whether they should or should not allow their child to use m-learning. Parents of STEM learners in rural areas are influenced by messages about m-learning. This was suggested by Venkatesh et al. [21] who stated that people internalize the beliefs of other people and make them part of their own belief system. If parents think that their community, children, and teachers are expecting them to accept the use of m-learning, they would have a positive attitude towards m-learning. Therefore, the hypothesis:

H9: Perceived social influence has a positive effect on perceived usefulness

H10: Perceived social influence has a positive effect on attitude towards the use.

On the basis of the theoretical underpinning, a hypothetical model is in Fig. 1.

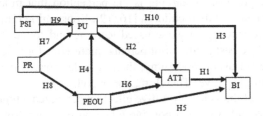

**Fig. 1.** The parents' acceptance of mobile learning model

# 3   Methods

## 3.1   Research Design

The research followed a quantitative approach, where survey demographic and opinion-related data were collected from parents using a questionnaire. Firstly, the data from parents were explored using descriptive statistics. Secondly, the partial least squares structural equation model (PLS-SEM) was used to test the hypothesized model.

### 3.2 Participants

The study adopted stratified sampling to collect data [35]. All high schools in rural areas in King Cetshwayo District were grouped using their quintiles. To ensure that homogenous elements form a stratum, schools in the same quintile were grouped. Three strata were formed. Simple random sampling was then used to select four schools in each stratum. Simple random sampling was also used to select 200 grade, 12 STEM learners, from the selected schools. The selected learners were given questionnaires to give to their parents and 129 (65%) valid questionnaires were collected. Using Chin's [36] recommendation of 10 times larger than the number of items of the construct with most items, the sample size exceeds the recommended 50.

### 3.3 Measures

Firstly, the parents filled in questions about demographical information. Secondly, respondents answered the main part of the questionnaire, which comprised of scales measuring the constructs of the model. The questionnaire was adopted from previous studies [19, 33] and modified to suit the needs of the current study. The measurement instrument consists of six constructs making a total of 25 items. The questionnaire was developed and translated into IsiZulu and distributed both in English and IsiZulu. The respondents were asked to choose the language they are comfortable with. All items were measured on a 7-point Likert-type scale with 1 corresponding to "strongly disagree" and 7 to "strongly agree."

### 3.4 Analysis Technique

Partial Least Squares Structural Equation Modeling (PLS-SEM) was used to analyze data making use of the software SmartPLS 3. One of the functions of PLS-SEM is the prediction of the target variable [10] in this case rural parents whose children are pursuing STEM's behavioral intention to allow their children to use m-learning. PLS-SEM was also used to assess the predictive power of antecedent variables. The study followed Chin's [36] two-stage approach of model analysis. First, the reliability and validity of different model variables were assessed to confirm the quality of the outer model. In the second step, the relationships within the structural model were assessed by testing the significance of the relationships, explained variance of the endogenous variables and predictive power of different variables [10].

## 4 Data Analysis Results

### 4.1 Measurement Model Assessment

The outer model describes the association between items and the latent variables. Convergent validity and discriminant validity of the outer model needs to be assessed [37, 38], in order to ascertain the goodness of fit of the out model. Convergent validity assesses the degree to which there is a high correlation between the latent variable which are theoretically identical, while discriminant validity assesses the degree to which a construct differs from other constructs [37, 38].

The results (see Fig. 2) show that almost all reflective indicators have loadings higher than 0.7 [37] except ATT1 (0.692), PR4 (0.612) and PU4 (0.671). The items were returned due to the exploratory nature of the study and removing them did not result in an increase in the composite reliability [37]. The results confirm item reliability. The results (Appendix 4) also confirm convergent validity as well, with Cronbach's alpha ($\alpha$) greater than 0.7, composite reliability (CR) above 0.6 and average explained extracted (AVE) values greater than 0.5 [37].

## Discriminant Validity

The heterotrait-monotrait ratio of correlations (HTMT) and the Fornell-Larcker criterion were used to assess discriminant validity [37]. Results (Appendix 1) show that all the root of AVE values were higher than inter-construct correlations and all the HTMT values were under 0.85 [37]. The results confirm discriminant validity. Overall, the indicator reliability, internal consistency reliability, convergent validity and discriminant validity tests conducted on the measurement model were satisfactory.

### 4.2  Structural Model Assessment

After ascertaining the suitability of the outer model, the inner model was examined, and the hypotheses were tested. Before assessing the inner model, the variance inflation factor (VIF) was used to assess collinearity issues. All the VIF values were less than 4 [39], indicating that there were no collinearity issues. Results in (Appendix 2) and Fig. 2 summarize the inner model and the hypotheses testing results. Figure 2 shows the $R^2$ of the model. The model explains 24% of PU 19% of PEOU, 43% ATT and 41% of the variance of rural parents' BI for their children to use m-learning. The variance explained in rural parents' ATT and BI is considered moderate, while, variance explained in PU and PEOU is considered small [36]. The results of Fig. 2 also shows the standardized path coefficients. The results show that all model's antecedents predict rural parents' behavioral intention to allow their children to use mobile learning for learning STEM. Results (Appendix 1) show the results of the bootstrapping procedure. The results show that all the hypotheses were supported except H3 and H5. Additionally, the results in (Appendix 1) show the effect size of these relations. Two relations (ATT -> BI and PEOU -> ATT) have large effect size, PR -> PEOU has a

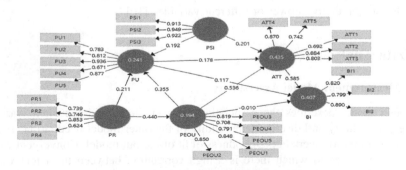

**Fig. 2.** Structural equation model analysis

medium effect size while the last five (PEOU -> PU, PR -> PU, PSI -> ATT, PSI -> PU and PU -> ATT) have small effect size. The $Q^2$ values range from 0.16 to 0.23, indicating a medium predictive relevance [37].

To answer research question 2, the observation of total effects (Appendix 3) was used. The results show that the best predictors of parents' BI to allow their children to use mobile learning to STEM-related subjects are ATT, PEOU and PR.

# 5  Discussions

RQ1: This study sought to examine the effects of PU, PEOU, ATT, PSI and PR on the behavioral intention to allow children to use m-learning for rural parents. The results show that the model was appropriate for determining the rural parents' acceptance of m-learning as it explains 41% of the variance in BI. It was found that all the antecedents predict behavioral intention to use m-learning. However, only parents' ATT has a direct effect on BI. It would be reasonable to infer that when rural parents have positive feelings towards the use of m-learning, these positive feelings will reinforce their intention to allow their children to use m-learning to learn STEM-related subjects. Parents' ATT mediates the effect of their PU, PSI, PR and PEOU on their BI. The results show some notable differences from prior adoption studies [10, 11, 13]. In contrary to the previous finding, PU has an insignificant effect on rural parents' BI [13, 19]. The results show that rural high school STEM learners' parents are not acquainted with the usefulness of mobile devices in the classroom. However, the results also confirm the finding of [19], who found that PU indirectly influences users' BI by the mediation of ATT. This might mean that even though rural parents have limited knowledge about the benefits that m-learning bring into STEM learning, that little knowledge they possess positively affects their attitudes towards the use of m-learning for STEM learning.

In contrary to the findings of Davis [11], the current study found that PEOU predicts ATT, better than PU. This shows that rural parents consider the effort needed to learn to use m-learning more important when adopting it than its utility. The finding might be due to parents belonging to the "digital immigrants" generation which struggle to use mobile devices to carry out specific tasks. The results also show that parents are not indifferent to what other people (teachers, society and children) think about m-learning, as their ATT towards m-learning was influenced by their PSI better than their PU. These results are line with the findings of Tsuei [19], who found that teacher-parent and children-parents communication influenced parents' technology acceptance. PSI also positively affect PU and BI by the mediating of ATT. The results suggest that rural parents value what people important to them say about the use of m-learning for STEM learning. Therefore, it is important for teachers and learners to provide rural parents with an awareness of the potential of m-learning for STEM-related subjects.

Regarding PR, the results show that it positively affects both PU and PEOU. The results also show that PR has an indirect effect on BI through PEOU and ATT. This finding was not surprising due to the rural environment in which the study was carried. Most of the families in rural areas are living in poverty and depend on social grants as their source of income [34]. It is also interesting to note that PR has indirect effects on ATT and PU by the mediating effect of PEOU. The results suggest that for rural parents, the availability of resources affects the usefulness and ease of use, which in turn affects parents' attitudes towards m-learning. The conclusion that can be drawn from these results is that, for a successful implementation of m-learning for STEM learning in rural areas, resources need to be provided. Based on the current findings, the following suggestions can be made to mobile developers and instructional designers and the Department of Basic Education (DBE), in line with Li et al. [13] and Nikou et al. [14] who studied learners' and teachers' acceptance of m-learning. Mobile developers should make m-learning platforms user-friendly and contain as much learning material and assessments as possible. This is because rural parents, teachers and learners consider utility and ease of use to be important when adopting m-learning. The DBE should provide resources needed for mobile learning. The researchers suggest that the DBE should supply rural STEM learners with tablets. Furthermore, the DBE should use offline portals to support m-learning in rural areas, make some partnerships with cellular network service providers to allow some educational platforms and websites to be accessed freely, this will remove the burden of buying data from rural parents.

RQ2: The ordinal strength of the predictors of rural parents' BI to use mobile learning is as follows: ATT ($\beta = 0.629$, $p < 0.01$), PEOU ($\beta = 0.374$, $p < 0.01$), PR ($\beta = 0.189$, $p < 0.01$), PSI ($\beta = 0.148$, $p < 0.01$) and lastly PU ($\beta = 0.113$, $p < 0.05$).

One limitation in the current study is that it focuses on parents of STEM learners. Therefore, the generalization of the findings of this study to all high school and primary parents of rural areas should be done with caution. Future studies should study perceived resources by clearly differentiating the different resources needed to support m-learning. It would be interesting to study perceived social influence to clearly determine the actual group (teachers, children or society) that affect rural parents' attitudes towards m-learning.

# 6  Conclusion

Based on the results of this study, contrary to the findings of Davis [11], only parents' attitudes towards m-learning have a direct effect on rural parents' behavioral intention to allow their STEM learners to use m-learning. Additionally, the results support the suggestion by Venkatesh et al. [22], who proposed that more variables that are context-related can be added to TAM to study the acceptance of an information system. In this study perceived social influence and perceived resources were added to TAM. The results showed that perceived social influence and perceived resources had a positive indirect influence effect on their behavioral intention to use mobile learning. The results also show that all the variables in the model predict behavioral intention to use m-learning. The predicting power of these variables is as follows: ATT, PEOU, PR, PSI and PU. The lessons that can be drawn from the study are that rural parents' attitudes towards m-learning and the perceived ease of use are the most important factors that they consider when accepting m-learning. This might mean that parents expect their children to be trained on how to use m-learning before its implementation. Furthermore, infrastructure, mobile devices and data need to be made available for mobile learning to be successfully adopted in rural areas.

# Appendix

**Appendix 1.** Discriminant validity analysis

| | Fornell-Larcker criterion | | | | | | HTMT | | | | | |
|---|---|---|---|---|---|---|---|---|---|---|---|---|
| | ATT | BI | PEOU | PR | PSI | PU | ATT | BI | PEOU | PR | PSI | PU |
| ATT | **0.802** | | | | | | | | | | | |
| BI | 0.630 | **0.837** | | | | | 0.748 | | | | | |
| PEOU | 0.600 | 0.392 | **0.805** | | | | 0.675 | 0.440 | | | | |
| PR | 0.243 | 0.160 | 0.439 | **0.744** | | | 0.288 | 0.192 | 0.527 | | | |
| PSI | 0.184 | 0.187 | 0.068 | 0.288 | **0.928** | | 0.204 | 0.208 | 0.084 | 0.365 | | |
| PU | 0.433 | 0.366 | 0.435 | 0.316 | 0.106 | **0.821** | 0.480 | 0.401 | 0.476 | 0.367 | 0.118 | |

**Appendix 2.** Path coefficient

| Hypothesis | Relation | Standard Beta | Confidence interval | | $f^2$ | P values | Result |
|---|---|---|---|---|---|---|---|
| H1 | ATT -> BI | 0.585** | 0.406 | 0.710 | 0.349 | 0.000 | Supported |
| H6 | PEOU -> ATT | 0.536** | 0.356 | 0.688 | 0.405 | 0.000 | Supported |
| H5 | PEOU -> BI | 0,01 | −0,171 | 0.176 | 0.000 | 0.922 | Not Supported |
| H4 | PEOU -> PU | 0.355** | 0.199 | 0.502 | 0.133 | 0.000 | Supported |
| H8 | PR -> PEOU | 0.440** | 0.294 | 0.553 | 0.240 | 0.000 | Supported |
| H7 | PR -> PU | 0.211* | 0.055 | 0.371 | 0.043 | 0.033 | Supported |
| H10 | PSI -> ATT | 0.201** | 0.073 | 0.314 | 0.070 | 0.006 | Supported |
| H9 | PSI -> PU | 0.192** | 0.078 | 0.264 | 0.044 | 0.001 | Supported |
| H2 | PU -> ATT | 0.178** | 0.037 | 0.313 | 0.045 | 0.034 | Supported |
| H3 | PU -> BI | 0.117 | −0,077 | 0.265 | 0.018 | 0.269 | Not Supported |

**Appendix 3.** Total effects

| Relation | Standard beta | Standard error | T-statistics | Confidence interval |
|---|---|---|---|---|
| ATT -> BI | 0.629 | 0.054 | 11.610** | 0.523–0.705 |
| PEOU -> ATT | 0.595 | 0.094 | 6.315** | 0.431–0.728 |
| PEOU -> BI | 0.374 | 0.075 | 4.977** | 0.246–0.492 |
| PEOU -> PU | 0.355 | 0.097 | 3.649** | 0.196–0.508 |
| PR -> ATT | 0.301 | 0.059 | 5.097** | 0.190–0.384 |
| PR -> BI | 0.189 | 0.046 | 4.098** | 0.109–0.254 |
| PR -> PEOU | 0.440 | 0.086 | 5.126** | 0.274–0.556 |
| PR -> PU | 0.371 | 0.090 | 4.130** | 0.217–0.505 |
| PSI -> ATT | 0.235 | 0.069 | 3.401** | 0.132–0.354 |
| PSI -> BI | 0.148 | 0.046 | 3.204** | 0.079–0.226 |
| PSI -> PU | 0.192 | 0.059 | 3.275** | 0.086–0.279 |
| PU -> ATT | 0.180 | 0.087 | 2.081* | 0.044–0.323 |
| PU -> BI | 0.113 | 0.058 | 1.966* | 0.027–0.218 |

Significant at $p^{**} = <0.01$, $p^* < 0.05$;

**Appendix 4.** Measurement model

| Construct | PR | PU | PEOU | PSI | ATT | BI |
|---|---|---|---|---|---|---|
| Cronbach's alpha (α) | 0.737 | 0.877 | 0.865 | 0.920 | 0.858 | 0.790 |
| CR | 0.831 | 0.911 | 0.902 | 0.949 | 0.899 | 0.875 |
| AVE | 0.554 | 0.673 | 0.648 | 0.861 | 0.642 | 0.701 |

# References

1. El-Deghaidy, H., Mansour, N.: Science teachers' perceptions of STEM education: possibilities and challenges. Int. J. Learn. Teach. **1**(1), 51–54 (2015)
2. English, L.D.: STEM: challenges and opportunities for mathematics education. In: Paper Presented at the Proceedings of the 39th Conference of the International Group for the Psychology of Mathematics Education, Hobart, Tasmania (2015)
3. Burke, L., Francis, K., Shanahan, M.: A horizon of possibilities: a definition of STEM education. Paper Presented at the STEM 2014 Conference, Vancouver (2014)
4. Chan, Y.L., Norlizah, C.H.: Students' motivation towards science learning and students' science achievement. Int. J. Acad. Res. Progressive Educ. Dev. **6**(4), 174–189 (2017)
5. Modisaotsile, B.M.: The failing standard of basic education in South Africa AISA POLICY brief: Africa Institute of South Africa (2012)
6. Makgato, M.: Factors associated with poor performance of learners in mathematics and physical science in secondary schools in Soshanguve, South Africa. Africa Educ. Rev. **4**(1), 89–103 (2007)
7. Criollo, C.S., Luján-Mora, S., Jaramillo-Alcázar, S.: Advantages and disadvantages of M-learning in current education. Paper presented at the 2018 IEEE World Engineering Education Conference (EDUNINE) (2018)
8. Kong, S.C.: Parents' perceptions of e-learning in school education: implications for the partnership between schools and parents. Technol. Pedagogy Educ. **27**(1), 15–31 (2018)
9. Pinker, S.: How the Mind Works. W. W. Nortan, New York (1997)
10. Sánchez-Prietoa, J.C., Hernández-Garcíab, Á., García-Peñalvoa, F.J., Chaparro-Peláezb, J., Olmos-Migueláñeza, S.: Break the walls! Second-order barriers and the acceptance of mLearning by first-year pre-service teachers. Comput. Hum. Behav. **95**, 158–167 (2019)
11. Davis, F.D.: Perceived usefulness, perceived ease of use, and user acceptance of information technology. MIS Q. **13**(3), 319–340 (1989)
12. Estrieganaa, R., Medina-Merodiob, J.-A., Barchino, R.: Student acceptance of virtual laboratory and practical work: an extension of the technology acceptance model. Comput. Educ. **135**, 1–14 (2019)
13. Li, R., Meng, Z., Tian, M., Zhang, Z., Ni, C., Xiao, W.: Examining EFL learners' individual antecedents on the adoption of automated writing evaluation in China. Comput. Assist. Lang. Learn. **32**(7), 784–804 (2019)
14. Nikou, S.A., Economides, A.A.: Factors that influence behavioral intention to use mobile-based assessment: a STEM teachers' perspective. Br. J. Educ. Technol. **50**(2), 587–600 (2019)
15. Saroia, A.I., Gao, S.: Investigating university students' intention to use mobile learning management system. Innovations Educ. Teach. Int. **56**(5), 569–580 (2018)
16. Bourgonjon, J., Valcke, M., Soetaert, R., Wever, Bd, Schellens, T.: Parental acceptance of digital game-based learning. Comput. Educ. **57**, 1434–1444 (2011)
17. Alshmrany, S., Wilkinson, B.: Factors influencing the adoption of ICT by teachers in primary schools in Saudi Arabia: teachers' perspectives of the integration of ICT in primary education. IJACSA **8**(12), 143–156 (2017)

18. Ford, M., Botha, A.: A pragmatic framework for integrating ICT into education in South Africa. Paper Presented at the IST-Africa 2010 Conference Proceedings (2010)
19. Tsuei, M., Hsu, Y.Y.: Parents' acceptance of participation in the integration of technology into children's instruction. Asia Pacific Edu. Res. **28**, 457–467 (2019)
20. Fishbein, M., Ajzen, J.: Beliefs, Attitudes, Intention, and Behavior: An Introduction of Theory and Research Reading. Addison Wesley Publishing, Reading (1975)
21. Venkatesh, V., Davis, F.D.: A theoretical extension of the technology acceptance model: four longitudinal field studies. Manage. Sci. **46**(2), 186–204 (2000)
22. Venkatesh, V., Morris, M.G., Davis, G.B., Davis, F.D.: User acceptance of information technology: towards a unified view. MIS Q. **27**(3), 425–478 (2003)
23. Park, S.Y.: An analysis of the technology acceptance model in understanding university students' behavioral intention to use e-learning. Educ. Technol. Soc. **12**(3), 150–162 (2009)
24. Teo, T.: Modelling technology acceptance in education: a study of pre-service teachers. Comput. Educ. **52**(5), 302–312 (2009)
25. Fang, C.S.O.Y., Kayad, F., Misieng, J.: Malaysian undergraduates' behavioural intention to use LMS for online English learning: an extended self-directed learning technology acceptance model. J. ELT Res. **4**(1), 8 (2019)
26. Dutota, V., Bhatiasevib, V., Bellallahom, N.: Applying the technology acceptance model in a three-countries study of smartwatch adoption. J. High Technol. Manage. Res. **30**, 1–14 (2019)
27. Cheng, E.W.L.: Choosing between the theory of planned behavior (TPB) and the technology acceptance model (TAM). Education Tech. Research Dev. **67**(1), 21–37 (2019)
28. Venkatesh, V., Bala, H.: Technology acceptance model 3 and a research agenda on interventions. Decis. Sci. **39**(2), 273–315 (2008)
29. Yorganci, S.: Investigating students' self-efficacy and attitudes towards the use of mobile learning. J. Educ. Pract. **8**(6), 181–185 (2017)
30. Mathieson, K., Peacock, E., Chin, W.W.: Extending the technology acceptance model: the influence of perceived user resources. ACM SIGMIS Database **32**(3), 86–112 (2001)
31. Lim, C.P., Khine, M.S.: Managing teachers' barriers to ICT integration in Singapore schools. J. Technol. Teacher Educ. **14**, 97–125 (2006)
32. Teo, T., Lee, C., Chai, C.S.: Understanding pre-service teachers' computer attitudes: applying and extending the technology acceptance model. J. Comput. Assist. Learn. **24**(2), 126–143 (2007)
33. Sivo, S.A., Ku, C.-H., Acharya, P.: Understanding how university student perceptions of resources affect technology acceptance in online learning courses. Australas. J. Educ. Technol. **34**(4), 72–91 (2018)
34. Mboweni, L.: Challenges and factors contributing to learner absenteeism in selected primary schools in Acornhoek. Master of Education, Unisa (2014)
35. Creswell, J.W.: Research Design: Qualitative, Quantitative, and Mixed Methods Approaches, 4th edn. SAGE Publications Inc., Thousand Oaks (2014)
36. Chin, W.W. (ed.): The Partial Least Squares Approach for Structural Equation Modelling. Lawrence Erlbaum Associates, Hillsdale (1998)
37. Hair, J.F., Hult, G.T.M., Ringle, C.M., Sarstedt, M.: A Primer on Partial Least Squares Structural Equation Modeling (PLS-SEM). SAGE Publications, Thousand Oaks (2016)
38. Salloum, S.A., Al-Emran, M., Shaalan, K., Tarhini, A.: Factors affecting the E-learning acceptance: a case study from UAE. Educ. Inf. Technol. **24**, 509–530 (2019). https://doi.org/10.1007/s10639-018-9786-3
39. Genc, Z.: Parents' perceptions about the mobile technology use of preschool aged children. Procedia Soc. Behav. Sci. **146**, 55–60 (2014)

# May the Change Be with You: The Need for New Roles to Support Flipped Classroom Development

Linda Blömer(✉), Alena Droit(✉), and Kristin Vogelsang(✉) ⓘ

Osnabrueck University, Katharinenstr. 3, 49074 Osnabrueck, Germany
{linda.bloemer, alena.droit,
kristin.vogelsang}@uni-osnabrueck.de

**Abstract.** The usage of digital media to provide learning content is becoming increasingly popular. One form of e-learning is the Flipped Classroom (FC). FC courses, however, are still heavily dependent on the commitment of individual teachers. Repeatable descriptions of approaches or institutionalized support are rare. The high amount of work involved discourages many teachers from using FCs. Strategic course development should therefore be conducted collaboratively by several stakeholders. Change management approaches offer a solution to deal with the integration of strategies for change and consider all stakeholder groups. This paper aims to combine an FC process model and a change management approach to include all stakeholders. Based on a literature review, we develop an integrative approach and summarize the necessary aspects of change. Our results show that for the successful integration and development of FC courses, we need new roles that support the process and assure the stakeholder's acceptance.

**Keywords:** Flipped Classroom · Change management · Stakeholder · Course development · Literature review

## 1 Introduction

The practice of teaching has undergone fundamental changes. The integration of technology for the supply of content and learning material leads to improved e-learning variants [1]. One method of so-called blended learning (BL) is the Flipped Classroom (FC). In an FC, the essential basic knowledge is supplied via online material and can be learned at home, while the in-class time can be used to train deeper understanding and application of the knowledge [2]. As the concept is rather new, much research only deals with siloed - and therefore, often heterogeneous case presentations [3]. Process models that present the development process are rare [4, 5]. Often, the FC is planned and proceeded single-handedly by the teachers. Supportive institutional structures are hardly ever available. The transformation of a traditional course is a time-consuming task [6] in which the teacher should be supported by a clear division of roles and tasks. The high amount of work involved discourages many teachers from using technology-enhanced approaches for teaching [7]. The role of the institution and its supporting duties are not defined [8]. Newly created FC design models fall too short, as they

© IFIP International Federation for Information Processing 2020
Published by Springer Nature Switzerland AG 2020
M. Hattingh et al. (Eds.): I3E 2020, LNCS 12066, pp. 532–544, 2020.
https://doi.org/10.1007/978-3-030-44999-5_44

assume a high intrinsic motivation of all stakeholders. However, research has already proven a resistance to change among students, teachers, and administration [9]. Change management (CM) that accompanies stakeholders and directs the change is often missing [10]. Due to the defined lack of applicable process models that include stakeholders and motivational structure, this paper links an FC process model with a CM approach. The aim is to present the possible connections between FC development and CM integration. Doing so, we will answer the following three research questions (RQ): (1) *Which CM approaches are considered in the current FC literature?* (2) *What tasks and recommendations to change, referred to as CM aspects, can be identified and linked to the FC development process?* (3) *What other CM aspects should be taken into account in a stakeholder-integrating FC development process in the future?*

Based on a literature review, we decide to link a CM model with an FC process model to disclose similarities between the FC development and the change process. We define how a successful CM can support the FC development process and foster the distribution of the tasks arising. Also, we emphasize which aspects cannot be directly assigned to the development process, but should nevertheless be considered in the sense of a successful change process. To achieve this, we have conducted a research process based on a systematic literature review described in Sect. 2. In Sect. 3, we will present the theoretical basis: The selected FC process model [11] as well as the underlying CM model from Kotter [12]. We then link the CM aspects derived from the literature review with both models in Sect. 4 and discuss supplementary aspects without direct reference to the FC development process in Sect. 5. Further research and limitations of our work are also covered in the section. The paper ends with a conclusion in Sect. 6. We regard the paper as a wake-up call for higher education institutions (HEI) to recognize the importance of a fundamental and managed change, involving all stakeholders, providing support and structure, and breaking down barriers.

## 2  Method

Our research process shown in Fig. 1 is based on a literature review [13] that leads to a merge of two different models.

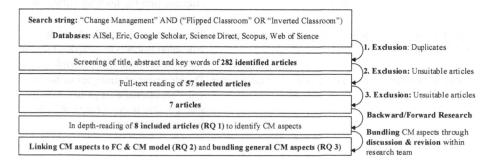

**Fig. 1.** Research process

The aim is to identify current articles and conference proceedings that deal with the consideration of CM during the development of an FC course and show which CM approaches have been applied (RQ 1) to identify CM aspects, that can be linked to specific checklist tasks (CTs) of the FC process model as well as to steps of the CM model (RQ 2) or be bundled to general CM aspects (RQ 3). We searched in six databases using the search string and limiting the results from 2015 to get only current sources. After deducting duplicates in the first exclusion, we identified 282 articles of which title, abstract, and keywords were screened for relevance. Reasons for the second exclusion were a lack of relevance to CM and FC or at least BL and a lack of quality when the source was not published as a journal or conference paper. We selected 57 articles for full-text reading rejecting 50 of them during the third exclusion which we carried out taking into account the criterion lack of relevance to CM and FC/BL, lack of relevance for HEI as well as lack of application of a CM approach. Afterward, we conducted a backward/forward research determining one more article as relevant for our study. Our findings are summarized in Table 1, in which the CM approach, the mainly addressed stakeholder (Ad. ST) and the primary goals of the paper are noticed.

**Table 1.** Considered CM approaches in current FC literature

| Author [Ref.] | CM approach | Ad. ST | Major goal |
|---|---|---|---|
| Berglund et al. [14] | Self-developed | Institution | Establishment of the role "pedagogical developer" to accompany the CM |
| Daniel et al. [15] | Self-developed | Teacher | Overcome challenges for teachers by training students as multipliers for digital learning |
| Collyer and Campbell [16] | CM model (Kotter) | Institution | Build a grounded theory for adequate technology adoption change support |
| Hurtubise et al. [17] | CM model (Kotter) | Teacher | Build a pedagogical strategy for FC implementation using CM methods |
| Hutchings and Quinney [10] | Triple helix model of change (Hutchings et al.) | Institution | Transform the learning experience and organizational culture to adopt technology-enabled learning |
| Quinn et al. [18] | CM model (Kotter) | Institution | Using CM principles to engaging students into the learning culture in e-learning |
| Van Twembeke and Goeman [19] | Self-developed | Institution | Examination of what leads adult education teachers to integrate FC and seeks to cultivate CM principles |
| White et al. [20] | Self-developed | Staff/teacher | Development of strategies to foster transformational change in teaching and learning using a range of active learning strategies |

The results of the literature review show that there are only a few articles taking into account a CM approach while developing a BL method like FC. This also corresponds to the results of other researchers for FC [17] and blended learning [18, 21]. In three of the eight articles, the well-known CM approach of Kotter was chosen. Most of the articles shown in Table 1 address the institution as a whole or at least teachers and further staff. We assume that an institutional anchoring and a distribution of tasks to clearly defined roles within the institution is needed. To identify such tasks, as well as recommendations to change, that should be considered in the FC development process, we continue to proceed our research as follows in this paper: First, we describe the FC creation process on the one hand and the CM process on the other hand. Therefore, we merge the FC process model [11] and Kotter's CM model [12], as Kotter's approach is the only one that is used in several included articles. The chosen models build the basis for assigning CM aspects derived out of the eight papers from the underlying literature review. To do so, we screened the articles for relevant CM aspects. We collected a total of 79 CM aspects, discussed the content within our team of three experienced FC researchers and assigned the aspects to the CTs of the FC process model as well as the steps of Kotter's CM model whenever possible. Doing so, we could link 46 CM aspects with both models (Sect. 4). 33 CM aspects could not be assigned to single CTs of the FC process. They were as well discussed within the team and clustered (Sect. 5).

## 3 Theoretical Basis

An FC is defined as a concept in which interactive, group-based learning activities take place in the classroom, while individual learning occurs outside the classroom [2]. Many studies prove the success of FC concepts [9]. Videos, podcasts, and reading assignments provide basic knowledge, which is studied individually by the students online [22]. The attendance time of the FC is arranged differently according to the needs; the main focus is on the application of the knowledge imparted online, problem-oriented and collaborative learning as well as discussions between the students and the teacher [23]. The implementation of the FC courses is heterogeneous and scientific findings, therefore, challenging to transfer. Many researchers and users in this field wish for uniform procedure models for the creation of FC courses [24]. First models for FC design came up, which primarily concentrate on content creation [4] and student learning [25].

**Table 2.** FC process model checklist [11]

| Phase | No. | Checklist task |
|-------|-----|----------------|
| Initiation | 1 | Define need and goals |
| | 2 | Estimate time, staff, and financial expenses |
| | 3 | Identify stakeholders (lecturers, students, institution) |
| | 4 | Weigh benefits and costs and make a decision whether FC is useful |

*(continued)*

**Table 2.** (*continued*)

| Phase | No. | Checklist task |
|---|---|---|
| Planning | 5 | Activate project team |
| | 6 | Train teachers |
| | 7 | Check if changes/plans are in accordance with university requirements |
| | 8 | Define learning outcomes and levels with the help of taxonomies |
| | 9 | Identify group of learners (context, diversity) |
| | 10 | Inform students in advance |
| | 11 | Prepare and produce material (choose media type) |
| | 12 | Choose in-class activities and prepare material |
| | 13 | Tune in-class and online courses |
| | 14 | Prepare learning analytics |
| | 15 | Check and provide resources (rooms, technical equipment, LMS) |
| Execution | 16 | Provide online material |
| | 17 | Continuous learning assessment |
| | 18 | Proceed in-class activities |
| | 19 | Monitor participants and learning success |
| | 20 | Steer according to students needs |
| Closing | 21 | Cany out exams |
| | 22 | Conduct formative evaluation (attitudes, perceptions) of stakeholders |
| | 23 | Conduct summative evaluation (learning success) of students |
| | 24 | Lessons learned |

For the instructional design of an FC that integrates CM, we chose an already existing FC process model [11]. As the FC process model has its roots in project management, we assume that further stakeholder can easily be included. Four successive project management phases initiation, planning, execution, and closing [26] describe the process and the activities of FC development. A supplementary checklist with CTs for each phase is shown in Table 2. During the initiation phase, the idea of the project comes up and has to be evaluated. Risks and impacts are considered for preparing the decision about the project execution. In the second phase, the planning, required resources are identified and plans for time, costs, and performance are developed. The third phase is often presented in two sections (testing and execution). Here the FC takes place. The closing phase includes an evaluation of the project and its output. Lessons learned are collected. Besides the practical implications of this model, we assume, the model profits from some enhancements to include stakeholder and their tasks from a broader perspective than the core teaching team.

The results of our literature research show that Kotter's eight-step process is the only established CM approach described in multiple articles. John P. Kotter's work is based on the experiences he made during the observation of several companies, which were dealing with the process of change. According to Kotter, mistakes can have a destructive effect on the whole change process. In his work, he focuses on eight errors, from which he derives the eight steps to transform an organization [12]. Figure 2 gives an overview of the steps.

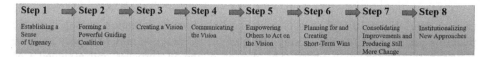

| Step 1 | Step 2 | Step 3 | Step 4 | Step 5 | Step 6 | Step 7 | Step 8 |
|---|---|---|---|---|---|---|---|
| Establishing a Sense of Urgency | Forming a Powerful Guiding Coalition | Creating a Vision | Communicating the Vision | Empowering Others to Act on the Vision | Planning for and Creating Short-Term Wins | Consolidating Improvements and Producing Still More Change | Institutionalizing New Approaches |

**Fig. 2.** Kotter's CM model [12]

Step 1 is based on current facts, communicated tactically to stimulate the formation of motivated collaborations. At the beginning of the change process, the acceptance to change from at least three-quarters of the management is critical to success for the whole change process. Excellent leaders with comprehension for the necessity of change are required. Step 2 underlines the importance of guiding coalitions, which rely on power. Numerous influential individuals are needed, breaking loose with former hierarchy structure and earlier formalities within their cooperation, working as a team – a steep challenge when they, until then, were used to reach goals on their own and therefore overlook the significance of such a coalition. Step 3 assumes responsibility to sketch and maintain the direction of change, defining a vision that is simple to communicate and easy to understand in a short time, inducing comprehension and interest and combining all single plans to a future perspective. The vision has to be spread through every communication channel, as step 4 demands. The change will fail without the support of many people, based on their trust in the change, willing to make concessions at their expense. Therefore, extensive and believable communication is indispensable, even if still not enough. Step 5 makes clear that in the following process, serious barriers to change have to be determined and removed so that people are enabled to adjust their organization on the vision. Step 6 deals with the relevance of diverse goals, that can be reached and celebrated in short steps during the change process. This short term wins have to be planned and created, e.g., to prevent people discontinuing or even start rejecting the change. However, once proclaiming a concluding triumph is dangerous, step 7 considers. In this process step, it is more advisable to go on with short term wins in broader contexts, taking care of organization parts that did not change yet, be aware of prospective recruiting and development and start new, more extensive projects. Step 8 anchors the change within the culture by communicating relevant circumstances that enabled the positive change and the resulting success and by anchoring the new approaches within the next generation [12].

We share Kotter's opinion that a vision of the change process can reduce the error rate [12]. Therefore, we link CM to an FC development to not just reflect the creation process, but also the process of change.

## 4 Consideration of CM During FC Development

We identified 46 CM aspects of which we were able to assign each of them to a single checklist task (CT) of the FC process model and to a step of the CM model by searching for parallels. This approach should be seen as a superior supplement to mere course development models. The focus here is not on imparting knowledge, but on the long-term integration of the FC course system, supported by institutional anchoring.

Table 3 illustrates the distribution of CM aspects and the connection between the two models. While 10 CM aspects could be linked to the initiation phase, 25 to the planning phase and 11 to the closing phase of the FC process, no CM aspect could be assigned to the execution phase. The phases of the FC process and assigned CM aspects are explained below.

**Table 3.** Linking CM aspects with FC and CM model

| | | | CM model (Kotter) | | | | | | | |
|---|---|---|---|---|---|---|---|---|---|---|
| | | | Step 1 | Step 2 | Step 3 | Step 4 | Step 5 | Step 6 | Step 7 | Step 8 |
| FC process model | 1. Initiation | CT 1 | 4 | | 2 | | | | | |
| | | CT 2 | 1 | | | | | | | |
| | | CT 3 | 1 | 1 | | | 1 | | | |
| | | CT 4 | | | | | | | | |
| | 2. Planning | CT 5 | 2 | 2 | | 5 | 2 | 1 | | |
| | | CT 6 | | | 1 | 1 | 5 | 1 | | |
| | | CT 7-8 | | | | | | | | |
| | | CT 9 | | | | | 1 | | | |
| | | CT 10 | | 1 | | 1 | 1 | | | |
| | | CT 11 | | | | | 1 | | | |
| | | CT 12-15 | | | | | | | | |
| | 3. Execution | CT 16-20 | | | | | | | | |
| | 4. Closing | CT 21 | | | | | | | | |
| | | CT 22 | | | | | | | 1 | 2 |
| | | CT 23 | | | | | | | | 2 |
| | | CT 24 | | | | | | | 4 | 2 |

1-5  Number of CM aspects linked with a particular CT of the FC model and a step of the CM model
     CT without linking to CM aspects

## 4.1  Initiation Phase

The first phase of the process model is the initiation phase, which starts as soon as a teacher considers to introduce an FC by converting an existing course or creating a new course. The phase includes all process steps from the first idea to the decision for or against the FC and the communication of the vision of the FC class (CT 1–4). Implementing CM is particularly crucial at the beginning of the FC development; Most of the CTs are closely linked to one or more steps of Kotter's CM model. At the very beginning, goals and needs for an FC (CT 1) have to be defined, which corresponds directly with the task to generate necessity for digital transformation in classrooms (step 1). The initiators should explain and justify the change [14] to all affected stakeholders at an early stage. Existing problems in teaching should be discussed in retrospect, and the need didactical change should be demonstrated [18, 20]. It is important to create awareness for the usefulness of the learning system, including the voices of industry leaders [16]. By creation an induction experience that allowed students to self-assess their needs and undertake development as required before the beginning of a course, teachers can motivate students for the FC [18]. The estimation of time, staff and expenses (CT 2) can be linked to Kotter's first step as well. From a CM perspective (step 1), Berglund et al. [14] recommend the establishment of pedagogical developers (PDs); Highly motivated teachers who work part-time as PDs to promote pedagogical development and facilitate cooperation and knowledge exchange among faculty members at the HEI [18]. The identification of all affected stakeholders (CT 3) can be linked to the first, second and fifth CM step. The FC initiators should demonstrate the benefits of FC teaching clearly and ensure teachers that support and training will be available for them and all other affected stakeholders (step 1) [16]. It is crucial to involve the relevant stakeholders for the FC transformation from an early stage. A guiding coalition should be formed, including not only teachers, students and administration but also technical support, faculty development leader and curricula designers (step 2) [17]. When involving the stakeholders, their diversity must be considered: Van Twembeke et al. found out, that teachers often feel frustrated when basic accomplishments were overlooked and not valued, especially because skills that seem self-evident for younger teachers might be hard to master for older or less digital literate teachers (step 5) [19].

## 4.2 Planning Phase

The planning phase includes all the tasks to organize the FC in general and in detail, involving the affected stakeholders in each stage (CT 5–15). Concerning the CTs, this phase is the most extensive. First, the project team must be activated (CT 5). Together they agree on an action plan, that can be subsequently adapted into a project management document, as a BL agreement (step 1) [18]. To connect a powerful stakeholder coalition (step 2) interdisciplinary networking should be promoted within and outside of the institution [10, 19] and connections should be formed between lecturers to share and extend knowledge and best practices [19, 20]. It can help to organize workshops to create and inform the stakeholders about the FC vision [18] (step 4). Also, peer-to-peer interaction is useful [19]. Peer assessment activities through platforms and peer-reflection about teaching and learning concepts and implementations between teachers have been proven beneficial for the change process [18] (step 4). To transplant the vision of the FC approach (step 5), regular meetings of involved stakeholders should be held at the institution [19] to exchange ideas, feedback, and knowledge. Furthermore, White et al. motivate stakeholders to overcome barriers (step 5) by constantly communicating "why" and "how" FCs should be implemented and point out the advantages and possible applications of FC methods [20]. To support teachers while planning and executing the FC (step 6), the institution can provide shared workspaces, where teachers can prepare new materials and have access to books and materials supporting technology-enhanced teaching [19].

The training of teachers plays an essential part during the CM process (CT 6). To assure the use of the systems, teachers, and students must have unrestricted access to the system (step 3). It implies that teachers, in particular, should be able to use the system in terms of content and technology [10]. Also shared vision and agreement on how the technical system will be used in teaching is needed (step 4). Therefore, the expected effort must be realistically estimated and communicated [19]. Specifically, the support and training opportunities for teachers should be developed and offered [14]. Training that focuses on teaching in the digital environment is particularly important [15]. The combination of technical and didactical training is a distinctive feature of FC [19]. These measures are necessary to remove potential barriers in advance (step 5). This also includes providing comprehensible materials, for example, in the first language [19], so that the necessary steps for electronic teaching are easy to understand [19]. To rely on existing, functioning technical tools and start learning the basics [15], can be an easy way to gather short-term wins (step 6).

To check if changes and plans are in accordance with university requirements (step 7) and to define learning outcomes and levels with the help of taxonomies are subsequent significant actions. These tasks refer to the instructional design of the FC. The underlying CM literature suggests no further actions taken focusing these stages due to the strong relation to the didactical part of the FC. When the learning goals are settled, the teacher should spend some time to classify the group of learners taking the content and the different preconditions (CT 9) into account. The consideration of the diversity of the students is a key to enable the overcoming of potential barriers (step 6) [19]. Now the focus is on involving the students. They should be informed in advance about the course and the requirements (CT 10). This also includes explaining the benefits of the course. In concrete terms, former students or practitioners can advertise and explain the benefits of the classes for their future careers [18]. The course can be advertised with these strong stakeholder alliances (step 2). Students are informed comprehensively through different channels [17] (step 4) and the information about the course is provided [18]. This step also serves to overcome potential barriers (step 5). Once the learning material has been created, and the corresponding media type has been selected (CT 11), the material can be made available to the students [18]. Here it is crucial to identify and remove potential barriers that make access to the material more complicated, such as technical barriers or language barriers (step 5).

The final CTs of the planning phase are again strongly focused on the interaction of the teachers with the students. Once the students' diversity is defined in advance, in-class activities can be selected, and the material prepared (CT 12). The current in-class activities will now be tuned to the online courses (CT 13). The preparation of the Learning Analytics (CT 14) is also based on the previous steps towards CM. The information used in step 7 is used here. This phase concludes with a final check of resources. Rooms must be booked, and the technical equipment should be available and accessible. The same applies to the learning management system (LMS) (CT 15).

### 4.3    Execution Phase

The execution phase is the most challenging part of FC development. Here most actions are taken that focus on the proceeding of the courses. It, therefore, seems somewhat surprising that we were unable to work out clear recommendations for action on CM from the selected literature. We see the reason for this in the fact that many CM measures have already been established at this point. Help structures regarding administrative activities and technical support should already be anchored. Stake-holders should already be informed at this point and follow a shared vision. New impulses from CM do not come to bear at this point. Instead, the team is now concentrating on the successful handling of the FC course. This includes above all the processing of CT 16–20: The online material is made available via existing systems. This is accompanied by opportunities for the students to continuously check their performance. The in-class activities take place at the same time. The teacher focuses on the participants and their learning success and steers his course according to the student's expectations and needs.

**4.4  Closing Phase**

The final phase of the FC development and implementation is the closing phase. This phase marks the end of the FC process. The teacher and the teaching team must choose an evaluation method (step 8) and decide whether formative (CT 21) or summative (CT 22) methods or a combination of both are appropriate. There is a need for the adaptation of evaluation and assessment methods [17] to the course settings. The collection, comparison, and dissemination of research results [17] (step 8) is proper preparation of the lessons learned (CT 23) from the past course. In forums, teachers can discuss recent events retrospectively [14]. For this purpose, however, a suitable framework for these meetings must be created. Within established sessions, teachers can share their experiences [19] and knowledge [15]. Networking should be enabled [18]. Also, the derived success factors are communicated to the stakeholders (step 7).

To raise the interests of future students, the opportunities that arise through the courses should be promoted. The arising advantages should be reported through appropriate channels [18]. The FC approach can then be expanded to other courses and programs within the universities (step 7). This means this phase is, on the one hand, the closing of the current course but also the first preparation for future courses.

# 5  Discussion

Besides those CM aspects that could be linked to the FC process, we found a total of 33 aspects which are more general and therefore cannot be clearly assigned to a single CT. Instead, they are ongoing tasks and recommendations that should accompany the whole development process of FC thus concentrate on the management of the stakeholders. We defined the following five categories for accompanying CM aspects that should be taken into account in a stakeholder-integrating FC development process: (1) *Care for the stakeholders:* Make circumstances for stakeholders as pleasant as possible [16], show appreciation [19], remove barriers like insufficient time and money [19] and compensate the additional burden of time on teachers through the use of trained students [15] or the support of Ph.D. students [20] during all phases; and also note the changes in the requirements of stakeholders during the various phases. (2) *Encourage teams:* Create a sense of community [14] and promote the presence of the guiding coalition [19]. (3) *Live the vision:* Create and use a vision [20] that gets a proper name and is distributed across different communication channels [18]. Consider an FC establishment from bottom-up [19], set and communicate goals [20], use motivational techniques [18] and activate committed stakeholders [10]. (4) *Offer permanent support:* Form a team for support [18] and provide necessary framework conditions [10]. Offer emotional support and encourage self-confidence of teaching staff [19]. Concentrate on established technological tools [16] and support voluntary participation of teachers [15]. (5) *Enable step-by-step procedure:* Implement FC step-by-step [20] by starting small, flipping one lecture at a time, executing pilots and preparing subareas [17]. Set intermediate goals [19], evaluate the progress [16] communicate the first results [18], and employ feedback loops [16]. Enable reflection [18] and promote presentations of cases and pilots [16].

In literature, it often remains unclear who exactly will take on the task to guide the change. As shown in Table 1, either the institution is addressed in general terms or tasks are assigned to the teacher. Thus, we call for new roles in HEIs, which overtake the task to guide the change and take into account the individual FC phases as well as the consideration of the entire CM process. Such a position could be located within the organizational development of HEI, initiate the change together, accompany stakeholders, and thus act as a present and responsive support.

## 6    Conclusion

By disclosing the relevant CM aspects for the change to digital teaching, we will show institutions how they can support relevant stakeholders in a targeted and holistic way during the change in the future. We combined two perspectives and merged them into one overview of how CM can be integrated to foster a successful FC development. Our literature research has shown that many authors have recognized the critical role of CM in the digital transformation of education.

Despite the merits of our model, we have to name some limitations. Although we based our research and the model development on well-prepared literature research, it is possible that models exist, that would be suitable as well.

The alignment of CM process steps and CTs to design an FC give hints for several stakeholders. Compared to the existing literature, we do not focus solely on the inclusion of the teachers and students in the FC implementation focus. We consider all different stakeholders. We assume the findings to be of value for teachers and teaching teams to implement new FC concepts or improve existing ones. The integration of CM to an FC process model is of particular relevance for researchers from the fields of e-learning, instructional design, CM, and Process Management, especially in HEI. For further research we would welcome reports about FC development projects, that rely on our findings. Furthermore, stakeholder specific action plans should be developed and tested. In the long-term, it could be of value to see how the strategic stakeholder-based FC development affects the satisfaction of the recipients.

Furthermore, the role and tasks of the institution are still somewhat unclear [8]. It would be the aim of future research to clarify the promotional and driving role of the institutions and to define the implications of the change for the stakeholders involved [21]. We claim here for the creation of new supporting roles like a teaching coach and teaching teams that are responsible for successful CM in FC course implementation.

## References

1. Güzer, B., Caner, H.: The past, present and future of blended learning: an in depth analysis of literature. In: Laborda, J., Ozdamli, F., Maasoglu, Y. (eds.) WCES 2013 (2013). Procedia - Social and Behavioral Sciences, vol. 116, pp. 4596–4603. Elsevier, Amsterdam (2014)
2. Bergmann, J., Sams, A.: Flip Your Classroom: Reach Every Student in Every Class Every Day. International Society for Technology in Education, Alexandria (2012)

3. Lundin, M., Rensfeldt, A., Hillman, T., Lantz-Andersson, A., Peterson, L.: Higher education dominance and siloed knowledge: a systematic review of flipped classroom research. Int. J. Educ. Technol. High. Educ. **15**(20), 1–30 (2018). https://doi.org/10.1186/s41239-018-0101-6
4. Lee, J., Lim, C., Kim, H.: Development of an instructional design model for flipped learning in higher education. Educ. Technol. Res. Dev. **65**(2), 427–453 (2017). https://doi.org/10.1007/s11423-016-9502-1
5. Oeste, S., Lehmann, K., Janson, A., Leimeister, J.M.: Flipping the IS classroom-theory-driven design for large-scale lectures. In: 35th International Conference on Information Systems, Auckland, pp. 1–12. Association for Information Systems (2014)
6. Karabulut-Ilgu, A., Cherrez, N.J., Jahren, C.T.: A systematic review of research on the flipped learning method in engineering education. Br. J. Edu. Technol. **49**(3), 398–411 (2018)
7. Gregory, M.S.-J., Lodge, J.M.: Academic workload: the silent barrier to the implementation of technology-enhanced learning strategies in higher education. Distance Educ. **36**(2), 210–230 (2015)
8. Shnai, I.: Systematic review of challenges and gaps in flipped classroom implementation: toward future model enhancement. In: Mesquita, A., Peres, P. (eds.) ECEL 2017, Porto, vol. 16, pp. 484–490. Academic Conferences and Publishing International (2017)
9. Bishop, J.L., Verleger, M.A.: The flipped classroom: a survey of the research. In: 120th ASEE Conference and Exposition, Atlanta, GA, pp. 1–18 (2013)
10. Hutchings, M., Quinney, A.: The flipped classroom, disruptive pedagogies, enabling technologies and wicked problems: responding to 'the bomb in the basement'. Electron. J. e-Learn. **13**(2), 106–119 (2015)
11. Vogelsang, K., Droit, A., Liere-Netheler, K., Hoppe, U.: Designing a flipped classroom course - a process model. In: Ludwig, T., Pipek, V. (eds.) Proceedings of the Internationale Tagung Wirtschaftsinformatik (WI 2019), Siegen, vol. 14, pp. 345–359 (2019)
12. Kotter, J.P.: Leading change: why transformation efforts fail. Harv. Bus. Rev., 60–67 (1995)
13. Webster, J., Watson, R.T.: Analyzing the past to prepare for the future: writing a literature review. MIS Q. **26**(2), xiii–xxiii (2002)
14. Berglund, A., et al.: The pedagogical developers initiative - systematic shifts, serendipities, and setbacks. In: Proceedings of the 13th International CDIO Conference, Calgary (2017)
15. Daniel, M., Hüther, J., Ohngemach, C.: Smile - Studierende als Multiplikatoren für innovative und digitale Lehre. In: Krömker, D., Schroeder, U. (eds.) DeLFI 2018, vol. 16, pp. 57–68. Gesellschaft für Informatik e.V., Bonn (2018)
16. Collyer, S., Campbell, C.: Enabling pervasive change: a higher education case study. In: Proceedings of EdMedia + Innovate Learning, Montreal, pp. 249–255. AACE (2015)
17. Hurtubise, L., Hall, E., Sheridan, L., Han, H.: The flipped classroom in medical education: engaging students to build competency. J. Med. Educ. Curric. Dev. **2**, 35–43 (2015)
18. Quinn, D., et al.: Leading change: applying change management approaches to engage students in blended learning. Australas. J. Educ. Technol. **28**(1), 16–19 (2012)
19. Van Twembeke, E., Goeman, K.: Motivation gets you going and habit gets you there. Educ. Res. **60**(1), 62–79 (2018)
20. White, P.J., et al.: Adopting an active learning approach to teaching in a research-intensive higher education context transformed staff teaching attitudes and behaviours. High. Educ. Res. Dev. **35**(3), 619–633 (2016)
21. Adekola, J., Dale, V.H.M., Gardiner, K.: Development of an institutional framework to guide transitions into enhanced blended learning in higher education. Res. Learn. Technol. **25** (2017). https://doi.org/10.25304/rlt.v25.1973

22. Said, M.N.H.M., Zainal, R.: A review of impacts and challenges of flipped-mastery classroom. Adv. Sci. Lett. **23**(8), 7763–7766 (2017)
23. McLean, S., Attardi, S.M., Faden, L., Goldszmidt, M.: Flipped classrooms and student learning: not just surface gains. Adv. Physiol. Educ. **40**(1), 47–55 (2016)
24. Giannakos, M.N., Krogstie, J., Chrisochoides, N.: Reviewing the flipped classroom research: reflections for computer science education. In: Proceedings of the Computer Science Education Research Conference, pp. 23–29. ACM, New York (2014)
25. Chiang, F., Chen, C.: Modified flipped classroom instructional model in "learning sciences" course for graduate students. Asia Pac. Educ. Res. **26**(1), 1–10 (2017)
26. Project Management Institute, P.M.: A guide to the project management body of knowledge: (PMBOK® guide). PMI, Newtown Square, Pa (2010)

# Preliminary Insights into the Nature of Graduate IS Programmes in Sub-Saharan Africa

Mark-Oliver Kevor, Richard Boateng[✉]🆔,
Emmanuel Awuni Kolog🆔, Acheampong Owusu🆔,
and Anthony Afful-Dadzie

University of Ghana Business School, Box LG 78 Accra, Ghana
Richboateng@ug.edu.gh

**Abstract.** Extant Information Systems (IS) curriculum research has focused on the nature of undergraduate IS programmes, particularly in the US and UK, eliciting calls for studies on graduate IS programmes and in regions beyond the US and UK. This study, consequently, looks at the nature of graduate IS programmes in Sub-Saharan Africa (SSA). Using a direct survey method, IS courses information were collected from the websites of top universities in SSA based on a 2019 webometric world ranking of universities. The course offerings from these universities are mapped to the competencies specified in the Global competency model for graduate IS programmes (MSIS 2016). The findings generally indicate, among others, non-adherence of graduate IS programmes in SSA to the MSIS 2016. The reasons for the non-adherence to the MSIS 2016 curriculum model is recommended for future research.

**Keywords:** MSIS 2016 adherence · IS curriculum · Adoption · Sub-Saharan Africa

## 1 Introduction

It is becoming well-accepted that the aim of information systems (IS) curriculum design and delivery is to prepare IS graduates with the skills required by organisations (Benamati et al. 2010; Topi et al. 2017). Recently, organisations have been concerned with the competencies of IS graduates due to the implications—financial and otherwise —of providing on-the-job (i.e. in-service) training to ensure employees can meet the organisations' competency demands (Anderson 2017). Stefanidis et al. (2013, p. 1) claim that 'there is an expectation that IS graduates possess sufficient skills to make their transition into graduate employment as seamless as possible'. As a result, organisations are gradually eliminating trainee positions and preferring to hire graduates with the relevant competencies (Anderson 2017). While this organisational dimension supports expansion and competitiveness, it poses a practical challenge for IS faculty and curriculum developers, who must work to meet the changing demands of businesses in the face of declining IS enrolment (Akbulut-Bailey 2012).

© IFIP International Federation for Information Processing 2020
Published by Springer Nature Switzerland AG 2020
M. Hattingh et al. (Eds.): I3E 2020, LNCS 12066, pp. 545–556, 2020.
https://doi.org/10.1007/978-3-030-44999-5_45

The IS community has responded to organisations' rapidly changing IS competency needs by developing IS competency models to guide the design and delivery of both graduate and undergraduate programmes in higher education institutions (Gorgone et al. 2006; Topi et al. 2017). While considerable research has examined the level of adoption of IS curriculum models at the undergraduate level (Andoh-Baidoo et al. 2014; Bell et al. 2013; Clark et al. 2017; Lo and Cruz 2014; Mills et al. 2012; Osatuyi and Garza 2014), there is less research on adoption and adherence at the graduate level (Apigian and Gambill 2014; Yang 2012). Moreover, much of the domain-specific research is predominantly conducted in the North American context (Helfert 2011), despite the fact that organisations' IS competency needs differ between regions and regional market factors influence the structure of IS curricula (Larsson and Boateng 2010; Kaiser et al. 2011; Clark et al. 2017). Yang (2012) suggested that researchers should investigate this topic in non-US universities, preferably in other regions of the world. However, in our preliminary investigation, we found no empirical research on the adoption of the IS competency model in Sub-Saharan Africa (SSA). Additionally, according to Yang (2012) and Apigian and Gambill (2014), few studies have been on the adoption of the IS competency model at the graduate level, only with the MSIS 2006 (Gorgone et al. 2006) and none with the global competency model for graduate degree programmes (MSIS 2016) (Topi et al. 2017) which is the latest of the curriculum guidelines developed by a joint committee of professionals specifying competencies required from an IS graduate. Quality graduate IS programmes in SSA presents an opportunity to develop contextual solutions to the myriad of problems challenging the region and other less developed countries (Syler and Venkatesh 2018). In view of these gaps, this paper seeks to understand the nature of graduate IS programmes in SSA and to assess the level of adherence of SSA IS curricula to the MSIS 2016 guidelines. The following research questions are posed: *What is the nature of graduate IS programmes in SSA? What courses are offered in graduate IS programmes in SSA to ensure that students attain IS competencies? What is the level of adherence of graduate IS curricula in SSA to the MSIS 2016 guidelines?*

The rest of the paper is organised as follows. Section 2 presents the background of the study, including an overview of the MSIS model and IS in higher education. Section 3 describes the research methodology. Section 4 presents the results and discusses them. Section 5 describes the relevant conclusions and suggests a direction for future research.

## 2    Background

### 2.1    Information System Programmes in Higher Education Institutions

Westfall (2012, p. 66) defines IS as a 'field that prepares students to interface between non-technical organizational employees and managers and very technical IT professionals, with a focus on functions that are unlikely to be offshored'. This definition, which we have adopted in the current study, underscores the relevance of understanding the content and curricula of IS programmes in higher education institutions. Research aiming to identify the nature of graduate IS curricula often starts by investigating the nomenclature associated with IS programmes in various institutions (Brooks et al. 2016; Cassel et al. 2008; Longenecker et al. 2015). IS programmes can be found within various departments of higher education institutions (Longenecker et al. 2015), and a benchmarking effort in the UK identified more than 6000 different names for computing-related programmes of study and over 150 different names for IS programmes (Cassel et al. 2008). Brooks et al. (2016) found that the terms IS, management information systems (MIS), computer information systems (CIS) and information technology (IT) refer to the same or similar disciplines, indicating that no effort has been put towards developing a naming convention or standard for IS education. Similarly, Pierson et al. (2008) compared the names of IS programmes in 2004 to 2007 to determine whether there was any convergence in the naming of IS programmes in higher education. They found that MIS, IS and CIS are the dominant names, but 20% of the programmes in the surveyed US schools did not use these names (Pierson et al. 2008). Given the aim of this paper, we believe it is critical to add to the debate on the identity of the IS field (Agarwal and Lucas 2005; Benbasat and Zmud 2003) and investigate the naming conventions of IS programmes in other regions. This will help researchers understand not only the identity of the IS discipline but also distinguish IS from other computing-related disciplines.

## 2.2  The MSIS Model in Perspective

In an attempt to maintain standards and work towards a core body of knowledge in the field of IS, a joint task force created by the Association for Computing Machinery (ACM) and the Association for Information Systems (AIS) developed a model curriculum for IS programmes in various higher education institutions. The most recent model for undergraduate programmes is the IS 2010 (Topi et al. 2010) and for graduate programmes is the MSIS 2016[1] global IS competency model (Topi et al. 2017). The MSIS 2016 model is a revised version of the MSIS 2006 (Gorgone et al. 2006), which was itself a revision of the MSIS 2000 (Gorgone et al. 2000). The MSIS 2000 and MSIS 2006 were developed based on the assumptions and principal characteristics regarding IS in the US and Canada. The MSIS 2016 was the first to consider the context of other regions, such as Asia and Europe. Moreover, whereas its antecedents provide specific recommendations, the MSIS 2016 is a meta-model that specifies necessary competencies and provides guidance for the development of IS curricula or models. This follows the recent emphasis on a competency-based approach to IS curriculum design and delivery (Sutcliffe and Chan 2004; Topi 2016; Topi et al. 2011). According to Sutcliffe and Chan (2004), this approach is more flexible than the course-based approach, which specifies that certain courses must always be taught.

The MSIS 2016 offers three categories of competencies: *IS*, *individual foundational competencies* and *core competencies* in a domain of practice. These categories cover broad areas of competency as well as specific competencies where appropriate. Nine IS

---

[1]  Heikki, T. et al. (2017) "MSIS 2016 Global Competency Model for Graduate Degree Programs in Information Systems," Communications of the Association for Information Systems: Vol. 40, Article 18. Available at: https://aisel.aisnet.org/cgi/viewcontent.cgi?article=3997&context=cais.

competency areas, 88 specific competencies (omitted in this paper), and 11 indicative foundational competencies are identified. Whilst previous models emphasised competencies in the business domain, MSIS 2016 recognises the applicability of IS beyond business and core competencies in other domains, such as health, law and government.

The MSIS 2016 specifies four levels of competency attainment expected from an IS graduate for each competency: *awareness* (i.e. the graduate is aware of the existence of the competency), *novice* (i.e. the graduate has enough knowledge and skills that s/he could perform tasks under supervision while developing the competency further), *support* (i.e. the graduate has sufficient knowledge and skills to work with others and support those with higher levels of competencies to achieve set goals) and *independent* (i.e. the graduate can achieve the desired competency outcomes without continuous supervision). A fifth level, *expert*, cannot be achieved with a graduate-level IS curriculum (Topi et al. 2017). Employees perform IS roles by applying their knowledge, skills and attitudes within organisational structures and processes (Peppard and Ward 2004). The MSIS 2016 prepares graduates to fill these roles by teaching specific competencies beyond the awareness level and provides curriculum profiles for the roles of Business Analyst, Business Information Manager, Enterprise Architect, IT consultant, IT Project Manager and Systems Analyst (CEN 2012).

Extant research has examined the IS curriculum model from various perspectives. One perspective looks at the presence (or absence) of a specific IS competency recommended by the model in a selected number of schools. Andoh-Baidoo et al. (2014) undertook such a study, examined business intelligence and analytics courses in 161 US schools accredited by the Association to Advance Collegiate Schools of Business. They found a considerable difference in the schools offering business intelligence courses and degrees in different departments. Another perspective looks at the IS courses offered by universities to provide students with specific IS competencies or promote certain career tracks. Studies adopting this perspective survey universities with IS programmes, and they can be exploratory in nature, be guided by a model or perform comparisons with existing IS model curricula. In separate studies of graduate IS programmes in the US, Yang (2012) and Apigian and Gambill (2014) compared a list of courses that universities required and deemed valuable with the MSIS 2006 graduate IS curriculum model. This study applies a similar approach, using the MSIS 2016 global IS competency model as the framework.

## 3 Methodology

To study the nature of graduate IS programmes in SSA, we adopted a direct survey approach (Andoh-Baidoo et al. 2014; Apigian and Gambill 2014; Bell et al. 2013; Yang 2012) and thus collected data directly from the websites of the participating institutions. Bell et al. (2013, p. 77) explained that direct surveys are advantageous because they focus on a 'specific program of interest, allowing systematic collection and quantification of data'. The top 50 universities in SSA were selected based on their rankings by Webometrics (2018), which is an initiative of the Cybermetrics Lab, a research group belonging to the Consejo Superior de Investigaciones Científicas, which ranks universities by region in order to improve the web presence of academic and research institutions. In this study, the university websites were accessed beginning in September 2018, when the academic calendar for most universities in SSA begin and updated course catalogues are provided. Only English-language websites were selected in this survey. The websites of two universities in the top 50 were in French and were therefore excluded. To fill this gap, we included the 51st and 52nd universities. Since our focus is on graduate programmes, only universities that offered graduate IS programmes were included.

Of the 50 universities included in the survey, 27 either did not offer a graduate IS programme or did not offer information about their graduate IS programme online. Furthermore, the Masters programmes of six universities are exclusively dissertation-based. Since such programmes do not detail the specific competencies a learner will acquire, it would be difficult to include them in this analysis. Five universities provided incomplete information about the offerings of their graduate IS programmes, and three were specialised universities focusing on, for example, health or agriculture. Nine universities offering graduate IS programmes provided complete data that was sufficient for this analysis.

The name of the programme, total number of courses/modules, minimum duration, presence of domain and IS bridge modules, university type, mode of instruction delivery and modules/courses offered within each broad competency category were recorded. These data were obtained from department websites, university yearbooks, rulebooks and programme catalogues. These descriptions were indicative of what broad competencies students were expected to acquire. The courses offered by the universities were mapped to the broad competencies specified in the MSIS 2016. Similar courses were combined into a common category (for example, systems analysis and design and information systems development). 'YES' was used to indicate that at least one course matching a broad competency category was found. For example, 'YES' was used for a university that offers only entrepreneurship courses, as these fit within the IOCE category, even if there are no courses teaching other competencies within the category. A descriptive analysis was performed on the collected data, and the results are presented in Sect. 4.

## 4 Results and Discussions

### 4.1 The Nature of Graduate IS Programmes in SSA

There is generally lack of graduate IS programmes in SSA. This may be as a result of IS being relatively new as compared to other traditional business and computing programmes and may be an indication of the maturity of the IS discipline in SSA. Nevertheless, the nine graduate IS programmes are offered by flagship universities in SSA. Flagship universities are "almost always public, often among the largest in the system or country, and a leading university in a country or an academic system which is looked to for influence and emulation" (Altbach and Balan 2007, p. 8) and relevant in the SSA context (Teferra 2016) to understanding the nature of graduate IS programmes. Again, Larsson and Boateng (2010) argue that different countries have different resources strengths, maturity and approach in offering IS programmes.

Consequently, of the 50 universities we surveyed, 9 offered a graduate IS programme or an equivalent programme with a different name. This result confirms other studies (Brooks et al. 2016; Pierson et al. 2008) suggesting that there is a lack of standards for the naming of IS programmes and emphasising the multidisciplinary identity of the IS discipline. The institutions and the names of the graduate IS programmes are summarised in Table 1. All are public universities offering different types of degrees, such as MSc, MBA, MCom and MIT, and they are located in six different countries in SSA.

**Table 1.** Summary of IS graduate programmes in SSA (Source: Authors)

| University | Type | Country | Programme name | Degree type |
|---|---|---|---|---|
| University of Pretoria | Public | South Africa | ICT Management | MIT |
| University of Kwazulu Natal | Public | South Africa | IS and Technology | Mcom |
| University of Nairobi | Public | Kenya | IT Management | MSc |
| Makerere University | Public | Uganda | IS | MSc |
| University of Ghana | Public | Ghana | MIS | MBA |
| University of the Free State | Public | South Africa | CIS | MSc |
| University of Dar Es Salaam | Public | Tanzania | Health Informatics | MSc |
| Mbarara University of Sci. and Technology | Public | Uganda | IS | MSc |
| University of Botswana | Public | Botswana | BIS | MBA |

The minimum number of modules offered is 6, and the maximum number is 20, with an average of 13 (12.88). This is not unlike the typical MSIS programme in the US, which offers 10 to 12 modules over three semesters (Topi et al. 2017). Three of the 9 graduate IS programmes offer bridge modules covering both IS and domain-specific competencies. Such modules are important to help learners from diverse backgrounds transition into the programme (Topi et al. 2017). However, this study did not consider the entry requirements for the programmes, and it is therefore difficult to interpret the absence of bridge modules as injurious. A summary of the number of modules and the presence or absence of bridge modules is presented in Table 2.

From Table 2, the minimum duration of a graduate IS programme is 1.5 years, and the average is 2 years for face-to-face (f2f) delivery (regular stream). In line with the recommendations for IS programmes to move beyond business domain (Gorgone et al. 2006; Topi et al. 2017), there is evidence that graduate IS programmes consider the education, geographic information systems (GIS) and health domains, although the business domain remains dominant.

**Table 2.** Summary of graduate IS programmes' characteristics in SSA (Source: Authors)

| University | Number of modules | Duration | Domain | Bridge modules | Instruction mode |
|---|---|---|---|---|---|
| University of Pretoria | 13 | 2 | Business | Present | F2F |
| University of Kwazulu Natal | 6 | 2 | General | Absent | F2F |
| University of Nairobi | 10 | 2 | Business | Absent | F2F |
| Makerere University | 13 | 2 | Business/GIS | Absent | F2F |
| University of Ghana | 20 | 2 | Business | Present | F2F |
| University of the Free State | 13 | 2 | Education | Absent | F2F |
| University of Dar Es Salaam | 14 | 2 | Health | Present | F2F |
| Mbarara University of Science and Technology | 11 | 2 | Health/GIS | Absent | F2F |
| University of Botswana | 16 | 1.5 | Business | Absent | F2F |

## 4.2 Courses and Adherence of Graduate IS Curricula in SSA to MSIS 2016

The results show that information systems development (ISD) and related courses are widely offered in graduate IS programmes in SSA. This supports Surendra and Denton's (2009) suggestion that the defining course in an IS programme is systems analysis and design, on which the core body of knowledge in the IS field depends (Baskerville and Myers 2002). The five most common courses providing IS competencies are ISD, IS Research, Strategic IS Management, IS Project Management and IS Security and Auditing. These findings are similar to those of other researchers (Apigian and Gambill 2014; Yang 2012). Yang (2012) identified IS Analysis/Modelling/Design, IT Infrastructure, Project and Change Management and Management of IS as the four courses most commonly offered in IS programmes by universities in the US, and Apigian and Gambill (2014) identified Database, Management of IS, System Analysis and Design, and Project Management as the most common courses.

We compared the courses offered in graduate IS programmes with the MSIS 2016 global competency model. To do so, we mapped the IS courses offered by the universities to the appropriate broad IS competency categories in MSIS 2016 (which are discussed in Sect. 3). The results are summarised in Table 3. The results show that courses providing competencies within the Data, Information and Content Management (DICM) and Systems Development and Deployment (SDAD) categories have a strong presence in graduate IS curricula in SSA. Fewer courses that cover competencies within the Ethics, Impacts, and Sustainability (ETIS) and the Enterprise Architecture (EARC) categories are provided. Moreover, little attention has been given to the categories Innovation, Organisational Change and Entrepreneurship (IOCE), Business Continuity and Information Assurance (BCIA) and IS Strategy and Governance (ISSG).

None of the graduate IS curricula completely followed the MSIS 2016 model. The most adherent curriculum differed by four broad competencies, and the least adherent differed by six. Four of the universities offer courses providing graduate IS competencies in five broad categories, three offer courses that provide competencies in four broad categories and the remaining two offer courses providing competencies in three broad categories. These results are not much different from those of Yang (2012) and Apigian and Gambill (2014) or from studies examining undergraduate programmes (Bell et al. 2013; Clark et al. 2017; Mills et al. 2012). Apigian and Gambill (2014) found that graduate IS programmes in US universities generally exhibited non-adherence to the MSIS 2006, and Yang (2012) found that course offerings differed from the MSIS 2006 in terms of one category. In a survey of undergraduate IS programmes in the US, Bell et al. (2013) found a wide range of non-adherence to the IS 2010 model. Moreover, a number of non-IS courses were required despite their absence in the IS 2010. Similarly, Stefanidis et al. (2012) found generally low adherence to the IS 2010 in a study of undergraduate IS programmes in the UK.

**Table 3.** Mapping of graduate IS curricula offered by universities in SSA to the broad IS competency categories in MSIS 2016 (Source: Authors)

| University | Core IS competencies (MSIS 2016) | | | | | | | | | |
|---|---|---|---|---|---|---|---|---|---|---|
| | IOCE | ETIS | EARC | BCIA | DICM | ISMO | ISSG | INFS | SDAD | Total |
| University of Pretoria | NO | NO | NO | NO | YES | YES | YES | YES | YES | 5 |
| University of Kwazulu Natal | NO | NO | NO | NO | YES | YES | NO | YES | YES | 4 |
| University of Nairobi | YES | NO | NO | YES | NO | YES | YES | YES | NO | 5 |
| Makerere University | NO | NO | NO | YES | YES | NO | YES | YES | YES | 5 |
| University of Ghana | YES | YES | NO | NO | YES | YES | NO | NO | YES | 5 |
| University of the Free State | NO | NO | NO | NO | YES | NO | NO | YES | YES | 3 |
| University of Dar Es Salaam | YES | NO | NO | NO | YES | NO | NO | YES | YES | 4 |
| Mbarara Univ. of Sci. and Techn. | NO | NO | NO | YES | YES | NO | NO | NO | YES | 3 |
| University of Botswana | NO | NO | YES | YES | NO | YES | YES | NO | NO | 4 |
| Total (YES) | 3 | 1 | 1 | 4 | 7 | 5 | 4 | 6 | 7 | |

The current study shows that IS graduates from SSA universities may not have the global IS skills specified in the MSIS 2016 and may require interventions to fill the gaps in their skills, which are associated with extra training costs and time to integrate into organisations, making these graduates less likely to be hired. This continues to be a subject of research, and relevant questions have been raised about the usefulness of the IS curriculum model due to the general non-adherence of universities and whether non-adherence can be further explored.

The results shown in Table 4 also reveal that IS curricula are beginning to move beyond the business and organisational domains, although these domains remain dominant. Previous studies on graduate IS curricula did not analyse domain competencies separately, but this study identified course offerings in non-business domains, such as health, GIS and education. No courses offered competencies in the law or government domains, as suggested by the MSIS 2016. One programme focused only on the core IS competencies, which we refer to as the general (GEN) domain.

No modules or courses provided individual foundational competencies, and it was not clear whether these competencies were embedded in other courses based on the course catalogues. Individual foundational competency modules were identified in a survey of undergraduate IS programmes in the UK (Stefanidis et al. 2012), but not they have not received much attention at the graduate level. A number of studies have advocated for the inclusion of courses in IS curricula that provide individual foundational competencies, including creativity and problem-solving (Martz et al. 2017), service learning (Jones and Ceccucci 2018), virtual teamwork (Chen et al. 2008), intercultural communication (Mitchell and Benyon 2018) and ethics and social responsibility (Harris and Lang 2011).

**Table 4.** Summary of domain competencies offered by IS graduate programmes in SSA (Source: Authors)

| University | BUS | HEALTH | LAW | GOVT | GIS | EDU | GEN |
|---|---|---|---|---|---|---|---|
| University of Pretoria | YES | NO | NO | NO | NO | NO | NO |
| University of Kwazulu Natal | NO | NO | NO | NO | NO | NO | YES |
| University of Nairobi | YES | NO | NO | NO | NO | NO | NO |
| Makerere University | YES | NO | NO | NO | YES | NO | NO |
| University of Ghana | YES | NO | NO | NO | NO | NO | NO |
| University of the Free State | NO | NO | NO | NO | NO | YES | NO |
| University of Dar Es Salaam | NO | YES | NO | NO | NO | NO | NO |
| Mbarara Univ. of Science and Techn. | NO | YES | NO | NO | YES | NO | NO |
| University of Botswana | YES | NO | NO | NO | NO | NO | NO |
| Total (YES) | 5 | 2 | 0 | 0 | 2 | 1 | 1 |

## 5   Conclusion and Future Studies

This research sought to identify the nature of graduate IS programmes in SSA and their adherence to the MSIS 2016. Notwithstanding a number of limitations of the study, the findings indicate that traditional business and computer science programmes dominate, although a few universities offer a two-year graduate IS programmes in SSA. The graduate IS programmes generally offer courses providing competencies in SDAD as well as DICM. Courses providing competencies in ETIS and EARC are rare in graduate IS curricula in SSA. Popular core IS courses include ISD, IS Research, Strategic IS Management, IS Project Management and IS Security and Auditing. Whilst this study did not consider specialised courses that provide competencies specific to certain career tracks, we found that the programmes included new domains beyond business. However, there were no specific courses providing individual foundation competencies. We observed different levels of adherence of graduate IS programmes to MSIS 2016. Due to the general non-adherence, many graduates of IS programmes in SSA may not have sufficient skills for the workplace. The reasons for non-adherence were not studied in this research and may be explored in future studies.

A descriptive survey like this, though valuable, does not provide rich insights into how faculties develop or revise graduate IS curricula. Future research could look at specific case studies of graduate IS curricula similar to those of Gupta et al. (2015), and Ramesh and Gerth (2015). Such a study would provide richer insight into the factors that enable or inhibit IS curriculum model adherence than provided by extant literature. These insights could help guide universities in planning graduate IS programmes in SSA. In addition, future research should use all specified competencies during mapping to provide a detailed view of which competencies are provided by courses in graduate IS programmes, moving beyond the broad competencies. Finally, although we compared graduate IS curricula to the competencies specified in MSIS 2016, it is important to understand whether those competencies are exhaustive and relevant to organisations in Africa, as this would guide its adoption or adaptation by universities (Larsson and Boateng 2010). A future study could consider the views of employers, employees and other stakeholders regarding the value of the competencies specified in MSIS 2016 in SSA.

## References

Agarwal, R., Lucas, H.C.: The information systems identity crisis: focusing on high-visibility and high-impact research. MIS Q. **29**(3), 381–398 (2005)

Akbulut-Bailey, A.: Improving IS enrolment choices: the role of social support. J. Inf. Syst. Educ. **23**(3), 259–271 (2012)

Altbach, P.G., Balan, J. (eds.): Transforming Research Universities in Asia and Latin America: World Class Worldwide. The Johns Hopkins Press, Baltimore (2007)

Anderson, D.L.: Improving information technology curriculum learning outcomes. Informing Sci. **20**, 119–131 (2017)

Andoh-Baidoo, F.K., Villa, A., Aguirre, Y., Kasper, G.M.: Business intelligence & analytics education: an exploratory study of business & non-business school IS program offerings. In: Proceedings of the 20th Americas Conference on Information Systems, Savannah, pp. 1–9 (2014)

Apigian, C.H., Gambill, S.: A descriptive study of graduate information systems curriculums. Rev. Bus. Inf. Syst. (Online) 18(2), 47–52 (2014)

Baskerville, R.L., Myers, M.D.: Is information systems a reference discipline? MIS Q. 26(1), 1–14 (2002)

Bell, C., Mills, R., Fadel, K.: An analysis of undergraduate information systems curricula: adoption of the IS 2010 curriculum guidelines. Commun. Assoc. Inf. Syst. 32(1), 72–95 (2013)

Benamati, J.H., Ozdemir, Z.D., Smith, H.J.: Aligning undergraduate IS curricula with industry needs. Commun. ACM 53(3), 152–156 (2010)

Benbasat, I., Zmud, R.W.: The identity crisis within the IS discipline. MIS Q. 27(2), 183–194 (2003)

Brooks, S., Gambill, S., Clark, J., Clark, C.: What's in a name? An examination of information system degree programs in AACSB international accredited schools. J. High. Educ. Theory Pract. 16(6), 66–76 (2016)

Cassel, L.N., Davies, G., LeBlanc, R., Snyder, L., Topi, H.: Using a computing ontology as a foundation for curriculum development. In: Proceedings of the Sixth International Workshop on Ontologies and Semantic Web for E-learning, pp. 21–29 (2008)

CEN: European ICT professional profiles (ver. 3), Brussels, Belgium (2012). http://www.ecompetences.eu/wp-content/uploads/2014/02/European-e-Competence-Framework-3.0_CEN_CWA_16234-1_2014.pdf

Chen, F., Sager, J., Corbitt, G., Gardiner, S.C.: Incorporating virtual teamwork training into MIS curricula. J. Inf. Syst. Educ. 19(1), 29–41 (2008)

Clark, J., Clark, C., Gambill, S., Brooks, S.: IS curriculum models, course offerings, and other academic myths/hopes. J. High. Educ. Theory Pract. 17(9), 61–68 (2017)

Gorgone, J.T., Gray, P., Stohr, E.A., Valacich, J.S., Wigand, R.T.: MSIS 2006: model curriculum and guidelines for graduate degree programs in information systems. Commun. Assoc. Inf. Syst. 38(2), 121–196 (2006)

Gorgone, J., et al.: MSIS 2000: model curriculum and guidelines for graduate degree programs in information systems. Commun. Assoc. Inf. Syst. 3(1), 1–63 (2000)

Gupta, B., Goul, M., Dinter, B.: Business intelligence and big data in higher education: status of a multi-year model curriculum development effort for business school undergraduates, MS graduates, and MBAs. Commun. Assoc. Inf. Syst. 36, 449–476 (2015)

Harris, A., Lang, M.: Incorporating ethics and social responsibility in IS education. J. Inf. Syst. Educ. 22(3), 183–190 (2011)

Helfert, M.: Characteristics of information systems and business informatics study programs. Inform. Educ. 10(1), 13–36 (2011)

Jones, K., Ceccucci, W.: International service learning in is programs: the next phase – an implementation experience. IS Educ. J. 16(4), 53–62 (2018)

Kaiser, K.M., Goles, T., Hawk, S., Simon, J.C., Frampton, K.: Information systems skills differences between high-wage and low-wage regions: implications for global sourcing. Commun. Assoc. Inf. Syst. 29(32), 605–626 (2011)

Larsson, U., Boateng, R.: Towards a curriculum adaptation model for IS undergraduate education in Sub-Saharan Africa. In: Molka-Danielsen, J. (ed.) Selected Papers of the 32nd IRIS Seminar. Tapir Academic Press, Sweden (2010)

Lo, A., Cruz, A.P.: The implementation of the AIS/ACM IS 2010 curriculum by top US universities: an analysis of catalogs and college websites. In: Proceedings of Twentieth Americas Conference on Information Systems, Savannah, pp. 1–13 (2014)

Longenecker, H.E., Babb, J., Waguespack, L.J., Janicki, T.N., Feinstein, D.: Establishing the basis for a CIS (Computer Information Systems) undergraduate program: on seeking the body of knowledge. Inf. Syst. Educ. J. **8**(2), 37–61 (2015)

Martz, B., Hughes, J., Braun, F.: Creativity and problem-solving: closing the skills gap. J. Comput. Inf. Syst. **57**(1), 39–48 (2017)

Mills, R.J., Velasquez, N.F., Fadel, K.J., Bell, C.C.: Examining IS curriculum profiles and the IS 2010 model curriculum guidelines in AACSB-accredited schools. J. Inf. Syst. Educ. **23**(4), 417–428 (2012)

Mitchell, A., Benyon, R.: Adding intercultural communication to an IS curriculum. J. Inf. Syst. Educ. **29**(1), 1–10 (2018)

Osatuyi, B., Garza, M.: IS 2010 curriculum model adoption in the United States. In: Proceedings of 20th Americas Conference on Information Systems, Savannah, pp. 1–11 (2014)

Peppard, J., Ward, J.: Beyond strategic information systems: towards an IS capability. J. Strat. Inf. Syst. **13**(2), 167–194 (2004)

Pierson, J.K., Kruck, S.E., Teer, F.: Trends in names of undergraduate computer-related majors in AACSB-accredited schools of business in the USA. J. Comput. Inf. Syst. **49**(2), 26–31 (2008)

Ramesh, V., Gerth, A.B.: Design of an integrated information systems master's core curriculum: a case study. Commun. Assoc. Inf. Syst. **36**, 301–316 (2015)

Stefanidis, A., Fitzgerald, G., Counsell, S.: A comprehensive survey of IS undergraduate degree courses in the UK. Int. J. Inf. Manag. **32**(4), 318–325 (2012)

Stefanidis, A., Fitzgerald, G., Counsell, S.: IS curriculum career tracks: a UK study. Educ. Train. **55**(3), 220–233 (2013)

Surendra, N.C., Denton, J.W.: Designing IS curricula for practical relevance: applying baseball's 'moneyball' theory. J. Inf. Syst. Educ. **20**(1), 77–85 (2009)

Sutcliffe, N., Chan, S.S.: A competency based MSIS curriculum. J. Inf. Syst. Educ. **16**(3), 301–311 (2004)

Syler, R.A., Venkatesh, V.: Growing doctoral education in Africa: the story of an online course at ICT University in Cameroon. Commun. Assoc. Inf. Syst. **43**(1), 1–21 (2018)

Teferra, D.: African flagship universities: their neglected contributions. High. Educ. **72**(1), 79–99 (2016)

Topi, H.: IS education: using competency-based approach as foundation for information systems curricula. ACM Inroads **7**(3), 27–28 (2016)

Topi, H., Helfert, M., Ramesh, V., Wigand, R.T., Wright, R.T.: Future of master's level education in information systems. Commun. AIS **2011**(28), 437–452 (2011)

Topi, H., et al.: MSIS 2016 global competency model for graduate degree programs in information systems. Commun. Assoc. Inf. Syst. **40**(1), 1–117 (2017)

Topi, H., et al.: IS 2010: curriculum guidelines for undergraduate degree programs in information systems. Commun. Assoc. Inf. Syst. **26**(1), 359–428 (2010)

Webometrics. https://www.webometrics.info/en/Sub-Saharan. Accessed 11 Mar 2018

Westfall, R.D.: An employment-oriented definition of the information systems field: an educator's view. J. Inf. Syst. Educ. **23**(1), 63–70 (2012)

Yang, S.C.: The master's program in information systems (IS): a survey of core curriculums of U.S. institutions. J. Educ. Bus. **87**(4), 206–213 (2012)

# Requirements for an eModeration System in Private Schools in South Africa

Vanitha Rajamany$^{(\boxtimes)}$ ⓘ, Corne J. Van Staden ⓘ,
and Judy van Biljon ⓘ

School of Computing, UNISA, Pretoria, South Africa
7232969@mylife.unisa.ac.za,
{vstadcjl, vbiljja}@unisa.ac.za

**Abstract.** Despite the growing importance of digitization in all aspects of teaching and learning, digital moderation (eModeration) has received little attention in research or practice. Considering the secondary school environment, no evidence-based requirements could be found for the development of a digital moderation system. This finding provides the rationale for this investigation into the requirements for an efficient eModeration system for IT and CAT assessments at grade 12 level in South Africa (SA). This study draws on eModeration literature as well as technology adoption literature to identify a set of pre-adoption eModeration requirements against the background of the challenges and benefits of eModeration. The research design involved a single exploratory case study with IT and CAT moderators as units of analysis. Qualitative data analysis using Atlas.ti V8 was conducted on the 61 responses received from an online survey and 4 responses received from a focus group interview. The findings confirmed the absence of customized eModeration systems. The main contribution is the eModeration requirements identified from literature and then refined by triangulation with the empirical findings of the survey. The research has practical value in guiding the design of eModeration systems for the school environment.

**Keywords:** eModeration · Quality assurance · Paper-based moderation · Technology acceptance · Annotation tools · Security

## 1 Introduction

eModeration can be explained as the use of electronic media to support moderation and the secure storage of student evidence; quality assure evidence of assessment; record results electronically and upload students' work to a secure site for moderation [1]. Van Staden [2] describes eModeration as an electronic quality assurance process using an online tool. The New Zealand Qualifications' Authority established the Digital Moderation Project for completing all external moderation online [3]. The objective was to submit assessments via an online digital platform by providing an application to support moderation practices [4]. However, there is no evidence of the successful implementation nor the efficacy of such a system within the New Zealand educational system.

© IFIP International Federation for Information Processing 2020
Published by Springer Nature Switzerland AG 2020
M. Hattingh et al. (Eds.): I3E 2020, LNCS 12066, pp. 557–568, 2020.
https://doi.org/10.1007/978-3-030-44999-5_46

In the SA context, Van Staden et al. [5] demonstrated the efficacy of an eModeration system which was successfully implemented at a higher education institution. However, despite the identified benefits of optimizing moderation procedures, reducing the time taken for moderation processes and decreased costs, the application of online moderation in the secondary school environment is limited. Paper-based moderation is still extensively used at academic institutions in SA [6].

Drawing on the existing work of Van Staden [6] and reports commissioned by the New Zealand Qualifications Authority [7], eModeration is defined as the electronic quality assurance of portfolio tasks by external moderators within a digital environment. This study draws on prevailing eModeration and technology adoption literature and empirical research in the private secondary school environment in SA to provide an evidence-based contribution to the requirements for an efficient eModeration system.

This study is structured as follows: an introduction to the study, a preliminary literature review of the requirements for an eModeration system and introduction to four existing technology acceptance models whose constructs formed the basis for this study, an overview of the data collection methods and the findings, an analysis of the qualitative data and the final section concludes this paper.

## 2  Preliminary Literature Review

*A preliminary literature review of the benefits, challenges and requirements from the literature are now presented.*

### 2.1  Benefits and Challenges of eModeration

The benefits of eModeration are directly related to the disadvantages of paper-based moderation. The latter is less efficient, both in terms of time and resources. For example, the resources required for transporting assessments to moderators and the space for archiving the scripts. Additionally, online moderation limits the loss of moderation reports and assessments (which are conventionally couriered [2, 9]), in transit.

Challenges and benefits identified from the literature are discussed in the context of participant responses in Sect. 3.3. The challenges relate mostly to the usability of the systems, e.g. judgements are impaired when moderators must manage different pages in documents [10]. Searching through different portfolios presents difficulties when viewing and comparing different candidates' work. Studies indicate that an annotation tool is invaluable in developing shared perspectives of standards in digital moderation [11, 12]. The limited accessibility of such tools increases cognitive demands on the educator and the process can become less reliable [11]. Additionally, teachers involved in eModeration must be confident in the use of the technology [1].

## 2.2    Requirements for an EModeration System

Technological developments offer the possibility of developing online tools for remote standardization of marking [13]. The following requirements for an eModeration system have been identified from literature [6, 14]:

- Reusability: existing content can be reused on different platforms.
- Manageability: refers to the ability of a system to track moderation procedures.
- Accessibility: stakeholders can access content without time or place constraints.
- Durability: unnecessary to redevelop content when new versions are installed.
- Scalability: minimal effort is expended to extend the system.
- Affordability: the system must be cost effective for the primary users of the system or based on free technologies so that the institution has no licensing issues.
- Security and reliability: each user should have her own space with email and discussion facilities. The privacy and confidentiality of each school's work must be guaranteed while all access to a student's private space should be denied.
- Usability: the tool should be user friendly and self-explanatory.
- Portability: possible to set up the system on another server without difficulty.
- Infrastructure: hosting institutions should have adequate infrastructure.
- Bandwidth: increased bandwidth will increase the efficiency of the system.

An important consideration is if the technology enhances task performance and if it will provide an e-Service to potential users. If there is a good fit between the task and the technology being used to complete the task, then there is increased probability of greater utilization which is important for online standardization. Online standardization has distinct characteristics and best results can only be obtained if the requisite processes are supported by the technology [15].

## 2.3    Technology Acceptance Models

Studies into the acceptance of technology stem from the sphere of information systems (IS). Various technology acceptance models for instance, Technology Acceptance Model (TAM) [16–18], Task-Technology-Fit (TTF) [17], Technological-Organizational-Environmental (TOE) [19] and the Human, Organization and Technology (HOT-Fit) model [20] exist in IS literature. A challenge is that technology acceptance models relate to existing system use while the context for this study is the pre-adoption of an eModeration system. The basic premise of these models is summarized in Table 1.

See Rajamany, Van Staden and Van Biljon [26] for a detailed comparison of the pre-adoption constructs of these models, namely TAM, TTF, TOE and HOTFIT. A table (cf. https://cutt.ly/NetW0jq) was created to determine the commonality of the constructs amongst the models as well as commonality with constructs mentioned by respondents to the survey and comments made by focus group participants. The constructs were prioritized by centrality, i.e. those occurring across all three data streams formed the basis for the extraction of final requirements for an eModeration system.

**Table 1.** Summarized Theoretical models

| Model | Fit between human and technology |
|---|---|
| TAM | Users will not readily accept a system, irrespective of how efficient the system is, if they cannot immediately identify tangible benefits in their job performance as a direct result of utilizing the system [23] |
| TTF | An IT system will be used only if the functionality supports the user's activities. Any system not offering sufficient support will therefore, by extension, not be utilized [24] |
| TOE | Technological, environmental and organizational factors influence ICT adoption [19] |
| HOT-Fit | The user, technologies and organizational contexts cumulatively affect the net benefits of using an IS. Human, organizational and technical elements should have a mutual alignment to ensure successful implementation [25] |

# 3    Data Collection and Findings

The pragmatist philosophy views research as a human experience based on the beliefs of individual researchers [27]. Pragmatism proposes a philosophy extending beyond "what works" [28] and encourages an inquiry based process of searching for knowledge with the aim of solving societal problems. Pragmatism is particularly suitable for the current study as it is envisaged that the resulting body of knowledge will inform future practices and policies within schools and assessment bodies.

The literature review informed the design of a customized questionnaire developed using Google forms and distributed via email to teachers at private schools in SA. The online survey captured qualitative and quantitative data. The responses to the open-ended questions (qualitative) provided a basis for the structuring of the questions for a focus group interview conducted with 4 moderators.

Focus group interviews explore the attitudes and perceptions of a homogeneous group of people focused on a given issue [29] and use a purposeful sample composed of information-rich participants resulting in a greater sharing of insights [27, 28]. The demographics of the survey population is depicted in Table 2. The survey was

**Table 2.** Participant *Demographics*

| Role (N= 61) | % |
|---|---|
| IT Educator | 53,20% |
| CAT educator | 24,20% |
| CAT and IT educator | 6.4% |
| Cluster moderator | 3,30% |
| Regional moderator | 4,90% |
| National moderator | 6,60% |
| Other | 1,40% |

| Technology Experience (N = 61) | % |
|---|---|
| < 1 year | 3,30% |
| 1 - 5 years | 8,30% |
| 6 - 10 years | 8,30% |
| > 10 years | 80% |

distributed to 122 IT and 145 CAT teachers in private schools via email; 61 of whom responded. Focus group participants (N = 4) were moderators who volunteered to participate after being contacted via email.

Both qualitative and quantitative data was collected, but due to space constraints only the qualitative data is reported on. The survey contained open-ended questions requiring participants to express their opinions on the challenges and benefits of current moderation practices and the perceived challenges, benefits and requirements of an eModeration system. The data from the survey and the focus group was analyzed thematically where a theme is considered to be a coherent and meaningful pattern in the data which captures an important aspect about the data in relation to the research question [31].

Section 3.1 presents the findings from the survey, Sect. 3.2 presents the findings from the focus group and Sect. 3.3 presents an integrated analysis of the findings.

## 3.1 Qualitative Findings from Survey

Participants' comments around the challenges and benefits of current moderation practices and the perceived challenges, benefits and requirements for an eModeration system were imported into Atlas.ti V8. Words which appeared most frequently were used to identify themes around which the discussion of the findings is structured.

- **Challenges of current moderation practices:** The greatest challenge is that it is time consuming to scan portfolios before uploading these documents digitally. Huge amounts of paper is wasted when moderating manually. A related challenge of paper-based moderation is that of *"inconsistent record-keeping"* and the fear of losing evidence of moderation. Together with the costs of paper, printing and other consumables, costs are incurred when portfolios are couriered to *"out of town"* schools.
- **Benefits of current moderation practices:** Participants' responses were mostly positive for those who use some form of digital moderation. The most frequent response was that Google Drive or Google docs are used for moderation processes. Respondents agreed that it is easy and effortless to use Google Drive. Feedback is timely and eModeration is especially convenient when the school is in a rural area. A related benefit is that eModeration reduces the costs of transporting or posting portfolios.
- **Challenges of eModeration:** The most common challenge was Internet connectivity. Additional challenges: differing file formats, access to necessary resources like scanners, a knowledge of the system, versioning problems, the time required to learn to use the system and the time consumed in scanning the necessary documents. A respondent mentioned *"Annotation of content."* However, it is not evident if the reference was to the availability of the tools or the knowledge required to use these tools. A significant finding is that although some respondents indicated using a digital moderation process as evidenced by the following: *"I have been using an eModeration system for the past 3 years and will never go back to a paper-based system again"*, other respondents responded as: *"I have only used Google Docs and am Will (sic) be honest to say I do not know what an eModeration system is."*

- **Perceived benefits of an eModeration system:** ease of use, faster feedback, cheaper than couriering portfolios, faster to find digital files, easy to upload files.
- **Requirements for an eModeration system:** Respondents mentioned Internet bandwidth, multiple access and reliability but did not expand on these aspects. The requirements for an eModeration system are summarized using the specific quotations of respondents:


- Connection availability: "A good internet connection and a secure drop site."
- Connection speed: "Fast connection speed."
- Additional resources: "Equipment. Good quality scanner which can handle bulk scanning."
- Attitude: "A positive attitude towards the use of this technology."
- Availability of system: "Being always available."
- Annotation: "Annotation that will allow for different moderation styles."
- Communication: "It should make communication easier."
- Ease of use: "An easy to use interface with standardized organization for files and folders."
- Flexibility: "Flexibility so one can moderate one section only or start at the back."
- Responsiveness: "The system needs to be responsive and not have huge amounts of latency."
- Security: "There should be sufficient security to ensure that the portfolios can only be seen by the school and relevant moderator."
- Timely feedback: "It should save me time. It should also give you feedback as to whether the other person is actively involved in the moderation process."

### 3.2   Focus Group Findings

The focus group interview was structured around themes that emerged from the responses to the open-ended questions in the questionnaire. Participants' responses were loaded into QDA Miner Lite and the various subthemes were analyzed. The significant findings for each theme are summarized as:

- **Challenges of current moderation practices:** turn-around time; more difficult to keep track of hard copies; physical waste of resources; security; slow and inflexible.
- **Challenges of manual moderation:** easier to lose hard copies; physical waste of resources; many drafts must be done on paper.
- **Challenges of eModeration:** resistance to change; competence; file formats; document formatting; time taken for feedback; slow to download files; need for many screens.
- **eModeration vs Manual Moderation:** easier to track, view and review changes on a digital version; eModeration takes longer than manual moderation.
- **Benefits of eModeration:** easier to contact the moderator.
- **Requirements for an efficient eModeration system**: more than one screen; multiple views; revision histories; easy to use and advanced annotation software; voice over to leave a comment; a call button for communication.

While the consensus was that scanning of documents is time consuming, participants acknowledged that *"the pen and paper connection"* is important. However, the issue of security pertaining to written assessments cannot be trivialized. Focus group participants agreed that security is the largest challenge posed by paper-based moderation. A qualitative analysis of the data indicates that the frequency at which security was mentioned in the context of paper-based moderation is 30%.

## 3.3    Integrated Data Analysis

*In this section, the challenges, benefits and requirements are synthesized from the literature and data obtained from the survey and focus group interview.*

*– Challenges.*

*Cost:* An electronic moderation system requires additional technology like scanners thus increasing the initial costs [6].

*Infrastructure:* The ICT infrastructure necessary to develop digital portfolios is a particular challenge [12, 32]. A good computer network capable of high-speed uploading and downloading of projects is essential. Instability in the network can create challenges for uploading projects. Having appropriate access to the schools' network systems is also important [1]. Focus group interviewees agree that the Internet connection hampers the process by slowing down the downloading of files as evidenced by participant B's response: *"the frustration is waiting for the assessment to load which slows down the process."*

*Technology and Availability of Resources:* Technological limitations can hamper the implementation of eModeration systems [33]. Focus group participants concur, indicating: *"At this stage technology is failing the process."* Although all participants are from private schools, the assumption that all schools are equally resourced cannot be made. Hence available resources at individual schools play a significant role in the efficacy of eModeration. It is therefore reasonable to assume that the lack of adequate resources could be a limiting factor in digital moderation.

*Training:* Making comparative and holistic judgements of students' work is a critical aspect of moderation [33]. Participants A and B stated that *"Having to highlight on a pdf or add a comment box to annotate a pdf requires the person moderating to be trained on the technology."* Additionally, participant C indicated that *"A challenge is that people are resistant to being trained on a new technology."* These statements confirm literature findings that assessors' approach to online standardization may be hampered by discomfort in using technology and the skills required to interact with an eModeration system [8, 34]. Contrary to literature findings, none of the survey respondents indicated discomfort in using technology. A factor in the contradiction between the findings of this study and the literature reviewed is that respondents were teachers whose professions require prowess in using digital resources. Whereas the literature generalized the challenges to all educators, the survey and focus group in this study isolated IT and CAT educators. It is thus not surprising that these teachers would either be proficient or possess the motivation to learn how to use unfamiliar technology.

*Confidentiality and Reliability:* Participants concurred with Van Staden [9] that physical copies can easily be misplaced leading to issues around confidentiality. If one misplaces a learner's work, then there is no evidence of submission which creates the added problem of reliability. With eModeration, proof of moderation is easily available with tracked changes.

*Time:* Turnaround time is a challenge of paper-based moderation. Many drafts must be done; involving rewriting information. Data from the focus group and the survey confirms Van Staden's [9] findings that moderators prefer to use an eModeration system. For instance, participant A indicated: *"tending towards digital because of poor security with paper"* while participant B indicated that *"digital moderation is preferable because there is an audit trail"* and a survey respondent stated, *"I prefer sending a digital portfolio for moderation that (sic) making endless copies for each student file."*

Contrary to the assertion that electronic development and storage of evidence results in greater flexibility, convenience and accessibility [34], participant A indicated that the *"loss of flexibility is huge with digital moderation."* However, upon further interrogation it was determined that this view was being expressed on current moderation practices as evidenced by: *"the way in which it is currently being done is slow and inflexible."* This result is not surprising given that there is no standard, usable dedicated eModeration system in place.

## – Benefits of eModeration

Summarized benefits are: typing comments is faster; easy to create a reusable bank of comments reducing the amount of work and time taken; better quality; eliminates the possibility of mistakes; easy to determine if changes have been made. Feedback is faster as evident by the comment *"reduces the time of couriering moderation documents and having to wait for the results to be delivered. With digital moderation, as soon as the submit button is clicked, all parties concerned receive notification."*

## – Requirements of an eModeration System

Based on the results from the survey and focus group interview, the perceived requirements for an eModeration system can be summarized as: need for multiple views, easy to use annotation tools, effective communication, security, availability and flexibility.

Responses from the focus group strongly confirm the literature findings; with participants mentioning multiple views and having *"more than one screen"* so that *"all relevant documents can be viewed side by side"* with great frequency. Additionally, participants indicated that *"these views should also show revision histories"* and that it would be useful to have *"one document with all changes made right from the first version."*

Consistent with the findings discussed in Sect. 2.1, focus group participants indicated that an eModeration system should include easy to use *"top tier"* annotation software; a sentiment echoed by respondents of the survey. For instance: *"Annotation has to be quick and simple to use."*

The privacy and confidentiality of each school's work must be guaranteed while all access to a student's private space should be denied [6]. This important theme of security recurs in the data extracted from additional comments provided by respondents to the survey. The statements *"Security - papers may not leak."* and *"Security for the documents using a per session key of suitable length that changes for each session"* are representative of statements made by these respondents.

Contrary to the results from the literature reviewed and the survey responses, and despite security being a recurrent theme during the discussion on manual moderation, it was surprising that security was not overtly mentioned when participants were asked to elaborate on the requirements for an eModeration system. A possible explanation for this contradiction is that while security is a huge issue from the organization's perspective; it is not necessarily an issue that directly impacts users of the system. The focus seems to be on convenience and flexibility of use rather than on essential aspects. It seems reasonable therefore to conclude that users focus on aspects that affect them directly as evidenced by the frequency of hardware requirements being mentioned. This evidence supports the technology adoption theories which form the theoretical basis for this study as summarized in Table 1.

Participants not overtly mentioning security as a requirement does not in any way detract from security being a critical requirement in eModeration. During the initial selection of constructs, security was recognized as a critical component. Despite no questions being structured around security, the lack of security in paper-based moderation was repeatedly discussed. Therefore, security is an essential requirement for an eModeration system.

Additional requirements which were not evident in the literature reviewed were phrased as follows by focus group participants:

- *"Should allow for a voice over so that it is easy for the moderator to leave a comment."*
- *"Have a call button for both the assessor and the moderator to "meet" instead of back and forth communication i.e. multi-user communication technology."*

## 4   Structured Requirements for an eModeration System

In determining the requirements for an efficient eModeration system, the broad categories of User Requirements (UR); Task Requirements (TR) and System Requirements (SR) were identified as depicted in Fig. 1 (see Rajamany, Van Staden and Van Biljon [26] for a full-sized diagram).

Based on the findings, it was deemed useful to replace *attitude* by *self-efficacy*. *Accuracy* was replaced by *audit trail* as this was the context in which participants viewed the accurate keeping of records. *Ease of learning* was removed as it was specific to literature. The assumption is that participants are skilled as well as experienced (cf. Table 2) in the use of technological resources. The survey results indicate that 70% of the participants believe that they have the capacity to learn to use a new system. The categorization of *flexibility* was based on the system supporting different file formats. It is thus necessary to support paperless work and other formats like videos [14].

Based on the context in which participants described constructs, *Productivity* and *Work* volume were merged into *Productivity*. *Job effects* and *Time consumed* were

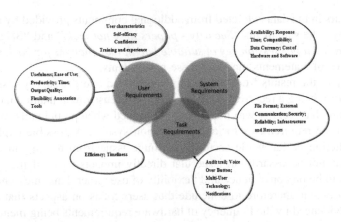

**Fig. 1.** Diagram depicting structured requirements

merged into *Time*. *Confidence* was removed and *Self-Efficacy* was retained and assumed to encompass confidence. After the analysis, core technological characteristics that were initially left out of the survey were added to the requirements. Context specific items, for instance a voice over button arising from the focus group interview, were added. The identified dimensions were then analyzed further. Dimensions present in 2 or more streams of evidence (literature review, survey and focus group) were included. These values were categorized under UR, SR or TR; with some overlap. For instance, file formats was categorized as both SR and TR. User characteristics inform UR. It was thus deemed necessary to include a separate dimension for user characteristics.

## 5    Conclusion

This paper addresses the lack of eModeration requirements for secondary schools. A single exploratory case study strategy was employed to determine the challenges, benefits and requirements of an eModeration system with the purpose of identifying requirements for an eModeration system. Empirical data was collected from a focus group interview and an online survey to investigate the current moderation practices of IT and CAT teachers at private secondary schools in SA and triangulate the findings with the challenges, benefits and requirements abstracted from literature. The requirements for an eModeration system (presented under the categories of UR, TR and SR) constitute the theoretical contribution of the study. The pre-adoption attributes could be useful to designers and developers of eModeration systems and hence constitute a practical contribution.

**Acknowledgement.** This paper is based on the research supported by the South African Research Chairs Initiative of the Department of Science and Technology and National Research Foundation of South Africa (Grant No. 98564).

# References

1. Lynch, G.: GCSE ICT E-moderation pilot case study. The e-Assessment Association (2014). http://www.e-assessment.com/category/resources/case-studies/page/3/. Accessed 25 Apr 2017
2. van Staden, C.J., van Biljon, J.A., Kroeze, J.H.: Using a user experience evaluation framework for eModeration. In: 2017 Conference on Information Communications Technology and Society, pp. 1–6 (2017)
3. New-Zealand-Qualifications-Authority: Digital Assessment Requirements for Post-Moderation. ServiceIQ (2016). http://www.serviceiq.org.nz/assets/Attachments/QA-Docume nts/SIQ-GUIDE-QA-PostModDigitalAssessment-Ed3-Aug16.pdf. Accessed 26 Apr 2018
4. Sorenson, A., Gill, L.: Digital assessment transformation: internal assessment and moderation. http://www.nzqa.govt.nz/about-us/publications/newsletters-and-circulars/assess ment-matters/digital-assessment-transformation-internal-assessment-and-moderation/. Accessed 21 Aug 2017
5. Van Staden, C.J., Van Biljon, J.A., Kroeze, J.: eModeration: towards a user experience evaluation framework. In: SAICSIT 2015, 28–30 September, pp. 1–11 (2015)
6. Van Staden, C.J.: User experience evaluation of electronic moderation systems: a case study at a private higher education institution in South Africa. UNISA (2017)
7. New-Zealand-Qualifications-Authority: Digital Moderation Discussion Paper, Wellington (2016)
8. AlphaPlus: Standardisation methods, mark schemes, and their impact on marking reliability (2014)
9. Van Staden, C.: IT moderation going green. In: SAICSIT 2010, pp. 426–428 (2010)
10. Johnson, M., Greatorex, J.: Judging text presented on screen: implications for validity. E-Learning 5(1), 40–50 (2008)
11. Adie, L.: An investigation into online moderation. Assess. Matters 3, 5–27 (2011)
12. Greatorex, J.: Moderated e-portfolio project evaluation, Cambridge (2004)
13. Chamberlain, S., Taylor, R.: Online or face-to-face? An experimental study of examiner training. Br. J. Educ. Technol. 42(4), 665–675 (2011)
14. Berger, D.: Supporting tool for moderation in the grading process of summative assessments. Graz University of Technology (2011)
15. Venkatesh, V., Bala, H.: Technology acceptance model 3 and a research agenda on interventions. Decis. Sci. 39(2), 273–315 (2008)
16. Venkatesh, V., Morris, M.G., Davis, G.B., Davis, F.D.: User acceptance of information technology: toward a unified view. MIS Q. 27(3), 425–478 (2003)
17. Goodhue, D.L., Thompson, R.L.: Task-technology fit and individual performance. MIS Q. 19(2), 213 (1995)
18. Zhou, T., Lu, Y., Wang, B.: Integrating TTF and UTAUT to explain mobile banking user adoption. Comput. Human Behav. 26, 760–767 (2010)
19. Ramdani, B., Chevers, D., Williams, D.: SMEs' adoption of enterprise applications a Technology-organization-environment model. J. Small Bus. Enterp. Dev. 20(4), 735–753 (2013)
20. Erlirianto, L.M., Ali, A.H.N., Herdiyanti, A.: The implementation of the Human, Organization, and Technology-Fit (HOT – Fit) Framework to evaluate the Electronic Medical Record (EMR) system in a hospital. Procedia Comput. Sci. 72, 580–587 (2015)
21. Pynoo, B., Devolder, P., Tondeur, J., Van Braak, J., Duyck, W., Duyck, P.: Predicting secondary school teachers' acceptance and use of a digital learning environment: a cross-sectional study. Comput. Human Behav. 27(1), 568–575 (2011)

22. Rienties, B., Giesbers, B., Lygo-Baker, S., Ma, H.W.S., Rees, R.: Why some teachers easily learn to use a new virtual learning environment: a technology acceptance perspective. Interact. Learn. Environ. **24**(3), 539–552 (2016)

23. Venkatesh, V., Davis, F.D.: A theoretical extension of the technology acceptance model: four longitudinal field studies. Manag. Sci. **46**(2), 186–204 (2000)

24. Goodhue, D.L.: Development and measurement validity of a task-technology fit instrument for user evaluations of information systems. Decis. Sci. **29**(I), 105–138 (1998)

25. Yusof, M.M., Kuljis, J., Papazafeiropoulou, A., Stergioulas, L.K.: An evaluation framework for Health Information Systems: human, organization and technology-fit factors (HOT-fit). Int. J. Med. Inform. **77**(6), 386–398 (2008)

26. Rajamany, V., Van Staden, C., Van Biljon, J.: eModeration requirements: a case study in private secondary schools in South Africa (2020)

27. Kivunja, C., Kuyini, A.B.: Understanding and applying research paradigms in educational contexts. Int. J. High. Educ. **6**(5), 26–41 (2017)

28. Morgan, D.L.: Pragmatism as a paradigm for social research. Qual. Inq. **20**(8), 1045–1053 (2014)

29. Dilshad, R.M., Latif, M.I.: Focus group interview as a tool for qualitative research: an analysis. Pakistan J. Soc. Sci. **33**(1), 191–198 (2013)

30. Krueger, R.A., Casey, M.A.: Focus group interviewing. In: Handbook of Practical Program Evaluation, 4th edn., pp. 506–534. Wiley (2015)

31. Clarke, V., Braun, V.: Teaching thematic analysis: overcoming challenges and developing strategies for effective learning. Psychologist **26**(2), 120–123 (2013)

32. Fatimah, S., Yassin, M., Mohamad, N.S., Yamat, H.: Developing W-Portfolio culture in computer. In: Proceedings of the ePortfolio 2007 Conference, 17–19 October 2007, pp. 327–332 (2007)

33. Raikes, N., Greatorex, J., Shaw, S.: From paper to screen: some issues on the way. In: International Association of Educational Assessment Conference, June 2004

34. ABC-Awards: eModeration Guide (2014). http://www.abcawards.co.uk/wp-content/uploads/2014/09/eModeration-Guide.pdf. Accessed 22 Mar 2018

# Ready to Go? Schools' Preparedness for Teaching and Learning Within a One-to-One Program

Cathrine E. Tømte[1]([⊠]), Markus M. Bugge[2], Sabine Wollscheid[3], and Frida F. Vennerød-Diesen[2]

[1] University of Agder, 4630 Kristiansand, Norway
Cathrine.tomte@uia.no
[2] University of Oslo, 0316 Oslo, Norway
markus.bugge@tik.uio.no, frida.vennerod@nifu.no
[3] NIFU, 0608 Oslo, Norway
sabine.wollscheid@nifu.no

**Abstract.** During the years there has been an increasing number of one-to-one programs around the world. In such programs all students are equipped with portable devices, such as laptops, tablets, smartphones for learning purposes. Even if these initiatives are increasing, our knowledge of the impact of such digital transformation of education is still little studied. Based on data from a three years longitudinal study on a large-scale implementation of Chromebooks in a municipality, this paper highlights teachers' experiences. Key findings suggest that this initiative has been successful when it comes to the administrative and technical implementation of the Chromebooks, but there is still a way to go to transform pedagogical practices to enhance student-active learning supported by the Chromebooks.

**Keywords:** One-to-One program · Implementation · Innovation · School · Teachers

## 1 Introduction: Implementation of One-to-One Programs

Since the 'one laptop per child-initiative', which originated from the U.S more than 10 years ago, there have been an increasing number of one-to-one programs around the world. Some have been quite successful, while others have failed, and there have been various reasons for the success and the opposite (Islam and Grönlund 2016; Zheng et al. 2016). In one-to-one (1:1) programs, all students are equipped with portable devices, such as laptops, tablets, smartphones and the like for learning purposes (Balankasat et al. 2013). Previous studies on 1:1 implementation suggests various efforts in order to succeed. For example, to ensure that changes are 'systemic and underpinned by pedagogical values' (ibid, pp. 7). Moreover, over the years, teachers' beliefs and views regarding the use of technology in classrooms have been studied by quantitative approaches (Scherer et al. 2019; Tondeur et al. 2012; Tondeur et al. 2016) and by qualitative approaches (Prestidge 2012; Tondeur et al. 2012; Genlott et al. 2019). Moreover, studies on such initiatives have looked at learning outcomes, and

M. Hattingh et al. (Eds.): I3E 2020, LNCS 12066, pp. 569–580, 2020.
https://doi.org/10.1007/978-3-030-44999-5_47

changes in workstyles for students and teachers. Findings suggest that one-to-one initiatives enhance student-centered teaching and learning (Hershkovitz and Karni 2018; Lindqvist 2015).

Even if 1:1 initiative in schools are increasing, we still have limited knowledge of the impact of such a digital transformation of education. Research has been directed towards the infrastructure, such as types of hardware and software use, Wifi-coverage and the like, and the prevalence of the number of pupils who have received their own digital devices, in English has often been referred to as 1:1 computing. or 1:1 coverage. Research has also looked at what is called 1:1 learning, that is teachers' pedagogical approaches and students learning in contexts where each student has their own digital device (Bocconi et al. 2013). In 2013, Bocconi and colleagues examined 29 1:1 programs in 19 countries in Europe to elucidate how such initiatives contribute to different types of innovation in education. One finding was that most of these efforts were primarily aimed at infrastructure, that is to equip schools with 1:1 coverage and to some extent also to contribute with competence development for the school's teachers. In such studies, much of the attention was focused on getting students more motivated for learning and technically competent. We also find such studies in the Nordic countries (Gilje et al. 2016). Later studies have confirmed that 1:1 coverage enables adapted training (Chauhan 2017). At the same time, some student groups may be more easily distracted from doing other things than learning (Zheng et al. 2016). Furthermore, 1:1 coverage will enable what is often called student-active teaching and learning (Genlott and Grönlund 2016). This means that the student is placed at the center of his/ her own learning and traditional instructor-driven teaching is given less space. Here, researchers disagree about what student-active teaching and learning in practice entails and what role a teacher should have. Such discussions are often colored by researchers' different pedagogical positions. For example, researchers who are concerned with socio-cultural approaches to learning work are more likely concerned with how technology can contribute as an artefact in such interactions, while researchers with a behavioral approach will increasingly use technology as a resource for repetitions. (Zheng et al. 2016; Tømte et al. 2018). Moreover, class leadership in technology-intensive classrooms requires different types of competence and skills than in classrooms where technology has less space (Genlott and Grönlund 2016). Researchers suggest that a holistic approach to change common to all schools in a municipality is important; it enables a larger network, and a shared understanding of the objectives of the change. In addition, it is easier to follow up for school owners, operating costs are kept under control by connecting user support to only one operating system and type of device. At the same time, the schools are different in technology maturity and professional digital competence and the initiatives can thus be experienced as demanding for some, but feasible for others (ibid). Several studies reveal an increased need for knowledge about governance, leadership and educational development work in schools with 1:1 coverage (Islam and Grönlund 2016; Genlott et al. 2019).

Based on how these previous studies have addressed what it takes to succeed with the implementation of digital technology for teaching and learning in schools and studies on one-to-one initiatives, the present paper will look at the role of school leaders and teachers within the implementation of one-to-one Chromebooks in a municipality in Norway. The research questions addressed are:

- How were schools prepared towards the one-to-one Chromebook initiative?
- How did teachers' digital competence influence this process?

As technology changes in a fast pace, our study might serve as an updated contribution to the growing body of studies on one-to-one initiatives in schools. With few exceptions, most studies that address one-to-one initiatives do not include longitudinal data, as we do here. Hence, we will present and discuss the results of various stages the one-to-one implementation, including the attitudes, readiness and perspectives of school principals and teachers.

Our study might bring new insights into how one-to-one implementation as pedagogical development/ change are understood and interpreted in schools and in the municipality. For example, knowledge about teachers' perceptions on how to lead classes in technology rich environments, how the digital devices may enhance learning within various subjects and the like can contribute to further understanding of such implementations and be further used in similar initiatives. Moreover, the roles taken by, and the communication with teachers, school leaders and stakeholders from the municipality will be discussed from the perspective of innovations.

## 2   Theoretical Framework

Rogers' Diffusion of innovation theory (2003) points to critical factors for success in implementing innovations. Such factors include the characteristics of the innovation, those who use the innovation, the communication channels the innovation is communicated through, the time perspective, and what Rogers calls the social system that surrounds those who use the innovation, such as where they live and where they work.

The theory has also gained ground in educational research, and especially in studies of the introduction of new technology. For example, Sahin (2012) studied teacher students' perspectives on the use of ICT in primary school, while Li and Huang (2012) studied implementation of game-based learning in primary school in light of Rogers' theory, and Akin (2016) reveals how school administration interpreted and used the authorities' ICT-based plans and strategies. Genlott, Grönlund and Viborg, explored Rogers' theory to shed light on how to introduce a new ICT-supported educational model in primary school. Through a survey of teachers who have taken a one-year course in the educational method WTL (Write to Learn), they highlighted three general implications: First, the method worked best when teachers use it as a reference point more than a set of standards. This way teachers would enable to use the method in the light of tailored training and student creativity, and to safeguard and further develop their own competence development. Second, Genlott and colleagues recommend establishing an extended social system involving more than one school. Larger school networks add more energy and allow for further dissemination and sharing of ideas and practices. Third, it is important to keep in mind that not everyone can be an innovator and therefore it is important to have a network large enough to handle discussions and knowledge about the new method/ innovation. In order to ensure dissemination, it is crucial to involve those with previous experience in using the innovation, and those who are good communicators, that is, who are good at communicating the method and the usefulness of the innovation to colleagues. It is also important to allow time for change, while ensuring continuous growth in the network. Of course, the quality of the innovation is decisive, and preliminary studies on the quality of the innovation are often carried out before starting to spread/ roll out. This again means that the school management also needs to be well updated on recent research in order to see the results of the innovation.

## 3     Research Context

Our study, which was designed as a formative dialogue design study comprises a municipality which initialized a large project on enrollment of one-to-one digital devices for all students in the 24 schools (16 primary schools; 1–7 grade, and 8 lower secondary schools; 8–10 grade). The students were provided with Chromebooks. The study run for three years and covered several aspects of the implementation process, such as teaching and learning with digital resources and devices, competence development, institutional learning, development of digital competence and the like. The present paper address' some distinct topics within the overall study.

## 4     Research Design, Methods and Data

The research questions for the present paper are illuminated by a case study design (Yin 2009). By looking at two distinct schools (8th–10th grade) which were equally exposed to the implementation from the school owner side, we are to identify local adjustments and efforts made in order to meet this new situation. We selected schools with different profiles in terms of socio-economic background of students, and with different geographical location in the municipality. Nonetheless, both schools are equal in size in terms of number of students. We conducted classroom-observations in Mathematics and Norwegian and interviews with teachers in these selected subjects and the school leaders from both schools. Table 1 summarizes our data from the schools.

**Table 1.**  Data collected from schools 8–10th grade.

| 8–10th grade | 2017 | | 2018 | | 2019 | | Total |
|---|---|---|---|---|---|---|---|
| | Norwegian | Mathematics | Norwegian | Mathematics | Norwegian | Mathematics | |
| Observation in class | 4 | 4 | 6 | 6 | 4 | 4 | 28 |
| Interview teachers | 4 | 4 | 6 | 6 | 5 | 4 | 29 |
| Interview school leader | 2 | | 2 | | 2 | | 6 |
| Total | **10** | **8** | **14** | **12** | **11** | **8** | 63 |

In order to grasp how the actual school owner prepared schools, we attended joint meetings organized for school leaders and teachers for 8th–10th grade. In addition to observation, we conducted group interviews with participants from these meetings. Moreover, we attended meetings with the coordinator of the one-to-one initiative in the municipality. This gave us insights about the overall processes within the implementation process; such as mutual challenges across schools. From each meeting we produced a short memo including observations notes addressing scope of the meeting, our role as observants and key takeaways including how people were reacting and acting throughout the meeting. Table 2 summarizes types of- and number of meetings attended.

**Table 2.** Overview meetings attended

| 2017 | 2018 | 2019 | Total |
|---|---|---|---|
| Meetings with resource-teams with teachers across schools (3) | Meetings with resource-teams with teachers across schools (1) | Meetings with resource-teams with teachers across schools (1) | 4 |
| Meeting with school leaders across schools (4) | Meeting with school leaders across schools (1) | | 5 |
| Meeting with coordinator from the municipality (10) | Meeting with coordinator from the municipality (10) | Meeting with coordinator from the municipality (10) | 30 |
| | Annual gathering for teachers at all schools (1) | Annual gathering for teachers at all schools (1) | 2 |

We analyzed the data by qualitative content analysis (Krippendorf 2004). Notes from interviews, the observation notes from class and memos from meetings were read with different reading techniques, such as wide and narrow reading. Based on this reading we developed several categories and sub-categories emerging as relevant to this study's overall aims and scope. The first and second author of this paper organised these categories, and these were later discussed with the research team and a shared understanding and categories were developed.

# 5 Key Findings and Discussion

The following section presents findings that illuminate our two research questions. In addition to presenting sole findings, we also discuss how these findings might be interpreted within our theoretical scope.

## 5.1 How Were Schools Prepared Towards the One-to-One Initiative?

A key message from the research literature is that institutional factors matters to succeed with the introduction of new technology in educational institutions. These include anchoring in management, adequate technological infrastructure and a holistic approach to 'get all teachers involved' (Tondeur et al. 2012). These elements are in line with Rogers framing of the users of the innovation, the communication channels, the time perspective, and the social system. In addition, researchers recommend to give individuals or smaller teams responsibility for implementation locally at schools (Genlott et al. 2019). In the 1:1 program studied here, the implementation of Chromebooks followed a step-by-step process. Students and teachers on 8–10 grade received their devices early spring 2017, students and teachers on 4–7 grade early autumn 2017, while students and teachers in 1–3 grade received Chromebooks fall 2018. Ahead of handing out the Chromebooks, the municipality had made preparatory work on technical facilitation and started a process of competence development of all teachers. The municipality had also allocated personnel resources and a binding collaboration with each school. The initiative was coordinated through regular meetings with school leaders and resource teams of teachers from each school. Few schools reported technical problems, such as the lack of broadband capacity or technical failures. Thus, much of what is referred to as "first order barriers" (Genlott et al. 2019) was avoided. Most teachers demonstrated positive attitudes towards the initiative, and many of them were well motivated when starting up with the program.

## Lessons Learned from the First Years (2017–2018)

As referred to in the theoretical section, researchers recommend establish an extended social system involving more than one school (Genlott et al. 2019). Larger school networks allow for the spread and sharing of ideas and practices. It is also important to allow time for change, while ensuring continuous growth in the network. In the municipality, resource persons were appointed at each school in addition to a central coordinator of the initiative centrally in the municipality. It was the school management who designated who should be the resource persons at the school. These formed teams of about two to four persons from each school. Initially, the resource persons/team often constituted persons with technical competence more than educational/professional didactic competence, but this changed during the years, so that awareness was raised to include the latter type of competence.

Through interviews and school visits, we found that peer-to-peer learning among teachers took place both unstructured (i.e. as chats in front of the coffee machine) and structured (i.e. in dedicated meetings and seminars) at schools, and in various arenas, such as at their own school and through gatherings organised by the municipality, and to some extent over the web, via the municipality's resource page.

In addition to organizing resource teams and project management for the initiative, the municipality also involved a national agency as knowledge provider. Employees from this agency were present in the initial joint gatherings for resource teams from the schools. Even if teachers reported to appreciate the contributions from representatives of this agency, the topics addressed were most likely to be generic (i.e. cyber ethics and copyright issues), or more technical oriented (i.e. how to share documents in google or shortcuts on the keyboard), and less linked to distinct subjects. This led to that some teachers reported to learn little, since the contents were too basic, while others experienced that the technical focus became too advanced. Moreover, some teachers expressed that due to the generic nature of these topics, they found it less relevant to their actual subjects and/or grades that they taught.

During the first one and a half years of the implementation, an overall impression was thus that despite the initial enthusiasm and positive attitude towards the initiative among most teachers and school leaders, many felt somewhat overwhelmed by the scope of the initiative, both technically and educationally. Several expressed that the implementation went too fast and that they did not have enough time to become acquainted with the potential of the Chromebook, whether technical or educational. This was also confirmed in that the schedule of the joint competence development program for all schools organized by the municipality became delayed. The municipality's aim was to implement two out of five modules during the first spring of implementation (2017), but as the process was delayed, the second module was launched half a year later. In the interviews, one of the resource teachers framed the situation as follows: "I am the captain on a boat floating on a tidal wave, it goes very fast!". Apparently, many principals and teachers experienced that they were given too little time to get used to the technical dimensions associated with the internal logic of the CB itself before they felt comfortable applying it in educational contexts. Interviews with teachers revealed for example that some were uncertain about how the Google versions of word processing tools and spreadsheets worked, and how other cheating and plagiarism functions worked.

## Lessons Learned from the Last Years (2018–2019)

During the last years of implementation, we observed that the organization of resource teams and local experience-sharing along with peer-to-peer learning among teachers had spread out and dominated the competence development practices at the schools. Technical and administrative issues linked to the use of the Chromebooks were less apparent, and a renewed attention towards the pedagogical integration of the Chromebook into the subjects were observed in the classrooms. One principal explains how competence development now had become systematically approached at her school:

> We have started with joint meetings with all teachers in where teachers who have done something new in terms of technology, i.e. the software, or done something innovative pedagogically with the help of the Chromebook can present their efforts and experiences in a 5–10 min time slot.

At several schools, we observed that teachers tested out various opportunities in the Chromebook as part of getting to know it and considered what opportunities it provided for student-active teaching and learning in the classroom. A teacher explains how she worked with video recordings with colleagues before trying them out with students:

> We teachers try out how to make video records linked to the topics and subjects we teach. It is very nice that we have tried it out ourselves before we throw the students into it.

We also observed the efforts in pedagogical change from the external bodies, such as the governmental agency mentioned above. Moreover, from the second year of implementation, an external company was engaged by the municipality to speed up the process of using the Chromebooks in for teaching purposes. The company run a fixed program that focused on getting student-active teaching and classroom management into technology-rich learning environments. The consulting company and the national agency had different roles in the implementation process. Where the national agency contributed with content and competence development, the consultancy had a more hands-on approach by implementing a practical scheme of using Chromebooks at each school. The municipality asked schools to provide feedback on the latter through a questionnaire. Although many teachers reported to be satisfied with their intervention, several were not, and the main reason they reported was that they felt they were exposed to an intervention that were either too difficult or to easy, since the consultancy adopted the same scheme to all schools without any adaption to the teachers' actual level of digital proficiency. Other teachers reported that they were given too little time to prepare themselves ahead of participating to the intervention, others were able to join, or they only got parts of it, while others did not think the arrangement was relevant, regardless of whether it was easy or difficult.

During the last period of the implementation, we thus observed that the one-to-one Chromebook-implementation had become integrated in teachers' daily work. Most teachers were using the Chromebook in their teaching, and competence development-practices have been set on regular basis in schools and across schools in the joint gatherings organized by the municipality. The technical and administrative efforts to make the Chromebooks work were solved, and teachers were exploring how the Chromebook might support their subject related didactics. However, these processes were colored by their actual professional digital competence.

### 5.2   How Did Teachers' Digital Competence Influence the Process?

At most schools, teachers' professional digital competence varied; from non-users, early adopters to teachers who liked to experiment with innovative teaching. These various types of competence and experiences with teaching with technology influenced the implementation at schools.

**Lessons Learned from the First Years (2017–2018)**
One year and a half after the implementation, we observed a technical-administrative change in the schools where most teachers highlighted that the Chromebook had contributed to better workflow and communication. In the interviews, teachers stressed that their workflow had been improved, in that all notes, files and submissions were stored within the Chromebooks, and not on diverse sheets of paper. However, as for pedagogical change, we observed only a slight development from teacher-directed teaching towards more student-active pedagogical approach, where Chromebook served as an integral part of the learning design. At the same time, we also observed that many teachers experienced challenges with class management in these new technology rich learning environments. One explanation was that such classrooms required a different pedagogical approach (Lindquist 2015). Teachers had to ensure that students used the Chromebooks for learning and not for non-schooling activities (Zheng et al. 2016). This required awareness of pedagogical use Chromebook, and a balance between digital and analogue teaching. While some teachers seemed eager in exploring new opportunities with the help of Chromebook, others were more hesitant about how Chromebook and digital resources could contribute in their teaching and learning. Some of these teachers called for more time to familiarize themselves with Chromebook and specific digital resources, others were less enthusiastic towards the

change of their own teaching that came with the Chromebooks. One teacher put it this way: "I would have started with Chromebooks and spreadsheets earlier, but I just noticed that I have postponed and postponed, because I always have something else that I can do." Nonetheless, some of the tech-savvy teachers were more enthusiastic towards the Chromebooks and stated that they often used their own free time, such as evenings, weekends and holidays to find new opportunities for teaching with the support of technology. One of them expressed his experience of the implementation as follows: "I think I might be an enthusiast about technical stuff, so I just find it fun to try new things." Another observation was the differences in the scope and use of digital resources between subjects; for example, in classes where the subject Norwegian were taught, a multitude of digital resources were explored, whereas in Mathematics, we observed a more traditional analogue teacher-led instruction.

Teachers professional digital competence thus varied a lot during the first years of the implementation. The efforts made by the municipality, the external agencies and the school leaders did not seem to work too efficiently in terms of raising the digital competence among teacher staff. One explanation might have been the way the implementation of the Chromebooks were communicated (Rogers 2003); as demonstrated, most gatherings and joint arenas for competence development were dominated by a 'one size fits all'-approach, which did not meet the actual competence need for teachers; not for the innovative digital competent ones, nor for those who were lagging behind. Following this, another reason could be that the competence development lacked a distinct connection with actual subjects and their distinct knowledge domains.

## Lessons Learned from the Last Years (2018–2019)

In 2019 late fall, three years after the implementation started, we observed that schools still needed more time allocated to 'get all teachers involved'. This means structural challenges along with challenges that comprise teachers' 'pedagogical beliefs' (Genlott et al. 2019), meaning that teachers must be convinced of the usefulness of conducting educational development as such, and of the opportunities that comes with digital resources in subjects, in order to change their teaching. The role of the school leader is central to this work (Tondeur et al. 2012). During the three years we observed increased involvement by the school leaders.

These processes mentioned here address what we have called 'second order change' (Genlott et al. 2019). During the last year of the implementation, we observed that teachers increasingly reported new opportunities to facilitate student-active teaching with the support of technology. At the same time, there was still a way to go to unleash the potential that lies in overcoming to teach as usual but with the use of the Chromebook, so called 'first order change' (ibid).

We observed the role of the professional, digitally competent teacher, and what it implied in practice. A central dimension of such teachers was how they managed to adopt varied and adapted teaching, and how they included various digital and analogue resources in this work. The good balance between analogue and digital was emphasized by many teachers, such as from this teacher:

*I have become more aware of when it is beneficial to use digital resources and when it is most beneficial to use handwriting on paper in teaching. Sometimes, when drawing graphs on the Chromebook, you can see trends and explore changes. This is nice when doing geometry.*

*Because then you can perform some changes and observe that the rule remains. It would have taken too much time to do the same tasks by hand. (teacher, 10 grade)*

However, some teachers let students choose themselves whether they wanted to work digitally or by analogy. This indicates that there is not yet enough awareness in the schools when it comes to awareness of a balance between analogue and digital learning. This could have unfortunate consequences in the form of being overweight by either analogue or digital teaching forms depending on the school and teacher and the preferences of the students. Several dilemmas thus emerge when teachers aim to reach out to all students. While some students quickly understand the technology, others may strive to make it work. This applies especially to software that is typical of school work, such as Excel and Geogebra in mathematics and word processing programs in other subjects. This way, teachers will have different starting points for taking the leap into new forms of teaching.

Moreover, some teachers referred to the new technical-administrative equipment as demanding, and that limited resources have been devoted to this development work beyond normal working hours. Given that there are considerable differences between teachers in terms of how tech savvy they are, one should not underestimate the challenge it will be to implement of new teaching methods based on the opportunities offered by 1:1 coverage of Chromebooks.

Furthermore, we also observed different practices in the competence development work regarding teaching and learning with the support of Chromebooks - both among teachers and across schools within the municipality. These differences reflect the organization and anchoring of the development work as well as the teachers' emphasis on digital versus analogue learning forms respectively.

## 6    Conclusion

The overall implementation process initiated and conducted by the municipality included a comprehensive approach for all schools in the district. This way all schools were offered joint competence development courses, and the teachers could benefit from networking across schools, in professional groups.

If we look to the concepts of 'first order' and 'second order barriers' (Genlott et al. 2019), where so-called first order barriers refer to putting the technical solution in place, while 'second order barriers' are about cultural change and teaching practice, it can be said that the comprehensive and coordinated commitment to the municipality has accomplished the first order barriers successfully. The introduction of the technical-administrative part that works on the Chromebooks went smoothly, and there were few technical issues related to infrastructure. We demonstrated how the research literature points out that understandings of change can also be seen as two-step processes, in which so-called 'first order change' is often about doing the same, but with new technology, while 'second order change', on the other hand, means that the activities themselves are redefined. In our study, we have shown that the work of addressing what we have called 'second order change' is in the form of an emerging maturation process in which teachers see new opportunities after they have begun to explore and understand the educational possibilities. by digital learning resources. At the same time, there is still a way to go to unleash the potential that lies in overcoming the 'power of analogue practice', i.e. 'first order change'. In the further development and implementation work in the schools in the municipality, this disparity between the teachers, the need for coordination and coordination across schools, as well as the extra work required to radically change teaching forms, should be considered. The work of addressing 'second order change' and new teaching methods will be even more demanding as 'first order change'. In sum, this is likely to represent a need for higher priority and increased resources for the further educational development work in the municipality.

# References

Akin, U.: Innovation efforts in education and school administration: views of Turkish school administrators. Eurasian J. Educ. Res. **63**, 243–260 (2016)

Balankasat, A., Bannister, D., Hertz, H., Sigillo, W., Vuorikari, R.: Overview and Analysis of 1:1 Learning Initiatives in Europe. Luxembourg Publications Office of the European Union, Luxembourg (2013)

Bocconi, S., Kampylis, P., Punie, Y.: Framing ICT-enabled innovation for learning: the case of one-to-one learning initiatives in Europe. Eur. J. Educ. **48**(1), 113–130 (2013)

Chauhan, S.: A meta-analysis of the impact of technology on learning effectiveness of elementary students. Comput. Educ. **105**, 14–30 (2017)

Genlott, A.A., Gönlund, Å., Viborg, O.: Disseminating digital innovation in school - leading second-order educational change. Educ. Inf. Technol. **24**, 3021–3039 (2019). https://doi.org/10.1007/s10639-019-09908-0

Genlott, A.A., Grönlund, Å.: Closing the gaps – improving literacy and mathematics by ict-enhanced collaboration. Comput. Educ. **99**, 68–80 (2016)

Gilje, Ø., et al.: Med Ark & APP. Bruk av læremidler og ressurser for læring på tvers av arbeidsformer. Sluttrapport. Universitetet i Oslo (2016)

Islam, S., Grönlund, Å.: An international literature review of 1:1 computing in schools. J. Educ. Change **17**(2), 191–222 (2016). https://doi.org/10.1007/s10833-016-9271-y

Hershkovitz, A., Karni, O.: Borders of change: a holostic exploration of teaching in one-to one computing programs. Comput. Educ. **125**, 429–443 (2018)

Krippendorf, K.: Content Analysis. An Introduction to its Methodology. Sage Publications, Thousand Oaks (2004)

Li, S.-C., Huang W.-C.: Lifestyles, innovation attributes, and teachers' adoption of game-based learning: comparing non-adopters with early adopters, adopted and likely adopters in Taiwan. Comput. Educ. **96**, 29–41 (2012)

Lindqvist, M.J.P.H.: Gaining and sustaining TEL in a 1:1 laptop initiative: possibilities and challenges for teachers and students. Comput. Sch. **32**, 35–62 (2015)

Prestridge, S.: The Beliefs behind the teacher that influences their ICT practices. Comp. Educ. **58**, 449–458 (2012)

Rogers, E.: Diffusion of Innovations. Free Press, New York (1962/2003)

Sahin, S.: Pre-service teachers' perspective of the diffusion of information and communication technologies (ICTs) and the effect of case-based discussion (CBDs). Comput. Educ. **59**, 1089–1098 (2012)

Scherer, R., Siddiq, F., Tondeur, J.: The technology acceptance model (TAM): a meta-analytic structural equation modeling approach to explaining teachers' adoption of digital technology in education. Comput. Educ. **128**, 13–35 (2019). https://doi.org/10.1016/j.compedu.2018.09. 009

Tondeur, J., van Braak, J., Sang, G., Voogt, J., Fisser, P., Ottenbreit-Leftwich, A.: Preparing pre-service teachers to integrate technology in education: a synthesis of qualitative evidence. Comput. Educ. **59**(1), 134–144 (2012)

Tondeur, J., van Braak, J., Siddiq, F., Scherer, R.: Time for a new approach to prepare future teachers for educational technology use: its meaning and measurement. Comput. Educ. **93**(3), 134–150 (2016)

Tømte, C.E., Wollscheid, S., Vennerød-Diesen, F.F., Bugge, M.: Digital læring i askerskolen. Midtveisrapport fra følgeforskning. NIFU-rapport 82/2018, Oslo (2018)

Yin, R.: Case Study Research. Design and Methods. Sage, London (2009)

Zheng, B., Warschauer, M., Lin, C.H., Chang, C.: Learning in one-to-one laptop environments: a meta-analysis and research synthetis. Rev. Educ. Res. **86**(4), 1052–1084 (2016)

# Agile Development of a Flipped Classroom Course

Linda Blömer$^{(\boxtimes)}$, Christin Voigt$^{(\boxtimes)}$, Alena Droit$^{(\boxtimes)}$, and Uwe Hoppe$^{(\boxtimes)}$

Osnabrueck University, Katharinenstr. 3, 49074 Osnabrueck, Germany
{linda.bloemer,christin.voigt,alena.droit,
uwe.hoppe}@uni-osnabrueck.de

**Abstract.** Digital course designs such as the Flipped Classroom (FC) are increasingly enriching university education. However, before implementing such an FC, teachers face the challenge of creating content in the form of materials and activities and finding a suitable development method. This is very time-consuming, which is why circumstances such as lack of time and personnel can make implementation difficult. In other areas, agile approaches have already proven to be effective in enabling flexible and efficient development. We use this opportunity to overcome different barriers in the context of FC development by creating an agile model for FC development. To achieve this, we first examined the previous research on agile development approaches concerning the implementation of an FC by a systematic literature review, concluding that no appropriate model exists yet. Building upon this, we designed an Agile$^{FC}$ Development Model, which can be used by teachers to create their FC. This model is very generally designed so that it can be easily adopted. On the other hand, it can be adjusted to a particular situation without effort. We also illustrate the application of the model using a small case study.

**Keywords:** Agile development · Case study · Flipped classroom · Model

## 1 Introduction

The Flipped Classroom (FC), also known as the inverted classroom, has become an increasingly popular teaching method in Higher Education Institutions (HEI) throughout the last decade. It can generally be described as the swapping of traditional attendance time activities with at-home activities [1]. Direct computer-based instructions like videos are used to convey knowledge at home before students apply and deepen their knowledge in interactive activities inside the classroom [2]. Many studies report positive effects of FC teaching, like improved learning performance and increased student engagement [3]. However, the development of an FC is a challenging task, where different barriers can occur, such as lack of time [4] or the need for technical and media didactic support [5]. FCs always contain an online and offline part, which has to be synchronized. The development of videos, self-assessment tests, and other online content is more time consuming than preparing a traditional lecture [3]. Also, for the interactive attendance part of a class, various active teaching methods

© IFIP International Federation for Information Processing 2020
Published by Springer Nature Switzerland AG 2020
M. Hattingh et al. (Eds.): I3E 2020, LNCS 12066, pp. 581–592, 2020.
https://doi.org/10.1007/978-3-030-44999-5_48

should be used, and new contents have to be created. Teachers can feel overwhelmed when they create FCs. A possible resistance of the teachers concerned about the effort and technical challenges involved should also be taken into account. In order to overcome these barriers, a feasible and efficient approach to FC development is required. At this point, agile methods can offer a solution. The concept of agility became quite common when the Manifesto for Agile Software Development was published in 2001. It stated that the development of software could be improved if the development process focuses on four principles: Individuals and interaction, working software, customer collaboration, and responding to change [6]. Even though some authors state that the current principles of agility often lack transferability outside the field of software development, the underlying concepts of agility, flexibility, and leanness, can be easily transferred to other fields [7]. Tesar and Sieber adapted the agile principles for the field of agile e-learning development, leading to the four core principles: Personalized learning process, the usability of learning utilities, learner-centered design, and flexible course design [8]. Agile methods can empower HEIs to implement new teaching methods in an efficient and cost-reducing way [9] and can lead to an improvement in the flexibility and reactivity of the capable stakeholders [10]. The added value of agile methods in teaching and pedagogy has already become clear in previous studies [11]. Besides, it is recommended to implement an FC step by step, starting with the transformation of single lectures as pilots instead of transforming the whole lecture at once [12, 13]. With this iterative procedure, teachers can assess, compare, and continually improve future FC lectures through regular evaluations [12, 14]. In order to limit the workload and consider students' opinions, teachers can also involve students to support FC development [13]. The Horizon Report highlighted the application of agile approaches as a long-term key trend to drive the change concerning technology adaption in 2014 [9]. Surprisingly, there has been very little isolated research on the use of agile methods to develop an FC so far. A transferable model showing an agile FC development process is still lacking. Therefore, it is our goal to give teachers and other stakeholders of different disciplines an overview and a recommendation on agile FC development to facilitate FC implementation and break down barriers. To achieve this, we give an overview of the previous research in this area, design a general model for agile FC development, and describe the application of the model in a case study. Thus, this paper addresses the following research questions (RQ): (1) *Which concepts of agile methods are already used in the context of FC development according to current research?* (2) *How could a process model for agile FC development look like?* (3) *How could an FC be implemented step by step, taking into account this agile development model?* Figure 1 shows an overview of the systematic procedure of this article, including the research process and the corresponding paper structure.

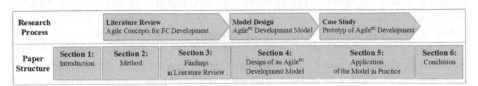

**Fig. 1.** Systematic procedure

As shown in Fig. 1, systematic literature research serves as the foundation of our paper, answering RQ1 in Sect. 2. Based on the results and current research about the determined agile concepts presented in Sect. 3, we then develop and explain our general Agile$^{FC}$ Development Model in Sect. 4, giving a response to RQ2. Afterward, we apply the model in practice by showing the use in a module of a bachelor's degree program at a German public university. By giving an insight into the current and planned implementation of this FC, we answer RQ3.

## 2 Method

In order to find out which agile methods have already been used for FC development in the current literature, we conducted a literature review and used the results to design an agile FC development model. This model was then applied in a case study. The literature review and its phases search and assessment, interpretation, synthesis, guidance and conclusion [15] build the basis of our work. While the search and assessment process are explained below and outlined in Fig. 2, the other phases of the literature review are included in the following sections.

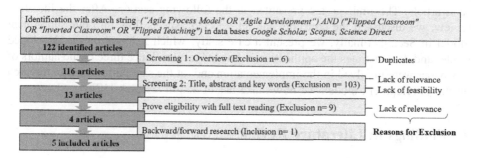

**Fig. 2.** Search and assessment process

The search was carried out systematically [16] under consideration of defining rules as reasons for stepwise exclusion. The search string shown in Fig. 2 leads to a total of 122 identified articles. We focused our search on the intersection between agile process models or agile development mentioned in research so far and the environment of the FC or similar. A focus on these topics in the investigated articles represents the inclusion criteria in our search and assessment process. On the other hand, we defined duplicates, lack of relevance, and lack of feasibility as exclusion criteria, which are explained in more detail below. We used the data bases Google Scholar, Science Direct, AISnet, Eric, Web of Science, and Scopus for our research. However, AISnet, Eric, and Web of Science did not deliver any results, which is why the results shown refer to Google Scholar, Science Direct, and Scopus. After the first screening, we removed all duplicates, which was necessary if an article was listed several times on different data bases. Thus, 116 articles remained for screening 2 in which title, abstract, and keywords are viewed. For the second screening, we defined the reasons for exclusion due to lack of relevance or lack of feasibility. We excluded articles due to a lack of relevance if they did not show reference to agile process models or agile development in the context of FC course development. However, we included those articles, which refer to agile process models or agile development in the context of blended learning or e-learning course development, if they show parallels, hints or outlooks on FC course development. Besides, reading the articles had to be classified as feasible. We excluded articles due to a lack of feasibility if they were written neither in English nor in German or were not available. As a result, 103 articles had to be excluded from screening 2 due to a lack of relevance or feasibility. Most of them showed a lack of relevance. After the second screening, 13 articles left for full-text reading to prove for eligibility, of which nine articles revealed a lack of relevance as stated above. In subsequent backward/forward research based on the remained articles, we looked for further sources dealing with agile process models or agile development in the context of FC, blended learning, or e-learning development. This search enabled us to identify another relevant article that we added to our study. Thus, the search and assessment process result in a total of five included articles. These articles form the basis for further development. In a team of three FC experienced researchers, we then carved out the used agile concept, the study design, and the primary goal mentioned in each text. Furthermore, we looked more closely at the concepts of agile development in each article. The findings are presented in the following section. After the literature review, we discussed the concepts and let selected aspects flow into our subsequent model in Sect. 4. Finally, we present a case study, which is based on the developed model and demonstrates the application in one FC lecture. Since three of the authors of this paper were involved in the implementation and, at the same time conduct research on the development model, we now make use of action research [17].

## 3   Findings in Literature Review

The literature review we conducted to answer our first research question resulted in five articles that deal with agile process models or agile development concerning FC course development. Table 1 gives an overview of the key aspects of the included articles, showing the agile concepts that have been used. It is striking how strongly most of the included articles differ concerning their concepts and their research background. The overview, sorted by year of publication, illustrates that no current articles could be found that were published after 2016. It seems surprising that no research has taken place in this field in recent years, although a need has been predicted [9]. Considering the agile concepts, it is also striking that just Scrum is used twice. The overview does not indicate that there is already an established concept or model for agile FC course development. The fact that most articles were conducted as case studies can be interpreted as further evidence that so far, mainly case-related models and concepts have been developed. The major goals of the articles shown in Table 1 focus on efficiency [6], individuality [18], flexibility [19], adaptability [20], and feasibility [4] of approaches or procedures creating digital media, digital materials or digital environments. The background and the implementation of the articles are versatile.

**Table 1.** Included articles and their applied agile approaches

| Author, Year [Reference] | Agile concept | Study design | Major goal |
|---|---|---|---|
| Tesar and Sieber [8] | Agile e-learning development | Literature analysis | Show an efficient procedure for responsible persons putting blended learning into practice |
| Meissner and Stenger [18] | JiTT | Case study | Demonstrate the use of digital media to support the individual integration of heterogeneous students at HEI |
| Vogel, Kilamo and Kurti [19] | Scrum & analogies to JiTT | Case study | Present a flexible approach to learning and teaching, considering issues of work from software employees |
| Gale et al. [20] | Scrum | Case study | Create a digital and adjustable learning environment to school health staff in Africa to fight against of Ebola |
| Bofill [4] | ADDIE & Rapid prototyping | Mixed methods | Present a feasible approach for medical schools on how to create digital learning materials |

Tesar and Sieber claim that changing teacher roles and new digital learning and teaching opportunities place new demands on the development of a digitally improved course. Based on a literature analysis, they derived a framework of agile e-learning development from the Manifesto of Software development, containing transparency of expectations towards learners, possibility for individual learning, adaptability and usefulness of digital learning material, alignment of teaching with the need of learners as well as flexibility and adaptability of the course [8]. Meissner und Stenger, on the other hand, reports about students that differ from beginners to repeaters and experienced professionals in the subject Electrical Engineering at TU Nürnberg. Using Just in Time Teaching (JiTT), they offer a learner-centered and individual learning process [18]. JiTT is a teaching design that is based on questions provided online by the teacher, which are answered by the students as preparation for the lecture. After planning the in-class activities, the teacher uses the answers just before his lecture to adapt his teaching agilely to the answers of the students. Thus, the students are recognized as essential participants in the development of face-to-face time [21]. Vogel, Kilamo, and Kurti describe the development of two courses closing the gap between academic education content and industrial demands in the field of software development. In one course, they used Scrum as a basis for the course structure. Scrum is based on the empirical process control theory. All participants included in the Scrum process are combined in the so-called Scrum Team: The Product Owner, the Scrum Master, and the Development Team [10]. The Scrum process has a specific sequence and begins with the Product Owner in a planning phase [22]. He or she is one person who is making the essential decisions of the project and is defining all the requirements [10]. The Product Owner's vision of the entire product is initially documented in the Product Backlog. The Product Owner now selects precisely those requirements that should be implemented in one Sprint, creating the Sprint Backlog [23]. Hereupon the Sprint starts, and the Development Team begins to evolve the product. One sprint takes about 30 days and has a fixed goal about what to fabricate [22]. It consists of a Sprint Planning Meeting, a Daily Scrum, the development work, a Sprint Review meeting, and a Sprint Retroperspective meeting. At the end of the Sprint there is the Product Increment, a functional intermediate product of the Product Backlog [10]. Vogel, Kilamo, and Kurti followed this process developing their FC. For the other course, they conducted an FC, in which online material for preparation as well as questions were previously addressed to the students. The answers of the students to these questions were then used to design the discussion that took place during face-to-face-time [19]. This procedure points to similarities with JiTT, even though the authors do not mention this method by name. The research of Gale et al. research is based on the Ebola outbreak calling for new learning methods because of time and place restrictions of training staff, difficult access to health staff, and limited financial resources. Using Scrum, the authors were able to produce training content as an online-simulation for three months. They adapted the Scrum process to their case-specific needs. Gale et al. point out that the resulting online material could be used within an FC by deepening important content in local workshops [20]. Bofill appoints time limit during the semester, missing adjustment of module contents and strong limitation of time for e-learning development as existing framework conditions at Florida International University Herbert Wertheim College of Medicine in the subject Radiology. She combined the instructional design (ID) model ADDIE with rapid prototyping to create e-learning material efficiently [4]. Along with this, other authors are also calling for important aspects of instructional design to be taken into account when developing an FC [12, 24]. However, it is a challenge to adapt existing ID models or to develop new ID models that seem suitable for the development of digital teaching concepts [25]. In Bofill's research, ADDIE delivers a framework to design a curriculum [26] while fast prototyping allows reverse loops and a corresponding adaptation during the development process [4].

As the findings show, a general model concerning the particularities of agile FC Development does not exist yet. Taking a closer look at the articles, it becomes clear that the minority explicitly deal with agile FC development. Instead, they deal with agile blended learning or e-learning development. Currently, literature provides only a few clues as to how agile FC development should take place. No holistic view of the development of an FC lecture has been taken into account yet, as some authors focus mainly on the development of online materials [4, 20], while others are primarily concerned with the design of the presence phase [18, 19]. In addition, general principles for agile development have already been addressed [8]. But a model for agile FC development in HEI considering both, the development of online materials and face-to-face time, is still pending. We, therefore, want to fill this research gap, answering our RQ2 in the next section.

# 4  Design of an Agile^FC Development Model

The results of the literature review and the more detailed investigation of the applied agile concepts lead us to the design of the Agile^FC Development Model. We claim that no agile concept listed in Table 1 is suitable on his own to design a general FC course nor a single FC Lecture. Although certain methods are suitable for particular phases of FC, such as video development, none of them have been used for the development of the entire course so far. We are instead of the opinion that those agile concepts should complement each user. Thus, we designed a model regarding key features of agile concepts used in the included articles. In order to allow teachers a flexible development of an FC course, the model refers to the development of individual FC lectures instead of the development of the whole course. Thus, teachers can decide whether they want to transform one, several or all events into an FC during one or more semesters. As a result, our Agile^FC Development Model for FC lectures is shown in Fig. 3. The model illustrates the creation of a single one-week session. Since an entire course consists of numerous sessions, the development model has to be run through several times in order to develop a whole FC course. Both, the agile principles [8] and the consideration of relevant ID aspects [4, 24], form the foundation of the Agile^FC Development Model. But since our model is designed to provide efficient and practical guidance for agile development of an FC, neither is considered in depth. Moreover, the model is a combination and generalization of Scrum and JiTT. The Agile^FC Development is to be separated into two parts: The online activities of the self-study phase and the in-class activities. For the first part, we made use of Scrum. In Fig. 3, this is shown by the first four steps of the model, starting with the Product Backlog and ending with the Finished Milestone. Unlike the classic Scrum process, roles in our model are distributed to stakeholders in the HEI. A Product Owner could be, e.g., a professor or a team leader of a special digitalization project. The Scrum Master could be a responsible researcher of the department. According to existing capacities, we claim for an interdisciplinary Development Team containing researchers, employed students, and IT-staff with knowledge concerning digital learning and technical implementation.

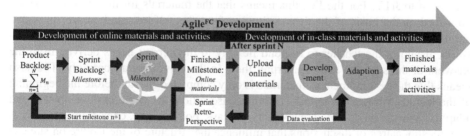

**Fig. 3.**  Agile^FC development model

The model itself starts with the Product Backlog of Scrum, given by the overall requirements for FC development. The Product Backlog is to develop the online materials for a single one-week long FC course. In the following, the requirements are divided into several milestones (M), which all have to be mastered in order to develop the materials. Each milestone represents a new Sprint Backlog. The Product Backlog is therefore given by $\sum_{n=1}^{N} M_n$ with n = 1, ..., N. A milestone is processed during each sprint sequence. For the development of an FC course, it is recommended to adopt Scrum by shortening the time of a sprint to one week, as the case study of Gale et al. shows [20]. Similar to the classic Scrum, the Sprint also includes daily Sprints. After a milestone has been completed, the Scrum Process starts again at the Product Backlog. The development of online materials is finished, when the last milestone N of the Product Backlog has been implemented, which means that the online materials for this single course are completely developed. Following the first phase, the materials produced are made available online to the students. The Sprint Retroperspective meeting will then take place hereafter. Due to the shortened sprint times and the fact that every sprint has a Review meeting itself, there is no need to do hold a Sprint Retroperspective meeting after every milestone- Sprint. Instead, the results of this meeting will be used for the online material development of the next Product Backlog at the next one-week session. Moreover, in this way, not only the evaluation of the Scrum Team but also an evaluation of the students and other stakeholders can flow into the next session production of online materials.

Once the materials are available online, the second phase of the Agile$^{FC}$ Development Model begins: The in-class material and activity development. This is aimed at the presence phase of the FC. Two of our included articles made use of JiTT or a JiTT similar procedure to adjust their presence phase on students' responses [18, 19]. JiTT is attributed with a positive effect on the learning success of students [18]. In order to use this effect and to ensure that agility is consistently applied in our model, we adopt this approach for the design of the presence phase, so that a flexible adaption to the respective students is possible. To apply JiTT in the following development process, it is necessary to produce at least one online-activity offering questions to the students that can be evaluated to adopt already developed learning activities according to student needs. At this point, the teacher is in charge of creating the content for in-class time. During this, he could make use of an ID, such as ADDIE. After evaluating the questions asked in the online phase before, he or she is able to adapt the materials according to JiTT. For the FC, this means that the materials for the in-class time are improved on the basis of the data evaluation from the self-tests and quizzes provided online. This has to be done short notice as a circle between development and adaptation. It allows the teacher to respond flexibly to the current needs derived from the answers of the students and to interpret them in the class time accordingly. This also means that the development of materials is only completed shortly before the beginning of the lecture. Further on, in-class activities also follow the circle of development and adaption and can be designed in a variety of ways. For example, open elements such as live questionnaires or discussions that influence the structure of the lecture on site can be integrated. During this phase, it lends itself to retain the roles previously defined. Thus, the Product Owner could set the essential goals, the Development Team could take over the data evaluation, and the Scrum Master could carry out the didactic implementation. Daily meetings are also recommended due to the fast-paced nature of the in-class time development. In a nutshell, the Agile$^{FC}$ Development Model is a combination of different agile approaches, most of all Scrum and JiTT, that has been transferred and adapted to the context of FC development at HEI.

# 5  Application of the Agile$^{FC}$ Development Model

In order to show one possible application of our Agile$^{FC}$ Development Model, we conducted a short case study by flipping one course as a prototype in which two of the authors were actively involved as Scrum Masters and one as a Product Owner. Within this case study, the module "Fundamentals of Organization" of the bachelor's degree program in economics at a German public university is supposed to be transformed from a traditional lecture into an FC course. This was carried out as part of a study project in the summer term 2019. As mentioned above, it is advisable to implement an FC step-by-step [12, 13]. Also, referring to our model, a stepwise implementation is recommended, as lecturers need some time to overcome barriers of change and get used to the new methods like JiTT [21]. Also, in our case, an abrupt change to an FC using the Agile$^{FC}$ Development Model for each lecture date does not seem feasible due to a lack of time and personnel. For this reason, we defined different levels of FC implementations to convert the module gradually. Four levels are required for the entire course transformation. Figure 4 visualizes level 1, conducted 2019 and explained below, as well as level 2, planned for 2020. The following levels will be continued accordingly until all sessions are transformed.

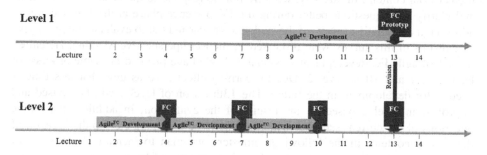

**Fig. 4.** Level 1 and 2 of Agile$^{FC}$ development

We started the application of our model in the middle of the semester using Scrum to develop videos and questions to generate online-activities and using JiTT to adapt in-class-activities to student's needs. The Scrum process of our model lasted five weeks until the 12th lecture when we uploaded the online material in our learning management system. JiTT was used during the 12th and 13th lecture, where the FC prototype took place. The Scrum Team of our development process consisted of the professor of the course, two research assistants, and three master students. The professor was the Product Owner of the project. He defined the Product Backlog, one session of FC course. He also decided about the type, scope, and design of the FC prototype. The research assistances, two authors of this paper, were the Scrum Masters, as they coordinated the activities of the Development Team and monitored the prototype development. We occupied this role twice to allow as many people as possible to benefit from the experience to facilitate the ongoing agile development process. Furthermore, the master students of the project seminar build the Development Team.

At the beginning of the process, an overview of project goals was formulated. We defined the milestones for each sprint as follows: (1) formulating learning objectives, (2) writing a storyboard for a video, (3) creating slides for the video, (4) formulating questions for online practice, quizzes, and online self-testing and (5) produce the video. At the end of each sprint, there was a weekly meeting with the whole Scrum Team, where the Development Team presented their results. Each meeting was related to one milestone. After discussing potential problems, the Scrum Teams adjusted the milestones as appropriate. In this way, the Development Team had a fixed date when which milestone had to be fulfilled. Since the meeting within the Scrum Team was held not daily, but rather weekly, we stayed in contact via social media to enable daily communication. In addition, Scrum Masters conducted every morning a short, approximately 15 min daily Scrum to support the Development Team whenever necessary. Short-term problems were solved in this way. After the last milestone, we held the Sprint Review meeting and reflected the project. This meeting concluded all five sprints we conducted for each milestone. After this, the production of the online materials for the prototype was finished, whereupon they were uploaded online. These were available to the students between the 12th and 13th lecture to prepare for the 13th lecture. Meanwhile, we developed the materials for the in-class time. In doing so, the online questions and quizzes were directly incorporated into the adaptation and influenced the focus of our content. In this way, we were able to respond to the needs of the students and clarify their questions better during the FC presence phase at the 13th lecture. In addition, a quantitative survey of the students was carried out to evaluate the prototype. The results of this survey were discussed in the Retroperspective Meeting. Hereafter, level 1 of agile FC development was finalized. We have planned the same process for lecture 4, 7 and 10 in level 2. Due to learning effects, we assume that less time is needed for development in the future. The 13th lesson of level 1 will be revised and improved in level 2 based on the results of the evaluation. In addition, the online questions of the current semester will continue to be incorporated into the revision of the course content. In the following semesters, we plan to increase the number of sessions to be developed, as shown in Fig. 4. At the end of level 4, the course is fully transformed into an FC, as illustrated in Fig. 5.

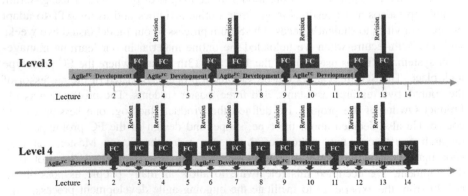

**Fig. 5.** Level 3 and 4 of Agile$^{FC}$ development

# 6  Conclusion

The aim of our work is to provide teachers with an understanding of the possible use of agile methods for designing FCs based on current research. For this purpose, we have developed a model that includes different agile methods. We assume that both teachers and students can benefit from our model, because following Scrum, a structured and time-saving development takes place, and following JITT, learner-centered and individual learning processes are made possible. To introduce the topic and an overview of the current state of research on the subject, we first conducted a structured literature review. Our review resulted in five research articles that make agile concepts in education a subject of discussion. There is no generally applicable agile model for FCs in current research. Thus, we filled the research gap evolving the $Agile^{FC}$ Development Model, referring to our findings. This model is a combination of different agile approaches, most of all Scrum and JiTT. To illustrate how to implement the $Agile^{FC}$ Development Model in practice, we introduced a case study of an FC development. We suggest a stepwise implementation of an FC course, beginning with one prototype of one single course and continuing gradually with the other sessions as a classic lecture.

Even though we conducted our research systematically and conscientiously, it may have limitations. Another research process could have led to other or more findings. Our model is based on the literature available through the literature review and our experiences as FC developers. Other experienced FC developers could have rated different concepts as relevant and suitable for an $Agile^{FC}$ Development Model. In addition, a general model, as we wanted to create, could be in contrast to the individuality of the course conditions. Depending on the course, further adjustments could be necessary. On the other hand, the shown application of the model is case-based and referred to our course and, therefore, not necessarily transferable to other HEI without adaptation. The boundaries of our work indicate the need for further research. During continuing the development process of our course, we would like to evaluate and adapt our $Agile^{FC}$ Development Model. In particular, we want to investigate whether an agile and stepwise approach to the development of an FC can increase acceptance by teachers and other stakeholders. We also plan to use the results of our evaluation for continuous improvement in the agile sense.

# References

1. Bergmann, J., Sams, A.: Flip Your Classroom: Reach Every Student in Every Class Every Day. International Society for Technology in Education, Alexandria (2012)
2. Bishop, J.L., Verleger, M.A.: The flipped classroom: a survey of the research. In: ASEE National Conference Proceedings, Atlanta, GA, pp. 1–18 (2013)
3. Giannakos, M.N., Krogstie, J., Chrisochoides, N.: Reviewing the flipped classroom research: reflections for computer science education. In: Proceedings of the Computer Science Education Research Conference, pp. 23–29. ACM, New York (2014)
4. Bofill, L.: The design and implementation of online radiology modules using the ADDIE process and rapid prototyping (2016)

5. Liebscher, J., Petschenka, A., Gollan, H., Heinrich, S., van Ackeren, I., Ganseuer, C.: E-Learning-Strategie an der Universität Duisburg-Essen - mehr als ein Artefakt? ZFHE **10**, 93–109 (2015)
6. Beck, K., et al.: The agile manifesto (2001)
7. Conboy, K., Fitzgerald, B.: Toward a conceptual framework of agile methods. Presented at the Conference on Extreme Programming and Agile Methods (2004)
8. Tesar, M., Sieber, S.: Managing blended learning scenarios by using agile e-learning development, vol. 5, pp. 125–129 (2010)
9. Johnson, L.: NMC horizon report: 2014 higher education edition. NMC (2014)
10. Schwaber, K., Sutherland, J.: The scrum guide-the definitive guide to scrum: the rules of the game (2013)
11. Sharp, J.H., Lang, G.: Agile in teaching and learning: conceptual framework and research agenda. J. Inf. Syst. Educ. **29**, 1 (2019)
12. Hurtubise, L., Hall, E., Sheridan, L., Han, H.: The flipped classroom in medical education: engaging students to build competency. J. Med. Educ. Curric. Dev. **2**, 35–43 (2015)
13. Harris, B.F., Harris, J., Reed, L., Zelihic, M.: Flipped classroom: another tool for your pedagogy tool box, pp. 325–333 (2016)
14. Owen, H., Dunham, N.: Reflections on the use of iterative, agile and collaborative approaches for blended flipped learning development. Educ. Sci. **5**, 85–103 (2015)
15. Schryen, G.: Writing qualitative IS literature reviews-guidelines for synthesis, interpretation, and guidance of research. Commun. Assoc. Inf. Syst. **37**, 286–325 (2015)
16. Webster, J., Watson, R.T.: Analyzing the past to prepare for the future: writing a literature review. Manag. Inf. Syst. Q. **26**, xiii–xxiii (2002)
17. Hult, M., Lennung, S.-Å.: Towards a definition of action research: a note and bibliography. J. Manage. Stud. **17**, 241–250 (1980)
18. Meissner, B., Stenger, H.-J.: Agiles Lernen mit Just-in-Time-Teaching. Teaching Trends, pp. 121–136 (2014)
19. Vogel, B., Kilamo, T., Kurti, A.: Teaching distributed agile development to software professionals: a flexible approach. In: Proceedings of the 2015 European Conference on Software Architecture Workshops, p. 31. ACM (2015)
20. Gale, T.C., Chatterjee, A., Mellor, N.E., Allan, R.J.: Health worker focused distributed simulation for improving capability of health systems in Liberia. Simul. Healthc. **11**, 75–81 (2016)
21. Novak, G.M.: Just-in-time teaching. New Dir. Teach. Learn. **2011**, 63–73 (2011)
22. Schwaber, K.: Scrum development process. In: Sutherland, J., Casanave, C., Miller, J., Patel, P., Hollowell, G. (eds.) Business Object Design and Implementation, pp. 117–134. Springer, London (1997)
23. Sharma, S., Hasteer, N.: A comprehensive study on state of Scrum development. Presented at the 2016 international conference on computing, communication and automation (ICCCA) (2016)
24. Hoffman, E.S.: Beyond the flipped classroom: redesigning a research methods course for eInstruction. Contemp. Issues Educ. Res. **7**, 51–62 (2014)
25. Enkenberg, J.: Instruction design and emerging teaching models in higher education. Comput. Hum. Behav. **17**, 495–506 (2001)
26. Hodell, C.: Instructional systems and the ADDIE model. In: ISD From the Ground Up, 2nd edn. Association for Talent Development, Alexandria (2006)

# Author Index